The Forméd Trace

The Later Poetry of Ezra Pound

The Forméd Trace

The Later Poetry of Ezra Pound

Massimo Bacigalupo

Columbia University Press · New York · 1980

Library of Congress Cataloging in Publication Data

Bacigalupo, Massimo, 1947–
    The forméd trace.

    Includes bibliographical references and index.
    1. Pound, Ezra Loomis, 1885–1972—Criticism and inter-
pretation.   I. Title.
PS3531.O82Z544   811'.5'2   79-12877
ISBN 0-231-04456-9

Columbia University Press
New York   Guildford, Surrey

Willing man look into that forméd trace in his mind
And with such uneasiness as rouseth the flame.
　　　　　　　　　　　—Canto 36

　　　　　nothing matters but the quality
of the affection—
in the end—that has carved the trace in the mind
dove sta memoria
　　　　　　　　　　　—Canto 76

Contents

Preface

The subject proper of this book, which Agostino Lombardo of the University of Rome suggested to me in 1971, is the verse written by Pound from 1945 to 1960, that is, from the *Pisan Cantos* to the end (for nothing was produced in the last twelve years of his life). However, in order to provide a somewhat thorough reading of this which is still the less explored section of the poet's work, it has been necessary to consider in the opening chapters the stages prior to the Pisan crisis, particular attention being devoted to the *Cantos,* of which even the early sections cannot be said to have been fully digested at this late date. Therefore this is also a book on the *Cantos,* though somewhat slanted towards the later ones.

I make no claim to having exhausted the subject and I am aware that my readings do not always keep up with the poet's often breathtaking gait—but I would hope to have exorcised it a little by eschewing the boundless admiration and frightened disregard (which amount to the same) of a good many of those who have printed their views on the matter, and by providing, through concentration on the text, all those interested with the means to judge for themselves.

My title points to the poet's obsession with the (previously) written, which is shared by not a few critics of the newer schools. His verse is essentially a transcription of traces which he reads in books, on leaves, in the sky, and—in his better moments—in the mind, "dove sta memòra." In turn the poem will yield its "revelations" only if closely read as trace, matter, graffito. "As to 'form' "—Pound wrote in "Cavalcanti" about the very "formato loco" which he transcribed as "forméd trace"—"you may here add the whole of medieval philosophy by way of footnote." Ultimately the word takes us to his peculiar brand of Neoplatonism. But all of this is beyond the scope of a foreword.

Should it be thought advisable that I state my general position in a few words at the outset, I will say that I concur with R. P.

Blackmur's statement of 1934 that Pound "is neither a great poet
nor a great thinker," though this should be qualified by a lengthy
consideration of the vicissitudes of modern poetry in America,
England, and Europe, in the context of which Pound's position as
a pathfinder and as an outstanding experimentalist is, I believe,
hardly assailable. He is also a rich and rewarding poet in his own
right, as this study should show.

There are other strictures harder to qualify. Pound was mili-
tantly pro-fascist and anti-Semitic from about 1930 onwards, to
what extent the following chapters will indicate. In many ways the
Cantos belong in those shops that sell swastikas and recordings of
Mussolini's speeches, for they are, among other things, the sacred
poem of the Nazi-Fascist millennium which mercifully never eventuated.

The only connection I see between Pound's stature as a poet
and his political aberrations is precisely the abnormality of both.
(Which is not to say that his poetics and his politics are not of
one piece.) A conventional mind in many ways, Pound broke off
malgré lui from the travelled roads of Western culture, which he
was not even equipped to understand, and dreamed up—for he
had that power or energy—another world, which, the West having come to where it is and seeking its antithesis (if that is how
Yeats puts it), turned out to be very attractive to all who in the
arts were intentionally and for better reason severing themselves
from the old tree. Pound, on the other hand, was never even
aware that his writing was different, he just did not know any
other way to go about his job. For all he consciously knew, he
was aiming at the effects of Rossetti and Swinburne. Like Colum-
bus, he was seeking the old and he found the new.

I am grateful to Olga Rudge and to the late Dorothy and Ezra
Pound for their friendship and some suggestions, to Mary de
Rachewiltz and Vanni Scheiwiller for granting access to original
material, to Eva Hesse and Guy Davenport for their correspondence, to my teachers and friends at Columbia, Quentin Anderson, Michael Wood, George Stade, Robert Gorham Davis,

Cary Plotkin, for their support and some careful reading of a previous version of this book, to the Fulbright-Hays Program, Columbia University, and Consiglio Nazionale delle Ricerche, Rome, for financial support. William F. Bernhardt and the staff at Columbia University Press have been most cooperative and patient in dealing with an intricate typescript and a transatlantic author. For last-minute checking of proofs I am indebted to my colleague at the University of Genoa, Maria Vittoria Gianelli Campana, and to Angela Kirsten.

                                                              M. B.

Abbreviations Used in This Book

Works by Ezra Pound

A   *Confucian Analects* (London: Peter Owen, 1956).

ABR   *ABC of Reading* (1934; rpt. New York: New Directions, 1960).

ALS   *A Lume Spento and Other Early Poems* (New York: New Directions, 1965).

CA   *The Classic Anthology Defined by Confucius* (Cambridge: Harvard University Press, 1954).

CC   *Confucius to Cummings: An Anthology of Poetry,* eds. Ezra Pound and Marcella Spann (New York: New Directions, 1964).

CEP   *Collected Early Poems of Ezra Pound,* ed. Michael John King (New York: New Directions, 1976).

CV   *Carta da visita,* 1942. Tr. as *A Visiting Card* by John Drummond and collected in *SPr* 306–35.

D&F   *Drafts & Fragments of Cantos* CX–CXVII (New York: New Directions, 1969).

GB   *Gaudier-Brzeska: A Memoir* (1916; rpt. New York: New Directions, 1974).

GD   *The Great Digest,* in *Confucius: The Unwobbling Pivot & The Great Digest* (Norfolk, Conn.: Pharos, 1947).

HSM   *Hugh Selwyn Mauberley,* 1920. Collected in *P* 185–204.

HSP   *Homage to Sextus Propertius,* 1919. Collected in *P* 205–30.

J/M   *Jefferson and/or Mussolini* (1935; rpt. New York: Liveright, 1970).

K   *Guide to Kulchur* (1938; rpt. Norfolk, Conn.: New Directions, 1954).

L   *The Letters of Ezra Pound, 1907–1941,* ed. D. D. Paige (New York: Harcourt Brace, 1950).

LE   *Literary Essays,* ed. T. S. Eliot (Norfolk, Conn.: New Directions, 1954).

LU   *Lavoro ed usura: tre saggi* (Milano: Scheiwiller, 1954).

OS   *Opere scelte,* ed. Mary de Rachewiltz (Milano: Mondadori, 1970).

P   *Personae: The Collected Shorter Poems of Ezra Pound* (1926; rpt. New York, New Directions, 1949).

PC   *The Pisan Cantos* (New York: New Directions, 1948).

PD   *Pavannes and Divagations* (Norfolk, Conn.: New Directions, 1958).

P&T   "Psychology and Troubadours," 1912; collected in *SR* 87–100.

QPA   *Quia Pauper Amavi* (London: Egoist, 1919).

RD   *Section: Rock-Drill 85–95 de los Cantares* (Milano: Scheiwiller, 1955).

SPr   *Selected Prose 1909–1965,* ed. William Cookson (New York: New Directions, 1973).

SR   *The Spirit of Romance* (1910; rpt. with additions Norfolk, Conn.: New Directions, 1959).

T   *Translations,* enlarged edition (New York: New Directions, 1963).

Th   *Thrones 96–109 de los Cantares* (Milano: Scheiwiller, 1959).

UP   *The Unwobbling Pivot.* See entry for *GD.*

WT   *Sophokles: Women of Trachis* (New York: New Directions, 1957).

Other

L'Herne   *Les Cahiers de l'Herne 6–7: Ezra Pound 1–2,* ed. Michel Beaujour (Paris: Editions de l'Herne, 1965).

M   *Mathews' Chinese-English Dictionary,* rev. American ed., 1944.

PL   J. P. Migne, *Patrologiae Cursus Completus: Series Latina* (Paris, 1844–80).

Studies Cited by Author's Name Alone

Julien Cornell, *The Trial of Ezra Pound* (London: Faber, 1967).

Nemi D'Agostino, *Ezra Pound* (Roma: Edizioni di Storia e Letteratura, 1960).

Donald Davie, *Ezra Pound: Poet as Sculptor* (London: Routledge, 1965).

George Dekker, *Sailing After Knowledge: The* Cantos *of Ezra Pound* (London: Routledge, 1963).

John J. Espey, *Ezra Pound's* Mauberley: *A Study in Composition* (Berkeley: University of California Press, 1955).

Donald Gallup, *A Bibliography of Ezra Pound* (London: Rupert Hart-Davis, 1963).

Marcel Granet, *La pensée chinoise* (1934; rpt. Paris: Albin Michel, 1968).

Eva Hesse, ed., *New Approaches to Ezra Pound* (London: Faber, 1969).

Hugh Kenner, *The Pound Era* (London: Faber, 1972).

Girolamo Mancuso, *Pound e la Cina* (Milano: Feltrinelli, 1974).

Charles Norman, *Ezra Pound,* rev. ed. (New York: Minerva Press, 1960).

William Van O'Connor and Edward Stone, eds., *A Casebook on Ezra Pound* (New York: Crowell, 1959).

Daniel D. Pearlman, *The Barb of Time: On the Unity of Ezra Pound's* Cantos (New York: Oxford University Press, 1969).

Boris de Rachewiltz, *L'elemento magico in Ezra Pound* (Milano: Scheiwiller, 1965). Abridged English version: "Pagan and Magic Elements in Ezra Pound's Works," Hesse 174–97.

Mary de Rachewiltz, *Discretions* (Boston: Little, Brown, 1971).

Forrest Read, ed., *Pound/Joyce: The Letters of Ezra Pound to James Joyce, with Pound's Essays on Joyce* (New York: New Directions, 1970).

Noel Stock, *The Life of Ezra Pound,* rev. ed. (Harmondsworth: Penguin, 1974).

J. P. Sullivan, ed., *Ezra Pound: A Critical Anthology* (Harmondsworth: Penguin, 1970).

Niccolò Zapponi, *L'Italia di Ezra Pound* (Roma: Bulzoni, 1976).

Numbers given with abbreviations indicate pages. Exceptions are as follows: *CA* and *HSP* (no. of poem); *A, GD, UP* (book and ch.); Gallup (code of entry); *HSM* (section [prefixed] and poem); *K* (ch.); *L* (no. of letter); *M* (no. of character); *PL* (vol. and col.).

Classical works have been abbreviated as is customary.

The text of the *Cantos* has been established by comparing *The Cantos of Ezra Pound,* new collected ed. (London: Faber, 1964), and *The Cantos of Ezra Pound,* 4th printing (New York: New Directions, 1973), with available first editions and typescripts. Departures from the current text (1978) have been noted, except in the following instances, where I have either *normalized spelling and punctuation, or §rejected an editorial emendation and/or followed the 1964 Faber text:

*page 30: line 28 (*current reading:* Ilion); *38:29 (il zaino); *38:33 (Gruss); *55:34 (Buccentoro); *63:19 (die Volkern); *§69:34 (NOUS); *69:35 (Karxèdoniōn); *89:21 (Cabrere); *116:28 (sotto le nostre scoglie); *117:19, 135:9, 188:12 (son'); *121:29, 122:17 (zecchin'); *140:18, 449:21 (Allegre); §151:19 ("Hay); §151:22 ("Yo . . . desaparecen"); §151:27 ("Come); §163:19 (Atreides); *165:36 (Reithmuller); *166:32 (Nicolo); *166:33 (la); *169:9 (*concret*); *281:36 (Pithagoras); *298:16 (parapernalia); *299:32 (charitas); *317:31 (calescemus); *322:14 (pien'); *341:34, 360:19, 363:20 (pervanche); §346:22 (Manuale); *360:15 (splendor' mondan'); *375:31 (Χρήδεμνον); *390:24 (Phaecia); *391:16 (EROTAS); §394:21 (Mihailovitch); *404:10 (keinas); *404:16 (Phaecians); *410:11 (pepneumenos); *415:12 (APHANASTON); *415:14 (KOSMOU); *419:11 (can "etcetera); *423:24 (kolschoz); *438:30 (phylotaxis); *438:31 (by hundred); *439:6 (caffaris, caltha palistris); *439:7 (herys); *439:13 (capitols); *466:19 (paion').

Acknowledgments

Farrar, Straus & Giroux, Inc.: From *Notebook 1967–68,* copyright ©
1967, 1968, 1969, 1970 by Robert Lowell. Reprinted by permission
of Farrar, Straus & Giroux and Faber and Faber Ltd.

Harvard University Press: From *The Classic Anthology Defined by
Confucius / The Confucian Odes /* by Ezra Pound, copyright © 1954
by the President and Fellows of Harvard College. Reprinted by permission of Harvard University Press and Faber and Faber Ltd.

Alfred A. Knopf, Inc.: From *The Collected Poems of Wallace Stevens*
and *Opus Posthumous* by Wallace Stevens, copyright © 1947, 1954
by Wallace Stevens; copyright © 1957, 1959 by Elsie Stevens and
Holly Stevens. Reprinted by permission of Alfred A. Knopf, Inc.

Macmillan Publishing Company: From "Down by the Salley Gardens"
and "The Moods" (copyright © 1906 by Macmillan Publishing Co.,
Inc., renewed 1934 by William Butler Yeats). From "The Circus
Animals' Desertion" (copyright © 1940 by Georgie Yeats, renewed
1968 by Bertha Georgie Yeats, Michael Butler Yeats, and Anne
Yeats). Reprinted from *Collected Poems* of William Butler Yeats by
permissions of Macmillan Publishing Co., Inc., New York, Macmillan Co. of London and Basingstoke, M. B. Yeats, Miss Anne Yeats.

New Directions Publishing Corp.: From *The Spirit of Romance,*
copyright © 1968 by Ezra Pound, All Rights Reserved. From
Gaudier-Brzeska, copyright © 1970 by Ezra Pound, All Rights Reserved. From *Literary Essays,* copyright © 1918, 1920, 1936 by Ezra
Pound. From *Guide to Kulchur,* copyright © 1970 by Ezra Pound,
All Rights Reserved. From *Pavannes and Divagations,* copyright ©
1958 by Ezra Pound. From *Selected Prose 1909–65,* copyright ©
1973 by the Estate of Ezra Pound. From *Selected Letters 1907–41,*
copyright © 1950 by Ezra Pound. From *Translations,* copyright ©
1926, 1954, 1957, 1958, 1960, 1963 by Ezra Pound. From *Confucius: The Great Digest, The Unwobbling Pivot, The Analects,*
copyright © 1928 by Glenn Hughes, copyright © 1957, 1950 by
Ezra Pound, copyright © 1951 by New Directions; published in England by Peter Owen, London. From *Women of Trachis,* copyright ©
1957 by Ezra Pound. From *The Cantos,* copyright © 1934, 1937,

The Forméd Trace

The Later Poetry of Ezra Pound

Part One

The Pisan Poem and Its Genesis

Those masterful images because complete
Grew in pure mind, but out of what began?
A mound of refuse or the sweepings of a street,
Old kettles, old bottles, and a broken can,
Old iron, old bones, old rags, that raving slut
Who keeps the till. Now that my ladder's gone,
I must lie down where all the ladders start,
In the foul rag-and-bone shop of the heart.

—Yeats, "The Circus Animals' Desertion"

The circumstances that brought Ezra Pound to the U.S. Armed Forces' Disciplinary Training Center near Pisa (24 May–16 November 1945) are well known. Indicted for treason by a federal jury in July 1943 on account of his broadcasts from Rome, he was arrested in May 1945, and interned at Pisa pending further decisions.

The writing there of the *Pisan Cantos* as a kind of testament of the poet's life and work, brings to mind Bertolt Brecht's version of the story of Lao-tzu and the customs officer.[1] Had not the obscure official insisted that the wise man leave a record of his knowledge behind him before he cross the border and vanish, the *Tao-tê-ching* would not have been written. The officer is a figure of the peremptory claims of history, to which even the ineffable *tao* owes its existence.

In fact there was quite a chasm between Pound and the history which he sought so insistently—a condition not uncommon in modern culture. It is enough to say that he witnessed *in situ* the twenty-year course of Italian fascism with scarcely any awareness

1. Bertolt Brecht, "Legende von der Entstehung des Buches Taoteking auf dem Weg des Laotse in die Emigration," in *Kalendergeschichten* (Hamburg: Rowohlt, 1963), pp. 121–24.

1

of the cruelty and barbarity of that regime—indeed, he took it for the embodiment of much of his political platform. This was not a mere error of judgement, for Pound belongs surely if erratically within a conservative strain of American social thought which has hardly ceased to exhibit its reactionary propensities.

The War did not alter but rather encouraged this confusion. Among conflicting worlds one could only rely on one's sense of things, and Pound spoke as a man alone to an invisible and imaginary audience—lack of feedback leading him to what would seem utter loss of reserve in checking his less honorable and untold night thoughts. In the earliest known draft of the *Cantos* he had written that "the truth is inside this discourse," and he was still working on this premise, though in the broadcast of 8 March 1942 he admitted with edgy wryness: "I lose my thread sometimes. So much that I can't count on anyone's knowing. Thread, as they call it, of discourse."[2]

Eventually the events of history tore this web of discourse as curtly as Brecht's customs officer. Only under the pressure of defeat and incarceration Pound was able to readjust his aberrant responses and produce his most lasting work, the *Pisan Cantos.* The turmoil once over, he was to return to what he called his "phantastikon," and accordingly remove himself from the scene of what has been termed the industrious despair of modern man.

Thus we may graph the *Cantos* as a curve that makes contact with historical time only in the middle section, and deflects from it at the ends. The point of contact, which corresponds within the poem to the *Pisan Cantos,* and in time to the summer of 1945, is the only place where the relevance of the whole may be ascertained. Here the poet's story is also that of man.

From the start Pound had set out to write "the tale of the tribe": the descent to Hades in canto 1 is meant to suggest a confrontation with the entire course of history-as-hell as a means of regaining history-as-paradise on earth. However, throughout the first part of the *Cantos,* the poet-hero (Ulysses) is at pains to

2. *"E.P. Speaking": Radio Speeches of World War II,* ed. L. W. Doob (Westport, Conn.: Greenwood Press, 1978), p. 57.

keep aloof of man's common lot: while his companions allow themselves to be bewitched and ordered to the pigsty (*hara*) by Circe, Ulysses, aided by the magic herb (moly) that Hermes has given him (roughly: by his intelligence), holds his own against— and beds—the dangerous sorceress:

> Came here with Glaucus unnoticed, nec ivi in harum
> Nec in harum ingressus sum.   [canto no. 39]

(Dante's Glaucus, the hero of Pound's early poem, "An Idyl for G.," also made use of a magic herb, thus becoming "fellow to the gods of the sea." Similarly Ulysses here is rather superman than man.) This situation is pointedly reversed at the outset of the Pisan sequence:

> ac ego in harum
> so lay men in Circe's swine-sty
> ivi in harum *ego* ac vidi cadaveres animae   [c. 74]

"And I have gone myself into the pigpen." On this occasion the descent to hell is for real, as the italics seek to point out, and the "souls out of Erebus, cadaverous dead"[3] of canto 1 actually materialize in the D.T.C. Yet Circe's swine and corpses were formerly Ulysses' companions, and they become manifest as such in the course of the ordeal recorded in the section. No longer "cadaveres" but "comites," they bring home to the poet (who now shares their experience) the fact that the true tale of the tribe is one of companionship in sufferance. Thus the gods and dreams esthetically described in earlier cantos gain human significance as metaphors for "the quality of the affection" or for "charity," which (as Paul of Tarsus claimed) is "the greatest," and yet best instanced by the black guard or fellow-inmate who, out of some discarded box, made the table on which the poem was probably written, though any assistance to the alleged traitor was forbidden and punishable:

> of the Baluba mask: "doan you tell no one
>   I made you that table"

3. "Animae ex Erebo cadaverum mortuorum" in P.'s Latin source. See "Translators of Greek," *LE* 260.

>   methenamine eases the urine
>   and the greatest is charity
>   to be found among those who have not observed
>   regulations   [c. 74]

In telling the story Pound sees that a justification for his own unobservance of regulations may be attempted on grounds of the charitable motives that inspired him in the first place, traces of which are in fact strewn throughout his work. Thus he invites a reading of the *Pisan Cantos* as a climax to the Education of Ezra Pound.

1. Lineaments of Space

From *Hugh Selwyn Mauberley* to the Early Cantos

Pound's was a long but purposeful apprenticeship. The sixty-year-old prisoner of Pisa is still bent upon fulfilling the promise, inspired by the *Vita nuova* and decadent ambience, formulated by the twenty-year-old graduate student, who believed he saw his "greater soul-self bending / Sibylwise with that great forty-year-epic" ("Scriptor Ignotus," *ALS* 38)—who wanted above all to be a poet in the line of Swinburne, Browning, the Pre-Raphaelites, early Yeats, and of the American (and Canadian) "artists of the Carman-Hovey period."[1] Among these models, Swinburne's intoxicating chant and Browning's discursiveness, the conversational and dramatic form of his personae, gained in those early days an ascendancy they would never lose.

Pound set out on his career with the uncommon lyric gift apparent in his first collection, *A Lume Spento,* went somewhat astray because of too much "mediaevalism" (another far-reaching inclination) in his subsequent volumes, *Exultations* and *Canzoni* (1909–11), then rallied his powers under the influence of "the prose tradition," and of the poets of France and Rome. In 1915, aged thirty, he brought out his last volume of short poems, *Lustra* (later added to), which has preserved over the years no little part of its freshness (as is the case with some of the very early verse). At about this time he set his hand to the long poem on his mind, three cantos of which appeared in 1917. These open with an address to Browning concerning the latter's *Sordello* (an attractive model for the young Romance scholar), proceed with an open-ended chain of semi-historical literary rev-

---

1. "What I feel about Walt Whitman" (1909, first pub. 1955), *SPr* 145. The decadent and symbolist movement of the American Nineties has been disregarded in studies of P. chiefly perhaps because Eliot and P. seldom admitted its influence or even its existence, enjoying as they did the role of strugglers in the desert. Yet magazines like *The Bookman, The Chapbook, M'lle New York,* and *The Bibelot,* tell a different story. See "Preludi americani," in D'Agostino 19–27, and John J. Espey, "The Inheritance of *tò kalón,*" in Hesse 319–30.

eries, and close with a scarcely reliable rendering of the opening
of *Odyssey* 11, the *nékuia*. Pound became quickly dissatisfied
with this beginning and revised it several times over the next few
years: at first he was content with tightening it up, but eventually
he reached a new understanding of the poem and of its structure
and redrafted the lot for the *Draft of* XVI *Cantos* of 1924. These
changes of mind were precipitated by the writing of the three climactic sequences of Pound's early period: *Mœurs Contemporaines* (1918), *Homage to Sextus Propertius* (1919), and *Hugh
Selwyn Mauberley* (1920).

The first and least successful of these seeks to convey the poet's
attitude toward his time by way of a set of heavily ironic vignettes. It is the first major instance of Pound's satire of modern
manners, which continues through many unattractive passages in
the first forty or so cantos—passages always brought in as a foil
to higher (usually medieval) things. In fact this is also the case
with *Mœurs Contemporaines,* which in Pound's collections follows upon a captivating set of imitations from the Provençal,
Langue d'Oc, which conveys the image of a world as integrated
and sensual as the other is void and sterile: the two sequences—
Pound insists—amount to a single "portrait." Despite the simple-
mindedness of this conception, and the slightness of the vignettes,
Mœurs Contemporaines is of interest because of its "extremely
peculiar cultural and historical integration," [2] in other words as a
pastiche of languages and cultures which anticipates the form
(and much of the content) of the *Cantos.* (P.'s proclivity toward
pastiche, however, is prominent as early as *A Lume Spento.*)

Propertius, a rather cavalier rendering of passages from the
Elegies, is a considerably more contemporary and more subtle
work. The jaded Roman poet is an apt mask of the modern condition as the problem he is concerned with in Pound's text (the
interference of poetry and politics, of private and public life) is of
immediate relevance—he is the bearer of Pound's ambiguous attitude toward the war in progress or just over. (This may be the

2. Edoardo Sanguineti, "I *Canti pisani,*" *Aut-Aut,* July 1954, p. 331. Quoted in Zapponi
192.

point of P.'s—probably inaccurate—dating of the sequence as of 1917.) As regards technique, Pound masters here the long and flowing line, both hieratic and colloquial, usually comprising a full sentence, which he will employ in the *Cantos*—and develops his poetics of translation or parody (taking the word etymologically, as "imitative song"), bringing to a head his inclination of old standing, to manipulate and distort, intentionally or not, the texts of others. (The first poem printed with P.'s signature is a "Belangal Alba" from the Provençal; "The Seafarer" and *Cathay,* which rank very high in the early work, are parodies.)

Mauberley is also a translation of sorts—not so much of extant matter as of patterns of form (Gautier's quatrains, James's paragraph, Bion's rhythms). Besides, it falls into two sections, the second of which may be read as an ironic translation of the first. The sequence displays the crisis which opened in the life of Pound, and more generally of Europe, at the close of the War—his disenchantment with the times and particularly with the literary establishment, which he can no longer dismiss, as Propertius had done, by flippancy and recourse to a lover's ministrations: in *HSM* the irony is harsher, and often passes into invective. Yet the protest against "the march of events" is but the projection of a deeper personal crisis: Pound is dissatisfied with his esthetic career, he feels that his vocabulary (particularly as exhibited in the *Ur-Cantos* of 1917, those uninhibited confessions of a "beautiful soul") is inadequate, "out of key with his time," and he seeks to redefine his role. The former part of the sequence belongs to the aggressive phase of the crisis, and is a critique (only more savage than heretofore) of the modern philistine, whom Pound berates first explicitly, then by throwing into his face (somewhat as he had done in *Langue d'Oc-Mœurs Contemporaines*) a masterly parody of a seventeenth-century poem. But in the second section the attack turns upon the poet, the Mauberley of the title, who enters only at this point, and is a transparent mask of Pound the beautiful soul. This concise (auto-) biography, molded expressionistically in its remarkable tension, is truly the birth certificate of a modern poet in the line of the French masters (Baudelaire, Rimbaud, Mallarmé) who paved the way several decades earlier, though Pound is essentially unaware of this precedent.

Mauberley weighs the alternatives of engagement and disengagement, of "impure" and "pure" art, and signifies a preference for the former, expectable in a writer who had proved himself from the start an eccentric critic of civilization—a choice which was to expose him to much obloquy and eventually to imprisonment. Today many are inclined to believe that the poet should not sully himself with the living, that it is enough that he provide formal models of a liberation to be carried out by others. This rationale for evasion Pound refuses to accept, like most poets of some standing, yet he does so with an insistence wholly his own, conceiving his work as the new gospel of liberation—while not forsaking an essentially esthetic perspective. Even so in *HSM* he insists that poetry is a public career, yet goes on to celebrate the oversubtle perceptions of the beautiful soul, the "phantasmagoria" of eyes and sea surge which will be just as central to the *Cantos*. Pound's messianic program cannot but bring to mind Whitman, who may have been (together with a Puritan strain)[3] a greater influence than the French decadents Pound was familiar with, who made claims as extravagant for their *Livres,* be they written or (as with Mallarmé) imaginary.

In a 1920 letter Pound accounted as follows for the book *Poems 1918–1921, including Three Portraits and Four Cantos* (the three portraits were of course the critical sequences we have been discussing):

I have sent the rest of copy for "Three Portraits"
It contains the Imperium Romanum (Propertius)
        The Middle Ages (Provence)
        Mauberley (today)
   and cantos IV–VII,
It is all I have done since 1916, and my most important book, I at any rate think canto VII the best thing I have done . . . At any rate the three portraits, falling into a Trois Contes scheme, plus the Cantos, which

3. See Herbert N. Schneidau, *Ezra Pound: The Image and the Real* (Baton Rouge: Louisiana State Univ. Press, 1969), pp. 173–87.

come out of the middle of me and are not a mask, are what I have to say, and the first formed book of poem [sic] I have made.[4]

The enlightening parallel with Flaubert's *Trois Contes* (which, we recall, are "Un Cœur simple," "Saint Julien l'Hospitalier," and "Hérodias"—that is, today, the Middle Ages, and Rome) testifies to Pound's care in appropriating the prose tradition of Europe, and to the epochal character of his vision, which is always a criticism of history. But when he comes to speak of cantos 4–7, which are actually concerned with the same three layers of time, and employ a method at least as objective as that of the portraits, Pound is eager to point out that these are no personae, but "the middle of me"—he points that is to the quality which had appealed to him in Whitman: "Camerado, this is no book; / Who touches this touches a man" (quoted in *Patria Mia, SPr* 123). In this connection one can do worse than recall the exceptionally candid statements of "What I feel about Walt Whitman" (1909):

I honor him for he prophesied me while I can only recognize him as a forebear of whom I ought to be proud. . . . I read him (in many parts) with acute pain, but when I write of certain things I find myself using his rhythms. The expression of certain things related to cosmic consciousness seems tainted with his maramis [sic].

. . . And yet I am but one of his "ages and ages' encrustations" or to be exact an encrustation of the next age. The vital part of my message, taken from the sap and fibre of America, is the same as his.

What follows is curiously farsighted:

Personally I might be very glad to conceal my relationship to my spiritual father and brag about my more congenial ancestry—Dante, Shakespeare, Theocritus, Villon, but the descent is a bit difficult to establish. And, to be frank, Whitman is to my fatherland . . . what Dante is to Italy and I at my best can only be a strife for a renaissance in America of all the lost or temporarily mislaid beauty, truth, valor, glory of Greece, Italy, England and all the rest of it.

. . . I am immortal even as he is, yet with a lesser vitality as I am more in love with beauty (If I really do love it more than he did). Like

---

4. To John Quinn, 9 October 1920. Quoted in Pearlman 301.

Dante he wrote in the "vulgar tongue," in a new metric. The first great
man to write in the language of his people. [SPr 145–46]

This is the self-portrait of the artist at twenty-three, who is already certain that beauty comes in waves and that his task is to
resuscitate it, yet is also quite ready to place himself in the
shadow of rough father Whitman. For himself he only anticipates
"a strife for a renaissance in America."

We conclude that the *Cantos* are the product of a Whitmanian
urge to embrace the cosmos, to do away with the irony and removal of the three portraits, and to speak to all—especially to
America. Pound was justified in fearing that the position of the
portraits would at length prove sterile, yet the Whitmanian
choice also meant trouble, since it implied an authorial stance
(for and against something) that the personae had at best es-
chewed. Now the reader was to be repelled by esthetic and ideo-
logic attitudes he could not share, but he was also to be presented
with a work more direct and appealing, a poem as indistin-
guishable from the man and as remarkable as *Leaves of Grass*.

We now turn to the momentous acquisitions of method signified by *HSM* (and—to a slightly lesser extent—by the contemporary cs. 4–7 and by the previous two portraits). Chief among
these is the "ideogramic method" (as Pound was to call it later),
a discussion of which may playfully open with Carlos Williams'
remark on his fellow-student: "Never explain anything, was his
motto. He carried it off well—and in his verse too, later" (Norman 6). The method calls for the "heaping up" within a structure
(a haiku, *HSM,* the *Cantos,* everything P. has written) of the materials for a closely reasoned exposé and for the omission of discursive links, that is of all external indication of what the speaker
is aiming at. Thus nothing, with the possible exception of the
title, *tells* the reader that *Mœurs Contemporaines* is an ideogram
of today, and *Langue d'Oc* an ideogram of the Middle Ages, and
nothing but juxtaposition suggests that the two build a larger
ideogram concerning the respective merits of the two epochs. The
method is clearly an offshoot of the persona form of drama,
which also avoids telling the reader what to think; it should

result in the vividness of thinking something out at first hand, as against following someone else's train of thought. If we bear in mind that Pound's exhibits are usually "objective" bits of reality, we see how this allows him to believe that what speaks through his verse is nothing less than the real. He does not form conclusions, except insofar as he rises to vision, or as he shows us through repeated juxtaposition that one of his "facts" is a detail so "luminous" that it governs a good number of the others. The same applies to the reader, who is not meant to commute Pound's juxtapositions into logical form and into ideas, but should be content with a sensuous perception eschewing the dryness of thought, or with ideas in action. In other words, he would mistake Pound's intention if he came to the conclusion that *Langue d'Oc-Mœurs Contemporaines* "means" that life (i.e., poetry and sex) was richer in Provence, 1200, than in London, 1900. This is in fact what the "portrait" amounts to, but he is not supposed to know it with his mind, he is not supposed to exchange an idea for an instinctive perception of "fact." Otherwise (as all artists would agree), why write the poem (or paint the picture)? (This may also serve as a warning to the reader, as in this essay what P. has wisely left unsaid will occasionally have to be made explicit.) So after all the ideogramic method is the method of all art. What is peculiar to Pound is the very inventive application of the juxtapository technique, and the primitive belief that the word can be at one with the real.

Encouragement in the latter train of thought and a name for the "method" he found in Ernest Fenollosa's fanciful explication of the Chinese written character as a cluster of images of actual things, a sort of photographic language intuitively understood (sky + drops = rain, sun + horizon = dawn, man + word = sincerity), and in fact undistinguishable from the processes of nature. This is scarcely more true for Chinese than it is for Egyptian hieroglyphs, which no one would attempt to read on the strength of the owls and cats so misleadingly recognizable on the old obelisks.[5] In other words language, whether Chinese or English,

5. The comparison is in Mancuso's valuable discussion of Fenollosa and P. (pp. 17–26). Only a handful of Chinese characters can be called ideograms without impropriety, as

is a product of society and not of transcendentalist nature, as in
Fenollosa's hiddenly mystical conception. No wonder that to
George Santayana Fenollosa's essay (submitted by P. in 1940)
seemed to contain little but "romantic metaphysics" (Stock 477).
This romanticism, coupled with an insistence on the particular,
was bound to appeal to Pound, who rather boasted of his powers
of vision, and would have centered his long poem around these
concerns even without Fenollosa's aid.

It need only be added that Fenollosa's linguistic fallacies do
not invalidate the *Cantos,* though they may invalidate as translations Pound's imitations from the Chinese. (But then, the Loeb
Classical Library and the *Homage to Propertius* perform different functions.) In fact, the ideogramic method (whose father
was Browning and whose mother was Fenollosa, the best man
being probably Wagner) should not be confused with Pound's
Chinese studies, which entered upon their ideogramic phase only
about twenty years after *HSM* and the first cantos were written:
in the portrait, as in the first fifty cantos, there is little trace of
China, and no Chinese sign. As applied in the *Cantos* the ideogramic method is Pound's own structural invention, an answer to
his need for a non-narrative form that could hold the poem
together, and a very remarkable answer indeed.

Ideogramic writing is narrative insofar as it presents epiphanic
flashes in the life of one or of many individuals, and critical insofar as these flashes always pretend to "reality" or historicalness, and as the reader is asked to consider them both as an
experience in progress and as exhibits to be assessed. Yet narrative and logical links are nearly always replaced by relationships
of contiguity and similarity. In other words, to establish a connection between exhibits the poet must either place one in the immediate neighborhood of the other (in the *Cantos* every transition is a comparison, as within certain limits in all poetry),[6] or

most include phonetic signs the original meaning of which has no bearing on the meaning
of the characters which they form. Fenollosa's papers came to P. from the amateur orien-
talist's widow in 1913. The essay "The Chinese Written Character as a Medium for Poetry" he included in *Instigations* (1920), and reprinted (with a disastrous appendix, the
"Notes of a Very Ignorant Man," as he wryly called them) in 1936.

6. See Roman Jakobson, "Closing Statements: Linguistics and Poetics," in *Style in Language,* ed. T. A. Sebeok (New York: Wiley and M.I.T. Press, 1960), pp. 350–77.

have them run parallel. (Thus, for example, the inferno of cs. 14–15 is understood to be in relation with the *nékuia* of c. 1.) The latter technique is reminiscent of the recurrent themes and variations of the sonata form or of the fugue, an analogy which Pound takes further by often paring down his statements to easily recognizable foreign tags and to set phrases which he then repeats with scarcely any change. When this happens the resurgent segment recalls its original context as well as the other clusters in which it has been introduced, and this allows a gradual buildup of effects (as a tag becomes increasingly rich in associations), and the intimation that all that has been experienced in the poem bears on the present moment: in the later cantos Pound will get most sections of his plotless epic into delightful resonance within a few lines.

Pound first employed the method with consistency and caution in late 1919, in the writing of *HSM* and of cs. 4–7. The contiguity of the vignettes in 1 *HSM* calls for inferences on the state of England (as in *Mœurs Contemporaines*), while the contiguity of first and second part demands that we investigate the connection between E.P. and Mauberley. The latter is of course also a case of parallelism, though what the "Ode" states but ironically of E.P. ("He passed from men's memory in *l'an trentiesme | De son eage;* the case presents | No adjunct to the Muses' diadem") is quite accurate as bearing on Mauberley (though the evidence of the "Medallion" suggests that the latter was no mean poet). The parallelism is underscored with the quotational and thematic method of the *Cantos:* both men are Ulysses to Flaubert's Penelope, both are faced with "a beastly and cantankerous age,"[7] both are "excluded from the world of letters" (1 *HSM* 1, 2 *HSM* 3), and both admire rather too poetically a singer ("Envoi" and "Medallion" are parallel, the work of the two related poets, who are really two aspects of P.'s psyche).[8]

7. Ur-canto 1, *Poetry,* 10 (1917), 115. I am referring to the tag "The Age Demanded"—1 *HSM* 2 and 2 *HSM* 3. On the ideogramic method in *HSM* see Mancuso 85–87.

8. It has recently been maintained, on biographical grounds (P.'s admiration for Raymonde Collignon, the singer), that "Medallion" must "be taken as spoken with pride *in propria persona*" by P. and not by the fictitious Mauberley. See Donald Davie, *Ezra Pound* (New York: Viking, 1976), p. 54*n.* Yet the poem's punctilious fidelity to Gautier's program, the comparison of the woman with an image in a book, the relationship with

The Penelope reference brings us to the second acquisition of method accomplished in *HSM,* namely the "mythical method" (as Eliot was to call it in his 1923 review of *Ulysses*). Myth provides novelist and poet with an archetypal pattern through which he may arrange and assess the materials of his experience, somewhat as in parody (*Ulysses, HSM,* and the *Cantos* are all parodies of the *Odyssey*) and in Pound's ideogram (both the mythical and the ideogramic method seek to preserve impersonality, and have recourse to quotations and "bricolage").[9] But whereas Joyce and the Eliot of the *Plays* employ the myth which they have in mind as an ever present yet unstated point of reference, Pound, as is apparent from his Paris Letter "in praise of Ulysses," has no use for these "mediaevalisms" (*"Ulysses," LE* 406): he employs the mythical *Weltanschauung* purely as a structural instigation, the mythologem as such as an explicit material among others, though at times a privileged one. In "Hades" Bloom follows Paddy Dignam's hearse and constructs a whole *sottisier* on the subject of death, while in canto 1 Ulysses descends in person to the netherworld: Pound's criticism is not aimed at the *nékuia* (of which he seeks to recover the original flavor) but at the texts in which the old story is told: Homer's Greek, Andreas Divus' fifteenth-century Latin crib, and (for sidelight) the Anglo-Saxon *Seafarer,* which he had rendered in 1911. "I have tried," he told a correspondent in July 1916, "an adaptation [of the *nékuia*] in the 'Seafarer' metre, or something like it, but I don't expect anyone to recognize the source very quickly" (*L* 102).

---

the difficult second poem of 2 *HSM* (which bears upon Mauberley's erotic insensitivity), and lastly the ironic contrast with the "Envoi" to 1 *HSM*—all point unambiguously to the (metaphorical, of course) authorship of Mauberley. I cannot see how the fact that both "Envoi" and "Medallion" may have been written with Collignon in mind can reverse the textual evidence.

9. Claude Lévi-Strauss, who with his structuralist method pursues the ancient project of determining the world's syntax, writes that the primitive's mythic perception interprets all he sees of animal and vegetal life as if part of a message, to be read by "signatures": "Mythical thought for its part is imprisoned in the events and experiences which it never tires of ordering and re-ordering in its search to find them a meaning. But it also acts as a liberator by its protest against the idea that anything can be meaningless, with which science at first resigned itself to a compromise." *The Savage Mind* (Chicago: Univ. of Chicago Press, 1969), p. 21. Quoted in Schneidau, *The Image and the Real,* p. 84n.

Pound made an early acquaintance with Leopold Bloom over a year after this letter was written, in December 1917. However, though he was attracted to the *Odyssey* quite independently of Joyce, the older writer's work may well have cast a new light on his interest, stimulating him to more radical departures from convention and establishing the Ulysses theme as a major non-narrative chord both in *Mauberley* (in which the poet dissociates within himself the Ulysses from the Elpenor type) and in the *Cantos,* the opening of which was redrafted around 1923 to accommodate the *nékuia* as a first theme of the great fugue, and to assure the reader that the longer poem would have (unlike *HSM*) a happy ending, parallel to the "original":

> . . . "Odysseus
> "Shalt return through spiteful Neptune, over dark seas,
> "Lose all companions." Then Anticlea came.
> Lie quiet Divus. I mean, that is Andreas Divus,
> In officina Wecheli, 1538, out of Homer.
> And he sailed, by Sirens and thence outward and away
> And unto Circe.
> > Venerandam,
> In the Cretan's phrase, with the golden crown, Aphrodite,
> Cypri munimenta sortita est, mirthful, orichalchi, with golden
> Girdles and breast bands, thou with dark eyelids
> Bearing the golden bough of Argicida. So that: [c. 1]

"Lie quiet Divus." This injunction, the first splice in the poem, lays to rest not only Divus and Homer (also "divine"),[10] but also

10. See the original induction to the *nékuia* in ur-canto 3, as printed in *Poetry,* 10 (1917), 250:

> . . . Doughty's "divine Homeros"
> Came before sophistry. Justinopolitan
> Uncatalogued Andreas Divus,
> Gave him in Latin, 1538 in my edition, the rest uncertain,
> Caught up his cadence, word and syllable:
> "Down to the ships we went, set mast and sail,
> Black keel and beasts for bloody sacrifice,
> Weeping we went."
> I've strained my ear for *-ensa, -ombra,* and *-ensa*
> And cracked my wit on delicate canzoni—
> > Here's but rough meaning:
> "And then went down to the ship, set keel to breakers, . . .

Tiresias (conjured up by Ulysses as Divus by P.), and Ulysses himself, who is telling Alcinous of his journey to the dead. And it is Pound who speaks: first of the tradition of his text, of the Renaissance, and of the circulation of the classics brought about by the invention of printing ("In officina Wecheli, 1538"); then of a *nostos* which, contrary to Homeric tradition, goes from Sirens (the "chopped seas" [1 *HSM* 1] of the first XXX *Cantos*) to Circe (the presiding goddess of the middle cantos), and thence to a Penelope sumptuously adorned with gold, orichalcum,[11] Cyprian muniments, and sensual "Cretan phrases," lifted from the *Homeric Hymns* (second Hymn to Venus) as translated by Georgius Dartona Cretensis and appended to Divus' *Odyssey* in the volume of 1538.[12] This Penelope is none but Venus, presented in the close as a dark-eyed seducer, as a sibyl who, "bearing the golden bough" of Hermes (see Virgil and Frazer—P. has picked up a line from the first Hymn to Venus), guides the hero to Hades and to *Hermetic* knowledge—and also perhaps as a mother, an amplification of Anticlea, who makes so brief an appearance between the last words of Tiresias and the first of Pound (her son?).[13]

---

11. The "orichalchi" of the current text returns, from the more correct "orichalci" of the *Poetry* and *QPA* drafts, to the spelling of P.'s source (see next footnote). The London 1964 and Milan 1961 (below, n. 29) texts read "oricalchi."

12. See "Translators of Greek," *LE* 259–67, and ur-c. 3:

> Lie quiet Divus, plucked from a Paris stall
> With a certain Cretan's "Hymni Deorum";
> The thin clear Tuscan stuff   [i.e., Divus]
>   Gives way before the florid mellow phrase,
> Take we the goddess, Venerandam   [*QPA* 31]

The reference to the Paris stall on which, "in the year of grace 1906, 1908, or 1910" (*LE* 259), that is, at the outset of his European venture, P. found Divus' *Odyssey,* does not occur in the earlier *Poetry* draft, and may have been introduced as a reference to *The Ring and the Book* (Browning having picked up his Book from a Florentine stall). P. clearly attaches an arcane significance to the fateful encounter with the prototype of the *Cantos* as soon as he reaches Europe, and this is why he waxes poetic and vague about the "year of grace" in which it occurred, though a later note (265*n*) indicates that it was in fact 1910.

13. The second encounter of mother and son (*Od.* XI.152 ff.) is recounted at greater length in ur-canto 3 (*QPA* 31), and referred to again in c. 99, but in all versions Anticlea is harshly received at her first appearance (ll. 84–89) by P.'s Ulysses, and this suggests an

The sudden transition from the shadowy netherworld to the environs of the goddess indicates that the mythical method of the *Cantos* bears upon at least two further archetypes (besides Homer): the *Metamorphoses,* which are to be central in the next canto, and which account for the present shuffling of texts (Divus, Dartona) and characters (Ulysses, P.; Circe, Venus); and the *Divine Comedy,* already brought to mind by Pound's choice of a descent to hell for an opening: the *nékuia* conflates the two literary traditions in which he is most interested. At the source of the Greek and of the European renaissance there are two descents to the shades, Ulysses' (or Homer's) and Dante's; and in his first canto Pound (who also, like Ulysses, has but emerged from a great war) is thinking of nothing less than a Second (or Third) Coming. This accounts for the final fading of the *nostos* of Ulysses into Dante's ascent to the stars—to the paradise of light, eros, and art. (The Latin tags are taken from the description of the *birth* of Venus, as we learn from the earlier versions, and this is of course a symbol of artistic creation.) It also accounts for the crucial placing of the word "venerandam," which is made to refer both to Circe and to Venus, to the woman of earth and of heaven, and to define an attitude of reverence which is to be Pound's touchstone throughout the poem.[14] The quick shift from hell to purgatory ("spiteful Neptune," "lose all companions"), and thence to paradise, anticipates ideogramicly the structure of the *Cantos* (shortly reproduced in the sequence Sirens-Circe-Venus), without departing, be it noted, from the order of the magic source printed "in officina Wecheli," the *Hymns* following the *Odyssey.* In other words, Pound's metaphorical, critical, and poetical work is but a corollary to (or an extrapolation from) what is essentially a capsulated account of the sections of a cer-

---

oedipal disturbance. According to Victor Brenner Reed ("Towards the *Cantos* of Ezra Pound," Diss. Columbia 1964, p. 154), she is "banned because the counterforce to the harsh vacancy of P.'s Hades is sensual love and as mother she must be banned from participation in love's rites." In life P. appears to have been more at ease with his father ("the naïvest man who ever possessed good sense"—*Indiscretions, PD* 8) than with his mother. He was an only child.

14. Reed, "Towards the *Cantos* of Ezra Pound," p. 158.

tain book. The final conjunction and colon indicate that the long poem to follow is in fact encrypted in its first few pages, and that the traveller is quite confident of the outcome of his periplus of "100 or 120 cantos" (*L* 189: 1922).

Let us now return to the "four cantos" included in *Poems 1918–1921*, which antedate the final version of c. 1 by at least three years, and are thus the oldest part of the poem as we read it today, ur-cantos become, with relatively few changes—cantos. The breakthrough from the discursive form of the *Ur-Cantos* to the apocalyptic presentation of the definitive text is unmistakable in c. 4 (pub. Oct. 1919), which is a medley of Provençal, Classical, and Oriental scenes exhibited without comment (but with much decadent rhetoric); the following three cantos, however, return to the convention of subjective vision; that is, the author, in order to hold his disparate materials together, feels that he must tell us that he "sees" them. Canto 6, the only one of the four to have been revised drastically, is, in its early version, particularly unfortunate and significant, as Pound incorporates here for the first time lengthy documentary matter (obscurely concerned with the Provence of Richard Cœur de Lion)—a first indication that the *Cantos* are intended as a historical poem based on original documents. (In the final version this becomes apparent from the start, as Divus' *Odyssey* is the first of the countless documents considered in the poem.) This first confrontation with "history" is unsuccessful because the poet has not made up his mind whether he is going to let the document stand for what it has to say or whether he is going to write a belated historical romance in pentameter ("Richard to Tancred: / That our pact stands firm, / And, for these slanders, that I think you lie").[15] Thus in the 1924 *Draft of XVI Cantos* most of the historical matter is excised and a new finale, concerning Sordello, is added, with the result that c. 6 in its final version is one of the most satisfactory of the early cantos. This transitional sequence, wholly parallel to the contemporary three portraits, closes with c. 7, considered by Pound in 1920 his best work to date (see above). This is an uncomfortable

---

15. "The Sixth Canto," *Dial*, 71 (1921), 203.

description of the fallen world of *Mœurs Contemporaines* and *HSM,* studded with estranged literary quotations, and reminiscent in mood and technique of *The Waste Land,* still two years ahead.[16] It is constructed on two planes: a critique of representation from Homer to the present importing that the true poets of modern times are Flaubert, James, and Joyce, and consequently that Pound's attempt is out of tune, so much so that no new canto was to be written until 1922; and an account of the poet's disenchanted journey through a sinister metropolis: Paris, to which he returns after the seven war years, somewhat in the fashion of Spencer Brydon returning to New York in James's "The Jolly Corner":

> We also made ghostly visits, and the stair
> That knew us, found us again on the turn of it,
> Knocking at empty rooms, seeking for buried beauty;   [c. 7]

The beauty which he seeks (Eleanor of Aquitaine, the Ione of an earlier poem, the very possibility of a new poetry) is "buried," and the past to which he is sentimentally attached weighs him down:

> Dido choked up with sobs, for her Sicheus
> Lies heavy in my arms, dead weight
>   Drowning, with tears, new Eros,   [c. 7]

This is the self-critical man who wrote *Mauberley* and who, two years later, in a letter congratulating Eliot on *The Waste Land,* was to add self-deprecatingly: "I go into nacre and objets d'art."[17] Pound's obsession with the past is often the object of censure in the *Cantos,* a poem which advocates a ruthless doing away of all

16. *The Waste Land* was written in good part in 1921, at Margate and Lausanne. P. sent cs. 4–7 to the editors of the *Dial* on 24 March 1920 (letter pub. in Pearlman 301), but publication of 5–7 was delayed until August 1921. On the making of the early cantos see Nemi D'Agostino, "Sulle origini dei *Cantos,*" *Nuova Corrente,* 5–6 (1956), 92–104; Miles Slatin, "A History of Pound's Cantos I–XVI, 1915–1925," *American Literature,* 35 (1963), 183–95; John L. Foster, "Pound's Revisions of Cantos I–III," *Modern Philology,* 63 (1966), 236–45; Read, passim; and Ronald Bush, *The Genesis of Ezra Pound's* Cantos (Princeton: Princeton University Press, 1976).

17. *L* 181, dated (according to the new Poundian calendar, of which more below) "24 Saturnus, An 1," i.e., 24 January 1922 (not 24 Dec. 1921, as it is dated editorially in *L*).

that in the past is dead ("Pity spareth so many an evil thing"—c. 30) in order to preserve the vital part, yet seldom escapes the false alternatives of cruelty versus sentimentalism, in the light of a more mature and compassionate vision. In fact Pound's bewilderment is expressed in c. 7 only through opacity and atonality; on the surface the poet is already far too certain that he is different from the men-as-locusts of Gourmont (whose dubious estheticism is as important to c. 7 as to *HSM*)—that he is (as in c. 1) "the live man [in the] world of Dead" (*L* 222):

> The live man, out of lands and prisons,   *Desmond*
>   shakes the dry pods,   *Fitzgerald* [18]
> Probes for old wills and friendships, and the big locust-casques
> Bend to the tawdry table,
> Lift up their spoons to mouths, put forks in cutlets,
> And make sound like the sound of voices.   [c. 7]

In the "Cavalcanti" essay Pound would again contrast "the definite act of absorption," which becomes a favorite subject for painters "somewhere about 1527," with "the body of air clothed in the body of fire" of troubadour, Tuscan, and (we may add) Pre-Raphaelite vision. Just so in c. 7:

> Eleanor!
>   The scarlet curtain throws a less scarlet shadow;
> Lamplight at Buovilla, e quel remir,
>   And all that day
> Nicea moved before me
> And the cold grey air troubled her not
> For all her naked beauty, bit not the tropic skin,
> And the long slender feet lit on the curb's marge
> And her moving height went before me,
>   We alone having being.
> And all that day, another day:
>   Thin husks I had known as men,
> Dry casques of departed locusts
>   speaking a shell of speech . . .   [c. 7]

---

18. "One of the Hulme circle, afterwards a member of the Irish Free State Government" (Norman 114). The fact that the subject of the vignette is Fitzgerald does not, of course, lessen its personal bearing. In the American text the marginal note is excised.

The "thin husks I had known as men" stand between the poet and his eros, depicted rather clumsily in the descriptive lines (the Provençal lady looks rather like the courtesan in Flaubert's *Novembre*). More suggestive (and characteristically Poundian) are the previous allusions to blushing Atalant (precisely correlated by Ovid with the shadow thrown by a red curtain on a white wall) and to the nude woman (the wife—P. suggests—of William of Bouville) whom Arnaut Daniel contemplates (remir) against the lamplight ("contra·l lum de la lampa") in the canzone "Doutz brais e critz," where he also refers to a "mantle of indigo" under which the lady has hidden him.[19] These allusions are not erudite ornaments (à la Des Esseintes) of an erotic revery, or not only this; they point to details of the most salient in the Poundian universe: traces of the highest stylistic accomplishment (compare the role of James, "the great domed [punning, perhaps, on 'doomed'] head," in this canto), but also indications of something more hidden, namely the visionary tradition cryptically reconstructed in the *Cantos'* archeological romance.

To clarify this central motif of the poem it is necessary to review Pound's contacts with the geography and culture of Provence. These began with formal Romance studies from 1903 to 1907 and with travels on a fellowship through France and Spain in 1906. In Paris the young would-be poet came across *Le Secret des troubadours* by Joséphin Péladan (the author of grotesque pseudo-mystical novels on related subjects), where it was sug-

---

19. Atalanta's simile is quoted in "Notes on Elizabethan Classicists," *LE* 235–36; Arnaut's line in *SR* 34 and elsewhere. P. mistakenly understands the latter to mean "with the glamour of the lamplight about it (the body)," for he reads "remir" as a noun (cf. again "the body of air clothed in the body of fire"— *LE* 153). In the *vida* Arnaut is said to have made songs to the wife of Guillem de Bouvila. See Arnaut Daniel, *Canzoni,* ed. Gianluigi Toja (Firenze: Sansoni, 1960), p. 166.

P.'s uncanny awareness of "husks I had known as men" is illumined by one of the "Affirmations" of 1915: "You find a man one week young, interested, active, following your thought with his thought . . . And the next week (it is almost as sudden as that) he is senile. He is anchored to a dozen set phrases. He will deny a new thought about art. . . . You look sadly back over the gulf, as Ut Napishtim looked back at the shades of the dead, the live man [cf. Fitzgerald in c. 7] is no longer with you" (*GB* 108). The reference to the Gilgamesh Epic turns up again in c. 25. For Gourmont's "shells of thought" see *GB* 87.

gested that the mysteries of Eleusis had come down to the poets
of *trobar clus,* and that these belonged to "a mystic extra-church
philosophy or religion, practiced by the Albigenses, and the cause
of the Church's crusade against them"—as Pound reported in his
earliest book review.[20] After settling in London in 1908, he
toured Provence in 1912, and was to tell of what he had found
there in "Provincia Deserta" and in the Browningesque "Near
Périgord"—poems that are the necessary and immediate premise
of the *Ur-Cantos;* but the first yield of that tour was an essay of
the utmost relevance as a key to Pound's work, "Psychology and
Troubadours," published October 1912 and later included in
reprints of *The Spirit of Romance* (1910). Here Péladan's theory
is presented with the freshness that marks Pound's early writing:

> Consider the history of the time, the Albigensian Crusade, nominally
> against a sect tinged with Manichean heresy, and remember how Pro-
> vençal song is never wholly disjunct from pagan rites of May Day.
> Provence was less disturbed than the rest of Europe by invasion from
> the North in the darker ages; if paganism survived anywhere it would
> have been, unofficially, in the Langue d'Oc. That the spirit was, in
> Provence, Hellenic is seen readily enough by anyone who will compare
> the *Greek Anthology* with the work of the troubadours. They have, in
> some way, lost the names of the gods and remembered the names of
> lovers. Ovid and *The Eclogues* of Virgil would seem to have been their
> chief documents. [*P&T* 90]

This is Pound's rationale for insistently splicing Provençal stories
and Greek myth in cs. 4–7, much of the material being quarried
from *SR* and from "Troubadours—their Sorts and Conditions"
(1913), another product of the 1912 *Wanderung*. For example,
canto 4 may be diagrammed as follows:

    a. Fauns and nymphs revel in the dawn. (Cf. "the pagan rites
of May Day.")

    b. Guilhelm de Cabestanh's lover commits suicide after her
husband has given her the poet's heart for food; Philomel sets
before Tereus the flesh of their son Itys.

---

20. "Interesting French Publication," *Book News Monthly* (Philadelphia), Sept. 1906.
Quoted in Stock 31. Péladan's influence is also noted in Schneidau, *The Image and the
Real*, p. 120.

c. Actaeon surprises Diana as she bathes with her cohort of nymphs, is converted into a stag and destroyed by his dogs; Peire Vidal walks the woods playing the wolf (he loves Loba, the she-wolf) and muttering Ovid. (See above, and "Peire Vidal Old," *P* 30–32.)

d. The marriages of Vinia Aurunculeia and of Danae; Catholic Virgin-worship in Provence, and troubadour-Tuscan lady-worship.

Let us only look at the baroque finale of the canto:

> Vidal, or Ecbatan, upon the gilded tower in Ecbatan
> Lay the god's bride, lay ever, waiting the golden rain.
> By Garonne. "Saave!"
> The Garonne is thick like paint,
> Procession,—"Et sa'ave, sa'ave, sa'ave Regina!"—
> Moves like a worm, in the crowd.
> Adige, thin film of images,
> Across the Adige, by Stefano, Madonna in hortulo,
> As Cavalcanti had seen her.
>   The Centaur's heel plants in the earth loam.
> And we sit here . . .
>   there in the arena . . .   [c. 4]

The centaur, an image of poetry (cf. "The Serious Artist," *LE* 52), canters in fertile loam; in Greece, Provence, and Tuscany, religion and sexuality coalesce, the former taking the latter as its object:

The rise of Mariolatry, its pagan lineage, the romance of it, find modes of expression which verge over-easily into the speech and casuistry of Our Lady of Ciprus, as we may see in Arnaut, as we see so splendidly in Guido's "Una figura della donna mia." And there is the consummation of it all in Dante's glorification of Beatrice. [*P&T* 91–92]

Let us now spell out the allusions in Pound's lines. Vidal, the new Actaeon of episode *c*, enters once again not only on account of Pound's "fugal" technique but also as the author of the line, "Good Lady, I think I see God when I gaze on your delicate body." This, in *P&T* 96, is cited as an example of medieval refinement of sexuality, and contrasted with Aurunculeia's epithalamium (*d*), where "the bride is what she is in Morocco today, and the function is 'normal' and eugenic. It is the sacrificial concept." The same dissociation is to be found in c. 4, where Morocco is replaced by Ecbatan: here, on a gilded tower, that is within the last of the seven polychrome and concentric walls erected by Deioces (Hdt. 1.98), a Median Danae awaits Zeus' impregnating rain[21]—the symbol of immemorial light and fertility rites, which are continued after thousands of years on the banks of the Garonne, in forms scarcely less primitive (as suggested by the image of the procession edging worm-like its way through the crowd). Out of this torpidly sexual and ecstatic hinterland comes the transparence of Tuscan song and Renaissance painting, the *Madonna in the Rose Garden* by Stefano di Giovanni d'Arbois (better known as Stefano da Verona), worshipped "by Adige" (see c. 42)—in Verona. By referring to Stefano's enclosed rose garden as "hortulo" Pound telescopes Mary, Aurunculeia (whom Catullus—also a Veronese—likens to a "flos hyacinthinus in vario hortulo"—LXI.91–92), and Cavalcanti's lady, an image of whom is said—in the very sonnet spoken of in the *P&T* paragraph quoted above—to be adored ("s'adora"—c. 20) in Florence's San Michele in Orto, today Orsanmichele. In the three instances woman is associated with vegetal renewal. The passage amounts no doubt to a collection of objets d'art, yet it is brought to life by an impassioned imaginative coherence, which will occasionally have a single word—here "hortulo"—cover a dizzying cultural span. In the close the maker detaches himself from his work and falls in with the audience on the tiers of the Arena (Verona's, as intimated by context), one spectator among others of the foregoing apocalyptic series of images-events. And the elliptical lines sound a poignant and purely musical chord often to be heard in the sequel.

21. P. may be thinking of Mandane, daughter of Astyages, the king of Media, and mother of Cyrus, the founder of the Persian empire (Hdt. 1.107–08). Astyages forbade Mandane's marriage to any Mede, and later sought to kill Cyrus, having been warned that he would become king in his place. Likewise Acrisius, being told that the son of Danae his daughter would kill him, detained her in a chamber (where she was visited by Zeus), and later committed her and Perseus to the waves. Cf. Pearlman 56.

If Adige is a metonymy for Verona and Italy, Garonne is Pound's shorthand for Provence and Toulouse, a city that Cavalcanti visited in the course of his pilgrimage (apparently never completed) to Santiago de Compostela (ca. 1292):

> . . . "I remember in Toulouse
> I saw a woman in tightly knit bodice,
> whom Love called Mandetta . . ."
>
> Go to Toulouse, my little ballad,
> and quietly enter the Daurade:
> and there call out, that by courtesy
> of some fair woman, you may be brought
> to her I have told you of . . .[22]

In 1910 Pound remarked that "Mandetta of Toulouse is an incident,"[23] yet he was intrigued enough by these lines to seek out, in the course of his 1912 tour, "the ruined 'Dorata' " ("Provincia Deserta," *P* 122), alias Notre-Dame-la-Daurade, built in the fifth century on the site of a temple dedicated to Minerva, and at present a baroque edifice. In 1919, when he first returned to the Continent after the War, Pound made his way again to Toulouse, and was stimulated by the new contact with Provence to rework his concerns of 1912 into cantos 4–7, completed shortly after his return to London. By this time he had come to suspect that "the young lady of Toulouse" (cf. "Sonnet xii," *T* 48–49) was something more esoteric than a casual affair, that the girl (like the daughter of Otreus in c. 23) concealed a "golden" goddess. Ten years later, Luigi Valli's suggestion that Mandetta (like Guido's and Dante's other ladies) is a lodge of "love's faithful" with which Cavalcanti came in contact during his journey, must not

---

22. Guido Cavalcanti, "Era in pensar d'amor quand'i' trovai." In P.'s upholstered translation of 1912 the first three lines are transmogrified as follows:

"Maid o' the wood," I said, "my memories render
Tolosa and the dusk and these things blended:
A lady in a corded bodice, slender
—Mandetta is the name Love's spirits lend her—   [*T* 113]

23. Introd. (dated 15 November 1910) to *Sonnets and Ballate of Guido Cavalcanti*, *T* 22.

have come as a surprise.[24] (P., however, was wary—as the "Ca-valcanti" essay shows—of Valli's allegorizing, there being to his mind no contradiction between the manifest and the latent con-tent, i.e. between eros and the mysteries, in troubadour and Tus-can poetry.) In the 1919 version of c. 4 it is suggested that the Daurade is to Toulouse what the gilded tower is to Ecbatan;[25] Guido is also encrypted in the scene of Diana's bathing (c) by way of his perception, "E fa di clarità l'aer tremare,"[26] which is the all but obliterated leitmotiv of the passage:

> Bathing the body of nymphs, of nymphs, and Diana,
> Nymphs, white-gathered about her, and the air, air,
> Shaking, air alight with the goddess,
>   fanning their hair in the dark.   [c. 4]

This allusion to Guido may amount to a suggestion that in the Daurades and woods of Provence the poet encountered the

24. See Luigi Valli, *Il linguaggio segreto di Dante e dei "Fedeli d'amore"* (Roma: Biblio-teca di Filosofia e Scienza, 1928), p. 218.

25. The earlier version is distinctly "softer," closer to the language and moods of the *Ur-Cantos,* than the 1924 text. And the "Madonna in hortulo" is, interestingly enough, an afterthought. I quote from the *Dial,* 88 (1920), 692; the ellipses are P.'s, the italics mine:
> Vidal tracked out with dogs . . for glamour of Loba;
> Upon *the gilded tower* in Ecbatan
>   Lay the god's bride, lay ever
> Waiting the golden rain.
>   Et saave!
> But to-day, Garonne is thick like paint, *beyond Dorada,*
> The worm of the Procession bores in the soup of the crowd,
> The blue thin voices against the crash of the crowd
>   Et "Salve regina."
> In trellises
>   Wound over with small flowers, beyond Adige
> In the but half-used room, thin film of images,
>   (by Stefano)
> Age of unbodied gods, the vitreous fragile images
> Thin as the locust's wing
> Haunting the mind . . as of Guido . . .
> Thin as the locust's wing. The Centaur's heel
> Plants in the earth-loam.

26. "Sonnet VII," *T* 38–39. The usually accepted reading is, "e fa tremar di chiaritate l'àre."

goddess or a vision, as was again to happen to Pound in 1912 and 1919. In fact there was always an air of legend and mystery connected with the customary pilgrimage to Santiago and to the Atlantic.

After Toulouse the way lay through the Pyrenees, where, in 1244, the last Albigenses defended the citadel of Montségur to the end; following the Garonne upstream the pilgrims came to the village of St-Bertrand-des-Comminges, with its cathedral and dramatic cloister, on a hill overlooking the remains of the old Roman capital, Lugdunum of the Convenae. Here, fifty years after the sack of Montségur, Guido may well have met survivors of the massacre. In 1919 Pound inspected these sites, and soon he began to incorporate allusions to the Montségur "vortex" into the *Cantos,* intimating that the same track had been beaten by his medieval fellow poets. Whatever we may think of this fantasy, it is certain that those roads had seen more recent travellers, for the supposedly erotic and mystical "secret of the troubadours" could hardly escape the occultists of the late nineteenth century, who are Pound's true contemporaries, though the allusive and metaphorical fashion in which the archeological fiction of the *Cantos* is constructed keeps its implausibility and fin de siècle connotations in the background. Likewise the poet's eccentric but impassioned acquaintance with Occitanic and Stilnovo texts leaves little room for the lurid reveries of his fellow worshippers, like Péladan, whose novel *La Vertu suprême* (1900)—the last of the "éthopée" *La décadence latine*—closes with its hero, who is none but Péladan, journeying

to the Abbey of Montségur, which is dedicated to the cult of the Rosicrucians—a copy of Monsalvat with aesthetic refinements, Flemish tapestries, Renaissance seats . . . but the Grand Cross of the Great Rose is made of artificial rubies, and in its centre, to hold the Host, is a chemical diamond. A Holy Grail of pinchbeck—in fact, an epitome of the whole of Péladan's pathetic "éthopée." Images of various divinities adorn the pilasters around the altar: "l'Oannès de Kaldée, le Dieu mitré à la queue de poisson, l'Ammon Ra du Nil, la Mayâ de l'Inde et l'Athéné grecque . . . une décoration panthéonique des religions." Parsifalism is mixed up with Legitimism: the Rosicrucians cultivate the dream of "the last of the Bourbons." Inside the temple the organ gives forth the notes of *Parsifal*.[27]

This description could well apply to the pantheon and the ideology of the *Cantos,* but for Wagner, who on the other hand must have influenced, directly or not, Pound's leitmotiv technique. However, it must be noted that in rehearsing the poem's "plot" we have committed an indiscretion, bringing to light themes that in the author's intentions have a subliminal function; furthermore Pound's esoteric inclinations are always checked by his more conspicuous pragmatism, and are accordingly to be distinguished from the fantastical constructs of "initiates" such as Yeats and Péladan:

I believe in a sort of permenent basis in humanity, that is to say, I believe that Greek myth arose when someone having passed through delightful psychic experience tried to communicate it to others and found it necessary to screen himself from persecution. Speaking aesthetically, the myths are explications of mood: you may stop there, or you may probe deeper. Certain it is that these myths are only intelligible in a vivid and glittering sense to those people to whom they occur. I know, I mean, one man who understands Persephone and Demeter, and one who understands the Laurel, and another who has, I should say, met Artemis. These things are for them *real*. [*P&T* 92]

Let us now see how the Albigensian theme is articulated in the poem. Canto 5 collects the following material:

a. Again Ecbatan and Aurunculeia in a Neoplatonic context, centered around the words "Et omniformis," already quoted in ur-c. 3.

b. An imitation of Sappho's fragment 98 Diehl, in which the poet speaks to her friend Atthis of a common girl friend who has left Lesbos for Lydia.

c. The troubadour Gaubertz de Poicibot, after escaping from his monastery "per volontat de femna," is knighted and provided with a revenue by the patron Savaric de Malleon. He marries the

27. Mario Praz, *The Romantic Agony,* tr. Angus Davidson (London and New York: Oxford Univ. Press, 1970), pp. 340–41.

woman he loves, leaves her to go to Spain, and on the way back seeks out a prostitute only to discover that this is his wife, whom in the meantime an English knight has seduced "with slow-lifting eyelids"[28] and abandoned.

   d. A Provençal Paris, the singer Peire de Maensac, elopes with the wife of Bernart de Tierci. The latter seeks to retrieve his Helen by force, besieging Peire's hold, to no avail. This story Pound had already told in "Provincia Deserta."

   e. The assassination of Giovanni Borgia and of Alessandro de' Medici, and Renaissance "decadence."

   In Poicibot's story Pound stresses the theme of patronage, as at about this time he was much concerned with financial schemes in favor of artists such as Eliot and Joyce. But also the encounter with the prostitute/wife appears to carry a recondite significance:

> "Came lust of woman upon him,"
> Poicebot, now on North road from Spain
> (Sea-change, a grey in the water)
>   And in small house by town's edge
> Found a woman, changed and familiar face;
> Hard night, and parting at morning.   [c. 5]

Poicibot is on the road of St-Bertrand and Montségur when he undergoes the epiphany suggested by the parenthetic flash of sea water, the element of Venus. The decadents were fond of remembering that in certain pagan cults (e.g., the worship of Adonis at Biblos, and of Venus at Corinth) young women were prostituted to strangers. It is not clear how Pound can reconcile the essential eroticism of his "mysteries" with the chastity demanded of the Cathars, yet as early as 1912 he spoke of "a cult stricter, or more subtle, than that of the celibate ascetics, a cult for the purgation of the soul by a *refinement* of, and lordship over, the senses" (*P&T* 90, my italics).

28. An allusion to the eyes of Venus, who is said to be *élikobléphare* in the 2nd Homeric Hymn dedicated to her, but "nigras habens palpebras" in the "Cretan" 's mistranslation followed in c. 1 ("thou with dark eyelids"). By interpolating this detail into the *vida* (which makes no mention of the knight's eyes) P. suggests that he is aware of the Cretan's inaccuracy. The discrepancy in c. 1 (but not the scolium in c. 5) has been remarked by John Peck, in "Pound's Lexical Mythography: King's Journey and Queen's Eye," *Paideuma*, 1 (1972), 17–18.

This reading is corroborated by canto 23, the structure of which indicates that it is intended as a companion piece to c. 5. It starts with the quotation, (a) "Et omniformis omnis intellectus est," attached to the Renaissance Neoplatonist Gemistus Plethon and to the otherwise "omniform" Pierre Curie, and continues with the following sections:

b. A parsing of the fragment in which Stesichorus describes the nightly voyage of the sun in his golden boat, with allusions to Ulysses, whom Pound identifies with the sun. (Cf. Sappho in c. 5.)

c. A beautiful erotic scene involving "Fa Han and I," where the speaker telescopes Pound, Ulysses, the Sun, Paolo Malatesta (of *Inf.* 5), Ugo Aldobrandino (lover of his stepmother Parisina), and Gaubertz de Poicibot, who goes back to his wife as the Sun to his own (the latter being an inference of ours based on the parallelism with c. 5).

d. An extended version of the tale of Paris-Peire de Maensac, as told by his landed brother, with the following apochryphal appendage:

> And he went down past Chaise Dieu,
> And went after it all to Mount Segur,
>   after the end of all things,
> And they hadn't left even the stair,
> And Simone was dead by that time,
> And they called us the Manicheans
> Wotever the hellsarse that is.
>
> And that was when Troy was down, all right,
>   superbo Iliòn . . .   [c. 23]

Peire[29] journeys through Chaise Dieu and south to Montségur after the death of the "crusader" Simon de Montfort (1218) and

---

29. According to Pearlman 106 the subject is not Peire but the cuckold Tierci, but this does not seem to fit P.'s (admittedly confusing) syntax nor his intention. Pearlman's reading, however, is indirectly corroborated by Mary de Rachewiltz's translation of this canto: E. P., *I Cantos* [I–xxx] (Milano: Lerici-Scheiwiller, 1961), p. 235. This may be the place to mention that this is the best text of cs. 1–30 available at present (1977), and that De Rachewiltz's translations (which often incorporate the documents P. has used) are invaluable for an understanding of P.'s intentions.

the fall of the citadel (1244). Thus the parallel with Troy, a little strained though it is in connection with Peire and Tierci (who, unlike Menelaus, does not win back his unfaithful wife), acquires a significance more extensive, accurate, and tragic. Troy was destroyed because it upheld the rights of Venus, and the same fate was to be visited on Montségur and Provençal culture at the hands of the uncouth barons of the north.

The last section of c. 23 departs from the parallelism obtaining so far to enlarge upon the theme of the mysteries. Pound brings home the junction of Venus and "superbo Iliòn" (*Inf.* I. 75—haughtiness is one of the goddess's attributes) by recalling the rites of Adonis and a less tragic (in fact quite Boccaccesque) escapade of the goddess: her seduction, under an assumed name, of Anchises, as told in the first Homeric Hymn in her praise. Out of their union will come "that rightful son of Anchises" (*Inf.* I. 74) whose offspring is to found a new Troy, Rome, which in later cantos is identified with love, *amor*.

If we compare these glosses with the poem they refer to we perceive not a few contradictions: Pound's subtly allegorical (rather than symbolic) scheme is executed with a good deal of clumsiness (for instance in the lines last quoted); his quest for an expression both clear and concise results in cryptic traces oblivious of the requisites of communication, or of the fact (as P. once put it) that "the importance of the matter will never outweigh the difficulties or the value of living men's time" ("Cavalcanti," *LE* 176). This is not to say that Pound can be charged with intentional obfuscation: his calligraphy is of a primitive kind, the immensely elaborate construct of a naïf, a provincial inventor. A curious proof are certain corrections he made with the purpose of clarifying his writing.[30] Primitivism and decadence are

---

30. In his valuable 1934 essay R. P. Blackmur ("Masks of Ezra Pound," Sullivan 168–69) complained that no one could be expected to recognize Venus and Anchises in the close of c. 23: "King Otreus, of Phrygia, / That king is my father" (this is in fact the fib Venus tells her lover in the Homeric Hymn, and probably the rationale for P.'s reticence). P. had probably his critic in mind when he corrected the 1954 London text to read: "And she said: 'Otreus, of Phrygia, / *That king is my father* . . .' / and I saw then, as of waves taking form . . ."—no doubt an improvement, as it avoids repeating "king," while the italics suggest the epiphanic quality of the goddess' words. (This correction, like others, is

in fact the headings under which his work is situated, like contemporary art in general, though Pound's is an extreme and strangely fascinating case.

We may now return to our chronicle of the early cantos. Canto 7, it will be remembered, closes with the announcement of the time of the assassins: while deferring to James, "eternal watcher of things," somewhat awkwardly travestied as Alessandro de' Medici (see c. 5e), Pound sympathizes largely with his murderer Lorenzino, who is none but the poet and stands for vitality and action, which are to Pound valuable for their own sakes: he is "more full of flames and voices." That Pound produced much sound and fury between 1910 and 1960 can hardly be denied.

In early 1920, however, while giving the final touches to cs. 5–7 and drafting 2 *HSM,* Pound was suffering a crisis testified to by these works and by a letter Eliot wrote John Quinn on 25 January:

The fact is that there is now no organ of any importance in which he can express himself, and he is becoming forgotten. It is not enough for him simply to publish a volume of verse once a year—or no matter how often—for it will simply not be reviewed and will be killed by silence. . . . As I consider that Pound and Lewis are the only writers in London whose work is worth pushing, this worries me. I know that Pound's lack of tact has done him great harm. But I am worried as to what is to become of him.[31]

A reviewer of *Quia Pauper Amavi* (which includes *Langue d'Oc-Mœurs Contemporaines,* the rather beautiful ur-cantos 1–3, and *Propertius*) had announced a fortnight earlier in the *Observer*

unfortunately ignored in the New York text, at present the only one available.) The same applies to the "Mount Rokku" of c. 4: one infers from *L* 189 that Felix E. Schelling, P.'s teacher at Pennsylvania, thought the phrase "on Rokku" (of the *Dial* and *Poems 1918–21* text) ambiguous.

Today these complaints of the poem's early readers appear rather groundless, as P.'s text is not meant to be grasped at sight, but to give up its secret in the course of a lengthy perusal.

31. T. S. Eliot, *The Waste Land: A Facsimile and Transcript of the Original Drafts Including the Annotations of Ezra Pound,* ed. Valerie Eliot (New York: Harcourt Brace, 1971), p. xix.

that "In himself Mr Pound is not, never has been, and, almost I might hazard, never will be a poet" (Stock 287). It was not long before Pound answered to the point: "His case presents no adjunct / To the Muses' diadem." It may have been at this time that present cantos 14–15, Pound's excremental hell for the English, were drafted.

Through the good offices of Quinn Pound was appointed correspondent of the *Dial,* and this (Eliot wrote Quinn on 10 May) "had a great effect in raising his spirits." [32] The *Dial* was to publish between 1920 and 1923 the early versions of cs. 4–8, and the twelve *Paris Letters,* which deserve to be reprinted. Disenchanted with England and doubtful of the value of his work, Pound returned to Venice and Sirmione, where he wrote (as a serial for the *New Age*) the estranged account of his infancy, *Indiscretions.* In spring 1921, after a brief return to England and a stay on the French Riviera, he moved to Paris, where at first he occupied himself with music, sculpture, and with a translation of Rémy de Gourmont's *Physique de l'amour, essai sur l'instinct sexuel.* In a "Postscript" to the latter he followed up certain remarks thrown out in *P&T* by enouncing the fantastical and somewhat chauvinist view of sexuality which we find in the *Cantos,* particularly in those of the twenties. The Postscript is dated 21 June 1921, close upon Midsummer Day—probably no coincidence as at this time Pound's mind was sensibly veering toward the occult. A few months later he announced that on 30 October 1921, his thirty-sixth birthday and the day on which *Ulysses* was completed, a new pagan era had commenced, and to this he alludes explicitly in his 1922 reports on *Ulysses:* "L'année du centenaire de Flaubert, première d'une ère nouvelle." [33] This we

32. Ibid.

33. "James Joyce et Pécuchet," Read 201. See also "Ulysses," *LE* 408. The Calendar of the new era, offered anonymously in the *Little Review,* VIII, 2 (Spring 1922), 2 and 40, and noted in Read 192*n*, is partly a joke, partly an integrated scheme of the mythical universe of the *Cantos.* Thus it is worth quoting at length:

"The Christian era came definitely to an END at midnight of the 29–30 of October (1921) old style.

There followed the Feast of ZAGREUS, and a Feast of PAN counted as of no era; the new year thus beginning as on the 1st November (old style), now HEPHAISTOS."

would take as unoffensive metaphor if we did not know that
Pound always, whether in poetry or in prose, wants to be understood literally.

These speculations were encouraged when, sometime around
New Year's Day, 1922, Eliot appeared in Paris with the *Ur-
Waste Land,* on which Pound went to work in a somewhat editio-
rial capacity, and with much excitement. This was accompanied
by a personal breakthrough, which, after a two-year stalemate,
resulted in the writing of an "eighth canto," soon to be relocated,
in a slightly revised form, as c. 2—manifesto of the new era and
celebration of its god, Dionysus. By rehearsing (*a*) the grudging
admiration of Troy's old men for the beauty of Helen, (*b*) the
marine intercourse of Neptune and Tyro (a new borrowing from
the *nékuia,* where Tyro's story is told), and (*c*) Dionysus' epiphany to the pirates who wanted to sell him into bondage—
Pound tells us in three ways that the godhead cannot be fettered
by the world, that it triumphs over all obstacles, and goes on to
announce the establishment of his own libertarian reign:

> And Lyaeus: "From now, Acœtes, my altars,
> Fearing no bondage,
>   Fearing no cat of the wood,
> Safe with my lynxes,
>   feeding grapes to my leopards,
> Olibanum is my incense,
>   the vines grow in my homage."   [c. 2]

The new months, replacing the old months: of cold months HEPHAISTOS (for November), and then in the following order ZEUS, SATURN, HERMES, MARS, PHOEBUS APOLLO; and
the warm months: KUPRIS, JUNO, ATHENE, HESTIA, ARTEMIS and DEMETER, the male months
being also under ISIS, and the female months two by two, under PAN, POSEIDON and
BACCHUS.

The following feasts are instituted: to ZAGREUS on the 30th Demeter; to PAN on the 31st
Demeter; Feast of Figures on the 14th Hermes; Feast of Political Buncomb, ancient feast
of fools or feast of the ass; Mort de Caesar, Jules, 15th Mars; PRIAPUS, 1st Kupris;
EPITHALAMIUM, ancient Corpus Domini, 15th Juno; FAUNUS, 6th Artemis; AUSTER and
APELIOTA, 14th Artemis.

The year turns upon HORUS."

In the diagram drawn by P. (p. 2) the year is conceived as the dial of a clock and the
months follow one another clockwise, winter beginning at 9 (Feast of Zagreus and Pan),
and summer at 3.

Thus in the *Cantos* Pound seeks to reverse the march of events decried in *HSM* ("Christ follows Dionysus"): the god of leopards regains the throne usurped by Christ. This program has little novelty (one need only think of Nietzsche and of his scarcely profound decadent followers), but for the pre-cultural immediacy and vigor with which Pound picks up the old standard. The involvement, however, is kept out of sight by the detached quality of his writing at this time: little prevents us from taking c. 2 as a very fine erudite variation on mythic themes, which the poet considers as coolly as Ovid. As with Homer, Divus, and "The Seafarer" in c. 1, we are chiefly aware of a process of layering: the principal inspiration is Ovid, yet he is also but one link in a textual chain reaching back to the Homeric Hymn to Dionysus (a logical follow-up to the quotations from the Hymn to Venus in c. 1) and forward to Ovid's translator Golding, whose *Metamorphosis,* "the most beautiful book in the language" (*ABR* 127), Pound has particularly in mind—for what is he after but the utmost beauty? In fact c. 2 is a great advance on cs. 4–7, bringing into the poem a new clarity, which one is tempted to call French. Yet we must correct the statement about beauty, since E.P., unlike Mauberley, is after something more, nothing less than the new (pan-esthetic) era, and this will make the *Cantos* both formidable and tragic.

So it happened that the discouragement of 1919–20 gave way to enthusiasm and to a sense of omnipotence: Pound conceived his own image *sub specie aeterni,* believed himself a reincarnation of Dionysus (30 October, according to the new calendar, is the Feast of Zagreus), and appropriated the god's feline totems—leopards, lynxes, and cats. This theophany is anticipated by a group of poems published in 1918, which includes "Glamour and Indigo" (a version of Arnaut's "Doutz brais e critz," the source of "remir"), the unfortunate but significant "Phanopoeia" ("The swirl of light follows me through the square"—phanopoeia, according to a letter to Joyce [Read 102] was P.'s aim in the *Ur-Cantos*), and "Cantus Planus," which in 1926 Pound was to use, disregarding chronological sequence, as an envoi to *Personae,* his collected shorter poems:

The black panther lies under his rose tree
And the fawns come to sniff at his sides:

Evoe, Evoe, Evoe Baccho, O
ZAGREUS, *Zagreus*, Zagreus,

The black panther lies under his rose tree.

// Hesper adest. Hesper // adest
Hesper // adest. //   [P 231]

By way of Catullus' (and Sappho's) address to the evening star, Zagreus (as Dionysus was called at Eleusis) is identified with Hymenaeus; the word, at the close of the first plentiful "day" of Pound's poetry, is resolved into music, anticipating the nuptials to follow (and the tri-syllabic meter of the *Cantos:* "Aňd thě fáwns cŏme tŏ sníff ăt hĭs sídes").

In c. 5 (where Catullus' poem is quoted again) there is a further reference both Dionysiac and authobiographical: "Fracastor had Zeus for midwife, / Lightning served as his tweezers."[34] In a letter of 1916 Pound rehearsed his early life as follows:

Biographical or otherwise: Born in Hailey, Idaho. First connection with vorticist movement during the blizzard of '87 when I came East, having decided that the position of Hailey was not sufficiently central for my activities—came East behind the first rotary snow plough, the inventor of which vortex saved me from death by croup by feeding me with lumps of sugar saturated with kerosene. (Parallels in the life of Fracastorius.) [L 84]

On the authority of c. 5, it would seem that Pound sees a connection between his rescue from death during the blizzard and Fracastor's delivering through the lightning of the "midwife" Zeus. But these are motifs of the myth of Dionysus, whose mother Semele was "shot to atoms" (c. 92) by the lightning of Zeus, who saved the infant god by sowing him into his own thigh—hence Dionysus' epithet "binatus" (*dígonos* in c. 74).

The theme is clarified by the final arrangement of cs. 1 and 2:

34. London text of 1954. The original reading, preserved in the American editions and preferred in the authorized Italian text (see footnote 29), is, "Fracastor (lightning was midwife)."

on the one hand Ulysses, the poet as man; on the other Dionysus, the poet as god. The two are again contrasted in the first lines of the second sequence of cantos, which links up with the elliptic finale of c. 1 and goes on to the "divine or permanent world" (*L* 222):

> So that the vines burst from my fingers
> And the bees weighted with pollen
> Move heavily in the vine-shoots:
>   chirr—chirr—chir-rikk—a purring sound,
> And the birds sleepily in the branches.
>   ZAGREUS! IO ZAGREUS!   [c. 17]

The Greek cry *ió* is also the Italian "I." "God am I for a time," was Pound-Propertius' comment on his nights with Cynthia. The exclamation signals the Panic moment in which man is at one with the cosmos; it is the cry of orgasm:

> By prong have I entered these hills:
> That the grass grow from my body,
> That I hear the roots speaking together,
> The air is new on my leaf,
> The forked boughs shake with the wind.   [c. 47]

It is worth remarking that in c. 17 birds and bees produce, in their drunken stupor, the "purring sound" of the creatures dearest to the god. Later in the same canto we find "Zagreus, feeding his panthers." And in the middle cantos:

> When I lay in the ingle of Circe
> I heard a song of that kind.
>   Fat panther lay by me
> Girls talked there of fucking, beasts talked there of eating,
> All heavy with sleep, fucked girls and fat leopards,
> Lions loggy with Circe's tisane,
> Girls leery with Circe's tisane   [c. 39]

These are all variations of a single scene constructed ideogramicly by the addition of new brushstrokes every time it recurs. In the lines last quoted, primitivistic (or rather harshly British—à la Wyndham Lewis) as they are, there is a novel foreboding of danger: everything about Circe induces sleep, yet Ulysses (we recall) will stay alert.

Before letting rest for the time being this figure in the carpet of the *Cantos* let us watch Ezra Pound bearing up in all humbleness to his divine calling for the benefit of W. B. Yeats:

Sometimes about ten o'clock at night I accompany him to a street where there are hotels upon one side, upon the other palm-trees and the sea, and there, taking out of his pocket bones and pieces of meat, he begins to call the cats. He knows all their histories—the brindled cat looked like a skeleton until he began to feed it; that fat gray cat is an hotel proprietor's favourite, it never begs from the guests' tables and it turns cats that do not belong to the hotel out of the garden; this black cat and that grey cat over there fought on the roof of a four-storied house some weeks ago, fell off, a whirling ball of claws and fur, and now avoid each other.[35]

At Rapallo, where he made his home in 1924 (but he had discovered the place at the latest in 1921), Pound imagined he was safe with his lynxes. Yet his Dionysiac fate was not to be accomplished until September 1943, when he fled northwards from Rome before the advancing Allied armies, a satchel (*zaino*) on his back, the ruins of his world about him:

> the man out of Naxos past Fara Sabina
> "if you will stay for the night"
> "it is true there is only one room for the lot of us"
> "money is nothing"
> "no, there is nothing to pay for that bread"
>   "nor for the minestra"   [*soup*]
> "Nothing left here but women"
>   "Have lugged it this far, will keep it" (lo zaino)
>   No, they will do nothing to you.
> "Who *says* he is an American"
>   a still form on the branda, Bologna [*folding bed*]
> "Grüss Gott," "Der Herr!" "Tatile ist gekommen!"   [c. 78]

This is the "Provincia Deserta" of Pound's last and most dramatic walking tour, as it flashes in the mind of the D.T.C. pris-

---

35. W. B. Yeats, *A Packet for Ezra Pound* (written 1928, pub. 1929), in *A Vision* (London: Macmillan, 1969), pp. 5–6; quoted in Norman 297–98.

oner, who also is (or was) "the man out of Naxos."[36] As in the older poem, a deep sympathy, nearly an oceanic feeling, unites him to the people that aid him. At Pisa he will finally be reunited with his feline love: "O lynx, my love, my lovely lynx" (c. 79).

After the breakthrough of the Dionysian canto Pound made rapid progress on his poem. During July 1922 he drafted five cantos on different topics, the first of which, concerned with Sigismondo Malatesta, was to occupy the poet (who inspected the sites of the condottiere's feats and searched Italian libraries for documents) until April 1923, expanding in the process into the present four Malatesta cantos, perhaps Pound's most complex persona, and the model of the subsequent historical-poetical ventures of the *Cantos*. At bottom Malatesta is but a blown-up Lorenzaccio, unscrupulous yet full of flames and voices—of the din of battle, the majesty of art, and the beauty of Isotta degli Atti—all of which (the latter having precedence) he celebrates with a curious monument, the Tempio Malatestiano, whose aborted grandeur is to Pound an apt correlative of the *Cantos*. In fact it is not difficult to see the bearing on the poem of the following description, by Paolo Portoghesi, of the interior of the Tempio:

The unifying subject of this complicated exhibition is the pathetic story of the provincial squire who dreams of conquering, through his military prowess, unlimited glory and power, and considers religion, rite, and the language of art, so many means of self-deception and evasion by which to build around himself a fictitious world of symbols and to deform everyday reality so that it may conform with an individualistic "heroic ideal."[37]

Pound's narrative is not strictly chronological but moves backwards and forwards, from one scene to another, seeking to

36. In the *Metamorphoses* and in c. 2 Bacchus is taken aboard the pirate ship at Scios and asks to be brought to Naxos: "Illa mihi domus est, vobis erit hospita tellus" (iii.67). See also *Oro e lavoro* (1944): "On the 10th of September last, I walked down the Via Salaria and into the Republic of Utopia, a quiet country eighty years east of Fara Sabina" (*SPr* 336). In the last line P. reaches his destination and is greeted by the Tirol family with which his 18-year-old daughter Mary was staying. See M. de Rachewiltz 184–90.

37. Paolo Portoghesi, *Il Tempio Malatestiano*, Forma e Colore 26 (Firenze: Sadea-Sansoni, 1965), [p. ii].

suggest the flurry and the *virtù* of the man of action. At the same
time it aims at formal autonomy, structuring a small and tense
intertextual ideogramic complex, disseminated with references
(thematic phrases, allusions to the matter of Provence and of Ferrara, parallel episodes) to other parts of the poem. For instance,
c. 8 is articulated as follows:

   a. A letter in which Sigismondo promises work and leisure to
a "maestro dipintore" (1449).

   b. A contract for military services stipulated between Sigismondo and Florence (1452).

   c. A poem by Sigismondo.

   d. A picturesque description of the triumphal reception given
in Rimini to Francesco Sforza and Bianca Visconti (1442).

   e. Gemistus Plethon in Italy for the Council of Florence
(1438–39). He speaks of Poseidon and Plato (cf. the Neopla-
tonists of c. 5).

   f. Sigismondo at war. This anecdote will be echoed as late as
c. 53.

   g. The confused alliances of the time, in spite of which Sigismondo "templum aedificavit" (as remarked by Pius II in his
Commentarii). The latter tag is to become a correlative of one of
the chief themes of the *Cantos,* the building of the poem-temple.

   h. Digression: William of Poitiers (c. 6), the origins of the
Malatesta as mentioned in Dante, the similar destiny ("for this
tribe paid always") of Paolo il Bello and Parisina Malatesta, the
subject of later cantos.

   i. An epic rehearsal of the commencement of Sigismondo's
dramatic career.

   In this largely documentary context Pound inserts glimpses of
the landscape of Romagna, the fruit of what (in a February 1923
letter to John Quinn) he called "geographical verification, cross
country in wake of S. M. to see how the land lay"[38]—and interludes of pure revery, also concerned (as customary in P.) with
geography. These inserts suggest the emotion aroused in the poet-

---

38. Quoted in Pearlman 303. Cf. Benedetto Varchi, who, "wanting the facts," seeks out
Lorenzino (c. 5).

historian by the events he records, as well as their recondite significance:

> And the wind is still for a little
> And the dusk rolled
> to one side a little
> And he was twelve at the time, Sigismundo,
>
> And that year he crossed by night over Foglia, and . . . [c. 8]

The incisive diction (e.g., note the sequence of dentals in the first lines) and the accomplishment of the phrasing are signatures of Pound, and not a little fascinating. For instance, the central enjambement carries a powerful suggestion of the dusk suddenly clearing and allowing us to *see*. The canto is cut short on an upbeat, and so ushers us into the wholly diverse (trochaic) measure of the first lines of c. 9:

> One year floods rose,
> One year they fought in the snows,
> One year hail fell, breaking the trees and walls.
> Down here in the marsh they trapped him
> in one year,   [c. 9]

The robust marching cadence of the first line (one, two, one, two) is elaborated in the second (which interpolates three unaccented syllables), reproduced in the third, which adds a new segment parallel in part to the previous line (*fóught ĭn thĕ snóws, bréaking thĕ trées*) and attached to it by the final assonance, and is finally abandoned in the fourth line, quite unexpectedly as this seems to open with the same metre and middle rhyme. The fifth line picks up the opening words in an entirely different key: we enter the changing world of chronicle and anecdote, in which pronounced rhythms and rhymes (rose, snows, walls) would be out of place.

In such a way Pound gives new life to antiquarian matter, and inserts it in an epic frame which preserves in part its historicalness. His intention to do so he announces at the outset of the enterprise:

These fragments you have shelved (shored).
"Slut!" "Bitch!" Truth and Calliope
Slanging each other sous les lauriers:
That Alessandro was negroid. And Malatesta
Sigismund:
                Frater tamquam
        Et compater carissime: tergo
                        . . . *hanni de*
                        . . *dicis*
                        . . . *entia*
        Equivalent to:
                        Giovanni of the Medici,
                        Florence.   [c. 8]

In *The Waste Land,* and in part in c. 7, the transmitted fragments are the residue of an irreversible enthropic process ("These
fragments I have shored against my ruin"). Now however Pound
is going to take them (as he does with Sigismondo's letter) as a
point of departure in order to reconstruct a viable image of the
past, unhampered by the superannuated conflict between history
and the epic, as here by Truth's protest that the Alessandro de'
Medici invoked in the previous close was negroid, hence scarcely
comparable to Henry James, who was "biondo" (c. 7). Henceforth Pound is to defer to the authority of the text, in the presence of which the quarrel between Truth and Calliope is revealed
to be nothing but a vulgar brawl. Having completed the *Malatesta* Pound will cite the same authority to put an end to his
seven-year-old discussion with Browning (which also takes place
"sous les lauriers" of poetry) by showing up its slovenliness:

Hang it all, Robert Browning,
        there can be but the one "Sordello."
But Sordello, and my Sordello?
Lo Sordels si fo di Mantovana.
So-shu churned in the sea.
Seal sports in the spray-whited circles of cliff-wash,   [c. 2]

Browning's endless psychologizing is cut short by a peremptory
reality, the text as history: the Sordello of the *Cantos* will live as
writing (the true protagonist— *my* Sordello—of the poem), as a

fragment not to be done away with, yet juxtaposable with other such fragments in which Sordello may bear the name of So-shu,[39] and Mantova change places with the sea, churned by the poet so as to condense the fluid of experience into the solid stuff of poetry. (All the images of this canto take form in the ebbing waves of the sea; they include the presiding gods of the *Cantos,* Dionysus and Aphrodite.) Truth has no more reason to complain, as Sordello and So-shu, though vaguely homonymous, are clearly distinct; they are, however, contiguous in the text, as are Provence, Tuscany, Greece (within a few lines we find Homer listening to the sea), and China in the entire poem and as early as c. 4—ideogramic segments of the mysteries of sea, light, and sex.

By the time he wrote these lines (ca. summer 1923) Pound had in fact produced a *Sordello* of his own, the *Malatesta,* furthering (as he believed) Browning's "impersonal" strategies. In the latter portrait there is likewise a secret tension, an ideogramic image of the mysteries. The man of war who erects a TEMPLE (the small caps. are P.'s, see c. 9) to his lady, and has Gemistus buried there, aims at a pagan renaissance; his conflict with "that monstrous swollen swelling s.o.b. Papa Pio Secundo" (P.'s alliterations scarcely blind us to the fact that this was the humanist Piccolomini, another builder of cities and temples) becomes fully significant only if we think of the Cathari of Montségur. With a storyteller's instinct Pound delays the account of Malatesta's victory over the papal army (1461) to the last of the four cantos. Within a few years Sigismondo is in turn defeated, and dies (1468) leaving the temple half-done, but the people celebrate him as a patron of fertility, and Pound tells us, by way of one of the key lines of the poem, that this was a deliverer, a golden glimmer in the dark:

> And the castelan of Montefiore wrote down,
> "You'd better keep him out of the district.

39. This may be, ironically, the Taoist Chuang-tzu, who is called So-shu in "Ancient Wisdom, Rather Cosmic" (*P* 118: 1915). In *J/M* 100, however, we hear that "So Shu, king of Soku, built roads"—and in "Affirmations" Li Po is quoted to the effect that "Yoyu and Shojo stirred up decayed (enervated) waters" (*New Age,* 28 January 1915; *SPr* 376). In sum, So-shu appears to be a composite image of the poet-renovator-king, an oriental kinsman to Sordello and Homer.

"When he got back here from Sparta, the people
"Lit fires, and turned out yelling: 'PANDOLFO!' "

In the gloom, the gold gathers the light against it.   [c. 11]

Yet it is clear from these lines that Pound does not overindulge
his esoteric bent, or swerve from a vigorous and unselfconscious
narrative which leaves us with the impression of a fresh and un-
dogmatic mind, fully in control of its means of expression. Thus
he is careful not to close the sequence (as he could) upon the
finely alliterating gold, but goes on to show Sigismondo in a
playful mood and to quote the Latin source for this anecdote—a
highly meaningful return to the textual authority invoked at the
outset.

Pound's intense involvement with the *Malatesta* brought about
a confirmation and clarification of his epic intent. It was only
after he had dispatched the sequence that he quarried from the
Ur-Cantos the present cs. 1 and 3, and substituted his new
address to Browning for the first fourteen lines of the "eighth
canto," relocating it as c. 2. By 1924 he had published the close
to definitive (the title notwithstanding) *Draft of XVI Cantos for
the Beginning of a Poem of Some Length,* which can be divided
as follows: 1–3 (main themes); 4–7 (*langue d'oc*); 8–11 (Malatesta). Of the following, 12–13 form a jarring diptych: on the
one hand several mediocre vignettes of adventurers and usurers;
on the other a quiet mask of Confucius, who enjoins a rather liberal and hedonistic ethic, is concerned for the welfare of artists,
and commends the historical method of the *Cantos:*

"And even I can remember
"A day when the historians left blanks in their writings,
"I mean for things they didn't know,
"But that time seems to be passing."   [c. 13]

How much Western man has to learn from the East is imported
by the subsequent descent (14–15) into a Christian (and, as
noted, English) hell, from which Pound ascends to a Pre-Raphaelite purgatory (16), where he hears an account of the War and

remembers friends who "went to it." This final triptych brings out the contemporary import of the *nékuia* of c. 1, of which it offers a threefold parody, in turn grotesque (the inferno), elegiac (purgatory), and tragicomic (war). The hell section, a brilliant appropriation (or "criticism in new composition"—"Date Line," *LE* 75) of the aspects of Dante less savoury to modern readers, is the most compelling, while the purgatory canto lapses at points into bathos ("And Augustine, gazing toward the invisible") and essentially rounds out the section on an intentionally unlyrical chord.

The *Malatesta* also sets the scene both for the XVI *Cantos* of 1924 and for cs. 17–30, which are structurally more closely integrated than the previous group, yet poetically more uneven. (The two groups were brought together in *A Draft of XXX Cantos,* 1930.) This scene is the Quattrocento, which Pound takes as a model for his new era, despite the fact that the ground had already been covered by such Victorians and decadents as Browning, Swinburne, Ruskin, and Pater. In 1915 he had remarked of the Renaissance that "no student, however imperfect his equipment, can ever quite rest until he has made his own analysis, or written out his own book or essay" (*GB* 111)—and this is borne out by the XXX *Cantos,* which are in fact Pound's *Studies in the History of the Renaissance,* or his *Italienische Reise* (a title which could be extended to the sum of the *Cantos,* though of course these have little of Goethe's suavity and attention to significant detail.)

That Pound shares the image of the Quattrocento entertained by the decadents is shown by his choice of themes, of which the most important is also mentioned in the 1915 article: "Never was the life of arts so obviously and conspicuously intermingled with the life of power." The first Malatesta fragment brought to our attention is (we recall) the letter concerning the "maestro dipintore," which is about enough to justify Pound's loyalty to the ambiguous condottiere. After all, Pound—like Joyce and Eliot—made in his best years only a precarious living. Another form that the great theme takes is the emergence of Venice (cs. 17, 25, 29), a case of near symbiosis of artist and ruler. Likewise in c. 27 we hear of cathedral building in the Middle Ages, and this is favorably contrasted with the labours of a "Tovarisch" who can "wreck the house of the tyrants" but cannot build—an ideogram which suggests that Pound's feeling for the people who built the cathedral does not go very deep, and is quite consistent with his abhorrence of the mob, like the irrational and mystical feeling which is the customary façade of fascism.

The builder of the temple is also the lover of Isotta: the other recurring decimal of Pound's Quattrocento is sensual love. The story of Ugo and his stepmother Parisina, familiar to readers of Byron and D'Annunzio, is alluded to throughout the section, after having been introduced with much drama in c. 8h. It forms the background of c. 20, the subject of which (P. tells us in L 222) is the (fictional) delirium of Parisina's husband, Niccolò d'Este III, after the execution of the adulterous couple—a curious relapse into historical romance, though this bit of psychologizing is so estranged that it is far from clear where Niccolò's stream of consciousness ends and Pound's customary presentation follows. The arras associated with the lovers as early as c. 8 suggests their presence in c. 23c, although their names are not mentioned, and indeed c. 24 opens with a letter of Parisina and provides the most extended treatment of the episode,[40] besides following Niccolò on his trip to the Holy Land. Unlike Bernart de Tierci in the previous canto, Niccolò is a positive symbol of princely prowess, and (as his voyage suggests) a type of Ulysses.

Other stories of passion (Inés de Castro and Peter the Cruel, Cunizza da Romano and Sordello) turn up several times in the course of the sequence, c. 29 being an extended meditation, uneven but highly representative, on this theme. It includes scenes from the early Renaissance (Cunizza, Pernella), the Middle Ages (Arnaut), and modern times; and introduces a new allegorical figure, Lusty Juventus, a persona of Pound. The curious allegorizing of cs. 17–30, reminiscent of courtly poetry (Pity being personified in c. 30), is abandoned in subsequent sections, though on the whole the poem is allegorical in character.

---

40. P.'s chief source (as noted in I Cantos [i–xxx], p. 321) is Alfonso Lazzari, "Ugo e Parisina nella realtà storica," Rassegna Nazionale, Anno 37, Vol. 201 (1 Feb. and 16 Feb. 1915), 261–71, 389–400; Vol. 202 (1–16 March and 1 April 1915), 75–91, 240–53.

In sum there is nothing novel about Pound's interpretation of the Renaissance, but for his descriptive and poetic strategies— which are indeed of contemporary interest. He aims at presenting a complex image of the period, not as history, but as news of events *in fieri,* occurring at the same time, patterned and yet irreducible. These events are not arranged in chronological sequence but in spatial configurations, outlining "the numerous vortices of the Italian cities" ("The Renaissance," *LE* 220). The Rimini of the Malatesta, the Florence of the Medici, the Ferrara of the Este, and above all Venice, are the loci from which we receive the dispatches of the poem, and these are strongly flavored by locality, and construct as it were circles of geographic experience which by intersecting structure the poem and hold it together. Instead of the "absolute" chronology of handbooks we find a movable time geared to separate points in space towards which and from which people and events come and go (which is approximately P.'s definition of "vortex"—see *GB* 92). This conception is barely hinted at in cs. 1–16, yet we find there many glimpses of the poet-reader reclining "on the Dogana's steps," in Venice (c. 3), and on the "quarante-trois rangées en calcaire" of Verona's Arena (4, 12, 21, 29), as he follows a drama which has been in progress over "forty four thousand years" (11)—an astrological number (mysteriously recalling the forty-three tiers of Verona) which is probably to be understood with reference to the Era of Zagreus. A spatial reading is also called for by the fragment "Lo Sordels si fo de Mantovana," and by the quotation from Dante ushering us into the inferno of c. 14: "Io venni in luogo d'ogni luce muto"—I came to a place devoid of all light. This recalls the personal opening of c. 3, "I sat on the Dogana's steps," and suggests an analogy between Venice—the City—and hell, to be developed in c. 17 (the description of a locus—Venice—where the light is "not of the sun"), and in c. 26, which opens again with an "Io venni":

> And
> I came here in my young youth
>   and lay under the crocodile
> By the columns, looking East on the Friday,
> And I said: Tomorrow I will lie on the South side

And the day after, south west.
And at night they sang in the gondolas
And in the barche with lanthorns;   [*boats*]
The prows rose silver on silver
    taking light in the darkness. "Relaxetur!"

   .   .   .

And hither came Selvo, doge,
    that first mosaic'd San Marco

   .   .   .

And that year ('38) they came here
Jan. 2. The Marquis of Ferrara
    mainly to see the Greek emperor,   [c. 26]

Thus space becomes the controlling fact of cs. 17–30. It is an
ambiguous presence which, having elicited the carefree esthetic
response registered in the opening lines (in which, however, the
possible allusion to the last days of the Holy Week brings to
mind another descent to hell), threatens to destroy, in Circean
fashion, the visitor. This is put quite clearly in the first canto of
the sequence, an intentionally hypnotic account of a voyage from
a countryside peopled with Renaissance gods to the anti-nature
of Venice (the attempt on Borso is first recorded in c. 10):

Thither Borso, when they shot the barbed arrow at him,
And Carmagnola, between the two columns,
Sigismundo, after that wreck in Dalmatia.
    Sunset like the grasshopper flying.   [c. 17]

From the vantage point of his "green clear and blue clear" Italian
sea Pound reconsiders the perils of his city dwelling, which (like
his friend Joyce) he is apt to exaggerate. Still, Circe's threat is as
fascinating to him as to other decadents, as these dreamy lines (in
which the heroes are quite overshadowed by the city, by place)
suggest. The evil of the civitas is brought out more stridently by
the shady traffics of cs. 18–19, and by the maggot world of c. 28.
But Pound's thumbnail sketches of contemporary estrangement
seldom rise above shallow caricature, whereas the mythic reveries
of cs. 20, 21, 23, 25, and 29, carefully juxtaposed with Renaissance documents (they are—P. stresses—Greek originals seen
through Quattrocento—and Novecento!—eyes), are born of a

genuine admixture of fascination and repulsion, reminiscent (let us say) of *The Waste Land*. The lotus eaters of c. 20 (again an allegorical image), followers of Des Esseintes given to murmuring medieval poetry ("My young bridegroom has put me into the fire of love"), renouncing all for the sake of "beauty," could well have dreamed up these stuporous visions, the work of Pound at his most esthetic. (In mingling eroticisim and medieval "mysticism" he follows two epigones, Péladan and Gourmont—see *P&T* 97–100.) Yet these passages also imply a critical and detached attitude, as is the case (for example) in Baudelaire, or—again—in dramatic poetry.

As these remarks suggest, besides being the subject of the poem, space accounts for its structure, its figurative form. In an essay on W. C. Williams written at about this time (1928) Pound disclaimed any interest in major form, that is in the structuring of necessary elements, and suggested a preference for the relatively formless constructs of Montaigne and Rabelais:

Art very possibly *ought* to be the supreme achievement, the "accomplished"; but there is the other satisfactory effect, that of a man hurling himself at an indomitable chaos, and yanking and hauling as much of it as possible into some sort of order (or beauty), aware of it both as chaos and as potential. ["Dr Williams' Position," *LE* 396]

This sounds like an ex post facto rationalization of the method of the *Cantos,* a poem in which the problem of making "order (or beauty)" out of flux is ever present, yet (despite several guiding principles) can only receive ad hoc solutions. Any other method would imply imposing an a priori form on the material and ipso facto abandoning all claims to exact portrayal, reality being in fact in Pound's view an "indomitable chaos" which assumes the aspect of order only in flashes of epiphany. The structure which we discern in the poem only signifies the consistency of Pound's instinct or "ear"—of his attitude to the givens of experience. The success of the xxx Cantos largely rests in their touching upon and getting into "some sort of order" or of poetic suspension all the elements of the poet's world, and thus bringing into the picture no little part of the European tradition.

Yet at this very time Pound provided Yeats with two explicit
indications of method: on the one hand the well-known analogy
with the fugue, which bears both on the grand themes of the
work, such as *nékuia* and metamorphosis, which recur and are
variously combined throughout the poem, and on such leitmotifs
as the arena and the arras; on the other hand the comparison of
the *Cantos* with the pictorial cycle of Schifanoia, at Ferrara, in
which every month is allotted a vertical panel in three compartments: above, the triumph of a god; in the center, the appropriate sign of the Zodiac; below, the seasonal activities of Duke
Borso, who is also (we recall) a character of some importance in
the poem.[41] Like the *Cantos,* Cosmè Tura's and Francesco
Cossa's Hall of the Months combines space and time, circular or
seasonal recurrence and ascent from the quotidian to the divine,
Ulysses' periplus and Dante's linear rise to the stars. But above all
it is worth noticing that the ideogramic juxtaposition of blocks of
cantos, single cantos, and sections of cantos, is in fact pictorial in
nature: Pound thinks of his work as a series of panels placed side
by side in a figurative Hall of Months. The narrative forma
mentis is wholly alien to this poet: the *Cantos* are that curious
thing, a very long poem in which nothing "happens"—or rather
everything is happening in so "indomitable" a fashion that ante-
cedents and consequences cannot be established. This explains
why the poem consistently withholds (to the distress of some
readers) information essential to the understanding of its subjects
(a good example is the story of Poicibot). It is not customary for
a painter to provide semantic and iconographic information on
his work—the job of the viewer and of the critic, who is not
always in the position to give a definitive answer. (Actually, it is
not unusual for P., especially in the early sections of the poem, to
aid the reader by providing in the margin a title for his vignettes—as with the Desmond Fitzgerald of c. 7.)[42] In sum, the

---

41. See Yeats, *A Packet for Ezra Pound,* pp. 4–5 (quoted in Sullivan 99–101).

42. Most of these marginalia have been omitted in subsequent printings, yet P. never for-
sook the method. In the typescript of *PC* at Columbia, the lines, "So Miscio sat in the
dark . . . ," and "Roi je ne suis, prince je ne daigne," both in c. 77, are glossed with the
names "Ito" and "degli Uberti," P. adding in his own hand, "Italic in margin." Likewise
in the 1954 London text the reference "hagoromo" is given opposite a line of c. 36,

Cantos demand a previous acquaintanceship with their iconography, that is to say a reader equipped with enough curiosity and time to identify the subjects treated, largely by reference to Pound's further works, and to the criticism and memoirs that have accrued to the corpus. (In a 1929 letter, quoted in Read 244, P. advises that "my one volume of prose is no more a series of . . . vols than my cantos are a series of lyrics . . . the components need the other components in one piece with them.") Nothing prevents us from appreciating a single compartment or detail of Pound's fresco, and the loss of entire panels or sections (as at Schifanoia) would not modify to any great extent our understanding and appreciation of the whole, though it would still be a loss: there is no part of the *Cantos* which we would gladly do without, and to consider the sum with the mind's eye is to undergo an uncommon architectonic and scenographic experience.

Benedetto Croce ridiculed on one occasion Mallarmé's contention that great poetry should not be vulgarized in cheap editions but protected by "the golden clasps of old missals" or by "rolls of papyrus with their inviolate hieroglyphs."[43] Yet it is true that Pound's scenographic writing can scarcely be appreciated in the clumsy editions available at present. The "sacred book" of the *Cantos* (which—like other sacred books—consists of sections dreary in the extreme and of breathtaking lines) should be read in a "de looks edtn . . . of UNRIVALLED magnificence" (*L* 195), on the model of the 1924 and 1928 *Drafts*. It is no coincidence that the subject of Renaissance printing runs the span of the XXX *Cantos*, from the "officina Wecheli" (c. 1) to Gerolamo Soncino with his "cutters of letters / and printers not vile and vulgar" (c. 30)—the same "vulgarity" against which Mallarmé directed his protest. At the very end of the great venture Pound was to look back, from the distance of thirty years, to "la faillite de François Bernouard," the "maître imprimeur" of the first edition of *A Draft of* XXX *Cantos*.

"Being divided, divided from all falsity"—another afterthought, omitted from American editions.

43. Benedetto Croce, *Letture di poeti e riflessioni sulla teoria e la critica della poesia* (1950; rpt. Bari: Laterza, 1966), p. 152.

2. "Absolute" Timeliness

The Case of the Middle Cantos

The middle cantos are an allegory of good government as Pound understands it, the celebration of an ideal ruler bearing many faces and of the serene customs of his flock. Concurrently, they seek to establish the nature of "the crime" which cuts off modern man from this utopia of which history apparently offers not a few examples. In a poem which "begins 'In the Dark Forest,' crosses the Purgatory of human error, and ends in the light, and among the 'maestri di color che sanno,' "[1] this is clearly the purgatorial section, and shares with Dante's second canticle a certain quiet serenity: Pound attempts to overcome haste (*la fretta,* censured in *Purg.* 3), however painful the process of slow cleansing, the *maestro dipintore*'s search for a definitive portrayal of error.

His allegory is composed with robust simplicity, falling into four compartments nearly equal in size (the first of eleven cantos, the three following of ten). These depict, left to right, the memorabilia of Jefferson (31–41), of Siena and Leopold I of Tuscany (42–51), of China's emperors (52–61), and of John Adams (62–71). The two outer compartments are parallel on account of their American subjects, while the two middle ones refer us back from the eighteenth-century foreground of the entire section to a timeless, ritualistic, and communal hinterland. However, more evident than these large-scale correspondences of theme is the close formal relationship obtaining on the one hand between the first and the second compartments, which are constructed with the combinatorial or fugal technique of the XXX *Cantos,* and on the other hand between the third and fourth, which were written and published together, and are—unlike previous cantos—solely concerned with their chosen themes, China and Adams.

So within the static and circular fresco of the middle cantos a clear line of formal progress may also be traced, along which

1. E. P., *Introduzione alla natura economica degli Stati Uniti* (1944), *SPr* 167. See *Inf.* IV.131.

themes are developed, positive and negative standards defined, and Pound's definitive ideological stance determined. As we have seen, the story thus told is meant to retrace Dante's ascent to heaven, yet to the reader it rather looks like a tale of regression leading to a forest considerably darker than the esthetic Hades of the xxx *Cantos:* the unconditional surrender to the Circe of fascism consummated in canto 52 (1939) and in the Italian coda to Pound's intended purgatory, cantos 72–73 (1944), chiefly a celebration of the nazi and fascist final days of terror in North Italy.[2] In other words the poem does not vindicate Pound's program, its journey leading from the *phantastikon* of the early sections to a desolate and occasionally repulsive mental landscape, the setting of the sorrowful and very human ebb and tide of ecstasy and terror of later cantos. It can hardly be disputed that during the thirties Pound's mind became increasingly obsessed, and that his language—poetic and otherwise—disintegrated to an unprecedented degree; yet his uneven powers of poetic vision and expression were not impaired but rather increased, to climax in the Pisan sequence, which is an outstanding intellectual, poetic, and human document.

The *Cantos,* therefore, are not a *commedia,* but the tragedy of a mind generous yet exacerbated, ready to underwrite half-truths and superficial formulas in order to satisfy its vanity and prejudice. The enquiry conducted in the poem, far from being dispassionate, is governed by gross preconceptions, and by a persecution complex which seeks to expose and destroy the enemy by means of the arrogance and hatred peddled (in Yeats's phrase) in the thoroughfares. Pound, under the delusion that he had been hunted out of the United States in 1908, and out of England in 1921, fabricated with materials of an often inferior kind a theory

2. P. sent cs. 72–73 to Fernando Mezzasoma (Minister of Popular Culture of the Salò Republic, executed at Dongo, 28 April 1945) on 13 November 1944, with the interesting comment, "I do not know whether the enclosed Cantos are useful in any way. No doubt they are too crude for the refined and too complex for the simpleminded." Quoted in C. David Heymann, *Ezra Pound: The Last Rower: A Political Profile* (New York: Viking, 1976), p. 335. The two cantos appeared in the periodical *Marina Repubblicana* for 15 January and 1 February 1945, but have so far been discretely omitted from collected editions of the poem.

of history that would avenge the insult he had suffered, and did
not hesitate to embrace fascist Anglo- and Franco-phobia, and in
the end nazi anti-Semitism. It was in fact the break with England,
his second home, which provided him with the subject of the
Cantos he had been vainly seeking. The new Ulysses had identified his Suitors.

In summer 1919 the London weekly the *New Age,* edited by
A. R. Orage, began to serialize C. H. Douglas' *Economic Democracy,* which Pound judged to be an accurate diagnosis of—and
therapy for—the intimate and collective discontent he had become aware of in the aftermath of the War. Douglas sought to
prove with his "A+B Theorem" that "the power to purchase can
never / (under the present system) catch up with / prices at large"
(c. 38), and suggested that this state of affairs, which could only
deteriorate with time, was due to the banking system. Individuals
(he maintained) should not pay "rent" for the credit which is
their social asset to exploiters who have illegally cornered it;
rather, the State should allot credit where and when needed
through "national dividends," and fix the prices (to avoid infla-
tion), while letting free enterprise do the rest. Pound responded
to Douglas' "protest against the wastage of human beings"
("Economic Democracy," *SPr* 211): had not the best minds of *his*
generation been hampered with hack work in order to make
good the unfortunate gap between purchasing power and prices?
He was also satisfied, as a conservative, that Douglas did not ad-
vocate any social change, and (as a pragmatist, a lover of shortcuts) that the solution of the world's problems was as simple as
emitting dividends and exposing profiteers: not the capitalists
(who may have been free entrepreneurs, like his grandfather
Thaddeus Coleman Pound), but the socially and racially differentiated type of the Jewish banker. Marx's economic interpretation
of history was to Pound an exciting discovery, even if under the
travesty of Social Credit, yet his contact with Douglas and his
anti-democratic background discouraged all serious investigation
of the problems involved, and directed his attention wholly to the
question of money, and thence to racist myth. His response was
immediate: before the end of 1919 he drafted, in 1 *HSM,* his first

major attack on the age and on its supposed gray eminence,
"usury age-old and age-thick."

The subsequent most critical years brought about the decision
that the *Cantos* would address the "particulars of the crime," investigating the cause of Ulysses' and Pound's exile from home,
and of modern man's expulsion from the earthly paradise which
is his birthright. The pirates who capture Dionysus in c. 2 are
"mad for a little slave money"; like Alberich they sin against the
godhead and (as becomes apparent in c. 12) forsake love for
gold. But the true starting point of the poem's economic work is
the final version of c. 3, the materials of which are quarried from
the *Ur-Cantos* yet given a wholly new meaning by juxtaposition
and a few additions. Having been introduced to Ulysses and
Dionysus in cs. 1–2, we now meet two more heroes in exile,
together with a vision of paradise lost, and a murdered heroine.
In ur-canto 1 Pound had playfully compared the Venice he came
to in 1908 with the city in which Browning had "mused" his *Sordello* "upon a ruined palace step," his attention straying to attractive local girls: [3]

> . . . Your palace step?
> My stone seat was the Dogana's vulgarest curb,
> And there were not "those girls," there was one flare,
> One face, 'twas all I ever saw, but it was real . . .
> And I can no more say what shape it was . . .
> But she was young, too young.   [*QPA* 21]

"Vulgarest," a Jamesian qualification added in the *QPA* text,
does not make this sentimental attitudinizing any less mawkish.
Pound seeks again to clear himself in the final version, only to fall
(as often in the early cantos) into mechanic parataxis—a self-
conscious anti-romanticism ill at ease with its esthetical contents:

> I sat on the Dogana's steps
> For the gondolas cost too much, that year,
> And there were not "those girls," there was one face,
> And the Bucintoro twenty yards off, howling "Stretti,"

3. Robert Browning, *Sordello* III.676 ff. Quoted in John Peck, "Pound's Idylls, with
Chapters on Catullus, Landor, and Browning," Diss. Stanford, 1973, pp. 142–43.

And the lit cross-beams, that year, in the Morosini,
And peacocks in Koré's house, or there may have been.   [c. 3]

The words of a popular song ("Close, close together, in the ecstasy of love"),[4] referred to again in c. 27, suggest that the scene
is set early in the century, and appear to comment sardonically
on the young poet's love of "one face," which turns out to
belong to D'Annunzio's Core.[5] But the most relevant addition is
the reference to the gondolas, too dear for the purchasing power
of Pound's $80 capital (c. 80), a part of which he will wisely in-
vest in the printing of A Lume Spento. Lack of funds and erotic
deprivation appear thus for the first time in subliminal conjunction.

This is the place to review the poet's social background. The
Pounds were Americans of long standing. Ezra's paternal grandfather was an affluent lumber merchant and a member of
Congress; his mother, Isabel Weston, was a descendant of the
patriot Joseph Wadsworth (cs. 74, 97, 109, 111), hence distantly
related to Longfellow. Yet the family fortunes had been waning,
and we know from Pound's biographers that as a boy he was
painfully aware that some of his friends were better off. Eventually he came to believe, like other members of his class, that his

4. "Known to Italians as 'La Spagnuola' this celebrated warble was known to the ignorant foreigner not by the title on the printed MUSIC, but by the more intelligible refrain, as
sung:

　　　Strr/ètti/Strééé . . . TI
　　　nel ezstasai' damn or
　　　Ya spaniolar sa 'mar così
　　　wookah! wuukaaah, la nott Edi!"

Letter to Carlo Izzo, 19 October 1935, from Rome. Quoted in Carlo Izzo, "23 lettere e 9
cartoline inedite," Nuova Corrente, 5–6 (1956), 128. The song's text reads: "Stretti,
stretti, nell'estasi d'amor. La spagnola sa amar così, bocca a bocca la notte e il dì."

5. "In Koré's house there are now only white peacocks. I see only the great stone base,
and the trees of the hidden garden, and a strip of luminous water." Quoted by P. in his fa-
vorable review of Il notturno (1921), in the "Paris Letter" for October 1922, Dial, 73
(1922), 553. It is interesting to note that P.'s expectably high estimate of the "poet hero"
(see for example "Cavalcanti," LE 192) was shared, less expectably, by James Joyce and
Henry James, who borrowed from Il Fuoco (1900) respectively the concept and term
"epiphany," and the symbol of the golden bowl. See Giorgio Melchiori, "Cups of Gold for
the Sacred Fount: Aspects of James's Symbolism," Critical Quarterly, 7 (1965), 313 and 316.

impoverishment (the consequence of competitive capitalism) was due to the waves of immigrants, who could be seen thriving in their "vulgarity," and perverting the pristine American stock. Hence his contemptuous attitude to minorities, particularly to Jews. "Race prejudice," he once remarked, "is . . . the tool of the man defeated intellectually, and of the cheap politician" (K 44). He was not aware that he had diagnosed his own affliction, and these words of 1937 were soon to be forgotten. Considered in this perspective, the casual allusion to poverty in c. 3 (after all, young poets are supposed to be poor), acquires its true and ominous significance.

The following lines depict a lost paradise, clearly distinct from the ambiguous Venetian Hades (see chapter 1): "Tuscan" (or Pre-Raphaelite) gods sit upon clouds overlooking Garda, and in the waters of the lake are to be seen nymphs with "the upturned nipple" (again the motif of eros).[6] Thereupon the image of Pound at Venice fades into a picture of the Cid at Burgos, where the great hero learns from a little girl that he has been proscribed. He has left the seat of his ancestors in disrepair:

> And he came down from Bivar, Myo Cid,
> With no hawks left there on their perches,
> And no clothes there in the presses,
> And left his trunk with Raquel and Vidas,
> That big box of sand, with the pawn-brokers,
> To get pay for his menie;
> Breaking his way to Valencia.   [c. 3]

If Bivar is America, and Burgos Venice, then Valencia is the city of the future whereto the exiled poet is directed, the site of his victory, which is also a return: Ithaca. More compelling versions of the Cid's story are to be found in SR, and in one of Pound's earliest published articles, "Burgos, a Dream City of Old Castile" (1906; quoted in Norman 16); later it became a part of ur-canto

6. The source seems to be Catullus (LXIV.16–18), associated with Garda because of his villa at Sirmione. In the canto P. gives the remark to the humanist Poggio Bracciolini because, as usual, he wants to *date* the vision. He probably has in mind his imaginary conversation "Aux Etuves de Wiesbaden, A.D. 1451," in which Poggio speaks to a gentleman, and its source. See Kenner 143.

2. The present version follows the ur-canto closely, but for a second highly meaningful interpolation, the story of the Cid's treacherous treatment (cf. Ulysses' reputation for mischief) of the usurers Raquel and Vidas, fooled into accepting as pawn a sumptuous "box of sand" (two boxes in the original and in *SR* 68). Like the pirates of c. 2, Raquel and Vidas are the obstacles which the divine poetic intelligence must overcome, they are the immigrants who beset the Anglo-Saxon race, impoverishing the poet and expelling him from his land.

In the last lines of this crucial, if poetically uneven, canto, economic malpractice is again associated with the repression of sex—and of art (cf. Douglas' "protest against the wastage of human beings"). Persephone reenters as Inés de Castro, who (according to Camões' tale, also recounted in *SR*) was killed by jealous courtiers and exhumed when her lover, Peter the Cruel, became king, that the peers may do her homage, thus "becoming a queen after dying":

> Ignez da Castro murdered, and a wall
> Here stripped, here made to stand.
> Drear waste, the pigment flakes from the stone,
> Or plaster flakes, Mantegna painted the wall.
> Silk tatters, "Nec Spe Nec Metu."   [c. 3]

Ideogramic parallelism calls for a comparison of these lines with the final tableau of canto 1. There Venus is born against a background of Cyprian temples, here she is destroyed in the shade of a ruined Renaissance mansion, Mantova's Gonzaga palace with its bridal chamber frescoed by Mantegna—a macabre allusion to Inés' marriage of death. Pound's lady, however, is not really dead, but a sleeping beauty he trusts he will awaken after vanquishing enemies and murderers with the shrewdness and unscrupulousness of Ulysses and Ruy Diaz. Elsewhere in the desolate ducal halls he finds, among tatters of silk to be reassembled subsequently, a Nietzschean motto for his enterprise: "Nec Spe Nec Metu."[7]

7. Originally placed in the ceiling of Isabella d'Este's "Grotta" at Mantova, the panel containing the motto was moved to another room (where P. must have seen it) after the 1630 sack of Mantua. See Peck, "Pound's Idylls," p. 330.

In the fifties Pound was to tell an interviewer that "there is a turning point in the poem toward the middle; up to that point it is a sort of detective story, and one is looking for the CRIME."[8] Actually by c. 3 we have both crime and corpse, and what is left to be discovered in mid-journey is the criminal, *Mauberley's* usury. Pound's bill of indictment is read twice, in cantos 45 and 51, which may be taken as two versions, pictorially redundant, of one theme. Both return with notable felicity of structure to the setting and motifs of c. 3:

> *With usura*
>
> With usura hath no man a house of good stone
> each block cut smooth and well fitting
> that design might cover their face,   [c. 45]

"No man" is *Oûtis,* the name Ulysses gave as his own to the Cyclops, as well as Pound and the Cid—heroes who have been expelled from their houses (even as Pound takes architecture to decay with industrialism), and from their erotic paradise:

> with usura
> hath no man a painted paradise on his church wall
> *harpes et luz*
> or where virgin receiveth message
> and halo projects from incision,   [c. 45]

We are familiar with Pound's notion that the worship of Mary is a continuation of the ritual of Our Lady of Cyprus, indeed it may be taken as a development both communal and arcane, for it introduces the new "mystery" of virginal conception, of which Pound is particularly fond. The references to sculpture, architecture, light, sex, and music (the "harps and lutes" of Mother Villon's "painted paradise"), amount to a description of the medieval cosmos, which Pound contemplates with the vigor of an Eric Gill (both poet and sculptor are in the line of the more energetic among the Pre-Raphaelites), and more generally, to an "ideogram" of the integration of art, sex, and religion, cham-

8. D. G. Bridson, "An Interview with Ezra Pound," *New Directions in Prose and Poetry,* 17 (1961), 172.

pioned in the *Cantos*. We now learn that Mantua's fresco (like Schifanoia of c. 24) has been allowed to decay because not readily marketable (Kenner 314–15):

> with usura
> seeth no man Gonzaga his heirs and his concubines
> no picture is made to endure nor to live with
> but it is made to sell and sell quickly
> with usura, sin against nature,
> is thy bread ever more of stale rags
> is thy bread dry as paper,
> with no mountain wheat, no strong flour
> with usura the line grows thick
> with usura is no clear demarcation
> and no man can find site for his dwelling.   [c. 45]

Pound's chief concern is always for art, his summum bonum: "age-thick" usury (1 *HSM* 4) debauches the painter's line, erases the trace (cf. "The house too thick, the paintings / a shade too oiled" of c. 7). And yet these lines also touch upon the more general alienation of man under capitalism, who sees his productions, his food, his love objects, all equally reduced to commodities. And we note the ambiguity of the Gonzaga line: it is not only Mantegna's fresco that is destroyed, but also the princely fertility of which it is the celebration; the ducal palace (we recall) has become a "drear waste"—or at best a museum. (In the sequel this is put very graphically indeed for whoever will pause to consider the meaning: "usura / blunteth the needle in the maid's hand.") Pound is well aware that in one gyre (the third of the seventh circle) Dante punishes together violence against God, against nature (sodomy), and against "art" (usury—by "art," human productivity in general is understood). So much is indicated by the entrance of Geryon, the "foul image of fraud" that carries the poets on its back down from the seventh to the eighth circle (*Inf.* 17), at the end of c. 51, the second reading of the indictment against usury. The sin against eros, or the theme of Inés, is very much in the foreground of the savage close of 45, which makes a dramatic transition from the description of the

cosmos which usury has lost us, to the expressionistic hell of
which she is the master:

> Usura slayeth the child in the womb
> It stayeth the young man's courting
> It hath brought palsey to bed, lyeth
> between the young bride and her bridegroom
>   CONTRA NATURAM
> They have brought whores for Eleusis
> Corpses are set to banquet
> at behest of usura.   [c. 45]

The mystery of wheat and sex celebrated at Eleusis and by medieval Christianity has degenerated to whoredom (i.e., a love that
can be bought), to a macabre banquet of corpses. (P.'s repulsion
for the "definite act of absorption" has been noted in connection
with c. 7.) [9]
    Pound's hatreds, however, tend to be less to the point than his
affections: the last lines, implicitly scolding against abortion and
contraceptives, are alarmingly in accord with the demographic
policies of fascism, and worse. (Repulsion for the marriage of the
"healthy" to the "diseased" was likewise evoked by Nazi propaganda.) The impression is corroborated by canto 51, which
repeats the usury theme in language less archaic, and further
defines its ideological implications. The world which, according
to c. 45, Ulysses has lost, is soon regained in the course of the
memorable sexual rites of c. 47, and this is also the intended message of c. 51, in which the theme of usury is checked without
delay by the forces of "nature"—and of politics. The canto opens
with a brilliant syntactic turn, actually a verbatim rendering of
two lines from Guido Guinizelli: "Splende in la intelligenza de lo
cielo / Deo creator, più che 'n nostri occhi 'l sole." [10] Then, from
the Neoplatonic *nous* of heaven, we descend to mud, which in

9. For an authorial gloss see *L* 338, and the additions in Izzo, "23 lettere e 9 cartoline
inedite," pp. 139–41.

10. From the canzone "Al cor gentil ripara sempre Amore," usually considered the manifesto of the "Dolce Stil Novo."

the same thirteenth-century text is said to "remain vile" though
the sun beat on it all day: [11]

> Shines
> in the mind of heaven   God
> who made it
> more than the sun
> in our eye.
> Fifth element; mud; said Napoleon
> With usury has no man a good house
> made of stone, no paradise on his church wall . . .   [c. 51]

What of Napoleon? In 1917 the author of these lines had delivered himself otherwise on the subject: Bonaparte was the incarnation of "the ever damned spirit of provincialism," governed by
"an idiotic form of ambition" ("Provincialism the Enemy," *SPr*
201). All of this had changed, under the influence of Mussolini's
"Napoleonic ideas," [12] by the time of the *Fifth Decad of Cantos*.
For example, c. 44 offers on the subject the pithy remark,
" 'Thank god such men be but few' / though they build up human
courage," and c. 50 includes a futuristic account of Waterloo.
Within a few years Brooks Adams' *Law of Civilization and
Decay* was to provide Pound (who read the book in 1940) with
further proof that Napoleon had fought for the good of all
against the bankers. (In c. 80 he is mentioned in one breath with
Jackson and Lenin, elsewhere he is compared to Mussolini.)

Taking us by surprise, Pound places after the new indictment
of usury an amusing and colorful set of instructions on the making of flies and on the periods in which these are to be used. Thus
the degeneracy of usury in counteracted by the craftsman's cosmos, simple yet attentive in the extreme to the signs, colors, and
times of nature. This is also the cosmos of "the precise defini-

---

11. Cf. E. P., "Notes (Parts of which have been used in later drafts)," *Agenda*, VIII, 3–4
(1970), 3: "The sun, as Guinicelli says [,] beats on the mud all day / and the mud stays
vile."

12. See P.'s letter to Mussolini of 12 February 1940, quoted in Zapponi 53: "Ten years
ago I received an order, I do not know whether authentic or apocryphal [i.e., whether it
actually came from the Duce]: 'Tell Mr. Pound his ideas on Napoleon are rotten.' . . . I
have thought it over, and I hope I have made amends . . ."

tion" (imported by the two Chinese signs at the end of this canto, the first to appear in the poem),[13] Pound's well-chosen weapon against Geryon's fraud. (In this matter at least he had been of one mind over the previous twenty-five years.) His ammunition are such words as "grizzled yellow cock's hackle."

So far the first section of the canto. A blank detaches it from the second, which repeats (in very abbreviated form) the structure of the first. But the role formerly played by God in the mind of heaven is now given to the "adept" intellect of poet, craftsman, and ruler, which "habet lumen agentis ut formam sibi adhaerentem," and is (always according to Albertus Magnus as quoted by Renan) "Deo quodam modo similis" ("Cavalcanti," *LE* 186):

> That hath the light of the doer; as it were
> a form cleaving to it.
> Deo similis quodam modo
> hic intellectus adeptus
> Grass; nowhere out of place. Thus speaking in Königsberg
> Zwischen den Völkern erzielt wird
> a modus vivendi.   [c. 51]

This canto terminates the second of the four middle compartments of the poem, the one concerned eponymously with the founding, in the early seventeenth century, of Siena's Monte dei Paschi, a bank which (in P.'s view, colored not a little by Douglasite and Gesellite doctrine) made credit on the surety of the community's "real capital"—its pastures or *paschi*. The theme is brought into c. 51 by the image of the grass which (like the fisherman's words and actions) is "nowhere out of place" (cf. c. 43), and by the reference to another *monte*: Königsberg, the King's Mount. Elsewhere Pound tells us that "Antoninus, Constantine and Justinian were serious characters, they were trying to work out an orderly system [cf. 'nowhere out of place'], a modus vivendi for vast multitudes of mankind" (*K* 3). This is effected here by the Prince of the Mount, in the way prescribed by Confucius:

13. The character *hsin* ("Fidelity to the given word," *UP* 35) at the close of c. 34 is a later (and somewhat distracting) afterthought.

"The proper man acting according to conscience is wind, the lesser folk acting on conscience, grass; grass with wind above it must bend" (*A* xii 19). Thus Pound's pithy defense of the precise and ordered word turns out to be a step towards a mystical and authoritarian (hence uncontrollable) conception of power—towards the worship of counterfeit gods, who are rather envoys of hell: in the second section Napoleon is replaced (as suggested by the German words) by Adolf Hitler.

Pound probably wrote these lines in 1936, under the influence of the invasion of Ethiopia, and of early gestures towards the Rome-Berlin Axis. It is no coincidence that Mussolini should appear in c. 41, last of the previous section (1934): the parallel entry of Hitler encrypts the Axis in the structure of the poem.

As in the first section, the charismatic leader is faced with his enemy, usury:

> circling in eddying air; in a hurry;
> the 12: close eyed in the oily wind
> these were the regents; and a sour song from the folds
>   of his belly
> sang Geryone: I am the help of the aged;
> I pay men to talk peace;
> Mistress of many tongues; merchant of chalcedony
> I am Geryon twin with usura,
> You who have lived in a stage set.
> A thousand were dead in his folds;
> in the eel-fishers basket
> Time was of the League of Cambrai:
>   [*cheng ming*]   [c. 51]

Unlike the patient fisherman, Geryon is in a hurry ("to sell and sell quickly"—c. 45), as he swims "through the thick and dark air," a sexless merchant speaking many tongues and endorsing peace and pity "when they are quite dead" (*Inf.* xvi. 130, xx.28). Though the lines also carry anti-Semitic implications (the unctuous merchant), Geryon is chiefly an allegory of the Bank of England with its "greasy-mugged regents" (*K* 52), which in the *Fifth Decad* plays hell to the Monte dei Paschi's paradise. Thereupon Pound quickly "repeats" the third and last part of the canto's first section, referring us to the fisherman, who by timely action will capture the serpent Geryon and defeat the enemies who have rallied against him: at Cambrai in 1508 and at Geneva in 1936.

The parody with variations brings out, as has been claimed, the implications of the first statement in c. 45. Canto 52, the first of the subsequent compartment, continues in the same vein, for it touches upon the Sienese bank, Axis economy, and the "sanctions" of 1936—goes on with the poem's most hysterical anti-Semitic tirade—and closes with an extensive ritualistic account of the sequence of the seasons or of the fisherman's natural time, based on a Chinese text. The following cantos rehearse the annals of the rulers of that distant region.

In such a way the liberal individualist Pound, a stronger opposer of socialism than he was of authoritarianism, became by imperceptible degrees an endorser of the most repellent dictatorship and an indirect accomplice of genocide. The process was gradual, yet in this perspective the *Cantos* are truly of a piece, for a mystical view of history obtains throughout, open to dangerous misjudgments. As early as the *Malatesta* Gemistus Plethon reports that

> . . . Plato went to Dionysius of Syracuse
> Because he had observed that tyrants
> Were most efficient in all that they set their hands to,
> But he was unable to persuade Dionysius
> To any amelioration.   [c. 8]

The defense of tyranny is significantly based on the criterion of efficiency: strikes cease and trains keep time. But this is only a screen for an irrational inclination—the tyrant is called Dionysus. It is easy today to see in the lines a prefiguring of Pound's tragicomic and unsuccessful attempts to interest in economic reform and in his work as a poet and as a propagandist Mussolini, whom he was seriously to compare, in July 1945, to Dionysus and Christ.

Yet it is precisely when Pound is at his most improbable, unabashedly venting his irrationalism (esthetic, political, religious), that his work rings rich and genuine. For we would gladly dis-

pense with the Pound who plays cops and robbers in verse: it is
curious that he should have been unaware of the inadequacy of
certain "studies" of his (both in the way of general interest and
of coherence of form and sentiment), even in comparison to
many unassuming critical artifacts. However, these shortcomings
follow upon the poem's pictorial approach, which is alien to all
rational strategy—and indeed Pound's prose, e.g. the "Cavalcanti" essay, is often quite compelling. We should also beware of
rejecting the "documentary" cantos in summary fashion, for the
consideration of documents or texts occasions some of the
poem's outstanding successes. By far more objectionable are
those sections of Pound's investigations which are handled by the
anecdotal and autobiographic approach, like the vignettes of cs.
18–19, or the controversy among Douglas, Pound, and John
Maynard Keynes, reported in c. 22 and ominously juxtaposed
with recollections (friendly yet mechanical) of a service in a syna-
gogue of Gibraltar—or again the (intentionally) vacuous c. 28
with its bathetic conclusion à la D'Annunzio, and the discomfort-
ing Mitteleuropa of c. 35. One is tempted to remark that few
other major poets have nodded so often, but then one thinks
again of that kindred spirit of Pound, D'Annunzio, who,

like other serious characters who have taken seventy years to live and to
learn to live, . . . has passed through periods wherein he lived (or
wrote) we should not quite say "less ably," but with less immediately
demonstrable result.

This period "nel mezzo," this passage of the "selva oscura" takes
men in different ways, so different indeed that comparison is more
likely to bring ridicule on the comparer than to focus attention on the
analogy—often admittedly far-fetched. ["Cavalcanti," LE 192–93]

Pound's problem is familiar. When he attempts to portray what
he considers to be the bourgeois vacuum ("You who have lived
in a stage set"), he becomes prey to the imitative fallacy and
writes badly. Which shows once again that his disgust is obtuse
and insecure, whereas his affection is clear-sighted. A remark in
the "Henry James" essay of 1918 applies: "Most good prose
arises, perhaps, from an instinct of negation . . . Poetry is the as-

sertion of a positive, i.e. of desire, and endures for a longer period" (*LE* 324*n*). Only at Pisa Pound comes around to write autobiography that reveals a rich inner life, heretofore unsuspected.

On the other hand, the American and Sienese documents of cs. 31–34 and 42–44 are worth the reader's time, particularly the latter, which were taken down in a happy condition of emotional suspension, apparent from several fresh lyrical interpolations. In fact, this second compartment of the middle cantos, the *Fifth Decad*, is one of the more notable poetic and structural successes of the poem. Unlike the somewhat bewildered progress of the previous (or Jeffersonian) compartment (1930–34), which opens with a liberal, anti-authoritarian, and anti-capitalist chord (Marx is quoted at length in c. 33), and closes with the suggestion that Mussolini is the modern Jefferson or Hanno who will sever the Gordian knot of Mitteleuropean decadence (c. 35), and of the shady transactions of banks and arms-merchants (37–38), the trajectory of the *Fifth Decad* stands out clearly and proceeds with a feeling of inevitability to its conclusions, which are those we have found in c. 51, extremely questionable but at least not lacking in expressive coherence. Siena is again a vortex of a city that produces history (cf. the local distribution of credit) and a point of view through which general history is perceived ("and this day came Madame Letizia, / the ex-emperor's mother, and on the 13th departed"—c. 44). The descriptions of the Palio, of the "kallipygous" women climbing the steep streets, and of the roofs overgrown with grass, which the poet interpolates in his documentary transcription, which is both hasty and easeful, make the city rather more real to us than Jeffersonian America. In this local context we are quite prepared for the transition from the establishing of the "Mount" (42–43) to the eighteenth-century tax reforms of Leopold I and Ferdinand III (44), which concern wheat, thus pointing directly to the theme of Eleusis. The enlightened ruler, sensitive to his people's needs, is celebrated (like the Sigismondo of c. 11) with bonfires and crackers. Subsequently c. 44 records the passage of Napoleon, who is also Malatestian insofar as he is concerned for the welfare of artists (as duly noted

by P.), only to return in the end to the principal theme, the
"Mount": "The foundation, Siena, has been to keep bridle on
usury." This leads, with perfect timing, to the invective against
usury (c. 45), and to its expository counterpiece, c. 46, in which
the poet pauses in avuncular attitude to consider the journey he
has gone:

> And if you will say that this tale teaches . . .
> a lesson, or that the Reverend Eliot
> has found a more natural language . . . you who think you will
> get   through   hell   in   a   hurry . . .
>   That day there was cloud over Zoagli
> And for three days snow cloud over the sea
> Banked like a line of mountains.
> Snow fell. Or rain fell stolid, a wall of lines
> So that you could see where the air stopped open
> and where the rain fell beside it
> Or the snow fell beside it. Seventeen
> Years on this case, nineteen years, ninety years
>   on this case   [c. 46]

The setting has changed to Rapallo; the day in which nature
(always the witness of visionary breakthrough) seemed to frown
may have been the one in which the poem came to its "turning
point," and the usury canto was drafted. The charge of imparting
a didactic narrative, made by those who want to get through hell
in a hurry (Geryon—we recall—is also "in a hurry" in c. 51), is
both corroborated and denied by the pictorial train of thought
firmly adhered to over the span of these five cantos. Unfortunately the preachiness of the rest of c. 46 strengthens the case for
the prosecution. But before we hear the harangue a flashback
takes us seventeen years into the past, to the inception of Pound's
investigations, in the *New Age* office, 1918. The speakers are
Pound (whose very body rebels against bourgeois clothing) and
Douglas:

> An' the fuzzy bloke sez (legs no pants ever wd. fit) "IF
> that is so, any government worth a damn can
> pay dividends?"

> The major chewed it a bit and sez: "Y—es, eh . . .
> You mean instead of collectin' taxes?"
> "Instead of collecting taxes." That office?
> Didja see the Decennio?
> ?
> Decennio exposition, reconstructed office of Il Popolo,
> Waal, ours waz like that . . .   [c. 46]

So it was the poet after all who suggested to the economist what
his theories finally implied. And here we find the instructive parallel with the office of the *Popolo d'Italia,* from which Mussolini
launched another "revolution."

A few pages on Pound suggests that in fact his monetary enquiries are now coming to an end. Yet they are subsumed to a
larger investigation:

> This case is not the last case or the whole case, we ask a
> REVISION, we ask for enlightenment in a case
> moving concurrent, but this case is the first case:
> Bank creates it ex nihil. Creates it to meet a need,
> Hic est hyper-usura. Mr Jefferson met it:
> No man hath natural right to exercise profession
> of lender, save him who hath it to lend.   [c. 46]

The creation of money out of nothing, that is usury, is the murderer the poet has been tracking down over the previous seventeen or more years; but at the same time ("moving concurrent")
he was establishing the foundations of positive economic
thought, the principle of credit upon real capital, and this second
case is to bring to an enlightenment, or to a *re-vision.* In fact it is
barely necessary to remark that the inferno of the *Cantos* is not
particularly gloomy, but points as early as c. 1 to its paradisal
destination: Aphrodite, the quiet reign of Dionysus, the vital
struggle of Malatesta, the quick intelligence of Jefferson:

> To the high air, to the stratosphere, to the imperial
> calm, to the empyrean, to the baily of the four towers
> the νόος, the ineffable crystal:
> Karxedoníon Basileos
>   hung this with his map in their temple.   [c. 40]

The story of Hanno's journey of exploration in c. 40 ends thus—
in a temple/crystal/*nous,* and upon a geographic chart. The *nékuia*-
Aphrodite pattern of c. 1 recurs often in the first two compartments of the middle cantos: the first part of c. 40 offers a negative image of Hanno's journey by way of the oil monopoly of a
"most glorious Mr D'Arcy." Likewise c. 35 opens in the Mitteleuropa (read Freud-land) so hateful to Pound, and goes on to the
"wise" economic planning of fifteenth-century Mantua, and to
the sensuous St. John's Eve Pound has been concerned with from
the time of the *Ur-Cantos:*

> It juts into the sky, Gordon that is,
> Like a thin spire. Blue night pulled down about it
> Like tent-flaps or sails close hauled. When I was there,
> *La Noche de San Juan,* a score of players
> Were straddling about the streets in masquerade,
>
> [urc. 2, QPA 25]

> Blue agate casing the sky (as at Gourdon that time)
> the sputter of resin,   [c. 4]

> When the stars fall from the olive
> Or with four points or with five
> Toward St John's eve
> Came this day Madame ὕλη, Madame la Porte Parure
> Adorned with the Romancero,
> foot like a flowery branch.   [c. 35]

The Sylvan Lady (also perceived as she enters our local horizon)
is ambiguous, the Circe of the middle cantos (in c. 30 she is the
Lucrezia Borgia of the decadents), yet she also has access to nature (the star-formed olive flowers, the branch-like foot). The
Ulysses-Pound of this purgatory seeks to reestablish contact with
the nature-Circe (the "real capital") lost to modern man without
being swept away by bestiality. Though he failed, he had correctly perceived the problem. The story of Ulysses is continued in
c. 39, where Circe's somnolence (cf. c. 17) is exorcised with a
propitiatory dance, and chiefly in memorable c. 47, which picks
up the themes of Adonis and of the mysteries from c. 23 (Venus
and Anchises, Fa Han and I), placing them in the same Ligurian

setting, "Toward St John's eve." Actually Pound intergrafts two different ritual customs: the setting up of symbolic gardens in the churches on Maundy Thursday to represent the Holy Sepulchre, and the placing in early summer nights in the waters of the Tigullio Bay of floating candles which the mountain wind (or, to P., "the sea's claws") pushes away from land. The first ceremony he associates with the gardens of Adonis, the second with the reddening of rivers ascribed in antiquity to the spilling of Adonis' blood:

> The sea is streaked red with Adonis,
> The lights flicker red in small jars.
> Wheat shoots rise new by the altar,
>   flower from the swift seed.   [c. 47]

The flower and the wheat of Eleusis are born from a "swift seed," which (we learn farther on) is also the seed of man, whose orgasm is figured by the death of the vegetation god—a death to be followed by rebirth. Thus c. 47 is a lyrical vindication of what had been suggested in *P&T* and c. 4—that ancient mystery cults have survived in Provence and environs, also if Mary and Christ have nominally replaced Venus and Adonis: the "forty days" of Lent, which Hesiod allots to plowing, prove that Christ is a vegetation god. It is also clear that to Pound the paganizing Christianity of the Mediterranean is an offspring not wholly degenerate of the rites of antiquity. The ultimate objects of worship are natural fertility and human sexuality, as correlated by sympathetic magic.

Here again the substantial agreement with Mussolini's "Grain Battle" and demographic fixations, cannot be wholly coincidental. For example, in 1927 the Duce spoke as follows in the Chamber of Deputies of Italy's declining birthrate:

Do you believe that when I speak of the ruralization of Italy I do so out of love for fine phrases, which I abhor? No! I am the clinician who does not overlook symptoms, and these are symptoms upon which we must seriously reflect. What are we to conclude from these remarks? Firstly, that industrial urbanization brings about the sterility of the population. Secondly, that the same is to be expected from small rural

property. Add to these two economic causes the infinite cowardice of
the socalled upper class of society. If we lessen, gentlemen, we shall not
create an empire—we shall become a colony.[14]

One need only go on to the next canto to find (as in the earlier
"mixed" cantos 35, 40, and 46) the sterility of urbanization and
"the cowardice of the socalled upper class" contrasted with primitive vigor—with the instinct of the sexual and territorial explorer
and conqueror (see Hanno):

> They say, that is the Norse engineer told me, that out past
>   Hawaii
> they spread threads from gun'ale to gun'ale
> in a certain fashion
> and plot a course of 3000 sea miles
> lying under the web, watching the stars   [c. 48]

From this, however, we gather that Pound's fondness of the ritual
and natural world in which he is most at home (his legs—we
recall—do not fit into pants) is not different from Hemingway's,
and that he is usually well aware of the difference between instinct as regression and instinct as an essential complement of intelligence. Like Ulysses, the Pacific islanders, according to these
lines fraught with wonder, plot their course by watching the
stars—the stars which mere instinct (as represented by Circe) will
ignore:

> The bull runs blind on the sword, *naturans*
> To the cave art thou called, Odysseus,
> By Molü hast thou respite for a little,
> By Molü art thou freed from the one bed
>   that thou may'st return to another
> The stars are not in her counting,
>   To her they are but wandering holes.
> Begin thy plowing
> When the Pleiades go down to their rest,   [c. 47]

14. 26 May 1927. Quoted in Luigi Salvatorelli and Giovanni Mira, *Storia d'Italia nel
periodo fascista* (Milano: Mondadori, 1972), I, 575–76. In connection with the "Grain
Battle" (1926–33), Mussolini circulated a "poem" of his own on the subject of bread, of
which the author of the *Cantos* may well have been aware: "Love bread / heart of the
home / perfume of the table, / joy of the hearths. / Respect bread / . . . Honor bread / . . .
Do not waste bread" (ibid. I, 563).

The generative instinct (*naturans*)[15] is as blind as the bull running to his death: it cannot be thwarted (P. tells us), but it must be illumined by the intelligence, the moly herb which makes Ulysses immune to Circe's potion and allows him to proceed beyond her to a more exalted "bed"—social work (plowing as regulated by the motion of the stars), and the ecstatic bed of Penelope-Aphrodite. Intercourse understood as the *other* bed, that is, not as regression, is revealed in the course of the initiate's instruction as "the greatest mystery" (CV 317), the one which epitomizes life and death of man and of the cosmos:

> Hast thou found a nest softer than cunnus
> Or hast thou found better rest
> Hast'ou a deeper planting, doth thy death year
> Bring swifter shoot?
> Hast thou entered more deeply the mountain?
>
> The light has entered the cave. Io! Io!
> The light has gone down into the cave,
> Splendour on splendour!   [c. 47]

Death leads to rebirth, Pound has told us as early as c. 6 (" 'Tant las fotei com auzirets / Cen a quatre vingt et veit vetz . . .' / The stone is alive in my hand, the crops / will be thick in my death year"),[16] but a swifter shoot (in both senses) and a greater rest is affected by the sexual act, the splendor of which is experienced by a sort of collective first person: the cry "Io" indicates at one time the instant of orgasm and the possible recovery of a "divine" I, the healing of the wound which separates us from the all:

>   that hath the gift of healing,
>   that hath the power over wild beasts.   [c. 47]

In the background of this canto are of course the words of Ulysses to his men in *Inf.* 26, "Consider your seed—You were not made to live as brutes, but to pursue virtue and knowledge":

15. This is not, of course, "in accord with nature; natural action" (*Annotated Index to the Cantos of Ezra Pound*), but *natura naturans* (as distinguished from *natura naturata*) of theology.

16. The Provençal words come from the close of William of Aquitaine's bawdy *vers* of the red cat: "I shall tell you how often I fucked them: one hundred and eighty-eight times."

               Knowledge the shade of a shade,
   Yet must thou sail after knowledge
   Knowing less than drugged beasts . . .   [c. 47]

Pound's subsequent actions, clearly prefigured in the anti-Semitic
and Hitlerite passages of the *Fifth Decad,* cast a fatefully ironic
light upon the announcement that he has acquired "the power
over wild beasts." This is reiterated in the close of c. 49, which
shifts the Ligurian themes to a Sino-Japanese landscape, anticipating the Chinese subject matter of the subsequent compartment, and indicating the common naturalistic background which
links the latter to the Siena section. In the context of the section,
and of the entire poem, this "Seven Lakes Canto" (as it is often
called), balances the equally brief usury canto by depicting a distant and motionless *locus,* impermeable to the time of history yet
also in agreement with what small part of history it comes into
contact with. The "no man" of c. 45, who (a fine pun suggests) is
both the author of these lines and but an anonymous voice,
comes here after a journey through the desolation of history
(equivalent to the *nékuia* of the "fertility cantos," 39 and 47).
This journey or desolation is barely touched upon in the opening
of the canto, yet it is alluded to twice in the sequel and thus
becomes a recurrent and shaping motif of the type we have noted
in cs. 47 and 51:

   For the seven lakes, and by no man these verses:
   Rain, empty river; a voyage,   [c. 49]

The opening words refer with intentional vagueness to the source
of the first and chief section of the canto, a Japanese manuscript
said to contain seven of "the eight famous scenes in the Sho-Sho
area of China, the region where the Rivers Sho and Sho (Hsiang
and Hsiang in Chinese) converge," each scene being glossed by
two poems, one in Chinese and one in Japanese (Pearlman
304–11). This genre of verse *for* place, Buddhist and Taoist in
background, is deeply attractive (as we may well expect) to
Pound, a master of the verse of landscape: c. 49 is very close in
tone (though more refined) to the 1915 poems of Provence in
which Pound developed the elegiac style he was to use in render-

ing Li Po (*Cathay*) and (supremely) in the Pisan cantos. (*Poetry* for March 1915 offered "Provincia Deserta" and "The Gypsy," as well as "Exile's Letter," one of the chief personae of P. the exile—yet P. was to insist in a 1917 letter [*L* 114] that "Provincia Deserta" was written before *Cathay*.)

> The wind came, and the rain,
> And mist clotted about the trees in the valley,
> And I'd the long ways behind me,
>   gray Arles and Beaucaire,   ["The Gypsy," *P* 119]

"And the wind is still for a little"—we were told in the *Malatesta*. Wind and rain, quickened by every emotional gradation while purely elemental and non-human, are to become, particularly at Pisa, the chief ministers of vision.

By the canto's second "stanza" we are firmly placed in epiphanic territory, within the painting, watched over by moon and sun and by a religion—a reverence—which is wholly unobtrusive, a bell carried by the wind:

> Autumn moon; hills rise about lakes
> against sunset
> Evening is like a curtain of cloud,
> a blurr above ripples; and through it
> sharp long spikes of the cinnamon,
> a cold tune amid reeds.
> Behind hill the monk's bell
> borne on the wind.
> Sail passed here in April; may return in October
> Boat fades in silver; slowly;
> Sun blaze alone on the river.   [c. 49]

Autumn, evening, bell (P. was fond of quoting the first lines of *Purg.* 8)—all signify the quiet and repose which follow upon the fruitful and agitated day of sexual and agricultural plowing celebrated in c. 47. "Dryad, thy peace is like water / There is September sun on the pools"—Pound was to write in a fine Pisan canto which develops this theme. As remarked above, time and history enter but slightly in Pound's world of space, also for the good reason that the rural community is quite self-sufficient, and

that the best government (in Jefferson's phrase) "is that which
governs less" (*J/M* 15): the only connection with the world at
large is the boat which passes within "our" horizon at the spring
and autumn equinox, "perhaps to collect taxes in due season"
(Pearlman 198)—an image impressionist in mood (we think of
Debussy's *En bateau*). One occasion on which the emperor, or
some representative of his, visited this remote part of his land is
also recorded:

> In seventeen hundred came Tsing to these hill lakes.
> A light moves on the south sky line.   [c. 49]

These lines prefigure the setting of later cantos, in which the
mind of Artemis is said to contain a beauty "as of mountain
lakes in the dawn" (c. 110). The light on the southern horizon
may well be the dawn. "Tsing" is the Manchu Dynasty (established 1616), celebrated for its "splendid administration" in
later passages, likewise ecstatic.

Yet history cannot enter the poem, however unobtrusively,
without recalling the "crime": presently Pound returns briefly
and (as remarked) explicitly to the *nékuia*, bringing out its "economic" import:

> State by creating riches shd. thereby get into debt?
> This is infamy; this is Geryon.
> This canal goes still to TenShi
> though the old king built it for pleasure   [c. 49]

The harsh abbreviation aptly suggests that Pound's query belongs
to a wholly different context, to the struggle for Social Credit
("The State should lend, not borrow"). The fraud of Geryon (to
be dealt with at length two cantos on, in the passage already
quoted) is contrasted with the enlightened measures of the old
king, whose canal is a symbol of communication and of work
which is not alienated—it is done "for pleasure." Pound is asking
the reader to recall Jefferson's project for the Erie canal, recorded
at the opening of c. 31, and is to make more of the theme in the
subsequent compartment, though there the poem's incipient authoritarianism becomes apparent:

> 1600 leagues of canals 40 ft wide for the
> > honour of YANG TI of SOUI
> the stream Kou-choui was linked to Hoang Ho the river
> > great works by oppression
> > > by splendid oppression   [c. 54]

Which takes us to the friendly suggestions offered to Stalin by the
Pisan prisoner:

> and but one point needed for Stalin
> you need not, i.e. need not take over the means of production;
> > > > > [c. 74]

(This notion of the abolition of property was clearly not to P.'s
liking.)

> But in Russia they bungled and did not apparently
> grasp the idea of work-certificate
> and started the N.E.P. with disaster
> and the immolation of men to machinery
> > and the canal work and gt/ mortality
> > > (which is as may be)   [c. 74]

Stalin's oppression is not as splendid as Yang Ti's, though the
end of the two rulers is the same, the building of a canal.[17] It is
amusing to note that after Mussolini's debâcle Pound was quite
prepared to try his luck with another "tyrant." What may seem
opportunism is actually a basic indifference to power, exhibited
in *Propertius* and finely restated in the close to c. 49. Here the instructions quoted from Hesiod in c. 47 are paralleled by a poem
traditionally assigned to the emperor Yao, and work in the
fields is attended by political equanimity and by the peace which
has control over such brutes as Geryon:

> Sun up; work
> sundown; to rest
> dig well and drink of the water
> dig field; eat of the grain
> Imperial power is? and to us what is it?

17. The instructive inconsistency is noted in Mancuso 39–40. See also *Oro e lavoro, SPr*
342.

The fourth; the dimension of stillness.
And the power over wild beasts.   [c. 49]

Dawn and sunset, work and rest, water and wheat—these things
are real. Power is of no concern to *us*—the inhabitants of this
landscape and the readers of these lines. Beyond the day's cycle
yet linking up with it ("sundown; to rest") is Pound's fourth
dimension—not time but a motionless space, coveted by a poet
whose entire life was spent in a flurry of activity.[18] Again we note
that this ataraxia is somewhat inconsistent with Pound's exclu-
sive passion for agenda—and more in accord with Taoism and
Buddhism (so often abused in the *Cantos*) than with the narrow-
minded Confucian pragmatism which we are asked to admire.

This is not to say that Pound ever calls a truce in his fighting,
as we can gather from c. 49, which is clearly not the detached
revery on oriental themes which the unwary reader may take it to
be, for (even overlooking its inner dialectic) the beauty of the
verse is not an end to itself but has a precise structural function.
Further proof of Pound's engagement is to be found in the line
before last ("The fourth; the dimension of stillness"), which
should be placed in the context of Wyndham Lewis' attack upon
the "time philosphy" of Einstein and Whitehead, and upon
Joyce, Stein, and Pound himself—all guilty of participating sentimentally in "the general indefinite wobble" (c. 35) of *mœurs
contemporaines,* and of not implementing the classical (and reactionary) programme of T. E. Hulme.[19] Joyce was so hurt by the

18. Cf. P.'s letter of 7 June 1942 to his translator Luigi Berti, published in *Tempo,* 26
November 1972, and quoted in Mancuso 33: "Stillness—the word is more concrete than
IMMOTO [the motionless], for it also suggests silence. What is still is motionless and sound-
less. But the concept of motionlessness is more important in this line. In Dante, above the
primum mobile there is the motionless, the sphere which does not turn. I conceive of a
dimension of stillness which compenetrates the euclidean dimensions."

19. Wyndham Lewis, *Time and Western Man* (1927; rpt. Boston: Beacon Press, 1957).
See Pearlman 203–10. Of course since 1927 P. had accumulated other reasons, quite
unspeculative, to oppose Einstein. It is enough to recall that on 26 December 1936 the
Ministero della Cultura popolare advised the Italian press never to mention Einstein (Salvatorelli and Mira, *Storia d'Italia nel periodo fascista,* ii, 325). Canto 49 was first published in June 1937.

attack of his "nephew" Lewis[20] that he referred to it several
times in *Finnegans Wake*; Stein retaliated by ridiculing in *The
Autobiography of Alice B. Toklas* the "Enemy" 's painting (which
is in fact uneven in the extreme, though it was to have a follower
of genius, Francis Bacon); Pound alone was not offended, as he
shared his friend's anti-democratic sentiments and had embraced
as early as 1911 a poetry "austere, direct, free from emotional
slither" ("A Retrospect," *LE* 12)—and after all Lewis' critique
had placed him in superior company. However, the three cantos
of 1930 acknowledge Lewis' *rappel à l'ordre* by professing contempt for "the female" (c. 29), and by damning the sentimentalism which passes for pity, and time itself, which is shown to be
subversive of all order: "Time is the evil. Evil" (c. 30). Did we
not take *Time and Western Man* for gloss we would not be able
to follow Pound's association of time with the deadly sentiment
suggested by the story of Venus who leaves Mars for lame Vul-
can, and by Peter the Cruel's demand that homage be rendered to
the corpse of Inés. This "time" is nothing else but usury, that
"hath brought palsey to bed, lyeth / between the young bride and
her bridegroom" (c. 45). A page on the XXX *Cantos* end with a
reference to the year (a *date*) in which Soncino's Petrarch was
printed (see above) and Pope Borgia died: "And in August that
year . . . Il Papa morì." We have found in c. 45 that in the era
of usury (connected by P. with the Reformation and with the dis-
placement to the north of the centers of power) sexuality and
religion meet a joint death: "Whores for Eleusis."

Yet our reading of cs. 47, 49, and 51, suggests that to Pound
beyond time-as-death there is time-as-life, the natural and cul-

20. "I am afraid poor Mr Hitler-Missler will soon have few friends in Europe apart from
your nieces and my nephews, Masters W. Lewis and E. Pound"—Joyce to Harriet Shaw
Weaver, 28 July 1934, quoted in Richard Ellmann, *James Joyce* (New York: Oxford
Univ. Press, 1965), p. 687. Lewis brought out his book on *Hitler* in 1931, and P. (who
wrote *J/M* two years later) was to praise him for this in *K* 18: "Form-sense 1910 to 1914.
15 or so years later Lewis discovered Hitler. I hand it to him as a superior perception. Superior in relation to my own 'discovery' of Mussolini. I was after all living in Italy where,
however, the decayed upper bourgeoisie and pseudostocracy in great part, and the weak-
ling litterati, sic 'not wops, more pseudofrogs,' did NOT sense the resurrection."

tural cycle which makes things new and to which man is to defer
in order to recover from his wound, from his being (unlike the
grass) out of place. In fact the middle cantos may be taken as a
quest for true time, which is at one time cyclic or seasonal, and
historical. Hence the twofold concern with the seasons and their
activities,[21] and with matters of the present historical moment,
which are to become increasingly obsessive. It follows that fascism
should have seemed to Pound the ideal solution, as it purports to
bring history into accord with an "order" supposedly absolute.

Pound takes time for his subject in the opening lines of the
middle cantos, which also make two statements, one general
("To every thing there is a season"), and one topical: it is fitting
that the poet of the thirties be silent, and attend the lesson of history:

> Tempus loquendi.
> Tempus tacendi.
> Said Mr Jefferson: It wd. have given us
> time.   [c. 31]

By bringing together the dictum from Ecclesiastes, its order reversed as on Isotta degli Atti's tomb in the Tempio Malatestiano,
and Jefferson's consideration for time (cf. Mauberley's "Asking
time to be rid of . . . / Of his bewilderment"), Pound suggests the
continuity of his inferno and his purgatory in the persons of their
chief heroes: on the one hand Malatesta with his renaissance
cohort, on the other hand Jefferson and his fellow illuminists
Leopold I, Mailla, and John Adams, as well as Martin Van

---

21. "Intention of Cantos / To run parallel / This found later / The Triumphs / The Seasons /
The Contemporary with activities of the seasons."—P.'s note on the verso of a photograph of the Schifanoia frescos. Seen at Sant'Ambrogio (Rapallo), 1964. The following
discussion of time in the middle cantos is indebted to Pearlman's valuable essay *The Barb
of Time,* the conclusions of which, however, I do not agree with. Pearlman believes that
time is the figure in the carpet of the *Cantos,* and that three versions of the theme (time as
disorder, time as order, time as love) provide the poem with the major form it needs to
satisfy Pearlman's esthetics. This, however, is in contrast both with P.'s poetics (which
seek to replace major form with ideogramic relationships, the language of reality), and
with his text, which pays little attention to the subject after the middle cantos. P. is hardly
concerned with time in the abstract, but only with the cycle of the seasons, or with the
pastness (and the resurrection) of the past.

Buren and Mussolini, considered by Pound (not wholly without
justification) to be Jefferson's followers. In *J/M*, a pamphlet contemporary with and parallel to cs. 31–41, Pound stresses his two
subjects' awareness of time: Jefferson is credited with "the opportunism of the artist," while Mussolini is said to conduct a
"continual gentle [!] diatribe against all that is 'anti-storico,' all
that is against historic process" (15, v). In this connection the
final paragraph of "Date Line" (1934) is worth recalling:

> I am leaving my remark on *anagke* in the H. James notes, but the Act
> of God alters with time. . . . Some infamies in the year XII are as
> needless as death by thirst in the city of London. There is a TIME in these
> things.
> It is quite obvious that we do not all of us inhabit the same time. [*LE*
> 87]

These words throw some light on the laconic close of the Jefferson cantos, "ad interim 1933" (c. 41)—and we should note that
the opening and closing lines of the poem's sections, as of single
cantos, are of particular structural importance. Having discarded
narrative form Pound must rely heavily on such pictorial strategies. So it is no surprise that the bad timing of the English is
censured in the very first lines of c. 42, that is, of the *Fifth Decad:*

> "And how this people CAN in this the fifth et cetera
>   year of the war, leave that old etcetera up
> there on that monument!" H.G. to E.P. 1918   *Wells*
>   [c. 42]

Pound's vow of silence is strictly kept through cs. 31–34,
which are almost entirely made up of quotations from Jefferson,
John and John Quincy Adams, and Van Buren, and are (as already noted) mostly liberal in tenor, having been written at the
time of the author's short-lived flirtation with the Left. (Canto 33
opens with Adams' condemnation of despotism and goes on to
quote the *Capital* on the iniquity of the labor of minors; in c. 34
John Quincy Adams mourns the "wrongs of the Cherokee nation.") After this American survey, to be resumed in c. 37, Pound
returns to the principal themes of his poem by contrasting, in c.

35, Mitteleuropa and the Middle Ages, and going on, in c. 36, to
a version (followed by a cryptic commentary) of Guido Cavalcanti's canzone "Donna mi prega":

> A lady asks me
>   I speak in season
> She seeks reason for an affect, wild often
> That is so proud he hath Love for a name   [c. 36]

The second line, interpolated by Pound into what is otherwise a
relatively close, if obscure, rendering, assures the reader that the
silence enjoined in c. 31 is not broken without good reason (the
quest for the love of Circe and Aphrodite), and that this block of
medieval discourse is inserted after much thought among the
American chronicles and in the context of the poem, in which the
canzone has a thematic function nearly equal in moment to that
of *nékuia* and metamorphosis. Already the pun on "season" and
the reference to stillness as the ultimate nature of love (in the
fourth verse), tell us that Pound is not only translating a text
which he has recently edited and glossed at length, but also going
on with his poem. In speaking of love "as an intellectual instigation" ("Rémy de Gourmont," *LE* 343) Cavalcanti lights the way
toward an unprimitivistic return to nature; besides, Pound, while
preparing his edition of the canzone, had come to consider it (like
several troubadour lyrics) a document of intellectual freedom and
of the secret religion which Guido may have gathered on the
roads of Provence:

His truth is not against *"natural dimostramento"* or based on authority. It is a truth for elect recipients, not a truth universally spreadable or
acceptable. The *"dove sta memoria"* is Platonism. The *"non razionale
ma che si sente"* is for experiment, it is against the tyranny of the
syllogism, blinding and obscurantist. . . . It seems to me quite possible
that the whole of it is a sort of metaphor on the generation of light . . .
["Cavalcanti," *LE* 159, 161]

Thus "Donna mi prega," though linked by literary history and by
secret affinities (Guido's pilgrimage) to Occitanic culture, stands
in the *Cantos* for something which no single Provençal text, with
sparse references to indigo mantles, solar rains (c. 4), and nudity

in the lamplight, could have been made to represent: a medieval-
ism "untouched by the two maladies" (fanaticism and asceticism,
LE 154), the source of Europe's greatest verse and the foundation of the Renaissance. These are some of Pound's reasons for
introducing Cavalcanti, who according to Boccaccio sought to
prove that God does not exist, among the enlightened thinkers
who proved the latter point to their satisfaction, and in the context of one of the first modern anti-authoritarian revolutions.
Pound tells us so much in his verse postscript to the canzone,
which introduces medieval free thought in the person of John
Scotus Erigena, whose Neoplatonic writings were consulted by
the Albigenses and consequently suppressed by the Church:

> "Called thrones, balascio or topaze"
> Erigena was not understood in his time
> "which explains, perhaps, the delay in condemning him"
> And they went looking for Manicheans
> And found, so far as I can make out, no Manicheans
> So they dug for, and damned Scotus Erigena
> "Authority comes from right reason,
>   never the other way on"
> Hence the delay in condemning him
> Aquinas head down in a vacuum,
>   Aristotle which way in a vacuum?   [c. 36]

These references provide the context within which the canzone
acquires the import it carries in the *Cantos,* which is also (P. believes) its true bearing. The second point need not be dwelt upon
except to note once again that the poet's constructs are metaphorical and not wholly lacking in verisimilitude, and that,
though we may enjoy Mario Praz's brilliant castigation (1932) of
Pound's ill-fated Cavalcanti edition,[22] we must not share the nar-

---

22. Guido Cavalcanti, *Rime: Edizione rappezzata fra le rovine* [ed. E.P.] (Genova: Marsano, 1932). Praz wrote: "To believe in that curious character, Ezra Pound, one must see
him, speak to him, or read that unbelievable olla podrida, his edition of Cavalcanti's
Rime, printed partly in England and partly in Genoa, and finally published by Genoa's
Marsano in 1932, between fiery red covers. Dishevelled, unpredictable in his gestures . . .
Apollo out of Offenbach, tawny goatee, glistening eye, shirt à la Robespierre—this American of distant (but very conspicuous) Irish background who is rumored to be a Jew, very
cordial, a good smith of English lines and a stutterer of Romance languages, among these

rowmindedness of the victims of the *Propertius* trap. Pound has
thought himself into Guido with unique passion (in fact his edition is but a poet's transcription of a fellow poet, of the sort we
find in the early Renaissance), and the Italian reader going
through the canzone in his company finds it not a little exciting.
Furthermore, it is enough to look at the way in which the text is
articulated on the large-format pages of the 1932 edition, "pieced
together among the ruins," to become aware of a very interesting
experiment: while bringing out fully the intricate verse and
rhyme structure Pound reproduces (with minor exceptions) the
text as it is given in the manuscript of his choice, unlike editors of
critical editions, who of course parse words and add punctuation.
In this way Guido's writing remains as it were virgin, open to all
readings, excluding none. The very beautiful typesetting of the
pages imported from England (which include the canzone) is also
indicative of the ambivalence—the hesititation between avant-
garde and tradition—of Pound. (The same applies to Mallarmé's
Coup de dès.)

The first line of Pound's ideogramic comment to the canzone
functions as a *senhal* of the subtle medieval knot of poetry, mysticism, and love, of which the foregoing text is an example. In
particular, it refers us to the third heaven (Venus') of the *Commedia,* in which Cunizza da Romano speaks of the angels of the
third order ("Above are mirrors, you call them Thrones"—*Par.*
9), and (a few lines down) the troubadour and bishop of Toulouse, Folquet of Marseille, is depicted "as a fine ruby [*balasso*]
hit by the sun." Six cantos later the soul of Dante's forebear Cac-

---

an Italian flavored with Ligurian idioms, generous, fiery, savagely critic, prone to colossal
blunders, a lover of precision unfortunate in the extreme . . . no, I must give up, and say
in German, *Es gibt eine Welt Pound."* Yet he went on to say: "I believe Bertrand Russell
once remarked, to illustrate the extraordinary combinations of the universe, that if twelve
monkeys would work at typewriters over centuries, some day a Shakespeare sonnet would
emerge. In the case of Pound's *Cavalcanti* this seems to have been the method followed,
though the result is not as satisfactory." In the same 1932 article Praz shrewdly remarked
that the only P. poem "deserving mention in an accelerated course of world literature [of
the *How to Read* type]" could be "Provincia Deserta." See Mario Praz, *Cronache let-
terarie anglosassoni* (Roma: Edizioni di Storia e Letteratura, 1950), I, 176–78; and Zapponi 150–53.

ciaguida is called "lively topaz," but the gem is probably introduced into c. 36 as it is associated with love in c. 5 ("Topaz I
manage, and three sorts of blue . . . Gold-yellow, saffron . . .
The roman shoe, Aurunculeia's"), as well as in the "Medallion"
of *HSM* ("The eyes turn topaz"). In 1910 Pound wrote of a line
of Guido that " 'Il Paradiso' and the form of 'The Commedia'
might date from this line" (Introduction to Cavalcanti, *T* 25),
and this is what he is saying of the canzone with the tags from
the Third Heaven. Erigena, he goes on (quoting Francesco
Fiorentino's *Manuale di storia della filosofia ad uso dei Licei*),
was also ahead of his time:

The boldness of this lonely thinker is unequalled in his century, and in
many of the following, therefore it is no wonder that his work was
largely forgotten in the age of scholasticism. Nicholas I certainly disap-
proved of Erigena, on account of which work we know not; Honorius
III, having learned in 1225 that the *De Divisione Naturae* had been uncovered in connection with the enquiries against the Albigenses, com-
manded that it be burned directly. A historian of philosophy must point
at this work as an early example of free speculation produced at a time
in which nearly all bent under the yoke of authority.[23]

Pound covers this ground in his postscript by referring to the
charges of Manicheism brought against the Albigenses, mentioned in c. 23 in connection with the siege of Montségur and the
troubadour Peire de Maensac—and by denouncing in the end
"the tyranny of the syllogism, blinding and obscurantist," which
(we recall) Guido's canzone escapes. Erigena's thesis, "Auctoritas
ex vera ratione processit, ratio vero nequaquam ex auctori-
tate,"[24] would easily have been endorsed by the Congress of

23. Francesco Fiorentino, *Manuale di storia della filosofia ad uso dei Licei*, 2nd ed.
(Napoli 1887), p. 229. Walter B. Michaels quotes from "a footnote on page 221" of an
unidentified edition of the *Manuale* a version of these remarks closer to P.'s rehandling:
"Scoto sorpassa il suo secolo per la sua estesa cultura . . . Perciò non è da stupire se non
fu subito compreso e se giunse tardi la condanna." "P. and Erigena," *Paideuma*, 1 (1972),
43. He also points out that the (apocryphal) digging up of Erigena mentioned by P. is a
detail probably suggested by the fate of the pantheist heretic Amalric of Bena, who lived
short of four centuries after the Irishman, and is cursorily mentioned by Fiorentino (p.
250).

24. Fiorentino, *Manuale*, p. 225.

1776. Having already considered c. 46, we are also in the position to see a connection with the phrase which brings to a head Pound's indictment of usury:

> Bank creates it ex nihil. Creates it to meet a need,
> Hic est hyper-usura. Mr. Jefferson met it:
> No man hath natural right to exercise profession
> of lender, save him who hath it to lend.   [c. 46]

The syllogistic vacuum in which Aristotle and Aquinas lie head first (like Dante's simoniac popes—the position suggesting sodomy) is the same nonexistent capital upon which the banker makes credit, pocketing the interest. However confused Pound may be in matters of economics, he can graphically suggest the interrelation of structure and superstructure, of philosophic systems and their economic background. The antithesis to the Aristotelian vacuum [25] is of course the real capital of nature and of art-as-work (which Dante's usurer, we remember, sins against), and to this Pound turns in the close of c. 36:

> Sacrum, sacrum, inluminatio coitu.
> Lo Sordels si fo di Mantovana
>   of a castle named Goito.   [c. 36]

According to the "Cavalcanti" essay the concept of eros as an instrument of knowledge and of ecstasy is wholly a contribution of the medieval poetic renaissance, the feature which distinguishes it from the culture of antiquity, diagrammed as "plastic to coitus," "plastic plus immediate satisfaction" (LE 151; cf. Vidal vs the Moroccan bride in c. 4). Elsewhere in his commentary Pound quotes from Avicenna (whom he considers to have been one of Guido's sources) the dictum, "Amplius in coitu phantasia" (176). Therefore, after expressing with the Latin outburst the basic philosophy of the Cantos, Pound introduces a type of the Provençal-

---

25. In the 1954 Faber text P. (besides correcting the "Ierugena" of the first printing to "Erigena") added after the reference to Aristotle the line, "not quite in a vacuum," reason for which may be found in K. I omit the line (though it is interesting as further proof of P.'s naive attempt to get his history right, and of his willingness to correct "error") as it impinges on the flow of the passage—and after all Aristotle is given the benefit of doubt also in the earlier text.

Tuscan poet by way of Sordello, a Lombard writing in Langue
d'Oc, the first character to represent in the poem Pound's medi-
evalism. (This final appearance is anticipated by the quotation
from *Purg.* 6 in c. 32, and by the references to Mantua in the
previous canto.) The poet's birthplace, Goito, yields a pun not
overly subtle (on "coitus") which suggests the ancestry of his
verse. (P.'s lackadaisical Sordello is quite inconsistent, we note,
with Dante's character, a type of the engaged poet if there ever
was one.) There is a further reason for Sordello's standing in for
Guido in c. 36, namely the connection between their two stories
established in the person of Cunizza da Romano (her role being
very indirectly suggested by the earlier "thrones" line). Cunizza,
as we learn from cs. 6 and 29, took Sordello for a lover among
many others, yet made her peace with God in old age, manumit-
ting in 1265 (at the age of sixty-seven) her father's servants.
Pound, who calls attention to her generosity as early as the 1910
Introduction to Guido's poems, believes that Dante places her in
the heaven of Venus on account of it (in this he is in accord with
most commentators), or because Guido (who in 1265 was about
six years old) spoke to him

of beauty incarnate, or, if the beauty can by any possibility be brought
into doubt, at least and with utter certainty, charm and imperial bearing, grace that stopped not an instant in sweeping over the most violent
authority of her time and, from the known fact, that vigour which is
a grace in itself. [K 16]

In sum, Pound takes *Par.* 9 as proof that Dante also endorsed the
sacrum of the middle cantos. (Croce, on the other hand, once
suggested that Cunizza's pardon is a costly example of the sense
of humor the Florentine is usually supposed to have lacked.) [26]
Unfortunately, Cunizza has little poetic life in the verse of the
Cantos. At the time of the XXX *Cantos,* when Pound was still concerned with traditional portraiture, he gave her, in another nod-
ding moment, the traits of one of his mitteleuropean ladies
("Greatly enjoying herself / And running up the most awful
bills"—c. 29). Later (cs. 36 and 92) he will deem it sufficient to

26. Croce, *Letture di poeti,* pp. 23–24.

quote a few words from Dante. This failure of communication, not uncommon in the poem, is the more surprising as the passage quoted from *K* tells us that Pound was particularly fond of Cunizza, and that he had certainly imagined her in the full. Again, we find that our view of the *Cantos* must accommodate all of Pound's *œuvre*, if we are to make the bones live.

In the way of c. 2, and in accord with Pound's promise to be silent, Sordello is presented in the sequel by way of a document concerning the patronage (another familiar motif) accorded him by Charles of Anjou, which is somewhat hastily modernized ("And what the hell do I know about dye-works?"—cf. c. 35). There is also a latently adverse reference to the pope, the orthodoxy challenged throughout the canto. Sordello, Pound tells us, rids himself of castles, land, and dye-works, at the earliest opportunity, his inclinations lying in a quite different direction. In the last line of the canto, a quotation from his verse, we find him wrapped in consideration of his "rich thought," not unlike Propertius (the imagination's sacred fount is erotic in nature).

We may conclude from the above that the two first compartments of the middle cantos are among the most carefully and intricately structured in the poem. Further evidence may be submitted. The matter of America is brought into alignment with the matter of Siena by way of the identical openings of cs. 32 and 50, and of cs. 37 and 44; remarks by Adams and Marx quoted in c. 33 are reiterated in c. 48; and Napoleon's comment, in c. 51, on mud, the fifth element (which amounts to an inversion of the theme of the fourth dimension), is introduced as early as c. 34. Likewise in both sections one canto develops the theme of Ulysses and of "inluminatio coitu" (39, 47), and another canto is concerned with the poetic stillness which follows upon intercourse (36, 49). Finally, the Provençal myth presented in the postscript to the canzone as an antidote to the Mitteleuropa of the previous canto, is continued in c. 48, which covers both sides of the antithesis: opening (as mentioned above) with "the cowardice of the so-called upper class," it goes on to the instinctively intelligent Hawaiian seamen, and hence to the Catharist citadel in the Pyrenees, as described in c. 23 ("And they hadn't left even the stair"):

> Velvet, yellow, unwinged
> clambers, a ball, into its orchis
> and the stair there still broken
> the flat stones of the road, Mt Segur.   [c. 48]

Pound's elegy *for* the place of desolation (but the reference to the stair as "still broken" intimates that a reconstruction is to be expected) is signalled, and then counterpointed, by an image savagely instinctive, not easily deciphered for it is indomitably "there." Rather than telling us that the sun rises over the fortress of its Manichean worshippers, the poet insists that we submit to the godly (and animal: "unwinged") phenomenon, that we watch the ball of fire rise through the denser layers of the atmosphere to become a sensuous flower—a process correlated (if we recall the pun on *órchis* in 2 *HSM* 2) with the descent of the testes. This refers us at once to "inluminatio coitu" and to the medieval nexus mourned in the sequel—a culture rooted in antiquity, as suggested by the Roman remains in the valley of the Garonne under the hill of St-Bertrand-des-Comminges:

> From Val Cabrère, were two miles of roofs to San Bertrand
> so that a cat need not set foot in the road
> where now is an inn, and bare rafters,
> where they scratch six feet deep to reach pavement
> where now is a wheat field, and a milestone
> an altar to Terminus, with arms crossed
> back of the stone   [c. 48]

An invisible cat, a wheat field, an altar engraved with the image of hands (cf. c. 29)—the Ulysses-like traveller to many cities notices these signs, rich in contextual significance, within a landscape which anticipates the hauntingly familiar China of c. 49. As in "Provincia Deserta," he becomes aware of ancient and living presences:

> Where sun cuts light against evening;
> where light shaves grass into emerald

> Savairic; hither Gaubertz;
>> Said they wd. not be under Paris.
>>> [c. 48]

"Hither"—"on North road from Spain" (c. 5)—came Savaric de Malleon and his protégé, the troubadour Gaubert de Poicibot, who sought a prostitute and found his wife. Here also came Guido Cavalcanti, on his way to Santiago de Compostela, as intimated by the light "shaving" the grass (the "paschi" of the *Fifth Decad*), bearing out Pound's reading of a cherished bit of the canzone:

We appear to have lost the radiant world where one thought cuts through another with clean edge, a world of moving energies *"mezzo oscuro rade," "risplende in sé perpetuale effecto,"* magnetisms that take form, that are seen, or that border the visible, the matter of Dante's *paradiso,* the glass under water, the form that seems a form seen in a mirror [cf. "e quel remir"], these realities perceptible to the sense, interacting . . . ["Cavalcanti," *LE* 154]

No matter if commentators of the canzone tell us that "in mezzo scuro luce rade" means that love, situated in a dark space, "excludes light"[27]—if indeed "rade" is not an adverb, in which case Guido would be saying that love "shines forth but rarely."[28] To Pound—who takes "radere" to mean, as in modern Italian, "to shave"—"*Amor* moves with the light in darkness, never touching it and never a hair's breadth from it" (*LE* 191), i.e., "Grazeth the light, one moving by other" (c. 36). Having touched upon the central vision he goes on to point out that his poets-initiates did not "observe regulations," in defiance of religious, political, and economic authority. The troubadours do not submit to Paris ("and to us what is it?"), and the barons of the north, led by Simon de Montfort, retaliate with the Albigensian Crusade, supported by local clergymen, Folquet of Marseille among them. (P., however, did not know this.)

---

27. Gianfranco Contini, ed., *Poeti del Duecento* (Milano-Napoli: Ricciardi, 1960), II, 528.

28. Gustavo Rodolfo Ceriello, ed., *I rimatori del Dolce stil novo* (Milano: Rizzoli, 1950), p. 43.

In the sequel the suppression of Occitanic culture is in turn avenged by an instinctive agent which is clearly cognate to the flying ball which has lighted the vision of Montségur:

> Falling Mars in the air
> bough to bough, to the stone bench
> .   .   .
>
> Fell with stroke after stroke, jet avenger
> bent, rolled, severed and then swallowed limb after limb
> Hauled off the butt of that carcass, 20 feet up a tree trunk.
> Here three ants have killed a great worm. There
> Mars in the air, fell, flew.   [c. 48]

Again the image is undetermined, recalling "the small stars [that] fall from the olive branch" in c. 47, and Mars-as-Napoleon (c. 50). It is Pound's ideogramic intention to show us what things are by describing what they do—not by definition in the abstract. Of the present agent he spoke more openly on another occasion:

> The flying ant or wasp or whatever it was that I saw cut up a spider at Excideuil may have been acting by instinct, but it was not acting by reason of the stupidity of instinct. It was acting with remarkably full and perfect knowledge . . . .
> When a human being has an analogous completeness of knowledge, or intelligence carried into a third or fourth dimension, capable of dealing with NEW circumstances, we call it genius. [J/M 18–19]

By recording this act of war in c. 48 Pound is promising, as in c. 2, a rebirth, since the energies of intelligent instinct (or of "genius") cannot be beaten down very long. Unlike the author of c. 2, however, he is now prepared to rest his claim on force—Mars. Thus the scene from 1919 (the year of P.'s last Provençal walking tour) is spliced with a fresher image and another locus: "Here three ants have killed a great worm."[29] The opposition of "here" and "there" involves not only Excideuil vs. Rapallo, but also

---

29. In order to underscore this change of scene Pound changed the comma after "tree trunk" to a full stop in the 1954 Faber reprint. He also placed a comma after "Venezia" three lines down, and omitted "the" in the last line (spoken in what appears to be broken English by the "elderly lady"). All of these changes are unwisely ignored in the New Directions text.

(time being relative to space) 1919 vs. 1936—the time of the invasion of Ethiopia, of the novel League of Cambrai, and of the Anti-Comintern Pact. It follows that very probably the "three ants" that kill the "great worm" (Cerberus in *Inf.* 6, Geryon in P.) are intended as an image of Italy, Germany, and Japan—the countries which Pound took to be the champions of the natural economic order, of vision, and (ironically) of anti-authoritarianism: "Said they wd. not be under Paris."[30] As if to bear this out the three subsequent cantos are set in China as seen through Japanese eyes, in Napoleon's (or Mussolini's) Italy, and in Hitler's Königsberg. To encourage immediate action the canto's final lines assess the forces of "Paris," or of the Venice-Hades of the XXX *Cantos.* In Pound's view (as in that of Mussolini four years later) they cannot escape destruction at the first onslaught:

> Employed, past tense; at the Lido, Venezia,
> an old man with a basket of stones,
> that was, said the elderly lady, when the beach costumes
> were longer,
> and if wind was, the old man placed a stone.   [c. 48]

The old man's stones will hardly be enough to keep Mitteleuropean costumes or *mœurs* from being blown away for good by the gathering storm.

In the event, however, it was Pound who went under, with his three ants. Yet before losing contact he managed to draft a rambunctious postscript to cs. 31–51, and to the better part of the thirties as he had known them. This was *Guide to Kulchur,* the climax of many years of *ABCs* and his last extensive prose venture (he being fifty-one at the time of writing), torrentially compiled within a few weeks, between February and April 1937. Its aim is a comprehensive survey of culture and/or Poundland, inclusive of matters dealt with in the other pamphlets of the thirties (*J/M* and the two *ABCs*), the chief addition being a consideration of philosophic thought based on Fiorentino's respectable

30. This echoes the close of c. 16.

(but forty-year-old) textbook. Philosophy is covered chiefly in the early sections, literature in Parts 4–5, and the finale is characteristically assigned to a close textual scrutiny of the *Nicomachean Ethics*. Pound, however, follows no orderly scheme of exposition, preferring (as in his other pamphlets) the ideogramic method, which allows the "real" to express itself and define its own structure. Hence the book's air of extemporization, its confusions, and its many surprises and felicities. We may read it as an avant-garde artist's chapbook, as seminal and as funny as (say) John Cage's *Silence;* as an experiment in education; or as a diary, if we profit from Pound's inclination to note the date of his world-shaking pronouncements ("the grand ideas of the villages"—as Wallace Stevens called them), or of the correspondence which finds its way into the discussion, precisely as in an innovative school, in which teacher and class explore together whatever the day happens to offer. In the *ABC of Reading* Pound had insisted that the teacher should read *with*—not only *to*—his class, and he makes good his word beyond our expectations and his own intentions. In fact he sets out with the prospect of introducing us to the brave new world of Mussolini, Confucius, Frobenius, and Ezra Pound—but as he goes on he is continuously checking and revising his attitudes to an extent surprising in the author of cs. 48 and 51. But then the poetry of the middle cantos is a harsh thing which does not allow for nuances, but only for mystical all-or-nothing proposals; the prose of *Kulchur* is another matter, though it probably owes its assuredness to Pound's feeling that the *Fifth Decad* is a major success.[31] Thus in chapter 44 we find the rejection of racism quoted earlier, with its implied criticism of the rabid anti-Semitism of English fascists (Zapponi 38). Elsewhere the poet voices his disagreement "with some of the details of contemporary Italian and German views and proposed laws on conjugality" (23), and detects an "Aristotelic residuum" in Mussolini's mind (54). The Pound of 1937 is in fact very unlike the desperado of the war years—he is the poet and patron of the

31. "It takes a while till you get your bearings—like a detective story—and see how it's going to go. I hit my stride in the *Fifth Decad of Cantos*"—P., in the fifties, to Ronald Goodman. Quoted in Norman 444.

arts, the small Sigismondo Malatesta (an explicit parallel: "Federigo Urbino was his Amy Lowell, Federigo with more wealth got the seconds") who wants Rapallo to become a major "center of culture" (*Il Mare*, 2 May 1936), and endorses for the new fascist town hall a project of the futurist architect Antonio Sant'Elia (ibid., 28 March 1936). To the village he brings the music of Vivaldi and Mozart, and, on 5 March 1937, during the writing of *K*, Bartok's *Fifth Quartet*, composed only three years previously—all of this at a time of general cultural lag in the country.

Bartok's work, performed in conjunction with a Boccherini quintet, occasions several clear-sighted remarks on the role of contemporary art, since it has "the defects or disadvantages of my Cantos . . . the defects inherent in a record of struggle" (*K* 19)—whereas Boccherini's sovran simplicity speaks to Pound of a culture wholly integral to communal life, anteceding Eliot's "dissociation of sensibility," which he believes can be healed in the doubtful way we have seen. This chapter, despite its confusions (it is incredible that an intelligent person in the thirties could hold P.'s uncertain opinion of Beethoven), indicates that Pound is capable of self-criticism and that something is beginning to clear up in his mind, the effect (he tells us elsewhere) of music: "The magic of music is in its effect on volition. A sudden clearing of the mind of rubbish and the re-establishment of a sense of proportion" (50). Accordingly, another score, Jannequin's *Chanson des oiseaux,* transcribed for lute by Francesco da Milano, and finally for violin and piano by Pound's friend, the composer Gerhart Münch, elicits the memorable passage on the reemergence of "the *forma,* the immortal *concetto*" by way of a continuous process of transcription—one of the chief keys to the poetics of the *Cantos* (*K* 23).

Pound's reappraisal of his role and his work comes to a head in the two impassioned chapters which function as a close to the substance of *K*. (The subsequent reading of Aristotle is intended as verification of P.'s findings, and as proof that he has not "just gone butterflying around all the time"—*L* 327.) Their subject is a poet and novelist whom one would think least likely to interest

Pound, namely Thomas Hardy. Yet a careful reading of *K* and of the *Cantos* reveals that Pound's instrument, though it records with some accuracy the contemporary waste land, is actually more at home in the small and somewhat old-fashioned world inhabited by Kipling, James, Stevenson, Swinburne, Yeats, Hardy, and many others of lesser stature—a world in which "there can be honesty of mind / without overwhelming talent" (c. 80). (This of course does not apply to James and Yeats, though it may apply to those works of these writers which P. responded to.) The 1937 confrontation with Hardy brings out from under the shadow of the boisterous writer of *ABCs* an unexpected apparition, the painfully insecure disciple who in 1920 had sent Hardy his two major portraits with the comment: "The Propertius is confused—the Mauberley is thin."[32] Within a few pages Pound does away with modernist poetics and offers a strangely traditional definition of poetry:

> If I have, a few pages back, set a measure for music [see above], I set another for poetry. No man can read Hardy's poems collected but that his own life, and forgotten moments of it, will come back to him, a flash here and an hour there. Have you a better test of true poetry?
> When I say that the *work* is more criticism than any talk around and about the work, that also flashes in reading Hardy. In the clean wording. No thoughtful writer can read this book of Hardy's without throwing his own work (in imagination) into the test-tube and hunting it for fustian, for the foolish word, for the word upholstered.
>
> .   .   .
>
> Sero sero te amavi, pulchritudo tam antiqua, quam nova. There is a clarity like Hardy's in the best English sporting prints, in stray watercolours, anonymous of the period. [K 51]

China and Provence in the *Cantos* share at times this clarity, reminiscent of early Wordsworth. (It is a measure of Hardy's authority that P. is willing to listen to—and to transcribe—his quotations from the Preface to the *Lyrical Ballads*—a manifesto which prefigures P.'s and Eliot's "revolution" in not a few points.) But Pound's clarity is often dimmed by elegy, and by a

32. Quoted in Patricia Hutchins, "Ezra Pound and Thomas Hardy," *Southern Review* (winter 1968). Reference in Davie, *Ezra Pound*, p. 44n.

certain amount of self-pity, when it is not wholly concealed by
the loud pounding. Likewise in the present homage, which
praises Hardy, James, Swinburne, and the Pre-Raphaelites for their
"rebellion against the sordid matrimonial customs of England,"
the reader is aware of an intimate embarrassment, of the weight of
Pound's socially and existentially ambiguous private life.[33]

The following chapter continues in the same excited vein, turning ceaselessly from literature to sex, economics, and religion
("Cogitavi vias meas: 'That the greatest of things is Charity' ").
Here Pound sketches the rationale behind the *Cantos*. The old
masters, Hardy among them, "bred a generation of experi-
menters, my generation, which was unable to work out a code
for action. We believed and disbelieved 'everything,' or to put it
another way we believed in the individual case" (*K* 52). Subsequently, however, Pound felt the need to commit himself, with
the results that we know:

And a few serious survivors of war grew into tolerance of the "new synthesis," saw finally a need for a "general average" in law. There was, in
this, perhaps no positive gain save that, again, a few saw a dissociation
of personal crises and cruces, that exist above or outside economic pressure, and those which arise directly from it, or are so encumbered by,
and entangled in, the root problems of money, that any pretended ethical or philosophical dealing with them is sheer bunk UNTIL they be
disentangled. [*K* 52]

Hence the recurrent *nékuia* of the *Cantos:* "First must thou go
the road to hell" (c. 47). Beyond which is the unattainable vision:

When you get out of the hell of money there remains the undiscussa-
ble Paradiso. And any reach into it is almost a barrier to literary success.

33. "As the Pounds always struck us as being happy enough together, we had been
surprised to gather from the gossip of the small English colony that for some time Ezra
had been apportioning the seasons between Dorothy and the violinist Olga Rudge—or between Rapallo and Venice, if you prefer. Perhaps something I said to Ezra one evening betrayed the fact that I had got wind of the arrangement: he suddenly started to rave against
the 'middle-class mentality of this bloody English bunch.' When the outburst had subsided, I observed that Dorothy must have been a lovely girl when he had first met her in
England. He was silent for a moment before replying: 'Yes, she was. I fell in love with a
beautiful picture that never came alive.' " Daniel Cory, "Ezra Pound: A Memoir," *Encounter*, XXX, 5 (May 1968), 31. See also M. de Rachewiltz, *passim*.

Sì vid'io ben più di mille splendori
Trarsi ver noi, ed in ciascun s'udia:
"Ecco chi crescerà li nostri amori." [34]

There is nothing in modern critical mechanism to deal with, and I
doubt if there is anything handy in our poetic vocabulary even to translate, the matter of this and the following Cantos.

Vedeasi l'ombra piena di letizia
Nel fulgor chiaro che di lei uscia. [35]

Sober minds have agreed that the arcanum is the arcanum. No man
can provide his neighbour with a Cook's ticket thereto. [K 52]

The radiant world is unrecoverable and Pound's novel journey to
the stars must fail as it is not backed up by a holistic culture. For
a moment Pound seems to see through the rhetoric of the
glorious fascist future:

A gain in narrative sense from 1600 to 1900, but the tones that went
out of English verse? The truth having been Eleusis? and a modern
Eleusis being possible in the wilds of a man's mind only?
The requirements being far beyond those of merely an intelligent literary circle (which doesn't in any case exist). We lack not only the
means but the candidates. Think of any modern waiting five years to
know anything! Or wanting to know! If ever anything but a fanaticism
could? A collection of misfits? Not the flower of a civilization. Was it
ever possible save with conviction and a simplicity beyond modern
reach? now that knowledge is a drug on the market, said knowledge
being a job lot of odds and ends having no order, but being abundant,
superhumanly abundant. [K 52]

Here Pound's writing is truly made luminous by a sudden grace,
or by what he calls a few lines down, "the oblivions of pure curiosity," and he reminds himself of the choice he had made at the
inception of the middle cantos: "tempus tacendi." Yet this has
brought no relief to the dizzy dispersion of knowledge, and the

34. *Par.* v.103–05. "In such a way I saw plainly over one thousand splendors move
towards us, and in each I heard: 'Here is one who shall increase our loves.'"
35. *Par.* v.106–08. "[And as each came to us,] it appeared that the shade was full of happiness, from the clear effulgence that it emitted." P., as we shall find later on, understands
this rather to mean: "One saw the shadow replete of happiness within the clear effulgence
which it emitted."

result of over five years of waiting to know is *Kulchur,* called "a book of yatter" one page back, and the flawed *Cantos.* We may take this chapter on "The Promised Land" to signal the conception of the *Pisan Cantos,* as many of its phrases and attitudes are to recur in that poem of an Eleusis wholly phantastical, yet also real.

Eight years, however, elapsed, before *K* bore its fruit—the darkest years of Pound's inferno, though these had also their share of epiphanies. After the conclusions reached in *K* Pound could only, in all coherence, seek "a simplicity beyond modern reach," Boccherini's transparence, and reject Bartokian and Poundian intricacies. With this aim he set his hand in 1938 to compartments third and fourth of the middle cantos, *China-John Adams*—and produced a glaring example of regime art, or of what we could call "fascist realism." The result is quite surprising, as contemporary politics and ideologies are less in the foreground here (with the single exception of c. 52) than in previous "decads." But we have come to believe that it is the form of an art work that carries the greater ideological burden, and so we need not be taken aback by the fact that the Jefferson and Siena cantos make progressive use of largely reactionary content, whereas *China-John Adams* is indifferent in subject and backward in form. These twenty cantos amount in fact to two elephantine quotations, two episodes on the model of the *Malatesta,* but quite lacking in critical and combinatory strategies, intended as a tragicomical summary *ad usum ducis* [36] of the twelve volumes of Chinese annals translated in the late eighteenth century by Mailla, and of the ten volumes of the *Works* of John Adams, who (we are to infer from ideogramic contiguity) is a Confucian ruler in the line of the great emperors. Expanding to absurd lengths the method of c. 1, Pound strictly observes the original order of his sources, and so

36. P. sent the book to Mussolini on 12 February 1940 with a covering letter in which he said: "I hope I have done a useful job at least in summarizing certain historical events in my CANTOS 52/71. The book is so far from neutral that my publisher has excised the name of Rothschild from the first page." Quoted in Zapponi 53. (This was the time, it should be recalled, in which Mussolini proclaimed that he was not "neutral," rather "nonbelligerent.") In c. 55 there is another address to the Duce and his people: "TSONG of TANG put up granaries / somewhat like those you want to establish."

produces on the one hand a chronological account of Chinese history from 2837 B.C. to the eighteenth century, on the other hand a bewildering hodgepodge which we can only set right by checking Adams' volumes, which are arranged not chronologically but according to genre. It must, however, be added that the Chinese cantos are relatively successful as an epic narration, and make for amusing reading (P. thought of himself at this point as a popular storyteller, and insisted that they be read aloud—see *L* 363)—and that the Adams persona, whatever its faults, is a unique example of anti-poetry and of textual labor, which at least may be said to suggest something of the original's tone. Yet it is enough to compare this diptych with the documentary sections of previous and subsequent cantos to become aware of the disproportion between its tiresome mass and the small weight it carries in the grand fugue (or spiral) of the poem, in spite of such devices as the Cavalcanti tags and the Chinese characters inserted in the Adams section. In fact it is hard to believe that the poem would have ever recovered from this lethargic spell had it not been for the powerful shock that brought about the *Pisan Cantos*. The evidence points to an eclipse (or to a new "passage of the 'selva oscura' ") of the poetic instinct in Pound, who, increasingly obsessed with haste and with a nightmare of politics, economics, and racism, is willing to cover with mediocre materials a conspicuous surface of his fresco of about one hundred cantos. Yet there is no indication that he had lost interest in the poem (though he had in fact come to think of it as a job soon to be done), while the fact that on the average the China-Adams cantos are nearly twice as long as the ones of Jefferson and Siena would indicate absorption with the subject matter, and no lack of energy and material. Furthermore, from Pound's correspondence we learn that at this time he considered *China-John Adams* to be his best work to date—a shattering rebuttal to suggestions that he was not quite "an American writer," and a timely contribution to world peace.[37] (In the Adams section there are several

---

37. See *L* 355 and 358, and the letter of early 1940 to Lulu Cunningham of Hailey, Idaho, quoted in Norman 375: "I suppose my best book is Cantos 52/71 / and probably the one before it, '(Kulch, or Ez') Guide to Kulchur' which the publishers blush to print with its real title, is the best prose."

passages of isolationist import, one of them scored in the margin for emphasis.) In the spring of 1939, after drafting the sequence, Pound took it upon himself to communicate what he believed to be the point of view of Italy and of John Adams to the United States government, and made the crossing to Washington, where he was hardly welcome. (He also made a hysteric scene at Hamilton College, where, on 12 June, he was awarded an honorary D. Litt.) This unhappy exile's return (the first since 1911) only deepened his difference with his country and with democracy, and alienated sympathies in the United States. At any rate, it is significant that the trajectory of Pound's poetry should reach its nadir (as elsewhere the zenith of vision) precisely in the course of a confrontation with the text—an irrational absorption with the written. We may also note that, as he forsakes his more individual voice in favor of totalitarian commitment, Pound is well within the phenomenology of modernist culture, for this is a road travelled by many artists, including those of the opposite persuasion.

3. The Works and Days of Pisa

On 11 February 1940 Pound inscribed his wife's copy of the freshly issued *Cantos LII–LXXI* with the words:

> *To build up the city of Dioce*
> *(Tan Wu Tsze)*
> *Whose terraces are the colour of stars* [Stock 479]

Thirty years back he had written a friend about his wish "to build a dream over the world" (ibid.); now he was bent upon the dreamlike City of the *Cantos,* Ecbatan of c. 4, its seven differently colored walls mirroring as it were the heavens, and its present name (after the builder Deioces) suggesting that the poem's city was in the process of being realized here and now—by the Duce.[1] These claims, however, were hardly borne out by the drudgery of much in these cantos, which rather point to the moral we have elicited from *Kulchur,* namely that the poet's heart does not follow his will in the matter of "the totalitarian synthesis," being distinctly more fond of the twilit world of love unsatisfied. "Love thou thy dream," he had advised in *A Lume Spento,* "And here take warning / That dreams alone can truly be, / For 'tis in dream I come to thee."

Apparently quite oblivious of this (and much taken—as we have seen—with his chronicles of China and John Adams), Pound turned in 1939–40 to collecting in a funnily practical fashion the religious and philosophical materials of a "paradise" he planned to make short work of in one "final volume" of cantos.[2] (He was in fact only twenty-nine cantos short of the Dantesque hundred.)

I have also [he wrote George Santayana on 8 December 1939] got to the end of a job or part of a job (money in history) and for personal

1. Cf. Hugh Kenner, *"Drafts & Fragments* and the Structure of the *Cantos,"* Agenda, VIII, 3–4 (1970), 14.

2. "My best stuff is in *Cantos* 1 to 71 (so far pubd) & complete as it stands. Tho' there's a final volume to be done."—To Lulu Cunningham, prob. early 1940, quoted in Norman 376.

ends have got to tackle philosophy or my "paradise," and do badly
want to talk with some one who has thought a little about it. There is
one bloke in England, whose name escapes me, who has dropped an intelligent aside in a small book on Manes. Otherwise you are the only
perceivable victim. [L 365]

Pound's long strides, however, were checked by the War, which
persuaded him to put off the final installment of the poem until
matters be settled in favor (as he did not doubt) of his Deioces,
and to rally to the latter's aid, if necessary by reconsidering the
subject of "money in history." Thus it was that the incubation of
his "paradise" stretched out to five years, covering the most dramatic period of his life, and that the outline of 1939–40 was considerably altered by events (the final volumes were to become
four; the cantos nearly 120). Among intervening works—all valuable to an understanding of the later poetry—are *Carta da visita*
(a bewildering "visiting card" to a new Italian audience: 1942);
the three rather controlled Italian pamphlets of 1944, which are
Pound's final prose statements of his economics and history; the
crucial Italian Confucius of 1942–45 (later to be Englished at Pisa); the Rome broadcasts, which may be read as a long
and more often than not repellent analytical session; and finally
cantos 72–73, which have little bearing on Pound's "paradise,"
being (as mentioned earlier) a celebration (again in P.'s approximate Italian) of the fascist last stand in Northern Italy ("Glory!
Glory! / To die for one's fatherland / in Romagna! / [. . .] And
what a fine girl, / what girls, / what boys, / wear black!").[3] Significant events were Pound's coming to know Rome and what was
left of its intelligentsia, some of it genuine; the correspondence
and meetings with Santayana; the removal from the Rapallo flat
to the hill of Sant' Ambrogio close by, the scene of many visionary encounters to be related in the poem; the escape of "the man
out of Naxos past Fara Sabina" after the fall of the regime in
September 1943; and, twenty months later (a few weeks after
the hanging "by the heels" of Mussolini and his mistress Claretta

3. Canto 73, quoted in Piero Sanavio, *Ezra Pound* (Venezia: Marsilio, 1977), p. 180. The
"girl" is the swineherdess who (as Guido's ghost tells P. in this canto) led a company of
Canadian soldiers to their death in a mine field, thus giving her life for the "cause."

Petacci), his capture. (This is not to say that P. went into hiding: he did not think he had committed any offense and rather believed that his countrymen would take him on as consultant on Italy.) The rest of the story has often been told: Pound was detained at the American Counter Intelligence Center in Genoa from 3 to 22 May 1945, then driven to Pisa and put in a solitary confinement cell where he underwent physical and mental strain (not enough, however, to enfeeble his exceptionally healthy physique). Within a few weeks he was moved to a tent in the medical compound and here, early in July, he set his hand to what was to become the *Pisan Cantos,* taking as his point of departure the materials he had been considering in 1939–40—Manes and the city of Deioces—but placing them in the new light of the Duce's destruction, which recovered the City to the realm of dreams truer than actuality in which he was most at home:

The enormous tragedy of the dream in the peasant's bent shoulders
Manes! Manes was tanned and stuffed,
Thus Ben and la Clara *a Milano*
        by the heels at Milano
That maggots shd/ eat the dead bullock
DIGONOS, Δίγονος, but the twice crucified
          where in history will you find it?
yet say this to the Possum: a bang, not a whimper,
    with a bang not with a whimper,
To build the city of Dioce whose terraces are the colour of stars.[c. 74]

By aligning Manes and Mussolini (the two names alliterate) Pound confers upon the latter the status of an initiate and religious leader, and imports that Italy has been visited with the fate of Albigensian Provence and other agricultural societies (for instance the American South) at the hands of the bankers and the orthodox—hence the ultimate victim is the peasant of the first line. Yet the references to Dionysus as twice born (*dígonos*), to Christ (who was crucified but once—unlike Mussolini, perhaps), and possibly to the birth of tragedy from the sacrifice of the goat (here the dead bullock to which "Ben" is compared), remind us that the tragedy of death is germane to rural culture—a necessary step towards renewal and rebirth (c. 47). Thus what seems a

25

defeat is really a most exalted victory, as Pound triumphantly informs the Possum, a representative of the orthodox bankers and hollow men who have just defeated peasant Italy and Germany.[4]

So far Pound has only restated with novel forcefulness the wild philosophy of the *Fifth Decad*. It is only in the sequel that we learn that this is not only hell's ranting, as he takes in the full measure of the natural cycle, and juxtaposes Deioces' city with the central object of his verse—the eyes of the goddess:

> The suave eyes, quiet, not scornful,
> > rain also is of the process.
> What you depart from is not the way
> and olive tree blown white in the wind
> washed in the Kiang and Han
> what whiteness will you add to this whiteness,
> > what candour?
> "the great periplum brings in the stars to our shore."   [c. 74]

This continues the elegy for the dead hero (who advertised his scorn), and adds to the previous list of precedents Confucius, whose virtue was said to be as incomparably white as "an object washed in the Kiang and Han" (Mencius 3A.4). But the eyes of the Duce are readily metamorphosed into those of the lady as Athene *glaukôpis*, Ulysses' patroness, her presence suggested (as often in the *Cantos*) by the olive tree which replaces the "object" of Mencius' praise.[5] Athene and the city are linked by ideogramic contiguity, by the former's name, by their ability to rise over the ruins of forgetfulness and tragedy, and by the fact that they are

4. P. once told Charles Olson that he had "baptized" Eliot "Possum" because of the latter's "ability to appear to be dead while [he] is still alive." See Olson, *Charles Olson & Ezra Pound: An Encounter at St Elizabeths*, ed. Catherine Seelye (New York: Grossman, 1975), p. 113.

5. The theme of Athene's olive is already to be found in ur-c. 1 ("Not a-gleam, / But coloured like the lake and olive leaves, / GLAUKOPOS"—QPA 20), and turns up again in cs. 20–21. P.'s source is Allen Upward's *The New World* (1910) as quoted in "Allen Upward Serious" (*New Age*, 23 April 1914; *SPr* 407–8). See also *L* 290: "Poor old Upward [he had committed suicide in 1926, as mentioned in c. 74] had a lot to say about Athene's eyes, connecting them with her owl and with olive trees. The property of the glaux [owl], and olive leaf, to shine and then not to shine, 'glint' rather than shine. Certainly a more living word if one lives among olive yards." P.'s debt to Upward is discussed by Donald Davie in *Ezra Pound* (1975), pp. 63–72.

both creatures fully of the imagination. They speak to the poet, in the words of the *Chung-yung* (*UP* 1 2), of the providential order of things, then of the mysteries of light and sex earlier alluded to by the name Clara and suggested here by Cavalcanti's "white light that is allness" (c. 36), and finally of the pattern and of the love that move the stars. If the speaker is Athene, it is fitting that she should turn in the end to Noman, the hero and author of the poem, joining the great periplum (a key word of *PC*) of the universe to his individual and ill-starred (but finally not so) voyage:

> You who have passed the pillars and outward from Herakles
> when Lucifer fell in N. Carolina.
> if the suave air give way to scirocco
> OὛ ΤΙΣ, OὛ ΤΙΣ? Odysseus
>   the name of my family.
> the wind also is of the process,
>   sorella la luna   [c. 74]

The Pillars of Hercules are made to remind us of Dante's Ulysses (who when he reaches them must press his men to sail after knowledge), of Hanno (c. 40), and of Pound, who in 1939 sailed past Gibraltar "to keep hell from breaking loose on earth" (as he was to explain later in 1945 to the presiding judge at his first arraignment)—apparently the import of the reference to Lucifer.[6] The trip, he realizes, ended in disaster, the suave air of his Italian idyll giving way to stormy scirocco, but this has truly made him one of a kind with Ulysses and Hanno—he may quote Noman's words to the Cyclops to introduce himself to the reader. But soon we find that the "family" includes St. Francis' "sister Moon,"

6. Norman, who quotes P.'s statement about hell on p. 360 of his biography, remarks on p. 355 that in writing these lines P. may have misremembered a book by his fellow Hamiltonian Carl Carman, *Stars Fell on Alabama,* or the popular song. In Dante it is the fall of Lucifer that, by repelling the earth, creates the inverted cone of hell and (on the other side of the globe) the Mount of Purgatory.

    In his fine study *The Cantos of Ezra Pound: The Lyric Mode* (Baltimore: Johns Hopkins University Press, 1975), p. 76, Eugene Paul Nassar suggests a different and perhaps equally satisfactory reading of "You who have passed . . ." as P.-Ulysses' "brotherly" address to the sun (for they both travel west, as in turn Lucifer-as-morning star). Not only the city of Deioces but also myth shows "the color of stars."

and realize that Pound is speaking of a bond of affection between all men, and between man and process. The crudity of tragedy has elicited a humane *pietas* involving men and things. This is the final message of the eyes, which have yielded up their earlier esthetic aloofness (they are "quiet, scornful" in c. 20), and the sum of the peaceful invocation of the way, of the wind, and of the stars, which distinctly prefigures the mood and the syntax of the climax of the section and possibly of the poem: "What thou lovest well remains / the rest is dross."

So, as he seeks to establish what has survived apocalypse, Pound discovers the essential item which we miss most in his earlier verse. He had much lost time to make up for, and this may have been his last chance to speak out—so in the course of the summer and early fall, as energies returned after the shock and physical harassment of the "cage," [7] he wrote his longest "decad" (actually eleven cantos, amounting to 125 pages—the eleven Jefferson cantos cover 57 pages), and created an entire world of memory, observation, and comment. The technique of playing against each other past glory and present squalor is of course employed as early as c. 7, but this accounts for only a small part of *PC*, for Pound does not quarrel overmuch with his surroundings. If he has little sympathy for the army and its routine, the men of the D.T.C. are dear to him as they provide him with first-hand material for his construct, and with what a poet most relishes, a live language. Pound can hardly be considered a master of language, as his interest in the spoken tongue often results in faulty diction (we have met several examples, and cs. 52–71 are a glaring instance). But he can tell the live from the dead when he hears it—and as soon as he becomes exposed to idiomatic Ameri-

7. On this matter evidence is contradictory. Perhaps P.'s lawyer Julien Cornell exaggerated a little, for reasons quite understandable, when he wrote in his affidavit (November 1945) that "after about three weeks" in his cell P. "was stricken with violent and hysterical terror. He lost his memory" (Cornell 20–21), for a sympathetic eyewitness remembered in 1958 only that "because the dust and harsh sun in the cage inflamed his eyes, he was transferred to a tent in the Medical Compound" (Robert L. Allen, "The Cage," *Esquire*, February 1958, and O'Connor-Stone 35).

can (after many years of speaking and writing first in a compact
of assumed English and of Americanese, then in broken Italian),
the language of the poem comes alive—it is the social language of
men—and the pointless and embarrassing phonetic spelling of earlier cantos is used sparingly and to good effect. Besides all of this,
and more (a table to write on, charity), the present has to offer
the wonder of summer, of birds and lizards and ants, and of
vision. When he was about halfway through with the section
Pound commented usefully on what he was doing for the benefit
of the base censor, who (we gather) was not sure he wanted the
obscure typescript to go out with the mail:

Note to Base Censor

The Cantos contain nothing in the nature of cypher or intended obscurity. The present Cantos do, naturally, contain a number of allusions
and "recalls" to matter in the earlier 71 cantos already published, and
many of these cannot be made clear to readers unacquainted with the
earlier parts of the poem.

There is also an extreme condensation in the quotations, for example
"Mine eyes have" (given as mi-hine eyes hev) refers to the Battle Hymn
of the Republic as heard from the loud speaker. There is not time or
place in the narrative to give the further remarks on seeing the glory of
the lord.

In like manner citations from Homer or Sophokles or Confucius are
brief, and serve to remind the ready reader that we were not born yes-
terday. The Chinese ideograms are mainly translated, or commented in
the english text. At any rate they contain nothing seditious.

The form of the poem and main progress is conditioned by its own
inner shape, but the life of the D.T.C. passing OUTSIDE the scheme cannot but impinge, or break into the main flow. The proper names given
are mostly those of men on sick call seen passing my tent. A very brief
allusion to further study in names, that is, I am interested to note the
prevalence of early american names, either of whites of the old tradition
(most of the early presidents for example) or of descendents of slaves
who took the names of their masters. Interesting in contrast to the relative scarcity of melting-pot names.[8]

8. A photograph of this note accompanies Donald Hall's late interview with P. in *Writers
at Work: The Paris Review Interviews*, 2nd Series (New York: Viking, 1963), p. 36.

Clearly the man who wrote this was as much in control of his strategies as he had ever been, and not in a state of mental collapse. He took time to remind the poor fellow that he had published no less than seventy-one cantos (he conveniently omitted mention of the two last Italian cantos),[9] and to make fun of the piped patriotism of the Battle Hymn of the Republic. And he made it clear that the new cantos were the work of "the opportunism of the artist," who quickly sees and takes advantage of the possibilities of a situation—like Henri Gaudier carving a German rifle butt to please himself. The periplus having come to a stop which may well have been an end, the D.T.C. was the ideal persistent and striking background upon which to weave a web of reminiscence, as Ulysses had done (also in the first person) in Alcinous' halls. The *Cantos* are largely autobiographical throughout, but heretofore personal materials were used out of context in order to suggest some ideogramic inference. In *PC*, however, Pound gives us his world for its own sake, because he is attached to it, as Villon had done in *Le Grant Testament,* that we (and *he*) may know who our Ulysses was before the days of Circe's swine sty. Previously events were the coordinates defining some concept, now they define an individual. It is the Contacts of E.P. (1 *HSM*) once over, on a larger and more moving scale, and with less of an ax to grind. The moment the person stands revealed, we feel that through him we are dealing with an entire culture—whereas previously we had nothing to show for our canto reading but the figments of Pound's own mind.

One could question Pound's claim that the "main progress" of the poem "is conditioned by its own inner shape"—such being the weight of *PC* that the *Cantos* become quite a different poem through this adjunct. Yet the interplay of reminiscences and prison life does signal a novel, creditably paradisal, phase of "the main flow." And Pound does bring to a head many of the themes

9. It may also be that he had not yet made up his mind about including them in his count, but this is unlikely for on 7 February 1946 he spoke of them with pride to Charles Olson, referring to them mistakenly as nos. 71–72 (Olson, *Encounter at St Elizabeths,* p. 69; editor Seelye—usually anxious to point out P.'s lapses—repeats this one in her note on p. 128).

dealt with desultorily in earlier passages, giving us a better image of the good life, and going on to the celebrations of Venus, Dionysus, and other "eternal states of mind," which he had certainly intended for the "final volume" of the poem.

Thus we witness the apotheosis of Confucius, who enters the poem's spiral briefly but forcefully in c. 13, to become very prominent in the latter part of Pound's purgatory (cs. 49 and 52–71). But the Confucius of Pisa, the contemplator of a "way" which looks suspiciously Taoist, and of the "white light," is very different from the persona of c. 13 and even of the Chinese cantos, being largely the result of Pound's fresh perusal of the *Four Books* (and translation of the former two among these) during the war years. The Confucius of the twenties was chiefly a Voltairian foil for the fanaticism and asceticism of certain (Puritanic) types of Christianity, whereas later Pound sought in his texts support for his own fanaticism, and eventually a religion to believe in. As early as 1933 he looked long enough at the Chinese sign which he renders as "Make it new" to see in it a representation of "the fascist axe," and pointed to Confucius' respect for "intelligence, 'the luminous principle of reason' " (*J/M* 112–13). The latter was to become more than a metaphor when, in the late thirties, his mind full of Cavalcanti's alleged philosophy of light, he turned for intense scrutiny to the *Four Books*—and saw everywhere symbols of light. We shall mention only two characters which he took as tokens of Confucius' concern for light—an evidence tenuous in the extreme, for of course these signs occur in a good many Chinese texts, which can hardly on this account be said to anticipate the tenets of Guido. One of them is *ch'eng,* "sincere," a combination of signs meaning "words" and "to perfect." The latter Pound reads, very imaginatively indeed, as the picture of a ray of light falling through a focussing lens. Hence his gloss to the whole: "The sun's lance coming to rest on the precise spot verbally" (*GD,* "Terminology"). Here, we see, the metaphysics of light touches Pound's other great theme, the precision of the word, for which he also sought and found Confucian authority, chiefly in a disputed passage of the *Analects* (third of the *Four Books*), in which the master says that, were he in power

in Wei, the first thing that he would do would be "to call people
or things by their names," or *cheng ming* (A xiii 3, K 1, and c.
51). What Confucius was saying with this, commentators tell us,
is that in Wei, because of court intrigue, positions had been shuf-
fled around and were held by people who were not entitled to
them, and that he would try to set this right. However, the *cheng
ming* motif is of central importance in Chinese thought, if not
particularly in that of Confucius.[10]

Another image of light Pound is particularly fond of, and a
better choice than *ch'eng,* is the character *hsien* ("to manifest, to
be illustrious"—*M* 2692), which does contain the sign for "sun"
over the sign for "silk." Pound was reminded of Grosseteste's
light extending threadwise from source to object ("Cavalcanti,"
LE 161), and late in 1944 he rendered a passage in which the
character occurs (the final paragraph in his Italian translation of
Chung-yung, the second Confucian book) so as to suggest Cavalcanti's love which "resplende in sé perpetüale effetto" ("shineth
out / Himself his own effect unendingly"): "La purezza funge (nel
tempo e nello spazio) senza termine. Senza termine funge, luce
tensile." [11] In July of the following year, at Pisa, he took the further unwarranted step of linking this with the theology of the immaculate conception, and five pages into c. 74 glossed *hsien* as
follows:

> Light tensile immaculata
>   the sun's cord unspotted
> "sunt lumina" said the Oirishman to King Carolus,
>   "OMNIA,
> all things that are are lights"
> and they dug him up out of sepulture
> soi disantly looking for Manichaeans.

10. See Mancuso 118–20; and Granet 47: "Aux premiers jours de la civilisation chinoise,
Huang-ti acquit la gloire d'un héros fondateur, car il prit soin de donner à toutes choses
une désignation (*ming*) correcte (*tcheng*), ceci 'afin d'éclairer le peuple sur les ressources
utilisables.' " Needless to say, *ch'eng* ("sincere") must not be confused with *cheng* ("correct"). The first can be seen in c. 76 ("the word is made perfect"); the second we have encountered in the close of c. 51.

11. *Ciung Iung. L'asse che non vacilla* (Venezia: Casa Editrice delle Edizioni Popolari,
1945). Quoted in Hugh Kenner, "The 5 Laws + Che Funge," *Paideuma,* 1 (1972), 83.

> Les Albigeois, a problem of history,
> and the fleet at Salamis made with money lent by the state to
>   the shipwrights
>   Tempus tacendi, tempus loquendi.   [c. 74]

—an ideogramic correlation of Cavalcanti, Confucius, Erigena (who flourished at the court of Charles the Bald), the Albigenses, credit on real capital (see Hdt. vii. 144), and speech after long silence (the phrase from Ecclesiastes being now returned to its original form). Having accumulated in the years of the "selva oscura" his material (his real capital) Pound now promises to have it out. All of these connections, with the exception of Confucius, we have already met in c. 36, and Confucius was in turn brought in with cs. 51 and 55.

So when, in October, still in the D.T.C., Pound came around to retranslating his Italian *Chung-yung* into English, he added the new specification: "The *unmixed* functions (in time and in space) without bourne. This unmixed is the tensile light, the Immaculata. There is no end to its action." [12]

Were we to assign a major source to *PC*, this would have to be the *Four Books*. They are quoted everywhere, in English and in Chinese—in fact the poem as printed preserves only a fraction of the characters occurring in the typescript. This is in keeping with the drift of the *Cantos*, in which, as we have seen, Confucius becomes increasingly prominent from the *Fifth Decad* on. As for Pound's heightened interest in Chinese characters, this follows upon his worship of the Word as the beginning of all. He has come to believe, like the ancient Chinese and other archaic peoples, that the signs of language and the signatures of nature secretly prefigure our actions, or tell us how we had better behave. Indeed, the Word has it within itself to affect things—for instance, a soldier will have a certain character, say "courage," embroidered upon his chest, and this will get him through the battle. The Chinese in the poem performs a similar function. Yet we need not call in magic to account for the use of characters in

12. *UP* xxvi 10. Reprinting the Italian version in 1955 P. also changed it accordingly: "La purezza funge (nel tempo e nello spazio) senza termine. Immacolata. Senza termine" (*OS* 597).

ideogramic clusters: it is sufficient to note that these make their
point quickly, for they are easily recognized with a little practice—that they project a visual image, which the reader of the
Cantos learns to make out as the poet's glosses would have
him—and that they evoke without need of verbalization all the
associations accrued to them previously (in the text). There is,
therefore, nothing gratuitous or merely exotic about Pound's use
of Chinese, though it has only a very tenuous connection with
China and Confucius. Religious thinkers and poets, however, will
often think nothing of historical accuracy—and Pound may be
considered with some reason the inventor of an American Confucian sect of which he is the only member, and allowed to quote
his sacred writ as he pleases.

The outline of the *Pisan Cantos* is clearly marked: beginning
with tragedy and with a summing up of the poet's beliefs, it rises
to the climax of cs. 79–83, and closes with the cavalier envoi of
c. 84. In the former part of the sequence the unsavory materials
of Pound's broadcasts are freely combined, as in its prelude, with
compelling flashes of paradise, or of the ambience of Venus. Thus
in the long canto 74 the goddess emerges "as by Terracina rose
from the sea Zephyr behind her," attended by the hours of love
fully recaptured—the Hours who dress the nude goddess in the
Homeric Hymn, in ur-c. 1, and in Botticelli's *Birth of Venus:*
"Time is not, Time is the evil, beloved / Beloved the hours."
Pound gradually develops a roughly Neoplatonic theory, suggesting that the timeless type (for instance, the city of Deioces) becomes manifest quite independently of the "subjective" ordeal
which he is undergoing. (This, it will be recalled, is also the import of the prelude.)

> one day were clouds banked on Taishan
>   or in glory of sunset
>   and tovarish blessed without aim
> wept in the rainditch at evening
>   Sunt lumina
> that the drama is wholly subjective
> stone knowing the form that the carver imparts it

> the stone knows the form
> sia Cythera, sia Ixotta, sia in Santa Maria dei Miracoli   [c. 74]

In the words of a fellow Neoplatonist, Michelangelo, "There is no concept of the master / that one marble block does not contain." For Pound—the Chaplinesque tovarish who attempts to forget his troubles by telling himself that "ALL THINGS are lights"—art, unlike usury, does not create out of nothing but reveals what is already "there," within the live stone (and, perhaps, "in the mind of heaven"), the goddess (Venus, Venice) being "like a great shell curved / In the suavity of the rock" (c. 17). The distinction is quite clear in c. 76:

> bricks thought into being ex nihil
> suave in the cavity of the rock la concha
> ΠΟΙΚΙΛΟΘΡΟΝ', 'ΑΘΑΝΑΤΑ
>   that butterfly has gone out through my smoke hole
> 'ΑΘΑΝΑΤΑ, saeva. Against buff the rose for the
> background to Leonello, Petrus Pisani pinxit
> that a cameo should remain   [c. 76]

Immortal (athánata) Venus is reborn from the sculptor's rock, which Pound equates first with the cockleshell ("concha") of the tradition which came down to Botticelli, then with the "many-colored throne" (poikilóthron') assigned to the goddess in Sappho's ode.[13] Like the butterfly, Venus appears and exits of her own will, in herself immortal, and yet terrible, "saeva," to the beholder, who can do nothing with his subjectivity about her coming and going—unless he make a work of art, a permanent sign, a token of presence in times of absence. Such a token is the rose in the background of Pisanello's portrait of Lionello d'Este (at Bergamo), or his medallions, or this verse. In his discussion of the *Chanson des oiseaux* of Jannequin-Da Milano-Münch, music which seeks to "represent" the sound of birds, Pound had men-

13. Venus is said to be "ex concha nata" in Plaut., *Rudens* 704. See Edgar Wind, "Aphrodite's Shell," in *Pagan Mysteries in the Renaissance* (Harmondsworth: Penguin, 1967), p. 263. "It is not surprising," Wind writes, "that the primitive idea survives in elegant Roman wall paintings which show a luxurious Aphrodite stretched out in her shell like a living pearl."

tioned "the floral background" of another Pisanello portrait as
an example of "the representation of visible things," and spoken
of the rose pattern

> driven into the dead iron-filings by the magnet, not by material contact
> with the magnet itself, but separate from the magnet. Cut off by the
> layer of glass, the dust and filings rise and spring into order. Thus the
> *forma*, the concept rises from death
> >   The bust outlasts the throne
> >   The coin Tiberius.   [K 23; cf. ABR 54]

The circular process described in this passage includes the Neoplatonic type (or the intellectual love of the lady), its becoming
manifest through the stonecutter's or poet's art, and its survival
as a sign (imported by the rehandling of Gautier's "L'Art") or a
transcription thereof, from which we may always return to the
original pattern. The image recurs in the well-known finale of c.
74, emerging from a free flow of reminiscences, suggesting that
these, the "iron-filings," yield a perceivable pattern—that the
haphazard contents of experience, under the influence of the invisible magnet, are molded into enduring form—and that from
purgatory we have come—by way of the river of memory and
forgetfulness (as in *Purg.* 31)—to paradise:

>   Hast'ou seen the rose in the steel dust
> >   (or swansdown ever?)
>   so light is the urging, so ordered the dark petals of iron
>   we who have passed over Lethe.   [c. 74]

Order is not imposed upon matter, but is perceived as a possibility within the real, and this to the poet is a sufficient consummation. It is scarcely surprising that the following canto should con-
sist of a brief but memorable portrait of Gerhart Münch, and of
the violin score of his transcription from Jannequin-Da Milano,
in the hand of Pound's companion Olga Rudge, who performed
it in a Rapallo concert of 1933. ("If the piano obscures the
fiddle, I have a perfect right to HEAR Jannequin's intervals, his
melodic conjunctions, from the violin solo"—K 23.)

Out of Phlegethon!
out of Phlegethon,
    Gerhart
       art thou come forth out of Phlegethon?
with Buxtehude and Klages in your satchel, with the
Ständebuch of Sachs in yr/ luggage
               —not of one bird but of many   [c. 75]

The dark chiming of the thrice repeated opening line, the fine
counterpoint of *Gerhart-art-forth* and of *thou-out,* and the ecstatic dactylic measure of the *Cantos* (aŕt thŏu cŏme fórth oŭt ŏf
Phlégĕthŏn), come together in what is indeed a noble bit of
music. Gerhart is a happy persona of Pound the seeker after old
masters who has but emerged "out of hell" (c. 74) or out of
Phlegethon. In fact Pound's joyful question is related by theme
and form to the previous interrogation concerning the rose. A
satchel on his back, Pound is again ready for a walking tour of
Provence, where Arnaut set down the song of birds, and passed
his perceptions on to Jannequin and followers. The final line
before the music gives us the remark of the dear violinist (also
recorded in *K* 23), and this comes to stand epiphanically for
Pound's poetics: as Gerhart recovers from Hades and forgetfulness the clear voices of medieval composers, so the *Cantos* are
the work "not of one poet but of many"—"and by no man these
verses."

The Neoplatonic theme is presently restated in the opening of
c. 76, which points to Cavalcanti ("The *'dove sta memoria'* is
Platonism"—*LE* 159) as authorizing Pound's recourse to the gifts
of memory—a new departure in which he was to be followed by
that other major objectivist, William Carlos Williams:

And the sun high over horizon hidden in cloud bank
lit saffron the cloud ridge
         dove sta memora
"Will" said the Signora Agresti, "break his political
but not economic system"   [c. 76]

The function of the magnet is now performed by the sun, which
produces in the cloud-scape a rose of light, diaphanous and saf-

fron. "Where memory liveth, / [love] takes its state / Formed like a
diaphan from light on shade" (c. 36). Saffron, we recall, is love's
own color ("Topaz I manage . . . gold-yellow, saffron"); and
Guido's "diafan" Pound takes as the penumbra both organic and
intellectual in which the generative process occurs ("eater of
grape pulp / in coitu inluminatio"—c. 74). In this passage Pound,
in a fashion as intellectual as it is primitive, goes a step beyond
the Chinese "ideogram" and confronts directly nature's handwriting.

The following lines state the canto's second theme—war as a
suppression of vision—and its resolution: there is something, real
capital (love and good economics), that cannot be destroyed. (Oli-
via Rossetti Agresti, a staunch fascist, is of course speaking of
Mussolini.) On account of its thematic perspicuousness this is an
exemplary opening—from which we may learn always to note
with care the first lines of cantos. After the quotation (another
habitual feature of P.'s beginnings) vision continues its course
with a cortège of fair women, opening with Alcmene (a *nékuia*
character) and closing with Cavalcanti's Primavera, recalled with
words from the *Vita nuova*. Pound seems to have met these mystical and medieval ladies when he was staying at Sant'Ambrogio,
before or during the war, and recalls his wonder:

> that they suddenly stand in my room here
> between me and the olive tree
>   or nel clivo ed al triedro?   [*on the slope or at the trihedron*]
>   and answered: the sun in his great periplum
> leads in his fleet here
>   sotto li nostri scogli
> under our craggy cliffs   [c. 76]

The women answer with the words quoted in the prelude to
c. 74: they are the stars, the Heliads, the flock or fleet of the sun
and of Ulysses, who has led them to the Ligurian shore. Noman
appears presently as Sigismondo, also encountered near Sant'Ambrogio, "by the old Aurelia under San Pantaleone" (cf. "The sex-
ton of San Pantaleo" in the canto fragment in *L* 384):

> Sigismundo by the Aurelia to Genova
>   by la vecchia sotto S. Pantaleone
> Cunizza qua al triedro,
> e la scalza, and she who said: I still have the mould,   [c. 76]

First Cunizza recalls the interaction of Provence and Tuscany; then the Barefooted ("la Scalza," who had already joined Cunizza in c. 74) and the mother who told the executioners of her (fascist) son that she still had the *forma* to make others of the same ilk,[14] point to the (second) theme of destruction and survival. But now the Italy of 1945 is replaced by the Provence of 1244:

> and the rain fell all the night at Ussel
> *cette mauvaiseh venggg* blew over Tolosa   [*that rotten wind*]
> and in Mt Segur there is wind space and rain space
>   no more an altar to Mithras
>
> from il triedro to the Castellaro
>
>   the olives grey over grey holding walls
> and their leaves turn under Scirocco
>
>   la scalza: "Io son la luna   [*I am the moon*]
>   and they have broken my house"
>
> the huntress in broken plaster keeps watch no longer   [c. 76]

Wind and rain are the sole inhabitants of the places once frequented by the adepts: Cavalcanti's Toulouse, Gaubertz' Montségur. The import of the ideogramic conjunction of cs. 47–48 is now made explicit: also in the valley between Rapallo and Zoagli, between the (unidentified) "trihedron" (a trivium?) and the Castellaro (a toponym common to sites of former cliff-settlements—here the one near S. Pantaleone), were altars for the gods of light, dedicated to "Sol invictus Mithras," or "to Jupiter and Hermes"—altars of which at present there is "no vestige save in the air" (c. 74). The evidence is the apparition of the

---

14. Noel Stock, *Reading the Cantos: A Study of Meaning in Ezra Pound* (London: Routledge, 1967), p. 89.

Heliads (mentioned above), and a vision of Pound recounted a few pages later. But the air—the glaucous leaves in the scirocco blowing from the sea—is enough to bring back Scalza, who looks like a "lunatic" Wordsworthian beggar (a sister to the gypsy of 1912) and speaks of her *broken* house (picking up Agresti's earlier comment)—a beggar concealing a goddess, the waxing and waning moon, the huntress Diana.[15]

This to-and-fro dialectic is continued throughout the canto, at the center of which Cavalcanti enters again ("Descendeth not by quality but shineth out"—c. 36):

> nothing matters but the quality
> of the affection—
> in the end—that has carved the trace in the mind
> dove sta memoria   [c. 76]

"Willing man look," c. 36 continues, "into that forméd trace in his mind." Memory, we gather, is yet another form of writing. (Freud once used the same simile.) Its traces remain and shine forth—like busts and coins. There follows the vision visited upon the poet near the Old Aurelia, where the hill falls steeply off to the sea—a world of crystal, water, fawns, and panthers, "the flower and the green"[16]—leading to the celebrated reprise of the theme of destruction ("broken"), attended once again by its elemental witnesses:

> As a lone ant from a broken ant-hill
> from the wreckage of Europe, ego scriptor.
> The rain has fallen, the wind coming down
> out of the mountain
> Lucca, Forte dei Marmi, Berchtold after the other one . . .
> parts reassembled.   [c. 76]

Like Leopold Berchtold after the other war Pound feels "as if been blown up by dynamite" (c. 87), about him a whirl of names and images to be reassembled. From here, leaving out the inter-

15. A plaster Diana stood in the courtyard of P.'s Paris studio at 70 bis rue Notre Dame des Champs. The full meaning of the line is brought out in c. 107: "Diana crumbles in Notre Dame des Champs / but the bronze must be somewhere / or stone."

16. Cavalcanti, "Sonnet xv," T 55.

mediate passages, we come to the close of the canto, where the vision of Venus as shell and butterfly (see above) is immediately followed (as in the opening) by images of economic war, reminiscent of "the poor devils"—Sigismondo's men—"dying of cold, outside Sorano" (c. 10), and of Ulysses' companions as memorialized in c. 20 ("Give! What were they given? / Ear-wax. / Poison and ear-wax, / and a salt grave by the bull field, *neson amumona*"):

> po'eri dia'oli sent to the slaughter
>> Knecht gegen Knecht
>> to the sound of the bumm drum, to eat remnants
>>> for a usurer's holiday to change the
> price of the currency
>> ΜΕΤΑΘΕΜΕΝΩΝ. . . .
>>> ΝΗΣΟΝ ΑΜΥΜΟΝΑ
>> woe to them that conquer with armies
>>> and whose only right is their power.   [c. 76]

These are the Allied armies (P. conveniently forgets that fascists are firm believers in the right of the strongest), and those of Simon de Montfort—yet to the reader the statement has a larger and truer meaning than to the author.

In c. 74 Pound reminds us that this is "by no means an orderly Dantescan rising / but as the winds veer"—ascent combined with circularity. So, after the steady climb of cs. 74–76, we return, as anticipated by the close of the latter, to the world of armies, of Confucian ethics, and of Pound's broadcasts—which is largely the subject of cs. 77–78, and all but overshadows the world of art and myth. Pound drafts something like an apologia for his wartime activities ("Pallas *Díke* sustain me") and prophesies a future for fascism, bringing to the fore the more rhetorical aspects of the theme of the city "now in the heart indestructible" (c. 77): "I believe in the resurrection of Italy quia impossibile est / 4 times to the song of Gassir / now in the mind indestructible." [17]

17. Canto 74. For P.'s source, the legend "The Lute of Gassir," see Leo Frobenius and Douglas C. Fox, *African Genesis* (London, 1938), as quoted in Stock, *Reading the Can-*

As customary with Pound, one cannot tell in these lines where
the passion finishes and the mere histrionics begin. Both may be
present, the latter certainly is. But these attempts at justification
are not wholly satisfactory to the speaker, who must go on from
abstract "justice" to the erotic revelation which alone can guarantee the exactitude of perception:

> "Just like Jack Dempsey's mitts" sang Mr Wilson
>
> > so that you cd/ crack a flea on eider wan
> > ov her breasts
> sd/ the old Dublin pilot
> > or the precise definition
>
> > bel seno (in rimas escarsas, vide sopra)
> > 2 mountains with the Arno, I suppose, flowing between them
> > so kissed the earth after sleeping on concrete
>
> > bel seno Δημήτηρ copulatrix
> > > thy furrow
>
> > in limbo no victories, there, are no victories—   [c. 77]

It is passion that suggests to Wilson (probably a D.T.C. character) a simile, worthy of a troubadour's rare and conceited rhyming, between his love's bosom and a pair of boxing gloves—and
to the pilot his imaginative remark, glossed in the typescript with
the *ch'eng* sign—the sun's ray hitting the word on the head. On a
flight of fancy of his own Pound identifies as the earth's (or
Demeter's) breasts two hills in the Pisan landscape (another
mountain, we recall, is renamed Taishan in the passage about
poor tovarish), and treats us to a further quite moving bit of histrionics, his kissing the earth after the weeks in the cage. From
the breasts and "furrow" of Demeter *copulatrix* (an epithet of
Venus from *Pervigilium Veneris*) he impetrates an impossible vic-

---

tos, pp. 76–77. The relevant passages are: "For really, [the city] Wagadu is not of stone,
not of wood, not of earth. Wagadu is the strength which lives in the hearts of men and is
sometimes visible because eyes see her and ears hear the clash of swords and ring of
shields, and is sometimes invisible because the indomitability of men has overtired her, so
that she sleeps. . . . Should Wagadu ever be found for the fifth time, then she will live so
forcefully in the minds of men that she will never be lost again . . . Hoooh! Dierra,
Agada, Ganna, Silla! [the names of the four incarnations of Wagadu] Hooh! Fasa!"

tory to set against his defeat, "quia impossibile est." (The latter is of course a slightly gratuitous reference to Tertullian.)

Close upon the opening of c. 74 *Oûtis*-Pound is spliced with another motif out of Frobenius, the Australian god Wondjina, who made things by naming them, and, having overproduced, lost his mouth at the hands of his father,

> as you will find it removed in his pictures
> in principio verbum
> paraclete or the verbum perfectum: sinceritas
> from the death cells in sight of Mt Taishan @ Pisa   [c. 74]

Pound's punishment (the "death cells"), like that of Wondjina and (latently) of Christ (the Logos sacrificed by the Father), testifies to the power of the word, which from tragedy may be reborn to perfection, as the Paraclete. (Here again, opposite "in principio verbum," P. has written into his typescript the sign *ch'eng*.) However, after the revelations of memory as writing of cs. 74–76, Pound is for a while deprived of the luminous word, as he indicates at the end of 77, the Confucian canto, by returning to Wondjina and going on to a sequence of discrete perceptions or images, separated by blanks—parts to be reassembled:

> and Tom wore a tin disc, a circular can-lid
> with his name on it, solely:
> for Wanjina has lost his mouth,
>
>   .   .   .
>
> mind come to a plenum when nothing more will go into it
>
> the wind mad as Cassandra
> who was as sane as the lot of 'em
>
> Sorella, mia sorella,
> che ballava sobr'un zecchin
>
> [*ch'eng*]   bringest to focus   [*ch'eng*]
>
> Zagreus
>
> Zagreus   [c. 77]

The loss of mouth and word is further illustrated by the arresting references to Pound's over-saturated mind and to prophetic Cas-

sandra, the wind's voice, believed to be mad and carried off as a
slave by Agamemnon—a counterpart of the Sister (cf. "sorella la
luna"—c. 74) of the broken house (Troy). Yet through his
brotherhood to this mystic and sensual character, who (as we
recall) claims to be the moon, or through "inluminatio coitu"
("bringest to focus"—the Chinese signs depict the converging
rays), the "man on whom the sun has gone down" of c. 74 is
reborn as the perfect word or Paraclete, Zagreus, his secret divine
self.

The Dionysian focusing, however, is little but an augury, as
suggested by the disconnectedness of the previous lines, and
Pound must play the Cassandra through another canto:

> By the square elm of Ida
> > 40 geese are assembled
> (little sister who could dance on a sax-pence)
> > to arrange a pax mundi
> > > *Sobr'un zecchin!*
> Cassandra, your eyes are like tigers,
> > with no word written in them
> You also have I carried to nowhere
> > to an ill house and there is
> > > no end to the journey.
> > > .The chess board too lucid
> the squares are too even . . . theatre of war . . .
> "theatre" is good. There are those who did not want
> > it to come to an end   [c. 78]

The exceptional momentum of the Pisan poem is made apparent
by the frequent rehandling in the opening of one canto of the
themes of the previous close, of which this is a particularly moving instance. Pound scorns the geese that negotiate peace, on
Troy's Ida or in New York (the United Nations Charter was
signed in June 1945 by fifty countries), and resumes the dialogue
among vanquished peasants, lovers, and prophets, with a chilling
sequence of negative images ("no word," "nowhere," "no
end"),[18] not without suggesting that in his folly he knows more

18. Cf. Cassandra's lament in *Agamemnon* 1095 ff.:
    Apollo, Apollo!
    My guide and ruin!
    Where have you led me? To what house?

about the true causes of war than others. It is the sixpence or
"zecchino" in the small compass of which the imagination can
dance that moves the knights on the chessboard.[19] The war is at
the center of this canto, which records the journey of "the man
out of Naxos past Fara Sabina," and makes it known that
Pound's "tyrant" would have implemented Douglasite and Gesellite reform ("Said one would have to think about that / but was
hang'd dead by the heels before his thought in proposito [in this
matter] came into action efficiently"). Even here, however, there
is no lack of surreal humor ("Be welcome, O cricket my grillo,
but you must not sing after taps"), of the awareness of approaching vision, and of the quiet of finding one's place in a process
which also includes the oxen passing by the D.T.C., on which, as
Pound's friend Williams would have said, so much depends:

Cunizza's shade al triedro and that presage
                    in the air
which means that nothing will happen that will
      be visible to the sergeants
Tre donne intorno alla mia mente   [*Three women about my mind*]
      .   .   .

and as for the solidity of the white oxen in all this
            perhaps only Dr Williams (Bill Carlos)
                        will understand its importance,
            its benediction. He wd/ have put in the cart.
The shadow of the tent's peak treads on its corner peg
marking the hour. The moon split, no cloud nearer than Lucca.
In the spring and autumn
      In "The Spring and Autumn"

CHORUS
To the Atrides' house . . .

CASSANDRA

Thus to a house hateful to the gods,
Aware of the slaying of brothers,
To a gory slaughterhouse.

In the subsequent exchange the chorus refers to the myth of Itys, as P. does five lines
below our quotation.

19. Cf. "The Game of Chess" (*P* 120), the source of which may be read in *SR* 236. In
Italian the lenis form of "sopra" is "sovra," of which P.'s "sobra" is a mnemonic reconstruction.

                              there
                              are
                              no
                          righteous
                          wars   [c. 78]

Under Pound's intent scrutiny this epical landscape yields its message—first, the abjuration of war (parallel to the close of c. 76),
then the related column of words at the end of the next canto,
"aram / nemus / vult"—the grove demands an altar. With c. 79 we
enter a different emotional sphere, which looks back to the matter
of love and to the bird song of cs. 75–76, and forward to ceremony. There are several references to music, the focuser, in the
meditative prelude:

          present Mr G. Scott whistling Lili Marlene
                    with positively less musical talent
                    than that of any other man of colour
                          whom I have ever encountered
          but with bonhomie and good humor
                       ·   ·   ·

          some minds take pleasure in counterpoint
                    pleasure in counterpoint
                       ·   ·   ·

                    4 birds on 3 wires, one bird on one
          the imprint of the intaglio depends
                    in part on what is pressed under it
          the mould must hold what is poured into it
                              in
                          discourse
                                what matters is
          to get it across e poi basta
                    5 of 'em now on 2
                       on 3; 7 on 4
                          thus what's his name
          and the change in writing the song books   [c. 79]

In c. 76 Pound deciphers the handwriting of light; now—as he
considers the intimate relationship of form and circumstance of
which he was to speak in the "Note to Base Censor"—he begins

to read the score written by birds as they perch on the wires en-
circling or crossing the D.T.C., and suggests that of such chance
observation may have sprung present-day musical notation,
which is also (we gather) an ideogram, a representation of visible
things. The mood is playful, but with an undercurrent of serious
concern for the ethical burden of writing and music ("the re-establishment of a sense of proportion"—*K* 50). To Pound's
seriousness we owe the relevance and interest of these experiments in concrete or objective poetry: as a Stravinsky writing
serial music, Pound will use or initiate novel and unconventional
techniques without overlooking the basic imperative, "to get it
across e poi basta." In the sequel there is again a comparison between Athene and Aphrodite, justice and love; in the previous
close Pound was visited, as Dante before him ("Tre donne intorno al cor mi son venute"), by "three women"—and now
something like the judgment of Paris seems to take place:

> Athene cd/ have done with more sex appeal
> caesia ocula
> "Pardon me, γλαύξ"
>   ("Leave it, I'm not a fool.")
> mah?
>   "The price is three altars, multa."
>   "paak you djeep oveh there."
>   2 on 2
> what's the name of that bastard? D'Arezzo, Gui D'Arezzo
> notation   [*huang*]
>   3 on 3
>   chiacchierona   the yellow bird   [*niao*]
>   to rest   3 months in bottle
>   (auctor)
> by the two breasts of Tellus   [*chih*]
>   [c. 79]

Incensed by the decision against her the gray- (or glint-) eyed
goddess exacts an "equitable" reparation, the erection of three
altars (one for each of the "tre donne"), and possibly the three
months of prison already served by the *auctor*, guilty (like Wondjina) of talking too much ("chiacchierone"). Thus these lines,

which look rather like certain scores produced in later years by contemporary composers, are again subtly concerned with the chastisement of the word, which is resurrected (on the third day) as a definition both precise and loving: Gregorian notation as perfected by Guido d'Arezzo (P. can now remember the name), and the breasts of Tellus in the environs of which the *auctor* is bottled. All of this Pound learns from the D.T.C. birds, and from the yellow bird of *GD* III 2 (whose flight is graphed in the margin of his score), said to be "chiacchierone" in the 1942 Italian translation (*OS* 449):

> *The twittering yellow bird*
> *The bright silky warbler*
> *Talkative as a cricket*
> *Comes to rest in the hollow corner of the hill*
> —*Shi King,* II, 8, 6, 2 [CA 230]

Kung said: comes to rest, alights, knows what its rest is, what its ease is. Is man, for all his wit, less wise than this bird of the yellow plumage that he should not know his resting place or fix the point of his aim?

Through graphic experiment Pound seeks and finds an accurate notation, a point of rest (*chih*)—the stillness following upon intercourse with the Earth.

In fact this musical and intellectual pointillism climaxes shortly in the triumph of the lynxes of Dionysus, of Venus, and of "Old Ez," who, as he looks up to the dawn sky (his magic hour), and writes of the landscape in the dry epic tone of the previous close, feels finally justified ("having root in the equities"), and—in his humbleness and old age—almost divine, a type of Dionysus instructing his totem animal. This passage emerges by analogy out of a reminiscence of Henry James as "cher maître," as the supreme artist who is always Pound's ideal—yet James' eccentric follower acknowledges more openly the bond of humanity, and art is not the entire burden of his dream:

> The moon has a swollen cheek
> and when the morning sun lit up the shelves and battalions
> of the West, cloud over cloud
>   Old Ez folded his blankets

Neither Eos nor Hesperus has suffered wrong at my hands

        O Lynx, wake Silenus and Casey
        shake the castagnettes of the bassarids,

the mountain forest is full of light
    the tree-comb red-gilded
Who sleeps in the field of lynxes
    in the orchard of Maelids?

     .   .   .

    Salazar, Scott, Dawley on sick call
        Polk, Tyler, half the presidents and Calhoun   [c. 79]

The Laforguian teasing of the moon and Homer's epic topos
("But when the young Dawn showed again with her rosy
fingers"—Lattimore's translation) dramatically made new, set the
scene for Old Ez (named only at this point of *PC*), who goes
about making his bed in a fashion both Chaplinesque and Ho-
merically exposed. (E.g., see *Od.* IV. 296: "And Helen of Argos
told her serving maids / to make up beds in the porch's shelter
and to lay upon them / fine underbedding of purple, and spread
blankets above it / and fleecy robes to be an over-all covering.")
He then shifts abruptly but naturally enough to the first person
singular for his most stirring, perhaps, defense—he has lived in
agreement with the times and seasons, the morning and evening
star, Homer's Eos and Sappho's Hesperus—and for the address
(in which humor is again blended with emotion) to the lynx, who
is to make sure that Pound's mythical and actual fellow-sleepers
also hear the news that the dawn is coming on. We may take the
lynx as a figure of the very *vis poetica,* bristling with wakefulness
and awareness, and converting the D.T.C. into an immemorial
setting—the field and orchard of Maelids (the apple-nymphs of c.
3, "my one bit of personal property in greek mythology")—
where Casey and the other "trainees" on sick call join "the gay
chorus singing, for three full nights amid the herds . . . / And the
whole night long will be watched out with continuing song."
Thus Pound's 1910 rendering of the *Pervigilium Veneris* (*SR* 20),
a memorable version of Midsummer Night of which he and other
late romantics were especially fond (Eliot quotes it in *The Waste*

Land), and to which the present recovery of the magic moment central to the *Cantos* is indebted even more than to the Albas of Provence (a continuation in fact, according to *SR,* of the sentiments of the *Pervigilium*):

> We are here waiting the sun-rise
> and the next sunrise
> for three nights amid lynxes. For three nights
> of the oak-wood
> and the vines are thick in their branches   [c. 79]

The poet's single voice has merged with the chorus of a rural (and initiate) community celebrating its lusty (Priapus is honored) and melancholy rites and seeking protection from its minor gods—and chiefly from the attention of the lynx—for the vine and the hearth. There is little of the redundant primitivism of the middle cantos in this fresh singing—and Pound takes his time for good-humored asides and exposures of what others— "crusaders" of various denominations—call religion ("and you can make 5000 dollars a year / all you have to do is to make one trip up country / then come back to Shanghai / and send in an annual report / as to the number of converts"). Eventually the chorus takes the entire stage and, as the sun "comes to *our* mountain" (my italics), Venus is brought in by the Graces (the arts) on a "cell . . . drawn by ten leopards" (more "ferae familiares"). The canto closes (somewhat like c. 1) with a polyglot litany which intones the many names and attributes of the goddess in brief, chiefly dactylic, ejaculations of English, Latin, and Greek. She is in turn "a petal líghtĕr thăn séa fŏam" (the element of her birth) and "líghtĕr thăn aír ŭndĕr Héspĕrŭs" (her own star, mentioned earlier); "terrible in resistance" as regards her worshippers ("saeva" in c. 76) and—a final musical analogy— "tríne ăs prăelúdiŏ" (and as the Christian Trinity, see Dekker 73), for she appears first as *"Kórĕ kăi Déliă kăi Máia"* (or as girl, virgin, and mother) before becoming fully manifest as *"Kúprĭs Ăphródĭtĕ"* and *"Kúthĕră."* But the canto's final gesture, affectionate and most resonant (a near-perfect dactylic hexameter), is devoted to the lynx, whom the poet invokes as a puma, servant of the sun (as is always the case with his cats) and dedicated to the god of mysteries:

O púmă, sácrĕd tŏ Hérmĕs, Címbĭcă sérvănt ŏf Hélĭŏs.

The poetic ritual cannot but climax with a lovely instance of the precise definition ("bringest to focus")—the securing (at a twenty-five-year remove) of the name and good offices of W. H. Hudson's South-American puma, "Chimbica, friend of man, the most loyal of wildcats." [20]

Pound's definitive celebration of St. John's Eve (or of the Eve of St. Venus Genetrix) terminates the former of the two large divisions of the Pisan periplus, and signals the acquisition of a novel "sense of proportion" ("Amo ergo sum, and in just that proportion"—c. 80), and of a novel emotional availability. Pound is now ready for a more intimate journey through his past and his dream world, and on this he sets out in c. 80, which is as long and as comprehensive as c. 74—a new prelude and summary—yet on the whole is less strained and less given to the sublime in the old sense, being sustained by a continuous undercurrent of controlled emotion which never falters, not even when it is again time to reminisce about "poor old Benito" and his sorry end—in fact this may be the only place in the *Cantos* [21] in which Pound qualifies his sympathy for the Duce: "but on the other hand emphasis / an error or excess of / emphasis / the problem after any revolution is what to do with / your gunmen" (apparently an allusion to such events as the assassination of Giacomo Matteotti). The joyous retrieval of ritual and song in the lynx chorus

20. E. P., "Hudson: Poet Strayed into Science," *Little Review*, vii, 1 (May–June 1920), rpt. *SPr* 429–32: 431. For another cat doing obeisance (like Cimbica and Old Ez) to the sunrise see the opening lines of c. 39 ("Desolate is the roof where the cat sat, / Desolate is the iron rail that he walked / And the corner post whence he greeted the sunrise"), and Dorothy Pound's gloss in *Etruscan Gate* (Exeter: Rougemont Press, 1971), p. 11: "The black cat . . . sunned himself on the roof of the house across the narrow street and we threw him bits of eatables. We named him Schwartz." (The mystic black cat was to return in the fine fragment of *L* 384 (1941) and in *Thrones*.) P.'s coalescence with his lynx may be seen in the light of his theory that he and Frobenius belonged to one "cat family" (Olson, *Encounter at St Elizabeths*, p. 103).

21. But see c. 116: "Muss., wrecked for an error."

having restored his self-confidence, Pound can now afford to speak openly of sorrow, fatigue, and discouragement—emotions which he had previously taken care to minimize. With little further reference to Neoplatonic memory he allows himself to be carried wherever the bittersweet flow of reminiscence will take him: on the opening page he speaks longingly of a gone "era"; elsewhere he demands to be "put down for temporis acti," and adds sadly (and a little mysteriously), "OU TIS / áchronos / now there are no more days"; a few lines later, after a reference to the "eminent armies" of which he is a prisoner, we find the following:

> così discesi per l'aer maligno
> > [*thus I descended through the evil air*]
> > on doit le temps ainsi prendre qu'il vient
> or to write dialogue because there is
> > no one to converse with
> to take the sheep out to pasture
> to bring your g.r. to the nutriment
> > gentle reader   to the gist of the discourse
> > to sort out the animals   [c. 80]

The passage is typical in its quick alternation of mood, from caustic and didactic humor to elegy—a combination reminiscent of such heroes of Pound as Laforgue and Heine. After telescoping two lines from *Inf.* 5 Pound quotes the opening of a roundel by Froissart—perhaps the most memorable exhibit in the unsatisfactory "Arnaut Daniel" essay:

> On doit le temps ainsi prendre qu'il vient:
> Tout dit que pas ne dure la fortune.
> Un temps se part, et puis l'autre revient:
> On doit le temps ainsi prendre qu'il vient.
>
> Je me conforte en ce qu'il me souvient
> Que tous les mois avons nouvelle lune:
> On doit le temps ainsi prendre qu'il vient:
> Tout dit que pas ne dure la fortune.   [*LE* 113]

The lines recur elsewhere in c. 80 (the second in c. 76). (Farther on, the words, "Les mœurs passent et la douleur reste," recall another Froissart line: "Le corps s'en va, mais le coeur vous demeure"—*LE* 113.) Other cherished passages from the lyrical tradition tell in these pages of Pound's plaintive mood: Lope de Vega's "A mis soledades voy / De mis soledades vengo" (*SR* 208), and Ronsard's "Quand vous serez bien vieille, au soir, à la chandelle"—which suggests the fine address of the poet to his dearly loved daughter:

> before the world was given over to wars
> Quand vous serez bien vieille
>   remember that I have remembered,
>   mia pargoletta   [*my little girl*]
>   and pass on the tradition   [c. 80]

Finally, the words from Augustine ("Sero, sero te amavi"—*Conf.* x. 27) Pound had quoted in *K* (and in c. 20, where the charge of lateness is expectedly aimed at *others*) are central to the canto's finale:

> repos donnez à cils
>   senza termine funge   Immaculata Regina [22]
>   Les larmes que j'ai créées m'inondent
> Tard, très tard je t'ai connue, la Tristesse,
> I have been hard as youth sixty years   [c. 80]

This brings home the meaning of a previous, apparently disgressive, remark: " 'The evil that men do lives after them' / well, that is from Julius Caesar." Pound cannot resolve the conflict between the eternal "lumina" on which his vision dwells, and sorrow and time. This is also the import of another rather difficult passage situated about one-third into the canto, a "vision" which breaks through the flow of reminiscence, which then continues uninterrupted to the powerful close. It opens with the well-known autobiographical lines which pick up the terminal "So that" of c. 1:

> so that leaving America I brought with me $80
>   and England a letter of Thomas Hardy's
>   and Italy one eucalyptus pip
>   from the salita that goes up from Rapallo   [*climb*]
>   (if I go)   [c. 80]

22. "Functions without bourne   Immaculate Queen." See above, n. 12.

As early as c. 74 the poet tells us that eucalyptus "is for memory," and as c. 80 opens we are advised of a "eucalyptus bobble"
which may have the same virtue, but is also somehow connected
with Eleusis: "and the eucalyptus bobble is missing / 'Come pan,
niño!' / that was an era also, and Spanish bread / was made out of
grain in that era." The aromatic bobble is said to bear mystical
signatures (a cat's face, a Maltese cross) some pages later, in the
course of a fantasy suggested by Beddoes' *Death's Jest Book or
the Fool's Tragedy,* and perhaps by Eliot's peculiar interpretation
of *Pericles:*

> Curious, is it not, that Mr Eliot
> has not given more time to Mr Beddoes
>   (T. L.) prince of morticians
>   where none can speak his language
> centuries hoarded
> to pull up a mass of algae   [*ho*]
>   (and pearls)
>   or the odour of eucalyptus or sea wrack   [*yuan*]
>   cat-faced, croce di Malta, figura del sol
>   to each tree its own mouth and savour   [c. 80]

Pound remembers the lines he had quoted from the play in an article of 1917:

>   and I utter
> Shadows of words, like to an ancient ghost,
> Arisen out of hoary centuries
> Where none can speak his language.[23]

—and dwells on the *arcana* brought to light by the poet (misunderstood like Cassandra): the pearls of Ariel and of *The Waste
Land;* the odor of sea wrack Eliot (in an unguarded moment)
said he perceived when reading *Pericles*—possibly the source of
"Marina";[24] and Pound's feline, solar, and mystical eucalyptus.

23. "Beddoes and Chronology," collected in *SPr* 378–83 (where it is mistakenly dated
1913). In another of P.'s excerpts we read of "a mighty destiny, / Whose being to endow
great souls have been / Centuries hoarded" (*SPr* 379).

24. Cf. T. S. Eliot, "Shakespeare's Verskunst," *Der Monat,* ii, 20 (May 1950). This is the
German version of an unpublished lecture, "Shakespeare as Poet and Dramatist," deliv-

(The Chinese characters in the margin, translated in c. 77 as "How is it far, if you think of it?,"[25] suggest a full recovery of the mysteries in the imagination.) But none can understand the language of the poet-ghost in the world of the D.T.C. (a sample of the world at large), where the "god-damned," or rather (P. shrewdly notices) "man-damned" trainee must perform intellectual exercises like the one mentioned close upon the reference to the subtle signatures borne by every tree:

> "Hot   hole   hep   cat"
> or words of similar volume
>   to be recognized by the god-damned
>   or man-damned trainee
> Prowling night-puss leave my hard squares alone
>   they are in no case cat food
>   if you had sense
> you wd/ come here at meal time
>   when meat is superabundant
> you can neither eat manuscript nor Confucius
>   nor even the hebrew scriptures
>   get out of that bacon box
>   contract W, 11 oh oh 9 oh
> now used as a wardrobe
>   ex 53 pounds gross weight
>   the cat-faced eucalyptus nib
>   is where you cannot get at it   [c. 80]

The address to the cat (also mentioned in the excursus on "the army vocabulary" [c. 77], a riding seriocomic concern of *PC*)

ered by Eliot in 1937 and 1941, and quoted in part by G. Wilson Knight in *Neglected Powers* (New York: Barnes and Noble, 1971), from which book I have taken the previous reference. "In reading Pericles," writes Eliot, "I have a sense of a pervading smell of seaweed throughout" (p. 490). He may have informed P. of this apropos of "Marina" (pub. 1930).

25. Cf. A ix 30: "The flowers of the prunus japonica deflect and turn, do I not think of you dwelling afar? He said: It is not the thought, how can there be distance in that?" The more common reading of the Master's remark is as follows: "Les hommes ne pensent pas à la vertu. Ont-ils à surmonter la difficulté de la distance?"—Séraphin Couvreur, *Les Quatres Livres* (1895; rpt. Paris: Cathasia, n.d.), p. 173. In the above quotation from c. 80 I have, as always, replaced Chinese characters with the standard transliteration, italicized and in brackets.

echoes colloquially the lynx chorus a few pages back; it allows us
to look into Pound's tent, with its boxes serving as wardrobe and
table:

> What counts is the cultural level,
>   thank Benin for this table ex packing box   [c. 81]

(Culture, we learn from P.'s *Guide* to the same, is not bookish
learning but what penetrates existence until it becomes second
nature; thus the black guard who made P.'s table operates within
the African "Paideuma" studied by Frobenius, and not—
ironically—as an American.) Upon the "table" we see the manuscript of *PC* and its chief sources so far: *The Four Books* and the
prisoner's Bible—a book Pound had virulently abused in previous
years ("Not a letter of the Hebraic alphabet can pass into a text
without danger of contaminating it"—*CV* 320), but which in his
new mood he is ready to accept as an authority against usury (cs.
74 and 76) and for religious tolerance (Micah's phrase, "Each
one in his god's name," recurs throughout *PC*)—to the point of
speaking of rebuilding Jerusalem's Temple, among others ("Why
not rebuild it?").[26] Finally we come to the eucalyptus bobble, the
secret charm Pound had in his pocket when he was arrested, or
which he picked up from the "salita" as he was led downhill.
And we note the crescendo: from America he brought away only
some money, and little at that; from England his correspondence
with the poet and novelist whom he worshipped; and from Italy
(though he is not sure he will come out of it alive) nothing but
the pure signature of the initiate.

26. Canto 76. Cf. Eliot's remark to Robert Lowell, as reported in the latter's poem "T. S.
Eliot," *Notebook 1967–68* (New York: Farrar Strauss & Giroux, 1969), p. 71:
> Then on with warden's pace across the Yard,
> talking of Pound, "It's balls to say he isn't
> the way he is. . . . He's better though. This year
> he no longer wants to rebuild the Temple at Jerusalem.
> Yes, he's better. 'You speak,' he said, when he'd talked two hours.
> By then I had absolutely nothing to *say*."

(In the revised *Notebook* of 1970 Lowell is at pains to tone down this bit of gossip, and
replaces the candid first remark with the opaque: "It's balls to say he only / pretends to be
like Ezra.")

The autobiographic meditation which started us on the eucalyptus theme is followed by a vision which brings out the arcane
significance of the "pip"; this is set again upon the sacred hills
behind Rapallo, namely at San Bartolomeo, an attractive and rus-
tic seventeenth-century chapel:

> "a S. Bartolomeo mi vidi col pargoletto,
> Chiodato a terra colle braccia aperte
>   in forma di croce gemisti.
>   disse: Io son la luna."
> Coi piedi sulla falce d'argento
>   mi parve di pietosa sembianza
> The young Dumas weeps because the young Dumas has tears
>   Death's seeds move in the year
>   semina motuum   [c. 80]

It is difficult to make sense of Pound's broken Italian and untrustworthy punctuation—and the obscurity may be intentional,
as these are matters "not to be spoken of save in secret" (K 22).
The speaker may be the poet, who sees himself crucified with a
little boy, or rather with the "pargoletta" addressed six pages on,
hears her say, "I am the moon," and describes her sorrowful appearance and her feet "on the silver scythe." Or the girl herself
may speak in the first four lines about her meeting the little boy
on the cross and about her being the moon,[27] and Pound adds a
description of her in the two subsequent lines. The passage is cor-
rupt beyond recovery: "mi vidi" can be taken as "I saw myself"
or "I met"; "chiodato" can modify either the speaker (P.?) or the
"pargoletto"; "gemisti" can be construed as an aborted attempt
to write "gemetti" or "gemesti" (I cried, you cried), or as a qualification of the Maltese cross on the eucalyptus ("the cross of
Gemistus"?). At any rate we are made aware of such recurrent
themes as sacrifice (cf. c. 74), the broken house of the waxing
and waning moon, and (ironically) the precise definition which

27. In this case we would have to prefer the original reading, "diss'io: Io son la luna" ("I
said: I am the moon"), to P.'s later correction, "disse: Io son la luna" ("he/she said: I am
the moon"). On the other hand, if we take all the Italian to be spoken by P., we must
change about the inverted commas to suggest that "Io son la luna" is a quotation within a
longer quotation. But the passage had better stay as it is, with its multiple possibilities.

comes after the "bang." (The last two Italian lines, besides por-
traying Diana, recall the sister dancing on a sixpence.) Accordingly, in the revery that follows grief is once again shown to be
consistent with process, young Dumas' vaunt ("Je pleure parce
que j'ai des larmes"—Pearlman 276) suggesting that *lacrimae
rerum* or "death's seeds" are from the beginning among the
"semina motuum" referred to in *GD* ix 3. This, the burden of the
section's prelude ("What you depart from is not the way"), is
presently reiterated in connection with the Nô *Hagoromo,* the
story of a fisherman who, having found a moon nymph's magic
feather mantle, promises to return it on condition that she dance
for him; she says that she must have the mantle to dance with,
and the fisherman is afraid she may deceive him: "If you should
get it, how do I know you'll not be off to your palace without
even beginning your dance, not even a measure?" To which she
rejoins: "Doubt is of mortals; with us there is no deceit" (*T* 312):

> "With us there is no deceit"
>> said the moon nymph   immacolata
>> Give back my cloak, *hagoromo.*
>> had I the clouds of heaven
>>> as the nautile borne ashore
>> in their holocaust
>>> as wistaria floating shoreward
> with the sea gone the colour of copper
>> and emerald dark in the offing
> the young Dumas has tears thus far from the year's end   [c. 80]

As he telescopes several passages of the play in a sort of synthetic
chorus suggesting the collective mood of the characters,[28] Pound
equates his neo-Confucian "Immacolata," the Japanese moon
nymph, and Venus borne ashore upon (or like) a "concha"/nau-
tilus through a sea dyed with the color of her jewels ("ori-

---

28. Cf. *Hagoromo, T* 311 and 314: "Enviable colour of breath, wonder of clouds that
fade along the sky that was our accustomed dwelling . . . Plover and seagull are on the
waves in the offing. . . . The clouds lie in . . . heaven like a plain awash with sea."
    P. had referred to this Nô as early as ur-c. 1: "Whom shall I hang my shimmering gar-
ment on; / Who wear my feathery mantle, *hagoromo;* / Whom set to dazzle the serious
future ages?"—*Poetry,* 10 (1917), 117.

chalci"—c. 1)—it is no chance that in the lynx canto she is called
Kúpris Aphródite. The three goddesses have a common luminous
substance, underscored by the reference to the clouds' holocaust
in which the nautilus drifts ashore—or in which (as in c. 76) love
carves its writing. The iconography from Botticelli is previously
introduced in c. 74—

> but this air brought her ashore a la marina
> with the great shell borne on the seawaves
> <div align="center">nautilis biancastra</div>   [c. 74]²⁹

29. Cf. ur-c. 1:
If Botticelli
Brings her ashore on that great cockle-shell,
His Venus (Simonetta?), and Spring
And Aufidus fill all the air
With their clear-outlined blossoms?
World enough.   [QPA 23]
(It is strange that the pair of Zephyrs propelling Venus in the painting should become
"Spring and Aufidus"—the latter being Latin for the river Ofanto. However, a footnote to
"Occidit" [CEP 83] glosses "Aufidus" as "the West Wind." See Peck, "Pound's Idylls,"
p. 324n.)
    We hear more of Sandro's *Birth of Venus* in 2 HSM 2, where (as noted in Dekker
161–62) P. takes to task his effete alter ego for responding to the painting somewhat as he
had done in ur-canto 1, i.e. for being content with a painted Venus ("World enough"—
QPA 23) while overlooking the sexual implications of the "Botticellian sprays" (Lucre-
tius' "genitabilis aura favoni," Politian's "Zefiri lascivi"), and those of the widening (or
distance—"diastasis") of "Simonetta's" eyes:
    —Given that is his "fundamental passion,"
    This urge to convey the relation
    Of eye-lid and cheek-bone
    By verbal manifestations;

    To present the series
    Of curious heads in medallion—

    He had passed, inconscient, full gaze,
    The wide-banded irides
    And botticellian sprays implied
    In their diastasis;

    Which anaesthesis, noted a year late,
    And weighed, revealed his great affect,
    (Orchid), mandate
    of Eros, a retrospect.   [2 HSM 2]
This is the poem in which P. follows James's strategies to describe in "endless sentences" a hallucinated Strether—the poem which Eliot deemed obscure: P. appears to
have corrected the manuscript slightly and returned it to his confrère with the outburst:

—and connected several pages on with Cavalcanti's psychology
and with the Immaculata:

> . . . . cheek bone, by verbal manifestation,
>   her eyes as in "La Nascita"   *[The Birth—of Venus]*
>   whereas the child's face
> is at Capoquadri in the fresco square over the doorway
>   centre background
> the form beached under Helios
>   funge la purezza,
> and that certain images be formed in the mind
>   to remain there
>   *formato locho*
>   Arachne mi porta fortuna
> to remain there, resurgent ΕΙΚΟΝΕΣ
> and still in Trastevere[30]

"Cher T: Now, 'n' be DAMN this thing MUST be comprehensible???!!!" (Stock 287). He
may have been irritated because he had put much of his vision and secret language into it,
and in fact many of its puns and phrases recur in the *Cantos* (e.g., "orchid" in c. 48;
"irides" in c. 110).

It is difficult to accept Espey's claim (pp. 71–72) that P. took his "wide-banded irides"
and his "diastasis" from Politian's

> *bagna Cipresso ancor pel cervio gli occhi*
> *con chiome or aspre, e già distese e bionde*   [*Stanze* 1.82]
> (Cyparissus' eyes are still wet for the stag,
>   his hair is now bristly, which was smooth and blond)

According to Espey P. confused Cyparissus with the Cyprian (whose birth is described
twenty stanzas later), and took "distese e bionde" as modifying "occhi" (eyes) rather than
"chiome" (hair, foliage). The evidence from c. 7 submitted by Espey (who misunderstands
"già distese e bionde" [formerly even and blond] as "already divided and yellowish")
suggests that P. had if anything a better grasp of Politian's meaning than his (usually accurate) critic, without quite proving that he had this passage in mind rather than *Inf.* XII.
110. I am of course referring to the description of James:

> Eyes floating in dry, dark air,
> E biondo, with glass-grey iris, with an even side-fall of hair
> The stiff, still features.   [c. 7]

If the splicing of James's cool eyes and those of Venus (or *glaukópis* Athene) takes us by
surprise, we must remember that to P. a bond of sympathy connects the subject to the object of perception, and that (like Poe) he is more interested in the teeth than in the girl.

30. Cf. the opening of c. 74 ("but a precise definition / transmitted thus Sigismundo / thus
Duccio, thus Zuan Bellin, or trastevere with La Sposa / Sponsa Christi in mosaic till our
time"), and CV 320: "The mosaics in Santa Maria in Trastevere recall a wisdom lost by
scholasticism, an understanding denied to Aquinas." The "Sponsa Christi" is portrayed in
the apse mosaic of the basilica.

for the deification of emperors
and the medallions
                    to forge Achaia   [c. 74]

Here Pound notices the resemblance between the beloved's eyes
and those of Botticelli's Venus—and between his daughter's face
and that of a putto in a fresco at Palazzo Capoquadri, Siena.[31]
We gather that the timeless type emerges of its own accord in nature and in art, even as the shell of Venus (a pure "form") is
beached under Helios. When this love establishes itself as a "forméd trace" in the artist's mind, it can be reborn out of that "formato loco"[32]—as with the Birth of Venus and Pisanello's medallions (one of which serves as a frontispiece to K). It is hardly
necessary to remark the connection between this cluster and such
themes as the rose in the dust (which is both the mental image
projected by the artist and the real form within the rock, waiting
to be uncovered)—and as the city of Deioces, which also is "resurgent." In the background there is the religious conception of
art which comes down to Pound from the decadents and which is
central to the Cantos, where these scarcely novel attitudes are
enriched by fantastical metacultural intimations, and (in PC) by
genuine emotion. Thus we are prepared for Pound's harking back
to such projects à la Mauberley as "To forge Achaia," and "To
convey the relation / Of eye-lid and cheek-bone / By verbal manifestations" (the sequence of eye and cheek being subtly inverted):
Achaia can truly be forged anew, for Venus and her "form" are
always "the same eternal beauty" (as the essence of the Chanson
des oiseaux is called in K 23). Canto 80 picks up from c. 74 a
leitmotif—"Beauty is difficult."

Yet in the passage concerning the hagoromo and weeping
Dumas we are aware of an unfulfilled yearning ("had I the

31. See Mary de Rachewiltz 165–66.

32. The usually accepted reading of Cavalcanti's phrase, P. notes in his commentary (LE
187–88), is "non fermato loco," the whole line importing that the lover is to wonder (not
"look"—as P. has it in both his translations) at an object unstill. But of course P. is following his attractive notion that under the pressure of love the mind becomes a locus endowed with form (somewhat like a computer tape), and thus may reproduce the original
stimuli, or offer them up for contemplation.

clouds of heaven"). However confident that time can hide the eternal type only temporarily (if the tautology will be allowed), i.e., not at all, the poet cannot avoid a sense of loss, and the suspicion that he may be deceived in his faith. Accordingly, as he conflates Venus and Diana (the Japanese nymph and Scalza are both lunar Venuses), he recalls the latter's compassion for the craftsmen of Ephesus and for the young Pound, who saw larks rise in flight at Allègre (near Le Puy), in Provence, and was reminded of Bernart de Ventadorn's poignant song: "When I see the lark a-moving / For joy his wings against the sunlight . . ." (*SR* 41). The sister who dances in the sixpence or the moon, "reveals the paraclete"—the word made perfect and the methods of art:

> At Ephesus she had compassion on silversmiths
> > revealing the paraclete
> standing in the cusp
> > of the moon et in Monte Gioiosa[33]
> > as the larks rise at Allègre
> > > > Cythera egoista
> > But for Actaeon
> > of the eternal moods has fallen away
> in Fano Caesaris for the long room over the arches
> > olim de Malatestis
> > > wan   caritas   ΧΑΡΙΤΕΣ   [c. 80]

Yet vision is followed by loss: after surprising the goddess Actaeon was slain (c. 4c); the Fair is in turn compassionate and terrible ("egoista"); moods are eternal, yet they fall away.[34] Accordingly Pound, having begun this effusion by recalling his setting out from the United States in 1908, closes it with allusions to the decadence of Malatesta (the long room and the mournful Latin

33. This may be a place name, as suggested in the *Annotated Index,* but the actual import of the words is probably more relevant: "and in the Mountain [she being] Joyous" (the feminine adjective "gioiosa" may not be an accident). An allusion to Montallegro (behind Rapallo), mistakenly mentioned in the *Index* in the gloss to Allègre, may also be intended.

34. "What one in the rout / Of the fire-born moods / Has fallen away?"—W. B. Yeats, "The Moods," *Collected Poems* (London: Macmillan, 1965), p. 63. (Reference noted in Pearlman 279*n.*) But P. does not seem to share his friend's confidence.

inscription are borrowed from c. 8). All of this has passed beyond recovery; yet he reaffirms that culture (*wên*),[35] Pauline charity, and Hellenic art (*Chárites*) are one and the same.

Dejection gives way to a stream of reminiscence for about ten pages; then Pound begins to prepare the canto's finale by returning to the contrast between absence in time and presence in the trace (mental or poetic):

> Nancy where art thou?
> Whither go all the vair and the cisclatons[36]
> and the wave pattern runs in the stone
> on the high parapet (Excideuil)
> Mt Segur and the city of Dioce
> Que tous les mois avons nouvelle lune   [c. 80]

The vair and gowns of Provence are gone like the snows of yesteryear, yet the wave pattern cut in the stone at Excideuil (an image familiar from cs. 29 and 48)[37] is still there to remind us of

---

35. Cf. *A* xiv 19. In the typescript the character *wên* ("Literature; literary accomplishments; polite studies"—M 7129) is inserted between "wan" and "caritas."

36. "Gowns." Cf. "Troubadours—Their Sorts and Conditions," *LE* 107.

37.   So Arnaut turned there
             Above him the wave pattern cut in the stone
             Spire-top alevel the well-curb
             And the tower with cut stone above that, saying:
                  "I am afraid of the life after death."   [c. 29]
Excideuil is a small town northeast of Périgueux, some 100 kilometers east of Chalais and Aubeterre-sur-Dronne (of "Provincia Deserta"). It has been suggested that "Arnaut" is T. S. Eliot, who visited Excideuil with P. in August 1919 (Kenner 336, 582), and who appears to have been present in the following Verona scene (also mentioned in c. 78—see Stock 306–07). This may be P.'s way of reversing the *Waste Land* dedication, equating Eliot with the better craftsman, though the sum of the passage is critical of the Eliotic utterance, "I am afraid of the life after death"—the eternal wave pattern being there to show that personal survival is irrelevant. In fact P. would have hardly given a "pagan" troubadour such a remark, so it may be wise to dissociate the man who "turned" from the person who made it. Arnaut is brought in to qualify the wave pattern, and this cluster is in turn contrasted with Christian concern over hell-fire. For evidence we may go to Mary de Rachewiltz' authoritative translation, where "saying" is rendered as "lei disse" ("she said"—*I Cantos* [1–30], p. 311). From all of which we gather how unsatisfactory some of P.'s writing can be from the point of view of communication.
    As for the wave pattern, this is probably the motif photographed by Kenner near the chateau gate (p. 337), though it smacks rather of baroque decoration than of Albigensian carving. Excideuil's other *senhal*, the well-curb on the castle's grounds, said to be "alevel"

a "cult founded on the waves,"[38] and of a whole culture. The juxtaposition (also anticipated in c. 48) of Excideuil and Montségur suggests that the wave pattern is a trace of the Cathars' "Manicheism," which in turn "rhymes" with the city of Deioces, associated by Pound with Zoroastrism and Manicheism and chiefly with the metaphysics of light. (We recall that the seven terraces of Ecbatan are "the colour of stars," an image of the heavens, and in fact the same has been claimed for the structure of the Montségur citadel.) In the myth of the *Cantos* all of these cultures may be graphed as a single wave resurgent in time at regular intervals, always different yet always the same eternal beauty. Thus the wave pattern is not only an archeological trace of the Albigenses but also a powerful image of the secret tradition and of its main concerns—water, stone, and light. And the sorrowful poet can be comforted, like Froissart, "en ce qu'il me souvient / Que tous les mois avons nouvelle lune." The absence of the wave, tragedy, is itself an indication that it is to reappear shortly—or that spring is not far behind.

The sources of Pound's mytho-cultural construct are clearly to be sought in his poetics of translation or parody, concerned as it is with reemerging patterns (*nékuia, Chanson des oiseaux*). A few lines later he illustrates his meaning by referring to Rossetti's discovery of FitzGerald's "still born" *Rubáiyát* (1 *HSM* 6), itself a translation or an instance of beauty forgotten and retrieved:

> lay there till Rossetti found it remaindered
>   at about two pence
> (Cythera in the moon's barge whither?
>   how hast thou the crescent for car?   [c. 80]

---

the spire of the village below (see also cs. 48 and 107), appears to be an image of the temporal and spatial "layerings" of the poem ("where they scratch six feet deep to reach pavement"—c. 48), and links up with the other "anti-materialistic paradoxes" (Pearlman 109) of c. 29 ("Light also proceeds from the eye"—cf. the "Postscript" to Gourmont, *PD* 210: "Let us say quite simply that light is a projection from the luminous fluid, from the energy that is in the brain, down along the nerve cords which receive certain vibrations in the eye"). The well of the initiate is as high as the steeple of the common; still higher up is the wave, the "cut stone," the supreme touchstone in Poundland (Davie, passim).

38. " 'Blandula, Tenulla, Vagula,' " *P* 39.

The Cytherean Diana "standing in the cusp of the moon" of the earlier passage (now echoing *Antony and Cleopatra:* "The barge she sat in . . .") reminds us again of the periodical nature of the lady, who became manifest to Rossetti in the guise of FitzGerald's melancholy and sensuous quatrains, and now confronts once more the imagination of the Pisan poet as a natural ideogram: his exquisite address (cf. the earlier "Nancy where art thou?") appears in fact to be directed to the planet Venus, which he sees in the morning sky over the moon's sickle or "barge." (Eos and Hesperus, i.e. the morning and evening star, are also referred to in the epic dawn scene of c. 79, clearly because Venus was then visible in the early morning.)[39] This is supported by the subsequent variation of the astronomical image, which refers to the planet both as "Eos of the rosy fingers" (we remember Venus' rose)[40] and as "savage *Kúthera,*" a torch unconcerned with the moth it kills (as in Arthur Symons' poem):[41]

So very difficult, Yeats, beauty so difficult.

39. As first suggested by Wendy Stallard Flory in "The 'Tre Donne' of the *Pisan Cantos,*" *Paideuma,* 5 (1976), 45–46. However, she goes on to claim, at odds with elementary geography, that P. saw Venus both in the morning *and* in the evening. Actually, in summer 1945 Venus rose at 1:45 AM and culminated at about 9 AM. The chief thesis of Flory's overconfident article—that the "tre donne" are Dorothy Pound, Olga Rudge, and Bride Scratton—is rather doubtful and uselessly autobiographic. A more subtle critic, Walter B. Michaels, reminds us of a passage in the 1910 Introduction to Guido: "Commentators, in their endless search for exact correspondences, seem never to suspect [Dante] of poetical innuendo, of calling into the spectrum of the reader's mind associated things which form no exact allegory" ("Pound and Erigena," 44; cf. *T* 22–23).

40. P. uses the Aeolic form of the Homeric epithet, *brododáktulos* (perhaps from Sappho fr. 98 Diehl, cf. c. 5b)—as noted in Frederic Peachy's thoughtful Appendix on Greek words to the *Annotated Index.* P.'s response to this useful but uneven companion volume to the *Cantos* may be worth quoting at this point: "The Universities of California and Cambridge England, which would not sponser [sic] new composition, have E-mitted a large and expensive index to Cantos / the greek well done . . . but the Italian part merely illiterate / or worse. Now considering that Edwards could have consulted you or various educated Italians this gives a chance for constructive criticism of la trahison des clercs." Letter to Carlo Izzo, 10 January 1958, reproduced in *Italian Quarterly,* XVI, 64 (Spring 1973).

41. "Modern Beauty," quoted by P. in the Preface to *Poetical Works of Lionel Johnson,* 1915, *LE* 367. See also Espey, "The Inheritance of *Tò Kalón,*" pp. 322–24.

"I am the torch" wrote Arthur "she saith"
in the moon barge βροδοδάχτυλος Ἠώς

with the veil of faint cloud before her
    Κύθηρα δεινὰ as a leaf borne in the current
pale eyes as if without fire

all that Sandro knew, and Jacopo
      and that Velásquez never suspected
lost in the brown meat of Rembrandt
      and the raw meat of Rubens and Jordaens   [c. 80]

What it is that Jacopo del Sellaio "knew" when he painted his *Venus Reclining* we are told by a poem of *Ripostes,* in which the same dialectics obtain—of fading women and times, and enduring artifacts and eyes:

Of Jacopo del Sellaio

This man knew out the secret ways of love,
No man could paint such things who did not know.
And now she's gone, who was his Cyprian,
And you are here, who are "The Isles" to me.

And here's the thing that lasts the whole thing out:
The eyes of this dead lady speak to me.   [P 73]

It is hardly surprising to find that, in the avowedly Pre-Raphaelite context of c. 80, Jacopo and Botticelli (or rather Rossetti and Burne-Jones, whose Beggar Maid's "yeux glauques"—"Thin like brook-water, / With a vacant gaze" [1 *HSM* 6]—are not easily distinguished from the "pale eyes" of *Kúthera deiná*) fare much better than Velasquez and Rembrandt. This bears out Pound's earlier comments on the decadence of painting after 1527, his remarks on the entrance of "the dinner scene" producing the witty definition (which of course is also partial to the point of superficiality) of Rembrandt and Rubens as, respectively, meat broiled and raw.

    There follow some of Pound's more transparent "watercolors": Abelard's Paris, Confucius' China (fading to Provence's roads: Montségur, the Aliscans of Arles), and an America as distant and near as these in which Pound, at the age perhaps of thir-

teen, after a game of tennis ("on the quais of what Siracusa? /
. . . near what pine trees?"), is confronted for the first time with
Homer's Greek. As he retrieves time past the poet encompasses in
an epiphany the sum of his career: the young man was to become
a modern Ulysses or Everyman, a being similar to the gods because of his fine mind. (This is how he understands Zeus' comment in *Od.* 1. 65–67.) But it is in his capacity to suffer that he is
the more typically human—or godly:

> with a mind like that he is one of us
>   Favonus, vento benigno
>   Je suis au bout de mes forces/   [c. 80]

Ulysses and Pound, third and first person, intelligence and
dejection—these are brought into relation through benignity,
Venus' Zephyr, which is in part a correlative for memory. The
process recurs in the subsequent lines, in which, however, the
voices of Ulysses and of Pound coalesce in a first person singular
very like the psalmist's ("Save me, O God; for the waters are
come in unto *my* soul"—Psalm 69):

> That from the gates of death,
>   that from the gates of death: Whitman or Lovelace
>   found on the jo-house seat at that
> in a cheap edition! [and thanks to Professor Speare]
> hast'ou swum in a sea of air strip
>   through an aeon of nothingness,
> when the raft broke and the waters went over me,   [c. 80]

Venus reapproaches the hero out of obscurity, precisely as with
Rossetti: between the covers of a cheap discarded book which he
picks up in the D.T.C. outhouse, *The Pocket Book of Verse,*
edited in 1940 by the platitudinous ("Men cannot live by bread
alone") M. E. Speare, "A.B., M.A., *Harvard University,* Ph.D.,
Johns Hopkins University,"[42] and including (besides the poets
saluted by P. and many others), the entire *Rubáiyát,* first edition.
As she appears shipwreck gives way to flight, and to a syntactic

---

42. *The Pocket Book of Verse,* ed. M. E. Speare (New York: Washington Square Press,
1940), pp. iii and x.

and metric pattern which we recognize and of which we are to have more: "Hast thou found a nest softer than cunnus?," "Hast'ou seen the rose in the steel dust?," "how hast'ou the crescent for car?." It is the cadence with which Ben Jonson's Cyprian is wonderfully praised:

> Have you felt the wool of beaver,
> Or swan's down ever?
> Or have smelt o' the bud o' the brier,
> Or the nard in the fire?
> Or have tasted the bag of the bee?
> O so white, O so soft, O so sweet is she!

In c. 74 Pound follows up the tag "swansdown"—the only quotation from "The Triumph" in the *Cantos*—with the ecstatic, "So light is the urging, so ordered the dark petals of iron," the metre of which is somewhat more predictable than Jonson's jagged anapests. (It is difficult to resist smoothening the arresting first line by reading "the wool of the beaver").[43]

As the quest for the goddess comes to a head in the already quoted invocation of "Immaculata Regina," whose trinitarian prelude is now quite orthodox (but the names of the three martyrs mean, "eternal," "good," and "reborn"), we realize that vision, entrance to the mysteries ("introibo"—we should not overlook the sexual implications of this Joycean ingress), is bestowed only upon those who suffer:

> Immaculata, Introibo
> for those who drink of the bitterness
> Perpetua, Agatha, Anastasia
> saeculorum
> repos donnez à cils
> senza termine funge   Immaculata Regina
> Les larmes que j'ai créées m'inondent
> Tard, très tard je t'ai connue, la Tristesse,
> I have been hard as youth sixty years   [c. 80]

43. The course of this motif in the *Cantos* is discussed by Donald Davie, *Ezra Pound* (1975), pp. 77–98.

The crisis is followed by a sense of calm (the "repos" Villon prays for) and of brotherhood with the ants of the D.T.C., be they men or insects. Pound lists their names with gratitude, as earlier he had given thanks to the anthologist Speare (whose *Pocket Book* includes poems by Sandburg, Amy Lowell, and Frost—but not by P., Williams, or Eliot):

> if calm be after tempest
> that the ants seem to wobble
>   as the morning sun catches their shadows
>   (Nadasky, Duett, McAllister,
>   also Comfort K.P. special mention   [*Kitchen Police*]
>   .   .   .
>   White gratia Bedell gratia
>   Wiseman (not William) africanus.   [c. 80]

(The latter a warning not to confuse black Wiseman of the D.T.C. with William Wiseman, head of British Intelligence and member of a New York banking firm, who played a significant role in P.'s conspiracy theory—see Stock 467.) The African and his companions are so many candidates for initiation:

> with a smoky torch through the unending
>   labyrinth of the souterrain
> or remembering Carleton let him celebrate Christ in the grain
> and if the corn cat be beaten
>   Demeter has lain in my furrow
>   This wind is lighter than swansdown
>   the day moves not at all
>   (Zupp, Bufford, and Bohon)
>
> men of no fortune and with a name to come[44]   [c. 80]

Tiresias' prophecy that Ulysses would "lose all companions" has been accomplished, as we find in Pound's earlier threnody for Yeats, Ford, Joyce, Plarr, Hewlett, and others ("these the companions"—c. 74; the implicit reference to Tiresias is noted in Pearlman 247n). Now, however, Ulysses finds himself many new companions and promises them (as to Elpenor in c. 1) "a name

44. In the Butler Library, Columbia University, typescript of *PC* to which I have been referring, this is followed by the note, "bis in gk."

to come" by way of his permanent verse, or perhaps through the arcane voyage hinted at previously, which brings together Christianity and Eleusis ("Christ in the grain . . . Demeter has lain in my furrow") [45] and leads once again to Venus' swansdown (or to the soft nest of cunnus), but only after the beating of the corn cat, or of the shipwrecked prisoner.

In the last part of c. 80, which develops the theme of memory and affection, Pound makes a formal pact with his second country, which he has been aspersing with youthful hardness over twenty-five years, by picking up at length the verbal music of two English poets. As he encounters father Browning in Speare's paperback he playfully breaks out with, "Oh to be in England now that Winston's out"—to go on in a more thoughtful vein:

> to look at the fields; are they tilled?
> is the old terrace alive as it might be
> with a whole colony
>   if money be free again?   [c. 80]

The day begun with thanksgiving to the D.T.C. companions is coming to an end: "Only shadows enter my tent / as men pass between me and the sunset." He remembers other shadows he became aware of in 1911 in immemorial Salisbury Plain:

> and for that Christmas at Maurie Hewlett's
> Going out from Southampton
> they passed the car by the dozen
>   who would not have shown weight on a scale
>   riding, riding
>   for Noel the green holly   [c. 80]

As elsewhere in PC the associative writing answers a precise expository strategy: the "vision" aligns Salisbury Plain with the numinous haunts of France and Italy (when first recounting it in ur-c. 2 P. had added: "Ply over ply of life still wraps the earth here"—QPA 25); it is also a correlative of the Cantos' communing with the disembodied voices of the English lyric, a major in-

45. See also "Date Line," LE 76: "Mark Carleton 'the great' improved American wheat by a series of searches. I see no reason why a similar seriousness should be alien to the critic of letters."

stance of which is the new imitation to follow shortly, its text the *Rubáiyát*, that exquisite compendium of estheticism, which has functioned a few pages earlier as a metaphor of Venus. Pound's three quatrains in the characteristic *aaba* rhyme scheme, also adopted by Swinburne in "Laus Veneris," amount to a score parallel to the *Chanson des oiseaux* of Daniel-Jannequin-Da Milano-Münch—the *Rubáiyát* of Khayyam-FitzGerald-Swinburne-Pound. It is, therefore, no surprise that they should start off from FitzGerald's fifth verse, "Iram indeed is gone with all his rose," and that they should go on to sing of what passes and of what remains, of the two Roses of England, and of a more exalted (swansdown and steel dust) "rose":

> Tudor indeed is gone and every rose,
> Blood-red, blanch-white that in the sunset glows
> Cries: "Blood, Blood, Blood!" against the gothic stone
> Of England, as the Howard or Boleyn knows.
>
> Nor seeks the carmine petal to infer;
> Nor is the white bud Time's inquisitor
> Probing to know if its new-gnarled root
> Twists from York's head or belly of Lancaster;
>
> Or if a rational soul should stir, perchance,
> Within the stem or summer shoot to advance
> Contrition's utmost throw, seeking in thee
> But oblivion, not thy forgiveness, FRANCE.   [c. 80]

In the sunset the red and white roses cry blood, not only for the war fought in their name (referred to again in the second verse), for Henry VIII's wives, and for Mary Stuart and David Rizzio (mentioned but a few lines earlier)—i.e., for "the sordid matrimonial customs of England"—but also for the War which is now coming to its gory end (these lines were written in the days of Hiroshima), for which (as we recall) the poet holds England jointly responsible, to say the least. However, the following verses deny that "the white bud" has any knowledge of its murderous roots, and suggest that "contrition's utmost throw" (even now undergone by P.) is to be followed not by "rational" forgiveness but by spontaneous oblivion. Deferring to natural pro-

cess ("is the old terrace alive as it might be / with a whole colony?"), England is reconciled with "FRANCE," a symbol (as the
capital letters suggest) of the Romance world and perhaps of
Italy (which may be to modern England what France was to the
England of the Roses), and essentially of love.

This imitation is ideally a companion to HSM's "Envoi," and
performs within c. 80 and PC a like function, proudly announcing that the writer is the rightful heir of a noble race ("and pass
on the tradition"), a function which we may wish to dissociate
from the content of the verse, as in both lyrics the syntax is ambiguous if not confused, and one does not get very far by attempting to unravel it. When using "closed" forms more than
when extemporizing, Pound avails himself of the freedom which
he detected in Aeschylus: "One might almost say that Aeschylus'
Greek is agglutinative, that his general drive, especially in
choruses, is merely to remind the audience of the events of the
Trojan war; that syntax is subordinate, and duly subordinated,
left out" ("Translators of Greek," LE 273). Did we not bear in
mind this indication of method, we would judge the third quatrain much too loose. (It is difficult to forgive a poet the clumsy
padding of "perchance.") Instead we must respond pre-logically
to the interaction of grief, the oblivion of Lethe, and the pact
with England, and recognize so important a leitmotif as the ra-
tionality of plant life ("Or if a rational soul should stir, perchance, / Within the stem"), which the syntax rather seems to rule
out than to posit. (I take the subject of "seeking" to be the white
bud rather than the rational soul.)

In the last lines of the canto, elegy (now quite explicit) for
"our London / my London, your London" is spliced with a fine
glimpse of the D.T.C., the present ambience in which the section's new mood has arisen and in which it is reflected. A "green
lizard" extends upon a grass blade to capture a small "midge,"
but the poet, who has come to dissent with the right of the
strongest (even though the latter may be cat-like), interferes so as
to save the insect's "green elegance," as long as it may remain
this side of the ditch around his tent ("and they digged a ditch
round about me / lest the damp gnaw thru my bones"—c. 74):

> and if her green elegance
>> remains on this side of my rain ditch
>> puss lizard will lunch on some other T-bone
>
> sunset grand couturier.   [c. 80]

Linguistic zest ("T-bone") and indirect presentation give the passage the necessary robustness: the affectionate and esthetic rescue (it is prompted by the insect's beauty) remains to be inferred by the reader, thus preserving an unsentimental freshness. With this clear chord, and with an homage to the sun (its sartorial accomplishment rhyming with the midge's elegance), the long day's work of c. 80 comes to an end.

The following morning (in the narrative of the poem, of course, though this may well reflect the actual sequence of events) the poet casts his eye upon the Pisan landscape, which has become familiar and conceals "ply over ply" of life:

> Zeus lies in Ceres' bosom
> Taishan is attended of loves
>> under Cythera, before sunrise
> and he said: Hay aquí mucho catolicismo—(sounded
>> catoli*th*ismo)
>> y muy poco reliHión"
> and he said: Yo creo que los reyes desparecen"
> (Kings will, I think, disappear)   ·
> That was Padre José Elizondo
>> in 1906 and in 1917
> or about 1917
>> and Dolores said: Come pan, niño," eat bread, me lad
>> [c. 81]

In the quiet dawn the hills identified as earth's breasts conceal Zeus (the sun?), or the act of love from which Core and wheat will be born; farther on is Mount Taishan, attended of loves which could be the sensuous clouds of c. 76, and dominated by the planet of the Cytherean. The pagan cosmos—the Eleusis "possible in the wilds of a man's mind only"—has been reattained under our eyes in the course of the sequence, which on account of this may be said to tell a paradigmatic story—the poet

acting out the drama for the benefit of all. Remote voices return
as if to warrant this "religious" experience both modern and antique: Father Elizondo, who cares for religion more than for Catholicism or for "Imperial power" (c. 49)—and Dolores of c. 80
with her Eleusinian bread. They initiate the relaxed flow of reminiscences which takes up over half of the relatively brief canto.
From his very first independent *Wanderung* through Europe and
Spain in 1906 Pound goes on to other instances of spontaneous
faith (equated, it will be recalled, with "the cultural level"), his
concealed passion and affection for these reminiscences being
several times at the point of breaking through his reserve:

                    . . . and in Alcázar
       forty years gone, they said: go back to the station to eat
       you can sleep here for a peseta"
              goat bells tinkled all night
              and the hostess grinned: Eso es luto, *haw*!
       mi marido es muerto
              (it is mourning, my husband is dead)
       when she gave me paper to write on
       with a black border half an inch or more deep,
              say 5/8ths, of the locanda
       "We call *all* foreigners frenchies"   [c. 81]

It is clear that memory, even before it coalesces around examples
of ancient benevolence, soothes the troubled mind. These lines
have nothing very particular about them (but for P.'s unusual
readiness to speak in the first person)—yet they are as soft as
"the wind under Taishan" (c. 74), and ideogramicly relevant to
the burden of the canto. Thus the mourning hostess is rhymed
later on with the woman in Theocritus' poem who prays that her
husband be returned to her, and this leads to the mention of
Pound's sexual deprivation at the central juncture of the canto.
(In c. 76 there is also an apparent allusion to the masturbation of
prisoners, juxtaposed with medieval tolerance: " 'Just playin' '
ante mortem no scortum / that's progress.") Likewise Pound's insistence on providing us with the exact width of the black border
on the writing paper reminds us that in the *Cantos* exactitude of
perception is the basis of all culture and religion, insofar as it

does away with the muzziness of usury (cf. the fisherman of c. 51). A relevant passage of *K*, which announces concisely the program of Pound's paradise, may be quoted in this context:

Discrimination by the senses is dangerous to avarice. It is dangerous because any perception or any high development of the perceptive faculties may lead to knowledge. The money-changer only thrives on ignorance. . . .

You can, by contrast, always get financial backing for debauchery. Any form of "entertainment" that debases perception, anything that profanes the mysteries or tends to obscure discrimination, goes hand in hand with drives toward money profit.

It might not be too much to say that the whole of protestant morals, intertwined with usury-tolerance, has for centuries tended to obscure perception of degrees, to debase the word moral to a single groove, to degrade all moral perceptions outside the relation of the sexes, and to vulgarize the sex relation itself. . . .

Against which Grosseteste (I suppose the one who wrote on the nature of light)

> The virtu of the harpe, thurgh skyle and right
> Wyll destrye the fendys myghte,
> And to the cros, by gode skylle
> Is the harpe lykened weyl.
> > Robt. de Brunne, trans.   [*K* 50]

The poet-musician must teach us to see and to dissociate, he must "re-establish a sense of proportion" (this definition of music, which we have quoted often, follows shortly De Brunne's lines), placing us free of fetters in the presence of that which is in no need of further explication:

Both jocundity and *gentilezza* are implicit in nature. There is plenty of propaganda for exuberance, plenty of support for Rabelais and Brantôme. But that does not by any means exhaust the unquenchable splendour and indestructible delicacy of nature. [*K* 50]

An intelligent revisitation of natural process as Pound is aware of it in the D.T.C. microcosm, is the main burden of cs. 79–83, the climax of *PC*. This has reminded some readers of the hypersensitive annotations of Ruskin and Hopkins (Davie 176), but a comparison with Thoreau and some Transcendentalist trends is probably even closer to the mark (Pearlman 289*n*).

The accuracy of the inn scene is contrasted with the inaccuracy of the little boy mentioned by Pound in his 1906 article on Burgos, but his remark is chiefly a playful epiphany:

The hill crest itself is covered with fallen fortifications of various times. At the gate . . . my guide, a boy of eleven, called: "Open! Open! for I come, and with me a Franthes"—spelled frances, and meaning French. I explained that I was not "Frances" but "Americano"; to which the boy replied: "It is all one. Here we know no other name for strangers save 'franthes.' "

And then there came a pair of very big black eyes, and a very small girl tugging at the gate latch; and I knew of a surety that she had sent away the Campeador at the king's bidding. ["Burgos: A Dream City of Old Castile," quoted in Norman 18.]

It may be that Pound is using, intentionally or not, the boy's pronouncement as a formula to bring about a similar apparition of very big black eyes. He is not to be disappointed.

In form this prelude is an orchestration of voices from the past, their quality registered with care until a dominant chord be sounded (in 95 lines there are 11 instances of "to say"): Elizondo, Dolores, hostess and boy, Possum, John Adams, Malatesta ("Te caverò le budella"—see c. 10), Mencken (cf. *K* 28), the black table-maker (" 'It'll get you offn th' groun' / Light as the branch of Kuanon"), and finally George Santayana, whose "faint *cecear*" echoes subtly the priest's "catolicismo," and the boy's "frances":

> and kept to the end of his life that faint *thethear*
> of the Spaniard
>   as a grace quasi imperceptible
> as did Muss the *v* for *u* of Romagna
> and said the grief was a full act
>   repeated for each new condoleress
> working up to a climax.
> and George Horace said he wd/ "get Beveridge" (Senator)
> Beveridge wouldn't talk and he wouldn't write for the papers
> but George got him by campin' in his hotel

and assailin' him at lunch breakfast an' dinner
                          three articles   [c. 81]

The basic theme of religion-benevolence-culture is insistently connected with the notation of "quasi imperceptible" vocal traits,
which can go far in suggesting the flavor of a personality and its
"cultural level." So, after Santayana, we are made to hear Mussolini (whose lisping—already noted in c. 41—connects him with
Sigismondo's Romagna), and then—an instance of cultural poverty—the journalist George Horace Lorimer, who tells of a siege
to obtain an interview—a comic equivalent of the difficult quest
for "beauty." (The often-quoted remark, "to break the pentameter, that was the first heave," occurs earlier in this canto.) The
latter scene, as we discover presently, is set in Wyncote, the Philadelphia suburb where Ezra lived with his parents from 1891 to
1907, and Lorimer has a silent listener, Homer Pound, of which
this is the only portrait to be found in the poem (Isabel, P.'s
mother, is mentioned in the close of c. 83):

          and my ole man went on hoein' corn
              while George was a-tellin' him,
       come across a vacant lot
                where you'd occasionally see a wild rabbit
       or mebbe only a loose one
              AOI!
              a leaf in the current
                        at my grates no Althea   [c. 81]

At the farther end of time's corridor is an image bound to
impress a child, a glimpse of a wild rabbit, "or mebbe only a
loose one." This suddenly brings the poet (Rabbit to his friend
Possum)[46] up against the full terror of his present plight, and he
breaks out in a cry. For a moment he feels like a thing lost in the
current, a needle blindly seeking to be oriented. But presently
new major voices claim his attention.

46. See Stock 435: "For Christmas one year Eliot sent P. a copy of C. P. Nettels's *The
Money Supply of the American Colonies before 1720,* published by the University of Wis-
consin in 1934. The book was inscribed: 'Rabbit from Possum / for Canto XCI / Noel
Noel!' "

To the grates of a fellow prisoner, Lovelace, Love, "with un-
confinèd wings," brought his "divine Althea," as recorded in a
poem included in *The Pocket Book of Verse* (cf. "Whitman or
Lovelace / found on the jo-house seat"):

> When I lie tangled in her hair
>   And fettered to her eye,
> The birds that wanton in the air
>   Know no such liberty.   ["To Althea, from Prison"]

After lamenting the absence of such a visitation the prisoner of
the D.T.C. appropriates it by way of "the virtu of the harpe,"
preparing the "libretto" of a liberating song:

---

libretto   Yet
              Ere the season died a-cold
              Borne upon a zephyr's shoulder
              I rose through the aureate sky
                        Lawes and Jenkyns guard thy rest
                        Dolmetsch ever be thy guest,
              Has he tempered the viol's wood
              To enforce   both the grave   and the acute?
              Has he curved us the bowl of the lute?
                        Lawes and Jenkyns guard thy rest
                        Dolmetsch ever be thy guest   [c. 81]

Before the end of summer (these lines were probably written late
in August) and of this "season" of poetry, the wind of Venus lifts
the poet through a sky of gold—to the paradise of the Meister-
singer of all time. "There I heard such minstrelsy," he had originally added in the typescript after the first refrain, "as mocketh
man's mortality." In the second verse the deserts of the new-
comer are weighed by his forerunners, and the art of verse is
equated with the carving of wood and of stone. It now appears
that the couplet is not addressed to the reader but to the poet, anticipating from the outset the form of the third and crucial verse,
which falls into the Jonsonian cadence of the rose in the steel
dust. After passing his first exam the candidate is questioned by
the goddess herself:

> Hast 'ou fashioned so airy a mood
>   To draw up leaf from the root?
> Hast 'ou found   a cloud   so light
>   As seemed neither mist nor shade?
>   Then resolve me, tell me aright
>   If Waller sang or Dowland played.   [c. 81]

The questions are of a type with those that Jahweh asked of Job; they intimate that "certain colours exist in nature though great painters have striven vainly" (*K* 52), and that what Pound's instrument has in fact accomplished (and it certainly responds memorably to plant life and *diaphaneité*) is as much its own doing as that of earlier singers ("not of one bird but of many") and ultimately of Venus, who is in fact the only begetter of song: poet and sculptor can "find" her in air and stone only if she consent to become incarnate. So to the riddling irony of the challenge in the final couplet (which makes a transition from trochees to iambs in view of the subsequent pentameters) [47] the candidate can only answer with Chaucer's words, and declare his absolute submission to the "merciles Beaute":

> Your eyen two wol sleye me sodenly
> I may the beauté of hem nat susteyne

> And for 180 years almost nothing.   [c. 81]

Beauty is difficult: after the vanquishing of Chaucer "180 years" elapsed before the muse of the lyric was heard again in the age of Shakespeare and Waller—and a darker and longer lapse was to follow. Pound, we see, is both recounting an actual experience—his conjuring of Venus in the D.T.C.—and providing an idiosyncratic history of the lyric by comment and "exercise in the style of a given period" ("Date Line," *LE* 74), somewhat as he had done in that earlier version of the "libretto," *Mauberley's* "Envoi" (which parodies Waller, mentions Lawes, and addresses "her that sheds such treasure in the air"—*che fa di clarità l'aer tremare*). This takes us to the next *ricorso* of the goddess, Pound's summoning of the rose by a return to the Romance fore-

47. Davie, *Ezra Pound* (1975), pp. 97–98.

runners of Chaucer and Shakespeare. The vision now to be visited upon him in the Pisan tent is a correlative of this: it is prefaced by a few Italian words and depicts what on one occasion, "to avoid writing a folio in 900 pages," Pound called "the medieval dream" (*ABR* 104):

> Ed ascoltando al leggier mormorio
>   there came new subtlety of eyes into my tent,
> whether of spirit or hypostasis,
>   but what the blindfold hides
> or at carneval
>   nor any pair showed anger
>   Saw but the eyes and stance between the eyes,
> colour, diastasis,
>   careless or unaware it had not the
>   whole tent's room
> nor was place for the full εἰδώς[48]
> interpass, penetrate
>   casting but shade beyond the other lights
>   sky's clear
>   night's sea
>   green of the mountain pool
>   shone from the unmasked eyes in half-mask's space.   [c. 81]

The eyes Chaucer had seen now confront the modern poet. They have put away mercilessness and are recognizable as a fuller realization of earlier experiences: "The wide-banded irides / And botticellian sprays implied / In their diastasis" of 2 *HSM* 2; the "Eyes floating in dry, dark air" of c. 7; and above all "the suave eyes, quiet, not scornful" of this sequence's prelude.[49] They are the word—"mormorio"—made flesh, if "subtlety" be flesh; a metaphor of perception, like the lynx; but also an apparition to be questioned with tools vaguely Cavalcantesque. As in c. 76 ("spiriti questi? personae?") Pound would like to know (or perhaps he would rather not: "whether of . . ." indicates also indifference to hair-splitting definition) if these pairs of eyes attended

48. "Knowing" (from *eídomai*)—*Annotated Index*. But P. may well be thinking of *eîdos*, "form."

49. See also c. 39: "Can see but their eyes in the dark / not the bough that he walked on."

by intimations of faces are entities personal or universal (hypostasis); [50] but, as stated, he is content to let them "interpass, penetrate" in the tent's small compass, for this is the quality of Dante's *Paradiso* that he had sometime despaired of regaining. (In an earlier draft he had been more particular and less suggestive: "but if each soul lives in its own space and these / interpass, and penetrate as lights not interfering / casting but shade beyond the other lights / nor lose own forms. . . .") [51] It is the great good place where the embittered and tragic mind can, supremely, rest. In the end three colors gleam at him from three pairs—or one pair—of eyes, and it may not be amiss to connect this with the "tre donne" and the triune Venus of cs. 78–79 (and even with the "three sorts of blue" of c. 5): [52] perhaps Pound is indeed at the brink of recognizing three beloved pairs of irides, for this rather leads up to the message they carry here as in the prelude ("What you depart from is not the way"):

> What thou lovest well remains,
> > the rest is dross
> What thou lov'st well shall not be reft from thee
> What thou lov'st well is thy true heritage
> Whose world, or mine or theirs
> > or is it of none?
> First came the seen, then thus the palpable
> > Elysium, though it were in the halls of hell,   [c. 81]

After the closed song-form of the libretto and the free ecstatic notation of vision these slow and muted pentameters carry the conviction of a hymn the sounds of which move sensually on the reader's lips, as if anticipating the two lines by which the query was followed in the earlier draft: "So thinking of Althea at the grates / Two rose-like lips pressed down upon my own." Pound omitted these as perhaps too pat, but not the sequence by which

50. Cf. the perhaps different vision of c. 76: "nor are here souls, nec personae / neither here in hypostasis, this land is of Dione [i.e., Venus] / and under her planet." In "Cavalcanti," *LE* 177, there is a reference to "the then opinion, or ten dozen opinions regarding hypostasis."

51. For P.'s Dantean text see above, chapter 2, n. 35.

52. See Flory, "Tre Donne," pp. 50–51; above, n. 39.

this world "of none" becomes increasingly tangible: from music to vision to touch—the ultimate consummation made available in the very "halls of hell" through none of the worshipper's doing. (Pound's Calvinistic background is here strangely in evidence.) This brings home the burden of much of the previous development, which is voiced in the short berating of vanity so often quoted that it is not easy to read with fresh eyes:

> The ant's a centaur in his dragon world.
> Pull down thy vanity, it is not man
> Made courage, or made order, or made grace,
>   Pull down thy vanity, I say pull down.
> Learn from the green world what can be thy place
> In scaled invention or true artistry,
> Pull down thy vanity,
>   Paquin pull down!
> The green casque has outdone your elegance.   [c. 81]

The sentiment here clearly goes back to Ecclesiastes (whose statement on vanity is included in Speare's anthology), though the experience of making oneself humble and naked is common—as Pound would point out—to many religions and mysteries. As in the previous passage the poet is not the speaker (a role for which he is unqualified) but the person addressed by an unusual godhead, half Jahweh and half Venus, and finally by the Goddess Natura. The ants and "green midge" introduced narratively in the foregoing canto return as the paradigm of exquisite elegance and intelligence, from which such worldly couturiers as Paquin and Pound (the common initial is no coincidence) have all to learn, for, as we have found, art is but the manifestation of what is already "there," not invention but "finding." Pound's good counsel (which includes an adapted quotation from Chaucer's "Balade"—also in Speare) falls into two stanzas interspersed with the refrain-injunction, "Pull down thy vanity" (seven occurrences), answered by "I say [or Paquin] pull down" at the start, middle, and end. The strict pentameter of the opening is dismembered in the second stanza in accord with the shift in sentiment from quiet morality to an invective reminiscent of fire and brim-

stone, cannily constructed with elements borrowed from Villon's
Ballade des Pendus ("La pluye nous a büez et lavez, / Et le soleil
dessechiez et noircis"):

> "Master thyself, then others shall thee beare"
>   Pull down thy vanity
> Thou art a beaten dog beneath the hail,
> A swollen magpie in a fitful sun,
> Half black half white
> Nor knowst'ou wing from tail
> Pull down thy vanity
>   How mean thy hates
> Fostered in falsity,
>   Pull down thy vanity,
> Rathe to destroy, niggard in charity,
> Pull down thy vanity,
>   I say pull down.   [c. 81]

Line 2 announces the quickening of tempo, which reaches an extreme in the syncopated finale, chiming with half-lines equivalent
to (and rhyming with) the chief chord. From this fitful climax we
pass with a feeling of release to the quiet and elegiac movement
of the closing reaffirmation, in which Pound, carefully eschewing
the first person singular, claims indirectly the value of works, if
undertaken with due deference. After all, he has only put himself
to the masters' school, sought them out in the course of "ghostly
visits . . . Knocking at empty rooms, seeking for buried
beauty":[53]

> But to have done instead of not doing
>   this is not vanity
> To have, with decency, knocked
> That a Blunt should open

53. Canto 7. The emergence of Wilfrid Scawen Blunt is again imputable to Speare, who
prints the double sonnet "With Esther." The latter may have been a source of the previous
stanza, for it speaks of "what dole of vanity / Will serve a human soul for daily bread."
(Be it noted, however, that P. employs "vanity" in the modern way, rather than—as the
Bible and Blunt—in the older sense of something useless.) P. visited Blunt on 18 Jan. 1914
with his fellow-poets Yeats, Sturge Moore, Flint, Aldington, Plarr, and Manning (see photograph in Norman 79). He returned in April with Aldington; Blunt received them in the
garb of an Arab sheik, and "his toast was: 'Damnation to the British government' " (Norman 142).

> To have gathered from the air a live tradition
> or from a fine old eye the unconquered flame
> This is not vanity.
>   Here error is all in the not done,
> all in the diffidence that faltered . . .   [c. 81]

The masters—always unconventional like Blunt and Pound himself—have spoken to—and through—the seeker, as this canto has
shown. It is interesting that these lines, which plumb very deeply
Pound's feelings (and consequently the reader's), should be
chiefly concerned not with woman, the mother-goddess, but with
the eye of the father (as is the case with James in c. 7), who
agrees to bestow his blessing on his first-born. However, the burden of the canto is not forgotten: Blunt and Pound and the "fine
old eye" (James, Yeats, Hardy . . .) are finally concerned not
with themselves ("Then resolve me, tell me aright / If Waller sang
or Dowland played") but with "passing on the tradition" (c.
80)—a "live tradition," an "unconquered flame," a beauty only
"buried" so as to be brought back into the air. But the statement
is subdued, and it is further dampened by the final gesture towards the negative, the shadow, appreciation of which is not the
least lesson imparted by the days of Pisa.

   In 1938 Pound had advised Laurence Binyon (who was translating the *Commedia*) that "an opening shd. be as near normal
speech as possible and a heightened or poetic diction can be slid
into later if necessary or advisable" (*L* 349). He took his own advice in cs. 79–81, all of which open with the recitativi of memory
and meditation and climax with mythical and lyrical arias, and
again in c. 82, which pays homage to more masters (Swinburne
and Whitman) and goes on to celebrate the "mysteries" of earth
and eros, following up the previous confrontation with Venus. In
the opening lines we are allowed a glimpse of the D.T.C. and
we hear (as in c. 80) the names of soldiers and convicts, this
being Pound's way of thanking his new companions. But presently we are back in the London of 1908:

> Swinburne my only miss
> and I didn't know he'd been to see Landor
>   *and* they told me this that an' tother   [c. 82]

From the stories he heard of Swinburne (and from his reading of the latter's work) Pound gathered the image of a fellow of Villon, a man "who kept alive some spirit of paganism and of revolt in a papier-mâché era," and a master of the music of language worthy of Chaucer, like him a representative of a culture not insular but European (as suggested here by the reference to his meeting Landor).[54] So this homage is in keeping with the previous breakthrough, and pertinently introduces the "mystery" to follow, an anecdote (largely apocryphal) being made to impress us with Swinburne's Hellenism:

> When the french fishermen hauled him out he
> recited 'em
>   might have been Aeschylus
>   till they got into Le Portel, or wherever
> in the original
>   "On the Alcides' roof"
> "like a dog . . . and a good job
>   ΕΜΟΣ ΠΟΣΙΣ . . . ΧΕΡΟΣ
>   hac dextera mortus
>   dead by this hand
>   believe Lytton first saw Blunt in the bull ring   [c. 82]

Pound's concessive interjections ("might have been," "or wherever") indicate at what points he has rehandled the material to fit his plan. In the 1918 review of Edmund Gosse's biography quoted above, Pound had contrasted the "epileptic" and (for his taste) much too unromantic Swinburne portrayed there with "the glory of a red mane, the glory of the strong swimmer, of the swimmer who when he was pulled out of the channel apparently drowned, came to and held his French fishermen rescuers spellbound all the way to shore declaiming page after page of Hugo" (*LE* 291). In the next paragraph we see the poet in his room,

54. See "Swinburne Versus His Biographers" (1918), *LE* 293.

"hair on end and stark naked, [striding] backwards and forwards howling Aeschylus"—and may again have trouble in distinguishing him from his champion Pound, also a redhead and a good swimmer. This accounts for the substitution of Aeschylus for Hugo, and for the emergence of Swinburne as an alter ego of Ulysses ("hast'ou swum in a sea of air strip?"—c. 80), whom French Phaeacians carry to a "port" par excellence, Le Portel, already mentioned among the English themes of the finale of c. 80, clearly because of some cherished memory associated with the place:

> That would have been Salisbury plain, and I have not thought of
>   the Lady Anne for this twelve years
>   Nor of Le Portel   [c. 80]

Incidentally, the brief recollection of Anne Blunt is the necessary antecedent of the apparition of her husband, a few pages later, as the old master par excellence—a ghost not entirely laid as c. 82 opens: we see him a last time in the bullring, a figure as adventurous and heroic as Swinburne.

The quotations from the *Agamemnon* perform the double function of lighting up Swinburne's paganism and of introducing the theme of ritual murder, the latent sexual import of which is significantly suggested in Greek, the language of the mysteries ("of my husband . . . by this hand"). The other tags refer to the guard who, at the end of another war, awaits the signal of the fall of Troy sitting "on the Atrides' roof" ("Alcides" is an oversight) "like a dog"—a simile perceptively transferred by Pound to the murdered king, "dead by this hand," as Clytemnestra says in his tentative version, "and a good job." [55]

In the *Cantos,* as in the *Odyssey,* the homecoming of Agamemnon serves as a tragic double to Ulysses' *nostos,* the two stories coming to the same in the end: the murder committed by Clytemnestra is but a violent variant of the reunion with lawful Penelope. Cassandra's prophecy (which in the play immediately precedes the queen's murder and confession) is also quoted, it

---

55. See "Translators of Greek," *LE* 269–70, also for P.'s Greek and Latin sources.

will be recalled, in cs. 77–78—as well as in c. 2: "Eleanor, *helénaus* and *heléptolis.*" It reminds the Chorus of "the nightingale
crying, 'Itys, Itys!' "—which may account for the reprise of this
theme of c. 4 in c. 78 ("ter flebiliter: Ityn / to close the temple of
Janus bifronte"), and, more indirectly, in the finale of c. 77,
where Cassandra is addressed as "Sorella, mia sorella," that is, as
"Sister, my sister, O fleet sweet swallow"—the words spoken by
Philomel to Procne in Swinburne's "Itylus." As we may expect,
the theme turns up again in this Swinburne and Aeschylus canto,
together with the birds' "notation," and with the closing statement of the investigation of war conducted in c. 78:

> 8th day of September
>   f   f
>   d
>
>   g
>   write the birds in their treble scale
> Terreus! Terreus!
>   there are no righteous wars in "The Spring and Autumn"
> that is, perfectly right on one side or the other
> total right on either side of the battle line
>   and the news is a long time moving
>   a long time in arriving
>   thru the impenetrable
> crystalline, indestructible
>   ignorance of locality   [c. 82]

The birds protest against cruel (or "terrible"?) Terreus, and their
voices overlap (in a way reminiscent of c. 4: "Ityn! / It is") with
another indictment, the Confucian adage we have spoken of.
Thereupon Pound suggests that war and the unrighteousness it
works are due to a lack of proper communication or notation
among peoples, a dearth of the swift news for which the poet is
always struggling, a striking image of which is again to be found in
the *Agamemnon:*

> The news was quicker in Troy's time
> a match on Cnidos, a glow worm on Mitylene,
>   Till forty years since, Riethmüller indignant:

"Fvy! in Tdaenmarck efen dh' beasantz gnow him,"
        meaning Whitman, exotic, still suspect
    four miles from Camden   [c. 82]

It follows reason that, after recalling the beacons that brought
Clytemnestra the news that Troy was taken (see *LE* 274–75),
Pound should choose for an example of the "ignorance of locality" that makes war the unreceptiveness of American academe to
Whitman (another transparent mask for the equally "exotic" P.),
even after his becoming known to the "peasants" of Europe. And
of course rural man is much in the mind of the author of the
Cantos, and stands at the beginning of this section, even as (P.
would insist) he is the audience most fit to grasp the meaning of
an Aeschylus or a Whitman. Taking for a sounding note two
snippets from "Out of the Cradle" (another of Speare's offerings,
cf. "Whitman or Lovelace / found on the jo-house seat") Pound
launches once again into the earthy mystery of plowing-coition-
death, which was hardly unfamiliar to Whitman's sensibility. The
king has returned to his lady, and receives full illumination from
her—a communication even faster than the beacon's light:

> "O troubled reflection
>   "O Throat, O throbbing heart"
> How drawn, O GEA TERRA,
>   what draws as thou drawest
>   till one sink into thee by an arm's width
>   embracing thee. Drawest,
>   truly thou drawest.
>   Wisdom lies next thee,
>   simply, past metaphor.
> Where I lie let the thyme rise
>   and basilicum
>   let the herbs rise in April abundant
> By Ferrara was buried naked, fu Nicolò
>   e di qua di là del Po,   [c. 82]

The teaching of the previous canto ("Learn of the green world
what can be thy place / In scaled invention or true artistry") has
caught on, as this answer to the teacher that spoke there shows.

The priest-king who has yielded to the universal appeal of love-death ("To that is she bent, her intention / To that art thou called . . . / Never idle, by no means by no wiles intermittent"—c. 47) sees, as the William of Poitiers of c. 5, "the stone alive in my hand, the crops thick in my death year." Niccolò d'Este who, after sowing multitudes of "sons of Niccolò" on the near and far side of the Po, as the ditty has it, went to his death as to a last embrace (see c. 24), envisages its yield as a conjunction with the process of April (thyme, basilicum, herbs) but also as a furtherance of cultural aims (readers have noted the puns on time, basilica, urbs). Again, the sexual and the creative act are linked by Pound, the virile "founders gaz[e] at the mounts of their cities" (c. 16)—or their wives. The theme of reunion with the spouse is made explicit in the gradually quickening sequel through Greek tags from Theocritus ("my man") and Aeschylus ("my husband said"—a page back is a passing reference to Renaissance MSS "with the greek moulds in the margin"), and is graphically presented by the image of the perfectly fitting "halves of the seal," which Mencius (4B.1) uses to suggest the striking agreement of two rulers who lived in different ages and parts of the Empire but still worked to a single purpose (the *Cantos* are of course full of similarly "perfect"—and improbable— "rhymes").[56] Soon the poet communicates impressionistically his ebbing with the ocean of life, his yielding to "the souse upon me of my lover the sea" (Whitman, "Spontaneous Me"), the earth having become in the interim, for reasons easily intuited, liquid:

> fluid ΧΘΟΝΟΣ o'erflowed me
> lay in the fluid ΧΘΟΝΟΣ;
>   that lie
> under the air's solidity
>   drunk with ΙΧΩΡ of ΧΘΟΝΙΟΣ
>   fluid ΧΘΟΝΟΣ, strong as the undertow
> of the wave receding   [c. 82]

After the climax, the "bridegroom night of love working surely and softly into the prostrate dawn" ("I Sing the Body Electric"),

56. See "Mang Tsze (The Ethics of Mencius)" (1938), *SPr* 89–90, and c. 77.

or Pound's drunkenness and "strong undertow of the wave," the
speaker comes up suddenly against a wholly different face of
death (Whitman's "word from the sea" in the poem that
prompted this meditation)—the death not of Niccolò or Walt but
of Christ, the savior figure with which the sequence opens:

> but that a man should live in that further terror, and live
>   the loneliness of death came upon me
>   (at 3 P.M., for an instant)   δαχρύων
>   ἐντεῦϑεν
>
> three solemn half notes
>   their white downy chests black-rimmed
> on the middle wire
>   periplum   [c. 82]

It is death not as reunion but as separation, the butchering of
Agamemnon, the hour—3 P.M.—when the resurrection is far off.
It is not song of the body electric but silence, only punctuated by
stage directions calling for "tears" with the discretion of the
remote language. But then (enteûthen) the hour is made vocal by
the symbolical notation of the birds (it should be recalled that
birds are also the subject of "Out of the Cradle"), and as it
solemnly rings in the mind the announcement that "It is finished," it is answered by the three syllables of "periplum," indicating the conjunction of crucifixion and resurrection, tragedy
and process.

The latter theme is prominent in the following canto, invocation (81) and orgasm (82) passing into a watery dimension of
stillness, which emerges with scarcely an interruption out of the
previous traffic with chthón or earth as fluid—and with swim-
mers, hellenists, and conversationalists (Ford and Yeats in c. 82):

> ὕδωρ
> HUDOR et Pax
> Gemisto stemmed all from Neptune
>   hence the Rimini bas reliefs
> Sd Mr Yeats (W. B.) "Nothing affects these people
>   Except our conversation"
> lux enim
>   ignis est accidens   and,

wrote the prete in his edition of Scotus:
Hilaritas   the virtue *hilaritas*   [c. 83]

Pound's subjective mood, which is again of the type defined in *K* as "ecstatic-beneficent-and-benevolent," will as customary seek correlatives in cultural history, or in an external landscape inhabited by the Neoplatonic shadows of the poem's archeological romance: Gemistus Plethon who, being of the following of the Byzantine emperor at the Council of Ferrara-Florence (1438), brings to Italy his Platonism, centered upon "POSEIDON, *konkret Allgemeine*" (c. 8e), and on this account influences, through his conversation, Renaissance thought and art, as well as (by extension) Agostino di Duccio's fluid bas-reliefs in the Tempio Malatestiano, where he is buried (see again "Neoplatonicks Etc.," *K* 39); and Scotus Erigena, who grafts Greek culture (and in particular the Neoplatonism of the Pseudo-Dionysius, whom he translated into Latin) upon the Carolingian renaissance, and is dear to Charles the Bald (as biographers tell us) because of his sense of humor and his brilliant talk.[57] Pound is fond of the notion that "The culture of an age is what you can pick up and/or get in touch with, by talk with the most intelligent men of the period" (*K* 37)—a quick hint can go a longer way than the perusal of much printed matter. The anecdotal form of the *Cantos* is clearly based on this assumption, cognate to Pound's early theory about "the luminous detail . . . governing knowledge as the switchboard governs the electric circuit."[58] The tales of Gemisto, Erigena, Cunizza, and so on, told or half-told in the *Cantos,* are shortcuts which would lead us to the center of complex cultural phenomena, and are in fact to Pound seminal paradigms and, on

57. "Regi hilaritas ejus et facete ingenioseque dicta magnopere placuerunt."—C. B. Schlueter, Preface to Erigena's *De Divisione Naturae,* PL CXXII 101. P.'s actual (remembered) source, however, would seem to be the "Pietate insignia [sic] atque hilaritate," he quotes (apparently from Schlueter) in a letter to Eliot of 18 Jan. 1940 (of the period, that is, in which he was "tackling philosophy"). Michaels ("Pound and Erigena," p. 50) indicates that he has indeed found the quotation in Schlueter, but withholds chapter and verse. By "the prete" (priest) P. seems to mean Jacques-Paul Migne, the editor of *PL* but not of Erigena's single works, or Schlueter himself. For the previous Latin quotation see c. 55 and the *De Luce* of Grosseteste (the other medieval translator of Pseudo-Dionysius), as quoted in "Cavalcanti," *LE* 161.

58. "I Gather the Limbs of Osiris: A Rather Dull Introduction" (1911), *SPr* 21–23.

account of their vividness, good matter for poetry—the last being
the claim with which we are more likely to agree. The canto continues as follows, after one of several blanks breaking up its
leisurely progress:

> the queen stitched King Carolus' shirts or whatever
> while Erigena put greek tags in his excellent verses
>   in fact an excellent poet, Paris
>   toujours Pari'
>   (Charles le Chauve)
>   and you might find a bit of enamel
>   a bit of true blue enamel
>   on a metal pyx or whatever
>   omnia, quae sunt, lumina sunt, or whatever
>
> so they dug up his bones in the time of De Montfort   [c. 83]

The bit of enamel to be found on the old chalice (see K 16—and
Gautier's *émaux* and medallions) is a correlative of the luminous
detail—the fragment (like "omnia, quae sunt, lumina sunt")
through which we grasp a whole culture, or the Greek word
which, "in the margin" of Basinio's manuscripts (see above) and
in the texts of Erigena and Pound, preserves its original flavor
(like pre-Socratic *húdor*) and indicates that certain correlations
have been made. Erigena, for instance, celebrated as follows, in
couplets of doubtful excellence, the domestic deserts of Charles
the Bald's wife, Irmintrud:

> Ingens ingenium, perfecta Palladis arte
>   Auro subtili serica fila parans.
> Actibus eximiis conlucent pepla mariti,
>   Gemmarum serie detegit indusias.
> Miratur fugitans numquamque propinquat ἀράχνη
>   Quamvis palladios aequiperat digitos.[59]

59. "Laudes Yrmindrudis Caroli Calvi uxoris," *PL* xcv 1227 (Floss's edition, used by P.).
The text, as emended by Traube (*M.G.H., Poetae* iii, 533), may be translated as follows:
"Greatly intelligent, perfect in Pallas' art, she interweaves silken threads with subtle gold.
Her husband's cloaks shine with her noble efforts, many gems cover his clothes. As she es-
capes, Arachne the spider is taken with wonder, nor does she dare to approach, though
she be equal to the fingers of Pallas."

—lines which may account for the references in cs. 74 and 76 to "Arachne che mi porta fortuna" ("who brings me luck"), and, perhaps, for the juxtaposition of the girl-spider with the "serica fila" of the Immaculate ("funge la purezza"—c. 74)—though the latter association is rather self-explanatory. The radiance of such luminous details as Erigena's statement is proved indirectly by the destruction visited upon them, as intimated by the last line, which looks back to cs. 23 and 36, and refers us obliquely to Albigensian arcana, which also may "stem all from Neptune," as we have found when speaking of the wave of Excideuil.

The entry of Yeats in line five as the bearer of the news about conversation is no accident, however antithetical his spiritualism may be to Pound's sensual immanentism. In "Sailing to Byzantium" he had spoken of rising from the transience of organic life to "the artifice of eternity"—the perfect world of art. To Pound art may be an even more central concern, yet it does not stand in opposition to the cycle of life and death, it is an extension or emanation of nature. The carving of Rimini or of Santa Maria dei Miracoli in Venice emerges from *húdor* by way of a cultural impulse (Gemisto) which is only accessory to the process, as is the case with Waller and Dowland in c. 81:

> Le Paradis n'est pas artificial
> and Uncle William dawdling around Notre Dame
> in search of whatever
>   paused to admire the symbol
> with Notre Dame standing inside it
> Whereas in St Etienne
>   or why not Dei Miracoli
> mermaids, that carving,
>
>   in the drenched tent there is quiet
>   sered eyes are at rest   [c.83]

Notre Dame is not a symbol, but a type fully manifest in the carver's stone; she is a "terrible" revelation ("Your yën two wol slee me sodenly"), not the subjective revery subtly implied by the portrait of Yeats, who first "dawdles" with little care for the object and eventually "pauses to admire" (the pompousness is intentional) what is in fact but a figment of his imagination. Of course with this friendly nagging Pound does not quite hit the mark, while laying himself open to the retort that his own allegedly objective world is notably more abstract than his mentor's—for instance, in this matter of Notre Dame, there is little doubt that the cruel fairs of the *Cantos* are less real (in the flesh and in the imagination) than the forward girls of the later Yeats. This is not to deny that Pound can be an unequalled witness of presence, as in the closing lines of our excerpt, which return us to the Pisan tent and to the "subtlety of eyes" within it—but now it is the poet's eyes which, having been wounded by the dust and glare of summer, are soothed by the rain: "HUDOR et Pax." Thus the first chord of the canto is placed against the background which originally suggested it—a September shower:

> the rain beat as with colour of feldspar
> blue as the flying fish off Zoagli
> pax, ὕδωρ   ΥΔΩΡ
> > the sage
> delighteth in water
> > the humane man has amity with the hills
>
> as the grass grows by the weirs
> > thought Uncle William   *consiros*
> as the grass on the roof of St What's his name
> > near "Cane e Gatto"
> > > soll deine Liebe sein
> it would be about a-level the windows
> > the grass would, or I dare say above that
> > when they bless the wax for the Palio   [c. 83]

As if taking back his earlier censure Pound shows us Uncle William as he befriends—like the "humane" Confucianist—the water and the hill,[60] and chooses as a paragon for his love not an

60. *A* VI 21. See also the catalogue of epiphanies in *K* 9:
   "Against this a few evenings in Brancusi's old studio, wherein quiet was established. 'The quality of the sage is like water.'
   I don't know the source of Allan Upward's quotation.
   A few evenings in the Palazzo Capoquadri listening to Mozart's music."
Even so in c. 83 P. goes on from *húdor* to the view from (and frescoes of) Palazzo Capoquadri.

artifact but a phenomenon as natural as the blue flying fish's leap that the younger poet recalls from the familiar Ligurian landscape:

> She bid me take love easy . . . as the grass grows on the weirs;
> But I was young and foolish, and now am full of tears.
>
> ["Down by the Salley Gardens"]

The regret attached to the memory of grass growing at water's edge is signified by the single word "consiros," from Arnaut Daniel's melancholy lines in *Purg.* 26 ("consiros vei la passada folor," sadly I look upon my past folly)—the very word which early in *PC* signals the sequence's quest for things past: "e'l triste pensier si volge / ad Ussel. A Ventadour va il consire, e'l tempo rivolge."[61] Yeats's elegiac image fades to one of Pound's own finding, the grass springing from the roof of Siena's San Giorgio in Pontaneto,[62] which prompted—early in the Monte dei Paschi cantos—the memorable lines in which Pound confidently submits to life's cycle:

> wave falls and the hand falls
> Thou shalt not always walk in the sun
> or see weed sprout over cornice
> Thy work in set space of years, not over an hundred.   [c. 42]

—lines which already establish a connection between man's hand ceasing from work and the wave that falls, but only (as we have seen) to rise anew. (In the next canto—43—we find a funny account of the preparations for the Palio referred to again in the "consiros" passage.) In c. 83, as earlier in 74 ("and this grass or whatever here under the tentflaps / is, indubitably, bambooiform / . . . whereas the child's face / is at Capoquadri in the fresco square over the doorway"), grass comes to be associated with the timeless—wavelike—renewal of mental icons:

61. "And the sad thought returns / to Ussel. To Ventadour goes desire, retrieving time." I have added apostrophes, for P.'s "el" looks like a contraction of "e il." In drafting the lines P. first wrote, significantly: "el triste pensier si volge in lontananza / e al passato."

62. See Vittorugo Contino, *Ezra Pound in Italy: From the* Pisan Cantos: *Spots & Dots,* w. notes by Olga Rudge (Venice: Gianfranco Ivancich, 1970), n.p.—a book of photographs of P. and of his haunts.

Olim de Malatestis
        with Maria's face there in the fresco
        painted two centuries sooner,
        at least that
before she wore it
                    .   .   .

        or πάντα ρει   [c. 83]

The poet's daughter "wears" the ancient traits[63]—and the additional pre-Socratic reference (also to be found in a fine passage of c. 80, likewise concerned with water) does not import so much that All flows but rather that All returns.[64]

The canto's sequel offers a captivating description of the Pisan landscape, pellucid after the September shower, together with recollections of Venice, city of waters, the latter allowing us to think of Pound's meditation on *húdor* as a companion piece to the equally moving and elegiac canto 76. The whole is informed by a feeling of sympathy in sufferance, by gratitude for men, plants, animals:

Nor can who has passed a month in the death cells
        believe in capital punishment
No man who has passed a month in the death cells
        believes in cages for beasts
                .   .   .

(have I perchance a debt to a man named Clower)
                .   .   .

mint springs up again
        in spite of Jones' rodents
as had the clover by the gorilla cage
        with a four-leaf

When the mind swings by a grass-blade
        an ant's forefoot shall save you
the clover leaf smells and tastes as its flower   [c. 83]

63. The lines I have omitted allude to Thomas Hardy's "Heredity": "I am the family face; / Flesh perishes, I live on, / Projecting trait and trace / Through times and times anon, / And leaping from place to place / Over oblivion" (CC 283).

64. In fact, where the printed text of c. 80 reads "*Pánta hreî,*" the typescript offers "not *pánta hreî.*"

It is perhaps not an accident that the name of the printer of *Lustra*, Clowes, should be made to resemble the clover which produced by the poet's cage a lucky four-leaf—an apt token of his fortunate fall.

In a well-known passage Pound watches "Brother Wasp," who turns out to be a lady, "*la* vespa," build "a very neat house" of mud on his tent roof, from which "an infant, green as new grass," emerges and descends to the earth, performing again the chthonian ceremony of the previous canto, now openly connected with the *nékuia* and Passion:

> begotten of air, that shall sing in the bower
>   of Kore, Περσεφόνεια
> and have speech with Tiresias, Thebae
>   Cristo Re, Dio Sole
>
> in about ½ a day she has made her adobe
> (la vespa) the tiny mud-flask
>
>   and that day I wrote no further
>
> There is fatigue deep as the grave.   [c. 83]

The poet compares his writing to the insect's work ("½ a day," "that day"); but while the latter becomes a positive symbol of reunion with the earth, of the *nékuia* ("bower" and "Thebae" point back to Circe's speech in cs. 39 and 47), and of the resurrection, human labor must face (as in c. 82) a "further terror," "deep as the grave"—and not in the erotic sense of the earlier passage ("lie into earth to the breast bone").[65]

It appears from the typescript that Pound originally intended to finish the canto with the words "and that day I wrote no further"—but this would have been too close a parallel to the previous finale. So the sun rises again, a few lines on, upon another day, and Pound fills out the homage to Yeats with which his "song" opened, by way of an extensive and playful recollection of the days spent as the master's secretary "at Stone Cottage in Sussex" in 1913–15. (The otherwise obscure lines "Summons

---

65. "Deep as the grave" looks like a reminiscence of Swinburne's "A Forsaken Garden," anthologized by Speare: "What love was ever as deep as a grave?"

withdrawn . . ." refer to some trouble with local authorities because P. was an "alien in prohibited area" [Stock 238]. They are the shorthand of memory.) The making of the wasp's mud-bottle and of c. 83 is thus placed side by side with the writing of "The Peacock":

> sun rises lop-sided over the mountain
> so that I recalled the noise in the chimney
> as it were the wind in the chimney
> but was in reality Uncle William
> downstairs composing
> that had made a great Peeeeacock
> in the proide ov his oiye
>
>   .   .   .
>
> as indeed he had, and perdurable   [c. 83]

The lines in the process of being written ("What's riches to him / That has made a great peacock / With the pride of his eye?") are clearly not without bearing upon the "fine old eye" and the more fugitive triune eyes, "whether of spirit or hypostasis," of c. 81, which return some twenty lines on, but as if internalized, placed not before but behind the proud eye of the poet, who now thinks of them as of "my world." (Elsewhere he speaks of "a sense of [the] presence [of gods] as if they were standing behind us"— "Religio," *PD* 97.)

> The eyes, this time my world,
> But pass and look *from* mine
> between my lids
> sea, sky, and pool
> alternate
> pool, sky, sea,   [c. 83]

Gods are, again, states of mind, ways of looking *at* things—here in the perspective of *pánta hreî*, of the world of water, to which this is the final reference in the canto. (Cf. "sky's clear / night's sea / green of the mountain pool / shone from the unmasked eyes.") Returning to the thought cluster suggested earlier by the grass, the poet refers us in one breath to the transience of human life ("Mir sagen / Die Damen / Du bist Greis, / Anacreon") and to the permanence of nature, art, and religion ("And that a Madonna novecento [i.e., twentieth-century] / cd/ be as a Madonna quattrocento / This I learned in the Tirol")—and we note that the quotation (by way of an untold number of parodies) of Anacreon brings together both aspects of the question, because the complaint has lasted, whereas Anacreon-Pound and his *Damen* have vanished, à la Villon.

The final lines transfer us to the United States, "in my mother's time," when "respectable" people deigned "to sit in the Senate gallery / or even in that of the House," to hear out their representatives; a custom discontinued, to the regret of Pound, who makes ready for a new round of political banter, though he takes care to mention that in such a way he has come to hear of speeches made sixty years before he was born (Nimian Edwards held office in the 1820s):

> but if Senator Edwards cd/ speak
> and have his tropes stay in memory 40 years, 60 years?   [c. 83]

Which may well be a last echo of one of the canto's opening chords—enlightenment through conversation.

Pisa's concise finale, canto 84, takes us from the timeless ambience of *húdor* and peace to the turmoil of contemporary events, and sums up—in a fashion bracing if occasionally irritating—the tale of which it provides the last chapter. In fact it sums up a good deal of the entire uneven poem:

> "when we came out we had
>   80 thousand dollars' worth"
>   ("of experience")
>
>   .   .   .
>
>   Under white clouds, cielo di Pisa   [*Pisa's sky*]
>   out of all this beauty something must come,[66]   [c. 84]

At the close of his soliloquy the speaker sees fit to review his position, which has changed little since the days of the Rome broadcasts, but for the playfulness with which he refers to Roose-

66. In the margin of the typescript: "(17 Oct.)."

velt, Churchill, and Stalin. (It was in fact at this time that P. wanted to study Georgian in order to communicate his worth of experience to "dear Koba.")[67] Accordingly, between final respects to Apollo and to Henry and Brooks Adams,[68] he breaks out with a hysterical farewell to Mussolini ("il Capo"), Alessandro Pavolini, and Fernando Mezzasoma (notorious officials of the puppet Salò regime)—and to fellow-collaborators Laval, Quisling and Philippe Henriot. (The two reputable trios are absurdly compared to the "three men full of humanitas" of Yin dynasty—A xviii 1.) That the canto is essentially a threnody for fallen comrades is apparent from its powerful overture:

> 8th of October:
>   Si tuit li dolh el plor
>   Angold τέθνηκε
> tuit lo pro, tuit lo bes
>   Angold τέθνηκε   [c. 84]

The poet J. P. Angold had contributed, like Pound, to the pro-fascist and anti-Semitic *New English Weekly,* edited from 1932 by Orage; he fell, on the Allied side, in 1943. But what is more relevant is the reprise (together with Bertran de Born's dirge for Henry Plantagenet, which P. had translated and quoted in the early version of c. 6) of the Greek perfect which in c. 23 introduces for the first time the theme of the death of Adonis: " 'Téthneke,' said the helmsman, 'I think they / Are howling because Adonis died virgin.' "[69] Thus the passage bears on the opening theme of *PC,* the sacrifice of Manes-Ben-Dionysus. There follow, developing the previous close, some recollections of what Pound was told (by isolationist senators) in Washington, after he had passed, in 1939, the Pillars of Hercules. A final reference to matters dealt with in the prelude of the section is to be

---

67. Canto 74. However, on the page before last P. sketches an irate and obscure comparison between himself and F.D.R., in which, as in the previous valediction (see below), there is an utter lack of sense of proportion and humor. Yet he adds with the utmost confidence the fine meaningless line: "These are distinctions in clarity / ming these are distinctions."

68. "Adams" in the typescript; "Adam" in the printed text.

69. The source here is Plutarch, *De Defectu Oraculorum* 17.

found on the last page of this troubling manifesto, which records
an Italian conversation of the poet with a "sorella della pa-
storella dei suini," [70] a young Circe clearly cognate to the "sorella
luna" and to Scalza of other passages:

> e questi americani?
>> si conducono bene?
> ed ella: poco.
>> Poco, poco. διὰ ὑφορβά   [divine swineherdess]
> ed io: peggio dei tedeschi?
>> ed ella: uguale, through the barbed wire   [c. 84]

In other words, there are no righteous wars.

Canto 84 is meant to remind us of the historical and topical
circumstances and of the confused yet integrated personality out
of which the lyric breakthroughs of the Pisan sequence originated. This it accomplishes with confidence and some detachment, striking an attitude at least not open to the charge of unc-
tuousness and uncandidness. In the couplet which terminates the
long monologue the tent in which it was written is also on view:
it is no longer visited by the Bassarids of midsummer or by the
mild Heliads of early autumn, but attacked by the frost of October's nights:

> If the hoar frost grip thy tent
> Thou wilt give thanks when night is spent.[71]   [c. 84]

The season is now finally "dead a-cold," but it has been made to
yield fruit. The reader is charged with the remembrance—and
pity—of the foregoing "record of struggle."

In typescript the canto's opening threnody was preceded by a
valediction notably different in tenor, which Pound may have excised as too "soft" and conventional in metre. (Besides, its foreboding of death had been happily disproved by the time he prepared PC for publication.) The lines are surely worth recovering

70. "Sister of the little swineherdess" (of c. 73, see above, n. 3), i.e., P.'s daughter, who as
a child tended sheep in Tirol, and who visited her father in the D.T.C. on 17 Oct. 1945
(Stock 524). P.'s account was written shortly after (see n. 66).

71. In the Columbia typescript the couplet (perhaps a reminiscence of the close of Samson Agonistes) is missing, being replaced by the date, "Oct. 1945."

for what they tell us of Pound's ultimate hope that his verse and
possible execution may lead to reconciliation and peace, and for
the playful and poignant chord (that of the lynx chorus) they
strike: of the poet's tomb there is to be no mark, "no vestige save
in the air," [72] and yet the spot will be easily told by the number of
cats and girls that will flock, eyes alight, to their former boon
companion:

> Yet from my tomb such flame of love arise
> that whoso passes shall be warmed thereby;
>   let stray cats curl there
>   where no tomb stone is
> and girls' eyes sparkle at the unmarked spot
> Let rancours die
>   and a slow drowse of peace pervade who passes.

72. Canto 74. Cf. "And thus in Nineveh" ("Aye! I am a poet and upon my tomb / Shall
maidens scatter rose leaves"—*P* 24: 1909), and *HSP* 1: "And I also among the later
nephews of this city / shall have my dog's day, / With no stone upon my contemptible
sepulchre; / . . . There will be a crowd of young women doing homage to my palaver."

Part Two

Loyalty and Disloyalty to the Text: Poetics of Translation

Just as a tangent touches a circle lightly and at but one point, with this touch rather than with the point setting the law according to which it is to continue on its straight path to infinity, a translation touches the original lightly and only in the infinitely small point of the sense, thereupon pursuing its own course according to the laws of fidelity in the freedom of linguistic flux.

—Walter Benjamin,
"The Task of the Translator," tr. Harry Zohn

But then all translation is a thankless, or is at least most apt to be a thankless and desolate undertaking
—Pound, "Translators of Greek," *LE* 268

To Pound, a full correspondence between reality and discourse is possible; this elementary mimetic hypothesis he never questions overtly. From the much quoted definition of "image" (it "presents," that is imitates, "an intellectual and emotional complex in an instant of time"—*LE* 4), to the recurrent discussions of the ideogram (advocated as a model for thought-processes), to the fragmentary statements of poetics scattered through the *Cantos,* Pound relies consistently on an uncritical theory of *mimesis* (however this may be refuted by his practice), for he avoids investigating the status of the vehicle of expression and of the object as such. But as a matter of fact, in his nonmetaphoric universe, signs are contiguous to phenomena—not placed between these and man as instruments of knowledge. Thus it is not possible to determine the presumptive object of Pound's mimesis as a concrete entity, and his "realism" (like that of others) often appears to be but a roll call of *pre*judices concerning things. The dumb show offered at Montjouvain by Miss Vinteuil and her friend to Proust's troubled narrator, savors of a nondiscursive experience that discourse cannot (and would not) fully explore, as it is the center of a constantly expanding structure of significance. The real is barred instead from the *Cantos*, not because it is "vile," as Mallarmé would have said, but because the page is the sole actuality, Pound's world is all told in his lines, it is all present, explicit, equally lit—though no doubt it will wholly revert to *absence* as soon as we set the book aside. In other words Pound's poetry is primarily *matter:* not thought and not even description or, worse, instruction. His words, rather than conveying a content, attach themselves to memory in the manner of musical phrases, handsome or trivial as the case may be.

This situation holds for Pound the translator, who seeks a total imitation of a particular object that is already a sign, namely another work of literature. His is the method he commended to a prospective translator of his own work: to interchange single words with their equivalents and trust that the tenor will come to light of itself. ("It's easy. Find the Hungarian equivalent of my English words, and put it down. For example, when I say *tree,* write the Hungarian for *tree.* It's as simple as that.") [1] The literary work is primarily but one occurrence among many of universal denotation, and the translation is contiguous to it; a discussion of the correlation of the two is irrelevant because to undertake it we would be digressing from the space in which alone both have being. Their bearing upon each other is as immediate and arbitrary as is the inclusion of history in the "epic" of the *Cantos:* history is but a row of events, of forms carved in an amorphous continuum, which are fully expressed within a certain verbal unit (the *Cantos'* line); in the same way the original is principally *text,* to the exclusion of its historical *context.* Here again all is discourse, the rest is unimportant and is not even taken into account. The translation is not the end product of a comparative study; it does not make remote authors such as Sophocles and Confucius more accessible—because the true ma-

1. Reported by Guy Davenport, personal communication, 9 July 1967.

teriality of their work does not allow penetration, nor does it call
for it. As such they belong already to our cultural present, though
"obscurantists" may have excluded them from it, by suggesting
that these texts, with the civilizations that produced them (their
contexts), are irretrievable, and by instituting partial relationships with them. So Pound's translation is *apocalyptic,* as L.S.
Dembo first suggested: it *reveals* an identity where one saw only
distances, and does so—I will add—by making that distance absolute. In this way it becomes impossible to distinguish original
from translation, and it is paradoxically the latter, e.g., the
Women of Trachis, that designates itself as the rightful "original," because it discloses layers of meaning that have been concealed by the "closed" readings of which the text has been the
object, and perhaps also because Sophocles in turn was the translator of an ur-text to which Pound is more "faithful." The "laws
of fidelity" determining translation bear but lightly on the sense,
as stated by Benjamin in my epigraph. Imitation is concerned
with forms, with (Jannequin's) "intervals" (*K* 23) within "linguistic flux"—not with a supposed definite meaning. It is an act of
perception, not of definition. This point is clearly seized by Jorge
Luis Borges. "Les érudits—he writes—accusent Pound de tomber
dans des erreurs crasses, démontrant son ignorance du saxon, du
latin ou du provençal; ils ne veulent pas comprendre que ses
traductions réfléchissent les formes insaisissables et non le
fond." [2]

2. Jorge Luis Borges, "Note sur Ezra Pound, traducteur" (July 1965), tr. Jean de Mil-
leret, *L'Herne* 233.

4. Confucius

The Integral Study

The *Pisan Cantos* were not the only testament to come out of the D.T.C. In the fall Pound prepared an English translation of the two Confucian books he had published in Italy during the war (*Studio Integrale*[1] and *L'asse che non vacilla*[2]) and dated them as follows:

> D.T.C., Pisa; 5 October—5 November, 1945
> "*We are at the crisis point*
>   *of the world.*"
>   —*Tami Kume, 1924*

The quotation suggests that he thought of his version as a cornerstone on which to build after the wreckage of war. In fact, as we have found in *PC*, the meaning and the relevance of Confucius became increasingly evident to the poet as the crisis approached its climax. "I do not know I would have arrived at the centre of his meaning if I had not been down under the collapse of a regime," he wrote, a little ambiguously insofar as his own stance was concerned, to his father-in-law's firm on that very 5 October (Cornell 11).

Let us recapitulate Pound's career as a Confucianist, at the risk of repeating matters stated earlier. In ur-canto 1 we find that

> Confucius later taught the world good manners,
> Started with himself, built out perfection.[3]

—and this is essentially the Voltairian Confucius of c. 13 and of its prose companion piece, *Ta Hio, The Great Learning* (1927), a rendering which, be it noted, relies wholly on Pauthier's French.

1. Hence the title of this chapter.

2. People have been amused by the notion that this book was destroyed because suspected of containing Axis propaganda. But the reference in the title is doubtless intentional, and both versions use words popularized by the fascist regime.

3. *Poetry,* 10 (1917), 119.

At this time, however, Pound began to acquire his bad manners, and we may already sense something shrill and uncompassionate in the platitudes presented as profound verities in c. 13—in fact, the shrillness of Voltaire. The next step was the making of the Master into a forerunner of fascism, and a closer look at the "ideograms." As already noted, Pound made one of his very first attempts at an etymological reading of Chinese on the "Make it new" text (GD 1 2) in 1933, as follows:

> Confucius on "La rivoluzione continua."
> King Tching T'ang on Government. . . .
> The first ideogram (on the right) shows the fascist axe for clearing away of rubbish (left half) the tree, organic vegetable renewal. The second ideograph is the sun sign, day,
> "renovate, day by day renew."   [*J/M* 113]

Hsin (axe + tree) is probably the sign Pound is most fond of, and we should not allow ourselves to forget that it implies throughout the *Cantos* a bow towards fascism.

By the time of *Kulchur* Pound thought of himself as a Confucian and used the Chinese as a beating stick for Western philosophers and religions—which was after all the point of c. 13. In the *Fifth Decad* and in the China cantos we find the first signs of an alignment of the Master with the metaphysics of light, but on the whole Pound's interpretation progresses little in depth, though it becomes (in the poem) virulently partisan. In 1937 he began to state his belief in the magic power to do away with malnutrition residing in the first forty-six characters of the *Ta-hsüeh* (which alone are attributed to Confucius), and told readers of the *Criterion* that he had gone on retreat with the *Four Books* [4]—yet nothing came of this until 1942, when the *Studio integrale* was first published, and in fact the full conversion of Confucius into a mystic was not accomplished until 1945, with *L'asse che non vacilla* and the Immaculata passages of *PC*. It is perhaps in late 1944 that Pound pasted sayings of Guido and Confucius onto the walls of Rapallo: his being a poetry of reality, there was nothing to forbid that dialogue in Tuscan, Chinese, and

---

4. "Immediate Need of Confucius" (*SPr* 80), and "Mang Tsze" (*SPr* 82).

American, to his fellow townsmen. Yet this reminds us of Rousseau trying to convince Parisians of the plot upon him by writing out a long appeal in many copies and attempting to hand it out on the street, unsuccessfully of course. (Everyone was party to the plot, he explains. See *Rousseau juge de Jean-Jacques*.)

The Confucius of the war years is wholly a new invention of Pound, based on his supposed findings among the ideograms. His notions of the mystical import the signs could carry to the ancient Chinese were on the whole correct, his etymologies only a little more fanciful than those provided by the old authors to please themselves—in fact they are but extemporary reveries, often fascinating; he could have found as much in a Rorschach.

Let us take as an example the following passage, biblical in flavor, and possibly a source for "the great periplum" of *PC:*

In the heavens present to us, there shine separate sparks, many and many, scintillant, but the beyond [what is beyond them] is not like a corpse in a shut cavern.

(This sort of farfetched metaphor is always a sure sign of etymological wandering—a corpse somewhere among the signs.)

Sun, moon and the stars, the sun's children, the signs of the zodiac measuring the times, warners of transience, it carries all these suspended, thousand on thousand, looking down from above the multitude of things created, it carries them, now here, now there, keeping watch over them, inciting them, it divides the times of their motions; they are bound together, and it determines their successions in a fixed order. The visible heaven is but one among many. [*UP* xxvi 9]

If we turn to the original, we find that this vision has been suggested by a mere twenty-three characters, which Legge—Pound's source—construes as follows:

The heaven now before us is only this bright shining spot; but when viewed in its inexhaustible extent, the sun, moon, stars, and constellations of the zodiac, are suspended in it, and all things are overspread by it.[5]

5. James Legge, "The Doctrine of the Mean," *The Chinese Classics,* 2nd ed., 1 (Oxford, 1893), 420.

Clearly Pound, carried away by his own visionary and rather Whitmanian cosmic consciousness, has paused to bring out all the implications he finds in the characters, as if these were parcel of Confucian ideology. But of course, as noted, the signs used by the Confucian school are also to be found in the texts of Taoists and others, and the meaning they carry in any particular persuasion cannot be inferred by "etymology" but only through careful comparative and historical scrutiny.[6]

Of course all of these objections are no more as soon as we see Pound as a Confucian prophet speaking for the spirit and both seeking the mystical word and rejecting the word of philology. The translations of the war years are doubtless an extreme case, later ones being more wary and to the point. At that time the spirit seems indeed to have come down upon him, with the excitement of the discovery that—

Confucian metaphysics is born of light and can be compared with the metaphysics of light apparent in Guido Cavalcanti's "Donna mi prega"; it conceives of all things as containing lights and energies inseparable from their essences, and demands that terminology be defined, that one struggle to find the precise word. [*L'asse che non vacilla*, OS 504]

But it is only in *PC* that we find a Confucius whom we would worship, and then he looks suspiciously like a Taoist and esthetic saint:

> as he had walked under the rain altars
> > or under the trees of their grove
> > or would it be under their parapets
> in his moving was stillness
> as grey stone in the Aliscans   [c. 80]

This should be compared with Kung's walk in c. 13. It is clearly much finer and emotionally richer. Earlier in the section Pound tries his hand at the opening paragraphs of the *Analects,* and comes up with this:

6. As remarked by Mancuso (p. 43), who also points out that occasionally P.'s etymologies (e.g., "takes the bird in its net" in the last paragraph of *UP*) will be wholly obscure to readers of current Italian and U.S. editions printed opposite the "Stone Classics" text, for here some characters appear in a variant form different from the one P. parsed in his source, Legge.

To study with the white wings of time passing
        is not that our delight
to have friends come from far countries
        is not that pleasure
nor to care that we are untrumpeted?
              filial, fraternal affection is the root of humaneness
              the root of the process
nor are elaborate speeches and slick alacrity.
        employ men in proper season
            not when they are at harvest
            E al Triedro, Cunizza
        e l'altra: "Io son la Luna."   [c. 74]

Here there is but one etymological addition (Legge has: "Is it not pleasant to learn with a constant perseverance and application?"),[7] and this is sustained by a truly poetic intuition, the flying of time as one is engrossed in study. It is the ambience of the poet-scholar-bureaucrat of the "Exile's Letter" of Li Po/Pound, where we also hear of friends coming from afar. In the context even the platitudinous acquires significance: laborers must be employed in proper season not because we are to respect an abstract totalitarian order, but out of humanity. As in c. 1, the translator's work is rewarded with an epiphany of Venus, the first entry of the goddesses and beggars of the Mediterranean hills, Cunizza and Scalza. Confucius has now become their improbable prophet.

Pound was to return to the *Analects* in the early Washington years, his full translation of the "third" book being the first work of the period at St. Elizabeth's Hospital (1945–58). Here the mood is entirely different, a "rappel à l'ordre" has intervened, the savage forties have passed into the arduous fifties:

I

1. He said: Study with the seasons winging past, is not this pleasant?
2. To have friends coming in from far quarters, not a delight?
3. Unruffled by men's ignoring him, also indicative of high breed.

7. Legge, "Confucian Analects," *Chinese Classics*, I, 137.

II

1. Few filial and brotherly men enjoy cheeking their superiors, no one averse from cheeking his superiors stirs up public disorder.

2. The real gentleman goes for the root, when the root is solid the (beneficent) process starts growing, filiality and brotherliness are the root of manhood, increasing with it.

III

1. He said: Elaborate phrasing about correct appearances seldom means manhood.

V

1. He said: To keep things going in a state of ten thousand cars: respect what you do and keep your word, keep accurate accounts and be friendly to others, employ the people in season. [*Probably meaning that public works are not to interfere with agricultural production.*] [A I 1–5]

Less given to revery, Pound again seeks compression, to the point that there are now sometimes fewer words in the translation than characters in the text. The language has toughened under the influence of American speech, prominent throughout the work of this period. Ideologically Pound has retraced his steps, he is again a man of "order" who "keeps his word" and is concerned with "high breed," believing that mysteries and real thinking are only for the few—such as the small group of pupils surrounding Confucius, or the band of acolytes which Pound gathered about himself in the hospital. The voice is no longer that of Li Po, but that of the sententious and occasionally obscure village explainer. The result is often bracing:

If a man keep alive what is old and recognize novelty, he can, eventually, teach. [II 11]

To see justice and not act upon it is cowardice. [II 24]

He said: Hear of the process at sun-rise, you can die in the evening. [*Word order is:* morning hear process, evening die can? may, you may, it is possible that you may.] [IV 8]

He said: Those who know aren't up to those who love; nor those who love, to those who delight in. [VI 18]

To be able to take the near for analogy, that may be called the square of humanitas, and that's that. [VI 28]

In Ch'i he heard the "Shao" sung, and for three months did not

know the taste of his meat; said: didn't figure the performance of music
had attained to that summit. [vii 13]

He said: the proper man: sun-rise over the land, level, grass, sun,
shade, flowing out; the mean man adds distress to distress. [vii 36]

He said: the miracle bird has not arrived, the river gives forth no map
(of turtle-shell), I've only myself to rely on. [ix 8]

He said: In hearing litigations I am like another, the thing is to have
no litigation, *n'est-ce-pas?* [xii 13]

Confucius, referred to by his pupils as "the boss" and "the big
man," has wholly become a persona of Pound, and can be alter-
natively languorous, terse, bromidic, and afire against what he
takes to be injustice. But Pound the apostle wears also the
scholar's mask, he checks and quotes previous versions, he has finally access to a modern Chinese dictionary, Mathews. In working out his translation he alights upon themes and characters he
is to incorporate in future cantos, for instance *ching*, "To reverence; to respect; . . . Reverent attention to" (*M* 1138). In *A* xiii
19 Pound renders this as "honest procedure," but then, noticing
that it contains the radicals for "beat" and "grass" (besides another sign of "various meanings," *M* 1541), he suggests that it
may bear upon a ceremony of his own imagining, "beating on
the earth to propitiate the grain spirits."[8] Meeting the sign again
in the next book Pound simply sums its accepted meaning
("reverent attention to") with the "grass" radical, writing, "(The
proper man) disciplines himself with reverence for the forces of
vegetation."[9] Later on he returns to "reverence" unqualified, but
takes care to add in brackets, "I do not think this ideogram can
be too far separated from the original source, it has to do with
vegetative order" (xvi 10). Within a few months the concept of
"reverence for the intelligence working in nature" (which recalls
the line, "Learn from the green world what can be thy place,"
but places more weight upon hierarchy and upon discrimination

8. Cf. Granet 50: "L'emblème graphique enregistre (ou prétend enregistrer) un geste
stylisé. Il possède un pouvoir d'évocation *correcte,* car le geste qu'il figure (ou prétend
figurer) est un geste à valeur *rituelle* (ou, du moins, senti comme tel). Il provoque l'apparition d'un flux d'images qui permet une sorte de *reconstruction étymologique* des notions."

9. *A* xiv 45. Legge's translation: "The cultivation of himself in reverential carefulness"
(*Chinese Classics,* i, 292).

of intelligence) had become central to Pound's ideology: he wrote
Santayana that it was the token of "a tradition that runs from
Mencius, through Dante, to Agassiz, needing no particular
theories to keep it alive," and launched the Square Dollar Series
("Basic education at a price every student can afford"), a collec-
tion of texts mainly of interest for the light it throws on the later
Cantos (it includes writings by Thomas Hart Benton, Alexander
Del Mar, and Louis Agassiz), stating that its purpose was to
foster such a spirit (Stock 550–51). *Rock-Drill* and subsequent
cantos are full of it:

> "We have," said Mencius, "but phenomena." [10]
> monumenta. In nature are signatures
>   needing no verbal tradition,
> oak leaf never plane leaf. John Heydon.   [c. 87]
>
> And from this Mount were blown
>   seed
> and that every plant hath its seed   [c. 92]
>
> To Kung, to avoid their encirclement,
> To the Odes to escape abstract yatter,
>   to Mencius, Dante, and Agassiz
>   for Gestalt seed,
> pity, yes, for the infected,
>   but maintain antisepsis,
> let the light pour.   [c. 94]

In the last lines, far from qualifying (as has been maintained) the
Complaint against Pity of c. 30, Pound condescends toward the
infected and urges that they be cut away from the healthy, missing the dark irony that such a scheme should be urged by one
who had in fact been judged infected and had been put away by
society. We may well gather that with the Washington cantos we
are back in the company of such champions of light and of unstained blood as the speaker of Königsberg (c. 51)—the "Mount"
from which seed are blown, the phrase being also a reference to
Dante's Mount Purgatory and its garden.[11] Yet the hard lesson of

10. "All who speak about the natures *of things,* have in fact only their phenomena *to
reason from,* and the value of a phenomenon is in its being natural." Legge, "The Works
of Mencius" (4B.26), *Chinese Classics,* II (Oxford, 1895), 331.

11. See the Postscript to Gourmont, *PD* 207.

Pisa is not entirely forgotten, and occasionally Pound's deep urge
to be reunited with process by way of sorrow and repentance will
break through:

> The shrine seen and not seen
> From the roots of sequoias
> > pray   [*ching*]   pray
> > There is power   [c. 110]

Through reverence and prayer man may partake of the secret
power to be reborn.

Of the context in which the later work was done enough has
been written at the time and since. If the Government may have
been generous to the poet in choosing to consider him irrespon-
sible, the controversy over this and the Bollingen award was in
the main uncompassionate, and in perspective a book like the
Analects, which amounts to an apologia, rings one of the few
decent notes in a whirlwind of opinion in which Pound might
easily have lost what remained of his balance. Confident of his
mission, he attended to the work to be done, he saw whoever
cared to come, and corresponded with untold numbers. Unhap-
pily only a very few of these contacts proved intellectually fruitful, as those who went to Pound were chiefly outcasts, whereas
the intelligentsia preferred to stay aloof from so scorching an
issue.

Pound had been the master of several generations of writers,
and his influence continued through these and through his work,
though few grasped its relevance as it appeared. But personally
he had become a bad teacher, imparting *idées fixes* of the worst
sort with ever-increasing insistence as the years went by. To
American culture (which owed him not a little) he became an un-
approachable skeleton in the closet—a situation best presented in
Elizabeth Bishop's poem, "Visits to St. Elizabeth's."

Po-niu was ill. Confucius went to ask after him and took hold of his
hand through the window. Said: he's lost, it is destiny, such a man, and
to have such a disease. Such a man, such a disease. [*A* vi 8]

5. A World Fit to Live In

The Classic Anthology

"To the Odes to escape abstract yatter." The Confucius of the *Analects* often recommends to his pupils, for much the same reason, the *Odes* or *Shih Ching,* a collection of over three hundred poems from different parts of China (which he is supposed to have arranged), and this, Pound tells *his* pupils in *Kulchur,* "lifts him above all occidental philosophers. It avoids the blather of rhetoric and the platonic purple patch" (*K* 18). Unlike philosophical and religious writing, even the passage on the Immaculata in *UP,* poetry does not speculate about the mysteries, it signifies them without ever departing from Mencius' phenomena:

1. He said: Mes enfants, why does no one study the great Odes? [*Or more probably:* these Odes.]
2. The Odes can exhilarate (lift the will).
3. Can give awareness (sharpen the vision, help you spot the bird).
4. Can teach dissociation. [*Legge takes it as:* exchange, sociability.]
5. Can cause resentment (against evil).
   L. regulate feelings?? katharsis?? means of dealing with resentment. I mistrust a soft interpretation.
6. Bring you near to being useful to your father and mother, and go on to serving your sovran.
7. Remember the names of many birds, animals, plants and trees. [*A* XVII 9]

Pound, the compiler of a ragbag for modern thought (ur-c. 1, *QPA* 19), an "apex" (and "a monumental failure") like the Tempio Malatestiano (*K* 24), was bound to respond to this encyclopedic notion of the function of poetry, the didacticism of the *Cantos* being but an extension of the extravagant claims made by the decadents for their *livres* (see ch. 1). In fact another passage of *K* (22) refers us in one breath to Kung, Mussolini, poetry as the only true education, and the mysteries or Eleusis. Thus the full translation of the *Shih* is the climax of Pound's career as a Confucian and as a translator, and is intended to provide us with a model by which to assess the *Cantos,* or with an anticipation of what the later poem will look like when all the available space in Pound's Schifanoia has been frescoed. But if we look into this ideogramic juxtaposition we find that it is faulty, for the *Shih,* like those other poems of civilization, the Homeric epos, the *Metamorphoses,* and the *Commedia,* is a fully realized image of a world integrated beyond its contradictions, whereas much in the unfinished *Cantos* is confusion and nightmare, a world of signs let loose and referring only to itself. However, Pound's *Classic Anthology Defined by Confucius,* fitfully composed on the basis of Bernhard Karlgren's Chinese text and English translation, shares many of the flaws of the *Cantos,* and these (as we shall see later) are in some ways the apex, however aborted, Pound aimed at.

Marcel Granet may have been the first (1934) to point out the true poetic content of the *Shih,* by way of a sociological consideration of the situations it presents. He remarks that the "Folk Songs" of Part 1 (the most extensive of four, comprising 160 poems) chiefly take their cue from natural phenomena and return to these at the beginning of every verse (usually in the number of three). These references to the world of nature specify (he suggests) the time of year, chiefly spring and autumn, in which certain great festivals were held, and of these the songs are so many libretti, improvised by choruses of young people upon given themes:

Tous les êtres . . . concourent à la fête. Celle-ci se passe en chants et en danses. . . . Hommes et choses, plantes et bêtes . . . semblent, unis par le désir d'obéir de concert à un ordre valable pour tous, s'envoyer des signaux ou répondre à des commandements. Ce sont ces signaux et ces commandements qui, enregistrés dans les vers, valent tout ensemble comme thèmes poétiques et comme dictons de calendrier. . . . A tous et depuis toujours, le même paysage rituel propose impérieusement les mêmes images. Chacun les réinvente et croit improviser. . . . Ce sont des emblèmes vivaces, débordants d'affinités, éclatants de puissance évocatrice, et, si je puis dire, d'omnivalence symbolique. [Granet 56–57]

This description may well apply to the choral world of the middle cantos, and to the more arcane but more genuine celebrations

of Pisa, and suggests that, in translating the *Shih,* Pound under-
took, not to render a few poems, but to recreate a world. This
aim he did not fully achieve, yet the fresh folk singing to be heard
occasionally in the *Classic Anthology* is a valuable acquisition,
and some of the later cantos were to benefit from its trenchancy.
In 1964, looking back with extreme disenchantment upon his
life's work, Pound was to single out his ear for the people's
speech as a saving trait. At the publication of the Italian version
of *CA* he remarked, before reading a few of his translations:
"I've written some [compulsive?—word unclear] third-rate poetry; at times perhaps I have found some sentiment of the people's melancholy." [1]

Having perceived the folk nature of the *Odes* Pound went on
to translate them in clearly stressed metres, reminiscent of the
ballad and other popular forms, often rhymed and leisurely in
tone. He had never outgrown an inclination towards established
verse forms and was pleased to have recourse to such playful motions, like the well-tempered craftsman he was. For actually it
would be difficult to find a wholly regular poem among the odd
three hundred—Pound being concerned rather with the feel of
tradition than with its precise mechanism. He is, again, the improvisor who finds his rhymes as he goes along—easy rhymes, as
against the harsh play of *HSM,* where traditional devices were
used to sardonic effect, while here the poet is wholly at home,
and masterfully careless and simple. [2] So the exoticism of *Cathay*
is replaced by a more resilient archaism. An instance would be
Ode 11 ("Kylin's foot bruiseth no root, / Ohé, Kylin"), which

1. "Ho fatto un po' di poesia [per forza?—word unclear], di terz'ordine; qualche volta
forse ho trovato un po' di sentimento di melanconia popolare." From a recording made
by RAI, the Italian network.

2. It is strange that Charles Olson should have missed the fun, as shown by his obtuse
criticism of *CA,* the poem "I, Mencius, Pupil of the Master"—in *The Distances* (New
York: Grove Press, 1960), pp. 61–63. Horrified by "the dross of verse. Rhyme!," he did
not see that P., having exorcised the enemy, could now use him to his purposes—to write
300 poems that a modern reader would enjoy and that would preserve some of the flavor
of the original. But pupils do not always see the spirit of the law set by their masters. One,
for example, thought that Confucius studied and memorized a lot, and got the answer:
"No, I, one, through, string-together, sprout [*that is:* unite, flow through, connect, put
forth leaf]. For me there is one thing that flows through, holds things together, germinates" (*A* xv 2).

may be compared with Archilochus' little hymn to Heracles: *"Ténella / ô kallínike chaîr' ánax Heráklees, / ténella kallínike."* If this is a correspondence of mood which the poet had not necessarily in mind, in many other odes he borrows freely rhythms and phrases from the poems he cherishes, be they "Unter der linden" ("Mid the bind-grass on the plain"—94), Charles d'Orleans' "Le temps a laissié son manteau" ("The year puts on her shining robe"—214), or a Shakespeare sonnet ("Whenas my heart is filled with kings and deeds"—289). The result is a stereoscopic impression of reading two texts at the same time, which places the translation in historical and emotional perspective. More frequently it is difficult to determine a precise model, yet the cadence has a familiar air and the remote poem comes alive. What details Pound has chosen not to assimilate stand out strongly in such a context (Davie 11–12).

Parts 1–2 are chiefly indebted to English forms of the fifteenth to seventeenth centuries, very freely rehandled. Or perhaps we should look at such modern words after old music as Yeats's late verse (similar in its rhythms and clear rhymes to some of P.'s), or as the "Alba" in *Langue d'Oc:*

> Lies a dead deer on younder plain
> whom white grass covers,
> A melancholy maid in spring
> > is luck
> > for
> > lovers.
>
> Where the scrub elm skirts the wood,
> be it not in white mat bound,
> as a jewel flawless found,
> > dead as doe is maidenhood.
>
> Hark!
> Unhand my girdle-knot,
> > stay, stay, stay
> > or the dog
> > may
> > bark.   [CA 23]

Besides giving an archaic and popular flavor to the text, the song form relates to the original, adding the variety which it lacks.[3] For the metre and rhyme schemes of the *Shih* are of extreme regularity, while Pound, with his characteristic pressure, can scarcely keep up one metre through a poem. Besides, as remarked by Granet, not infrequently every verse of the original opens with the same calendar proverb, while the translator is never short of variations:

> In the South be drooping trees,
> long the bough, thick the vine,
> Take thy delight,
> my prince, in happy ease.
>
> In the South be drooping boughs
> the wild vine covers,
> that hold delight, delight, good sir,
> for eager lovers.
>
> Close as the vine clamps the trees
> so complete is happiness,
> Good sir, delight delight in ease,
> In the South be drooping trees.   [CA 4]

What may be merely a ceremonial statement is made to yield an endearing sensuality and the gentleness of the roundel, reminiscent of Froissart as quoted in *PC*. Another memorable example of the repetitive form, perhaps the one regular poem in the book, is the following:

> What hour is this? the court-yard flare burns bright,
> we hear a chink of bit-bells thru the night.

3. For a closer discussion of P.'s handling of the originals, see L. S. Dembo, *The Confucian Odes of Ezra Pound* (Berkeley: Univ. of California Press, 1965), and Mancuso 54–60. To give one instance, the ode last quoted has three verses, rhyming abab, ccdd, eee—the first and second comprising four lines of four syllables, the third three lines of five syllables. In Bernhard Karlgren, *The Book of Odes* (Stockholm: Museum of Far Eastern Antiquities, 1974), p. 13, the second verse comes out as follows: "In the forest there are low shrubby trees, in the wilds there is a dead deer; with white grass one wraps it up and binds it; there is a girl like a jade." P. somewhat confusingly telescopes girl and doe, and brings in the traditional theme of sterile maidenhood.

We hear it faint: "chin-chink" across the night,
he comes not yet, the court-yard flare flicks bright.

What hour of dawn, the lanthorn wick smokes still
to greet his flag that crests yon eastward hill.   [CA 182]

Perhaps carried along by the memory of Spanish "goat bells [tin-kling] all night" (c. 81) Pound moves on ecstatically to an epiphany of sun-worship, for which he chooses the words of "the great past-master of pastiche" ("Cavalcanti," *LE* 199), linking China to Elsinore.

Often the translator must make up his mind as to the speaker of the lines. He must construct, on small evidence, a believable persona—like the Uncle Remus of the following:

> Ole Brer Rabbit watchin' his feet,
> Rabbit net 's got the pheasant beat;
> > When I was young and a-startin' life
> > I kept away from trouble an' strife
> But then, as life went on,
> Did I meet trouble?
> > > > Aye, my son;
> Wish I could sleep till life was done.
> > > > [CA 70—alternative version]⁴

If, in transcribing a nobleman's disaffection, Pound will occasionally use the meditative rhythms of *Cathay* ("On declining office," 184), it is enough to compare the first poem of the old collection, "Song of the Bowmen of Shu," to Ode 167, to see with what different results he confronts the same text at the two

---

4. Compare this with the first verse of Arthur Waley's translation, from his *Book of Songs* (1937), which is an eminently readable and reliable work, but not that new thing, both exciting and occasionally dreary—P.'s *CA:*
> Gingerly walked the hare,
> But the pheasant was caught in the snare.
> At the beginning of my life
> All was still quiet;
> In my latter days
> I have met great calamities.
> Would that I might sleep and never stir!
Arthur Waley, *Chinese Poems* (London: Allen & Unwin, 1976), p. 33.

ends of his career. In CA the speaker is usually a man of the people, not a melancholic poet or soldier, Pound being reminded of an American hillbilly, a black slave (16, 187), and so on; or the speaker may be a nobleman, a king, or a bureaucrat, who has not forgone contact with the rural world, and whose language is not unlike the people's. Always an anti-intellectual, Pound is at home in this strongly colored ambience, where inwardness or existence is quite absent, as it is in his other work. The people are reticent in venting their feelings (and the prince of course looks down upon sentiment), unless they can give them traditional form, yet the use of stereotypes does not make their utterances any less spontaneous, as in the poem quoted above—or in the *Cantos*. The accuracy and lack of redundancy of these verses needs no comment:

> Town Life
>
> Sun's in the East,
> her loveliness
> Comes here
> To undress.
>
> Twixt door and screen
> at moon-rise
> I hear
> Her departing sighs.   [CA 99]

Frequently we find Pound in a more thoughtful vein than heretofore. Yeats and many after him have suggested that he can approach excellence only when rehandling another's work, real or imaginary. We know that this is true only in a very particular way, that scarcely casts a shadow upon Pound's creativity (quite the contrary, in fact), and that his translations have little in common with what the word is usually understood to mean (e.g., Waley's impeccable work). Pound's "originals" are little more than cues—nor are his responses in any way predictable or of the same quality. He gives us sketches on given themes, impressions that throw light upon the original without being in any way equivalents or substitutes, quotations rather than translations. And, all said, there is no denying that Pound's corpus, whatever

its perhaps frequent opacities, is sustained by a vital undercurrent
that makes for a coherence of sorts—and that it must be studied
as a whole.

"Rumours as to the death of Süan's sons"

A boat floats over shadow, two boys were aboard.
There is a cloud over my thought
and of them no word.

The boat floats past sky's edge, lank sail a-flap;
and a dark thought inside me: how had they hap?   [CA 44]

Meditative interludes such as this are integral to Pound's experiment in folk music, and point to a sympathy which would be impossible, for example, in Eliot. The latter can only propound a
regressive theory of the people, as he does in his political writing,
dissociating the social world from meditation; when he tries his
hand at a poetry available to all he comes up with the practical
cats. Yet the quest for a collective repossession of nature is common to both poets, and a central theme in the *Quartets*.

The Waste Land and the fertility cantos have a common
source, *The Golden Bough*. Yet Pound is influenced not only by
the moderately anti-Victorian Frazer but also by the more radical
and stimulating findings of Leo Frobenius. Even Confucius he
takes, on account of his interest in the past and in folklore (*K*
49), to be an anthropologist.

Frobenius holds Pound's interest because, anticipating more
recent developments, he criticizes positivistic ethnology and pro-
pounds a cultural model not categorical but (as is the case in the
Cantos) relational: an "autonomous organism" within which geography, myth, behavior, art, and so on, modify each other, and
may be understood only as functions of one another: "intuitively," as Frobenius somewhat equivocally maintained; *structurally*, as we would say today:

It is not the will of men that produces culture but rather culture that
lives upon men. (I would now say: it lives *through* men.) Culture is connected by way of its forms to specific fields or cultural domains; forms

change as they are transplanted and by intergrafting produce new forms.[5]

Even so the *Cantos* are meant to portray *Kulturkreise* (e.g., the teeming Quattrocento of the XXX *Cantos*) in their superpersonal complexity and in their interrelation, and to provide an account of the autonomous change and renewal of modes of feeling and action, recording the frequency with which a certain pattern becomes manifest in time, be it ten times to the minute (in music) or to the era (in culture).[6] Such an enquiry is not retrospective but seeks to reveal a past breaking into the present, which is in turn actively bent upon defining the Paideuma of the future:

Example: the peasants opposed a railway cutting. A king had driven into the ground at that place. The engineers dug and unearthed the bronze car of Dis, two thousand years buried.

It wd. be unjust to Frazer to say that his work was *merely* retrospective. But there is a quite different phase in the work of Frobenius.

"Where we found these rock drawings, there was always water within six feet of the surface." That kind of research goes not only into past and forgotten life, but points to tomorrow's water supply.

We do NOT know the past in chronological sequence. It may be convenient to lay it out anesthetized on the table with dates pasted on here

5. Leo Frobenius, *Das Paideuma*, Erlebte Erdteile, 4 (Frankfurt am M., 1925), p. 40. Karl Kerényi called Frobenius "the elementary and protean spirit of ethnological research." In the same letter (to Thomas Mann, 24 December 1938) he adds: "In the last years . . . he only collected materials for the extensive and scientific universal mythology. . . . This fall . . . passing through Frankfurt, I looked over the immense quantity of mythological extracts he left behind, and understood . . . that I should courageously investigate the non-antique sources of the great mythologies." Karl Kerényi—Thomas Mann, *Romandichtung und Mythologie* (Zurich: Rhein Verlag, 1945).

6. Cf. *K* 42: "[In music] the sense of high order and clarity is not due to sense [of] pitch . . . alone but to the sense of proportion between all time divisions from 10 to the minute or era up to top harmonic 8vo and 32mo above treble stave." To P. music is melody and rhythm, not harmony: the composer's metronome indication gives the chief note, the "great bass" on which the piece is constructed. Hence the theory of the "absolute rhythm," according to which all poems "[connote their symphonies], which, had we a little more skill, we could score for orchestra" (Introduction to *Sonnets and Ballate of Guido Cavalcanti*, *T* 23–24).

and there, but what we know we know by ripples and spirals eddying
out from us and from our own time.

> .   .   .

When a given hormone defects, it will defect throughout the whole
system.
Hence the yarn that Frobenius looked at two African pots and, observing their shapes and proportions, said: if you will go to a certain
place and there digge, you will find traces of a civilization with such and
such characteristics.

As was the case. In event proved. [K 5]

This is what Pound understands under "raising the dead," an activity which he holds to have been pursued alike by Frobenius,
Browning, Ovid, and Confucius.[7] The latter is said to have compiled not only the *Shih,* but also the *Shu Ching,* the Annals often
referred to in the notes to *CA,* and the object of close scrutiny in
the first Washington cantos (85–87). Odes and Annals—it is the
admixture of myth and history which Pound is fond of, and
which may also be found within both collections: in the epic sections of the *Shih,* and in the mythical concept of history which
underlies the *Shu* and traditional Chinese thinking in general, a
concept so ubiquitous that today we are very much in the dark as
to the ancient history of China—a nation of which the annals
volunteer "exact" accounts of events five thousand years back.

> and as to the nature of sorrow
> there are men who do not strive to grasp the antique. [CA 265]

These are the final lines of Part 3 of *CA,* the "Great Odes," epic
narratives of the splendour of Chu, the third dynasty, and of its
decadence, which sets in when the tradition affirmed by its
founders becomes exhausted. This kind of big bang theory of history, positing a heroic impulse followed by slow decay or entropy, is strikingly similar to the doctrine of the dissociation of
sensibility held by Eliot and Pound, and (ante litteram) by the

---

7. See *SR* 16. Yet we know that P., while conversing with the dead, loses, in spite of his
intentions, access to the living: "In meiner Heimat / where the dead walked / and the living
were made of cardboard" (c. 115). An unhistorical consideration of tradition, like the one
propounded by P. and Frobenius, passes easily into nostalgia. Hence the reactionary attitudes of both men.

ideologists Henry and Brooks Adams. Both Pound and Eliot claimed (like Frobenius) that tradition was something "eddying out" from the present, constantly reassessed, yet their deeper allegiance was to a timeless, absolute tradition—to the fancy that once upon a time the world was not out of joint, that the age of gold obtained. Their great theme is paradise lost, plenitude versus despair. We may disagree with their history, yet must respond to the "popular melancholy" of the *Quartets* and of *CA*, which, insofar as it expresses a collective chagrin, is not a regressive trait. Confucius may have meant something of the kind when he remarked of Ode 1, the fish-hawk song, that "its melancholy does not hurt (does not wound)" (*A* III 20). A moving instance of lamentation in the waste land is the Drought Ode, spoken by the bewildered ruler, Pound abandoning his sprightly sprung rhythms for the long unrhymed line of the *Cantos*:

> The drought has parched into the depth,
> I struggle, I labour and dare not retire.
> Why comes this affliction upon us, mad with the heat,
> We know not the reason.   [CA 258]

The epic verse of Part 3, the "Great Odes," differs in its lack of a sustaining narrative from *Iliad* and Pentateuch, which were written at about the same time.[8] The hypnotic odes honoring Wenn Wang, founder of the dynasty (235 ff.), seem to move in a circle about a single mythic concern, which Pound (as if preparing the palette of *RD*) renders with a profusion of images bearing upon light. See for instance Ode 268, of which two versions are given—a frequent occurrence in *CA*, indicating both the experimental and tentative spirit of the translator, and his absorption with levels of meaning in the original. Often he will feel his way into an ode by prefacing it with a title which is in fact a small verse anticipating some of the themes. *CA* has all the accoutrements of a Poundian text—it is jumpy and inconsistent yet it teems with interrelations and suggestions, many of which may be

8. Emilio Cecchi, "Ecco l'antica poesia cinese," *Corriere della Sera*, 27 Sept. 1964. A review of E.P., *L'antologia classica cinese*, tr. Carlo Scarfoglio (Milano: Scheiwiller, 1964).

decoded only by readers of the *Cantos:* "nondum orto jubare,"[9] "per plura diafana" (247; see also 240 and 255), "molu" (42, 287), "olim de Malatestis" (247), and so on. Pound's footnotes, some private, some obscure, and his irregular capitalization of lines (a kind of shorthand for their relations) may also be cited to show how very personal his approach is.

Elsewhere the Chinese ruler is made into a courtly Western figure (or reminds us of certain Iranian miniatures):

> The king stood in his "Park Divine,"
> deer and doe lay there so fine,
> so fine so sleek; birds of the air
> flashed a white wing while fishes splashed
> on wing-like fin in the haunted pool.   [CA 242]

In 1918 Pound had written Margaret Anderson:

Chère amie . . . I desire to go on with my long poem; and like the Duke of Chang, I desire to hear the music of a lost dynasty. (Have managed to hear it, in fact.) And I desire also to resurrect the art of the lyric, I mean words to be sung, for Yeats' only wail and submit to keening and cha*u*nting (with a *u*) and Swinburne's only rhapsodify. And with a few exceptions (a few in Browning) there is scarcely anything since the time of Waller and Campion. AND a mere imitation won't do. [*L* 142; cf. c. 81's version of the history of the lyric—"And for 180 years almost nothing."]

In CA this intent is accomplished in a fashion, and in fact not through imitation but experiment—drafts which allow us to discern the traits of the old masters. The lines last quoted, for instance, may well appear overadorned with internal rhyme and alliteration, yet the extempore quality of the music makes them acceptable.

We saw that according to the Master the *Shih* is also a means of focusing ethical censure. Pound, as we may expect, responds readily to such passages:

> The "people" are not in the least perverse
> the high-ups rob, cheat 'em and do worse,

9. CA 96 and c. 29. From the Latin-Provençal "Alba" translated by P. as "Belangal Alba," quoted in Norman 12.

then tell you they haven't sufficient power,
polite while you're there, jip you next hour,
and then say calmly: It wasn't me.

I have therefore compiled
this balladry.   [CA 257]

Often enough resentment gets the better of him, and then the
"changed odes" become improbably violent and slangy (L.S.
Dembo), but this matters less than the falling off in tone on such
occasions. Likewise in the longer odes Pound deals with static
subject matter in a jumpy and inconsistent fashion, and the poem
accordingly falls to pieces. Pound's constant pressure to get
something out of the text and his impatience make for difficult
reading and unevenness of tone—but these are constants of his
work. He is at his best with little ditties, loving or mocking (the
mood, say, of "Cino"), and with the world of marvel and ecstasy, as in this Chinese genesis—or "Donna mi prega":

Water above, fire beneath
so man had, from heaven, his breath,
                          a vapour,
matter and form compact,
seed and cord held intact
                   to love
natural heart
              shown in act.   [CA 260][10]

Pound's inclination towards the sacred it also attested by the
unwonted consistency of style of Part 4, the "Odes of the Temple
and Altar." The temple is the perfect and fragrant locus of vision:
"The secret temple is still and consecrate, / solid the inner eaves."
It is the site of an event most appealing to Pound, the worshipper
of the Immaculata: virginal conception (300).

It is significant that, as we move on through CA, we move
backwards in time, Part 4 being the oldest (perhaps 11th century
B.C.). The last poem celebrates the deed most exalted in Pound's

10. Karlgren's version: "Heaven gave birth to the multitude of people, they have (concrete objects =) bodies, they have (moral) rules; that the people hold on to the norms is
because they love that beautiful virtue" (The Book of Odes, p. 228).

world, retrojecting it in the "holistic" civilization of the Bronze
Age: a temple is erected after a victory over the enemy—a victory
which, however, seems to have been (like the city of Deioces)
wishful thinking on the side of the remote poet, for in fact the
Yin-Shang which he glorifies was defeated at the hands of the
rising Chu dynasty:

> They went up to the King mountain,
> straight trunks of pine and cypress
> they cut and brought here,
> hewed pillars and rafters
> carved pine beam-horns ornate
> contrived pillars and sockets
> to the inner shrine, perfect
> that his ray come to point in this quiet.   [CA 305]

Pound stays close to his text, though the reader of the *Cantos*
cannot but recall the people of Ferrara, who

> All rushed out and built the duomo,
> Went as one man without leaders
> And the perfect measure took form;   [c. 27]

Yet in the last line, which Karlgren translates, "The temple hall
was achieved, it was very still," the poet records an epiphany of
"the sun's [or king's] lance coming to rest on the precise spot,"
having alighted upon *ch'eng* (see c. 77), the *Shih*'s third character
before last. Poetry is, once again, the handmaid of the mysteries,
as Pound also suggests at the other end of CA, in Ode 1. This
opens with a bird's cry, *kuan-kuan*, onomatopoeic signs in which
the "gate" radical may be discerned—the doors of poetry,
"beyond [which] are the mysteries. Eleusis. Things not to be
spoken save in secret" (*K* 22). Hence the translation: " 'Hid!
Hid!' the fish-hawk saith."

Also the final word, "quiet," which emerges from a finely
drawn-out cadenza, points to one of Pound's central concerns.
Scarcely interrupted by the solemn drums of Ode 301, quiet
reigns over this remote society, envisaged as resting in essential
harmony:

> **Wu royal**
> **if we inherit**
> **age-old quiet**
> **'tis by his merit.**
>
> Not by envy in his zeal
> Wu king'd the Imperial rule;
>
> Wen by his learning won
> what has been from that time on.
>
> Wu had the heritage;
> layed low Yin-Shang's rage by arms
> and left to us our world of quiet farms.   [CA 285]

The quiet farms point the way back to the folk songs of Parts 1
and 2. Besides the caption which sets the mood, the poem offers
a good example of Pound's metrical zest: he keeps our attention
by never relaxing with an established pattern, and the final pentameter comes as a token of great quiet beauty.

This extensive attempt to recreate a world has been assessed
with justice by L. S. Dembo as a work highly representative of its
time and of Pound's poetry. It is less difficult than the *Cantos*
(though it cannot in the end be understood without them) and af-
fords much insight into Pound's cultural and ideological leanings
in these decisive years. If we now return to the translator's statement quoted early in the chapter we may want to admit that "the
substantial lack of historical *pietas*" imputed to Pound by one of
his more perceptive critics and fellow poets, Eugenio Montale,[11]
is not without exceptions:

> Le Paradis n'est pas artificiel
>   States of mind are inexplicable to us.
>   δακρύων   δακρύων   δακρύων
> L.   P.   gli onesti   [*the honest ones*]
>   J'ai eu pitié des autres
> probablement pas assez, and at moments that suited my own
>   convenience

11. "Il moralismo 'naturale,'" *Corriere della Sera,* 19 December 1965. A review of
L'Herne.

> Le paradis n'est pas artificiel
>   l'enfer non plus.   [c. 76]

As remarked by Baudelaire (in "Au Lecteur"), we demand a high price for our confessions, Pound's fees being among the most outrageous (the initials stand for the collaborationists Laval and Pétain). Still, we have seen that in *CA* Pound has spoken for "the sentiments of the people"—or at least has done so in its better moments.

> Nor shall effacèd be,
> once known, from memory.   [CA 83]

6. Sophocles and the Tragic Dance

The Trachiniae *presents the highest peak of Greek sensibility registered in any of the plays that have come down to us, and is, at the same time, nearest the original form of the God-Dance.*

With this statement, and with a footnote to the effect that Sophocles was sixteen when Confucius died, Pound introduces and accounts for his version of the *Trachiniae*.[1] In the new imitation two of his concerns are grafted, the sacred theatre as he has known it in the Nô, and classical antiquity and its interpretation. Furthermore, the tragedy functions as a metaphor of a situation which he recognizes as his own.

Pound always considered conventional theatre a derivative form, loosely symbolic and mimetic. In the Nô, on the other hand, he found a *Gesamtkunstwerk* employing wholly stylized means to constitute an emotional and intellectual whole:

In the Noh we find an art built upon the god-dance, or upon some local legend of spiritual apparition, or, later, on gestes of war and feats of history; an art of splendid posture, of dancing and chanting and of acting that is not mimetic. . . . I find these words very wonderful, and they become intelligible if, as a friend says, "you read them all the time as though you were listening to music." . . . These plays are also an answer to a question that has several times been put to me: "Could one do a long Imagiste poem, or even a long poem in vers libre?" . . . When a text seems to "go off into nothing" at the end, the reader must remember "that the vagueness or paleness of words is made good by the emotion of the final dance," for the Noh has its unity in emotion. It has also what we may call Unity of Image. At least, the better plays are all built into the intensification of a single Image: the red maple leaves and the snow flurry in Nishikigi, the pines in Takasago, the blue-grey waves and wave pattern in Suma Genji, the mantle of feathers in the play of that name, Hagoromo. [*T* 214, 237*n*, 237]

Forty years after writing this, Pound approaches the *Trachiniae* as if it were a Nô, or rather as if the unity of image and of emotion

1. *Sophokles: Women of Trachis*, a version by Ezra Pound, *Hudson Review*, 6 (1954), 487.

which he detects in the tragedy had the same sources that were to produce the noble art of Japan, which, unlike our interpretation of classical antiquity, has remained virtually unchanged from the Middle Ages (Japanese) to the present. The unconventional methodology which prompts Pound to approach the Greek text by way of a code borrowed in part from a wholly diverse cultural ambience anticipates investigations undertaken at present by advanced critics. Yet he defines his method as he immediately confronts the text, and so avoids the sterility which at times attends critical practices of this kind. He is, rather than a critic, a *dancer;* the text—and the cultural vortex of which it is the center—is his partner in the celebration.

The god-dance is the sunken forma, still to be found in the Japanese plays but not in the Greek, or in the reading to which we are bound by bimillenary conditioning. It follows that a code closer to (though more recent than) the primary dance will bring it out where it is concealed by an obsolete code. The latter is the cause of the fracture which divides the modern reader from the classics: an improper use of the literary artifact deadens it, allowing it to appear as a completed process, no longer capable of development. Even Pound, attempting years earlier to translate the *Agamemnon* of Aeschylus, could not overcome this barrier:

There are, to the best of my knowledge, no translations of these plays that an awakened man can read without deadly boredom. . . . I twisted, turned, tried every elipsis and elimination. I made the watchman talk nigger, and by the time you had taken out the remplissage, there was no play left on one's page. There was magnificence; there was SENSE of play, the beacon telegraph stuff is incomparable. [K 12]

In *PC,* we recall, the image of the fire racing from mountaintop to mountaintop in the night is made into a metaphor of the very process of communication, and introduces the Whitmanian "connubium terrae" (c. 82), the communication of identity, the mythical union toward which Pound's imitations gravitate.

While the intention of exposing the institutional use of the classics is common to Sartre, Anouilh, Brecht, Pound, and others, the means employed and the ends envisaged diverge sharply.

Pound does not seek to rationalize myth but to make its obscure conflicts newly operative. His use of particularly strident modern-isms in this *Women of Trachis* (as, less insistently, in *A* and *CA*) is not intended to bring the play up-to-date by revealing its latent present-day mediocrity. Rather than transposing myth into the present, Pound retrojects the present into myth, in order to re-cover the savage impact of the original. The use of language frequently coarse is preeminently archaizing in import.

As he confronts the god-dance in 1953, Pound commands means more novel than in 1916 and in the twenties. Like Yeats he has been progressing through the years from a faded spiritual-ism to the strong flavor of the real. His Heracles talks slang because aware of pre-Sophoclean and even pre-Hellenic roots. He wears a terrible beauty:

The Apollo at Villa Giulia [the Roman museum of Etruscan antiquities] gives tip to Mediterranean gods; startling, sudden, none of that washy late stuff done by sculpting slave models, nor afternoon-tea Xtian piety. Gods tricky as nature. [L 294: 1935]

The spirit of tragedy appears to resist the domestication (or dis-placement) of such gods *sive natura*, already prevalent in the Periclean commonwealth, as suggested by Nietzsche. The Diony-siac refutes the academic interpretation of antiquity as a model of bourgeois existence. The tragic hero confronts his acts as they become charged with meaning and collide with the absolute. In the ensuing struggle he is inevitably vanquished, yet his being is as if lighted up, made perfect, by the difference.

Such an approach (which, as stated, P. does not theorize but allows to emerge through textual practice) is more outgoing and fruitful than—and very different from—the attitude to antiquity displayed in *HSP*, a work but little concerned with the archaic. Pound's Propertius makes light of imperial power, Roman and British, and disbelieves everything (to use the phrase from *K*) but Cynthia's favors and his own wit ("ingenium nobis ipsa puella facit"). But this urbanity and detachment, more appealing per-haps to the general reader, would be quite out of place in the world of primary pigment to which Pound increasingly turns from the twenties on, setting engagement before facile flippancy, the aftermath of adolescence.[2]

So begins a voyage backwards to be pursued even in spite of Sophocles, for the *Trachiniae,* especially the character of the heroine, probably owes something to psychological Euripides. Deianira's plight is told in the first part of the tragedy, Pound showing little sympathy for "Madame d'Oineus," whereas the entrance of Heracles in his death throes takes us into deeper waters. This is also, in Pound's view, the relation obtaining between the *nékuia* and the rest of the *Odyssey.*[3]

The Chorus of the women of Trachis delivers itself in a wholly musical and oracular language. Pound notes in the margin the instruments that are to accompany its ecstatic hymn:

> APOLLO
> and Artemis, analolu
> Artemis,
> Analolu,
> Sun-bright Apollo, Saviour Apollo
> analolu,
> Artemis
> Sylvan Artemis,
> Swift-arrowed Artemis, analolu
> By the hearth-stone
> brides to be
> Shout in male company:
> APOLLO EUPHARETRON.   [WT 12]

Thus the Chorus responds to the news of Heracles' return (ll. 205–09 of the Greek). The refrain is drawn from the first word it says, instructing the "brides to be," i.e., the Chorus itself, "to cry with joy [*anololuxáto*] by the hearth of the home." Before reporting this message, Pound offers us the very cry and the names of the gods addressed beyond all syntax—we remember his state-

2. Robert Lowell has developed with intelligence the themes of *HSP* in *Near the Ocean* (New York: Farrar, 1967), where he attempts to define an attitude toward "Rome, the greatness and horror of her Empire" (p. 9), model of present-day technocracy.

3. See *L* 296. Actually the *nékuia* is held to be a later addition to the body of the *Odyssey,* as noted by Reed, "Towards the *Cantos* of Ezra Pound," p. 137.

ment about the choruses in Aeschylus "merely [reminding] the audience of the events in the Trojan war" (*LE* 273). Before long, enlarging upon the cries of "Evoë!" and the references to Bacchic dance in the text, he is calling upon "ivied Zagreus" in person. It will be remembered that only in recent years have we had Dionysian interpretations of Greek tragedy of the sort implied by *WT*, for instance the Living Theater's 1966 production of *Antigone*, in which the social and ritual import of the text was made apparent. Likewise the gestural and choral music underlying Pound's lines is cognate to experiments undertaken by composers like Karlheinz Stockhausen in later years. But the Chorus of *WT*, besides stuttering the names of the gods, can articulate sentences and melodies that flow:

(*accompaniment* PHOEBUS, Phoebus, ere thou slay
strings, mainly   and lay flaked Night upon her blazing pyre,
cellos)   Say, ere the last star-shimmer is run:
                    Where lies Alkmene's son, apart from me?

(*drums, quietly*   The shifty Night delays not,
added to music)   Nor fates of men, nor yet rich goods and spoil.
                    Be swift to enjoy, what thou art swift to lose. [*WT* 9]

The first phrase is not wholly at odds with the opening of the first chorus in the play, but that in Sophocles the Night is said to give birth to the Sun at dawn, and to lay him to rest as he blazes at sunset (ll. 94–96). Pound, however, is glancing through F. Storr's Loeb translation:

> Child of star-bespangled Night,
>   Born as she dies,
> Laid to rest in a blaze of light,
> Tell me, Sun-god, O tell me, where
> Tarries the child of Alcmena fair[4]

—and, judging "laid to rest" to modify Night, takes the whole as denotation of his favorite time of day, the dawn. The reader scarcely needs to be told what is in the offing—nor would it have

4. *Sophocles*, tr. F. Storr, Loeb Classical Library (London: Heinemann, 1913), II, 265.

made much difference had Pound grasped (or chosen to follow) Sophocles' meaning. Another poet who worshipped the sun is to be discovered (cf. "APOLLO EUPHARETRON"), as well as another text which may be taken, like "Donna mi prega," as "a sort of metaphor on the generation of light." In c. 87 of RD we find the gloss: "The play shaped from *phlogizómenon*," i.e., the word rendered by Pound as "blazing." This insight may have lain behind his decision to translate the whole.

In the final verse Pound bypasses Storr's flight of fancy ("The sheen of night with daybreak wanes") and goes to the original: "For flaked night does not wait upon mortals, nor does fate, nor wealth, but quickly they go" (131–34). Well acquainted with loss, he singles out the elegiac theme of the *Fifth Decad* ("Thou shalt not always walk in the sun"), and has night and fate approach (rather than depart) with steps barely perceived yet ubiquitous, like the drums called for in the margin. This is significant for, as we shall see, the message spelled out in WT is that the secretive processes of fate, no matter whether ostensibly just or unjust, are revealed as totally luminous, assigning coherent meaning to all, if only man can contemplate them from without the human condition.

Heracles' love for Iole (also known as "Tomorrow") [5] is presented by Pound as a low affair, a "letch," an unexplained occurrence which, like all tragic action, must forsake worldly nobility in favor of *amor fati*. (We do not miss the similarity between Heracles' plight and Pound's private history.) The character of Deianira suffers a corresponding diminution, her irrelevant psychological motivation being underscored sardonically ("rêveuse"—WT 28), that it may be rejected, as it were, by the linguistic context. [6] The Chorus wonders whether her attempt to secure her husband's love will succeed, and presently she reenters

5. WT 4. In "Redondillas, or Something of that Sort," a long and chatty poem excised from *Canzoni* (1911) and looking forward in tone to the *Ur-Cantos*, P. had written: "I would sing of my love 'Tomorrow,' . . . Would turn from superficial things for a time, into the quiet, / I would draw your minds to learn of sorrow in quiet, / To watch for signs and strange portents" (CEP 216–17).

6. See H. A. Mason, "*The Women of Trachis* and Creative Translation" (1969), Sullivan 295–96.

"in the tragic mask" (29) to learn from her son that her act of love is in fact a murder. She speaks no more, but briefly becomes, through the words of the Chorus, one of the delicate Japanese characters that Pound has in mind:

> (DAYSAIR *exit.*)
> KHOROS: Why does she go so quietly?
>   Has she no answer?
> HYLLOS: Let her go. And a nice wind take her far enough
>   . . . out of sight,
> and another label to keep up her maternal swank,
> fine mother she is, let her de-part
>   in peace . . .
> and get some of the pleasure she has given my father.
>
>   [*WT* 35]

In Storr's translation ll. 819–20 read: "Let her depart in peace, and may she share / Herself the happiness she brings my sire!" With customary free hand Pound does not hesitate to adopt the commonplace phrase (also to be found in the Greek) to vent Hyllus' resentment, reminding us of Ulysses' animus against his mother in c. 1. The same end is reached in the previous line with different means, namely by willfully overlooking the syntax of the Greek ("Why vainly augment the brilliance of a mother's name?"), and by employing the affected modernity of *HSP* (and of Laforgue).

The chorus that follows shortly points to Venus as the first mover of the tragedy (ll. 860–61), but Pound, in a long stage note, insists on the indifference of the *belle dame sans merci*. He wants her to appear on the stage as a sort of wax figure, somewhat like a character in a Minoan fresco. This, and the account of Deianira's suicide (almost a hara-kiri), refers us back to the theatricals of Nô: whereas the Nurse merely tells us of the heroine's death, "2000 years later the Minoru had developed a technique which permitted the direct presentation of such shades by symbolic gesture" (*WT* 39*n*).

The climax comes when Heracles enters "in the mask of the divine agony," introduced by the Chorus. Now begins the older

drama concealed under Sophocles' lines, the agony in which the
hero gives his full measure (as in the first lines of *PC*):

> Brother of God, Sweet Hell, be decent.
> Let me lie down and rest.
> Swift-feathered Death, that art the end of shame.
>
> .   .   .
>
> Go, pick up your courage. Get going and
>   have mercy on me
> or pity, that's it: pity.   [*WT* 44–45]

In the course of the soliloquy, broken by curses and written in an
often savage jargon, Heracles slowly becomes aware of his situation, apprehending that a long oracular sequence of events has
resulted in Deianira's apparently thoughtless act. When he realizes that "it is finished" (see l. 1174) he becomes witness to the
splendor of the tragic structure which it has been given him to accomplish. The oracle of Dodona had an unforeseen import, as
the oracle in *Macbeth*. He had been promised rest after his final
labor:

> I heard it and wrote it down
>   under my Father's tree.
> Time lives, and it's going on now.
> I am released from trouble.
> I thought it meant life in comfort.
> It doesn't. It means that I die.
> For amid the dead there is no work in service.
> Come at it that way, my boy, what
> SPLENDOUR,
>   IT ALL COHERES.

[*He turns his face from the audience, then sits erect, facing them without the mask of agony; the revealed make-up is that of solar serenity.
The hair golden and as electrified as possible.*]   [*WT* 49–50]

As with the images of the Nô plays, Pound points to one key line
("*taut'oûn epeidè lamprà sumbaínei,*" "since this [oracle] has
clearly come to effect") as to the seed of the work, holding it all
together: "This is the key phrase, for which the play exists, as in
the *Elektra*: 'Need we add cowardice to all the rest of these ills?'

. . . And, later: 'Tutto quello che è accaduto, doveva accadere.' " [7] And on the face of Heracles/Pound we discern the smile of the Apollo of Veii.

The tragedy continues after the illumination, the unyielding sequence of events being in any case but the drawing out in time of a central instant which has been seized definitively. Hyllus is to cremate his father's corpse, and marry his father's lover. In WT Sophocles' father-son conflict is censored in accord with Confucianism ("This is the great rule: Filial Obedience"),[8] and Hyllus pronounces a formal conclusion, reproaching the gods as blind and inequitable, for he has not yet come to tragic serenity.

It is clearly difficult to share several of the chief assumptions of this version, as elicited by our reading. There are also a number of less successful passages in which Pound's familiar uncertainty of tone is in evidence. Deianira, for instance, speaks indifferently like a Jamesian lady and in brutal slang. Yet it is just this linguistic freedom, intentionally careless of psychological verisimilitude, that makes WT the vital thing that it is.

Pound has given us a radically novel reading of the *Trachiniae* as the "splendid" myth of the sun, occurring (as he goes on to say in *RD*) "from the dawn blaze to sunset"—that is, between the dawn of the first chorus and the sunset in which "Helios is the king." [9] (In fact, in the table of personae, P. identifies the hero with "the Solar vitality.") Within the compass of his work the theme of the recurrence of history (which in the world of actuality can become a reactionary ideology) mirrors the depths of the

7. "All that has happened was bound to happen." This is the opening remark of a *Notebook of Ponza and La Maddalena,* said to have been written by the captive Mussolini in 1943, an English version of which was published at P.'s instigation in the Australian little magazine *Edge* for March 1957. For the other quotation see Sophocles, *Electra* 351.

8. WT 50. Commentators usually interpret this as a sarcastic reference to the misleading oracle of Zeus, Heracles' father.

9. WT 4 and 50. In *Töchter der Sonne* (Zürich: Rascher, 1952), p. 58, Karl Kerényi tells us that at sunset the Greek peasant or shepherd is likely to say, "Helios is now the king!," and suggests that this is because at sunset the sun joins his queen, thus becoming truly a king.

real. Jean-Paul Sartre has spoken of the reactionary bent of all art, for this, like Clytemnestra after the killing of Agamemnon, coolly states: "These, gentlemen, are the facts." [10] The feature which distinguishes Pound's translations from other perhaps more articulate products (e.g., Yeats's Sophocles) is the untold violence of facts which called them into being, facts among which are texts and their irregular relationships. [11]

10. "Translators of Greek," *LE* 270. Cf. J.-P. Sartre, "L'artiste et sa conscience," *Situations, IV* (Paris: Gallimard, 1964), p. 26: "La révolution sociale exige un conservatisme esthétique tandis que la révolution esthétique exige, en dépit de l'artiste lui-même, un conservatisme social."

11. Other translations of value produced in the Washington years are the four "Guides to the Montanari poems" (*PD* 238–41: 1951—P. took an interest in the undistinguished Montanari because he died in 1943, a young soldier in Albania, though his poems are far from political), the versions of early Rimbaud and Tailhade, among them the "Lice-Hunters," and three imitations of Horace. The poignant "Conversations in Courtship," from the Egyptian, were apparently written after P.'s return to Italy.

At the time of his release (1958) P. was planning an anthology of world poetry, *Confucius to Cummings*—a Book of Odes for the West and a definitive version of his "canon." He wrote several interesting notes for it, stressing the social function of literature, and perhaps made a few translations ad hoc, but lost interest in the project before long. As a consequence, the book published in 1964 cannot be considered wholly his, and is, at any rate, quite disappointing.

Part Three

Rock-Drill

The wind scatters the leaves on the ground, but the live timber
Burgeons with leaves again in the season of spring returning.

—*The Iliad,* tr. Richmond Lattimore

Die Welt zerfällt in Tatsachen.
—Wittgenstein, *Tractatus
Logico-Philosophicus* 1.2

Put your hand on my forehead for a moment to give me courage.

—Kafka, *Aus den Gesprächblättern*

To the *Cantos,* which (in Eliot's ambiguous phrase) "are wholly
himself," [1] Pound returned with the attitude of objectivity and
professionalism he had taken in planning his paradise at the out-
break of the War. His confidence, we recall, had been severely
tried at Pisa, yet poetry had won the day in the face (or with the
assistance) of the onslaught of events. Now a captive in Washington, D.C., he responds to the violence of the community that has
passed judgment upon him with the violence of his uncompromising poem, of which he is sole master. In no way apol-
ogetic, he chooses again the role of "driller" versus the world's
ignorance, of the exorcist of demons, and of the mentor of vision,
covering the ground between the war to the death against
usury—

Bellum cano perenne . . .   [c. 86]

. . . between the usurer and any man who
wants to do a good job   [c. 87]

—and contemplation:

1. T. S. Eliot, Introduction to Ezra Pound, *Selected Poems* (1928), Sullivan 104.

Above prana, the light,
                              past light, the crystal.
Above crystal, the jade!   [c. 94]

Section: Rock-Drill 85–95 de los Cantares [2] is another record
of digressive soliloquies, of anecdotes worth the telling ("That
Queen Bess translated Ovid, / Cleopatra wrote of the currency"),
of invectives ("The total dirt that was Roosevelt, / and the farce
that was Churchill"), of visions more or less induced, and of
mornings spent leafing through the documents suppressed by the
bankers' conspiracy, with an intensity which frequently infects
the reader, as long as he has the same sources at hand: " 'One of
those days,' said Brancusi, / 'when I would not have given / 15
minutes of my time / for anything under heaven.' "

As the poet comes to this new sphere he is greeted by several
contemplative spirits new to the *Cantos* though often retrieved
from remote spots of Pound's corpus: in the first place Richard of
St. Victor, the patron saint of the section, and then (briefly) the
neo-Pythagorean Ocellus, and the seventeenth-century alchemist
John Heydon (a persona of ur-c. 3, also mentioned in the "Neoplatonicks" chapter of *K*), and finally the neo-Pythagorean divine
Apollonius of Tyana. These and other "initiates" (in *RD* P.'s
verse veers markedly to the esoteric) are accompanied by less
remote characters, apparently impressed during an eccentric
revisitation of seventeenth- and eighteenth-century history,
which in one instance at least brought about a change of mind in
the absolute despot of this universe. Picking up the scatological
language of cs. 14–15, canto 50 (of the Siena and Napoleon
"decad") informs readers that "Two sores ran together, Talleyrand stank with shanker, / and hell pissed up Metternich." In *RD* and *Thrones* Pound's admiration for Napoleon
does not cool (we hear of "Wellington's peace after Vaterloo"—
the spelling suggesting Belgian pronunciation—at the outset of
RD), but Talleyrand he now takes for a paradigm of political
acumen and good conversation ("Van Buren already in '37 un-

2. *The Rock Drill* is a vorticist sculpture by Jacob Epstein. Wyndham Lewis retrieved the
name for the title of his review of *L* (*New Statesman and Nation,* 7 April 1951). P.
adopted it a little later.

smearing Talleyrand"—c. 89). Accordingly, in the 1954 London text, Metternich's secretary is damned in lieu of Napoleon's turncoat minister: "Two sores ran together, Gentz, Metternich, / Hell pissed up Metternich."[3]

Among relatively recent historical characters entering the poem with this late levy are Bismarck, the enlightened despots (the motif is familiar) Maria Theresa and Joseph II of Austria, Edward VIII (another change of mind, the former "non-sovereign Edwardus" of c. 74 being imparadised because of his lenience towards fascism), and—from the U.S.—Thomas Hart Benton, John Randolph, and Louis Agassiz—the Swiss-American naturalist who fought against Darwin a long backward battle not unlike Pound's rock-drilling.

So unauspicious a platform warrants the assumption that *RD* will end in disaster, as had the dynastic cantos (52–71), or at best rehearse the obsolete ideologies of the Jefferson and Siena compartments. But the Pisan experience has not passed for nothing, and in the new "decad" a continuous dialectic is established between Pound's questionable intentions and "the freedom of linguistic flux" (Benjamin), which is, as we have found, the emergent datum in *PC* and in the later translations. This counterstress of language generously immerses in the shadow of formal doubt Pound's peremptory statements and corroborates his pathetic proffers of love.

The actual rock-drilling is done by an amorous and subtle force which is like that of the seed that penetrates in a fissure and germinates there ("pine seed splitting cliff's edge"—c. 87). Pound may want to employ his terroristic methods to climb to the third heaven, but the rock of language resists this grosser impulse and brings about its conversion into a secret process of poetic germination which can work through both the rock of language and the rock of Pound's intentions, and thus set the tone of the section:

---

3. The editors of the more recent New York editions have, as usual, disregarded P.'s emendation, and have simply omitted the half-line, "Talleyrand stank with shanker," leaving the reader to wonder who the two sores may be. Probably the best solution in such cases is to preserve the original reading.

The rock is the gray particular of man's life,
The stone from which he rises, up—and—ho,
The step to the bleaker depths of his descents . . .

Thus Wallace Stevens.[4] And who does not remember the program
of William Carlos Williams?

—through metaphor to reconcile
the people and the stones.
Compose (No ideas
but in things) Invent!
Saxifrage is my flower that splits
the rocks.[5]

4. "The Rock," *The Collected Poems of Wallace Stevens* (New York: Knopf, 1957), p. 525.

5. "A Sort of Song," *The Collected Later Poems of William Carlos Williams* (Norfolk, Conn.: New Directions, 1950), p. 7.

7. An American Tradition

I offer, in explanation, a quote:
si j'ai du goût, ce n'est guère
que pour la terre et les pierres

   —Charles Olson,
   "The Kingfishers"

The major American poetry to appear since the War may still be the work of the old modernist masters. *The Rock, Paterson* and Williams' later poems, the *Pisan Cantos* and a few of those to follow—these were among the very best fruits of poetic careers extending over many decades. It is clearly no accident that this exceptional cluster (to which Eliot's *Quartets* may be added) should have occurred at a critical turn of world history, yet the poems tell us of this only indirectly, and Pound alone recorded at Pisa the full shock of events. (The London after the air raid of *Little Gidding* is still chiefly the sign of a different desolation.) Likewise, it is difficult to allocate them in literary history, on account of the strongly personal stance of the individual writers, though we are at once aware of a distinct American flavor, despite the prominent influence of Europe, especially of medieval Italy and modern France. They are all poems in the first person, held together by a meditative and image-making self, an heir to Puritan introspection and to Whitman's universal self. The latter is the stronger influence (as we have seen in ch. 3), though Whitman's double, Poe, has also contributed his genetic store. On the other hand, the immediate heirs of the Puritans, Melville and Dickinson, are mythical figures wholly disregarded by the modernists, for these are quite impermeable to the question of evil, as we find if we go, for an a fortiori proof, to the more "religious" poet of the lot, Eliot, whose chief ambition is to be lost in the all, into the good night. Rather than of Mallarmé, the *Quartets* remind us of Verlaine.

Among these the path followed by Pound is the more hazard-
ous, the more so because of the swagger with which he intends to
proceed. Williams and Stevens, on the other hand, would be
quite at home in a poetic Elysium.

Stevens appears to have apprehended all things in their in-
timacy, as they become thought—to have become aware of pure
presence:

> The palm stands on the edge of space.
> The wind moves slowly in the branches.
> The bird's fire-fangled feathers dangle down.[1]

Williams is more direct, his tenet (shared by Stevens) that
imagination is the sole reality more disarming, because it is not to
evade but to approach the real that he records it, intact, in his
verse, adding but one of his delicate exclamation points. Whereas
Stevens cerebrates upon the "Ding an sich," Williams is confident
that the ultimate is Eros, of which things are phenomena but also
sole witnesses. Brueghel's painting, Dr. Williams' breakfast on
the terrace, his daughters-in-law, a picture postcard—it is enough
to render these in a metre which he holds to be his chief contribution to poetry (the variable foot), and their import is revealed to
be light, love. (Williams' senile sensuousness is reminiscent of
Yeats's, yet it is less postured and heroic—a gentle virility which
does not take woman by storm.)

> It is ridiculous
> what airs we put on
> to seem profound
> while our hearts
> gasp dying
> for want of love.[2]

The words of the poets, though avoiding contact with the
chronicle of the day in which they were written, were nonetheless

---

1. "Of Mere Being," *Poems by Wallace Stevens,* ed. S. F. Morse (New York: Vintage
Books, 1959), p. 169.

2. "Asphodel, That Greeny Flower," *Pictures from Brueghel and Other Poems* (New
York: New Directions, 1962), p. 170.

timely, and even anticipated the attitudes with which a section of American culture was to respond in the sixties to technocratic alienation. The nascent counterculture was to reject the language of the establishment, well aware that this would only validate the status quo, and was to seek, often in bewildered fashion, new signs for new sensations.[3] With Thoreau, Whitman, and Eliot, it made its way to nature and India; with Pound it sought to recover the magic essence of language and the pantheon which it implies; with Stevens it conceived of the world as meditation, heightened consciousness; with Williams (and Blake) it affirmed the holiness of all that lives, particularly of sexuality. So these are the more responsible spokesmen of the tide of "vulgar" spiritualism of these years, their followers being often minor poets concerned with the fabrication of a *Gebrauchsdichtung* which quickly loses its gloss: today the lyrics of certain popular songs seem more pointed than their lines. This is why poets of different heritage, like Lowell and Berryman, were to become the leading voices of the sixties. This is not to deny the achievement of such writers as Creeley, Olson, Levertov, Corso, Ferlinghetti, Ashbery, and so on, who are all indebted to the Whitman-Pound-Williams mainstream (at any rate, it is still early for a confident assessment), but to note a significant swing of the pendulum in poetic sensibility, which has now come around to Melville and Dickinson, masters for which negation, the shadow, is not easily reabsorbed within the One.[4]

An erotic apprehension of the world must, on pain of losing its bite, take into account the discontents of civilization, it must sharpen rather than dull the critical faculty, or it will surrender to

3. See Theodore Roszak, *The Making of a Counterculture: Reflections on the Technocratic Society* (New York: Doubleday, 1969).

4. This outline is, of course, only of very general use. Lowell, for example, openly claimed descent from P. and Eliot, like the avant-garde (which, however, tends to ignore Eliot). On the other hand Olson has written a well-known essay on Melville (*Call Me Ishmael*, 1947) but this in the end may prove our point, as it consistently belittles the conflictual and religious Melville. As for P.'s attitude to Melville (largely shared, so far as we know, by James and Eliot), his incautious comment on *Call Me Ishmael* is indicative: "I read with joy—made it unnecessary to read Melville" (quoted in Charles Olson, *Encounter at St Elizabeths*, p. 138).

the first haranguer—vide the *Cantos* and other such equivocal reports on history, the valid part of which can be rescued only through a cautious reading. Let us follow for instance the family tree which grows out of Whitman's Prefaces and *Democratic Vistas,* branching out into Williams' *In the American Grain* and Pound's *Kulchur,* and eventually bringing forth Olson's writings. (D. H. Lawrence's *Studies* are a not too distant relation.) Whitman's messianism is checked by his democratic instinct, but this is not always the case in the sequel, when estheticism blurs the issues at stake: Pound in China, or Olson among the Maya, can only uncover their own baggage, or at least they do not command a method capable of dissociating this from the genuine find. Of course this problem is germane to all enquiry, yet, as someone has remarked, the student's task is to distinguish, not to heap all together in one mass.

Williams, possibly because of continuous exposure to the New Jersey proletariat, is more suspicious of cultural intergrafting (and of all "internationalism"—hence his diffidence towards Eliot) and more restrained in his speculations, to the effect that his book of myth and history provides a compelling image of America.[5] In one of his last poems he criticizes his friend Pound both from a humane and from a linguistic point of view:

> If I were a dog
> I'd sit down on a cold pavement
> in the rain
> to wait for a friend (and so would you)
> if it so pleased me
> even if it were January or Zukofsky
>
> Your English
> is not specific enough
> As a writer of poems
> you show yourself to be inept not to say
> usurious[6]

5. However, Williams was also sympathetic for a while to Social Credit. In Books 3 and 5 of *Paterson* he includes two letters from P., economic in subject, with implicit agreement. These letters are representative of the tenor of P.'s correspondence after the War.

6. "To My Friend Ezra Pound," *Pictures from Brueghel,* p. 66.

The generic charge of creative ineptitude is surely unfounded—in fact Williams' verse, apparently all made of things, is often less robust than his friend's—it is poetry about poetry, or about the romantically idealized Poet. Yet Williams senses that the world of the *Cantos* is foreign, at odds with his everyday gestures, and is irritated by their synthetic language, though Pound had been a champion of the precise word even more strenuous than himself. He overlooks the coherence of the development of Pound, whose unappealing language is a largely intentional choice, and the parallelism of their two *œuvres*. Pound, for his part, in a late introduction to the reprint of *A Lume Spento* (1964), readily concedes that Williams, without departing from his time and from his deliveries, has run the lesser risk to go astray into no-man's-land, and has been the first to emerge from the mists of the Nineties, at least in point of language (for the message of both poets never wholly emerges from its nineteenth-century background):

A collection of stale creampuffs. "Chocolate creams, who hath forgotten you?"
At a time when Bill W. was perceiving the "Coroner's Children." [7]
As to why a reprint? No lessons to be learned save the depth of ignorance, or rather the superficiality of non-perception—neither eye nor ear. Ignorance that didn't know the meaning of "Wardour Street." [ALS 7]

American poetry as we have it—and modern poetry at that—is in fact to no small extent the work of these "foolish and ignorant m[e]n" (Yvor Winters passing judgement on Williams): [8] for all his internationalism, Pound was to remain unconversant with "that poetry of Vergilian and Petrarchan origin which by way of Leopardi and Baudelaire remains the secret of the European lyric." [9]
The poet, at least in this European version, is "the man who

7. "The coroner's merry little children / Have such twinkling brown eyes"—"Hic Jacet," *The Collected Earlier Poems of William Carlos Williams* (Norfolk, Conn.: New Directions, 1951), p. 30.

8. *Forms of Discovery: Critical and Historical Essays on the Forms of the Short Poem in English* (Chicago: Swallow, 1967), p. 319.

9. Eugenio Montale, "Uncle Ez" (1953), tr. Angela C. Yung and Guido Palandri, *Italian Quarterly*, xvi, 64 (Spring 1973), p. 25.

engages himself to lose." [10] But the American lyricist, Whitman and Pound, though he is as much of an invalid as Virgil, Petrarch, Leopardi, and Baudelaire, sets out to win, and his defeat comes from without—from the world, from his deeper instinct, or from his writing:

Ez's epic solves problem by his ego: his single emotion breaks all down to his equals or inferiors (so far as I can see only two, possibly, are admitted, by him, to be his betters—Confucius, & Dante. Which assumption, that there are intelligent men whom he can outtalk, is beautiful because it destroys historical time, and

thus creates the methodology of the Cantos, viz, a space-field where, by inversion, though the material is all time material, he has driven through it so sharply by the beak of his ego, that, he has turned time into what we must now have, space & its live air [11]

Olson's words, inscribed within the tradition they seek to discuss, provide unintentionally its diagnosis. If the flattening out of time on the space of the page reminds us of certain formulas of advanced criticism, it becomes equivocal as soon as we think of the actual web of experience, in which historical time is to be constructed, rather than destroyed. Besides, as he wrote this letter, Olson did not know *RD* or the *Odes* (the significance of which

10. Jean-Paul Sartre, *Situations, II* (Paris: Gallimard, 1948), p. 87: "Si donc l'on veut absolument parler de l'engagement du poète, disons que c'est l'homme qui s'engage à perdre. . . . Il est certain de l'échec total de l'entreprise humaine et s'arrange pour échouer dans sa propre vie, afin de témoigner, par sa défaite singulière, de la défaite humaine en général." This is doubtless the case also with the Imperial Self of America, however strong his confidence in the resources of the future: he is drawn unwillingly into the common defeat, and refrains from acknowledging this.

11. Charles Olson, *Mayan Letters* (letter of 8 March 1951), *Selected Writings* (New York: New Directions, 1966), pp. 81–82. The influence of P.'s style is as prominent here as in Olson's attempted epic (also epistolary in form), *The Maximus Poems*. It is interesting to compare Parts 4–6 of this poem with *RD* and *Th,* for (as we shall see) they have some sources in common. However, Olson abandons also P.'s ultimate convention, the unity of the "canto," which is always a sort of soliloquy, banal or impassioned as the case may be, though always inscribed within "the terroristic complex" (Sartre) of writing. In Olson only the latter obtains, as he progressively forsakes the form of the letter (equivalent to the canto), placing sparse phrases in an undetermined space (the pages are unnumbered), seeking to evoke cosmological implications—the final outcome of Walt's soliloquizing.

will escape him, as mentioned previously), yet he had access to
PC, which is precisely the section of the poem which takes cognizance of historical time, which is identified with narrative time.
However, the definition of the peremptory American self is of significance: in the equation of self and world the former is stressed,
thus preventing all verification and letting in the arbitrary. Therefore the "precision" sought by Pound turns out to be an uncon-
trolled allusiveness, just as Olson's language implies a context in
which it may be understood—an assumption questionable in the
extreme. And in the later cantos Pound cannot (or does not want
to) distinguish between private and common experience. Hence
the magic quality of the poem, also in the derogatory sense: it
carries messages which cannot all be deciphered and eventually
leads an autonomous existence, bearing witness to a presence
destined to absence, to *a* world vastly unqualified to become *the*
world, but presented as such to the reader in the encompassing
space of the page—*Song of Myself.* The text becomes an original
undecipherable in part which must be freely recreated, as Pound
has done with Confucius and Sophocles. Its closeness is a function of this irreparable distance, which is not relative to the reader's point of view, but inheres in the work from its very conception. Eugenio Montale has pointed out this removal in
connection with the interviews given by Pound in 1959–60:

They are the memories of a man alive, but chiefly alive in his memories.
At no time, not even when he was casting the seed that awoke many
minds, was Pound a man of the present; he was always a little on this
side or on that of current history—and history itself, when it unfolded
in his imagination, became a universal chronicle, an endless sequence of
"diverse facts." . . . In fact, the *Cantos* are a prodigious medley of
quotations, indicating the poet's formidable memory and the thematic
essence of his vision of life. To him history is a musical score which he
opens at one point or another for his own amusement or to extract new
themes for his poetry.[12]

Montale does not mention the fact that this removal from history
arises precisely from the insistent questioning with which the

12. Montale, "Il moralismo naturale."

American self (unlike other, more lyrical, invalids) confronts history—to the point of becoming an involuntary presence. We
know that in support of his estheticism Pound maintains that
good government and good art are synonymous. While pursuing
his "excessive idea of literature," [13] he has stumbled upon Marx-
ist ground: "Lot of damn rot and 'psychology,' people fussing
with in'nards which are merely the result of economic pressure"
(*L* 271).

13. Gérard Genette, *Figures: Essais* (Paris: Seuil, 1966), p. 126, as quoted by Umberto
Cianciòlo in Jorge Luis Borges, *Carme presunto e altre poesie* (Milano: Mondadori,
1972), p. 13: "Mais l'idée *excessive* de la littérature, où Borges se complaît parfois à nous
entraîner, désigne peut-être une tendance profonde de l'écrit, qui est d'attirer fictivement
dans sa sphère l'integralité des choses existantes (et inexistantes), comme si la littérature
ne pouvait se maintenir et se justifier à ses propres yeux que dans cette utopie totalitaire."

8. Stone Annals and Atomic Facts

> Other masters may conceivably write
> Even yet in C major
> But we—we take the perhaps "primrose path"
> To the dodecaphonic bonfire.
>
> —Hugh MacDiarmid, "In the Fall"

Vision cannot be severed from dross. Within the compass of the *Cantos* this means that vision must be sustained by an enquiry into the world of history that will supply ethical standards and revisitations of key events, sometimes forgotten, of the past. Pound, however, far from constructing a system, à la Yeats, does not even clarify his systematic program to himself, being wholly absorbed in the manipulation of the verbal object. At any rate his historical inclinations (which may also spring from the fascination with the written) account for the "unpoetic" texture of his last work, and for the singularity of the visions which it includes. Nothing is ineffable in this verse, harrowed as it is throughout by the contradictory impulses of its matter, and vital precisely by reason of this conflict. A sieving is therefore impossible: to extract the dross of history is to deprive the vision of meaning. The reading attempted in this study is to be distinguished both from the contention of Pound, or rather of his more unwary readers, that the *Cantos* are unified in a traditional way, and from the breaking up advocated by disintegrative critics, who overlook the fact that no part of the poem "functions" if removed from its context.

In letters written at this time Pound insists, in fact, upon the unity of his work: "Nobody can understand what the final cantares are ABOUT until they have read the earlier ones AND I doubt if anyone will have the necessary technique until they have been

231

thru the earlier parts of the POEM, POEM, not poems."[1] *RD* is planned as carefully as the prewar decads: "There are three different kinds of Cantos," Pound explained to Scheiwiller on 7 December 1954, announcing that he had mailed him the typescript, "3 chinese / 2 american / 6 paradise." Clearly, if there were a "system" of the *Cantos,* America and China would be its historical poles, and these would be as it were connected by Europe and Italy. Or we may say that the China-America diptych of cs. 52–71 is briefly recapitulated at this later stage of the "fugue." Thus vision is coherent with its premises in seeking out these foundations. But if we follow its workings at close quarters we see that the plan does not hold and rather gives way to the coherence of different order, irrespective of all programs, of which we have spoken in this part's opening remarks.

Cantos 85–86 usher in *RD* with an extreme instance of Pound's captivation with the word transmitted, with the textual source—a controlling concern throughout his work, which in turn captivates the reader precisely as a textual object. The confrontation with the source begun in c. 1 becomes more radical in the fifties: rather than interpreting the texts, the poet transcribes the nodes he has detected—a practice which he had in fact indulged as early as c. 1, in the word-portrait of Venus, which few Latinists could unravel did they not know about "the Cretan's phrase." Hence the footnote at the end of c. 85:

Kung said he had added nothing. Canto 85 is a somewhat detailed confirmation of Kung's view that the basic principles of government are found in the Shu, the History Classic.

1. November 1956, to Vanni Scheiwiller, the publisher of the first editions of *RD* and *Th.* For the associations of the word "cantares," used by P. in the fifties for the *Cantos,* see the blurb for *RD* on the dust jacket of *WT,* written by P. or under his direction: "This is the major theme as the *Cantos* move into their third and final phase: the 'domination of benevolence.' And, though no exact correspondence is intended, we think of the Thrones of Dante's *Paradiso,* or of the allegories of the virtues in the upper level of the frescoes in the Palazzo Schifanoia in Ferrara. Now the great poem has progressed into the realm of 'the permanent'; the poet has passed through 'the casual' and 'the recurrent' and come to the values that endure like the sea. [New par.] *Los cantares.* Compare Mallarmé's '*mots de la tribu*'—the tale of the tribe." The suggestion that P.'s paradise only begins with *RD* is of interest, as a case could be made for cs. 52–74 as an extended Confucian purgatory, the first part hellish, the second paradisal. But, "no precise correspondence is intended."

The confirmation is so detailed that canto 85 (and, to a lesser extent, the two following cantos of the Chinese triptych) cannot be deciphered without continuous consultation of the "score" employed by Pound to verify Confucius' view, that is, the *Shu Ching*, or Annals, in the trilingual text (Chinese, transliteration, French and Latin translations) prepared by Séraphin Couvreur in the last years of the 19th century.[2] The English text is overshadowed by large, silent, Chinese characters; it does not comment so much on their "religious" and graphic meaning (as so often in *PC*), but rather insists on their social implications. The characters, however, preserve their magic appeal: Pound places at the entrance of his later paradise this Rosetta stone inscribed with modern and extremely ancient languages (according to the traditional dating of the *Shu*, some of its chapters were written before the tenth century B.C.), its smaller and larger Chinese type accurately laid out on the space of the page. (The use of type is a happy innovation; formerly P. had used his and his wife's often unclear drawings.) The coupling of the totemic import of this stele with what is after all a meditation on a "historical" source can be taken as a further example of the method of the "school" to which Pound belongs.

As for the English text, its diction becomes compact and supple, shrinking to small bits of mosaic, very unlike Pisa's discourse-in-progress. The main unit of expression is the line-phrase, which can contract to a single word or occasionally expand into a continuous whole—most often it adds itself to and reacts against other like units, which are apparently irreducible atomic facts, often repeated in the cantos of one or more sections with minimal variation. Only very rarely does a gradual explication reveal the hidden sense of a statement as it recurs.

The syntactic and semantic form of these units is most simple and curt, its lack of perspective and articulation insistently recalling infantile and primitive thought. For an example the lines which open and set the scene of *RD* may be quoted:

> LING[2]   [*ling*]
> Our dynasty came in because of a great sensibility.

2. S. Couvreur, *Chou King, Les Annales de la Chine* (Paris: Cathasia, 1950).

All there by the time of Y Yin.   [*i*]
All roots by the time of Y Yin.   [*yin*]
Galileo index'd 1616,
Wellington's peace after Vaterloo
               [*chih*]   chih³
                  a gnomon
Our science is from the watching of shadows;
That Queen Bess translated Ovid,
         Cleopatra wrote of the currency,
Versus who scatter old records
         ignoring the hsien form
            [*hsien:* "virtuous, worthy, good"—M 2671]
                       [c. 85]

This side of the 1527 watershed is the age of usury, of the obscurantist (literally so) Reformation and Counter-Reformation, which places Galileo on the Index and scatters the old magic records—"the hsien form," *chih,* and *ling.* On the farther side of the dissociation of sensibility is the world of Elizabeth, Ovid, and Cleopatra (queen and metamorphic poetry)—of a sane interest in the currency—and of a science grounded on the watching of shadows, the shadow cast by the gnomon/*chih* ("to stop"—we have met this character, earlier glossed by P. as "the hitching post," and roughly similar to a gnomon, in the yellow bird passage of c. 79). Galileo (already taken as an example in c. 48), that is experimental science, watches the gnomon's shadow to establish the movements of the earth; and so do the Chinese, in order to discover (Granet tells us—p. 267) the locus where "at midday of midsummer, the gnomon casts no shadow"—here, at the world's center, they build "the Capital of the perfect sovran," Pound's City of Deioces. Pound calls this science, which (just as Fenollosa's method) is both experimental and mystical, "our science"—he speaks, that is, as a member in a community of initiates, referred to as "our dynasty" in the opening line, where the science is presented as "a great sensibility," and graphed by the character *ling.* This comes from a passage in the *Shu,* narrower in meaning as it refers to the Chu (third) dynasty alone: "Les empereurs de notre maison de Tcheou (Wenn wang et Ou wang), à cause de leur grande bonté, furent chargés d'exécuter l'œuvre du roi du ciel" (p. 285). Pound replaces goodness with sensibility and demands, by printing *ling* in a particularly large type (it is in fact the largest character in the poem), that we consider the precise import of the word. Now, *ling* contains at the top the sky radical, below which are three "mouths," and at the bottom a character meaning, "A wizard or witch; a medium. Magical arts. Dancing and posturing in order to induce the descent of the spirits" (*M* 7164). We gather that the sky speaks, that nature brings forth shadows, signs, and that these are interpreted by magic. Sensibility, we conclude, consists in reverent attention to the words and traces of nature. Later on in the same canto (and in *Th*) Pound is to suggest that it is in fact connected with "bonté" (but this is implicit in "the ecstatic-beneficent-and-benevolent [state]" which it graphs), and, (in cs. 90 and 104) that the witch in the bottom part is the Pythoness or Sibyl of Delphi— but its foremost concern is with the writing of the world. The theme is punctually restated at the inception of the paradisal section of *RD*, suggesting that the two parts of the "decad" bear upon a single mystery. The restatement is: " 'From the colour the nature / & by the nature the sign!' " By watching the colors or shadows we may come to the essence of things—and vice versa, nature brings forth the true sign.

Having opened *RD* with a reference to the coming to power of the Chu, the great central fact of these cantos (as of the Great Odes), Pound jumps six centuries back, to the time of Ch'eng T'ang (founder of the second dynasty, Shang) and of I Yin, minister to T'ang's grandson and successor T'ai chia, picking up from a note to "The Proclamation of T'ang" the doctrine of the "four foundations" (*tuan*) of Confucian ethics—love, duty, propriety, and wisdom.[3] In fact the *Shu Ching* appears to be (like the Annals paraphrased in cs. 52–61) a reconstruction of the past on the model of Confucian ideology, despite Couvreur's state-

---

3. *Chou King*, p. 109*n*; and M 6541: 7. Mancuso (pp. 50–51) notes that this doctrine is also developed in Mencius 6A.6, and that P. never reproduces in the *Cantos* the character *li*, "propriety," suggesting that P. is less interested in this than in the three other "cornerstones." This inference, however, is questionable, as P. was always very concerned with social accomplishement—with being (as he puts it) *salonfähig*.

ment that it acquaints us with "les idées qui avaient cours, sinon deux milles ans, au moins mille ans avant J.C." ("Préface"). If this is indeed how the book came to be written, we are not as surprised as the annotator Pound to find that it includes many statements also made in the *Four Books*. (The words "ta seu," on the second page of c. 86, are not one of P.'s many transcriptions of Couvreur's transliterations, but a reference to the *Ta-hsüeh*, called by P. in 1942, *Ta S'eu Dai Gaku;* cf. "I believe the Dai Gaku"—c. 88.)

Pound takes care to stress that the four *tuan* are innate ("ch'e' ditta dentro") [4]—that they are part of the native culture he had spoken of in *K,* and in his paper of 1939, "European Paideuma":

The people in Rapallo rushing down into the sea on Easter morning or bringing their gardens of Adonis to church on the Thursday before, have not learned it in school. Neither have the peasant women *read* anything telling them to bring silk-cocoons to church carefully concealed in their hands or under their aprons. [Quoted in Norman 373.]

Hence the image of organic ethics in the verse of c. 85:

> Not led of lusting, not of contriving
> > but is as the grass and tree
>
> .   .   .
>
> THE FOUR TUAN [1]
> > [*tuan*]   or foundations.
> Hulled rice and silk at easter
> > (with the *bachi* held under their aprons
> From T'ang's time until now)
> That you lean 'gainst the tree of heaven,
> > and know Ygdrasail   [c. 85]

"Le ciel ne se trompe jamais dans ses dispositions," we read in T'ang's Proclamation, "cette vérité brille come les fleurs au printemps [*Latin version:* herbae et arbores]. Aussi tous les peuples reprennent vie." The princes are instructed not to seek "ni le repos ni les plaisirs. Observez chacun vos règlements, pour mériter les faveurs du ciel" (pp. 111–12). The sign translated as "faveurs," the last in the paragraph, places side by side two radi-

4. Canto 85 (the tag is associated with *ling*). Cf. *Purg.* xxiv. 54.

cals, "tree," and "man"—and this suggests Pound's reference to
the world-ash Yggdrasil, which is not so farfetched after all, for,
according to Chinese speculation,

Au centre même de l'Univers—là où devrait être la Capitale parfaite—
s'élève un Arbre merveilleux: il réunit les Neuvièmes Sources aux Neuvièmes Cieux, les Bas-Fonds du Monde à son Faîte [peak]. *On l'appelle
le Bois Dressé* (Kien-mou), *et l'on dit qu'à midi rien de ce qui, auprès de
lui,* se tient parfaitement droit, *ne peut donner d'ombre.* Rien non plus
n'y donne d'écho. Grâce à une synthèse (qui est parfaite, car elle résulte
d'une hiérogamie), tous les contrastes et toutes les alternances, tous les
attributs, tous les insignes se trouvent résorbés dans l'Unité centrale.
[Granet 267–68]

Yggdrasil is the process as tree, as the forces of vegetation. *Ling,*
reverence for the words of the sky, implies *ching,* reverence for
the green world. (The latter character occurs for the first time in
the poem in this canto, ten pages on.) [5]
    There follow I Yin's instructions to profligate T'ai chia, whom
he has sent to meditate by his grandfather's tomb ("Avec ces trois
vertus (la diligence, la bienfaisance et la sincérité) on gouverne
bien; sans elles on gouverne mal"—p. 125). Pound enlarges them
to include the doctrine of signatures, as well as the tradition of
contemplation and action "needing no particular theories to keep
it alive":

> But if you will follow this process   [*te*]
> not a lot of signs, but the one sign
>   etcetera
>   plus always Τέχνη
> and from Τέχνη back to σεαυτόν
> Neither by chinks, nor by sophists,
>   nor by hindoo immaturities;

5. With the gloss, "and you can know the sincere." Cf. *Chou King,* p. 273: "Veillez at-
tentivement [*ching*] sur vous-mêmes, et il vous sera facile de discerner les princes qui vous
offriront (de coeur) leurs présents et leurs hommages de ceux qui ne vous les offriront pas
(de coeur)." In this painful period P., seeing everywhere accomplices of the bankers' plot
against him, is very much concerned with "knowing the sincere." Hence the paradigmatic
opening of c. 89: "To know the histories / to know good from evil / And to know whom to
trust."

Dante, out of St Victor (Richardus),
　　Erigena with greek tags in his verses.
Y Yin sent the young king into seclusion
by T'ang Tomb to think things over,
　　that they make total war on CONTEMPLATIO.　[c. 85]

The practice of virtue (*te*) is again equated with the watching of signs, in fact of "the one sign"—the innate movements of the heart ("ch'e'ditta dentro"). In 1945 Pound, noticing that *te* is formed by the radicals "eye," "heart," and "to pace," had provided the following etymology, which amounts to commentary on these lines: "the eye . . . looking straight into the heart [and] what results, i.e., the action resultant from this straight gaze into the heart. The 'know thyself' carried into action. Said action also serving to clarify the self knowledge" (*GD*, "Terminology"). Chinks, sophists, and hindoos are not "straight"; the true contemplatives have always returned to the givens of nature (human, vegetal, and other), and, having "known themselves" (Socrates' "*gnôthi seautón*") have gone on to act. Without *téchne*, or action, virtue is an empty word—in fact *téchne* and *seautón* are inseparable. Around this doctrine Pound gathers the tradition he has chosen for himself: Erigena with his Greek background (the foreign tags rhyming with P.'s use of Chinese), Richard of St. Victor (who defined contemplation as "a clear rational intuition accompanied by sentiment"),[6] and Dante, who took Richard to be "more than man in contemplation" (*Par.* x.132), and was much indebted to his philosophy. There are, we realize, patterns in nature, and, related to these, lines of descent in culture. T'ai chia must go both to his grandfather's example (as Erigena to the Pseudo-Dionysus, Dante to Richard), and to his heart.

But "discrimination by the senses," or "this process," "is dangerous to avarice," and the money-changer has declared total war upon it—the Albigensian crusade and the more recent obliteration of all silence and consideration of old records at the hands of the media, of the inventors of muzak. "They" are the

---

6. *Ben. major* 1. 4, quoted in Galvano della Volpe, *Eckhart o della filosofia mistica* (Roma: Edizioni di Storia e Letteratura, 1952), p. 49.

natural enemies of sensibility and of the "awareness" insistently referred to in the last part of the canto; "the pusillanimous / wanting all men cut down to worm size" castigated two pages on, after a further reference to *te* and immediately before a thrust against F. D. Roosevelt. Under "pusillanimous" Pound understands, literally, men devoid of all largeness of spirit, but he also uses the word for its more common suggestions, for in *RD* much weight is put upon courage, honor,[7] and resistance (fascist, of course) beyond defeat, Pound confusing the latter with the individual power of resistance to which it was necessary for him to appeal.

Thus in the close of c. 85 the sensibility of Brancusi (and of P. the reader of the *Shu*), referred to by way of the remark quoted earlier, is immediately contrasted with the opening image of *PC* ("Dead in the Piazzale Loreto"), which is to Pound an allegory of defeated sensibility, and with the first of many allusions to the trial of Orestes in the *Eumenides,* which was decided in favor of the avenger by Athene's additional vote (at this time P.'s trial was still pending). Returning to the *Shu,* the canto closes with a vindication of the old records and of the tale of the tribe by way of a final symbolic Chinese character, *chiao* ("To teach; to instruct"—*M* 719): to the right "old man" over "child," to the left "to beat," the radical of *ching.* Hence (in P.'s synthetic German, possibly an homage to Frobenius) the tag "Sagetrieb"—oral and written communication from one generation to another. This cryptic yet eloquent close is, however, preceded by a few Greek words, the "key phrase" from *Electra* quoted in the footnote to the climax of *WT:* "Need we add cowardice to all these ills?"

From the start of this introductory canto Pound had made clear his scorn for such as "jump to the winning side," yet it must be said that his persistance in the old errors, however predictable

7. Cf. P.'s letter to Julien Cornell, 26 October 1948: "No emphasis has been placed on Ital govt. promise that shd/ not be asked to say anything vs/ conscience and duty. After 12 years of frankie the perjurer who had sworn to support the const/ etc. the am/ people is too degraded to understand that I was dealing with men of honour (phrase as alien in U.S. as if it had been last used in the Morte d'Arthur) and that the promise was kept by them, as it wd/ NOT have been by Roosevelt or any of the men about him. However, that also will come out some day" (Cornell 109).

in a man of his relatively advanced age, is less suggestive of integrity than of sectarian obtuseness—of excessive resistance, characteristically increasing as the trauma of defeat becomes more distant in time, for in general the stance of *PC* is more nuanced and realistic. But in the "objective" world of *RD* (as, to a slightly lesser degree, in the Jefferson and Siena "decads") there is no place for exceptions and qualifications: every statement is desperately peremptory, impermeable to all objections, and as such hopelessly invalid. This obstinacy follows upon, and compensates for, the precarious status (increasingly in evidence through the fifties) of Pound's discourse, which proceeds warily one step at a time, from one small fact to the next, and cannot admit any hesitation, doubt, or self-irony, for then the whole shaky poetic-ideological edifice would collapse. In the end this defensive strategy may well prove to be expedient, for *RD* is certainly an important structural and poetic achievement. At any rate Pound's difficulty of articulation must be borne in mind in accounting for the suddenly more pronounced atomization of his ideogramic narrative, which is not so much the consequence of an intentional choice of method, as the naked transcription of an arduous and at times arid mental condition.

The seminal phrases mentioned in the footnote to Heracles' epiphany (among which is the alleged Mussolini quotation, "All that has happened was bound to happen"—rhyming with, "You do not depart from the process even for an instant") prove to be closely relevant to the central concerns of *RD*. We find them again in c. 86, spliced with the character which Pound understands to connote "fidelity to the given word" (*GD*, "Terminology"):

> All, that has been, is as it should have been,
>   but what will they trust in
>   [*hsin*: "Truth, sincerity, confidence"—*M* 2748] now?
> "Alla non della," in the Verona statement
>   οὐ ταῦτα . . . κακοῖσι
>   Section Rock Drill.
> Alexander paid the debts of his soldiery. . . .   [c. 86]

As he announces the section's title Pound throws a fragmentary yet coherent light upon it by way of Electra's "resistance," of a vindication of his doing that admits no discussion ("All . . . is as it should have been"), and of the economic "benevolence" of the leader—the author of the "Programma di Verona" (see c. 78), and Alexander who distributes credit. This benevolence is in fact the implicit guiding theme of c. 86, which opens with a handful of novel quotations on the subject, from Bismarck ("No more wars after '70"), Margaret of Savoia ("Dummheit, nicht Bosheit"; and, perhaps, "Sono tutti eretici, Santo Padre, / ma non sono cattivi"),[8] and Albert Reeder Ballin, 1857–1918 ("wd/ indeed have stuffed all Hamburg with grain")—and goes on with the first and most extensive display of Talleyrand's political acumen. The same cluster, with an additional reference to the "three years peace" which (we are told) Europe owes "to young Windsor" (c. 89), recurs just before the "Rock Drill" passage quoted earlier, and is joined further on by a similar sequence, only more "economic" in turn, which is juxtaposed with a new pass at Roosevelt ("HE talks"):

> "What" (Cato speaking) "do you think of
> .   murder?"
> But some Habsburg or other
>   ploughed his Imperial furrow,
> And old Theresa's road is still there in Belgium.
> Tree-shadowed
>   and her thalers
>   were current in Africa,
>
>   .   .   .
>
> Cleopatra wrote of her coinage.
>   (Joseph two, verify? ploughed his furrow)
> Up out of Tuscany, Leopoldine.   [c. 86]

As usual usury as murder[9] is weighed against nature's increase—the fertility which attends the sovran's prowess and plowing (P.

8. Later translated as, "They are all prots YR HOLINESS, / but not bad."

9. Cf. *Oro e lavoro, SPr* 347: "In Cato's *De Re Rustica* we find the following piece of dialogue: 'And what do you think of usury?' 'What do *you* think of murder?' "

having in mind both the Chinese emperors and Mussolini), and
the natural economy which builds roads and channels that last
("This canal goes still to TenShi"—c. 49), as old Maria Theresa's
tree-shadowed road—the qualification almost succeeding in converting the rock-drill to poetry. But the whole passage has a certain grace, and exhibits the customary structural acumen: Maria
Theresa's coinage brings back, from the first page of the previous
canto, Cleopatra; the "benevolence" of her son, the great enlightened autocrat Joseph II, is accounted for by way of the "Tuscan" background of his father and uncle (Leopold II of c. 44);
and the sequel happily clears the ground of all "natural" justification of war:

> "We don't hate anybody."
>   Quoted Konody,
> "We fight when our Emperor says so."
>   (Austrians 1914)
> "Decent chaps" (Schwartz '43)
>   "a shame we have to fight 'em."
> Mais le prussien!
>   Le prussien
>   c'est un chic homme."
> Said the aged femme de ménage with four teeth out.   [c. 86]

These are all instances of ling-as-benevolence, naive in the extreme, but nonetheless moving and rather funny, as when France
and Germany are reconciled at last thanks to the aged femme de
ménage, who—in Pound's strangely democratic world—takes her
place near Marshal Bismarck and the Emperor. Having brought
to an end on this note the canto's long central excursus (87 lines),
Pound returns to the *Shu Ching* at about the point where he had
left off (the first part of the canto covers pp. 305–21 and
361–85), pausing at the following:

Ce n'est pas que le ciel soit trop sévère; mais c'est l'homme lui-même
qui se précipite dans l'infortune. [*Latin version:* Non coelum non in
medio stat; sed homo stat in sorte (infelici).] Si les châtiments du ciel
n'étaient pas souverainement justes, jamais sous le ciel le peuple
n'aurait un bon gouvernement. [pp. 388–89]

This becomes a springboard for the introduction, as usual quite
sudden, of a theme supported (like *ling*/sensibility, *te*/téchne,
ching/reverence, and *chiao*/Sagetrieb) by a Chinese character, the
relevance of which is suggested by the type, which is nearly as
large as that of *ling*:

> non coelum non in medio
>   but man is under Fortuna
> ? that is a forced translation?
>   La donna che volgo
> Man under Fortune,
>   CHÊN⁴ [*chen*]
> Iou Wang, 770 . . .
>   killed by barbarians   [c. 86]

We realize that in these Chinese cantos Pound is preparing an entirely new palette for his final ascent, somewhat as he had done
thirty years earlier: "I *have to* get down all the colours or elements I want for the poem. Some perhaps too enigmatically and
abbreviatedly. I hope, heaven help me, to bring them into some
sort of design and architecture later" (*L* 189: 1922). He continues to write a poem projected towards the future, in a state of
becoming, increasingly quick: themes are filed down to single
words and characters (as early as c. 51 the precise definition is
capsuled into *cheng ming*), which function as novel indices of
thought complexes so far lacking in the atomistic definition
Pound seeks, a formulation maximally charged with meaning but
also reminiscent of the slogans of advertising. It is strange only
that, while undertaking all of this, Pound should still suggest to
visitors and correspondents that c. 100 will be the last.

The motif of Fortune is referred to, as an example of the continuity obtaining between paganism and Christianity, in a footnote
to *P&T*: "There is a magnificent thesis to be written on the role
of Fortune, coming down through the Middle Ages, from pagan
mythology, via Seneca, into Guido and Dante" (98). A few years
earlier, in the "Lingua Toscana" chapter of *SR*, Pound had
quoted the opening lines of a "canzone to Fortune" erroneously
attributed to Cavalcanti, along with Rossetti's translation; in

1930 he included the first verse in his edition of the *Rime;* eventually, in 1949, the whole canzone was edited by Olga Rudge in *Tre canzoni di Guido Cavalcanti, con i facsimili dei manoscritti senesi* (Gallup B27)—and Pound maintained that it was "certainly authentic" in a footnote added to "Cavalcanti."

> Io son la donna che volgo la ruota
> Sono colei, che tolgo e do stato
> Ed è sempre biasmato
> A torto el modo mio da voi mortali.   [SR 111][10]

With these elements in hand we can decipher the "thesis" which Pound has finally decided to write for himself, taking the further step (unwarranted even to him: "?that is a forced translation?") of reading as Fortune the Chinese *ming* ("sors" in Couvreur; "fate" in Mathews),[11] and, then, quite unexpectedly, identifying her with a character which does not occur at this point of the *Shu,* namely *chen,* "to shake, to excite, to tremble" (*M* 315). Possibly Pound came to this sign by accident, as on the same page (389) of Couvreur's *Chou King* there is a character (*M* 1167) which looks somewhat like it, and was arrested by its eloquent simplicity, for *chen* is the sum of two radicals: above, "rain" (as in *ling*), a symmetric glyph which he may have taken for a vertical section of Fortuna's wheel; below, "time." Combining again dictionary meaning and graphic content, Pound produces the tag, "timing the thunder" (c. 91; thunder = shake + rain), a condensation of "rain also is of the process" (c. 74). Fortuna gives assurance that grief is not meaningless, but according to pattern: "All, that has been, is as it should have been." She is not the blind and wicked agent many believe her to be (according to Pseudo-Caval-

---

10. "I am the woman who turneth the wheel, / I am who giveth and taketh away. / And I am blamed alway / And wrongly, for my deeds, by ye, mankind."—Rossetti's translation, quoted ibid. For a critical text see Natalino Sapegno, ed., *Poeti minori del Trecento* (Milano: Ricciardi, 1952), p. 435.

11. *M* 4537. Cf. c. 85: "Cdn't see it (ming) could / [*ming*] extend to the people's subsidia / that it was in some fine way tied up with the people." This for Couvreur's: "Dans sa folle présomption, [the last emperor of Hsia] se persuada que le roi du ciel ne lui retirerait jamais son mandat, et n'aida pas le peuple à se procurer des ressources" (pp. 312–13). Heaven's mandate, *ming,* follows upon sensibility to the needs of the people.

canti) but a benevolent enforcer of process: "Splendour, it all coheres." Pound's little thesis, to be continued, has (as we gather) nothing academic, but answers the urge of "a man of no fortune" to see meaning in his plight and enlist the protection of mother goddesses half Romance and half pseudo-Confucian: Immaculata/*hsien*, Fortuna/*chen*.

In c. 85 Pound reports Wu Wang's instructions to his soldiers before the momentous battle of Mu (B.C. 1122), "and do not chase fugitives," suggesting that this benevolence bears on the sensibility which brings to power the new dynasty; likewise c. 86 closes with one Pe-ch'in warning a few decades later the men he has "mobilized against insurrection," not to "traipse into peoples' fields / chasing fugitives." [12] Pe-ch'in's balance is contrasted with America preparing for the last war: Roosevelt who, at conference, does not allow anybody else to speak [13]—and, " 'hysteric presiding over it all' '39" (P. does not realize that the reader can scarcely help thinking that by 1939 he was quite hysterical himself). The quotations lead up to the breaking out of war, Pound insisting that this is part of the timeless war which is his subject, and ushering us rather elegantly with this statement into the third "Chinese" canto, which leaves the *Shu Ching* for a wider look at Poundland:

> Bellum cano perenne . . .   [c. 86]

> . . . between the usurer and any man who
> wants to do a good job
> (perenne)
> without regard to production—
> a charge
> for the use of money or credit.

12. See *Chou King*, pp. 285, 394. In both instances the leader makes it clear that the soldiers are not to chase (kill) fugitives not for humanitarian reasons but because he wants live slaves. P. disregards this to enforce the benevolence theme.

13. On 24 November 1954 P. wrote Scheiwiller that "the type for the HE [i.e., F.D.R.] must be high, but slim, some ridiculous font." He was trying, with his customary graphic experimentation, to suggest his contempt for the man who had committed the unpardonable sin of ignoring him. That all of this is the product of an unbalanced mind is hardly questionable.

> "Why do you want to
> "—perché si vuol mettere—
>   your ideas in order?"
>   Date '32
> Or Grock: Où ça?
>   (J'ai une idée.)
>   Grock: Où ça?
>   Berchtold as if been blown up by dynamite,
> Calm on the surface.
>   If I had known more then,
>   cd/ have asked him,
> as Varchi—one wanting the facts.   [c. 87]

Again Pound introduces himself both as poet ("cano") and as specialist in world affairs, the shrewd seeker—(like Varchi, who sought out Lorenzino—c. 5) of firsthand information from such makers of history as Mussolini ("he did not use *voi* if my memory is correct") [14] and Leopold Berchtold, a key figure in the Austrian declaration of war of 1914—the latter, admittedly, a lost opportunity to find out more about the nature of war. At any rate he puts his ideas in order to the extent of providing a broken definition of usury, "A charge for the use of purchasing power, levied without regard to production," [15] that is, without regard to the doctrine of Mencius (3A.3, "the great chapter"—c. 87) that taxes should be in proportion to the harvest—to the "seasons." But the whole passage, like all the later cantos, is in fact suggestive of a consciousness "blown up by dynamite," which pauses in the midst of its pseudo-history for a characteristically bewildered Poundian joke: to the small clown who says he has an idea, Grock answers: "Où ça?" The two clowns, Mussolini and Grock, have this in common: their question explodes a commonplace and invites further enquiry. At least, this is what Pound suggests, whereas it is clear that Mussolini's punch line, "Why do

14. To Vanni Scheiwiller, 28 March 1956. But when P. had his one interview with Mussolini, at the Ministry of Foreign Affairs on 30 January 1933, the Duce had not yet come upon the brilliant idea of eliminating the third-person address form, "lei," from the Italian language, for the sake of the more "Roman" "voi." See *Carta da visita, SPr* 335.

15. The definition has been clumsily introduced as a footnote to c. 45 in recent New Directions printings of the *Cantos*.

you want to put your ideas in order?," is but the product of a mechanical irrationalism, reminiscent of the ugly nonsense that he and his fellows (like the Rossoni mentioned in the *Cantos*) were wont to utter in Parliament, as upon the one occasion on which Antonio Gramsci spoke there.[16]

In this canto, very representative of the climate of *RD,* of which it begins to define with some fullness the central nodes, Pound goes on from the usury theme (which, like the references to John Randolph and James Buchanan, anticipates the economic matter of the subsequent American diptych) to his religious notions, or to "the mythologies" which alone, he tells us, can "establish clean values" (again, we suspect that this "cleanliness" is worse than much "dirt"). He lists the initiates:

"Cogitatio, meditatio, contemplatio." / Wrote Richardus, and Dante read him. / Centrum circuli.

Y Yin, Ocellus, Erigena: / "All things are lights." / Greek tags in Erigena's verses.

In short, the cosmos continues / and there is an observation somewhere in Morrison. / leading to Rémy? [c. 87]

—and hints at visionary experiences he and others have undergone:

> Baccin said: I planted that
>   tree, and *that* tree (ulivi)
> Monsieur F. saw his mentor
>   composed almost wholly of light.
> (Windeler's vision: his letter file
>   the size of 2 lumps of sugar,
> but the sheet legible. Santa Teresa . . .
> Butchers of lesser cattle, their villain the grain god.
> Fell between horns, but up . . .
>   and the murmur: "salta sin barra,"
> There is no such play for a goat.
> Tho' Mr Paige has described Ligurian butchery,

16. 16 May 1925. See Giansiro Ferrata and Niccolò Gallo, eds., *2000 pagine di Gramsci* (Milano: Il Saggiatore, 1964), pp. 748–61. Gramsci was arrested in 1926, and died, a prisoner, in 1937.

And the hunting tribes require some preparation.
Mont Ségur, sacred to Helios,
        and for what had been, San Bertrand de Comminges.   [c. 87]

Vision is granted to agricultural society (Baccìn is a S. Ambrogio peasant) and denied to nomads, who are "butchers of lesser cattle" (e.g., goats), and enemies of agriculture and of the grain god.[17] This is possibly the first intimation (significantly coupled with a reference to the Cathars of Montségur) of the metamorphosis of Pound's long-standing agricultural passion, and of *RD*'s "reverence for the powers of vegetation," into a sort of vegetarianism, presented as Pythagorean but chiefly reminiscent of the sickly "cleanliness" of *Parsifal* (and of Joséphin Péladan). Leitmotifs, vegetarianism, and anti-Semitism appear to be the three chief points of contact between Pound and that incomparably greater artist, Wagner. (Both also held unorthodox anticapitalist views.) It is most likely that, when speaking of nomads and Hyksos, Pound meant the Jews, holding them accountable, as other anti-Semites do, for their condition of migrating money-changers rather than farmers.

This longish passage, we note, suggests as usual a man musing out loud, in a fashion perhaps more condensed than in *PC* but finally quite clear, as long as we read with the rather unnatural attention demanded by Pound, who, as we have seen, will state a basic theme in one word. Thus the bullfight is neatly distinguished from the killing of goats, and the Ligurian butchers are in turn cleared on the evidence provided by D. D. Paige, the editor of *L*. We gather that the nomad does not fully perceive and love his world, and cannot therefore make art (which, Vlaminck tells us a few pages back, "is local"—however, P. was also a wanderer of sorts)—whereas Baccin is familiar with every tree he has planted and watched as it grew. Pound goes on:

            "Wherever"
    said Frobenius "we find these drawings, we
        find water at not more than 6 feet,
    And the headless clay lions leave place for the head."

17. For Windeler's vision see the Postscript to Gourmont, *PD* 211.

Squirrils white, perhaps before a hard winter, oak cats,
Indians say: when high weeds.
As the water-bug casts a flower on stone
                    nel botro,   [*in the pool*]
One interaction. Tê   [*te*]   interaction. A shadow?   [c. 87]

In the farmer's cosmos things interact, that is, they stand to one
another in the kind of spatial relation that obtains among the
segments of Pound's verse. The drawings import (to the structural enquirer—see ch. 5) the nearness of water; the water-bug
makes flower-like (rose-like?) shadows of light, water, and rock
(as P. had noted during the war); [18] eye, heart, and *téchne* com-
bine in the perfect virtue, *te*. These relationships are the
"shadows" which are the stuff of "our science."

More extensive information as to this community of "scientists" is to be found in the central passage of the canto, already
quoted in part in the earlier discussion of *ching* (ch. 4):

and the squirmers plunder men's mind,
          wanting all men cut down to worm-size.
"A few" said Jean C.
                    "gros légumes."
in pochi,
          causa motuum,
                    pine seed splitting cliff's edge.
Only sequoias are slow enough.
          BinBin "is beauty."
"Slowness is beauty.":
          from the
                    [*san:* "three"]   San
                    [*ku:* "lonely"]   Ku
                                        to Poictiers.

18. In the lines he sent Katue Kitasono on 12 March 1941 (which also mention Jannequin, San Pantaleone [of c. 76], and a black cat): "The water-bug's mittens show on the
bright rock below him"—P. adding: "I wonder if it is clear that I mean the shadow of the
'mittens'? and can you ideograph it; very like petals of blossom" (L 384). In cs. 87 and 91
P. was able to include the latter perception in the line. "Nel botro" may be a reminiscence
of Enrico Pea's *Moscardino*, translated by P. in 1941. See Scheiwiller's edition of P.'s
translation (Milano, 1956), p. 44; and Zapponi 122 (where it is compared with the original).

> The tower wherein, at one point, is no shadow,
>   and Jacques de Molay, is where?
> and the "Section," the proportions,
>   lending, perhaps, not at interest, but resisting.
> Then false fronts, barocco.   [c. 87]

Predictably, we have on the one hand the "total war on CON-
TEMPLATIO," led by "quelques gros légumes," [19] and vividly suggested by the new, half-rhyming, phrasing, and by the suggestion
that men are robbed of their minds—and on the other hand the
subtle but powerful seed-force of the "few" who (in the words of
Machiavelli P. has been quoting since 1912) truly "live." These
recognize one another in the "slowness" of millennia which only
three-thousand-year-old sequoias can compass: from the "Three
Solitaries" or *San Ku* appointed by Chen Wang (11th century
B.C.) to "illuminate the action of heaven and earth" (*Chou King*,
p. 333), and whom we should probably associate with the "tree
of heaven" at the Center where things cast no shadow—to those
other watchers of shadows who built the room in the Palace of
Justice of Poitiers (12th century A.D.) in which a similar phenomenon is said to occur. The latter Pound links with the Tem-
plars, who have left us many arcanely luminous monuments (like
Segovia's Chapel of the True Cross), and who were suppressed
by Philip the Fair on account of their economic power. (Jacques
de Molay, last Great Master of the Order, was burned at the
stake in Paris in 1314; Yeats, before P., demanded "vengeance"
for him in "Meditations in Time of Civil War.") On the strength
of the interaction of good art and good economy (also mentioned
in *K* 16, where P. refers to the Poitiers building), Pound conjec-
tures that the Templar bankers were distributors of credit ("Was
De Molay making loans without interest?"—c. 87), and goes on
to point out the consequences wrought upon European art by the
suppression of the religious-economic vision: the " *'section d'or'*
. . . that gave the churches . . . the clear lines and proportions"
("Cavalcanti," *LE* 154—so the "Section" in the title of *RD* has
architectonic implications, even as P.'s "proportions" have a mu-

19. Cf. Jean Cocteau, *Antigone,* as quoted by P. in "Jean Cocteau Sociologist" (1935),
SPr 436. Laurence Binyon's statement about beauty is quoted in *K* 18.

sical-ethical bearing) gives way to "false fronts, barocco," that is
to signs untrue (in P.'s view) to structure—to the primary and
natural code which is the true source of mystical architecture,
and which is spoken of in the subsequent lines, which we may
now go over again:

> "We have," said Mencius, "but phenomena."
> monumenta. In nature are signatures
>   needing no verbal tradition,
> oak leaf never plane leaf. John Heydon.
>   Σελλοί sleep there on the ground
> And old Jarge held there was a tradition,
>   that was not mere epistemology.
> Mohamedans will remain—naturally—unconverted
> If you remove houris from Paradise   [c. 87]

The leaf is a sign, a phenomenon, that does not deceive as to the
nature of the seed. And this tradition of sincerity the chosen symbol of which are "the forces of vegetation" cannot be suppressed,
even as the sensuous houris cannot be removed from the Maho-
medan's paradise: so much is imported here by the cultures of
China, Provence, Greece (the Selli who in the *Trachiniae* decipher
the messages of the "polyglot" [see c. 95] oak of Zeus), England
(the Neoplatonist Heydon, but also Laurence Binyon, who translated Dante, with P.'s assistance, and was much concerned with
the Orient), and America (George, or "Jarge," Santayana, who
had taken a friendly interest in P.'s enquiry, and had recently
died). It is an ideogram which picks up themes as old as the
poem (Greece, China, and Provence, are—we remember—already
aligned in cs. 4 and 23), with a certain simplicity which prepares
us for later more complex ventures.

"In short, the cosmos continues." Pound mourns (as in the
close of this canto) his many lost Sikandars (or Alexanders), yet
he is confident that a renaissance, both in the sphere of poetry
and in that of history, is in the offing, and this is not only the
sorry revanchism of the fascist (though it is also this). Certainly
RD is eloquent proof that his poetic cosmos continues and is renewed, like "the faint green in spring time," associated in this

canto with the *jih hsin* / make-it-new motto, which now, appropriately enough, reenters the poem.

A dramatic splice transfers us unhesitatingly from China to the
United States, or from the textual field of the *Shu* and its gloss to
another Book of Annals, Thomas Hart Benton's *Thirty Years'
View*, the intelligent and often compelling chronicle of thirty
years of American political life (1820–50), and the eponymous
text of cs. 88–89. Senator Benton is the perfect Poundian historian insofar as he participates in a position of some relevance in
the events which he records, and insofar as he champions the
populist and anti-monopoly reforms of Jackson and Van Buren,
already dealt with (in the wake of the latter's *Autobiography*) in
c. 37. Canto 89 vindicates its source as follows: "I need add
nothing, wrote Van Buren, to the description by Col. Benton"—a
reminder of the footnote to c. 85: "Kung said he had added
nothing." It is in fact Benton's voice that greets us at the gates of
the "nuevo mundo" of c. 88:

> It was Saturday the 1st day of April, toward noon,
> the Senate not being that day in session . . .
>   came to my room at Brown's asking was I
> Mrs Clay's blood-relation?   [c. 88]

From the opening sentence of Benton's Volume 1, chapter 26
(1826), Pound has omitted the decisive words, "that Mr Randolph" ("came to my room" etc.), thus assimilating his new hero
to the impersonal subject notably absent in the first line of the
poem: "And then went down to the ship." John Randolph of
Roanoke, the subject of a biography by Henry Adams, hostile to
John Quincy Adams and to his Secretary of State Henry Clay,
and to the Second Bank of the United States, an opposer of slav-
ery because unprofitable ("masnatosque liberavit"—c. 89), seeks
out Benton on April Fools' Day and asks him with much decency
to be his second in the forthcoming duel with Clay (whom Randolph has charged with forging an official letter). It is an ambience both cordial and Jamesian, and Pound, detained on the
very site of the events, is content to dwell on its precisely re-

corded details in a long narrative passage truly unusual at this late stage of the *Cantos:*

> Right bank, which is in Virginia *
>   above bridge of the Little Falls
> @ ten paces [20]
>   * where there was a law
>   against duelling.
> I alone knew how he meant to avoid that.
> I went to Clay's on the Friday, the youngest child
>   went to sleep on the sofa.
> Mrs Clay, as always since the death of her daughter,
>   the picture of desolation
> But calm and conversable.
>   Clay and I parted at midnight.
> Saturday, Randolph's, Georgetown,
> Could not ask him
>   but mentioned the child asleep on the sofa.
> He said:
>   "I shall do nothing to disturb its sleep
>   or the repose of its mother,"   [c. 88]

Randolph has secretly resolved not to fire on Clay, holding that he need not answer in private for a charge he has made as a speaker for the people. Benton guesses his decision, but can satisfy himself only indirectly, by referring to Clay's child. Randolph's answer corroborates Benton's surmise. Among the watchers of shadows engaged in the fight against usury a very few words will carry much import. (James is mentioned in the close of the previous canto.) To his friends Randolph wants to leave some special coins as a memento, and of these he possesses himself in the course of the amusing scene that Pound goes on to recount, which makes clear his attitude towards the bank system. When the duel (which will leave both contenders unhurt) is about to begin Pound interposes abruptly a resumé of the timeless war to which it belongs, first in an American setting (drawing upon the *Introductory Text Book* of 1939), then in that of world his-

20. Thus in the typescript (Scheiwiller, Milan). The lines refer to the site of the duel, on the bank of the Potomac.

tory ("That these are the Histories / OR / Thus recapitulate:"),
telling us of Ch'eng T'ang (the emperor who wrote *jih hsin* on
his bathtub, and who "opened the copper mine," quarrying the
metal of Venus), of Antoninus Pius (c. 42 etc.), of Erigena, St.
Ambrose, Thales,[21] Baccin, and so on. The recapitulation done,
he returns to Benton and refers openly to his source: the second
part of the canto transcribes in the customary atomic fashion
Benton's impassioned speeches against the Tariff, the renewal of
the Bank's charter, and an emission of paper money which he
deems illegal,[22] and closes with the theme of Fortuna, offering for
our consideration the relationship between a set of playing cards
and the days of man's life, "fifty 2 weeks in 4 seasons" (cf. the
1st of April). In 1833 Jackson was to pass to action, removing
funds from the Bank to the "pet banks," and was to be censured
for this (on Clay's motion) by the Senate—a resolution later ex-
punged from the record, as recorded in the close of the following
canto.

This second American canto continues, and enlarges upon, the
subject of the previous one in a fashion which may seem chaotic
because of the fragmentary writing, but which a more careful
reading shows to be worked out with some care.[23] At any rate
Pound does not cease, even at the doors or in the recesses of his
paradise, to recount the history which he believes to have been
unjustly forgotten, clearly indicating why this is germane to his
"vision," which seeks to be collective and grounded in society's
economic history: in 1834 "public debt was extinguished" (an
event glossed with a Chinese phrase extrapolated from the *Ta-
hsüeh*, see *GD* x 23), and Jackson and his allies are promoted
among "the founders, gazing at the mounts of their cities"
(c. 16):

21. Cf. *Introduzione alla natura economica degli S.U. d'America* (1944), *SPr* 176, 181.

22. 1828–31. See *Thirty Years' View: A History of the Working of the American Government for Thirty Years, from 1820 to 1850* (New York, 1854–56), Vol. 1, Chs. 34, 56,
60, 64.

23. An early draft of several passages may be found in E. P., *Versi prosaici* (Caltanissetta:
Sciascia, 1959).

And in the time of Mr Randolph, Mr Benton, Mr Van Buren
   he, Andy Jackson
      POPULUM AEDIFICAVIT
which might end this canto, and rhyme with
      Sigismundo.
Commander Rogers observed that the sea was sprinkled with
      fragments of West India fruit
and followed that vestige.
      Giles talked and listened,
more listened, and did not read.
      Young Jessie did not forward dispatches
so Frémont proceeded toward the North West and
      we ultimately embraced Californy   [c. 89]

The canto does not finish as it very well could, but goes on to
link the enlightened rulers with explorers like John Charles
Frémont, who, despite dispatches recalling him ("not forwarded"
by his wife Jessie, Benton's daughter), reconnoitered in 1843–44
Oregon, crossed Sierra Nevada, and descended into California:

He proceeded—soon encountered deep snows which impeded his progress upon the high lands—descended into a low country to the left (afterwards known to be the Great Basin, from which no water issues to
any sea)—skirted an enormous chain of mountain on the right, luminous with glittering white snow—saw strange Indians, who mostly
fled—found a desert—no Buena Ventura: and death from cold and fam-
ine staring him in the face.[24]

With Frémont the Homeric archetype of the *Cantos* is again
brought to light: Ulysses, who saw many men and cities
(*"d'anthrópon íden* / Frémont, with small arms and one howit-
zer"—c. 89), stands behind the explorer Pound, who seeks (as he
tells us again) to put his ideas in order. After reperusing, in the
first part of c. 89, Benton's speeches already quoted in the previous pages and other passages of *Thirty Years' View,* he
presents, at truly rock-drilling pace, his utopia of local art and
economy:

24. Benton, *Thirty Years' View,* Vol. 2, Ch. 134, p. 579. Cf. also Chs. 164 and 176–77.

"Benton has begun understanding me"
                                              (Randolph)
In Venice the bread price was stable,
        ship models still there in Danzig.
Alex said: set up the tables,
              any soldier's note will be paid.
Gold was under the Pontifex,
              Caesar usurped that.
Bezants were stable till Dandolo broke into Stamboul,
        there had been some arab uneasiness.
The forgery was from ignorance,
              Valla found it.
12 to one, Roma, and about half that at Karachi.
        And the Portagoose, as we cease not to mention,
              uprooted spice trees
Orage remarked upon the "recession of power"   [c. 89]

Instead of absconding, as in the age of usury, power must become the visible sign: self-government (Venice, the Hansa) and
distribution of wealth unfettered by monopoly (of the kind enforced at Goa by the Portuguese). In accord with an inclination
already noted but more prominent at this time, Pound is willing
to entrust the ultimate power to a pontifex-king, that is, to a man
of religion rather than of politics and coercion (in this view Caesar is a usurper of the sacred role): "that there be / no coercion,
either by force or by fraud, / That is the law's purpose, or should
be" (c. 89). The usual liberal position, willing to surrender to
charismatic power as long as bourgeois "freedom" is preserved,
is at the bottom of the ideological platform of the later cantos,
which is narrower than ever but also passionately bent on providing an "orderly" contribution, on the model of Benton and
Valla. (Yet note that, according to P., Valla, by exploding the
"Donation of Constantine," brings to light the ignorance of a
pontiff unaware of his rightful claim upon gold. That is, P. is
more royalist than the king.) [25] The poet wants to join the

25. Cf. a passage in D. G. Bridson's "An Interview with Ezra Pound" (p. 179), in which
P. (whose conversation was often modelled on his verse, and vice versa) goes over the
ground already covered in the lines under discussion: "The Roman Empire worked on the
principle of the light and the heavy [see c. 106], gold against silver, twelve to one in Rome

"peace" effort ("Without historic black-out / they cannot maintain perpetual war"), and is made to pay for his protest as
dearly as some of his fellows: "Tasso, Kidd, Raleigh, all jailed."
    The other explorer, Frémont, also faced a court-martial on ac-
count of his enterprise and his disrespect for his "betters"—a fact
Pound may have in mind when mentioning, in connection with
him, Fortuna, who "taketh away" ("Che tolgo lo stato"—c. 89).
But the goddess may also restore what has been lost, as when
"*Athéne* swung the hung jury," the jury which sat at Orestes'
trial. The justice sought by Pound for himself and other explorers
is not "impartial" but inclined to leniency even when the vote of
the people's jury (as ours in this matter of P.) must remain fifty-
fifty. We need these traitorous explorers to point the way to the
paradise which they may not be able to enter. So much is suggested by the final lines of this American diptych, in which
Frémont and the man who initiated Pound to the Orient, Ernest
Fenollosa (buried at Lake Biwa), are made to stand at the threshold of the "mountainous" heaven of cs. 90–95:

> And when "EXPUNGED," A.J. sent back the bullet,
>   which is, I suppose, part of parliamentary history
> dull or not, as you choose to regard it.
>   I want Frémont looking at mountains
>   or, if you like, Reck, at Lake Biwa,   [c. 89]26

To admit, after twenty-five pages of Benton, that parliamentary
history may be dull, is a typically Poundian sleight of hand, even
as this is a typically assured close—the final comma amounting to
a signature. (Also the last line of c. 81, in its earliest and perhaps
preferable reading, closes with a comma: "all in the diffidence
that faltered,.") It is interesting to note that Pound often takes

---

and six and a half to seven in Karachi—tipping that little balance and milking the public.
But the Empire stood and it stood by a balance between central power and local good
management. Gold was under the Pontifex—there was not the least need to forge the Donation of Constantine; it was done in ignorance because all the Pope needed to do was to
claim the pontificial right over gold. Caesar usurped it."

26. Michael Reck (a visitor, as we gather, to Fenollosa's tomb) is the author of *Ezra
Pound: A Close-Up* (New York: McGraw-Hill, 1967).

leave of us at the end of his cantos with a handful of open-ended, dream-like sentences, in which all attempts at reference trail off into an intimation of the universal possibilities of human experience.

9. In the Sibyl's Cave

You will find to the left of the house of Hades a wellspring,
and by the side of this standing a white cypress.
You must not even go close to this wellspring; but also
you will find another spring that comes from the lake of Memory
cold water running, and there are those who stand guard before it.
You shall say: "I am the child of earth and the starry heavens,
but my generation is of the sky. You yourself know this.
But I am dry with thirst and am dying. Give me then quickly
the water that runs wild out of the lake of Memory."
And they themselves will give you to drink from the sacred water,
and afterwards you shall be lord among the rest of the heroes.

—Inscription found at Petelia, tr. Richmond Lattimore.

Just as in the Jefferson, Siena, and Pisa sequences, the climax of
Rock-Drill occurs in the middle part of the section, in the remarkable diptych of cantos 90–91, of which the former is in fact
the sequence's still point and center of balance, whereas canto
91, more extensive, arresting, and problematic, comes as a bewildering flood of materials old and new, and is continuously send-
ing the reader elsewhere, into the poem's past and chiefly into its
future—the four "paradiso" cantos to follow, which are equally
composite and stirring in places, and the vast and disconsolate
reaches of *Thrones*.

Whereas at Pisa Pound had recovered the modes of tradition
under pressure from tragedy and affection, here his method is
more forbidding, fitful, cerebral, and makes for a text atonally
composed of broken-off micro-elements, to which, as we have
learned, the reader must attend with unprecedented care. In fact
the forty pages of cs. 90–95 may be taken as a single new *Canzone d'amore*, modelled upon Cavalcanti's (and Dante's) *poesis
docta* and on Provençal *trobar clus,* as these "medievalisms" may

259

be perceived from a fin de siècle vantage point, though this is up-
dated and "hardened" through the uncompromising 1950s poetics of the Rock—as in the deflated Swinburnian litany at the
center of c. 90. The haphazard exoticism à la Péladan which
inspired this Joycean feast of heteroclite esoteric matters (often
retrieved from P.'s remote contacts and readings in theosophy—
Yeats, G. R. S. Mead), will thus occasionally fall into the background leaving us to confront the sharply outlined world of
Averroistic Guido, encyclopedic Dante (the *Convivio* is made
much of in c. 93), and secretive troubadours. Following the practice of these latter (as outlined in *P&T* 89), Pound addresses his
canzone of paradise "to those who are already expert." But this,
ironically, may be held of all communication—and we have seen
that Pound, far from seeking—like Mallarmé—exclusiveness on
principle, truly wants to make his readers aware of experiences
attainable only "by an attrition of follies," if they are not to be
misrepresented.[1] In fact the difficulties of *RD,* as always in
Pound but unlike most modern poetry, are only of the surface—
indeed his writing is often so nakedly transparent that too hard a
look will evaporate the poetry: we must never allow ourselves to
overlook the concision and quiet humor of this text, which has
the quality of a subtle poliphony. (Incidentally, when Scheiwiller's first edition of *RD* came out, P. was delighted that the book
could fit into a pocket and be carried around—like the small Petrarch of Renaissance wooers.)

Far from being overly esoteric, Pound is most often making us
uncomfortable by being too explicit about his agenda, his un-
flagging engagement to bring about "movements" (or counter-
movements) in the social world. One of the chief limits of the
Washington cantos, as against the Pisan ones, is the deeper ideological coloring. Yet a serious concern for social issues is the
defining trait of many major artists, and surely Pound's engagement, whatever our quarrel with its particular type, is also a

---

1. "Science is hidden. The layman can only attain conic sections by labour. He can only
attain the secretum by greater labour, by an attrition of follies, carried on until perception
is habit. Every knowledge in our time has its outer courts and its portals. The pons
asinorum is but one bridge of many"—*K* 22.

thing of value, to which we owe not only his less savory pronouncements but also the force of his entire *œuvre*.

The theme that vision must go into action is the ideal (but not
"merely epistemological"—c. 87) cornerstone of *RD*. I Yin
rouses young T'ai chia to a contemplation not to be dissevered
from *téchne*—indeed the imperial pupil is told to consider the interaction of *téchne* and heart or self, the Socratic *seautón*. Richard of St. Victor, quoted on contemplation in this cluster of c. 85,
restates the theme in the epigraph of c. 90, which also serves as
an introduction to this entire six-canto canzone, and spells out
from the outset the difference between Pound's impassioned elysium and, for instance, Eliot's *Quartets,* ushered in by two metaphysical Heraclitean captions. In order to show how it is that the
Holy Spirit may be understood as the love of Father and Son
(*Quomodo Spiritus Sanctus Est Amor Patris et Filii*), Richard
avails himself, as is his custom, of a psychological simile:
"Animus humanus amor non est, sed ab ipso amor procedit, et
ideo seipso non diligit, sed amore qui a seipso procedit."[2] The
Father, though one with the Holy Ghost, may be distinguished
from the latter just as the human soul can be differentiated from
the love it emanates, through which alone the soul can—transi-
tively—love. In Poundian words, amorous contemplation is not
introverted and narcissistic, but extroverted and active, always
attended by signs, traces, *téchne*. Dante ("out of St Victor"—
c. 85) put this same theological idea and its practical lesson in
one of *Paradiso*'s memorable incipits:

> Looking upon his Son with the Love
>   that the One and the Other eternally breathe forth,
>   the first and ineffable Power
> made with such order all that revolves
>   in mind and space, that he who contemplates this
>   cannot but taste of Him.   [*Par.* x. 1–6]

In another passage of *P&T*, the essay written (we recall) after
the Provençal tour of 1912, and, significantly, first published in

2. *PL* cxcvi 1012. Quoted in D. James Neault, "Richard of St Victor and *Rock-Drill*,"
Paideuma, 3 (1974), 219–27.

G. R. S. Mead's theosophical quarterly *The Quest,* Pound had distinguished between the introverted contemplation of the monk and the extroverted passion of the lover, and gone on to dissociate within sexual love the "reproductive" from the "educational" ("one sort of vibration produces at different intensities, heat and light"), the latter being possibly refined in Provence to "mediumistic properties":

Did this "chivalric love," this exotic, take on mediumistic properties? Stimulated by the color or quality of emotion, did that "color" take on forms interpretive of the divine order? Did it lead to an "exteriorization of sensibility," and interpretation of the cosmos by feeling? [*P&T* 94]

A dissociation of the kind made in the essay seems to be encrypted in cs. 90–91, the first of which is predominantly concerned with ascetic contemplation, whereas the second is the luxuriant mantra (see *P&T* 97) of the Lady, both as a reproductive and a mediumistic animal. Moreover, the hazy but fresh pseudo-scientific language of *P&T*—a combination of an undergraduate acquaintance with science and of séance talk, of which Pound availed himself often (if more skillfully) in subsequent years (cf. the rose in the steel dust)—turns up to good effect in the first lines of both cantos, which present a single, if differently shaded, ecstatic experience, reaching back, through a reading of the signs or colors of *téchne,* to *seautón,* the inner self, or to *K*'s "*forma*" and "immortal *concetto.*" And vice versa:

> "From the colour the nature
>   & by the nature the sign!"
> Beatific spirits welding together
>   as in one ash-tree in Ygdrasail.
>   Baucis, Philemon.
> Castalia is the name of that fount in the hill's fold.
>   the sea below,
>   narrow beach.
> Templum aedificans, not yet marble,
>   "Amphion!"   [c. 90]

With the structural rigor we have learned to expect of him Pound subtly repeats in this prelude to the later *RD* the first bars of the section, and tells us (as noted) of sensibility and of the dynasty which is born of it, and of the emanation of the sign from inner and manifest nature as graphed by *ling* ("under the cloud / the three voices"—c. 104), the character being strongly implied. (Line 2 and *ling* are finally juxtaposed in a climactic passage of *Th.*) But these lines fit within an architecture which is vaster than *RD* and the entire *Cantos*, for they pointedly recall the poem that in 1926 Pound chose to place at the beginning of the collected *Personae*, or of his life's work—"The Tree" (1906–07):

> I stood still and was a tree amid the wood,
> Knowing the truth of things unseen before;
> Of Daphne and the laurel bow
> And that god-feasting couple old
> That grew elm-oak amid the wold.
> 'Twas not until the gods had been
> Kindly entreated, and been brought within
> Unto the hearth of their heart's home
> That they might do this wonder thing;
> Nathless I have been a tree amid the wood
> And many a new thing understood
> That was rank folly to my head before.   [P 3]

Though the language has a good deal of clarity already, we realize how direct the young poet is being about his epiphany only when we look back at the poem as readers of *RD*. We also see how faithful he has been to his central intuitions, seeking a novel way of communicating them and leaving us little doubt as to their genuineness. The somewhat undetermined "truth of things unseen before" is to be turned into the much more definite and striking "science" of "the watching of shadows"; Baucis and Philemon are to tell us of the literally "beatific," i.e. active, benevolence associated with vision and vegetation, and are to be cast as the loving ancestors of the "dynasty" one of the chief figures of which is the poet who has told their story ("Ovid . . . is one of the most interesting of all enigmas—if you grant that he was an enigma at all"—*K* 49): in the metapoetic design of c. 90 this allusion to Ovid and to metamorphosis is as significant as the invocation of "that god-feasting couple old"; finally, the trees into which the young lyricist and his symbolical parents are transformed,[3] fade into the single world-ash, Yggdrasil, as the knowing into the known, the dancer into the dance: Yggdrasil is at one time the tree of the "dynasty" which comes forth out of a stem not biblical (Jesse) put pagan, and the cosmos quickened by the inexhaustible train of correspondences as it becomes manifest to its "reader"; it is the "tree of knowledge"[4] and the Unwobbling Pivot of the Confucian canon:

That axis in the center is the great root of the universe; that harmony is the universe's outspread process (of existence).

From this root and in this harmony, heaven and earth are established in their precise modalities, and the multitudes of all creatures persist, nourished on their meridians. [*UP* ɪ 4]

Chu Hsi's note to this first chapter of the *Chung-yung,* as translated by Pound—

The main thing is to illumine the root of the process, a fountain of clear water descending from heaven immutable. The components, the bones of things, the materials are implicit and prepared in us, abundant and inseparable from us.[5]

seems to be the scriptural authority behind the transition, in itself quite logical, from Yggdrasil and Ovid to Parnassus, in the folds of which, not far from the temple of Delphi and high over the sea, Castalia pours forth its water. Like a painter of the Quattrocento or a Pre-Raphaelite follower, Pound draws a landscape which would not appear to call for gloss (cf. Botticelli's *Primavera*) and nevertheless conceals a complex Neoplatonic and contextual program. Castalia is a novel and compelling image of na-

---

3. P. is believed to have had in mind the lines in Yeats's *The Wind among the Reeds* (1899): "I have been a hazel-tree, and they hung / The Pilot Star and the Crooked Plough / Among my leaves in times out of mind" ("He thinks of his Past Greatness when a Part of the Constellations of Heaven," *Collected Poems,* p. 81).

4. "Theological taste good in Ric/s time. Animus humanus non est amor / dilexit in amore that pours from it. Tree of knowledge / error in that: RAPIT the knowledge, like Yeats always poking round seances etc/ instead of OBserving, let us say, blue jays"—P. to Boris de Rachewiltz, quoted in B. de Rachewiltz 77. This letter was written in 1954, that is at the time of the composition of *RD.*

5. *UP* ɪ 4. Here P. refers us to Ode 260 of the *Shih Ching,* the "Genesis" quoted in ch. 5.

ture bringing forth the color-sign, and of the "dynasty," for
whoso drinks of it is made a poet, or is given sensibility. But the
symbol has a yet more specific import, as we find in the "Cavalcanti" essay, where, criticizing Luigi Valli's decipherings of "the
secret language" of the Stilnovo poets, Pound recalls that the
commentary on the canzone wrongly attributed to Egidio Co-
lonna

> begins aptly for [Valli's] purpose with the secret fountain, obviously the
> source or font of tradition, the lady sends out her messengers, the first
> of whom is King Solomon, excellent for the mystic theory, but the sec-
> ond is Ovidius Naso . . . Would the eminent Aristotelian [Colonna]
> have chosen just these three men, Solomon, Ovid and Guido, as messen-
> gers from our lady of Paphos, or from the Divina Sapienza? Was Ovid
> also singing the yearning of the passive intellect for the active, and if so
> did he suspect it? [LE 179]

Pound, if I understand him, inclines to the belief that the poets
are messengers of Venus rather than of Divine Wisdom (as Valli
claimed); "Donna mi prega" would have lost much of its appeal
should the lady of the first line be an abstract entity instead of the
puella who is the poet's genius, a homely incarnation of our lady
of Paphos. However, the later Pound seems to come around in
some degree to Valli's view, and in fact we shall shortly find the
lady as Sophia or Wisdom. At any rate he will not give up Ovid,
the first of the messengers assembled around Castalia, the font of
tradition out of which c. 90 (and the following paradiso)
springs—the others being Dante, who refers to Castalia in the
ecstatic close of *Purg.* 31, and Homer, associated with the sea
and the sound it makes on the "narrow beach"—the sea which is
always somewhere in Pound's fresco:

> Castalia is the name of that fount in the hill's fold.
>   the sea below,
>   narrow beach.
> Templum aedificans, not yet marble,
>   "Amphion!"   [c. 90]

It is precisely the description of a figurative (or remotely real)
space, its features so much "there" that they can be pointed out.

A final hidden messenger may well be the author of *The Sacred Fount,* where "for perhaps the first time since about 1300 a writer has been able to deal with a sort of content wherewith Cavalcanti had been 'concerned' " (*ABR* 90).

Out of all this pouring forth there arises (by the sea, as in c. 1) the temple (perhaps Apollo's in the vicinage of Castalia), which is the very poem that Pound is in the process ("aedificans") of constructing, his song being of a kind with that of Amphion, who, wielding "the virtu of the harpe," erected the walls of Thebes. But it is a temple "not yet [of] marble"—a temple of water, wood, and sounds (the very "harmony" which is "the universe's outspread process of existence"). It is the temple as the architect may see it, "as the sculptor sees the form in the air" (c. 25)—or as the reader can follow this verse in the making and from within, on account (as P. believes) of the ideogramic method.

Building is central to the tradition of which the fountain is the symbol, and of which Pound now gives us again the capsulated account of c. 87:

> And from the San Ku   [*san*]
>   [*ku*]
>   to the room in Poitiers where one can stand
>   casting no shadow,
>   That is Sagetrieb,
>   that is tradition.
>   Builders had kept the proportion,
>   did Jacques de Molay
>   know these proportions?
> and was Erigena ours?   [c. 90]

The conversation of Sigismondo and Platina, and of Yeats and Pound ("Nothing affects these people / except our conversation"), is thematically (or algebraically) defined through the neologism "Sagetrieb" (see c. 85 and ch. 8), which covers the vast stretch of communication included between anecdote ("the oral tradition"— c. 89) and the pithy talk of the men for whom Pound believes he speaks when asking, "and was Erigena ours?"—the men who at Poitiers or in China watch the shadow cast by the gnomon, and "preserve the tradition," as Pound would have it (e.g., cf. c. 79: "So Astafieva had conserved the tradition / From Byzance and before that"). Clearly to Pound there is no distinction between knowledge and action: the proportions (of architecture and of music) which are handed down orally become inevitably manifest through signs, "monumenta." *Seautón* and *téchne* are thus placed side by side, as in the epigraph, when the object of secret knowledge becomes manifest: a female principle, timeless and amorous, but also terrible, though this it is only to those who cannot pass it on, or act upon it:

> Moon's barge over milk-blue water
> Kuthera δεινά
> Kuthera sempiterna
> Ubi amor, ibi oculus.
> Vae qui cogitatis inutile.
> quam in nobis similitudine divinae
> reperetur imago.
> "Mother Earth in thy lap"
> said Randolph
> ἠγάπησεν πολύ
> liberavit masnatos.   [c. 90]

In this Pisan cluster (Mother Earth, "Cythera egoista / But for Actaeon," the moon's barge bearing the divine planet) something has changed, and this is the insistence on the goddess's savagery (*deiná*), and the intimation that this is directed not upon "us" (as was at times the case in *PC*) but upon the "other people" of whom Eliot once spoke, upon the enemies of contemplation, the "sophists" and the "useless cogitators" ("Vae qui cogitatis inutile") of c. 85. Pound's discourse proceeds unflinchingly within this essential hubris, telling us with Richard that where there is love there also is the eye, the visible sign, and threatening such as disregard the image of the divine to be found "in nobis," within *us*,[6] or (in the words of c. 92) "turn from the manifest / overlooking the detail." In the same passage of c. 92 these defaulters are called "lice"—hence our suspicion that the quotation from Luke

---

6. "Bona voluntas . . . per quam in nobis divinae similitudinis imago reperetur"—*Benjamin Minor* 65, PL cxcvi 46. The omitted words are also relevant to the passage.

("for she loved much")[7] is being used inappropriately. (Tolstoi
once suggested that it usually is.) To the reader of the *Cantos* the
final lines import, at the side of George Randolph, the presence
of Cunizza da Romano, also a freer of slaves and (like Mary
Magdalen) a "great whore": in this instance it is the manumis-
sion that indicates the "usefulness" (P.'s customary pragmatism)
of the amorous meditation, otherwise attested by the fruitfulness
of the act of love.

Our unease in the face of this stolid "mystery" turns out to be
more than justified when, in the sequel, Cunizza and Randolph
are joined by Eva Braun and Adolf Hitler:

> Castalia like the moonlight
> > and the waves rise and fall,
> Evita, beer-halls, semina motuum,
> > to parched grass, now is rain
> not arrogant from habit,
> > but furious from perception,
> > > Sibylla,   [c. 90]

The timeless font of tradition ("Castalia like the moonlight")
gives way to the "waves" and "vortices" of history which the
Cantos seek to reconstruct. Among these variations on the theme,
or signs emanating from the nature, Pound confidently places
Nazism, of which the seeds were sown in obscure "beer halls," in
the presence of the "terrible beauty" of "Evita" (the diminutive
connotes affection; the reference to Evita Peron, if intended, is
only subsidiary). Pound defends that "furious" tempest by recalling the drought ("parched grass") against which it reacted, and
the intensity of the "perception"—or of the "sensibility"—from
which it originated (see c. 104: "Adolf furious from perception").
Fascinated by these flowers of evil he writes perhaps the most
compelling lines of the canto (the description of the storm, reminiscent of c. 7 and of *The Waste Land*), and takes them as a point
of departure for a *Laus Veneris* in which he celebrates his own
liberation, speaking also for the community which he believes he

7. Among the quotations from Richard selected by P. for Riccardo da S. Vittore, *Pensieri
sull'amore* (Milano: Scheiwiller, 1956), is "quoniam dilexit multum."

represents, and addressing his divine companion with the name
"Sibylla," which may be associated with the Delphic temple referred to in the opening, but also alludes to an obscure pamphlet
in comparative mythology, *La Sibylle,* by Thaddeus Zielinski.[8]
The chief thesis of the latter is that Christianity sprang from the
stem not of biblical but of pagan tradition—"teste David cum
Sibylla." It is also the burden of the usury canto and indicates at
this point Pound's continuing intention to make allowance in his
syncretic myth for some medieval Christianity—an ideological
justification, also, for his use of Richard in the present canto. But
the vocabulary of the syncopated litany is (as mentioned earlier)
essentially decadent, and is in fact largely borrowed from the
conjurations of "The Alchemist," a poem dated 1912 by Pound,
but not published until 1920:

> Anhes of Rocacoart, Ardenca, Aemelis,
> From the power of grass,
> From the white, alive in the seed,
> From the heat of the bud,
> From the copper of the leaf in autumn,
> From the bronze of the maple, from the sap in the bough;
> .   .   .
>
> Ysaut, Ydone, slight rustling of leaves,
> Vierna, Jocelynn, daring of spirits,
> By the mirror of burnished copper,
>   O Queen of Cypress,
> Out of Erebus, the flat-lying breadth,
> Breath that is stretched out beneath the world:
> Out of Erebus, out of the flat waste of air, lying beneath the
>   world;
> Out of the brown leaf-brown colourless
>   Bring the imperceptible cool.   [P 75–76]

The evocative juxtaposition within this Whitmanian mantra of
natural images of epiphanic clarity and of the abstract sounds of
the multitudinous names of the lady (woman to P. is always a
ritualistic, impersonal fact, whereas he responds individually to
the single leaf and breath of wind) cannot conceal the paucity of

8. 1925. An English translation was printed, at P.'s bidding, in *Edge* 2 (1956).

content and above all of humanity, which is still to be felt in the
more compact invocation of c. 90:

                              Sibylla,
          from under the rubble heap
                              m'elevasti   [*thou hast raised me*]
          from the dulled edge beyond pain,
                              m'elevasti
          out of Erebus, the deep-lying
               from the wind under the earth,
                              m'elevasti
          from the dulled air and the dust,
                              m'elevasti
          by the great flight,
                    m'elevasti,
                              Isis Kuanon
               from the cusp of the moon
                              m'elevasti
          the viper stirs in the dust,
                         the blue serpent
          glides from his rock pool   [c. 90]

What we find in this typically polyglot chant, and what was lacking in 1912, is a real experience of suffering, from which the
lady, now connoted as compassionate ("Isis Kuanon"), has
raised the poet—an experience of the death of sensibility and affection from which the terrible rain has awakened him. (In this
perspective the lines on the storm transcend the intended plea for
fascism.) Pound appears to pursue his crypto-Christian design by
picturing the Sibyl as the Immaculate who bruises the serpent's
head (said to eat the dust in Genesis); the viper, representing the
finally vanquished enemy, is contrasted with the luminous water
snake or *Natrix* of the rock pool—an image of the goddess. (P.
may be aware of the common origin of "pythoness" [see c. 104]
and "python.") Accordingly, with the following lines, a compelling instance of thematic reprise, we return to the Ligurian and
pagan-christian ambience of c. 47:

          And they take lights now down to the water
          the lamps float from the rowers

> the sea's claw drawing them outward.
> "De fondo" said Juan Ramon
>   like a mermaid, upward,
> but the light perpendicular, upward
> and to Castalia,
>   water jets from the rock
> and in the flat pool as Arethusa's
>   a hush in papyri.
> Grove hath its altar
>   under elms, in that temple, in silence
> a lone nymph by the pool.   [c. 90]

The lamps set afloat in the Tigullio on the night of 3 July are in fact intended as an homage to the Virgin. This is the first intimation of the communal ceremony brokenly presented in the last part of the canto. The present passage gathers together the theme of ascesis and the cognate theme of Castalia (reintroduced with a quotation from Jiménez, slightly at variance with the original, in which the poet states that he is "animal de fondo," an animal of the deep, rather than—as P. implies—rising *from* the deep);[9] and then the theme of metamorphosis in various forms and that of the construction of the temple. The grove is provided with the altar called for in the close of c. 79, and the statement is again inserted in an Ovidian context: with truly Alexandrian subtlety Pound alludes to the tale of Arethusa (*Met.* v. 577–641), who strips to bathe in waters "sine murmure euntes," "perspicuas ad humum," covered by willows and poplars (changed by P. to the elms of St. Elizabeth's), but is then embraced and pursued by the god of the pool, Alpheus, until Diana changes her into the "flat" fountain of Syracuse, in which papyri grow to this day:

>   Wei and Han rushing together
>   two rivers together
>   bright fish and flotsam
>   torn bough in the flood
>   and the waters clear with the flowing
>   Out of heaviness where no mind moves at all
>   "birds for the mind" said Richardus,

9. See Juan Ramón Jiménez, *Animal de fondo* (Buenos Aires: Editorial Pleamar, 1949).

> "beasts as to body, for know-how"
> Gaio! Gaio!
> > To Zeus with the six seraphs before him   [c. 90]

The mingling of Ovid's waters (a similar embrace is described in c. 2) is transferred to China, where it stormily pursues the "clearing of the mind of rubbish" celebrated in the litany of the Sibyl ("De fondo," "Out of heaviness," and, later, "out of Erebus"). The allusions to Ovid's tale may look like erudite play, but in fact they are there to remind us that the mind, once free of heaviness and "clear with the flowing" (cf. *CA* 251), arises with Richard's bird flight [10] to myth, or to a controlled religious vision; moreover they give further proof of the numinous nature of fountains and allow a glimpse of a "mermaid," adumbrating one prominent heroine of the poem's sequel.

The continuous ascent graphed by Pound leads, as in c. 40, "To the high air, to the stratosphere, to the imperial / calm, to the empyrean . . . the ineffable crystal"—in this instance to a Zeus singularly reminiscent of Isaiah's Jahweh, "sitting upon a throne, high and lifted up . . . Above it stood the seraphims: each one had six wings"—a description faithfully reproduced by Dante in Cunizza's canto (*Par.* ix. 78), where Pound met with it and (intentionally or not) misread it. His appeal to the jurist Gaius (similar to the earlier one to Amphion—the name Gaius is of itself eloquent enough) may be meant to suggest the social implications of the catharsis just undergone: having reestablished a "sense of proportion," the mind may create a just law, under Zeus's auspices.

Now Pound picks up again the "templum aedificans" motif, singling out the very instant in which (according to Alberti's theory quoted in one "Paris Letter"—*Dial* 74: 89) the painter's (or poet's) idea goes into the architect's "marble." Actually the stone appears to take form of its own accord, as the artist and "the virtu of the harpe" only call into existence a pattern which antecedes them—and the resulting altar is made to resemble the

---

10. "In avibus intellige studia spiritualia, in animalibus exercitia corporalia. *Watch birds to understand how spiritual things move, animals to understand physical motion.*" "Quotations from Richard of St. Victor," *SPr* 71.

truly pictorial Renaissance decorative work of the Lombardos
("stone knowing the form which the carver imparts it," "and
Tullio Romano [i.e., Lombardo] carved the sirenes"—cs. 74, 76):

> The architect from the painter
>   the stone under elm
> Taking form now,
>   the rilievi   [reliefs]
>   the curled stone at the marge
> Faunus, sirenes,
>   the stone taking form in the air
>   ac ferae,
>   cervi,
>   the great cats approaching.   [c. 90]

In order to visually emphasize the fulfillment of his dream of
stone Pound placed in the typescript, after the fifth line, the
rough graph of an altar, omitted in the first (Veronese) edition,
and, consequently, in subsequent ones. This pictorial insert is
among the devices Pound used to differentiate and scan his paradise. For instance, throughout the typescript of cs. 90–95 he
employed different spacings between lines to indicate their relationships, and set much store upon this innovation, which the
fastidious Veronese typesetter felt unable to carry through.[11] Accordingly, in the printed editions all spacings are unified, but in a
critical text at least the most important of these should be reinstated.

The fictitious stone space of the altar has the power to influence its real ambience—to produce about itself a valley surrounded by trees and to attract once again "the great cats"
sacred to the unnamed god and to his poet, among them Bagh-
eera of our infant reading ("Kipling suspected it"—P. remarks in
the chthonian canto of Pisa):

> Pardus, Leopardi, Bagheera
> drawn hither from woodland,

11. For example, in the foregoing excerpt lines 4, 5, 9, and 10 are single-spaced from the
lines previous; other lines are double spaced. The "altar" is drawn as a rectangle lying on
its longer side; there are three longer lines (for steps) under the base, and the upper side
curves at the corners to enclose offerings ("the curled stone at the marge").

woodland ἐπὶ χθονί
    the trees rise
      and there is a wide sward between them
οἱ χθόνιοι myrrh and olibanum on the altar stone
giving perfume,
        and where was nothing
now is furry assemblage
      and in the boughs now are voices
grey wing, black wing, black wing shot with crimson
and the umbrella pines
        as in Palatine,
as in pineta. χελιδών, χελιδών   [c. 90]

It is clearly enough a dream landscape drawn with but a few brushstrokes. Some light upon subject and method may again be cast by *P&T:*

Richard St Victor has left us one beautiful passage on the splendors of paradise.

They are ineffable and innumerable and no man having beheld them can fittingly narrate them or even remember them exactly. Nevertheless by naming over all the most beautiful things we know we may draw back upon the mind some vestige of the heavenly splendor. [*P&T* 96]

This is in fact what Pound proceeds to do (as formerly in "The Alchemist," which is set "under the larches of Paradise," cf. c. 94). He reviews meditatively the iridescence of birds, the Palatine's umbrella pines (and "la pineta in sul lito di Chiassi" of *Purg.* 28 and *SR* 139), the swallows spoken of in the *Pervigilium Veneris* and in Swinburne's "Itylus" (as well as in *The Waste Land*). The place "where no mind moves at all" has come alive with voices and supple feline entities, while meditation is aided by scents. A procession celebrating Dionysus-Christ, or chiefly the wafer, the grain god, enters the scene, somewhat like Dante's allegorical cortege in *Purgatorio*'s forest:

For the procession of Corpus
        come now banners
comes flute tone
      οἱ χθόνιοι

to new forest,
   thick smoke, purple, rising
bright flame now on the altar
            the crystal funnel of air   [c. 90]

Pound is hinting again at the Catholicism of the people, but is
also providing instructions for a peaceful offering of spices, a
paradisal repetition of the sacrifice performed by Ulysses in c. 1.
His specific sources, however, are the Chinese ceremonies recounted in several odes nobly rendered in CA:

to strum lute, archilute; beat drum;
come processional to meet the Lord of the Field,
so pray we rain be sweet   [CA 211]

"Processional" is glossed: "?Corpus Domini: 'La procession
va à travers les champs.' " And in the very beautiful Ode 209 we
find:

They have cleared the thorn from this place
how, here, in the old days? Here was grain sown in the old days
abundant, here was grain
for the rites, for the barns,
for distilling
that we offer up with corn and wine to the spirits
that they aid us aye and the more.
                         2
Here move we quiet in order
here be cattle spotless and rams
for the rites of winter and autumn,
flayers, boilers and carvers
and they who lay out and make ready
to invoke the spirit of banners,
to invoke the spirit of light,
to the spirits outspaced like banners,
to the glory of brightness,
to the source of the dynasty
here in his cartouche
white-shining, our sovran.
        .   .   .

4

We have gone thru with the fire rite
and no fault, the flamen has made the announcement,
he conveys this to the heir
             at the second stance by the altar,
the fumes of the filial incense are perfume,
the souls in the air lust after your drink and victuals,
your luck is an hundred fold.
As is the hidden so is the pattern,
as the service was orderly
there shall be early harvest.   [CA 209]

The latter statement distinctly anticipates c. 90's chief theme, the becoming manifest of "the hidden" as sign, "pattern." In the following stanza "the airy spirits," summoned by a familiar ceremony ("we have beaten the ground for the grain spirits"), drink their share of the feast. Then, with

> drum and gong sound: (nunc dimittis)
> the spirits, sustainers, have instantly ascended back to their
>   dwelling.

Which is what happens, in c. 90's final lines, to the spirits of "le donne antiche e' cavalieri" encountered by Dante (*Inf.* v. 70) and Ulysses in their respective *nékuias*:

> out of Erebus, the delivered,
>   Tyro, Alcmene, free now, ascending
> e i cavalieri,
>   ascending,
> no shades more,
>   lights among them, enkindled,
> and the dark shade of courage
>   'Ηλέχτρα
> bowed still with the wrongs of Aegisthus.   [c. 90]

Ascent and liberation through song [12] is also available to these shades of lovers, who are transformed into Dante's moving lights. Electra alone continues unreconciled with the king her fa-

12. Note the ritualistic recurrence of the hexameter clause (dactyl + spondee): *-lieri ascending, -mong them enkindled, courage Elektra, wrongs of Aegisthus.*

ther's assassination, suggesting Pound's own inability to fully
share, personal and historical circumstances being what they are,
the delivery he metes out to the heroes. His is a paradise that cannot but take reality into account, and this is perhaps the chief
source of its appeal. Electra's bowed figure recalls the bent peasant in the opening of *PC,* a passage which also lies in the background of the subsequent finale:

> Trees die & the dream remains
> > Not love but that love flows from it
> > ex animo
> > & cannot ergo delight in itself
> > but only in the love flowing from it.
> UBI AMOR IBI OCULUS EST.   [c. 90]

Tragedy proves "the dream," even as the death of trees is in fact
the premise of spring's rebirth. The canto's epilogue renders the
opening Latin caption more perspicuously than its sibylline introductory lines, leaving us with the sense of a generous "flowing"
(a happy choice for "procedit"), which will never cease (we
gather) to become "oculus," image, creation: "Ubi amor, ibi oculus, libenter aspicimus quem multum diligimus" (*Ben. Min.* 13).
As if bearing out this statement, *Paradiso*'s canto 10, the two
first tercets of which have been quoted earlier, proceeds to invite
the reader, as Pound would, to consider "the manifest":

> Therefore, O reader, lift with me your glance
> > to the high spheres, directly to the equinoxes,
> > where the one motion thrusts upon the other;
> and there begin delighting in the artwork
> > of the Master who loves it within Himself
> > so much as never to avert from it His eye.   [*Par.* x. 7–12]

10. Canto 91 and the Quest for the Queen

Enitharmon slept
Eighteen hundred years. Man was a Dream!
The night of Nature and their harps unstrung!
She slept in middle of her nightly song
Eighteen hundred years, a female dream.

—Blake, *Europe*

What was actually before me was the positive pride of life
and expansion, the amplitude of conscious action and design; not the arid channel forsaken by the stream, but the
full-fed river sweeping to the sea, the volume of water, the
stately current, the flooded banks into which the source had
swelled.

—Henry James, *The Sacred Fount*

Having considered love as contemplation and communal action,
we come to love as sensual and intellectual association with the
Lady: c. 91 is the mantra of the Queen, our lady of Paphos, who
"contains the catalogue" of beautiful things known (*P&T* 97)—a
mantra as florid and even overelaborate as that first catalogue of
the goddess's attributes, the finale of c. 1.

At the center of the canto we make out two model situations,
absolutely traditional: the variable confrontation of mortal man
(Actaeon in c. 4) with the divine woman whom he summons and
who in turn inspires him, punishes him, comes to his aid; and the
obverse case of the girl impregnated by the god of light, of the
virginal conception from which the messianic individual is born.
(Cf., again in c. 4, Danae and the "Madonna in hortulo.")

As in the essays on Cavalcanti, the troubadours, and Gourmont, Pound transfers wholesale this decadent mythology into
history, occasionally with such "systematic" elaboration as to
recall more insistently than elsewhere the constructions of Yeats's
Vision. The final paragraph of the esoteric Postscript to Gour-

mont already refers us to most of the cultural areas touched upon in c. 91:

> Perhaps the clue is in Propertius after all:
>> *Ingenium nobis ipsa puella fecit.*
>
> There is the whole of the XIIth century love cult, and Dante's metaphysics a little to one side, and Gourmont's Latin Mystique [see *P&T* 97–99]; and for image-making both Fenollosa on "The Chinese Written Character," and the paragraphs in "Le Problème du Style" [quoted in "Rémy de Gourmont," *LE* 353–55]. [PD 214]

But the address to the Queen implies also (and, perhaps, in the first place), a portrait of the deuteragonist, the man who addresses her. Canto 91 defines, cryptically yet unequivocally, the role of the poet-initiate, the lover of the lady of Paphos and the son of the Virgin—a role which is in fact messianic.

The canto begins with a material fragment (actually one of P.'s collages or misquotations) of "the XIIth century love cult": two rows of neumes (Amphion's music and Jannequin's birdcalls), both of them underscored by the words, "Ab lo dolchor qu'al cor mi vai." [1] This is a portmanteau line which brings together Bernart de Ventadorn's description of the lark joyfully rising towards the sun and then obliviously letting herself fall "per la doussor c'al cor li vai" ("on account of the sweetness that goes to her heart")—and the opening words of the *vers* "Ab la dolchor del temps novel" ("In the sweetness of spring") of William of Poitiers, the first troubadour, who "brought the song up out of Spain [by way of St-Bertrand-de-Comminges?] / With the singers and viels" (c. 8). We are again in the environs of *ling*, at the beginning (and—with Bernart—at the culmination) of the poetry of Provence, of the career of Pound (who at twenty-six saw "the larks rise at Allègre"—c. 80), of the year's cycle (springtime), and of poetry as such, insofar as this is written to love's inner dictation. And we are in the cognate ambience of the rose in the steel dust—the ever resurgent type best represented, as here, by the "intervals" of music. Accordingly the invocation of subsequent

---

1. Grammar demands *"la* dolchor"—but one hesitates to interfere with the vowel sequence that P. so delights in, as the imperfectly remembered lines return to him.

lines concerns (like c. 81) both Venus and the stylistic experience, the form, which Pound seeks to retrieve together with the conception of the world that it implies:

> AB LO DOLCHOR QU'AL   COR   MI   VAI
>> that the body of light come forth
>>> from the body of fire
>> And that your eyes come to the surface
>>> from the deep wherein they were sunken,
>> Reina—for 300 years,
>>> and now sunken
>> That your eyes come forth from their caves
>>> & light then
>>>> as the holly-leaf
>>> qui laborat, orat   [c. 91]

It will be recalled that in the age of the dissociation of sensibility flesh "is no longer the body of air clothed in the body of fire; it no longer radiates, light no longer moves from the eye," and there is no access to such perceptions as "the matter of Dante's *paradiso,* the glass under water, the form that seems a form seen in a mirror" ("Cavalcanti," *LE* 153–54). Pound is willing to specify that this deprivation has obtained for three hundred years—a reference to Chinese historical doctrine, which allotted three centuries to each dynasty[2] (this bears upon what has been said of the presence of the *ling* theme in these lines), and chiefly to the Elizabethan age, the last in which (as we found in c. 81) music and poetry were united under the aegis of an exalted "Reina," the Queen Bess of c. 85. Therefore the renaissance of art will also be the reemergence of this Lady from the deep of oblivion and imperception, the proceeding of the light of intellectual and visionary clarity from the fire of passion—and the lighting up of her emblematic eyes will be the sprouting of the new leaf on the timeless stem, the holly that Pound also associates with England's genius loci (see c. 80). The latter image returns us to the doctrine of signatures and to Pound's peculiarly antispiritualistic Neoplatonism, which is always stressing not the timeless

2. Cf. c. 85 ("Three hundred years until P'an"), and Mancuso 50.

type but the leaf which is born of it. We may also note the parallelism between the opening Provençal line and Richard's statement that the animus delights not through itself but only through the love, the "dolchor," pouring from it. The Benedictine saying which terminates this prelude is another fragment of the medieval *Weltanschauung* (the first to be quoted by P. in *SR*) and a mirror image of the fragment with which it opens: the same formal and semantic relationship obtains between *dolchor/cor* as between *laborat/orat*, one word containing the other as the leaf "contains" the information of the seed, or as "the colour" fully and singularly expresses "the nature." The motto imports the active or practical spirit of the prayer we have just heard, as well as (at a metacultural level) the convergence of monastic and courtly-erotic thought (both worship the Queen in her works; likewise the procession of c. 4 greets with "Salve Regina" both Danae and Mary). Finally, the juxtaposition of "orare" and leaf suggests rather clearly a transcription of the character *ching*, reverence for the forces of vegetation.

The lines that follow draw up in Pythagorean fashion a sequence of reincarnations of the queen and of her companion, signalled by an image both personal (the mermaid accosting the "rock" of the Section) and "historical": in the thirties Pound had celebrated the reclamation under Mussolini of the Pontine Marshes "by Circeo" (c. 41), by speaking of a statue of Venus reinstated "by Circeo, by Terracina," her "eyes to seaward" (c. 39)—and again in 1942 he claimed that "to replace the marble goddess on her pedestal at Terracina [in the temple of Jupiter Anxur?] would be worth more than any metaphysical argument" (*CV* 320). The best kind of prayer is, again, action:

> Thus Undine came to the rock,
>   by Circeo
> and the stone eyes again looking seaward
>   Thus Apollonius
>   (if it was Apollonius)
> & Helen of Tyre
>   by Pythagoras
>   by Ocellus

(pilot-fish, et libidinis expers, of Tyre;
Justinian, Theodora
                    from brown leaf and twig
The GREAT CRYSTAL
                    doubling the pine, and to cloud.
                    pensar de lieis m'es ripaus   [c. 91]

The "sempiternal" goddess of Terracina becomes manifest in history as Helen of Tyre, who, as her name indicates and as was claimed by Simon Magus (who took her from a brothel of that city to make her his carnal and mystical spouse), is also Helen of Troy, as well as "a thought which descended into the world for the salvation of men." So much we learn from the Fathers' denunciations of Simon, as quoted in G. R. S. Mead's revaluation of the heresiarch (*Simon Magus, An Essay*, London, 1892)—and Pound duly observes in the canonical *P&T* that

a recent lecture by Mr. Mead on Simon Magus has opened my mind to a number of new possibilities. There would seem to be in the legend of Simon Magus and Helen of Tyre a clearer prototype of "chivalric love" than in anything hereinafter discussed. I recognize that all this matter of mine may have to be reconstructed or at least re-oriented about that tradition. [*P&T* 91n]

This as a footnote to the "sheer love of beauty and delight in the perception of it," which, in Arnaut's "Doutz brais e critz" (whence "e qe·l remir"), may have "replaced all heavier emotion"—the body of light coming forth from the body of fire. Yet the fact that this Helen was a whore (like Cunizza—according to her detractors—and like Poicibot's wife) is certainly attractive to the bohemian Pound,[3] who in fact goes on to mention a probable colleague, Theodora.

The best-known treatment of Helen of Tyre is of course that in Flaubert's *Tentation de Saint Antoine* (1874), which may well have aroused the interest which Blavatsky, Mead, and Yeats took in the subject:[4]

3. See again the Gourmont Postscript: "The mystics have sought the gleam in the tavern, Helen of Tyre, priestesses in the temple of Venus, in Indian temples, stray priestesses in the streets, unprootable custom, and probably with a basis of sanity" (PD 214).

4. Cf. Giorgio Melchiori, *The Whole Mystery of Art: Pattern into Poetry in the Work of W. B. Yeats* (London: Routledge, 1960), p. 55.

Elle a été [Simon tells Anthony] l'Hélène des Troyens, dont le poète
Stésichore a maudit la mémoire. Elle a été Lucrèce, la patricienne violée
par les rois. Elle a été Dalila, qui coupait les cheveux de Samson. Elle a
été cette fille d'Israël qui s'abandonnait aux boucs. Elle a aimé l'adul-
tère, l'idolâtrie, le mensonge et la sottise. Elle s'est prostituée à tous les
peuples. Elle a chanté dans tous les carrefours. Elle a baisé tous les vis-
ages. À Tyr, la Syrienne, elle était la maîtresse des voleurs. Elle buvait
avec eux pendant les nuits, et elle cachait les assassins dans la vermine
de son lit tiède. . . . Je l'ai rachetée, te dis-je,—et rétablie en sa splen-
deur . . . Elle est Minerve! elle est le Saint-Esprit![5]

Of this voluptuous and sadistic phantasy Pound preserves only
the framework, but this he displays as a cultural paradigm metaphorically (and maybe not only so) trustworthy. In short, in the
Cantos the decadent world view, after a bracing transfusion of
barbaric blood, celebrates its final heyday, and goes on (as few
decadents would) to claim to be the annals, the "Sagetrieb," of
mankind.

With the slightest wink to the reader ("if it was Apollonius"),
Pound places at the side of his Helen Ennoia, in lieu of Simon, an
Apollonius, who, as a Tyrian, recalls the Greek personage whom
Shakespeare called Pericles, and, as an associate of Pythagoras, is
the Apollonius of Tyana whose exploits are summarized in c. 94,
a first-century conjurer revived in the second century as a foil
(some think) of Christ—Pound suggesting that he may have been
the contemporary Simon of the Acts of the Apostles. His actual
Pythagoreanism ("by Pythagoras / by Ocellus") invites a metem-
psychic reading of this "roll of honor" (Davie 223). Helen is his
undine or pilot fish (see c. 80), guiding him to the secrets of
Venus and of Gnosticism. (The tag "et libidinis expers" [see cs.
59 and 76] P. seems to take to mean precisely the opposite of
what it does mean—i.e., Helen is not "exempt" but "expert" of
all *libido*.)

The queen who gives birth to communal and arcane culture is
subsequently reincarnated as Theodora (whose lover built a tem-

5. Gustave Flaubert, *La Tentation de Saint Antoine* (1846–74), in *Œuvres,* eds. A. Thibau-
det and R. Dumesnil (Paris: Gallimard, 1951), ɪ, 123–24. Quoted in Praz, *Romantic
Agony,* pp. 222–23.

ple to "Divine Wisdom," Santa Sophia [c. 97], and sanctioned by
law marriage "from affection alone," regardless that is of social
status, to regularize his own marriage to a trapezist [c.
94])—and, later, as Eleanor of Aquitaine, queen of the troubadours, and (according to one tradition) addressee of Bernart's
verse, a snatch of which we have encountered above. With an eye
to Occitanic *trobar clus* and to its major exponent, Pound does
not refer openly to Eleanor, but by way of a canzone of Arnaut
Daniel which also may have inspired two lines of "The Alchemist": "Out of the brown leaf-brown colourless / Bring the imperceptible cool." In "En breu brisara·l temps brau"—a canzone
which in 1912 Pound thought fit to be compared to Sappho's ode
"Phainetai moi," and an anticipation of Guido's sonnet (mentioned in *P&T*) "Una figura de la Donna mia" (in which the lady
is said to heal the sick and give good sight to blind eyes)[6]—Arnaut had rendered onomatopoeically the whistling of the autumn
wind among the branches, "which all swish together with their
closed-over boughs of leaves,"[7] and had taken this as a cue to
make a song in which love is said to be "the garden-close of
worth, a pool of prowess (i.e., low flooded land) whence all good
fruits are born."[8] In the last verse are the lines said to anticipate
Cavalcanti:

> *Pensar de lieis m'es ripaus,*
> *e traga·m ams los huoills crancs*
> *s'a lieis vezer no·ls estuich;*

6. "I Gather the Limbs of Osiris, XI. En breu brisaral temps brau," *New Age*, 15 Feb.
1912 (Gallup C42); rpt. *SPr* 40-43. See also "Arnaut Daniel," *LE* 115.

7. *SPr* 40. "Qui s'entreseignon trastuich / de sobre rams claus de fuoilla." "Which already
take on different colors, because of the shrivelling of the leaves on the twigs"—U. A.
Canello, *La vita e le opere del trovatore Arnaldo Daniello* (Halle, 1883), quoted in E. P.,
Saggi letterari, tr. Nemi D'Agostino (Milano: Garzanti, 1957), p. 162*n*. "Which become
clearly outlined against the leafless twigs"—Arnaut Daniel, *Canzoni*, ed. Toja, p. 294. I
follow, as elsewhere, Toja's critical text. P. used the only previous edition of Arnaut,
Canello's.

8. *SPr* 40. "Amors es de pretz la claus / e de proes' us estancs / don naisson tuich li bon
fruich." "Claus" is literally a key; "estancs" can mean "pool" (Canello translates "reser-
voir"), but also trunk or shoot, and the latter meaning is more in accord (as Toja implies)
with the next line ("whence all good fruits are born").

To think of her is my rest
And both of my eyes are strained wry
When she stands not in their sight,[9]

Accordingly, "The GREAT CRYSTAL" peremptorily introduced by
Pound at this point is love's *estancs,* of which the unstained
transparence contrasts with the dying leaves ("Trees die & the
dream remains") and is born of them, even as c. 91 is born of the
hands of the sixty-eight-year-old poet.[10] Thus we find that the
crystal mirrors the pine (cf. the forms "seen in a mirror") and,
evaporating, becomes cloud—an aqueous dimension which, as in
c. 83, gives "pax," *ripaus.* The *senhal,* however, remains polyva-
lent and hermetic, as we know it from the more discursive visions
of c. 74 ("Serenely in the crystal jet") and of c. 76 ("the crystalline, as inverse of water . . . and within the crystal, went up
as swift as Thetis")—the image both of the poem in which every
element is being arranged in a tridimensional and transparent
thematic space, and of the "phantastikon" (or intellectual "body
of light") which Pound describes in ur-c. 1, and later in cs. 29,
76, and (perhaps) 48, as a sphere situated over his head:

"In the globe over my head
"Twenty feet in diameter, thirty feet in diameter
"Glassy, the glaring surface—
"There are many reflections
"So that one may watch them turning and moving
"With heads down now, and now up."   [c. 29]

It is hardly necessary to remark the gaucheness, perhaps intentional, of this picture, which is to be refined in the so very much
more suggestive hints of *PC.* (Still, the Gourmontian c. 29 is an
essential antecedent of c. 91.) The first explicit formulation of
this motif is to be found, once again, in the Provençal-theosophic
essay of 1912:

9. "Arnaut Daniel," *LE* 135. P. emends the text to fit his courtly notions, for "crancs" is
not "wry" but "cancer": "And may a cancer take both of my eyes / if I do not preserve
them to look upon her."

10. In the margin of the typescript of c. 91 P. has written the dates 26 June (at the
beginning) and 18 July (opposite "Democracies electing their sewage")—both referring to
1954.

The consciousness of some seems to rest, or to have its center more properly, in what the Greek psychologists called the *phantastikon*. Their minds are, that is, circumvolved about them like soap-bubbles reflecting sundry patches of the macrocosmos. And with certain others their consciousness is "germinal." Their thoughts are in them as the thought of the tree is in the seed, or in the grass, or the grain, or the blossom. And these minds are the more poetic, and they affect mind about them, and transmute it as the seed the earth. And this latter sort of mind is close on the vital universe; and the strength of the Greek beauty rests in this, that it is ever at the interpretation of this vital universe, by its signs of gods and godly attendants and oreads. [*P&T* 92–93]

The dissociation, if it be intended, seems to be essentially the one between Mauberley and E.P., or, to remain in the ambit of *P&T,* between ascetic and lover. Doubtless Pound thinks of his work as "semina motuum," close on the vital universe, as when (again in the Gourmont Postscript) he speaks of "driving any new idea into the great passive vulva of London, a sensation analogous to the male feeling in copulation" (*PD* 204). However he is to continue to speak until the very last canto of "the flimsy shell that circumscribes me" (ur-c. 1)—he will be true to the feminine, esthetic, component of his nature. (The tests he underwent at St. Elizabeth's Hospital revealed contempt for women and homosexual tendencies—both reminiscent of his associate Joyce.) But as time passes the "shell" is no longer flimsy, acquiring the hardness of crystal: "as diamond clearness" (c. 74), "The GREAT CRYSTAL." (It should also be noted that P. introduces the terminology of crystal, with a certain diffidence, in the Brancusi essay of 1921, the year of the Postscript and of the Zagreus era.)

We have said that "En breu brisara·l" refers us by way of Arnaut to Eleanor—presented as early as c. 2 as a second Helen of Troy, and associated in c. 5 with the "miglior fabbro"—and thus from Greece and Provence to England, where the courtly queen was to become Shakespeare's shrew ("she spoiled in British climate"—c. 7). But the very troubadour text he quotes is to Pound an intercultural event, of the type, let us say, of Erigena's Greek tags: in his final Arnaut essay (1920) Pound newly stresses the

onomatopoeia and insistent alliteration of the canzone and
suggests several times that Arnaut could have derived the technique from an "English jongleur" at the court of Richard Coeur
de Lion, son of Eleanor and (according to "Near Perigord")
friend to the poet, even though "the device dates at least from
Naevius." [11] This further (admittedly fanciful) patch of the ma-
crocosm freely floating in the *phantastikon* is of significance because a mediation between Mediterranean and Atlantic, between
nékuia and *Seafarer,* is precisely the task that Pound sets for himself in the *Cantos* in general, and more particularly in c. 91,
which is an elevated revisitation of the English theme of c. 80
(and in part of c. 81). Thus the woman who "brings rest" to the
poet's mind becomes by substitution the great Queen Bess mentioned as translator of Ovid on the first page of *RD,* and as Reina
lost over three hundred years in the first lines of this canto:

> Miss Tudor moved them with galleons
> from deep eye, versus armada
> from the green deep
>   he saw it,
> in the green deep of an eye:
>   Crystal waves weaving together toward the gt/ healing
> Light *compenetrans* of the spirits
> The Princess Ra-Set has climbed
>   to the great knees of stone,
> She enters protection,
>   the great cloud is about her,
> She has entered the protection of crystal
>   convien che si mova
>   la mente, amando   [c. 91]

The context of the tag from Dante would seem relevant to the essential world of light in which this section of the canto is set:

> Hence to the Essence so advantageous
>   that every good that is outside of It
>   is but a light (reflection) of Its ray,

11. *LE* 134. The *razo* of Canzone 7 ("Anc ieu non l'aic, mas ella m'a") tells of a poetic
contest, at Richard's court, between Arnaut and another "ioglars," said to be "engles" (P.
tells us) in some readings. See Daniel, *Canzoni,* ed. Toja, pp. 169–71.

> more than to any other *it is convenient*
> *that the mind* of all *move, loving* . . .   [*Par.* xxvi.31–35]

Yet, taken out of context, the words carry a different, peculiarly Poundian, suggestion, that mind must move—that love is flow, action. Likewise, in the opening lines, the eye of *Miss* Tudor, the virgin queen (incongruous modernity is again brilliantly used to retrieve myth)—the eye which (as its green depth suggests) has but emerged from the waters—lights up "as the holly leaf," that is, it is the source of movement in man's history, launching galleons against the Invincible Armada; the very vision which it discovers (together with the galleons) to the man who gazes into its iris—a vision of the past ("he saw it") which coalesces with the present vision of the poet—is the absolute in *fieri,* the rising and falling waves of c. 90 become "crystal waves weaving together toward the gt/ healing." The repetitive cycle of *ricorsi* and the poem in which it is outlined appear for an instant to have a termination, a kingdom of heaven on earth—Rimbaud's "Noel sur la terre."

This is, as imported by the compenetrating spirits of the next line, the neo-Dantesque paradise of c. 81: "but if each soul lives in its own space and these / interpass, and penetrate as lights not interfering." But the penetration carries also an erotic implication, and Pound links with the confrontation of the queen a scene, reminiscent of Gustave Moreau, in which a "Princess Ra-Set" (Ra is the Egyptian sun god, Set the principle of dampness and evil), after climbing "the great knees of stone" (knees were thought to be the seat of virility; the setting seems to be "The great alley of Memnons" of c. 17), is enfolded by a "great cloud" clearly similar to Danae's golden cloud, and becomes "protected," holy, possibly on account of her divine motherhood. (P. may also have in mind the cloud with which Diana envelops the Arethusa of c. 90.) Ra-Set is clearly a mythical projection of Miss Tudor: it is no accident that their names rhyme, nor that the virginity of the latter is stressed in the way we have seen, nor that the name of the former implies both good and evil, dark and light: Elizabeth (or Ele-Ra-Set—Aeschylus' pun on Helen as *he-*

lénaus, introduced in c. 2, recurs below) is a genuine type of the "belle dame sans merci." But the preeminent function of the scene of Ra-Set seems to be to describe, by way of its sexual and religious implications, the reconciliation and benevolence (*ling*) attendant upon "the great healing."

With the quotation from Dante we return to the crystal sea in which the incident of the Princess takes form—and to the queen in whose eye the entire vision is perceived by her worshipper ("he saw it"), who is now revealed as Francis Drake, the vanquisher of the Armada and circumnavigator of the globe—evidently a reincarnation of the Ulysses type. But the description of the "divine and permanent world," essentially a repeat of a Provençal vision of c. 4 ("The liquid and rushing crystal / beneath the knees of the gods"), tends to overrun the narrative frame (Drake looking at Elizabeth and seeing Ele-Ra-Set), to retrace, on the pattern of the previous canto, the lineage of the "nonverbal" tradition back to its center, to the great and amorous periplus of the stars:

> Light & the flowing crystal
>   never gin in cut glass had such clarity
> That Drake saw the splendour and wreckage
>   in that clarity
> Gods moving in crystal
>   ichor, amor
> Secretary of Nature, J. Heydon.
>   Here Apollonius, Heydon
>   hither Ocellus
>   "to this khan"
> The golden sun boat
>   by oar, not by sail
> Love moving the stars
> by the altar slope παρὰ βώμιον
>   "Tamuz! Tamuz!"   [c. 91]

The crystal (a key term, like "moving"/"flowing," of the passage and of the canto) is a *place,* whither (as in pre-war cantos) come the men of history—the familiar Pythagoreans (Ocellus punning, as usual, on "eye"), and their late and (in the view of many) spurious follower John Heydon, who introduces himself as "Secretary of Nature" on the title page of his *Holy Guide* (1662), a book in which (P. told his readers in 1916) he deals with "the joys of pure form . . . inorganic, geometrical form" (*GB* 127). These contemplators pay homage to a "khan," a sovran power which is revealed as "the golden sun boat," a solar variation of the "moon's barge" of the previous canto, drawing together "the golden cup" in which (according to Stesichorus and c. 23) the sun accomplishes his nightly voyage, and the vessel of Ra as figured in funerary papyri[12] and—a synthetic hieroglyph—in Pound's text a few lines below—where we see that it is drawn "by oar, not by sail," like a gondola, surely to suggest that (in Gaudier's phrase) not chance but "Will and consciousness are our VORTEX"(*GB* 24). This sovran is again the Cytherean, the love which "moves the stars" (*Par.* 33) in a great periplus about the altar erected a few pages earlier, as suggested by the subsequent invocation of Tammuz-Adonis (cf. c. 47) and by the new summoning of the rite of the floating lamps commemorating the spilling of his blood. This repeat indicates most clearly the close relation of this canto to the previous one, of contemplative love to the love of the lady:

> They set lights now in the sea
> > and the sea's claw gathers them outward.
> The peasant wives hide cocoons now
> > > > under their aprons
> > > > for Tamuz
> That the sun's silk
> > > hsien   [*hsien*]   tensile
> > > > > be clear
> 'Eλέναυς That Drake saw the armada
> > > & sea caves
> Ra-Set over crystal
> > > > [device]   moving
> in the Queen's eye the reflection
> & sea-wrack—
> > > green deep of the sea-cave
> ne quaesaris.   [c. 91]

---

12. See Boris de Rachewiltz, *Egitto magico-religioso* (Torino: Boringhieri, 1961), Pl. 21. The boat here is so similar to the one in P.'s text, that one would suggest that his son-in-law De Rachewiltz sent him either the photograph or a drawing based upon it.

Words scatter to form a terse symbolic constellation centered upon the glowing magical sign—and we sense that we have come upon an intersection and perhaps a consummation of the major strands of the poem: the naturalism of the middle cantos and the rarified theology of the fifties, the lovely and dangerous adventuress of the *xxx Cantos* and the messiah sacrificed in *PC* and reborn in the color of stars. We miss not a little, in this somewhat excessive clarity, a sense of tragedy, unless we are to see in the "wreckage" discovered by Drake, together with the splendor, in the eyes of Elizabeth, something more than the wreck of the Armada, namely the splendor of tragic structure disclosed to Heracles in *WT*. But on the whole Pound appears to be entirely absorbed in his wondrous *phantastikon*, in the meaningful interaction of fragments from Babylon, Greece, Liguria, China, Egypt, England. The love goddess for whom Tammuz dies is transformed, by way of the peasant women carrying cocoons under their aprons "from T'ang's time until now" (c. 85), into the "light tensile immaculata," *hsien*, and then into the queen who undoes ships (note the paronomasia *tensile/Helénaus*) and worshippers—Helen, Elizabeth, and Cleopatra (mentioned with Queen Bess in the section's prelude), in whose eyes Antony, according to José-Maria de Hérédia, saw "Toute une mer immense où fuyaient des galères." [13] Likewise Pound's Drake sees the galleons of the Armada, together with the queen's barge, which Shakespeare (in the passage imitated in *The Waste Land*) had already removed from Thames to Nile—and Pound provides us with an image of it, as of an Egyptian gondola, the boat of the underworld upon which Ra carries the deceased.

Yet silken clarity is attended, within the eyes, by the green deep of the sea, the incognita of the cavern. (Cf. the lines about another admiral, the Conde de Niebla [*SR 34n*], in ur-c. 2:

> Full many a fathomed sea-change in the eyes
> That sought with him the salt sea victories   [*QPA 26*].)

It is the mystery, the Mothers, which, as the poet has told us elsewhere and reiterates here lisping a line of Horace ("Tu ne

13. J.-M. Hérédia, "Antoine et Cléopatre," in *Les Trophées* (1893). Quoted in Dekker 105.

quaesieris, scire nefas"),[14] cannot be seized by force but must be attended reverentially as it becomes fragmentarily manifest. It was so, with reverence, that apparently Drake acted, as well as the Trojan Brut, who in Layamon's homonymous poem (and in Wace's *Brut*, its source) founds Albion, after invoking, in the course of his voyage, the protection of Diana. Pound's splicing is perfectly sound: on the one hand we have the two navigators, on the other the queen identified with Diana by the poets of her age:

> He asked not
> nor wavered, seeing, nor had fear of the wood-queen, Artemis
> > that is Diana
> nor had killed save by the hunting rite,
> > > sanctus.
> Thus sang it:
> > Leafdi Diana, leove Diana
> > Heye Diana, help me to neode
> Witte me thurh crafte
> > whuder ich maei lidhan
> > to wonsome londe.
> > > Rome th'ilke tyme was noght.
> So that he spread a deer-hide near the altar,
> Now Lear in Janus' temple is laid
> > > [*chen*]   timing the thunder
> > > > [c. 91]

Pound points to the *Brut* (1206), which he had studied at Hamilton College (he also placed Layamon with Heydon in ur-c. 3), as to an epic precedent of the *Cantos*, for it is also a tale of periplus and tribe, as well as of cultural synthesis, for Albion turns out to be the new Troy, the city of love earlier associated with Montségur. Availing himself of the old poem to bring to a head the English theme of c. 91, Pound extracts from it two episodes relating to the basic situations we have spoken of: Brut's prayer to Diana (man and goddess) and Merlin's immaculate conception (girl and god). The first functions as an archaic variation of the canto's

---

14. Translated by P. at about this time as "Ask not ungainly askings of the end / Gods send us, me and thee, Leucothoë." It is hardly surprising that there should be a reference to this ode in *P&T* 96.

opening address to Reina, and correlates the latter with the theme of hunting (cf. also the deer-hide near the altar) versus butchering: [15] Pound's ancestors Brut, Drake, Apollonius, Heydon, are all "clean," like the Cathars, or like Wagner's boys, Siegfried and Parsifal. After the references to Pound's persona Lear, buried (a martyr of peace?) in Janus' temple, and to the control wielded by Fortuna over the waves of history (and over the thunder visited upon the old king and the old poet), we come to Merlin's story, and with it to the kernel of the canto:

> Merlin's fader may no man know
> Merlin's moder is made a nun.
> Lord, thaet scop the dayes lihte,
>   all that she knew was a spirit bright,
> A movement that moved in cloth of gold
>   into her chamber.
> "By the white dragon, under a stone
>   Merlin's fader is known to none."   [c. 91]

Pound's Gabriel or Swan is, appropriately, a *movement* of light (again reminiscent of Danae); [16] it sires upon the bewildered girl the poet-magus who, Layamon tells us, is to build Stonehenge, a "monument" strongly suggesting that the Bronze Age dwellers of Salisbury Plain were acquainted with the watching of shadows, like the San Ku and the builders of the room in Poitiers. (It has been claimed that, when Stonehenge was built, "the axis through the Altar Stone and Friar's Heel pointed directly to the rising of the sun on midsummer day.") [17] Borrowing again from Layamon,

15. The prayer may be rendered as follows: "Lady Diana, love Diana / High Diana, help me in my need, / Counsel me through thy skill, / where I may go, / to a winsome land." See Layamon, *Brut, or, Chronicle of Britain, a poetical semi-Saxon paraphrase of the Brut of Wace*, ed. and tr. Frederic Madden (London, 1847), ll. 1198 ff., and Christine Brooke-Rose's canonic gloss, "Lay Me By Aurelie: An Examination of Pound's Use of Historical and Semi-Historical Sources," *Hesse* 259n. The following line, Brooke-Rose tells us, is by Robert of Brunne (cf. *K* 50), and P. has lifted it from Madden's footnote to l. 106; it has clearly the purpose of telling us, inter alia, how very far back Brut's prayer had taken us, to the days when Rome was not. Lear is lifted from ll. 3722 ff.

16. See Layamon, *Brut*, ll. 15643 ff. P.'s spelling "fader" refers us—as noted by Brooke-Rose—to the Tale of the Honest Sailor in c. 12.

17. *Columbia Encyclopaedia*, 2nd ed., s.v. "Stonehenge."

the poet-magus of c. 91 directs that this is where we are to inter him (like Lear in the temple)—towards the light of the east, beyond harm and hate, close by his king:

> Lay me by Aurelie, at the east end of Stonehenge
>   where lie my kindred
> Over harm
> Over hate
>   overflooding, light over light
> And yilden he gon rere
>   (Athelstan before a.D. 940)
> the light flowing, whelming the stars.
>   In the barge of Ra-Set
> On river of crystal
> So hath Sibile a boken isette.   [c. 91]

"So the Sibyl has set it in her book"—or, SPLENDOUR IT ALL CO-HERES. This is Pound's "prophecy" and apocalypse, somewhat bloodcurdling in its evocation of primitive burial rites, but finally very moving: the poet has it in himself to speak at such moments for a whole people, for by unrelenting superimpositions a number of voices merge in his: Layamon, Merlin, Aurelie, the Sibyl. Aurelie and his brother were involved in civil strife, on the background of the conflict of Britons and Saxons, and it is to a final reconciliation that Pound's "testament" points (as in "Yet from my tomb such flame of love arise / that . . . a slow drowse of peace pervade who passes"—see ch. 3), though the "over-flooding light" recalls the *Götterdämmerung* finale rather than the *Paradiso*. (Note the insistence on the "over," repeated four times.) [18] Yet we emerge from the flood with nothing less than the promulgation of the Law, by way of king Athelstan—and Pound takes the time to pause over the dating. Athelstan bridges the gap between myth, history, and the corporate economy Pound wants—as we will often be asked to remember henceforth: "And

18. Aurelie says: "& leggeth me an aest aende: inne Stanhenge. / [ware lith mochel of mine cun]." *Brut*, ll. 17842 ff.; Brooke-Rose, "Lay me by Aurelie," p. 267. By the way, the "white dragon" is a reference in Merlin's prophecy to Aurelie, and "Lord, thaet scop . . ." is from Aurelie's prayer before battle (*Brut*, l. 16274; Brooke-Rose, pp. 265–66). For Athelstan and the Sibyl see ll. 31989 and 32182 respectively, and Brooke-Rose, pp. 268–69.

to raise up guilds / in time of the moon kings" (c. 104). This final
achievement is framed by flowing light which settles in the quiet
Alexandrian image of "the barge of Ra-Set / on river of crystal,"
that is sun and moon, virgin and Queen, "on crystal": "light over
light." It is of some significance that "whelming the stars" picks
up the earlier allusion to the closing line of the *Commedia:* "Love
moving the stars." The poet-king is thus suggesting the fulfillment of his mission: the cultural unification of Europe and Eng-
land/America (and of East and West). Finally, the Sibyl recalls
that all of this is but one *écriture* over another.

But whereas at Pisa (in the cancelled lines quoted above)
Pound had been content with the benevolent vision and with
auguries of peace, here he angrily turns back upon the enemies of
contemplation, Gentiles and Jews of the intellectual establishment, among them those thinkers to whom modern man is most
indebted—Marx and Freud. Between glimpses of paradise that
we may sympathize with we are back in Pound's personal hell—a
strategy which has good precedent in Dante, who at the summit
of Paradise lets St. Peter berate "him who usurps my seat on earth"
in wording equally scatological ("he has made of my burial place a cloaca of blood and filth"—Par. XXVII. 22–26). But
the eight lines of italicized abuse Pound plants at the very center
of canto 91 lack moral authority and only succeed in exposing
"mean hate" (c. 81) as the actual core of the "love" he makes so
much of:

> *Democracies electing their sewage*
> *till there is no clear thought about holiness*
> *a dung flow from 1913*
> *and, in this, their kikery functioned, Marx, Freud*
> *   and the american beaneries*
> *Filth under filth*   [c. 91]

—and so on. This brings to the fore, and most unpleasantly, the
truculence the wary reader may have sensed in the celebration
through Layamon of the "uncreated conscience of the race." The
scurrilous language is constructed by conscious inversion of the
earlier affirmations: "no clear thought" takes up all preceding

references to light, and to clarity in particular; "Filth under filth" is the demonic inversion of "light over light." At this point the decision of how to respond to the old man's obsessions must be left to the individual reader. A slight gain may be reached if Pound's publishers followed the indication which he penned near these lines in the margin of the typescript: "carattere un poco più piccolo"—a somewhat smaller type.

Suddenly relaxing, Pound goes on from the total war between visionary and usurer to a set of personal reminiscences—not a divagation but the timely entrance (after the increasingly transparent personae Apollonius, Drake, Brut, Actaeon, Merlin) of the writer who intends this canto both as personal testament and summation of the poem. He carries with him, as usual, a world of memory, of sentimental traveling, chiefly through Italy, that will end in tragedy. (These personal reminiscences, however, are as much the product of transcription as the tribal ones taken from Layamon, for they pick up with little variation two passages of *PC*.) The setting is Verona, where for the last time we are made to sit on the Arena's tiers (be they forty-four or forty-three, as in c. 12), the spectators of a drama that may be coming to an end, or may well continue for another "forty-four thousand years" (c. 11):

> and damn all
> I wd/ like to see Verona again
> "ecco il tè"   *[here's tea]*[19]
> said the head waiter—
> en calcaire, quarante quatre gradins,
>   "Dodici Apostoli" (trattoria)
> and the affable putana wanting to adjust the spelling of Guido
> as it is *not* in the "Capitolare."

19. According to c. 74 the head waiter is "explaining" the mysterious beverage to "the piccolo," his assistant, in 1912. In the sequel the same boy remarks, after the War, on P.'s likeness "to the martyr"—Cesare Battisti who, having fallen into Austrian hands while fighting on the Italian side, was executed in 1916 because technically an Austrian citizen. So to P. the resemblance is not only physical. The trattoria "Ai Dodici Apostoli" is remembered in P.'s friendly dedication to Manlio Dazzi of his 1932 edition of Cavalcanti. As for the "affable whore," she belongs to the sisterhood of the great licentious ladies we have been hearing of, and her criticism of Guido is not to be taken lightly.

    "Come rassembra al martire! sd/ the piccolo
"there were french here, . . .
           (That was that war. Battista martire)
in Ortolo, San Zeno, San Pietro   [c. 91]

Pound insists that the distillations of the foregoing pages cannot be dissevered from his private odyssey of textual, sexual, and gourmet investigations—from the days "before the world was given over to wars" in which he learned to delight in the Romanic forms of San Zeno, discovered Guido's (and Catullus') "Madonna in hortulo," and was moved by a service in San Pietro Incarnario:

> And music as I heard it one clear night
> Within our earthly night's own mirroring,
> Cioè, San?—San Pietro by Adige,
> Where altar candles blazed out as dim stars,
> And all the gloom was soft, and shadowy forms
> Made and sang God, within the far-off choir.[20]

The tag "by Adige" was to ring through the *Cantos,* that "hard" poem concealing much softness.

These Italian reminiscences, which go on (as we may expect) to the years of Salò, and close with a note of thanks for two old acquaintances who assisted the poet in Washington ("the ladies from West Virginia" of c. 28), open, and establish the tone of, the latter part of the canto, in which the Lady shares the footlights with her beholder, who is indifferently Ulysses (who was bound to reenter in this summation), Apollonius, Heydon, and a small squad of poets.

Significantly, Pound goes on from his own history to Merlin's mother's reminiscences (the theme of memory is stressed) of her mystic impregnation, and hence by association to an allusive recapitulation of Ra-Set's adventure on "the great knees of stone," with the difference that now the princess bears the name of Rhea, the mother of Zeus, though Pound may also have in mind the

---

20. "Guillaume de Lorris Belated: A Vision of Italy" (1909), *CEP* 90. The experience P. refers to occurred in 1908 (Stock 66).

mother of Romulus (who also was impregnated by fire). She is portrayed as a Botticellian Beatrice:

That Rhea's lions protect her
(to the tough guy Musonius: honour)
Rose, azure,
            the lights slow moving round her,
Zephyrus, turning,
       the petals light on the air.
Bright hawk whom no hood shall chain,
They who are skilled in fire
       shall read   [*tan*]   tan the dawn.
Waiving no jot of the arcanum
       (having his own mind to stand by him)
As the sea-gull Κάδμου θυγάτηρ said to Odysseus
KADMOU THUGATER
                        "get rid of paraphernalia"
                                          TLEMOUSUNE
And that even in the time of Domitian
       one young man declined to be buggar'd.   [c. 91]

The rose and azure sky of dawn, the sunrise beheld by the eye, the petals falling about the lady—these are all taken from Dante's rapturous description of Beatrice in *Purg.* xxx. 22–33. Pound, however, gives the material a different turn, inclining on the one hand to Pre-Raphaelitism, on the other to "arcanum"—the latter connoted by the dawn character *tan* (sun over horizon) which only a few may read. In fact the lines offer several versions of the initiate or enquirer: "the tough guy Musonius" (a philosopher whom Nero incarcerated but could not bend, to be associated with the motif of Electra),[21] the unfettered hawk of which Dante speaks elsewhere (*Par.* xix. 34–36), and Ulysses struggling in the waves and aided by a seagull who is the dawn personified, Leucothea, "daughter of Cadmus," "known in Italy as Mater Matuta, 'mother of morning.' "[22] This encounter between the traveller and the white goddess is to be the leitmotif of what remains of

21. Philostratus, *Life of Apollonius of Tyana*, tr. F. C. Conybeare, Loeb Classical Library (London: Heinemann, 1912), i, 505 (v. 19).

22. Kerényi, *Töchter der Sonne*, p. 178. Cf. *Od.* v. 333–53.

the poem (hence P.'s capitals)—and it is fit that it should first appear in this climactic canto. Within a few lines we have gone (retracing backwards the progress of cs. 1–3) from Pound to Ulysses, whose epithet *polútlas*, "much-suffering," has probably led, by way of its derivation (from *tlênai*), to the *tlemósune* or "sufferance" of the text. As the story goes, Leucothea proffers her magic veil, the arcanum, suggesting that the man strip, dive from his raft, and swim ashore. In Pound's rendering her instruction to "get rid of paraphernalia" comes to echo the "Make it new" theme, for *hsin* (it will be recalled) is taken to be an image of "the fascist axe for the clearing away of rubbish." Defined by the two central signs, *tan* and *hsin* (the latter only implied), this daughter of the hero summoned at the outset of c. 4 is clearly a major character. In her speech she comments flatteringly on the voyager's understanding; Pound turns this around to mean that she bodies forth the very mind Ulysses is possessed of, a mind benevolent and conjuring a benevolent seagull or guardian angel in the storm. Yet the canny traveller is not immediately persuaded by the gull, always fearing mischief and "declining to be buggar'd." (He will act upon her advice, having no other choice, only when the sea god has finally destroyed the raft.) A smooth splice has Apollonius reenter at this point and voice the hero's perplexity; being instructed to enter Domitian's court (where he is to be tried), "with nothing on him," he asks (even while a line from Homer's description of the winds reminds us of Ulysses' similar predicament): [23]

> "Is this a bath-house?"
> ἄλλοτε δ'αὖτ Εὖρος Ζεφύρῳ εἴξασκε διώκειν
> "Or a Court House?"
> Asked Apollonius
>   Who spoke to the lion
>   caritas insuperabilis
> to ascend those high places
>   wrote Heydon
>   stirring and changeable
>   "light fighting for speed"   [c. 91]

23. *Od.* v.332. For the courthouse incident see *Life of Apollonius*, II, 277 (VIII.3).

The *Life of Apollonius* is largely a collection of trivial anecdotes of this sort, made nightmarish use of in Flaubert's *Tentation,* in which Apollonius appears shortly after Simon. But anecdote is precisely what appeals to Pound, who may have been introduced to the Tyanean, as to Simon, by G. R. S. Mead (the author of an *A. of T.,* 1901), and who takes him to be worthy of Ulysses and of St. Paul's statement about charity quoted in *PC* and in *K*. He resembles the voyager not only in his unwillingness to strip but also (as it turns out) in his benevolence toward animal life, for he "spoke to the lion." [24] As earlier in the canto, he is followed, not improbably, by the mystic and quack John Heydon, whom Pound presents, by way of a few well-chosen quotations, as a contemplator of light and of a "stirring and changeable"—or *flowing*—world, frequented by nymphs (cf. Leucothea) and glossed by the inevitable Greek tags. (The one quoted by P. Heydon attributes to Plato and translates: "Out of the Night, *both* day and skie *were born.*") [25]

In Book 6 of the *Holy Guide* Heydon tells of his initiation, at the hands of Euterpe in person, to the Rosicrucian mysteries. Pound, who had made a lot of this in ur-c. 3, associates Euterpe's vanishing before Heydon's eyes "into the Aether of Nature," [26] with the diving of Leucò (as she was nicknamed by Cesare Pavese) under the wave: he has her playful voice ring among Heydon's statements about the magic number four (cf. the four *tuan*) and about vegetal signatures as recognized by birds, and suggests that Heydon's "formality," unlike the sympathetically translated Apollonius, still needs "unpolluting," i.e., salvaging from detractors:

24. *Life of Apollonius,* I, 569 (v.42).

25. For sources and discussion of the Heydon material see Walter Baumann's informative paper, "Secretary of Nature, J. Heydon," Hesse 303–18. P., who had the *Holy Guide* (*Leading the way to Unite Art and Nature: In which is maide Plain All things past, present, and to come,* 1662) from Yeats (who in turn may have remembered the subtitle for the last line of "Sailing to Byzantium") at the time of their association, borrowed it back from George Yeats in the fifties, when writing *RD.*

26. Baumann, "J. Heydon," pp. 315–16.

Formality. Heydon polluted. Apollonius unpolluted
   and the whole creation concerned with "FOUR"
        "my bikini is worth your raft"
And there be who say there is no road to felicity
      tho' swallows eat celandine
   "before my eyes into the aether of Nature"
The water-bug's mittens
                petal the rock beneath,
The natrix glides sapphire into the rock-pool.
          NUTT overarching
"mand'io a la Pinella"
          sd/ Guido
               "a river,"
"Ghosts dip in the crystal,
            adorned"   [c. 91]

We can hardly miss the humor of Leucothea's line, and of its juxtaposition with Heydon's disparaging reference to such as believe
"there is no road to felicity." As long as there are bikinis, we
gather, such an opinion is manifestly absurd. Pound still holds
that man is perfectible through reverence and attention to na-
ture/culture and its jocund mysteries. All, in the "stirring and
changeable work" (Heydon) of the cosmos, is movement, interaction—and Pound offers again the image of the long-legged fly
gliding on the water and casting flower-like shadows onto the
pool's rock-bottom, an image which gathers together much of
RD: light, shadow, crystalline water, and the rock serving as a
screen for the delicate petals. The water-bug and the *Natrix*—the
huge, harmless, and elegant water snake—are Pound's own
seagulls, the signatures which have told him of the divine
world—of the Night from which (in the Greek of Plato-Heydon)
Day is born, and which the Egyptians called Nutt and showed
"overarching" Geb (earth), from whom she is separated by her
father Shu, the air;[27] in the end Night and *Natrix* are probably
one.

"What is the magic river 'filled full of lamias' that Guido sends

27. See B. de Rachewiltz, *Egitto magico-religioso,* fig. 24.

to Pinella in return for her caravan?"—Pound had asked in "Cavalcanti."[28] We may now answer that it is the vision of a splendid and coherent whole which the poet has attempted to retrieve
in this canto, as he suggests by bringing together Guido's lamias,
"bell'e *adorne* di gentil costume," and the earlier gods moving
"on river of crystal." In the close the poet, briefly picking up the
optative mood of the opening ("That—"), suggests that his
prayer has been fulfilled, if not by the rebirth of the queen, then
surely by the restitution of a lost mode of experience. The snows
of yesteryear are not, after all, beyond recovery, and the elegy (of
Villon, but also of P.) may well turn "to hymn":[29]

> That the tone change from elegy
> > "Et Jehanne"
> > (the Lorraine girl)
> A lost kind of experience?
> > > scarcely,
> O Queen Cytherea,
> > > che 'l terzo ciel movete.   [c. 91]

A last maiden and visionary queen, Joan of Arc (Villon's "bonne
Lorraine")—and the medieval sensibility which produced her and
worshipped her—open the way to the supreme Queen, whose
name Pound has held back for the end. The final words are borrowed from the major poet of the radiant world depicted at the
outset of the canto: "Voi che 'ntendendo il terzo ciel movete"
("O you who knowing move the third heaven"—*Par.* VIII.37).
Yet the old line is as it were rewritten through the vigorous context that Pound has provided for it: once again the Cytherean is
revealed as "sempiterna," eternally present, and as working like a
seed through time—and the canto refers us in the end to her
moving.

28. *LE* 180. See "Ciascuna fresca e dolce fontanella," *T* 58–59.

29. "Just think: / to transform the elegy into a hymn; / to renew oneself, to flag no more."
Eugenio Montale, "Riviere" (1920), in *Provisional Conclusions,* tr. Edith Farnsworth
(Chicago: Regnery, 1970), pp. 118–19.

11. Towards Shipwreck

Cantos 92–95

The theme of the dissociation of sensibility and the attack upon the culture and the usury of the establishment ("the enormous organized cowardice"—c. 95) are scarcely forgotten in the diptych which we have just read in some detail, but acquire greater prominence in the four last cantos of the section, which contaminate the matter of "love" with the language, attitudes, and some of the Chinese and American content, of cs. 85–89, that is, with "history," and allow us to detect in *RD* the circular (or sonata) form of Pound's "decads."

We are again made aware of an idiosyncratic Pound who drafts his paradise in a Washington summer of the mid-fifties,[1] alternating visionary attempts, often highly evocative, with scoldings of "the pusillanimous," and chiefly of the agents of "desensitization" (the *ling* theme inverted). The Pisan dialectics of despair and breakthrough has become exteriorized in a rather predictable conflict between powers of light and darkness, among which no reconciliation is conceivable, but only "total war." Hence the peril that the delicate flights inscribed in these pages should appear of a purely esthetic sort, void of the content which only a mature sentiment of love and suffering can provide. But we cannot demand of Pound that integrated vision of things the absence of which, experienced as an obscure unease, set him upon his journey; we can expect only the naked transcription of a revery of signs which not unfrequently turns to nightmare—the graph of a lacerate, and as such "absolutely modern," mental condition.

Especially notable is the verse—strongly connected to the central diptych—of cs. 92–93, enclosed by two quotations from Dante which set the scene in the Earthly Paradise, where "man-

1. Cantos 91–95 are dated in the typescript as follows: 91, 26 June–18 July [1954]; 92, 7–14 August; 93, 18 August–14 Sept.; 94, 16–29 Sept.; 95, "Oct. 16 or kalends," and (from "O World") 5 November. As mentioned earlier, P. had sent the typescript of *RD* to Vanni Scheiwiller, the publisher, by 7 December 1954. The little book was printed at Verona, "by the Arena," on 12 Sept. 1955.

kind's root was innocent" (*Purg.* XXVIII. 142). We have glanced
some chapters back at canto 92's inception, in which the mountains admired by Frémont are fittingly replaced by the Mount of
Purgatory (and of the *Fifth Decad*), at the summit of which is
"the divine forest, thick and alive," which (Matelda tells Dante)
casts throughout the earth its seeds, "ideas . . . capable of lodg-
ing and sprouting where they fall" (Postscript to Gourmont, *PD*
207), so as to produce "of different virtues, different plants"
(*Purg.* XXVIII. 2, 103–20):

> And from this Mount were blown
> > seed
> and that every plant hath its seed
> > so will the weasel eat rue,
> > and the swallows nip celandine   [c. 92]

Like Castalia and Yggdrasil, the image imports nature becoming
sign, and the inverse process of ascent through signatures to the
timeless. Dante's vision links up smoothly with Heydon on signatures by which animals ("swallows," "*chelidón*"—cf. *Purg.*
XXVIII. 14 ff.) recognize their food, and on numbers engraved
(according to the Pythagorean alchemist) on metals (cf. "and
the whole creation concerned with 'FOUR' "):

> and as engraven on gold, to be unity
> but duality, brass
> > and trine to mercurial
> shall a tetrad be silver
> > with the smoke of nutmeg and frankincense
> and from this a sea-change?
> And honour?   [c. 92]

The meditation on the *semina* turns questioningly in the end to
the actual *motuus* which the poet expects to follow upon his
alchemy (and upon the burning of spices of c. 90)—to the sea
change which, superseding "elegy," is to signal the renaissance of
the Queen and of an archaic world view centered upon "honour." (We have met an earlier reference to Ariel's Dirge when
discussing admirals and eyes.)

With this the canto comes to its second theme, and offers a
handful of naive examples of fortitude: Desmond Fitzgerald, an
Italian sentry "accused of not taking cover under bombard-
ment," Farinata degli Uberti ("Gran dispitto"),[2] Guicciardini's
"Nothing is impossible for him who thinks highly of honor."[3]
Then another swing of the pendulum returns us to more tasteful
matters: Natrix, Ra-Set ("in her barge now"), Pinella, Leucothea
("but the child played under wave"), virginal conception ("To
another the rain fell as of silver. / . . . Not gold as in Ecbatan").
As in c. 80, the city of Deioces, where Pound's Danae awaited the
golden rain, is associated with Montségur, and Pound goes on to
construct a synthetic rite of purification through water and light
with a fantastical collage of "details" from Egypt (the jackal
Anubis, known as "The one who is on his Mountain," become a
guardian of the sacred door),[4] Provence (a snatch of Bernart de
Ventadorn, the original of which is quoted in c. 20), classical antiquity (Aphrodite-Leucò "ex aquis nata"), and Italy (Dante's
"third heaven," from which P. borrows the "balasso" Folquet
[cf. c. 36]—still unaware, apparently, of the part the latter played
in the Albigensian Crusade—and the woman enclosed "within
this nearby light" [Par. ix. 112], namely the prostitute Rahab):

> O Anubis, guard this portal
>   as the cellula, Mont Ségur.
> Sanctus
>   that no blood sully the altar
> ex aquis nata
>   τά ἐκ τῶν ὑδάτων γενόμενα
> "in questa lumera appresso"
>   Folquet, nel terzo cielo.
> "And if I see her not,
>   no sight is worth the beauty of my thought."   [c. 92]

2. See c. 77 and Inf. x.36. Actually P. evokes Farinata so as to recall his friend Ubaldo
degli Uberti, who claimed to be Farinata's descendant, and was one of P.'s principal fascist
liaisons. Cf. also cs. 78 and 95, and Riccardo M. degli Uberti, "Erza Pound and Ubaldo
degli Uberti: History of a Friendship," Italian Quarterly, xvi, 64 (Spring 1973), 95–107.

3. Also quoted in L'asse che non vacilla, OS 599.

4. See c. 47, and B. de Rachewiltz, Egitto magico-religioso, p. 169.

The Cathars' alleged worship of the lady born of the waves implies, it is here suggested, benevolence to animals (the seagull) and a kind of sensual sublimation; in this it is a continuation of the religion of antiquity (the Latin and Greek tags), yet it is as different from it as the contemplation of Vidal and Daniel is different from "plastic to coitus" (*LE* 151)—Danae and the Moroccan bride. We are led back to the question Pound had ventured in 1912:

Did this "close ring," this aristocracy of emotion, evolve, out of its half memories of Hellenistic mysteries, a cult—a cult stricter, or more subtle, than that of the celibate ascetics, a cult for the purgation of the soul by a refinement of, and lordship over, the senses? Consider in such passages in Arnaut as, "E quel remir contral lums de la lampa," whether a sheer love of beauty and a delight in the perception of it have not replaced all heavier emotion, whether or no the thing has not become a function of the intellect. [Here, as mentioned earlier, we are sent to the footnote on Helen of Tyre.] [*P&T* 90–91]

The passage offered to our consideration in c. 92 is not from Arnaut but from Bernart, who, the lady absent, is satisfied with his thought (cf. "Pensar de lieis m'es ripaus"—that to P. the attitude is potentially dangerous is suggested in c. 20 by the juxtaposition of Bernart's line and the sirens' sharp song); the conjecture of 1912 is now taken for granted—in fact the reader must be aware of it if he is to perceive the pattern of the decadent incantation. Then Pound begins to describe the initiation scene, which (so far as one can gather from the intentionally blurred and broken syntax) parallels Ra-Set's coming under the protection of crystal: the rite (in accordance with troubadour "bipolarity") is entrusted to a woman, both "Coeli Regina" (the queen of the *third* heaven—our lady of Paphos) and a butterfly bewildered in love's furious tempest (see c. 90). The latter is a more humane and individual figure, though quickly lost in a magical assembly of her kind ("the gold wings assemble"—c. 91), among evocative Latin names of butterflies, which Pound recites even as in the next canto he is to intone the names of Venus (most of which he already had invoked in "The Alchemist"):

Then knelt with the sphere of crystal
That she should touch with her hands,
                    Coeli Regina,
The four altars at the four coigns of that place,
But in the great love, bewildered
          farfalla in tempesta
under rain in the dark:
                    many wings fragile
Nymphalidae, basilarch, and lycaena,
Ausonides, euchloe, and erynnis
And from far
          il tremolar della marina
chh   chh
     the pebbles turn with the wave
chh   ch'u
          "fui chiamat'
                    e qui refulgo"   [c. 92]

Dante's glitter of the surf, seen "from far" in the dawn; [5] Homer's pebble-turning *thálassa;* [6] a snatch of onomatopoeia (similar to, yet more evocative than, the transcription in c. 20)—this is
Pound's final (and truly "imaginary") "Audition of the phantas-
mal sea-surge" (2 *HSM* 3), splicing the coasts of Phaeacia and
Purgatory ("the sea below, / narrow beach"—c. 90) with the
heaven of light. As in c. 2 ("And the wave runs in the beach-
groove: / 'Eleanor, *helénaus* and *heléptolis!'* ") the sea brings
forth the name ("ch'u"—Cunizza) and the voice of the heroine of
"the great love," Folquet's companion in the "terzo cielo":
"Cunizza was I called, and here I shine / because the light of this
star o'ercame me" (cf. c. 29).

The waves are again the correlative of the *corsi* and *ricorsi* in
the history of a theme, an image—and of the coming and going
of vision according to laws of its own, not ours: vision cannot be
induced, it can only be accepted. The very nakedness of this
verse, forgetful of all but its own progress and its great personae

5. *Purg.* i.115–17.

6. E.g., see *Od.* vi.95. And cf. c. 7: "The sea runs in the beach-groove, shaking the
floated pebbles."

or *phares,* protects it from the mawkishness of too easy an escape—in fact within a few lines Pound is speaking of "agony."
Has not the Sibyl of c. 90 awakened him "from the dulled edge
beyond pain"? He reasserts that this paradise is not man-made
(c. 81) but immanent in the order of things: sea, woman, epiphanies all men have known ("certain times . . . when a man feels
his immortality upon him"—*P&T* 94); and that these "are perceptible in our own minds only with proper 'lighting,' fitfully and
by instants" (*K* 52). These are again themes from Pisa—and
imply a denial of any thinking (and economy) founded on "a vacuum":

> Le Paradis n'est pas artificiel
> > but is jagged,
> For a flash,
> > for an hour.
> Then agony,
> > then an hour,
> > > then agony,
> Hilary stumbles, but the Divine Mind is abundant
> > unceasing
> > *improvisatore*
> Omniformis
> > unstill
> and that the lice turned from the manifest;
> > overlooking the detail   [c. 92]

When he sings his *Laudes Creaturarum,* praising the divine *noûs*
as supreme artifex, restless improvisor ("moving," "flowing,"
"stirring and changeable"), Pound the primitive wins the day
over the decadent. Rather than a spurious and sentimental re-
ligiosity in medieval trappings, the last lines import the jocundity
and robustness of Rabelais, praised (it will be recalled) in *K* 50,
as well as in "An Anachronism at Chinon" (*PD* 85–95), where
he affably converses with the student Pound. The agony due to
the sign's discontinuity ("300 years"), to the spells of absence between all too brief flashes of paradise (aptly conveyed by the
stepped lines), turns out to be experienced not by the writer but
by a further Provençal persona—"stumbling" Hilary of Poitiers,

whom Pound may have read in *PL* because of his fondness for
the "proportion" of St-Hilaire-le-Grand (c. 51). By this sleight of
hand Pound can again write of absence as if from the point of
view of unceasing presence and divine creativity, of tragedy as
"part of the process"—only to fall back within a few lines from
the paradise of *noûs* and the purgatory of human enquiry to the
subhuman inferno of usury, which is "contra naturam" and "an-
tithetic to discrimination by the senses." This is the subject of the
final part of this concise canto, which takes care to mention what
Pound understands to be an instance of resistance against the
wave of insensitivity—the fascism of Carlo Delcroix, Giuseppe
Bottai, Marinetti, and the man of Königsberg (if in the obscure
line, "Nein! aber in Wolken," we are to see a distortion of
"Zwischen den Völkern" of c. 51). As in the canto of the Queen,
Pound estimates how long the "dung flow" (the flowing not of
signs but of excrement) has lasted, and increasingly amplifies his
denunciation without appeal until it includes all of Western history: entropy has set in since the days of Sophocles and Confucius, countered only by a few men "from the borders" of civilization, like the Irishman Erigena and the Scotsman Richard, as
well as the poet who was "born / In a half savage country" (1
HSM 1):

> For 40 years I have seen this,
>   now flood as the Yang tse
> also desensitization
>   25 hundred years desensitization
>   2 thousand years, desensitization
> After Apollonius, desensitization
>   & a little light from the borders:
>   Erigena,
>   Avicenna, Richardus.
> Hilary looked at an oak leaf
>   or holly, or rowan
> as against the brown oil and corpse sweat
> & then cannon to take the chinks opium
> & the portagoose uprooting spice-trees "a common"
>   sez Ari "custom in trade"   [c. 92]

The brown oil and corpse sweat would seem to stand for post-Raphaelite painting—a world in which there are no distinct shadows for *RD*'s scientists to measure, and consequently no light. Though submitting further evidence of the Crime (the Opium War and Portuguese monopoly, for which see c. 89), Pound is covering for an ending the same ground of c. 45's dramatic conclusion ("Corpses are set to banquet"), even as in the opening he reminded us of the sinister King's Mount of the other usury canto.

Appropriately, it is "the borders" both of space and time (third millennium B.C.) that provide the next canto, likewise centered upon Dante, with a springboard. Writing in 1954 to his son-in-law, Egyptologist Boris de Rachewiltz, of his admiration for Richard of St. Victor, Pound had promised: "If you can dig up a Richard of the Nile, I'll give him a canto."[7] On 14 August that year, the day in which the last twenty-six lines of c. 92 were written (or given final form), he received in the mail De Rachewiltz's little volume, *Massime degli antichi Egiziani,* and, searching it for forerunners of Richard, turned up the pronouncement of one King Kati, "Paradise for a man is his good nature."[8] This brought to mind the Pisan line, "Le Paradis n'est par artificiel," which (as he pointed out to De Rachewiltz) he had just repeated in c. 92; more generally, it seemed to agree with Richard's insistence (as he understood it) on contemplation (Kati's "paradise") and love going into action.[9] On 18 August, like the "unceasing *improvisatore"* he was, he inscribed Kati's words at the head of a new canto; later, to enforce the parallel with the Latin caption from Richard in c. 90, he was to add the hieroglyph original:

> "A man's paradise is his good nature"
>
> > > > > sd/ Kati
>
> "panis angelicus" Antef
> two ½s of a seal

---

7. Quoted in B. de Rachewiltz 77.

8. B. de Rachewiltz, ed. and tr., *Massime degli antichi Egiziani,* 5th ed. (Milano: Schei-willer, 1957), p. 19.

9. Cf. letters of 15 and 16 August, quoted in B. de Rachewiltz 26.

having his own mind to stand by him
                    Κάδμου θυγάτηρ   [c. 93]

Kati and Antef are the "beatific spirits" of this opening, whose
sayings echo one another as if they were the two halves of a seal
of the Mencian anecdote recounted earlier. Antef, who appears
to have lived a few centuries after Kati, and who tells the reader
of his stele: "I gave bread to the hungry, mead to the thirsty,"
and "I am a firm and thoughtful man," [10] brings out the active
import of the other's "good nature," while linking it with the
paradise of Eleusis, with the bread (and the tree) of knowledge
("pan de li angeli"—*Par.* II.11). Hence, in the next lines, Ulysses
and Leucò, the latter representing both the hero's good sense,
and arcane wisdom. She is also, of course, the seagull, "who can,
in any case, rest on water" (c. 95—this may be what she actually
taught the voyager, who was able to float two whole days upon
her "veil"):

> Apollonius made his peace with the animals,
>   so the arcivescovo fumbled round under his
>   ample overcloaks as to what might have been
> a left-hand back pocket of civil clothing
> and produced a cornucopia from "La Tour"
> or as Augustine said, or as the Pope wrote to Augustine
>   "easier to convert after you feed 'em"
> but this was before St Peter's
>   in move toward a carrozza
> from the internal horrors (mosaic)
>   en route to Santa Sabina
>   & San Domenico
> where the spirit is clear in the stone
>   as against
> Filth of the Hyksos, butchers of lesser cattle.   [c. 93]

Both Antef's giving of bread and Apollonius' peace with the animals wittily rhyme with the Archbishop's present of chocolates to

10. B. de Rachewiltz, *Massime*, pp. 27–28. In *Paideuma* 6: 181–82 Reno Odlin claims
that De Rachewiltz offers as individual utterances what are in fact stock formulas, but this
is hardly the case, as in *Massime* they appear under the generic heading "From the Stele of
Antef." At any rate such alleged inaccuracies scarcely invalidate P.'s "paradise," as Odlin
seems to suggest. The *Cantos'* Egypt is no more—and no less—"historical" than the
Odyssey's.

Pound's daughter (who thus comes to be associated with the daughter of Cadmus).[11] In this unusually ample, relaxed, and well-controlled passage (notice the sureness with which it returns in the end by way of the Hyksos to its Egyptian point of departure), Pound plays carefully his ideogramic pawns: on the one hand benevolence, Jamesian urbanity, good sense, mystical knowledge, fine architecture, Catholicism, his child; on the other the "false fronts" and bad mosaics of St. Peter's (imitations of the chiefly 17th-century paintings they replaced)—i.e., bad taste, co-terminous with bad manners and Hyksos butchering.

As in c. 90, if more colloquially, benevolence and proportioned temples open the way to contemplation of the lady of the waves (one of whose incarnations is Leucò):

> Narrow alabaster in sunlight
>   in Classe, in San Domenico
> (Yes, my Ondine, it is so god-damned dry on these rocks)
> "The waves rise, and the waves fall
> But you are like the moon-light:
>
> Always there!"   [c. 93]

The memories of Ravenna's Sant'Apollinare (or St. Apollonius?), preserving "la forme précise de Byzance" (Eliot, "Lune de Miel"), and of Rome's Santa Sabina and San Domenico (the latter an oversight, for no significant San Domenico exists in Rome), elicit the complaint (only half-mocking) to the mermaid, which parodies *The Waste Land* and alludes to the Rock that must be drilled. But Pound is quick to reassert, in words quoted from the Japanese,[12] his faith in the Sempiternal. One-half page down he addresses her with a little repetitive incantation, which picks up c. 90's Isis, *Natrix* (now identified with Kati's ureus), Castalia, rain, and "wide sward":

> corrent'attrattiva,
>
> > with the ureus, azure
> > that is from turquoise and gold,
> > Iside, out of turquoise and gold.

---

11. See M. de Rachewiltz 113–14, where we find that P.'s "arcivescovo" is the Monsignor Pisani of c. 97, and that the scene occurred around Christmas 1938.

12. See "D'Artagnan Twenty Years After" (1937), *SPr* 453. There is a chance that this haiku suggested the line of c. 42, "wave falls and the hand falls."

> Peitz trai pena d'amor   Que Tristans l'amador
>   Qu'a suffri mainta dolor
>   per Iseutz la bionda
> First petals   and then cool rain
>   sward Castalia again   [c. 93]

Like the Isis-Kuanon litany in c. 90, the lines are an extension of
"The Alchemist," less in form (this will be picked up later in the
canto) than in content, the woman being presented as elemental
power, magnet, "attractive current." As "corrente attrattiva," [13]
Isis gathers the limbs of Osiris and elicits the thoughts of the
lover, who "stands ever in unintermittent imagination of his lady
(co-amantis)" (*P&T* 97)—in fact Isis with the "turquoise and
gold" of her *Natrix* [14] is to become Isolde "la blonda" of Bernart's lovely lines [15] and of courtly thought. (P. was aware of the
spread of the cult of Isis in late Roman times—see *P&T* 95.) In
the sequel Pound rearranges on the page Provençal quotation and
Delphic landscape (for the petals see c. 91), as if to close his conjurer's circle.

The two early passages discussed so far account for much of
the substance of this discursive and longish canto. Thus the lines
that come between the last two excerpts return to social accomplishment and its more general implications:

> "non fosse cive"
>   Dant' had it,
>   Some sense of civility
>   & from Avon (whence they do not suspect it)
>   As in "dragons' spleens,"
>   or "a pelting farm,"   [c. 93]

13. See B. de Rachewiltz, *Egitto magico-religioso,* p. 179.

14. Of the background of this recurrent figure P. wrote his son-in-law as follows: "See no
reason to be hide re/ Ofids, especially as they aren't. The turquoise, that is to say white
belly turquoise shading, long diamond pattern, and sapphire back is a natrix, not a rock
viper . . . Som brute had needlessly slaughtered the one in memory, somewhere cross
country from Caserta, or thereabout and left it on a loose stone division wall, by foot
path or mulatiera . . . Certainly servant of Iside. I suppose olibanum standard for usage,
plus what else as salutation." Quoted in B. de Rachewiltz 34–35.

15. From "Tant ai mo cor ple de joya": "Plus trac pena d'amor / De Tristan l'amador, /
Que·n sofri manhta dolor / Per Izeut la blonda" ("More pain of love have I than Tristan
the lover, who suffered much grief for blond Isolde").

Attended by Shakespeare's, or rather Avon's (parallel to Castalia)
economic utterances (farther on we find: "The Bard of Avon
mentioned the subject, / Dante mentioned the subject, / and the lit
profs discuss other passages / in abuleia"),[16] Dante appears in person, a poet of paradise and of the body politic: it is precisely in
the third heaven that he discusses with Charles Martel the advantage of man's being *civis* (*Par.* viii.116)—and this points back to
Kati and forward to Pound's longish traffic with the *Convivio*,
which (the poet admits) "may be a little slow for the reader / or
seem platitudinous / und kein Weekend-Spass," but is in fact one
of his brightest textual exegeses. Finely weaving his Egyptian
themes into the medieval text, Pound begins, logically enough,
with Dante's own gloss to the line quoted at the end of c. 91,
"Voi che 'ntendendo il terzo ciel movete," which amounts to an
exposition of the system of the nine heavens and of their allegorical significance:

> Cortesia, onestade
> > out of the Ureus
> Nine knowledges about
> > [*chih*]   chih
> Avicenna and Algazel
> The 8th being natural science, 9th moral
> 8th the concrete, 9th the agenda,
> Agassiz with the fixed stars, Kung to the crystaline,
> To Queen Nephertari this incense
> > To Isis this incense   [c. 93]

Dante relates courtesy and honesty to the life of the court (*Conv.*
ii.x.8), and Pound takes advantage of this to repeat the Kati
(ureus) theme: benevolence, good manners. Thereupon he turns
the ureus into the center and gnomon, and Dante into a watcher
of shadows. Nine heavens turn around the center, nine knowl-
edges are to be had of the *chih* (ii.xiii.3). Skipping the trivium
and quadrivium Pound dwells upon the two last, respectively
physics and metaphysics (corresponding to the fixed stars) and
ethics (the crystalline—ii.xiii.8). Expectably, he ignores meta-

16. For "abuleia" see c. 5. In the previous quotation P. is citing *King John* ii.i.68, and
Rich. II ii.i.60.

physics and places his own heroes, the naturalist Agassiz and the moral man Confucius, in the most exalted positions. (Likewise, of Dante's list of authorities on the subject he omits Plato but quotes the more out-of-the-way Arab naturalist and philosopher, whom he associates with Guido.) Above all of these, Dante claims, is the sky that does not move, theology—an occasion for Pound to propitiate queen and goddess, Nephertari and Isis (who appear together on the dust jacket of the *Massime*).[17] Having thus graphed his three chief concerns—the natural and animal world, moral discourse, and the "attracting" queen—he enlarges upon the latter, predictably insisting upon the role of *téchne* in extracting *seautón*. Dante speaks of the union of the soul "with the goods of nature and reason, [which] is what we call love, through which it is possible to know what the soul is within, seeing without what it is that it loves" (iii.ii.8–9). That is, from the color one may know the nature. Pound annotates:

> To Isis this incense
> > > "quest'unire
> > "quale è dentro l'anima
> > > veggendo di fuori quelli che ama"
> > > > > > Risplende
> > From the sea-caves
> > > > degli occhi
> > Manifest and not abstract
> > > In the time of Numa Pompilius
> > > > che Pitagora si chiamò.
> > "non sempre" (in the 3rd of Convivio)
> > or as above stated "jagged"   [c. 93]

Without so much as departing (as is his custom) from the sequence of his source, Pound dexterously recapitulates the argument developed through previous cantos. From the epistemology of c. 90 he goes on to its pellucid illustrations—the ocular, marine, and Pythagorean splendors of c. 91. In the poet's imagination, the eyes surface from their underwater caves even as in

17. According to De Rachewiltz's caption, the tomb fresco shows "Queen Nephertari, wife of Ramses II, led by goddess Isis." P. remarked: "Dust jacket Isis behaving very nicely to N/tari" (B. de Rachewiltz 34).

Stilnovo psychology "the soul cannot feel any passion but its
semblance will come to the window of the eyes (*de li occhi*)" (III.
viii.10); the trisecular period of this event, "manifest and not abstract," is again defined by the Pythagorean school of which
Apollonius is a member: "At about the time of Numa Pompilius
. . . there lived a most noble philosopher, Pythagoras by name"
(xi.3). Picking up the name of the wise king, who was also coun-
selled by a nymph (and whom he had mentioned in *HSP* 1),
Pound fabricates, by dropping a few words, a new improbable
identification ("In the time of Numa Pompilius / who was called
Pythagoras"): having lived at the same time they may well have
been the same person. Finally, the phenomenal nature and the
periodicity of the vision are painfully vindicated by its fragmen-
tariness and absence, mourned in c. 92. "Those," Dante writes,
"who fall in love 'here,' that is in this life, behold the lady in their
thoughts not always (*non sempre*), but only when Love gives
them of his peace" (xiii.3). What "shines forth" ("risplende"—cf.
"Donna mi prega") in these gleanings, despite (or on account of)
their hastiness and discursiveness, insistently correlating statements scattered over centuries and millennia, is the non-verbal
tradition which Pound has chosen for a subject.

But, we recall, this *lectura Dantis* is essentially an enlargement
of "good nature" and "civility": soon we hear again of honor
("lealtà"), of valor (" 'd'udir . . . prode' both of antient times
and our own"),[18] of the just prince ("Alessandro & Saladin &
Galasso di Montefeltro"—see IV.xi.14), and of man's social and
companionable nature, the latter being illumined with Kati's hieroglyph cartouche:

> and on another point
> 600 years before Beaumarchais
> 38 hundred years after KATI
> "compagnevole animale"   [cartouche]
> or "Perché" said the Boss
> "vuol mettere le sue idee in ordine?"
> "Pel mio poema."   [c. 93]

18. See c. 11. P. probably understood "udire . . . l'altrui prode" (to hear what is of use
to others"—from Canzone 3, which opens *Convivio* 4 and is likewise the source of
the previous quotation) to mean, "to hear the worthy deeds of others." In fact, it means
"to hear what is of advantage to others."

Dante's rendering (iv.iv.1) of Aristotle's definition of man as *politikòn zôon* is in Pound's view an improvement for it leaves out the *polis* (with time the philosophy of the *Cantos* has become increasingly rural and Jeffersonian) and implies the courtesy and honesty of the ureus/good nature. (Cf. c. 95: " 'Not political,' Dante says, a / 'compagnevole animale.' ") So the canto's two heroes are brought up against each other, the "animal" of the one being answered by the pictogram of a bird which precedes (together with a symbol of the sun) the other's cartouche, importing as customary that the sovran is the son of Ra, the sun god of Heliopolis.[19] The correlation is also reminiscent of the association of good nature and peace with animals proper, while "compagnevole animale" amounts to a definition of the companionable—and conversable—hero of the *Cantos*. Having found that pharaoh, poet, and the dramatist of revolution (French and American) agree on the point, Pound is ready to answer proudly the Boss's quip: he is to put his ideas in order—"for my poem." Unsuccessful as it is, the poet's attempt to sort out the *Sagetrieb* in which we are all tossed about has its pathos—and of course it is this, the inquisitive and youthful spirit of Ulysses, not the tenor of the lines, that we respond to. It is just to this spirit that Pound turns, after some rather manic developments of the Hyksos (or bankers' conspiracy) theme, as he comes to the second, more lyrical, section of the canto, which picks up the earlier addresses to Ondine and Isolde. As at Pisa, the season of the year and of the poet's life is soon to "die a-cold," under the blast of Arnaut's gelid wind upon "the brown leaf" (c. 91), and the poet (who, as in "The Tree" and in "So that the vines burst from my fingers" of c. 17, identifies with the tree) prays for a last vision:

> The autumn leaves blow from my hand,
>   agitante calescimus . . .
>   and the wind cools toward autumn.
> Lux in diafana,
>   Creatrix,
>   oro.

19. The correspondence, however, may be coincidental, for it is unlikely that on 29 August, when he wrote these lines, P. could have been familiar with the form of Kati's cartouche, which must have been supplied later, by his son-in-law.

Ursula benedetta,
    oro
By the hours of passion,
      per dilettevole ore,
      guide your successor,
Ysolt, Ydone,
    have compassion,
Picarda,
    compassion   [c. 93]

Into the stirring and fully accomplished melody telling of the approach of winter comes a communal voice, the voice of the "scientists" whose spokesman is Ovid: "Est deus in nobis; agitante calescimus illo" ("A god is within us; by his moving we are warmed"—*Fasti* vi.5). The poet, like his Alchemist of 1912, addresses this warmth, this inner good nature, this brief light in the opacity of an entropic world, with names of women (in the earlier lyric he had written: "Picarda . . . Ysaut, Ydone, slight rustling of leaves"), working from this canto's early metamorphosis of mind-good nature into panis angelicus-Leucò, the white goddess (cf. "Lux in diafana") who—as Homer and the close of *RD* are to tell us—"had pity of wandering and suffering Ulysses" (*Od.* v.336). His rarefied bid for rescue, which cannot but retrieve in atomic fragments the lush language of forty years back, also incorporates a gleaning from Cavalcanti's sonnet "La forte e nova mia disaventura"—chiefly a cultural token aligning Guido and Arnaut—and the telescoping of Isis and Isolde (with a further allusion to the image in which the former, endowed with horns, leads by the hand the latter, her "successor"), as well as a reference to the psychopompos who presides over hermetic knowledge (cs. 1, 79):

By the wing'd head,
   by the caduceus,
      compassion;
By the horns of Isis-Luna,
      compassion.
The black panther lies under his rose-tree.
J'ai eu pitié des autres.
    Pas assez! Pas assez!   [c. 93]

Pound's insistent recourse to earlier themes in his new collage suggests that Washington's creative breakthroughs are less momentous than Pisa's, more complacent and ready to fall back upon patterns already tried-out—but in fact what little wine the old stock squeezes out at great cost turns out to be different but no less tasty than earlier vintages. The image of the panther under his rose-tree is familiar from *Personae*'s musical envoi, "Cantus Planus": it evokes Zagreus, perhaps the very poet and the pitiless feline narcissism which he shares. (In the "Introduction to Narcissism" Freud suggests that one is attracted to children, cats, and large wild animals because one would like to repossess their apparent autonomy and aloofness.) He is reminded then of the small claim to pity of whosoever has in turn been (and still is) short of it, and this moves him to renounce promptly what little grace his persistent poetic quest may have won him, in favor of others, the reader and the loved one, who this time appears to be not the *thugáter* of Cadmus but his own. (The daughter may in fact have moved the father to this act of renunciation by a poem written at the time she was living with him as a young girl, and quoted in her autobiography: "Nothing for me I desire, and / that life continue like this.") [20]

> J'ai eu pitié des autres.
>   Pas assez! Pas assez!
> For me nothing. But that the child
>   walk in peace in her basilica,
> The light there almost solid.
>   [*li hsing chin hu jen*]
> holding that energy is near to benevolence.   [c. 93]

We recognize the "clear" basilicas of the canto's inception (by now they belong to the child-goddess) and the solidifying of light of which Pound often speaks, and which is a metaphor of his own writing. The column of five Chinese characters which follows, with Pound's translation, in the text (see *UP* xx 10) is in fact an instance of luminous thought made solid; besides, it introduces Confucius into the ideogramic cluster and responds to the rejection of vanity somewhat like the last lines of c. 81:

20. See M. de Rachewiltz 151.

"laborare," "doing," the energy which throws off sparks in this
late autumn, is also a value pointing towards benevolence.

But the programmatic Pound, the would-be active and "male"
principle, jealously conceals a "feminine" sensibility which prays
for pity and yearns to be lost in the process, a leaf in the current.
The sequel dramatizes this bipolarity, taking up the form of Provençal albas and immersing us in a fairy-tale world of morning:

> Au bois dormant,
> > not yet . . . ! Not yet!
> > do not awaken.
> The trees sleep, and the stags, and the grass;
> The boughs sleep unmoving.
> "Krr! Krr!" from the starling:
> > "mai tardi . . .
> "per l'ignoto"
> > and the soul's job (Ocellus)
> > "Renew"   [c. 93]

Again a magic moment, very close to the purgatorial one ("And
from far / il tremolar della marina") of the foregoing canto: perhaps prayer and contrition have led to peace, to a love night
seized (with the aid of D'Annunzio—"It is never late to attempt
the unknown"[21]—, the Pythagorean Ocellus, China) in the keen
instant of wakening: "Oy Dieus, oy Dieus, de l'alba! tan tost
ve."[22] It is also the moment of creativity, of the birth of art and
of Venus:

> & there is no doubt that D'Annunzio
> > could move the crowd in a theatre
> or that the stone rose in Brescia,
> > > Amphion!

> > .   .   .

> Came then Flora Castalia
> > "Air hath no petal now,
> > where shall come leaf on bough

---

21. "Non è mai tardi per tentar l'ignoto." Quoted in "I Gather the Limbs of Osiris, IV.
A Beginning" (1911), *SPr* 25.

22. Rendered by P. as "Ah God! How swift the night. / And day comes on." "Langue
d'Oc: Vergier," *P* 77.

> naught is but air.
> "pone metum, Cerinthe,
>
> Nec deus laedit   [c. 93]

Autumn has changed to spring, and the latter *comes,* as Madame
Hule of pre-war cantos, into the poem's space, into an air still
void of petals (cf. Beatrice-Rhea in c. 91) but also soon to come
awake with leaves, stone (see c. 25, which deals with sculpture
and quotes the same lines from Tibullus on god's protection of
lovers), but chiefly music (Amphion) and verse (Castalia). If
Venus-Flora and her stone rise from the waters this is chiefly the
work of orphic song:

> tone, tide, tide
> if the tone draw the dolphin
>   [*hsien*]   hsien
>   nuova vita
> e ti fiammeggio.
>   Such light is in sea-caves
> e la bella Ciprigna
>   where copper throws back the flame
> from pinned eyes, the flames rise to fade
>   in green air.
> A foot-print? alcun vestigio?
>   thus saith   [cartouche]   (Kati).   [c. 93]

It is again the epiphany of c. 91, drafted upon quite a few Dantean points of reference (*Par.* v.1, 11; viii.2; *Vita nuova*), and
constructed like a fantastical musical score. We enter the submarine penetralia of Venus, luminescent with the copper of her earrings, and consider once again the mysterious relationship between this "eternal light"—Immaculata-*hsien*—and its "vestiges,
which shine through" into time (*Par.* v.7–12). Still, the quality of
the emotion and, to some extent, of the repetitive verse, has
remained that of "Praise of Ysolt," 1909:

> For in the morn of my years there came a woman
> As moonlight calling,
> As the moon calleth the tides,
>   "Song, a song."   [P 16]

Neoplatonic phantasy leads the way back to Kati-Richard and to their vestiges-signatures of a benevolent animal and solar essence—and with them to the count of the dark years and to the mockery of culture's wage-laborers, whom Pound would send, with little "courtesy" but with a finely timed allusion to the "filthy" Hyksos, to the slaughterhouse:

> A butcher's block for biographers,
>   quidity!
>   Have they heard of it?
> "Oh you," as Dante says
>   "in the dinghy astern there"
> There must be incognita
>   and in sea-caves
>   un lume pien di spiriti
>   and of memories,
> Shall two know the same in their knowing?   [c. 93]

This is nothing less than a romantic vindication of the irrational, the unknown, as against the mere gathering of information which overlooks a personality's "quiddity," its central thrust. The polemic can be traced back to Pound's early prose (which is often scornful of "Germanic" philology), and—it is here suggested—to Dante, who in *Par.* 2 warns his readers, "O voi che siete in piccioletta barca" (also quoted in c. 7), and who is joined by that other exponent of arcana, his "foremost friend" Guido ("Within my lady's eyes I see a light replete of love-spirits"—*un lume pien di spiriti d'amore*). Pound is no mean singer of "cosmic consciousness" and of its attendant perplexities (his course lies, as he puts it a few lines back, "amid stars / amid dangers; abysses"), though he lacks the sensibility and humility to discover cognate wonders within the reaches of philology, "whence they would not suspect it." Still, his complaint, however inarticulate and overfamiliar, would probably be endorsed by a majority of readers.

The secrets of initiation, be they what they may, and of arcane "societies," are dealt with, in appropriately obscure fashion, in the canto's coda. The second-person address to Ondine (see

above) is resumed as a dialogue between the poet and his "pargoletta" or puella, who does not seem any longer to afford him full
satisfaction:

> You who dare Persephone's threshold,
> Beloved, do not fall apart in my hands.
> E "chi crescerà"[23] they would be individuals.
> Swedenborg said "of societies"
> > by attraction.
> "Blind eyes and shadows"   [c. 93]

This is little more than shorthand, and is again indebted to earlier
perceptions: "The light became her grace and dwelt among / Blind
eyes and shadows that are formed as men" ("Ballatetta," P 38).
Approximately, what it amounts to is that "each knows his
own,"[24] and that others, the men who are but "blind eyes and
shadows," have no cognizance of these secret magnetisms. On
the one hand is "the narrow rast, / Half the width of a sword's
edge" (c. 15), on which the initiate must walk; on the other, "the
brown oil and corpse sweat" (c. 92) of the unenlightened:

> to enter the presence at sunrise
> up out of hell, from the labyrinth
> > the path wide as a hair
> & as to mental velocities:
> > Yeats on Ian Hamilton: "So stupid he
> couldn't think unless there were a cannonade going on." [c. 93]

A simplistic dissociation, it hardly needs telling. Could it be that
Pound is histrionically overstating his case as he both thanks and
dismisses his pretty one? In c. 92 he had queried: "And after this
a sea-change?" The hours of love are at an end:

> Without guides, having nothing but courage
> Shall audacity last into fortitude?
> > You are tender as a marshmallow, my Love,
> > I cannot use you as a fulcrum.
> > You have stirred my mind out of dust.

23. See chapter 2, n. 34.

24. Eugenio Montale, "Piccolo testamento," tr. Robert Lowell, *Imitations* (New York:
Farrar Straus Giroux, 1968), p. 129.

> Flora Castalia, your petals drift thru the air.
> the wind is ½ lighted with pollen
> > > diafana,
> e Monna Vanna . . . tu mi fai rimembrar.   [c. 93]

The farewell to the tender one takes us briefly back to the breakthrough of c. 90: "from the dulled air and the dust, / m'elevasti." And the final lines, subtly and intricately allusive, telescope Beatrice "within a cloud of flowers" (*Purg.* 30) and of diaphanous pollen (reminiscent both of "Donna mi prega" and of the "seed" of c. 92)—and Guido's "Monna Vanna" (as she is called in Dante's sonnet, "Guido, i' vorrei"), also known as "Primavera" (c. 76 and *Vita nuova* 24). The latter, it is suggested in the 1910 Introduction to Cavalcanti, reappears in the sacred wood at the summit of Mount Purgatory as flower-gathering Matelda, to whom Dante calls over Lethe:

> *Tu mi fai rimembrar* dove e qual era
> > Proserpina nel tempo che perdette
> > la madre lei, ed ella primavera.[25]

—a simile Pound has introduced earlier: "You who dare Persephone's threshold." The beloved of the troubadours and of the Stilnovo rhymers are to Pound both actual women and timeless symbols of nature's increase: "And perhaps Guido was enamoured as Dante has remarked of a certain Madonna Primavera, who, as Dante does not remark, had set the dance in Langue d'Oc and in Lemosi" ("Cavalcanti," *LE* 180). Accordingly the composite yet classical name which stands out in Pound's allusive web is Flora Castalia, the *Venus genetrix* of the *Pervigilium* and the source of all verse—"a fountain of clear water descending from heaven immutable."

In the two last cantos of *RD* "the tone" does in fact change—from lyricism to a discursiveness, "prosaic" but not unappealing, for which we are fully prepared by the previous pages. In

---

25. "You remind me of where and how Proserpine was at the time her mother lost her, and she the spring." *Purg.* xxviii.49–51, quoted in P.'s Introduction to Guido, *T* 22.

the first and very mixed section of c. 94, which serves as an introduction to the perusal at length of the *Life of Apollonius,*
Pound remarks: "Beyond civic order: / l'AMOR," and sketches (in
lines already quoted) the stages of his recurrent rising: "Above
prana, the light, / past light, the crystal. / Above crystal, the
jade"—that is, he is to go from "the animal spirits" to intelligence and thence to contemplation and to a secretum (jade)
not otherwise definable, even beyond light. Yet capitalized AMOR,
as readers of CV know, functions as an anagram for ROMA, and
in general this and following cantos are rather concerned with
civic or civil order, in the irrational and hierarchical ("that the
king shd/ be king"—c. 94) fashion which the very anagram
suggests, than with the late Stilnovo experience now come to an
end. Thus c. 94 not only puts on exhibit the feats of John Adams,
Justinian, Sargon the Great, Apollonius, certain Roman emperors, and Edward I Longshanks (whose expedition, "with an
Eleanor," to the Holy Land is mentioned among quotations from
Philostratus in connection with the union of Apollonius and
Helen Ennoia posited in c. 91); it also points to some of the principal subjects of the subsequent section, *Thrones,* the title of
which implies at once a religious concept of power: Yung
Cheng's *Edict* ("[*pen,* i.e., root] / That is of Thrones") and Edward Coke, the sources of cs. 98–99 and 107–09, respectively;
while c. 95 nearly exhausts the list of things to come by reminding us that "there were guilds in Byzantium," as we will learn at
length in c. 96.

As is clear from this list of its major characters, c. 94 enlarges
"historically" or "politically" upon the sequence of sovrans
sketched at the beginning of c. 91; even the gleanings from the
Life of Apollonius, which cover the Introduction by F. C. Conybeare (the translator who "unpolluted" the vegetarian conjurer)
and Books 1–6, and skip (but for an excerpt from the last chapter) Books 7–8, deal rather with the common sense of the itiner-
ant preacher who is said to have visited Egypt and India (the
usual Ulysses prototype), than with his religious pronouncements
(which, in any case, are hardly profound). (It is worth noticing
that Charles Olson, who broke with P. in 1948 but was to re-

main under his influence, makes even more extravagant claims for Apollonius in his "Dance" on the subject.)

Novel personae, as we have seen, are Edward I, who "brought the [Coronation] stone down to London" (P.'s interest in symbolic stones is shown by his letters of 1931–32 to Joyce [Read 241–44] on the Blarney Stone, which in fact he was later to associate in c. 74 with "Jim the comedian")—and Sargon the Great, the "hawk king" (inevitably attended by his Reina, "Queen Ash"), whom Pound identifies with Ka-ap, a predynastic Egyptian sovran whose cartouche (showing the "hawk") appears in the text. In this matter he follows the archeological fantasies of L. A. Waddell, who was led by his decipherings to date Sargon/Ka-ap "somewhere about 2704" and to assert that he was the father of the Egyptian Menes, who was the same person as Indian Manu and Cretan Minos.[26] All of which is clearly no less arbitrary than the telescoping of Apollonius and Simon Magus, and other such inventions, and in any case Pound does not so much borrow Waddell's absurdities (which also may have attracted his attention on account of their propounder's anti-Semitism), as transcribe (as is his custom) certain unadorned data, grateful for the opportunity, offered him by the date "on the black obelisk," to reach even farther back into the eddies of time, as far as "one thousand years before T'ang" (who in fact, according to tradition, ruled in the 17th century B.C.—see c. 97), and find there his type situation (King and Queen, father and mother?) and the healthy economy which is its inevitable appendage ("Manis paid for the land"). (Also in this connection we note that Charles Olson, in *Maximus* 4–6, made extensive use of this most questionable Poundian source.)

In the wake of the mytho-historical vortex of Sargon and Menes, to which he adds of his own accord an allusion to Frobenius' Wagadu (spliced with Sargon's Agdu) and to Isis (who is to protect both Nephertari and Queen Ash—Queen Yggdrasil?), Pound commences his life of Apollonius, having his new textual

26. Laurence Austine Waddell, *Egyptian Civilization, Its Sumerian Origin and Real Chronology, and Sumerian Origin of Egyptian Hieroglyphs* (London: Luzac, 1930), p. 53 and passim. See B. de Rachewiltz 35–38.

persona deliver himself in Chinese upon the proper use of riches [27] to "King Huey" (see Mencius 1A), for he sees a likeness between the Pythagorean's statements to the Indian king of Taxila (*Life of A.* II.26) and the *Four Books*. On the next page the magus strolls "under the larches of Paradise" (a phrase quarried, we recall, from "The Alchemist") and encounters the ghost of Achilles "in the summer lightning, close upon cock-crow," just as if he were at Elsinore (cf. IV. 16). The Chinese inserts clearly refer us back to "the basic principles of government" to be found in the *Shu Ching,* and in the close of the canto the Pythagorean Ocellus is made to reiterate the poet's invitation to renew—to renew by harking back to the prehistory of Sargon/Ka-ap.

Hence the final computation offered by the eloquent opening of the last canto of *RD:*

> LOVE, gone as lightning,
> > enduring 5000 years.
> Shall the comet cease moving
> > or the great stars be tied in one place!   [c. 95]

Love as experienced subjectively is but a flash gone before it is perceived, known primarily by its absence—yet it is also, in objective experience, a solid light which nothing can arrest, the eternal *moving* and *flowing* of the Galaxy. The Latin quotations from Bede that follow tell of the music of the spheres, of god as "anima mundi, / animal optimum [compagnevole?] et sempiternum," and of time become "non motus"—stillness.

Hence, also, the poet's need to measure in millennia, on the section's last page (and by way of a quotation from c. 25), his position in the great flow:

> And there is something decent in the universe
> > if I can feel all this, *dicto millesimo* [28]
> At the age of whatever.

27. P. splices characters from *GD* x 20 and 12: "[The humane man] uses his wealth as a means to distinction"; "[The Ch'u state] does not go in for collecting wealth (treasuring porcelain, jewels and money)."

28. "In the aforesaid year." The year is called a "thousandth" because it is customarily a four-digit figure. But P. appears to respond also to the millennial overtones.

> I suppose St Hilary looked at an oak-leaf.
> (vine-leaf? San Denys,
>   (spelled Dionisio)
> Dionisio et Eleutherio.
>   "the brace of 'em
> that Calvin never blacked out
>   en l'Isle.)   [c. 95]

In the end the enemy, Calvin, appears to have been vanquished by the "sensitive" (and somewhat self-congratulatory) poet, with the aid of saints as attentive to nature's signatures as Hilary (c. 92) or directly descending (if the vine-leaf but replace the oak-leaf) from the major god of liberation, Dionysus *eleuthéros,* as is the case with St. Denis, the supposed author of *The Celestial Hierarchy* (translated from the Greek by Erigena), whom no dung flow has succeeded in eradicating from the Île de France, the "Island of Paris" of Pound's letters to the *Dial.*

This c. 95 is a curt, frank, and somewhat arrogant finale, essentially autobiographical and a companion piece to c. 84 of *PC.* The "daughters of memory" (c. 74) reenter among many motifs from America (Adams, Van Buren), Europe (Talleyrand), China (the energy close to benevolence), Greece (the *Trachiniae*), Provence (St-Bertrand-de-Comminges), and Italy—the poet being clearly concerned with circular form, for instance picking up the "hindoo immaturities" of c. 85 in the rhetorical question: "Do not Hindoos lust after vacuity? / With the Gardasee at our disposition." (In c. 93 Garda is associated with St. Christopher "providing transport"—a "beatific" spirit.)

Yet the existential malaise running through these pages comes to a head in the section's last lines, putting again everything into question: for the first time since the writing of c. 1 Pound turns, with consummate epical skill, to Homer's text, and shows us his double and hero in the traumatic moment "when the raft broke and the waters went over me" (c. 80):

> That the wave crashed, whirling the raft, then
> Tearing the oar from his hand,
>   broke mast and yard-arm

And he was drawn down under wave,
    The wind tossing,
Notus, Boreas,
           as it were thistle-down.   [c. 95]

The oar, which in c. 91 has become the symbol of the intelligence
guiding the voyage, is shattered, and the wave covers Noman,
and the wind (not Zephyrus, but Arnaut's autumnal *bisa*) tosses
the raft as (Homer's simile) thistledown on the plain. It is at this
point that the inner benevolence becomes incarnate in a person
both human and divine, intentionally recalling Glaucus of *Par.* 1
(and of P.'s "Idyl"):

Then Leucothea had pity,
               "mortal once
Who now is a sea-god:
        νόστου
γαίης Φαιήκων, . . ."   [c. 95]

At the vanishing point of the white goddess's *pitiful* words there
appears a promised land, the country of the Phaeacians, "where"
(she says) "it is your fate to escape" (v. 345). Of this fate, however, Ulysses' modern counterpart is far from certain: for the subordinate clause Pound substitutes dots, projecting us at the end of
this remarkable poetic achievement towards a future wholly to be
discovered—and "built."

Part Four

Thrones

Think in the morning, Act in the noon, Eat
in the evening, Sleep in the night.
—Blake, *The Marriage of Heaven and Hell*

Et à l'aurore, armés d'une ardente patience,
nous entrerons aux splendides villes.
                    —Rimbaud, *Une saison en enfer*

" 'Called thrones, balascio or topaze.' "
In canto 36, published April 1934, this bare reference to
"thrones," qualified only by its context, follows directly upon the
last line of the imitation of Cavalcanti, as if to prefigure the relationship between *Rock-Drill* and *Thrones:* the "canzone
d'amore" which we have been reading is superseded by a different poetic landscape, preeminently masculine, at the center of
which is a view of sovranty both religious ("charismatic") and
thoroughly immanent. The transition from the former to the latter setting is, as we have seen, not sudden but gradual, for in the
very core of the amorous meditation (c. 93) such characters as
Kati and Antef are to be found; furthermore, there are in *RD* two
new references to the words of Cunizza used in c. 36 ("Above are
mirrors—you call them Thrones—by which the light of God as
judge is reflected upon us"—*Par.* ix. 61–62):

I believe the Dai Gaku. / Belascio or Topaze, and not have it sqush, / a
"throne," something God can sit on / without having it sqush; / With
greek tags in his excellent verses, / Erigena, / In reign of Carolus Calvus.
[c. 88]
[*pen*] / That is of thrones, / and above them: Justice [c. 94]

Of the common and of the celestial import of the term (which
thus may be said to comprise both aspects—the earthly and the

331

paradisal—of *Th*), the first appears to be foremost in Pound's mind, and to be connected with the "resistance," stubborn and linguistically coarse ("sqush"), which motivates, and presides over, both sections. In 1960 he will even seem to have forgotten that thrones are also celestial intelligences (indeed, according to the scheme set forth in the *Convivio*—later revised—those that "move" the "terzo cielo"):

The thrones in Dante's *Paradiso* [he told an interviewer] are for the spirits of the people who have been responsible for good government. The thrones in the *Cantos* are an attempt to move out from egoism and to establish some definition of an order possible or at any rate conceivable on earth. One is held up by the low percentage of reason which seems to operate in human affairs. *Thrones* concerns the states of mind of people responsible for something more than their personal conduct.[1]

This gloss, provided a few months after Pound had stopped writing, is not a little confused, for Dante's thrones-as-chairs (e.g., in *Par.* v. 115) are for God and all the Blessed in the Rose, whereas his thrones-as-angels preside (in the *Commedia*) over the "contemplative" spirits of Saturn. Still, it is accurate so far as Pound's poem is concerned, for "good government" is the subject of *Th*. Having quoted the poet's last recorded statement on the subject, let us look at a more revealing earlier one, which throws light on c. 36, for it was made one month after the publication of the latter, in a concert review ("La cantante Lonny Mayer") printed in *Il Mare* (Rapallo) for 5 May 1934:

Twice in my life have I heard church music of the required intensity—once at Burgos in Spain, and once at Cortona.[2] . . .
In this music of Telemann one feels the required intensity. One understands that the announcement to the Virgin was really "good news"—*incipit saeculum novum*, the new era begins. A "Hallelujah!" which truly expresses the joy of the celestial energies. "The more a thing is perfect, the more it acts, the less will it suffer." Those thrones, spirits, archangels of Dante's *Paradiso* have dominion, they are powers that move the great spheres of heaven. Religion is not only dejection, grief,

1. *Writers at Work,* Second Series, p. 58. Rpt. in Sullivan 279.
2. I give this paragraph because of the line of c. 52 which it illuminates.

sufferance—it is the eternal energy; it is even exuberance of energy. This quality is registered in music, in great music more than in any other art. In this field one can produce good criticism of music by beginning with good theology.

It will readily be seen how this links up with the sum of c. 36, that is, with "Donna mi prega," Erigena, Cunizza, Sordello, and the "inluminatio coitu." Nevertheless the canto's postscript (as noted in connection with Cunizza) appears rather grey if set beside the casual note, forgotten in the few extant files of *Il Mare*, of the Rapallo music critic—perhaps deliberately so (for c. 36 introduces only certain themes in an infernal setting), but also because Pound's best writing did not always find its way into the *Cantos* (as a comparison of *SR* with the cantos of 1917–20 will show): often enough we find there the rough outline of some idea, perhaps evocative, certainly undeveloped. In recompense *Th,* though scarcely concerned with angels and even with the fertility rites so conspicuous in the middle cantos, is to present us with several memorable visionary breakthroughs—but always of an unyielding, coriaceous, and fragmentary sort, the communal voice having cracked since Pisa.

In fact one can hardly speak of "canto" in connection with this verse which is all the time approaching silence, the unrelated rock splinter. It is true that occasionally, in the largos of cs. 96–99, we are aware of Pound's playful mutter, as he peruses, with inexhaustible curiosity which we cannot always share, the thick volumes of the *Patrològia Latina,* and the edicts of Leo the Wise and of Yung Cheng, lifting details more and less luminous into his tale of the tribe in annalistic or prescriptive fashion ("Teach kids to keep out of mischief"—c. 99); yet as soon as the writing approaches the secretum it disintegrates into a music which has little that is verbal about it, even though the Word is its ultimate object of contemplation; on those occasions (as in cs. 101 and 106) upon which the vision is sustained over a few pages, it calls for an atonal delivery quite indifferent to the content conveyed, like the readings given by Pound in his last decade, which (to be quite explicit) would not sound any different were their text the telephone directory: the "mystery" no longer involves certain words alone, but all discourse, of which an image is the breath or ethereal wind spoken of in *RD*.

But for some tracts of sorry weariness, more extensive than in *RD* (cs. 100, 103–05, 108), *Th* shows that Pound is capable of renewing his world, of structuring an entirely new field of poetic operations, and that he intends to pursue the quest after knowledge, even if this will almost inevitably lead to disaster. What could have been a telos, the hundredth canto, goes by with little to distinguish it from the rest, and we are again in open waters: clearly this was a wholly external and obsolete point of reference for a poem that has stronger ties of a different sort to Dante's precedent—and Pound has enjoyed some fun at the expense of the critics who, with little understanding of previous sections, were already prophesying the poem's end. Of internal reasons to prolong the poetic labor there is no lack, not least the fact that creation is life and that the poet cannot forswear it—a general truth to which in modern times we must add the coalescence of the writer with a particular work (from Montaigne's *Essais* to the *Recherche* to *Paterson*), in connection with the crisis of closed forms. (In Dante the closed form and the work as life coincide, for he appears to have died shortly after completing his great poem.) More particularly, as we have found in cs. 94–95, Pound has encountered in the writing of *RD* new and little known materials, which, as usual, he believes to be of extreme historical relevance, and good subjects for poetry. To us the former conviction (in itself scarcely defensible) is of concern only insofar as it bears upon the latter, the actual producing of "reading matter, singing matter, shouting matter, the tale of the tribe" (*L* 326). This occurs with some success in cs. 96–99, and, to much lesser extent, at the other end of the section, in the Coke cantos (107–09); the former, however, are enough to justify the bravado with which the poet rounds the hundredth buoy: we want an entire compartment to assimilate and balance out instigations so extensive and new. A compartment which reproduces the prescriptive character of the texts with which it is chiefly concerned.

The island, or rather the land (*gaîa*), of the Phaeacians sighted at the end of *RD* proves to be a promised land in which the poet-Ulysses establishes his seat and his good government: having accomplished the voyage which has taken him to many cities and men he gives out his Laws for commerce, ethics, and economics, extrapolating from the statutes of Byzance (c. 96), China (98–99), and England (107–09, cf. 91)—while in the middle cantos of the section there are indications of a liberal religious legislation (101–02, 106), derived from the mother cults of Greece (Eleusis) and from a lot more remote (but not extravagant) parts. In brief the *Cantos* terminate their extrovert career with an attempt to keep company with other books of the tribe, which, like the Koran and Bible, prescribe "a modus vivendi for vast multitudes of mankind" (*K* 3). The bid is scarcely novel in the history of the "Livre" of the decadents, a history of which Pound's tale of the tribe is in turn but a chapter of some interest, also because it may be the last; yet, unlike most decadents, Pound is a true primitive, as Blake was in different fashion, and this allows him to pursue his intent with some success where other better equipped minds (e.g., Mallarmé's) floundered in endless perplexity.

And all of this is, again, mere reading, the reading of chosen texts, pursued on occasion to dizzying irrational depths. In the ample web of *Th* are secret rents, through which we go beyond language, into a metalinguistic space where the panic passion for the word celebrates its final, luxuriant, and microscopic feasts. Nor is this without relation to the subject the poet has chosen, for he has told us for a long time that law must be grafted upon the precise definition, upon "a refinement of language" (as it is called in c. 96)—a refinement so extreme and rarefied that it is lost in a vast silence.

The outline of *Th* is affected to no little extent by the circumstances of its composition, which followed without interruption upon the completion of *RD* but progressed rather slowly, the preparation of the text from Pound's notes extending beyond his release from St. Elizabeth's on 19 April 1958. At his departure for Italy (30 June), cs. 96–99 were either in print or in the process of being published, and it is tempting to impute the disorder of some of the following cantos to anxiety connected with these events, a disturbance which was to increase after his return to Italy. The hospital routine had provided the man's sorely tried psyche with an undisputable basis upon which to fall back from his fluttered flights; suddenly he was left to his own devices, he was forced to choose and to be free, his hardly fresh energies diverted by insoluble intimate questions, as we shall see when discussing the subsequent, unfinished, "decad," which may be read as a record of the poet's trouble.

The chronology of *Th* is still to be ascertained: c. 100 terminates with the date, "1 Jan '58," but came out only in December; early in 1959 appeared cs. 101–02, of good quality but in poor textual shape; c. 105 opens with the date, "February 1956," and c. 106 appears to have been composed in 1957,[3] yet both were withheld until publication, on 12 September 1959, of *Th*. (P. had authorized the galleys for publication on 22 June.) It is likely, therefore, that cs. 100–09 were close to their present form when the poet left St. Elizabeth's, but clearly they still needed some ordering and revision which never eventuated. Consequently there is a void at the center of *Th:* between the two documentary "wings" of cs. 96–99 and 107–09 (the latter only roughly sketched in) we do not find the coherent core of previous decads (cs. 35–40, 45–49, 79–83, 90–93—approximately), but a confusion of unassimilated data, not wholly counterbalanced by the successes of cs. 101–02 and 106. Repayment of this, on the other hand, is to be found in the often referred to cs. 96–99, which cannot with justice be labeled "documentary," for they contain some of the most remarkable poetic breakthroughs that the section has to offer.[4]

3. See Stock, *Reading the Cantos,* p. 114.

4. Since the writing of the above, "La cantante Lonni Mayer" (pp. 332–33) has been translated and collected in the engaging *Ezra Pound and Music: The Complete Criticism,* ed. R. Murray Schafer (New York: New Directions, 1978), pp. 360–63.

12. The Edict

Roma and Byzantium

Il [Gautier] me demanda ensuite, avec un oeil curieusement
méfiant, et comme pour m'éprouver, si j'aimais à lire des dic-
tionnaires. Il me dit cela d'ailleurs comme il dit toute chose,
fort tranquillement, et du ton qu'un autre aurait pris pour
s'informer si je préférais la lecture des voyages à celle des
romans. Par bonheur, j'avais été pris très jeune de lex-
icomanie, et je vis que ma réponse me gagnait de l'estime.

—Baudelaire, *L'Art romantique*

The narrative of *Thrones* begins precisely where *RD* left off: the
two sections, hitching like dominoes or "halves of a seal," are
separated by an interval incommensurate and most brief, at any
rate predetermined, authorized by what is already written—the
interval between two lines of Homer, quoted (selectively) in
Greek. Having advised Ulysses to "get rid of paraphernalia" and
to try to swim for his *"nóstou / gaíes Phaiékon"* (c. 95 reproduces
the line division of *Od.* v.344–45), Leucothea makes the offer reported in cs. 91 and 95 ("My bikini is worth yr/ raft") stating that
her immortal veil (*"krédemnon"*—346) will preserve him from
sufferance and death. Twice the *krédemnon* is mentioned by
Homer (in the address and in the third-person narrative, when
the goddess hands it to the man), and twice the word is transcribed by Pound, as if to get a sure hold of the charm, and to
suggest the movement of the waves:

Κρήδεμνον . . .
κρήδεμνον . . .
and the wave concealed her,
                    dark mass of great water.
Aestheticisme comme politique d'église, hardly religion.   [c. 96]

The dark wave which blacks out the whiteness of the nymph-gull
becomes immediately charged with metaphorical significance, as

imported by the French insert: it is the "dung flow" mentioned several times in *RD,* and more particularly "estheticism" and "church politics," which (P. indicates) are a poor man's religion, quite unlike the dramatic and somewhat Manichean mysteries of the *Cantos,* and the extreme need which connects Ulysses to the arcane veil. We may consequently expect *Th* to deal with this truer religion, which is also, as we have seen, "eternal energy . . . even an exuberance of energy." Accordingly, a further borrowing from *Od.* 5 is used to sketch at once a bloodless offering of cedar and juniper reminiscent of c. 90,[1] which is to exorcize the threat quickly become apparent, and to allow the poet-hero to weather the sea between him and the island, as well as other opacities. (Already in the previous canto the daughter of Cadmus is implored to "bring light *per diafana.*") Clearly the double setting (the rough sea and Calypso's island) is not contradictory but constructs a composite image of the protagonist, and it is not even necessary to imagine a lapse of time that has allowed him to come to Alcinous' hearth:

> & on the hearth burned cedar and juniper . . .
>> that should bear him thru these diafana
> Aether pluit numismata
> Tellus vomit cadavera,
>> Thusca quae a thure,
> from the name of the incense, in this province is
>> ROMA *quae olim* . . .
> In the province of Tuscany is Rome, a city which formerly . . .
> And Sabines with a crow on their flag.
> Brennus came for the wine, liking its quality,
> Bergamo, Brescia, Ticino,
> & inviting his wife to drink from her father's skull
> (Cunimundus) a cup which I, Paulus, saw . . .   [c. 96]

The offering is not without effect but awakens, as in cs. 1 and 90, forgotten spirits or voices ("et j'entendis des voix"—c. 16): the voice, as we learn after the drift of the narrative has been established, of Paul the Deacon, himself a type of the poet-inves-

---

1. "A great fire was burning on the hearth, and from afar over the isle there was a fragrance of cleft cedar and juniper, as they burned." Homer, *The Odyssey,* tr. A. T. Murray, Loeb Classical Library (London: Heinemann, 1960), I, 175.

tigator of the *Cantos* who seeks out in person the people and things he is to speak of. (Cf. Varchi in c. 5; as late as c. 94 we hear of "an image that I, Philostratus, saw.") This voice speaks first of a rain of coins (a reference to P.'s subsequent economic labors, but also to Danae's impregnation); then of the earth giving up its dead, as is the case with Paul; then of Tuscany and of the supposed etymology of the name, which directs us to the incense burned for the courteous spirits of c. 93 and to the sacrifice of wood and spices a few lines back; and finally of Rome, "once," Paul writes, "the capital of the world" (*History of the Lombards* II. 16; the previous quotations are from I. 26). Pound capitalizes the name, for with this he has already come to his appointed destination: the city of Deioces, four times lost ("quae olim"—cf. c. 91: "Rome th'ilke tyme was noght") yet destined to be reborn, of which *Th* is to seek the "definition." The bikini of amor has already evoked its communal mirror image, the myth of the City.

Meanwhile the fragments of phrases which emerge from the depths of textual memory (P., as he tells us a little farther on, is reading the Deacon's *History of the Lombards* in Vol. 95 of the *Patrologia Latina*) begin to be deciphered by the poet-reader, who gives us snatches of translation, evocatively alternating English and Latin phrases superimposable in part, until, with the appearance of the city, the English voice becomes dominant, undistorted, and begins to give notice (as usual in the *Cantos*) of the travellers who *come* there (the Sabines with their crow, Brennus drawn by the wine, Alboinus with the inevitable skull-cup),[2] and of the just sovrans or "thrones" who attend to the city's government:

> that Tiberius Constantine was distributist,
> Justinian, Chosroes, Augustae Sophiae,
> lumina mundi, ἐπικόμβια . . . τὸν λαόν
> or a hand out. 586 chronologically
>   (more or less)
> Authar, marvelous reign, no violence and no passports,   [c. 96]

2. *History of the Lombards* II. 19, 23, 28. P.'s crow is actually a woodpecker, "pica," and it is borne not by the Sabines but by the Piceni (another of Paul's farfetched etymologies); Bergamo, Brescia and Ticino are *cities* mentioned among others as founded by the Gauls.

Paul recalls two occasions upon which good Tiberius Constantine (we have now come to the Rome of the Orient) handed out quantities of gold to the people, a forerunner (P. suggests) of Social Credit. From references in the same chapter (III. 12) to one Justinian, the empress Sophia, and wars upon Persians, Pound constructs a synthetic image of the royal couple, indicating that the queen, like Helen Ennoia, is an incarnation of divine wisdom, connected with Persian and Median lightcults. A footnote to chapter 15 mentions the fact that it was the custom of newly elected emperors to "throw bags of coins (*epikómbia*) to the people (*eis tòn laón*)," and this goes into the poem as a further instance of "distribution," well worthy of sovrans who are "the lights of the world" (same footnote). As for Authar, during his reign "there was no larceny, and all could go with no fear where they pleased" (ch. 16)—the latter being an important detail for our sentimental traveller, who never quite recovered from the introduction of passports after World War One.

This banquet of chronicle continues for another six pages, going on without notice to Paul's *Historia Miscella* (appended in P.'s source to the Lombard history), even though this familiar method implies a brief retrocession to the times of Diocletian, Vespasian, and Antoninus Pius. Pound's main purpose is to provide a background to the Byzantine "research" of the second part of the long canto—the background *in fieri* from which the word of the Law may emerge. But he is also carried along by the pure enjoyment of a world which is both "stirring and changeable" and materially textual—of the medieval universe which is his Byzantium, and through which in fact he sails to Constantinople ("Mr Yeats called it Byzantium," he remarks farther on). (Finally, the desire to investigate family history may not be alien to P., for his son-in-law claimed Lombard descent—see M. de Rachewiltz 269–70.) Nothing inspires Pound with so much confidence as the written word, and so he resumes the form of unfettered research and reading, not lacking in intelligence and humor, of the Siena cantos, to mention but one outstanding example, for it is also the form of c. 1 and essentially of the entire poem. These are new royal annals, quickened by a taste for the picturesque, for the precise date, for the names of antique places:

From the golden font, kings lie in order of generation
     Cuningpert elegant, and a warrior . . .
de partibus Liguriae . . . lubricus
Aripert sank, auro gravatus, because he was carrying gold.
Who shall know throstle's note from banded thrush
by the wind in the holly bush
Floods came in the Via Lata
     and from St. Peter's down to the bridge, Ponte Milvio
et quia Karolus followed Pippin,
     not Plectrude's son but Alpaide's
Wait, wait, Martel father of Pippin,
     Pippin of Charlemagne,
Alpaide's son, one of 'em, not Plectrude's
     empty grave outside San Zeno, to the right as you face it
                            [c. 96]

These gleanings, however hurried and imitative of the process of
reading (as with the erroneous reconstruction of Charlemagne's
genealogy),[3] are mostly in the nature of mythical emblems: Cun-
ingpert's epitaph (from a footnote to VI. 17—"Aureo ex fonte
quiescunt in ordine reges") calls forth an image reminiscent of
Aurelie's Stonehenge; Aripert's death rhymes with a passage in c.
77: "and they say the gold her grandmother carried under her /
skirt for Jeff Davis / drowned her when she slipped from the landing boat." Occasionally, between one tablet of annals and the
next, as here between Aripert and the record of a flood (VI.
36—Rome again), there comes a reference to a different, extra-
textual, world, and to the extreme attention upon which "our
science" is grounded: a couplet demanding that we distinguish
between the similar songs of similar birds as carried by Arnaut's
arcane wind (the holly bush, we have found in c. 91, is a *senhal*
of England, metempsychosis, and signatures)—or an epiphany of
Fortune, who presides over Byzantine and Lombard history, as
earlier over Layamon's chronicle:

    With eyes pervenche,
        all under the Moon is under Fortuna
            [*chen*]   CHEN,

3. See *History of the Lombards* VI. 37 ("De gente Anglorum, et rege Francorum Pippino
. . . et quia ei Karolus suus filius successit") and footnote in *PL* XCV 649. Alpaide's
Karolus is Charles Martel, the winner of Poitiers, not his grandson Charlemagne.

e che permutasse.
          With castled ships and images Dei Matris,   [c. 96]

Chen, a purely mental yet highly effective image in c. 91 ("timing
the thunder"), reenters here in the arresting format of its first occurrence (c. 86), and for the last time. Again we notice the *difference* (cf. the two birdcalls) between the radicals of which it is
the sum: rain (sky) over time, symmetry over asymmetry, order
over disorder, divinity over humanity. Hence the earlier gloss,
"Man under Fortune" (c. 86), and the similar one here, indirectly
suggested by the lines preceding Dante's momentous discussion
of Fortuna in *Inf.* 7. We recall that both Guido and Dante were
mentioned in the outline given in *P&T* for a "thesis" on the subject: having quoted the canzone spuriously attributed to Guido at
two points of *RD,* Pound is ready to consider Dante's treatment,
which is skillfully weaved into the subsequent canto. Meanwhile
he quotes (besides "under the Moon") a few words indicating
Fortuna as the goddess of changes ("e che permutasse")—of the
stirring and changeable Poundian world—and also tells us of her
periwinkle-blue eyes. We conclude that she is but the Queen of c.
91 under an assumed name: moonlike in her changes and in her
virginity (which also relates her to the Immaculate or "Dei Ma-
tris"),[4] associated with vegetation (as, again, Diana), and possessed of wondrous marine eyes.

   These and other asides lead us from the annals to the main
concerns of *Th.* So with the remark, "Laws aim? is against coercion"—and with two small untransliterated characters, the first
to appear in the section. The latter, *fa,* suggests "distribution";
whereas the former, *hsin,* which Pound lifts from the name of a
Chinese acquaintance ("Wang's middle name not in Mathews"—
it appears that dictionaries, like history books, are often silent at
crucial points), is an arrangement of radicals "wood" and "flames," and thus almost an ideogram of the initial burning of cedar
and juniper, and an ensign of the flamelike king of *Th* (hence P.'s
gloss, "verbo et actu corruscans"—see H. Witemeyer, *Paideuma*
4: 333–35).

4. See *PL* xcv 1023.

The sequence of Byzantine sovrans comes to an end ("we are getting to the crux of one matter") with a twelve-line prose excerpt fully given over to the Latin voice. This is the luminous find which the poet is always seeking, the historical correlative of the mystical ordering imported by the image of Fortuna. Predictably, it is economic in subject: caliph "Habdimelich," in the course of warring against Justinian II (692), mints his own coin and so attains independence from Byzance, illustrating another authorial aside ("and of course there is no local freedom / without local control of local purchasing power"), and indicating that economic autonomy is the necessary premise of art and religion: having coined his money the rebel presently turns to the building of the temple ("et voluit auferre columnas"). Moreover the quotation is supposed to pinpoint the instant in which the civilization which is to supplant the Eastern Empire gains the ascendant. Pound, who in fact intends a poetic chronicle of civilization, comments as follows:

> In fact this item, with that bit from the Eparch's edict
> which was still there for Kemal in our time,
>   PANTA 'REI, said Du Bellay translating,
> the base shall we say, and the slide of Byzantium,
> bags, baskets full of, presumably, coinage,   [c. 96]

Habdimelich's perception signals "the slide of Byzantium," which the tag from Heraclitus and Du Bellay (cf. "Rome, from the French of Joachim du Bellay," P 40: 1911) suggests we place in the context of Fortuna's permutations; whereas "the base" of the Empire was the distribution of *epikómbia* ("marsupium numismatibus plenum"—PL xcv 1060) to the people, and more particularly certain norms (perhaps economic) of the Edict of Leo the Wise (886–911) concerning the guilds of Constantinople, the subject of the subsequent final nine pages of this canto.

Clearly Pound was attracted to this obscure document,[5] as earlier to Athelstan, on account of his corporative leanings, which precede (and may in part explain) his infatuation with fascism,

---

5. *Le Livre du Préfet, ou l'édit de l'empereur Léon le Sage sur les corporations de Constantinople,* ed. Jules Nicole, Genève, 1893.

for they arise from his long-standing preoccupation with the writing (and more generally artistic) community. It follows that in his reading of Leo's edict he dwells at greater length upon such norms as concern artists or craftsmen: close upon the lines last quoted he turns abruptly to the "vestiarii" (ch. 4), whose important task is to "see that the white, black, green be in order" (c. 52), a function much like the poet's purifying the language of the tribe; a few characters in the margin of the transcription (*tzu,* "purple"; *chu,* "red"—cf. P.'s favorite illustration of the ideogramic method, the designation of "red") remind us of the similar interest in the "ordering" of color taken by Chinese tradition, an interest attested by the lines just quoted from c. 52. This collage of English, Greek, and Chinese, serving as a portal for Leo the Wise's and Pound's own edict, is actually quite confusing, for the terms on exhibit have no shared meaning, as their arrangement in three columns would suggest. Yet Mario Praz's "lover of precision unfortunate in the extreme" is as happy as a school boy with this show of learning, and does not hesitate to assure us that "Here, surely, is a refinement of language"—a remark as arresting as "these are distinctions in clarity" (c. 84), and equally meaningless. There follows a significant and thoughtful statement of poetics:

If we never write anything save what is already understood, the field of understanding will never be extended. One demands the right, now and again, to write for a few people with special interests and whose curiosity reaches into greater detail. [c. 96]

As already remarked, there is no reason to doubt Pound's intention to communicate and to extend the field of poetic understanding, that is, of the understanding "that matters." It must also be admitted that he introduced to contemporary culture-as-conversation many matters that would have otherwise remained beyond our compass, for he was able to sustain a passionate interest in these things and to infect us with some of it. The peril that his work be taken as a self-enclosed guide to culture remains, and it is not a mean one; yet of this misreading, however lacking in a sense of proportion he may himself have been, we cannot hold him accountable. Before going on, we would note the ambiguity of this interpolation in plain language, so out of keeping (and proportionally effective) with the hallucinatory context: the few interested people whom the poet claims, "now and then," for an audience, are actually much fewer than the bland statement would suggest, for they are Erigena and company, the "other few who turned in time to the bread of the angels," carefully distinguished in *Par.* 2 from the common crew of the "piccioletta barca," or dinghy.

In announcing a refinement of language Pound is speaking not only of his curious metalinguistic construct, but also of the text which he is perusing, for otherwise he would not give himself so much trouble in taking it down. In this matter he disagrees quite with his predecessor Jules Nicole, with whom in fact, as he goes on, he picks a number of quarrels on very poor grounds. Nicole mentions a "crainte puérile des répétitions des mots qui est un des caractères les plus frappantes du style de Léon." Pound, on the other hand, is so confident that the language of the Edict is superior, that his reading falls into two distinct sections, the former lexicographic, a consideration of single words, and the latter explicitly normative. Between these twin readings Habdimelich reenters in fugal fashion, his story being now translated into English and preceded by a poignant valediction to the sun:

> Good-bye to the sun, Autumn is dying
> Χαῖρε ὁ "Ηλιος
> whom the ooze cannot blacken
> Χαῖρε clarore.   [c. 96]

The autumn of c. 93 is turning to winter, yet the poet is sure of rebirth and addresses the sun as equal to equal. In context the salutation comments suggestively upon "the slide" of Byzantine civilization, and gives promise that other paideumas, like the Arab world, are to follow.

If we go on, with Pound, to the contents of Leo's edict, we find likewise that this is scarcely the enlightened document its reader-exegete would have us believe it to be, for it metes out such punishment as the loss of the hand for relatively slight offences (its subject being mercantile, not criminal, law); but Pound is cruel as all children and gloats upon the penalties for forgers and the like. (These, we hasten to add, are not extreme: "Whoso tries any monkey-shines / shall be put on a jackass and led through the streets quite / slowly, / flogged, shaved, and put out"—this for Nicole's "fustibus et tonsura et traductione et perpetuo exsilio afficitor"— x. 4.)

This clearly leads us back to the point that the poem is to be taken metaphorically, for what communicative tension it possesses, and not for its brute content. The Deacon's annals open the way to the discussion of the language, and this in turn to the law—a trajectory of remarkable structural perspicuousness and pregnancy, from which the occasional stoppage in the development should not be allowed to distract us. This is not to say that the actual writing does not at points have hidden significance (P. gives particular attention to jewellers and perfumers—the craftsmen of the Queen—and even more to bakers, more intimately connected to her than their fellow laborers), and that it does not contain engaging passages, like those concerning builders (of the temple, of course) and the guild to which the poet himself would belong:

> To be tabulary, must know the Manuel
>   to recite it, and the Basiliks, 60 books
> and draw up an act in the presence, and be sponsored
> by the primicier and his colleagues
>   and have a clear Handschrift
> and be neither babbler nor insolent, nor sloppy in habits
> and have a style. Without perfect style
>   might not notice punctuation and phrases
>   that alter the sense
>   and if he writes down a variant
>   his sponsors will be responsible.
> Give him time to show what he's got.
> And the smoke at his consecration,
>   incense θυμίαμα ἐνώπιον Κυρίου
> shows how his thought shd/ go. Upward, videlicet.   [c. 96]

It is an amusing genre vignette, which communicates indirectly a concern for the integrity of the given text and of its guardians (as if P. were warning future amanuenses who will copy the *Cantos* against introducing unauthorized variants or altering the sense), and an exalted conception of the mission of the artist, whose thoughts are to move "quam thus in conspectu Domini" (i. 3)—as *incense*. The unadorned simplicity of the writing aptly imports the conception of life both religious and practical held by Pound in his seventies.

The Arab rebel whose feats preceded by two centuries Leo's edict makes his third entrance to terminate the canto, and to awaken a remote echo. At the end of c. 20 we find: "Peace! / Borso . . . , Borso!"; and c. 21 goes on with, " 'Keep the peace, Borso!' Where are we?" Something vaguely similar occurs in the close of c. 96 and in the opening of the next:

> And before this was that affair of Habdimelich
> Anno sexto imperii, of the Second Justinian
>   "pacem."   [c. 96]

> Melik & Edward struck coins-with-a-sword,
> "Emir el Moumenin" (Systems p. 134)
>   six and ½ to one, or the sword of the Prophet,
> SILVER being in the hands of the people   [c. 97]

Borso's peace-making (reminiscent of P.'s: c. 103 closes with a reference to the letter he and Albert Mensdorff wrote to the Carnegie Endowment for Peace, suggesting investigation of the economic causes of war—see Stock 350) is echoed intentionally, for the fact that Habdimelich "rogabat ne pax solveretur" after Justinian II "pacem . . . ex amentiam dissolvit," is not essential to the story, and is consequently not mentioned in its second (English) version. The following canto begins with the same novel Borso, with the difference that his name is spelled as in the source Pound turns to at present, *A History of Monetary Systems* by Alexander Del Mar (an eccentric American historian of coinage and dilettante archeologist), who tells of the coins minted by Abd-el-Melik (Habdimelich), upon which the caliph or "Commander of the Faithful" ("Emir el Moumenin") appears, sword in hand. This "sword of the Prophet," Pound suggests, was in fact the revaluation of silver (which was "in the hands of the people"), as against gold, accomplished by the Arab mints. (The

ratio appears to have been 12 to 1 in Constantinople, 6.5 to 1 in
the Arab world.)[6] "The different rates of exchange between gold
and silver, as in imperial Rome and the Orient" (already mentioned in c. 89) are the alleged subject of c. 97 (as of Del Mar's
Systems), according to Pound's note for its first printing in 1956.[7]
On the other hand we have found better food for thought in that
hero's name suspended between two texts, two variants, and in
the radical reduction of the real to the written which this inconsistency or difference implies.

The would-be monetary discussion of c. 97 was likely to dis-
concert the reader of 1956—and also today, depending on the
passage we turn to and on our mood of the moment, we will
conclude that the author is a clown, a lunatic, or a poet of the
first water. The canto comprises fifteen pages among the most
rewarding and uneven in the entire poem: middle terms would be
inaccurate, for the imbalance has become too extreme. (But then
is it possible to deal reasonably with such abnormal works as the
Adams cantos?—a question which could be extended to the
poem as a whole.) The canto is in fact centered upon economics,
for its exasperating first seven pages are lifted with no discernible
scheme from Del Mar's *Systems*, pages 171–489 of the London
edition (P. apparently used a differently paginated American edition), while the heroine of the sequel is that most "economic"
goddess, Fortune, attended by a generous dose of not always
decipherable Poundiana. Yet what meets the eye is an incongruous sequence of graphic experiments in which genuine intuitions,
random thrusts, and playful winks to the reader that rarely come
off, coalesce so as to make analysis hopeless. However, the fact
that we can begin to discuss the canto and assess the relative intensity of passages and sections is already proof that this is not a
pointless game but the work of a mind seeking new ways and
leaving with us readable traces of a passion which is occasionally
worth the sharing.

A closer look reveals the first section to be a jumble of *names*
of coins, and of things and persons connected with them; it

6. Alexander Del Mar, *A History of Monetary Systems,* London, 1896, p. 167.

7. *Hudson Review,* 9 (Autumn 1956), 322.

presents a brute economic reality and provides a material sample of the verbal quality of Del Mar's work, from which most of the stuff is taken. Impatience, haste, and the intentional mystification of a man surrounded (like P. in the later Washington years) by sycophants who played up to his vanity, surely had their part in this aberrant construct, yet there must also have been a deeper obstacle, a sort of complex centering around the notion of money, which is the negative pole of Pound's world, the positive one being the magic word. In this connection it may be worth mentioning that Pound often called attention to the pun linking his name to the monetary unit, and that one's own name has a very special status among words, being in every respect separate, tabooed. At any rate, there is little doubt that the meditation of the word is the source of the poet's deepest intuitions, whereas all his obsessions center upon what he once referred to as the "toxicology of money." We know that as an adolescent he felt uncomfortable about his family's finances, and that he later suffered some penury, but his interest in the subject can be traced much farther back—to his visits to his father's laboratory in the "old" Philadelphia Mint, where he may have recorded the gold gathering the light about it in the gloom. "Silver I saw [he told a correspondent in 1935], as no Aladdin, for when Cleveland was elected [in 1893] there was a recount of four million in the Mint vaults, the bags had rotted, and the men half-naked with open gas flares, shovelled it into the counting-machines, with a gleam on tarnished discs" (Stock 9). An incidental reference to this experience of the eight-year-old Pound lies (as Stock notes) among the Del Mar jottings of c. 97:

> Octonary sun-worshiping Baltic.
> 371¼ grains silver in Del's time
> as I have seen them by shovel full
>   lit by gas flares.   [c. 97]

The descriptive flair of the letter has all but faded: private recollection receives no better treatment than "Del," and is in fact paler than the first line. (Del Mar refers incidentally to "octonary numbers and relations of the sunworship practiced in the countries of the Baltic.") [8] This one line is a good example of Pound's more successful "prosaic verse": a little historical poem in its own right, it suggests the metaphysics of light (and number) prominent in the second part of this canto. In the personal recollection what is most meaningful is the introduction of the self (cf. "a cup which I, Paulus, saw"). (A little earlier there is another authorial note: "And by curious segregation Brooks Adams ignores him, Del Mar, / and he, Adams, so far as I have met them, / despite stylistic resemblance.") The suggestion of direction, perhaps of an imminent breakthrough, is continued by a few other indications in the next page or so: "A disc of light over von Humboldt"; an allusion to Sophia and to the homonymous Gnostic treatise; [9] and the single word "abbreviare," italicized and in parenthesis. There is something that wants to be said. The carelessly dropped reference to the early boyhood experience is working through the money matter. Presently Pound puts away Del Mar with a mention of Geryon (see the *Fifth Decad*), and inscribes his central symbol *hsin*, "Make it new," at the head of the remarkable lines (if we may call them that) which signal the second part of the canto. Geryon is usury, death, and inversion— the dark wave of history and annals which, spilling over from the previous canto into this one, threatens to drown the swimmer and his veil. It is countered by the organic vegetable renewal graphed in the character and by Pound's Occamian axe which clears away "paraphernalia" and leaves us with a page through which the eye may freely wander:

> New fronds,
> novelle piante [*hsin*]
> > what ax for clearing?
> [*ch'in*] *ch'in* [1]   [*tan*] *tan* [4]   [*ch'in*] *ch'in* [1]
> [c. 97]

In an instant the poet rises from "the coil of Geryon" to the threshold of paradise: "born again, even as new trees (*piante*

8. Del Mar, *Systems*, p. 381. These, Del Mar adds, answer the "Gothic pagan ratio" (391). The second line refers to "today in the coinages of the U.S." (384).

9. Cf. G. R. S. Mead, *Pistis Sophia, a Gnostic Gospel (with extracts of the Book of the Saviour appended)* (London, 1896).

novelle) renewed with new foliage (*novella fronda*), pure and ready to mount to the stars." [10] He arranges, as if to cast a spell, three characters, each a stage in the contemplation of the new: the clearing away of the underbrush (*hsin*, tree [11] + axe), the "tender consideration of the growing" (*ch'in*, tree + "luminous eye"),[12] and the dawn, *tan*, graphically related to the eye, and a symbol of Leucò, Mother of Morning, whose injunction ("get rid of paraphernalia") we have already heard. What axe is he to use, he queries. The answer is reverence, the force of vegetation, and essentially the contemplation of the sign, the Word. To this he addresses himself explicitly in the sequel, picking up the color theme of c. 96 (and 90) and proceeding to a refinement of language. His subject is light, the reddish color of sea, wine, eye, and of the flames that rise from the latter "to fade in green air" (c. 93)—that is the "gas flares" and the "gleam on tarnished discs" he had seen as a boy:

> οἶνος αἰθίοψ the gloss, probably,
> not the colour. So hath Sibilla a boken ysette
> as the lacquer in sunlight ἁλιπόρφυρος
> & shall we say: russet-gold.
> That this colour exists in the air
> not flame, not carmine, orixalxo, les xaladines
> lit by the torch-flare,   [c. 97]

Pound is at first concerned, glossary-wise, with Dionysus' wine, Homer's *oînos aíthops,* also mentioned in the previous canto in connection with the taverners of Constantinople. He points out, rightly enough, that the adjective *aíthops* (from *aítho,* "I burn") refers not to the wine's redness, but to its gloss, "as the lacquer in sunlight." Likewise *halipórphuros* originally denoted movement (*porphúro,* "I move"), though after Homer it came to be associated with the mollusk, *porphúra,* and to mean "of sea-purple" ("russet-gold"). Yet this does not exhaust the lines, as

10. *Purg.* XXXIII.142–45, as translated in SR 140. Perhaps not all English readers know that all three sections of the *Commedia* close with the word "stelle"—a device as much medieval as modernistic.

11. Actually "tree" (radical 75) and "bitter" (rad. 160), i.e. hazel tree. Cf. Mancuso 179.

12. See c. 93, and (for the definition of *ch'in* just given) "Ideogrammario," *Studio integrale* (1942). The dictionary meaning is "related, relatives; parents; near to" (M 1107).

intimated by the entrance of the Sibyl (connected with the river-
eye of crystal and with Ra-Set's barge in c. 91), for Pound has
inserted into his matter-of-fact quest for the right color and word
an esoteric pun, by writing not *aíthops* but *aithíops,* i.e., an
"Ethiopian wine." The reason for this is to be found only three
cantos back, in the periplus of Apollonius, in *RD:*

> Ἠῴῳ Μέμνονι Memnon of the Dawn
> the one word meaning to burn and be warm
> ψυχὴ ἀθάνατος ἤ τί μετὰ ζωοῖσιν ἐὼν τιμητέον
>   [*pen*]
> That is of thrones,
>   and above them: Justice
> Acre again,
>   with an Eleanor   [c. 94]

We had looked at some of these lines as we were trying to establish what precisely "is of thrones." Part of the answer may be
in Pound's adaptation of what Apollonius tells his disciple in a
vision: "The soul is immortal . . . so why, being among the living . . . to be honored." [13] And yet it is the philological note in
the second line that *Th* picks up at once when it gets fully under
way in c. 97. The "word meaning to burn and be warm" is
aithíops (which, like *aíthops,* derives from *aítho*). This is what
Apollonius finds out after hearing the colossus of Memnon speak
and seeing its eyes glisten in the dawn (cf. "the great knees of
stone" of c. 91):

Now this statue, says Damis, was turned towards the sunrise, and was
that of a youth still unbearded . . . When the sun's rays fell upon the
statue, and this happened exactly at dawn . . . the lips spoke immediately the sun's ray touched them, and the eyes seemed to stand out and
gleam against the light . . . Then they say they understood that the figure was of one in the act of rising and making obeisance to the sun, in

13. Philostratus, *Life of Apollonius,* ɪɪ, 405 (vɪɪɪ. 31). P.'s Greek is selected from the hex-
ameters Apollonius recites in the vision, in order to stress both his spirituality and his
pragmatism: "So why, as long as thou art among living beings, dost thou explore these
mysteries?" The latter, however, was too much for P., who replaced *"peri tónde ma-
teúeis"* with *"timetéon"* ("to be honored")—if this is not a corruption that the scrupulous
Scheiwiller tried to set right.

the way those do who worship the powers above standing erect. They accordingly offered a sacrifice to the Sun of Ethiopia and to Memnon of the Dawn (*Helío te Aithíopi kaí Hóo Mémnoni*), for this the priests recommended them to do, explaining that the one name was derived from the word signifying "to burn and be warm," and the other from his mother.[14]

Pound, who dedicated his second book, *A Quinzaine for this Yule,* "To the Aube of the West Dawn," or to the earliest arfd more arcane dawn, and who directed fifty years later that his *Hieratic Head,* the work of Gaudier, face west,[15] must have been arrested by these lines. An indication of this is, I think, the wholly indirect transcription he gives of them in c. 94: they lie so close to the core of his "secret doctrine" that he would rather not call attention to them, but by a highly discrete echo three cantos later: the *difference,* one may well say, of an iota (and of a delayed accent: *aíthops* vs *aithíops*). "They who are skilled in fire," we were warned in c. 91, "shall read tan the dawn." What such readers may see is that Pound is completing, in accord with the ritual, the salutation of the sun of the previous canto; that the discussion of color furthers not only the metalinguistic concerns but also the tenor (dawn, renewal) of the lines that precede it; and that Pound, the poet who breaks into speech "when the morning sun [lights] up the shelves and battalions / of the West," *is* Memnon, the son of dawn. (The link is already established, subliminally, in "Octonary sun-worshiping Baltic . . . gas flares.")

"Le paradis n'est pas artificiel." "Certain colours exist in nature though great painters have striven vainly." "We appear to

---

14. Ibid. II, 15–17 (VI. 4). A footnote explains the pun.

15. See P.'s remarks (ca. 1959) about Gaudier's bust to D. G. Bridson ("An Interview with Ezra Pound," pp. 183–84): "Well, first they put it under the shadowing and symbolic pine tree, but I didn't want the sap to fall on it, so they put it properly facing the East, like the Sphinx. But that left one in the garden with nothing but the back of it, and then I remembered the old Greek story that Fontenelle has dug up of the man who got elected king because he saw the sunrise before the general mass of the people—his slave put him up to it—he saw the sunrise hitting the mountains in the West. Yes, that is the direction the statue now faces, and that's where the first gleam shows."

have lost the radiant world . . . *'mezzo oscuro luce rade'* . . .
the glass under water." These central statements resonate in the
background of the sequel of Pound's enquiry ("That this colour
exists in the air"), which gathers qualifications both negative
("not flame, not carmine") and positive ("orixalxo, les xaladines") in an excited revery reminiscent of earlier attempts to
define, in a flurry of alliteration and repetition, the colors of
Provence:

> and a valley,
> The valley is thick with leaves, with leaves, the trees,
> The sunlight glitters, glitters a-top,
> Like a fish-scale roof,
> > Like the church roof in Poictiers
> If it were gold.   [c. 4]

In c. 97 the flowing rhetoric is checked by the singleness of
words, that stand out unadorned, like pebbles churned at length
by the mind: "orixalxo" is an obliterated but pregnant trace of
Venus, who wears earrings "orichalchi preciosi" in the Homeric
Hymn which is among the sources of c. 1 ("mirthful, orichalchi"), and is associated with sea and caverns "the colour of copper" in cs. 80 and 93—the x's being the product of the churning,
of Pound's inclination to transcribe thus the chi of the Greek
alphabet, and of his temporary notion that *oreíchalkos* should be
written with two chis. The latter produce a purely visual alliteration with the subsequent "name," which is also brought to light
("to pull up a mass of algae / and pearls"—c. 80) from deep and
remote territory, not by an act of the will: it is important to bear
in mind that Pound, though a "poeta doctus" of sorts, is quite
alien to the quest for the precious word undertaken by other
decadents (for example D'Annunzio), but is always writing in a
hurry, gathering intuitively "a live tradition" from the air.

As for the "xaladines" (a feminine plural from Saladin?), twice
in *PC* Pound recalls Albert Mockel, editor of the Belgian magazine *La Wallonie,* and both times he quotes a line which he seems
to associate with Impressionism:

> . . . and Gluck's "Iphigénie"
> was played in the Mockel's garden
> Les mœurs passent et la douleur reste.
> "En casque de crystal rose les baladines"
> Mallarmé, Whistler, Charles Condor, Degas
> and the bar of the Follies
>   as Manet saw it, Degas, those two gents crossing "La
>   Concorde" or for that matter
> Judith's junk shop
>   with Théophile's arm chair
> one cd/ live in such an apartment
> seeing the roofs of Paris
>   Ça s'appelle une mansarde [16]

The poignant reminiscence concerns the somewhat Yeatsian world in which music is performed at garden parties, and the bohème world of attics, to Pound equally dear. What remains is sorrow ("la douleur reste"), but clearly also the art of the poet, and of the dancers wearing a "casque" or hairdo of rose crystal, as well as the art of nature: it seems to be no accident that this is referred to in the following canto as "the green casque."

On 18 August 1959 Pound responded to a query from his publisher in the matter of the *xaladines* as follows: "a French poem by Mockel, or I forget . . . Mallarmé, xaladines rhymes with baladines"—both association and "rhyme" pointing back to c. 80. Actually his source is Stuart Merrill's sonnet "Ballet," printed in *La Wallonie* in 1898 and given by Pound, with much praise for its music, in "French Poets," an article reprinted in *Make It New* but omitted from later collections because overly concerned with such epigones as Merrill and quite oblivious of Baudelaire, Mallarmé, and Rimbaud, whose poetics (as Montale has told us) were wholly alien to Pound. The sonnet is dedicated to Gustave Moreau and purports to describe his "pervers arcanes," the lurid colors of which may still be guessed in the background of Pound's mystical flames:

---

16. Canto 80. The other reference is in c. 78.

En casque de cristal rose les baladines,
Dont les pas mesurés aux cordes des kinnors
Tintent sous les tissus de tulle roidis d'ors,
Exultent de leur yeux pâles de xaladines.[17]

Thus the *xaladines,* scarcely perverse in these decorative lines, conceal (so far as c. 97 is concerned) a suggestion of eyes, the eyes of the goddess of the gleaming copper earrings, the "pale eyes as if without fire" mentioned in the same c. 80. Evoked by a verbal phantasy (and perhaps, unconsciously, by the rhyme with the "Aladdin" of P.'s 1935 letter), they stand in the torch- (or gas-) flare of the poet's childhood memory, connoting a homely version of Moreau's exoticism—these lines being in fact Pound's "Byzantium." The reader is reminded of Aurunculeia's nuptial torches melting "in the glare" in c. 4, and of the reprise of the theme in c. 5, where the flames become, as here, a symbol of creativity:

The fire? always, and the vision always,
Ear dull, perhaps, with the vision, flitting
And fading at will. Weaving with points of gold,
Gold-yellow, saffron . . . The roman shoe, Aurunculeia's
"Nuces!" praise, and Hymenaeus "brings the girl to her man"

[c. 5]

The erotic associations (e.g., the saffron) are no accident, as hinted in c. 97 by Venus' "orixalxo" and by the sequel.

For at this point Pound telescopes *RD,* printing *ling* as large as on the first page of the Section side by side with the second line of c. 90, which (it will be recalled) glosses a major part of the char-

17. *Make It New* (1935), p. 232—P. following (with a few slips) the *Wallonie* text. In Merrill's *Poèmes 1887–1897* (Paris, 1897), "rose" becomes "azur," and "xaladines," "Paladines"—thus suggesting, most ironically, a typo. At any rate the plangent sonnet, of which the tercets follow, is well worth adding to Mario Praz's collection: " 'Nous sommes, ô mortels, danseuses du Désir, / Salomés dont les corps tordus par le plaisir / Leurrent vos heurs d'amour vers nos pervers arcanes. // Prosternez-vous aves des hosannas, ces soirs! / Car, surgissant dans les aurores d'encensoirs, / Sur nos cymbales nous ferons tonner vos crânes.' " This may be where P. got the "heurs" (pleasures) of c. 74, which a New Directions editor tried to change to "heures," eliciting the rebuke (in the margin of the galleys): "it's not the word you think." Pearlman (p. 248) commits the same inadvertence.

acter's graphic content: the flowing of the sign from the natural essence ("under the cloud / the three voices"—c. 104). The witch-pythoness of the "small breasts" (ibid.) appearing at the bottom of the "ideogram" may be identified with the *xaladines* and the other personae who subsequently incarnate the type of Venus and of the Queen:

> & from the nature the sign,
> as the small lions beside San Marco. Out of ling   [*ling*]
> the benevolence
>
> Kuanon, by the golden rail,
>   Nile διïπετέος the flames gleam in the air
> and in the air άίσσουσιν
> Bernice, late for a constellation, mythopoeia persisting,
>   (now called folc-loristica)
> ⸙ reserpine clearing fungus,
>   Uncle William frantically denying his
> *most* intelligent statements (re/ every individual soul, per
>
> esempio)

δολιχηρέτμοισι
  [*jen*]   [*wei*]   [*ch'in*]
  [*ch'in*]   [*pao*]   [*i*]   [c.97]

The first line of the "paradiso" of *RD* ("From the colour the nature") is omitted because this is what Pound has been literally doing so far: working with color in order to close in on "nature"—the essential sensibility (skilled readership) and benevolence depicted by *ling,* and "the golden sun boat" of "Kuthera" ("Kuanon, by the golden rail"), the final object of contemplation in cs. 90–91. But as we reach the center the reverse process sets in, signs and love flow "out of ling": the good government of (Byzantine) Venice, and the captivating, tame, stone lions on the north side of St. Mark's ("ferae familiares")—as well as (in a mythical perspective) the golden rain of Zeus which impregnated Danae, suggested by the "rain" radical in *ling;* by the adjective *diipetés* ("sky-fallen"), which Homer always uses in the genitive and refers once to the Nile ("*diipetéos potamoîo*"—*Od.* IV. 477), connected with flames in the air; and, again, by "the golden

rail," a metonymy both of Ra-Set's barge and of "the gilded
tower in Ecbatan" (c. 4), situated (c. 5 tells us) south of Egypt
and of "the blue deep Nile." The Kuanon lines superimpose,
therefore, the two basic situations of c. 91: the confrontation
with the Queen's eye in which the arcane barge is to be discerned—and the nuptials of the girl with the flame (v. c. 39) or
luminous rain.

As if to draw all the threads of his poem together, Pound lifts
the final *mot juste* for his flames begotten of flame from Circe's
directions for Ulysses' *nékuia*, quoted in Greek, but for the final
line (whence *aissousin*—Od. x. 495), in c. 39: unlike Tiresias,
"Who even dead, yet hath his mind entire" (c. 47), the other dead
"*flitter* like shadows." But Ulysses is to give new life to the trem-
ulous dead through a sacrifice of beasts and later of spices, which
is also an act of translation (c. 1) or, more generally, metalinguistic traffic, as here. He will have them rise again, "free now, ascending . . . lights among them, enkindled" (c. 90)—and this is
precisely the suggestion of "in the air *aissousin*," presently
brought home by the reference to the lock of Berenice, another
queen of the Nile, becoming as late as 247 B.C. a constellation of
heaven. This, and the previous "alchimie du verbe," Pound glosses, putting suddenly in his usual way the dream in "historical"
perspective, as "mythopoeia persisting"—a persistent myth-mak-
ing or (punning on *poeia*) poetry of myth, the phrase alluding at
one time to the event, to its celebration by Callimachus and later
by his *translator* Catullus, and to the essence of Pound's quest. It
may be objected that Berenice's lock was transferred to heaven
from the temple of Arsinoe Zephyritis (where the queen had offered it as an ex voto for her husband's return from war), not by
mythopoeia but by the complaisance of a court astronomer, and
that Callimachus' urbane account of the story scarcely suggests
that he believed in it. (In fact a comparison of P.'s graffiti with
Catullus 66 and with what is left of Callimachus' poem will show
how primitive the art of poetry has become—at least in such admittedly erratic hands as P.'s—in the course of twenty-three centuries.) [18] Yet Carl Gustav Jung has shown in his discussion (*An-*

18. According to Callimachus-Catullus, the lock was flown to heaven by Zephyr, "the
brother of Ethiopian Memnon"—another link in P.'s associative sequence.

swer to Job) of so unlikely a mythopoeic feat as Pope Pacelli's dogma of the Assumption of the Virgin, that this mythical power is to be taken at face value if it is to be understood at all—and Pound makes the same claim for Ovid, who can hardly be credited with passionate belief in his tales.

Thus the vision closes with a protest against the degradation of vision to folklore: myth is the "ax for clearing" sought above, now presented as "reserpine [a drug P. probably became acquainted with at St. Elizabeth's] clearing fungus," the latter being associated with symbolist indifference to individuality. (Cf. c. 83; in *K* 9 Yeats is quoted to the effect that "God hath need of every individual soul.") "The mythological exposition," Pound had written in *K* 18, "permits . . . an expression of intuition without denting the edges and shaving off the nose and ears of a verity." The rubbish cleared away, the mind regains full possession of its faculty to dissociate—its antennae or "long oars" (*dolicherétmoisi,* a word lifted, like *diipetéos,* from *Od.* 4; cf. c. 91: "by oar, not by sail"). Geryon is vanquished by intelligence (and by no little conjuring), for the purified mind can see for itself the point of Confucius' adage (quoted conclusively in Chinese, as if to balance the opening ideographic cluster): "Manhood and the love of relatives are the true treasure" (*GD* x 13).

Pound's apparently disconnected jottings have yielded a perspicuous and compelling poetic trajectory, which derives its contextual parameters from the entire "field" of the Cantos, the nodes of which are touched upon with consummate mastery, "with long oars." But this is only a propitiatory ceremony, an introduction to the more discursive second section of the canto, a fragmented revery in which such themes as Fortuna, the initiate king, and the language, come repeatedly to the fore, in connection with graphic correlatives (characters, graphs), also recurrent.

On three occasions Pound takes up that conspicuous instance of persistent mythopoeia, the role of Fortuna in Dante's Thomistic heaven—a mirthful goddess reminiscent of Cunizza:

. . . to worldly splendors (*splendor mondani*) God appointed a general minister and guide, who should change in due time (*che permutasse a tempo;* cf. "timing the thunder") vain wealth from people to people

. . . according to her judgement, which is hidden like the snake in the grass. . . . This is she who is so reviled even by those who (being poor) should praise her, putting on her wrong blame and ill repute; but she is blessed and does not hear this: happy with the other primal creatures she turns her sphere and rejoices in her bliss (*beata si gode*). [*Inf.* vii.77–80, 83–84, 91–96]

The points which he draws from Dante Pound joins with themes of his own, as we have seen in c. 96: the contemplation of "the suave eyes" (which in *PC* intimate the process) and of their *color*, by which Fortuna is associated with vegetation and sea; the meditation or reading of the sign; and his hard-won experience of the apparent capriciousness of this new Cruel Fair. Yet he disagrees quite with such as wrongfully blame and slander her:

> All neath the moon, under Fortuna,
> >   splendor mondan,
> beata gode, hidden as eel in sedge,
> >   all neath the moon, under Fortuna
> hoc signo [*chen* ¹] *chen* (*four*), hoc signo
> with eyes pervenche,
> >   three generations, San Vio
> darker than pervenche?
> >   Pale sea-green, I saw eyes once,   [c. 97]

Although (as P. tells us below) "above the Moon there is order, / beneath the Moon, forsitan," the world of phenomena of which Fortuna is in charge is not a degraded thing (a view of which P. suspects the symbolists), but replete with *splendors,* eyes ("pale eyes as if without fire"), meaningful interactions, resurgent genes: "and the family eyes stayed the same Adriatic / for three generations (San Vio)" (c. 83)—the relation of Venice (cf. the small lions above) to the sea runs in the blood of the San Vio family, whose eyes are the closest approximation, among things seen, to those (unseen) of the goddess.

Yet it is a world in which things change, and not always for the better—and in which one must be prepared against Fortune's slings and arrows, armed with a shield and a sign. Hence Pound's unexpected sleight of hand, the replacement of Fortuna's *chen*[4]

(cs. 86, 91, 96) with man's *chen*[1] ("pure, virtuous"—*M* 346),
glossed in *A* xv 36, with regard to its radicals, as "a shell and a
direction," with the comment: "It is more than the ataraxia of
stoics, the insensitivity, ability to 'take it.' It implies going somewhere." Just as Fortuna is a force not blind but intelligent, so
man's attitude to her must be not passive but active, he must
keep going until the lady comes around—which is what Pound
did after his "enormous tragedy." The point made in *A* is restated in *RD:*

| [*tuan*] | tuan, there are four of them. | |
| [*chen*] | chen, beyond ataraxia | [c. 89] |

—and this throws light upon Pound's notation in c. 97: "chen
(*four*), hoc signo." The "four" suggests that the going will have
to be enlightened by the four Confucian cornerstones—in fact
one of the meanings of *chen*[1] is "four" ("as it is the fourth character in the *Book of Changes*"—*M*), and so the character may be
said to imply, for Pound, the *tuan*. At least one commentator[19]
has taken "(*four*)" as an indication of the tone in which *chen*[1] is
to be spoken—a blunder which suggests another possible point of
the aside. We do not know whether Pound was aware that the
earlier *chen* is spoken in the fourth tone (he transliterates the
character without indicating the tone in 86 and 96), but, granting
that he was, he may be implying that in the end *chen*[4] (Fortuna)
and *chen*[1] (beyond ataraxia) are interchangeable, for the trials of
fortune bring to light man's virtue. The goddess is to be praised,
never blamed.

"Pale sea-green, I saw eyes once"—the fine elegiac line could
be taken as a summation of Pound's sensibility: first the presentation of the color, then of that very dense act of perception: to *see,*
to see *eyes,* to see in time ("once")—the object of sight is the act
of seeing and poetry is "the daughter of memory." The poet's
"I" is at the conjunction of these vibrations, all these "I's." It is
from the Venetian vision that he has set out upon his expedition,

19. Daniel D. Pearlman, "The Blue-Eyed Eel Dame Fortune in Pound's Later Cantos,"
Agenda, ix, 4–x, 1 (Autumn–Winter 1971–72), p. 72. This is otherwise a perceptive
essay.

and always when the eyes revisit him they give him the exalted confidence of his vocation, pronouncing him a poet. "What soul boweth," he had demanded in "Praise of Ysolt," "while in his heart art thou?" Or, as another poet put it, "No mind can retain lightning / but who has seen the light does not renounce it."[20] Within the narrative frame of the *Cantos* the marine eyes are of course the source of Elizabethan sensibility:

> and Raleigh remarked, on Genova's loans non-productive,
>   that they had only their usury left,
> and there was that Führer of Macedon, dead aetat 38,
>   The temple [device] is holy,
>   because it is not for sale.   [c. 97]

Geryon reenters as the usury of Genoa (associated by P. with the Bank of England), which will fight the "nature" of Adriatic Venice, sell the temple, and eliminate the furiously perceptive Führers of Greek and German times. While Fortuna is good, natural, economics, the guarantor of process, usury is a departure from the order of things, more than faintly connected with such unpredictable "criminals" as F.D.R. (The quotation is only intended as proof of the articulateness of the obsession.)

> "No, George, don't you be with that fellow for president,
>   "We don't know what he'll do next."
> Some faint connection
>   between criminality and calamity,
>   lo jorn, Der Tag
> that at least a few should perceive this [*tan*] tan
> Arnaut spoke his own language, 26th Purgatorio,
> above the Moon there is order,
>   beneath the Moon, forsitan.   [c. 97]

Pound appears to quote himself to George Tinkham on the subject of unpredictable criminality, the confusion and hurry of Geryon, which is all that prevents the accomplishment of order also beneath the Moon-Fortuna. For the initiate (Arnaut, P.) can read the message of order of the dawn (the superlunar sun rising

20. Eugenio Montale, "Per album," *La bufera e altro* (Milano: Mondadori, 1957), p. 114.

over a sublunar horizon), and its promise of a better future ("E vei jauzen lo jorn qu'esper, denan"),[21] though he can communicate this knowledge only in his own language, the language of "our science," in which it is hardly surprising to find a bit of German. As Dante with Arnaut in the passage from *Purg.* 26 which *SR* brought into twentieth-century American poetry, so Pound will let people and things speak for themselves—and for the goddess who arranges their splendors.

Fortuna and the two signs printed in the previous lines (*tan* and the temple device) are the three recurrent motifs of the second section of the canto. The former, Pound playfully suggests by recalling a remark of Arthur Griffith ("Can't move 'em with / a cold thing like economics"),[22] is his own solution to the problem of making economics—the ratios of gold and silver—palatable, even as Dante was careful to introduce the popular goddess into his scheme of things:

> and you will certainly not convert them
> > if you remove the houris from Paradise.
> Even Aquinas could not demote her, Fortuna,
> > violet, pervenche, deep iris,
> > > beat'è, e gode,   [*she is blest, and rejoices*]
> the dry pod could not demote her, plenilune,
> > phase over phase.
> Dante had read that Canzone.
> > Birds, said Hudson, are not automata.
> Even Jonathan Edwards is said to have noticed trees,   [c. 97]

Fortuna, the houri of the paradise of this poet (who uses all his talent to convert us), is identified, through her ever-shifting vegetating eyes, with the signatures of nature,[23] the new fronds, which no Aristotelian or Calvinistic (Edwards) "dry pod" (see the close of c. 7) can possibly "black out" (c. 95); wholly unper-

21. *Purg.* xxvi.144, in the reading translated by P. in *SR* 25 ("Yet [I] see, rejoicing, the day which is before me"). The preferable reading is "lo *joi* qu'esper"—the joy which I hope awaits me, i.e., heaven.

22. See cs. 19, 78, and 103.

23. The unremovable houris first appear in c. 87, just after the major passage on signatures.

turbed, she rejoices, even "as in the clear nights of full moon (*ne'*
plenilunii sereni) Trivia smiles among the eternal nymphs," [24]
again undistinguishable from Diana of the Crossways, the moon-
goddess. Before relinquishing her (she is next to invisible in the
remainder of the poem) Pound provides a "philological" conclusion to what is after all his version of the "magnificent thesis to
be written on the role of Fortune, coming down through the
Middle Ages," spoken of in *P&T:* Dante, he tells us, had in mind
the canzone "Io son la donna che volto la rota"—"gauchely attributed," as a scholar puts it, "to Guido Cavalcanti." [25] The
scarcely convincing basis of Pound's statement is apparently the
recurrence in both his sources of the topoi of wrongful blame and
of the wheel.

Following up his exposure of the dry pods the lawgiver of *Th*
goes on to warn us against empty legalism—under the circumstances, a proviso for which we are grateful—though it is occasioned chiefly by his fear of censorship, which links up with the
persecutory notions ("dead aetat 38") ventilated a page back. But
if we read on we are rewarded with a striking esoteric representation of the arcane matters that the money changers have almost
entirely erased from their books, yet are to be preserved in this
record of *our* own:

> The Twelve Tables penalized satire,
>   and some one has wiped out most of Lucilius
> and there is, of course, very little about Antoninus
>   left in their records,
> Luigi, *gobbo,* makes his communion with wheat grain
>   in the hill paths
>   at sunrise
> ONE, ten, eleven, *chi con me*   [*tan*]   tan?   [c. 97]

From the *De Modo Usurarum* of Claudius Salmasius,[26] the humanist chiefly remembered for the *Defensio Regia pro Carlo I* to

24. *Par.* xxiii.25–26. Quoted by P. in *Hagoromo, T* 313*n.*

25. Giorgio Siebzehner-Vivanti, *Dizionario della* Divina Commedia, ed. M. Messina (Milano: Feltrinelli, 1965), p. 249*n.*

26. Leiden, 1639, according to the bibliography (useful for students of P.'s "economic
history") in *L'America, Roosevelt e le cause della guerra presente* (1944), *LU* 55. This is

which Milton replied (but the obscurity of the source is so much corroboration of the above theses), Pound learned of a "disputed text of Antoninus Pius,"[27] in which the emperor considers "the difference between Roman Law and the Law of Rhodes, between agrarian usury and maritime usury . . . concerned as to whether the Roman State shd. profit by sailor's misfortune and batten on shipwreck" [K 3]—as summarily reported in the *Fifth Decad* (cs. 42 and 46); and on this account Antoninus becomes, here and elsewhere, a symbol of successful resistance against the bankers, bearing out the formula (to be found among the Del Mar materials), "When the kings quit, the bankers began again." But on this occasion Pound goes on from the "bellum perenne" to the affirmative values of the "resistance"—to the grain-rite of Eleusis, performed at dawn, in the "hill paths" (see c. 39) above Rapallo, by a peasant double of the poet—the hunchbacked peddler Luigi. (In primitive thinking physical deformity is often considered to be a sacred sign.)[28] Thereupon the invitation of Pound-Luigi becomes most pressing: "Chi con me?" (Who with me?)—though he jealously claims in the same breath his birthright as Son of Morning by way of the arcane-looking sequence of numbers, the key to which may be found in the "Personal Note" to *L'asse che non vacilla* (1945): "The ideogram *tan,* the dawn . . . is to be found in the eleventh Ode of T'ang (*Shih Ching* I, 10, 11, 3) engraved in so splendid a fashion that the poetry of three millennia has not equalled it" (*OS* 600—this recalls Mallarmé's comments on the printing of masterworks). If, following this clue, we look up Pound's version (appropriately titled "Alba") of Ode 124 (or I.x.11), we may find in the third verse the motto of the initiate:

---

why, in reading the "Collation des extraits de Julien d'Ascalon transcrits dans le Genevensis" (appended to Nicole's *Livre du Préfet*), Pound takes note of the remark, "Ces leçons meilleures du Genevensis confirment certaines corrections des critiques modernes, de Saumaise et de Reitz en particulier" (p. 67), which turns up in c. 96, strangely enough, as "de Saumaise, de Reitz." (Salmasius' French name is Claude de Saumaise.)

27. "The Individual in His Milieu" (1935), *SPr* 272.

28. Luigi, I am told, was not a hunchback, but somewhat crippled. He would come in his round to P.'s house in S. Ambrogio, and call after "the poet" from a distance—then tell him of such wonders as the one recorded here.

> The horn pillow is white like rice,
> the silk shroud gleams as if with tatters of fire.
> In the sunrise I am alone.   [CA 124]

—where also the "tatters of fire" point to the magic of c. 97: "not flame, not carmine, orixalxo." [29]

The third recurrent symbol of this Wagnerian score is the temple with three columns, possibly signifying heaven, earth, and underworld—an image, like the gnomon *chih* and Yggdrasil, of the center of things.[30] It continues to occur and be expatiated upon after the themes of dawn and Fortuna have subsided, Pound indicating by juxtaposition that he has extrapolated it from the hieroglyph of the "hawk-king" Ka-ap (or of Sargon the Great, according to his authority, Waddell). The latter he prints in a more expanded form than in c. 94, together with a new sampling of pseudo-archeological data from Waddell, chosen on account of their contextual bearing. Thus we hear of "torchlight," of an offering of perfume, of a "lion head," graphed and associated with "Tyanu" (Apollonius, we recall, spoke to the lion with great charity)—and of the strangest of Waddell's tall tales: the voyage of Minos-Manu-Menes to Ireland, where he dies of a bee's bite, and is buried by "the Hill of Many," near Clogher: "By Knoch Many now King Minos lies."[31] Once again Pound, far from making a haphazard collection of materials, is indicating a pattern of recurrence: the periplus (of Ulysses-Brut-Minos), the interaction of cultures, particularly of the Atlantic and Mediterranean world—his chief concern. He wants to single out the constants of civilization, preeminent among which are "peace with the animals," and "reverence for the forces of vegetation": "From Sargon to Tyana / no blood on the altar stone." This Pound takes to be the message of Ka-ap's hieroglyph, which in its expanded form depicts the "hawk" perching (as if giving protec-

29. Karlgren's translation: "The horn pillow is beautiful, the brocade coverlet is bright; my beautiful one has gone away from here; with whom can I associate—alone I have my morning." *The Book of Odes*, p. 80.

30. Cf. B. de Rachewiltz 39, 50.

31. See Waddell, *Egyptian Civilization*, p. 69. Charles Olson recounts the story in *Maximus Poems* 4 (1968).

tion) over a cartouche which encloses the "temple" device; to the right are other hieroglyphs suggesting fronds and the Chinese radical for "field." It should be added that, though Pound's interpretation is as usual pure magic, the hieroglyph is in fact an undeciphered fragment of history dating back (as P. maintains) to "a thousand years before T'ang."[32]. Moreover the sign occasions lines that are their own justification—a compelling description of the royal tradition Pound is thinking of:

> Flowers, incense, in the temple enclosure,
>   no blood in that TEMENOS
> when crocus is over and the rose is beginning.
> PAUL, the Deacon, Migne 95.
>   Upsala, was the golden fane,
> ministrat virtutem, Fricco, pacem. Voluptatem,
>   ingenti Priapo.
> Dea libertatis, Venus.
>   Agelmund son of Ayon, reigned 33 years.
> PUER APULIUS
>   "Fresca rosa" sang Alcamo.
> Of Antoninus very little record remains
>   [device]
> That he wrote the book of the Falcon.
> Mirabile brevitate correxit, says Landulph
>   of Justinian's Code
> and built Sta Sophia, Sapientiae Dei
>   [*cheng ming*]   [c. 97]

Kings and cultures appear united in a timeless renaissance of civilization, intimately connected with the only valid model of rebirth: the new fronds, the instant "gone as lightning," yet "enduring 5000 years" (c. 95), in which "crocus is over and the rose is beginning"—an instant which Pound can sing with the transport of the major troubadours: "Ab la dolchor del temps novel." The revival of nature is juxtaposed with the myth of sensuality:

---

32. Waddell took it from W. M. F. Petrie's *History of Egypt* (1923–27). He gives the transliteration, SHA PA-RIN-BARA KAD GIN U-KUS, and the translation: "The shepherd of the (Sun-) Hawk, of the House of the Pharaoh, Kad (the lofty) Gin, the Ukus."

Fricka, Priapus, and Venus—the goddess of freedom.[33] The ideogram encompasses the civilizations of Egypt (the hieroglyphs), of
the far North (Upsala), of the Lombards (the reign, of mystical
length, of Agelmund, the son Ayon—father Time; cf. *History of
the Lombards* I. 14), of Swabish Sicily, of imperial Rome, and of
Byzance. The king's emblem is again the hawk (perched in the hieroglyph above the cartouche enclosing the temple and fronds),
the subject of "the book of the Falcon" by the "Apulian child"
Frederick II; and at his court the Song of the Rose is sung, by
Cielo d'Alcamo, one of the first to write an Italianate Sicilian
("Rose, fresh and most fragrant, that appears about the summer-
time"),[34] and by Pound. In this composite springtime "the golden
fane," the gilded "Dorata," is erected, in honor of a Gnostic
Sophia (Helen of Tyre)—and with it the Word of the Law, both
precise (*cheng ming*) and pithy (cf. "abbreviare"), is established.[35]

In the "Personal Note"—already quoted—which prefaces
L'asse che non vacilla, Pound wrote: "In editing his anthology
Confucius determined and perpetuated the meaning of the words
it includes. For example, the ideogram *tan* . . . [see above]. But
the odes are not only a source of delight, they are also a lexicographic source, the basis of an education which in many ways
is still valid" (*OS* 600). The close of c. 97 accomplishes the admirable trajectory of these two first cantos of *Th* by returning to the
text of "the Deacon, Migne 95" (the reference is appropriate in
the context of the "temenos"—the inner temple), i.e., to the point

33. In a footnote to the first chapter of the *De Gestis Langobardorum* the editor, Migne,
quotes "M. Adamus in Septentrionalium populorum Historia," on the subject of Wotan:
"In hoc templo (Ubsola patrio sermone vocato) quod totum ex auro paratum est, statuas
trium deorum veneratur populus: Thor . . . Wodan . . . Fricco. . . . Wodan fortior
bella regit, hominumque ministrat virtutem contra inimicos. Tertius est Fricco pacem,
voluptatemque largiens mortalibus, cujus etiam simulacrum fingunt ingenti Priapo" (*PL*
xcv 447–48). Later on, in connection with Woden and Wednesday, Migne remarks that
Friday is named for Freya and not for freedom, "quia Venus libertatis dea."

34. *The Penguin Book of Italian Verse,* ed. George R. Kay (Harmondsworth: Penguin,
1958), p. 33.

35. Migne appends to the *Historia Miscella* an "Adjunct" by Landulphus Sagax (*PL* xcv
1144)—whence the lines on Justinian, with the happy find: "Mirabile brevitate"—which
is of the essence of P.'s quest.

of departure, in accord with the pattern of allegiance to the actual source set definitively in c. 1. Migne appends to Paul's works
the latter's epitome of Sextus Pompeius Festus' *De Verborum Sig-
nificatione* (2nd cent.), which is in turn derived from a work by
Verrius Flaccus, and was brought to light by the humanist Pom-
ponio Leto—a tangle comparable to Divus' *Homeri Odyssea*.
Festus' book is a sort of glossary, rich in archeological and erudite materials of no little antiquarian interest; it is arranged in al-
phabetic order. In taking leave from his reader Pound turns, accordingly, to the meaning of words, extracting passages from the
glossary and suggesting that "the right word" is the kernel of the
mythological phantasy. The result is the image of a world of
humanistic *Sagetrieb* ("As from Verrius Flaccus to Festus . . .
All this came down to Leto")—a world of "dead words and
buried" (*PL* xcv 1626) from which such readers as are skilled in
fire can elicit demonic and benevolent energies:

> Deorum Manium, Flamen Dialis & Pomona
>   (seeking the god's name)
> "that remain in all aethera terrenaeque"
> Manes Di, the augurs invoke them
>   .   .
>
> & Spartans in Mount Taygeto
>   sacrifice a horse to the winds,
> as in Campo Martio, in October,
>   in Lacedaemon, dust to the uttermost
> and at Rhodos, the sun's car is thrown into the sea,
> rubbing their weapons with parsley,
>   Flamen Portualis
> "inter mortua jam et verba sepulta" [*pe ma tsu*]   [c. 97]

The scattered segments appear to crystallize a universe of individual gestures, of personal and communal attitudes to the sacred,
cognate to the "weaving with points of gold" of the *Cantos,* and
to single episodes and symbols: the fauns, dryads, and maelids of
c. 3; the Mount casting its seed everywhere (evoked by the ash of
the horse sacrificed on Taygetus to the winds, "ut eorum flatu
cinis ejus per finis quam latissime differatur"—1623); the boat
of the Sun and of his companion (Venus, to whom Rhodes, the

island of the rose, is sacred); and the vegetal vigor which sharpens the axe in the character *hsin* ("Persillum vocant sacerdotes rudiculum picatum, quo unguine Flamen Portunalis arma quirini unguet"—1625). The poet is not grieved that his Flamen Portunalis should receive him among words—in a harbor of writing—to the side of which he places three characters ("elder," "horse," "ancestors"): the search for analogies could be pursued, for instance in the "Horse Odes of Lu," the penultimate book of *CA*. For the time being, however, it comes to rest upon the image of the king who institutes "there" (in a textual space already familiar—*Brut*—or in a promised land still in the future) his guilds (cf. Leo the Wise)—and upon the names of other kinds of "persillum" particularly dear to the poet, who once hoped he would right Italian economy by introducing their cultivation, and who perhaps expected to be encouraged by a contemporary Athelstan: [36]

> And that Athelstan set up guilds there
> kadzu, arachidi, acero,
> > not lie down [*wu chüan*]   [c. 97]

The Confucian advice not to lie down (reiterated in Chinese—cf. *A* XIII 1) is but a variant reading of the message of renewal spelled out by the new fronds.

36. See his hilarious defense of peanuts in "Arachidi," *Meridiano di Roma,* 5 Oct. 1941, quoted in Zapponi 68; as well as *CV* 319 and the close of c. 74. In the following, "acero" is Italian for maple, "kadzu grass" (associated with peanuts in a letter to Scheiwiller of 15 Jan. 1954) perhaps short for a Japanese ivy that "would cover semideserted land, North Africa, Australia, etc.," making it cultivable (E. Hesse, *Paideuma* 8: 53–54). Always much concerned with agriculture, P. mentions in *Th* Giulio Del Pelo Pardi, fascist agrologist and inlaw of B. de Rachewiltz, who "came on cunicoli" (c. 101), i.e., channels which he took to be signs of prehistorical reclaiming in the Roman Campagna (cf. Mussolini in c. 41). Eventually, in c. 116, "cunicoli" becomes a symbol of the byways of communication in time of underground warfare or "resistance"—"a little light / in great darkness."

13. The Edict

China and Beyond the Center

What is the greatest hearsay?
The greatest hearsay is the tradition of the gods.
Of what use is this tradition?
It tells us to be ready to look.

> —"Religio, or The Child's Guide
> to Knowledge," *PD* 96–97.

One of my poems is called "Seagull: Bikini of God." We
cannot see God, He is not visible, but He is everywhere, He
exists, and we can only see His bikini. His bikini is a seagull
and it comes to us, we see God come to us, like Jesus walking on the water in the New Testament. Certainly it is a kind
of joke—the bikini, it's a little sexy—but there's a sense of
something serious too.

> —Andrei Voznesensky, in conversation
> with Stanley Kunitz, 1972

While the *China-John Adams* cantos and the *Rock-Drill* "histories" both move on from ancient China to pre-modern Europe
and America, *Thrones* reverses the pattern, for with its second
major episode we come from the confused Middle Ages of the
West dealt with in the cantos foregoing, to the model state, ca.
1700, of the enlightened despots of the East, K'ang-hsi and his
son and successor Yung Cheng, whose reigns are celebrated at
the close of the Chinese "decad." However, Pound's customary
mythicizing hardly allows us to notice this interesting structural
reversal or to distinguish in any way seventeenth-century China
from the prehistorical land of the *Shu Ching* and cs. 85–87—a
lack of historical perspective in keeping with Chinese thought (in
the Annals rendered by Mailla the first emperor Yao and
Yung Cheng come out, as has been remarked, much alike), and

of course with the method of the *Cantos,* in which Justinian, Malatesta, and Mussolini fit together as snugly as halves of a seal.

Cantos 98 and 99 are again an idiosyncratic gloss to a document of law, religious law in this instance, as suggested by its title, which one is tempted to extend to the entire body of *Th—Sheng Yü* or *Sacred Edict.* A summary of Confucian—or government—ethics (cf. P.'s insistence on "abbreviare"), it comprises sixteen pithy prescriptions said to have been written by the great K'ang-hsi (1670), and a commentary appended by Yung Cheng; Wang-iu-p'u, "salt-commissioner" of Shensi, translated it from the literary (Uen-li) to the colloquial tongue. The final link in the textual chain of transmission (cf. Divus' *Odyssea* and Jannequin's *Chanson*) leading to cs. 98–99 is F. W. Baller's 1892 edition of the Edict,[1] an unassuming little book which includes the Uen-li text and Wang's colloquial rendering, the latter with English translation, and which the editor intended as an introduction for fellow missionaries to the language and culture of China, little suspecting that sixty years on it would be taken as sacred writ. Unable to read the untranslated Uen-li text, Pound concentrates, with the aid of Baller's version, on Wang's colloquial rendering, which he approaches with the method brought to bear two cantos back upon Leo the Wise: first, in c. 98, which (he wryly remarked) "will be deemed the 'more poetic' " of the *Sheng Yü* diptych,[2] he considers closely Wang's "style," which is found to be as admirable as Leo's ("despite Mathews this Wang

1. F. W. Baller, *The Sacred Edict of K'ang Hsi,* with a translation of the colloquial rendering (Shanghai: American Presbyterian Mission Press, 1892).

2. E.P., "Servizio di comunicazioni," *Canto 98,* tr. M. de Rachewiltz (Milano: Scheiwiller, 1958), p. 9. "Canto 99 has appeared this month [July 1958] in the *Virginia Quarterly.* Canto 98 will be deemed 'more poetic,' but both—at least in the author's intention—indicate that the poem has a structure. That is, that the ten cantos of the emperors of Cathay, of the middle kingdom, 52–61, developing the theme of 13 (Confucian motif), lead to 98–99, which are a summary of Confucian ethics, as put into action and practice by the splendid administration of the Manchu, as State teaching. Si monumentum requiris. I cannot simplify it further." The note, in Italian, is dated from Brunnenburg (Merano), 22 July 1958. That not all was well with P. at the time of writing may be gathered by his forgetting to mention that essential occurrence of the Confucian motif, cs. 85–87; he also writes "51–61" (for "52–61").

was a stylist"—we recall an earlier lover's quarrel with the dictionary about another Wang); then, in c. 99, having satisfied himself in the matter of language, he incorporates at length the Edict's prescriptions within his *Thrones,* in a fashion almost as practical and unambiguous as the Salt-Commissioner's.

Canto 98, a rarefied but pregnant poem, and one of the most stirring in the sequence, is arranged in several sections. The prelude continues in the mythical vein of the foregoing reading of Festus' glossary, yet, being largely composed of Pound's own contributions, allows for a more direct and compelling presentation of the religiousness previously filtered through layers of text. Thereupon Wang-iu-p'u enters with a flourish of Chinese characters (let it be noted, however, that c. 98, unlike cs. 85–86, usually glosses these in English) and much emotion ("Until in Shensi, Ouang, the Commissioner Iu-p'uh . . . The King's job, vast as the swan flight")—and Pound introduces briefly the themes of the Edict he is most attracted to, chief among these K'ang-hsi's tenth prescription, "Let the people attend to their proper calling [*pen yeh,* 'one's original calling or profession'—M 7321: 23], that they may have settled determination," associated later in the canto with the adage, *Ne sutor ultra crepidam*—a theme clearly intended by Pound as a rhyme for Leo's and Athelstan's guilds. (See c. 94: "[*pen*] / That is of thrones.") This preliminary overview is followed by a fugal reprise of the theological themes of the canto's prelude, which in turn leads to a synthetic account of twelve of the Edict's clauses, anticipating the following canto's more relaxed treatment of these, and to a final ecstatic paean for King and immaculate Queen.

The prelude is centered upon Leucothea, whom we have just been able to make out in the sequence's opening lines, and who resurfaces as a gull a few pages on in a cryptic aside:

> After 500 years, still sacrificed to that sea gull,
> a colony of Phaeacians ϑῖνα ϑαλάσσης   [c. 96]

Speaking as Wagnerian exegetes, we would say that the lines encapsulate, besides the heroine, the following "themes": tradition and its transmission, peace with the animals, poetic sensibility

arising from "ear, ear for the sea-surge" (c. 7—P. had been long
concerned with Homer's line, see *L* 189 and 296, but this is its
first occurrence in the poem), sacrifice without bloodshed, and
Phaeacians as the tribe of sensibility—the initiate scientists. What
Pound is thinking of in terms of "history" is not easily discerned,
unless the pertinent gloss be found again in *P&T:* "At Marseille
the Greek settlement was very ancient" (96). In fact Massilia appears to have been founded by *Phocaean* colonists in the seventh
century B.C., some five hundred years after Ulysses' time. The
lines would then also provide a further instance of the continuity
of Greece and Provence.

Another quotation first found in *P&T* 98 ("loved her to make
her most fair"—Godeschalk by way of Gourmont), turns up in
connection with *thîna thalásses* and Phaeacians in c. 98's stirring
prelude to the Manchu edict:

> "Ut facias pulchram"
> there is no sight without fire.
> Thinning their oar-blades
> ϑῖνα ϑαλάσσης
> nothing there but an awareness
> In Byzantium 12% for a millennium
> The Manchu at 36 legal, their Edict
> the next pass.   [c. 98]

The body of fire of passion gives forth once again the body of
light of vision, of "awareness" (see c. 85), and this in turn perme-
ates the body politic, forming the law and the economy, in particular the slight degree of tolerance of usury obtaining in classic
antiquity, from Greece to Byzance, unsurpassed even by Manchu
China, to which we are to turn next. The oar-thinning Phaeacians (*"apoxúnousin eretmá"*—*Od.* VI. 269) are the poets who
pursue the refinement of language, like Mallarmé, Homer, the
troubadours, and the theologians summoned in the sequel; they
are watchers of shadows and of differences as subtle as those between "throstle's note" and "banded thrush," *aíthops* and *aithíops:*

> Anselm: that some is incarnate awareness
> thus trinitas; some remains spiritus.

"The body is inside." Thus Plotinus,
But Gemisto: "Are Gods by hilaritas";
        and their speed in communication.
        et in nebulas simiglianza,
                καϑ'ὁμοίωσιν Deorum
a fanned flame in their moving
must fight for law as for walls
—Herakleitos' parenthesis—   [c. 98]

This is the "hearsay," the *Sagetrieb,* of the gods, also closely connected with the word of the law, which a Heraclitean fragment
(44) compares to the walls of the city. The gods, "startling, sudden, tricky as nature" (*L* 294), are full of change, humor, communication—"They become other things by swift and unanalysa-
ble process" ("Arnold Dolmetsch," *LE* 431)—and this is why
they are to be seized only at the doors of perception. Following
suit Pound constructs his own complex mythologem, superim-
posing and *dissociating* Leucothea and her quasi-namesake Leucothoe, who was buried alive by Orchamus of Babylon, her father, out of anger for her love for Apollo (cf. Danae), and whom
the divine lover changed (as Ovid recounts) into an incense
shoot. (We now see the point of the references to incense, *thus*
and *thumíama,* in c. 96.)

And that Leucothoe rose as an incense bush
—Orchamus, Babylon—
        resisting Apollo.
Patience, I will come to the Commissioner of the Salt Works
        in due course.
Est deus in nobis.   and
        They still offer sacrifice to that sea-gull
est deus in nobis
        Κρήδεμνον
She being of Cadmus line,
        the snow's lace is spread there like sea foam   [c. 98]

The two Leucos are distinguished by way of their lineage (cruel
Orchamus vs heroic Cadmus) and of their metamorphoses (incense vs seagull, vegetal powers vs peace with the animals), and

yet they are associated "out of similitude" (*"kath'homoíosin"*)[3] as early as *RD,* Pound intentionally telescoping them in the line: " 'My bikini is worth yr/ raft.' Said Leucothoe."[4] Also here, though the distinction is maintained, the sacrifice to the seagull of Massilia's Phaeacians-Phocaeans calls to mind earlier offerings of cedar, juniper, and incense: the symbol of one lady is worshipped with the symbol of the other. There is good reason to do this for both are "incarnate awareness"—the mind standing by Ulysses in his trouble and "rising" at the tabulary's consecration. The connection is openly indicated by the application to both of Ovid's statement that "there is a god within us" (cf. c. 93)—"us" being mankind and more particularly the adepts' community, spoken of in the dramatic inception of the canto, which throws light upon what we have been saying. (It should be compared with the close of c. 94, that anticipation of *Th,* though it also acts upon the injunction immediately preceding: "not lie down.")

> The boat of Ra-Set moves with the sun
> "but our job to build light" said Ocellus:
> Agada, Ganna, Faasa
>   [*hsin*] hsin [1]

3. The words, hardly a quotation, would seem to have been added when the canto was in proof for publication in *L'Illustrazione Italiana,* Sept. 1958 (a photograph of the first proof page is included among the illustrations in *L'Herne,* after p. 328). The original reading was: "But Gemisto: 'Are Gods by hilaritas.' / and their communication. / in nebulas simil Deorum, / a fanned flame in their moving."

4. Canto 95. Christine Brooke-Rose, overlooking P.'s intention to portray his gods as they change into different things, has claimed, in *A ZBC of Ezra Pound* (Berkeley: Univ. of California Press, 1971), p. 151, that this is a mere typo, and her argument has convinced some editor to change the line in recent New Directions printings (a real typo— "Leucothae" for "Leucothea"—adding itself to the ill-advised urge to emend). But care should be taken before "improving" P.'s text to fit one's prejudices, especially when so delicate a matter as the tradition of the gods is at stake. Leucothea is the leitmotif of the later cantos, and the line is crucial to an understanding of the subject. Fortunately we have evidence that P. wanted it to stand precisely as he wrote it, for Vanni Scheiwiller was perceptive enough to notice the apparent inconsistency as he was publishing *RD,* and pointed it out to P., who wrote him on 21 June 1955: "Leucothea, Leucothoe, fatto con intenzione nel, medioevo NON si osservava questa uniformità" (". . . done intentionally; in the middle ages one did not observe uniform spelling"). Medieval precedent (a reference in itself significant) is cited as a screen, a warrant for the poet's central sleight of hand.

Make it new
Τὰ ἐξ Αἰγύπτου φάρμακα
Leucothea gave her veil to Odysseus
Χρόνος
Πνεῦμα θεῶν
καὶ ἔρως σοφίας
The Temple (hieron) is not for sale.
Getting the feel of it, of his soul,
while they were making a fuss about Helen   [c. 98]

The "great periplum," the love that moves the stars, is correlated
with the star-like city, Ecbatan and Wagadu,[5] to be built by
clearing away paraphernalia (hsin) and by taking as a model
vegetal rebirth—"reserpine clearing fungus," and the soothing
drug given by Helen to Telemachus and Menelaus (Od. iv.
219–32). This drug comes, like so many themes of the later cantos, from Egypt, land of compassionate Isis, and is a paradisal
rhyme for the "kakà phármaka" of Circe mentioned in c. 39. The
confrontation of Ocellus and Ulysses with Ra-Set, Helen, and
Leucò, suggests that the builder's job is to be furthered by the
lady's compassionate intervention, which gives access to the mysteries of "time, the divine breath, and the love of sophía"—to the
inner temple, which, like the veil (to be returned to Leucò on her
demand) is not for sale. Yet the lady is "incarnate awareness,"
"deus in nobis," as we find at the end: the Helen of the phármaka is not quite the Helen of the headlines, for she is the anima of
the much-enduring hero. (The lines enlarge upon Od. iv.
138–54.)

In the lines following the hearsay of the two Leucos, Pound as-
sesses his chief companions, and finds them wanting, not sufficiently Odyssean, unresponsive to the myth which is both of the
world and of the mind. The hero reaches Phaeacia alone, or almost so:

But the lot of 'em, Yeats, Possum and Wyndham
had no ground beneath 'em.
[pu]

5. See ch. 3, n. 17.

> Orage had.
> Per ragione vale
> Black shawls for Demeter.
> "Eleven literates" wrote Senator Cutting,
>   "and, I suppose, Dwight L. Morrow."
> Black shawls for Demeter.
> The cat talks—μάω—with a greek inflection,   [c. 98]

Yeats, Eliot, and Lewis lack the veil of sensibility, the ground for the building of light (*pu*, "no," underscores this with a visual pun, for the character has literally no ground beneath it)—unlike Orage, who was significantly both a visionary of sorts and an adherent of Social Credit. (A more likely choice would have been Williams, who, alone of P.'s poet friends, shared his economic views—but then he may have appeared to him to be too little the mystical type.) Orage is said to affirm himself by way of reason ("per ragione vale"), even as Ulysses had his own mind to stand by him; if we read the quotation from "Donna mi prega" in context ("Deeming intention to be reason's peer and mate"),[6] we see that it may also suggest a balance of reason and intention or vision—at any rate, the judgment does not change. The American political body, with its eleven or twelve "literate" senators,[7] is found equally wanting, and compares unfavorably with the inborn culture of the women of Venice, who commemorate with black shawls (variations of the white bikini) the mourning of Demeter (said to wear a *"kuáneon kálumma"* in the Homeric Hymn)—as well as with the learning of the cat which, in miaowing, shows some knowledge of Chinese (*mao*, a cat) and of Greek (*máomai*, I want). We are acquainted with the animal at least since *PC* ("and if the corn cat be beaten / Demeter has lain in my furrow"—cf. *Od.* v. 125–27); it is the Eleusinian (and Dionysian) totem of the poet, who in fact speaks in this canto an Esperanto of English, Greek, and Chinese. A last example of the political-natural culture that explodes bourgeois categories ("the

6. Canto 36. But "la 'ntenzione per ragione vale" means that love takes intention for reason—it rationalizes what is in fact mere impulse.

7. See *K* 47. P. is of course referring to Dwight Whitney Morrow. The name carries no special meaning, being only a "mnemonic" for Cutting's remark.

cowardice of the so-called upper class") is Mussolini's fascism, but soon Pound goes on to more likely Phaeacians:

> "Noi altri borghesi
>   could not speak efficiently to the crowd
>   in piazza,"
> said the Consigliere, "we thought we could control Mussolini."
>
> Uncle William two months on ten lines of Ronsard
>   But the salt works . . .
>   ψεῦδος δ᾽οὐχ ἐρέει
>   . . . γὰρ πεπνυμένος
> Patience, ich bin am Zuge . . .
>   ἀρχή
>   an awareness   [c. 98]

As if to qualify his previous censure (cf. c. 83) Pound admits Uncle William, the memorable "translator" of Ronsard ("When you are old and grey and full of sleep"), among the thinners of oar-blades, mankind's unacknowledged legislators. Once again he must remind himself of his intended subject, the *Sacred Edict* and its "translator," the Commissioner of the Salt Works. After the earlier reminder he had submitted that first the god within us was to be heard; now he quotes Athene's commendation of Nestor, "too intelligent to prevaricate" (c. 99, cf. *Od.* iii. 20), implying that the "truth" of the matter demands that we have patience and attend in the first place to his tale of metamorphosis (a request with which we are quite willing to comply), for the crucial point, the ground on which everything rests, the *arché*, is awareness. "Nothing there but an awareness"—he had remarked earlier.

Having brought the prelude to a close upon this key word, Pound turns to the *Sheng Yü*, reviewing the themes most appealing to him. He praises Wang for putting his text into "volgar eloquio" (a reference, of course, to Dante), in order (we gather) to "speak efficiently to the crowd"; commends the *pen yeh;* and turns to the evils of Buddhism and Taoism, as usual with much animus and at excessive length, for the heretics decried in the edict represent in these cantos (as in the Chinese decad) the ene-

mies of true contemplation and good government. However, one
point of Wang's refutation of unorthodox thought is worth quoting, for it is made much of in cs. 99 and 100, and provides the
poet with new evidence that "Great intelligence attains again and
again to great verity" (K 22). "If you recognize," we are told,
"that reason is true, and that the mind enlightened is heaven, the
mind in darkness is hell—you will then as a matter of course
have a ruling principle" (vii. 15). Consequently K'ang-hsi and
Kati ("A man's paradise is his good nature") are said to be like
"two halves of a seal." (P. is always interested in definitions of
heaven and hell because he is of course thinking of his poem.)

Ironically, after slighting Buddhists and Taoists, Pound singles
out for attention the ninth saying, "Elucidate courteousness, with
a view to improving the Manners (*feng*) and Customs (*suh*)," and
its explication, which is as Taoist as the more appealing parts of
the *Cantos* (cs. 49, 74, 76, 83)—those concerned with landscape
and with the process:

The principles of benevolence, right, propriety, knowledge, and sincerity, are in the hearts of all people. But of people born in different places,
some are vigorous, others are weak. . . . The people of one place do
not understand the talk of the people of another place. All this is the
result of climatic influences (lit. imbued with the wind breath of the
water and soil); hence it is spoken of as *"Feng"* (or Breath of Nature).
[ix. 1]

Baller points out that the character *su* "is composed of *man* and
valley," and that "the Chinese attach great importance to the influence of climate and locality on character."[8] Hence some of
Pound's variations in cs. 98–100: "Earth and water dye the wind
in your valley" (the mobility of the pronominal adjective should
be noted); "Manners are from earth and from water / They arise
out of hills and streams"; and, perhaps more beautifully: "Hills
and streams color the air, / vigor, tranquillity, not one set of
rules." This is the "world of quiet farms" of the *Classic Anthology;* the plea for the liberalization of the law does not arise from
a superficial determinism, but from a belief in the contiguity of

8. Baller, *Sacred Edict*, p. 99n.

nature and culture—a contiguity obtaining in *space* ("Art is local"—c. 97). A number of instances of culture *colored* by particular hills and streams or soil, follow fugally in c. 98, among them the *Odes* (culled, we remember, from different regions of the empire), Frederick's "Book of the Falcon" and Cielo's Song of the Rose (the Sicilian paideuma), and the talk of joyful gods of Plotinus, Gemisto, and Anselm, Pound suggesting a convergence of Eastern and Western theology by telescoping Jesus and China's vegetation god Hou Tsi (see CA 245) as "john barleycorn Je tzu"—the wheat god of Eleusis. After recapitulating the history of his text, another communal product ("Thought is built out of Sagetrieb . . . Iong-ching republished the edict / But the salt-commissioner took it down to the people"), he breaks off at the threshold of a final epiphany of locality:

> Baller thought one needed religion.
>   Without ^{2}muan ^{1}bpo . . . but I anticipate.
>   There is no substitute for a lifetime.   [c. 98]

Muan-bpo is yet another act of worship without bloodshed, concerned with the powers of vegetation. It used to be performed by the Na-khi of Southwest China in the Himalayan setting briefly glimpsed in the earlier traffic with Leucò: "the snow's lace is spread there like sea foam." However, Pound checks himself, as he intends to deal with the matter at a more advanced stage of *Th*'s religious quest. This is not the first time in the canto that the old poet acknowledges the pressure of so much that needs telling ("Patience, I will come to the Commissioner . . . Patience, ich bin am Zuge . . ."). In the last line he gives thanks for the flames and voices that have quickened his life, and indirectly prays for time enough (a familiar theme) to accomplish his life's work, of the form of which he appears for an instant to be fully the master.

The highly personal and compressed account of K'ang-hsi's sixteen clauses with which c. 98 draws to a close suggests that the *Sheng Yü* diptych is closely (if metaphorically) modelled upon its source: on the one hand (c. 98) the "sacred" text, the sixteen commandments; on the other (99) commentary and "vulgarization." However, as we know, both cantos come out of Wang's "volgar eloquio" and Baller's English, with the single exception of the jointure between them, the finale of the first and the inception of the second (cf. the transition from 96 to 97), for which Pound, after raising Yung Cheng and his father into his most exalted heaven, into the company of Confucius, Dante, and Pythagoras, goes to the original sacred fount of the Uen-li text:

> Deliberate converse
>   and with the colour of nature
> Iong Ching, Canto 61
>   of the light of [*hsien*]   hsien
>   [*ming*]   ming,
> by the silk cords of the sunlight,
> Chords of the sunlight (*Pitagora*)
>   non si disuna (xiii)
> Splendor
>   2nd year
>   2nd month
>   2nd day   as to the *Sheng*   [*sheng*]
>   The Edict.   [*yü*]   [c. 98]

Another ritualistic score, bent upon the audition of an unprecedented and stirring music. It is sustained by an awareness of unity—of the poem (P. reminds us that Yung Cheng is no novel character); of the tensile light, the cords (or—a masterly pun— chords) of which can extend to infinity, and which thus "does not separate (*non si disuna*) from its source, but is eternally one" (*Par.* xiii.56–60); and lastly of law and nature, by which the former is colored, as memorably stated by two lines of c. 99, which could serve as a summation of *Th:* "Heaven, man, earth, our law as written / not outside their natural colour." We have found in Pound's Note for the Italian translation of *Chung-yung* that "Confucian metaphysics conceives of all things as containing lights and energies inseparable from their essence" (*OS* 504). Just above the "non si disuna" lines of *Paradiso* Aquinas tells Dante that "What does not die and what may die / is but the *splendor* of the idea / which our Lord brings forth in love." Having come to this central light Pound returns once again to the beginning (*arché*) making ritual out of the title and the date of the Uen-li text of the Edict. Thereupon he begins to read, and to speak (like Wang-iu-p'u) for the King, who addresses the people in the season that seems to be associated with *Th*'s Edict, the time "when crocus is over and the rose is beginning":

> "Each year in the Elder Spring, that is the first month of it,
> The herald shall invite your compliance.
> There are six rites for festival
> and that all should converge!
> And not to lose life for bad temper.   [c. 98]

Under the quiet ease of the lawgiver's voice we detect an emotion, the excitement of speaking, as the poet does, to all. This comes to the fore in the advice he offers the rural audience and himself: it is time to draw the poem's *Sagetrieb* together, to have all threads converge, and not to waste time in acrimony. And with this the beginning joins the end, "Make up quarrels" being K'ang-hsi's sixteenth and last instruction. Canto 98 seeks again to offer not a reading but the very matter and form of the text— precisely as c. 1 with Dartona and Divus.

Having discussed the condition of his text and indicated its place in a vast historical and religious context, Pound goes on, as stated above, to transcribe it at length in his own juicy *volgar eloquio*, for ends that are openly prescriptive. The program of *Th* is accomplished in canto 99, the longest in the sequence, all of it a speech from the Throne: "CHÊN, *yo el Rey,* wish you to think of this EDICT." In the course of seventeen pages Pound "reads" the *Sheng Yü,* throwing out singularly few references to other fields of *Th* (Homer, Islam, Byzance, autobiography), and largely keeping, as is his custom, to the order of his original material. The irony he directs at those who will think c. 98 "more poetic" is not out of place, for he is as passionate a lawgiver as a theologian, though the former role brings out a different voice (the voice, for instance, of c. 46: "And if you will say that this tale teaches . . . / a lesson . . ."), and this has often a sinister ring on account of what is obsessive in his engagement. But this does not

seem to be the case in these entertaining pages, which allow us to
have part without misgivings in that most personal and doubtless
"poetic" invention, Pound's Americanized China. In fact Pound
is clearly addressing his compatriots, delivering his final instructions before leaving them for good: in the New York recordings
made a few days before sailing the only work representing the
fruitful Washington years is this long lecture, then still unpublished:

> Let a man do a good job at his trade,
>   whence is honesty;
>   whence are good manners,
>   good custom
>   this is tuan[1]   cheng[4]
>   good living
>   e basta
> There are five relativities: state, family and friendship,
>   amicitia.
>
>   .   .   .
>
>   You are not all of you idiots,
>   There are a lot of you who will not
>   fall for this hoakum.[9]
> But your females like to burn incense
> and buzz round in crowds and processions
>
>   .   .   .
>
> Buddha ipse is said to have been annoyed with such hoakum
>   [c. 99]

Humor, engagement, and Pound's customary jauntiness, make
for trenchant reading. The weight of the argument falls again,

---

9. I. e., Buddhism and Taoism. *Cheng,* Baller explains, means " 'upright' in a Confucian
sense" (p. 1*n*); and *"Cheng-king* as applied to books means those which are regarded as
orthodox by the Confucian school" (p. 65*n*—cf. c. 98: "That the books you read shall be /
cheng / king"). P.'s ambivalence towards the "sects" is, however, apparent from his transcription of vii. 3:
> But to live as flowers reflected,
>   as moonlight,
> free from possessiveness in affections
>   but, as Chu says, egoistical.   [c. 99]
Chu's puritan retort does little to dispel the fascination of the esthetic life evoked in the
lines previous, so very close to P.'s true (though often hidden) sensibility.

Jefferson-wise, on the dignity of agriculture ("Don't burn to abandon production and go into trading"), on the advantages of the small center as against huge conglomerates, on the harmony of the world of quiet farms:

> Small birds sing in chorus,
> Harmony is in the proportion of branches
>   as clarity (chao [1]).
> Compassion, tree's root and water-spring;
>   The state: order, inside a boundary;
>   Law: reciprocity.
> What is statute save reciprocity?
> One village in order,
>   one valley will reach the four seas.   [c. 99]

The whole is sustained by the robust and infectious rhythms of Pound's poetry, admittedly communal in sources and intent:

> This is not a work of fiction
>   nor yet of one man   [c. 99]

It is the work, we know, of *no man*—a word proceeding from the wind and streams of "our valley":

> But the four TUAN
>   are from nature
>   jen, i, li, chih
> Not from descriptions in the school house;
> They are the scholar's job,
>   the gentleman's and the officer's.
>
> There is worship in plowing
>   and equity in the weeding hoe,
> A field marshal can be literate.
>   Might we see it again in our day!   [c. 99]

Courtesy and the ritual tending of cocoons (cs. 85 and 91) are not to be learned in school; qui laborat, orat; culture concerns not the literati alone, but everyone (cf. Cutting's communication), though it is equally true that "You, soldiers, civilians, / are not headed to be professors. / The basis is man." Accordingly, the law-

giver's last thought is for the uncirculated classics ("To have masters in village schools / To teach 'em classics not hog-wash"—he
remarks earlier), and for academic curricula that lose sight of es-
sentials:

> All I want is a generous spirit in customs
> 1st/ honest man's heart demands sane curricula
> (no, that is not textual)
> Let him analyze the trick programs
> and fake foundations[10]
> The fu jen receives heaven, earth, middle
> and grows.   [c. 99]

The sage, as claimed in Confucianism, has "a transmuting and
operant power," limitless in its capacity "to effect changes" (*UP*
I 1*n*)—and to grow. The last word does in fact resonate, calling
to mind the first chord of this diptych ("Make it new") and the
final chord of the one previous ("Not lie down").

Yet canto 100 has no consummation in store: the bellum
perenne cannot come to an end in the poem as there is no sign of
a cease-fire in the world of which the poem is an image, and the
mind enlightened (*kuang ming*) of K'ang-hsi/Kati—the organic
community free from necessity—is sorely unable to check the
dung flow. It is a jarring irony that F.D.R., the villain of Pound's
scheme of things, should appear at the inception of the crucial
hundredth canto in the act of tampering with the law (and "the
Constitution") in order to bring America into the war which will
end, for the poet, in enormous tragedy:

> "Has packed the Supreme Court
> so they will declare anything he does constitutional."
> Senator Wheeler, 1939.
> —and some Habsburg ploughed his imperial furrow
> Eu ZoOn—
> [c. 100]

Two forms of government, that of usury and that of nature, of
the king who is literally "father" to his people (Joseph II of *RD*),

10. A reference to the Carnegie Endowment for Peace (see previous chapter) may be intended.

are immediately posited against each other. (The Greek "tag" could be interpreted as *eû zôon*—"compagnevole animale"?) But it is equally important to note the idiosyncracy and obscurity—in short, the ugliness—of the lines, which appear to rule out the very possibility of communication. In wartime one must use code, as Lenin (as much a favorite of P. as Mussolini) is made to tell us a few lines down: "Aesopian language (under censorship) / where I wrote 'Japan' you may read 'Russia.' " The obscurity, however, is not only a means to an end—it is also "the rubble heap" left by war, and the aim of the enemies of contemplation, who will allow no space for constructive effort. In the context law (Napoleon's Code), civilization, and temple, are at best a remote utopia:

PERENNE

BELLUM "not constructif"
but the Code out of Corsica
Civilization from Peloponnesus
Maison Quarrée, by greek workmen.   [c. 100]

Perhaps the lines will call to mind Jefferson choosing in c. 31 "for our model, the Maison Quarrée of Nismes," and the overlay of Greece and Provence. But this glimpse of a military paradise, of a warrior civilization, is not followed up, for the poet goes on to tell of enterprising financiers who died in poverty—and to some sarcasm at the expense of the earlier project (naive, it now appears), "that all should converge":

and the old bitch de Medicis died in miseria,
    '29, John Law obit
as you may read in San Moisé, in the pavement,
SUMBAINAI
Grevitch, bug-house, in anagram: "Out of vast
a really sense of proportion
                    and instantly."
wanted me to type-write his name on an handkerchief. [c. 100]

Instead of "paradise," the desultory talk of fellow-inmates. That there is no question of *sumbaínein*, utopic convergence, is imported also by the nature of these materials, which are wholly new to us, like the subsequent references to Cavour, Hohenlohe,

Madame de Staël, Peregrinus Proteus, and others. Before the
promised summing up we expect at least to be told who these
new ghosts are, and why they have waited so long before claiming Ulysses' attention—but Pound has no longer the time to explain, and is in fact burying his plan to conclude the *nékuia* with
the divine vision. True, most of the characters are lawgivers accountable "for something more than their personal conduct,"
and, perhaps, for a few years of "peace" (as claimed again, un-
convincingly, a little later, for Edward VIII). Moreover, the
cantos immediately previous are not lacking in novel materials
and in some forewarning of this accession of persons and events
from the nineteenth century ("Thiers a progress from Talleyrand,
/ less brain and more morals"—c. 99). But it makes all the difference whether Pound is considering Lombard history (or,
rather, experimenting with a Latin text), or whether he is passing
judgment upon things modern—a field in which he usually does
very poorly (as in the above praise of the brutal Thiers). Myth,
the utopia of "peace," does not translate well into the terms of
history schoolbooks—indeed, it is revealed to be essentially
equivocal in the attempt. This is not to say that the experience,
the attempt, is to be rejected as such (in this we are in agreement
with P.). On the contrary, it is an admirable thing that the poet
should feel so strongly about his responsibility to renounce "poetry" for "prose" (and rather poor prose at that) at this crucial
juncture.

Furthermore, several properly mythical flashes are to be found
in this uncaptivating canto—attempts, not fully successful on account of the context, to rise "Out of Erebus / Where no mind
moves at all." Such are the allusions to what Dante saw in the
Heaven of *Justice* ("Buona da sé volontà [cf. the *tuan*]. / Lume
non è, se non dal sereno / stone to stone, as a river descending / the
sound a jemmed light"); [11] and the scattered quotations from *De
Moribus Brachmanorum*, a work erroneously attributed to St.
Ambrose, which tells of Alexander meeting in India a happy people, who "neque aurum diligunt, neque mortem verentur" (*PL*
xvii 1775). Pound thought so highly of this tale that he had it

---

11. Sources for these and neighboring lines are *Par.* xviii.42, 60; xix.64; xx.16–27.

reprinted by Scheiwiller in 1956 (Gallup B58), apparently unaware that the Brachmani are Brahmins, i.e., the "vacuous" Hindus scorned elsewhere. In fact in c. 100 he seems to identify them with the Na-khi of Yünnan, who in one of their rituals recite the words: "We have not committed the wrong of not calling the objects by their proper names": [12]

> Coelum tecto, Deus nec vendit;
> Terra lecto, sed largitur
>   and that Caritas leads to serenity.
> Stead asked Douglas about the rupee . . .
>   with their own gods to lead them
> nor sin by misnaming
>   out of similitude into gathering
> "Mortal blame has no sound in her ears."   [c. 100]

The writing continues broken, though its subject is the ideal society of the Brachmani (or Phaeacians), one of whom remarks: "Coelum habeo pro tecto, terra mihi tota pro lecto est. . . . Nihil enim auro homini vendit Deus, sed sapientiam bonam eis qui noverint eam accipere, largitur" (*PL* xvii 1176–79). Their equanimity is born of a "caritas insuperabilis" (cs. 74 and 91) resembling God's, for He does not sell but gives. (Douglas' theory of distributions is mentioned in this connection.) The sequel establishes the connection with the Na-khi and other oarthinning people who "walk every one in the name of his god" (here Fortuna, summoned by the last line), and gather (like Swedenborg's "societies") "by attraction" (c. 93). But the last lines may also be construed to signify that it is no sin to make gods (like the double Leucò) by way of some "misnaming," for one is aware of the divine as "in nebulas simiglianza" (misty similitude, c. 98), and such errors and inconsistencies (of which the *Cantos* are replete) have no sound in the ears of those blessed creatures.

So we see that there is no lack of "points of gold" in these ostensibly dispiriting pages—to which should be added the "fugal" reprise of the *Sheng Yü,* which starts out with the case against Buddhism and Taoism—that is, in the negative—but goes on to

12. Joseph Francis Rock, "The Muan Bpo Ceremony or the Sacrifice to Heaven as Practiced by the Na-khi," *Monumenta Serica,* 13 (1948), 144. P. uses, in c. 98 and elsewhere, Rock's transliterations, with tone figures prefixed.

feng su ("*Peace* grips the earth in good manners"—my italics) and (as anticipated above) to the mind enlightened, *kuan ming*, and offers a portrait of the lawgiver as "verbo et actu corruscans" (c. 96):

> Nel mezzo [*chung*] the crystal,
> > a green yellow flash after sunset
>
> (Wang on the Sheng Edict,
> > and a blaze of light over Shensi)   [c. 100]

The heavenly sign gives testimony in favor of the poet and of his law. The telos towards which he has been travelling is revealed to be both the center ("mezzo") and the beginning of things ("Nel mezzo del cammin di nostra vita").

Finally, a snatch of the poem's chief narrative thread is necessarily involved in this attempted consummation. Ulysses has come to Phaeacia (like Swinburne to Le Portel in c. 82), and he returns the wonder-working scarf ("not for sale") to Leucothea, who, Homer writes (*Od.* v.462), receives it *"chersì phílesin,"* in her hands ("friendly hands" to P.). One line fully conveys the hero's languor as he awakens (*"agérthe"*—l. 458) and becomes aware of his surroundings, in a supreme setting—France, Luguria, or Phaeacia. (Note the crucial "So that.")

> So that the mist was quite white on that part of the sea-coast
> > Le Portel, Phaeacia
> > and he dropped the scarf in the tide-rips
> KREDEMNON
> > > that it should float back to the sea,
> > > and that quickly
> > > > > DEXATO XERSI
> > > > with a fond hand
> > > > > AGERTHE
> But their technique is two lies at once
> > so there be no profit in conflict,
> CODE functioned in all Latin countries
> > till even Bulgars had their Gesetzbuch
> > > in Justin's village
> "Non della" (Verona)   [c. 100]

Presently we are back at our law studies, which, like the *krédem-non,* may awaken and liberate from the subtly conflicting lies circulated by the enemy. Back in the world of the *Corpus Iuris Civilis,* and of Mussolini's Verona Program.

However, *krédemnon*-as-eros gains again the ascendant in the canto's envoi, a cluster of barely legible samplings from Caval-canti, Villon, and Plotinus, evidently gathered together that we may perceive their "simiglianza":

> "To avoid other views" said Herbert (De Veritate)
>   "their first consideration"
>   *come in subjecto*
>   *lisses*
>   *amoureuses*
>   *a tenir*
>   EX OUSIAS . . . HYPOSTASIN
>   III, 5, 3   PERI EROTOS
>   [device] hieron
>   nous to ariston autou
>   as light into water compenetrans
>   that is pathema
>   ouk aphistatai"
>   thus Plotinus
>   per plura diafana
>   neither weighed out nor hindered;
>   aloof.
>   1 Jan '58   [c. 100]

Strictly speaking, Herbert of Cherbury (another novel character in this canto) is brought in to indicate the unorthodox import of the sequel, and to relate it to the bellum perenne. However, the title of his work assures us that we are presently to arise from the Erebus of double falsehood to "the oblivions of pure curiosity" (*K* 52)—to the truth which "does not dis-unify" (c. 98). The first excerpt to follow indicates that Pound is still considering the second verse of "Donna mi prega," with its "dove sta memora," "diafan," and the statement that love

> Cometh from a seen form which being understood
> Taketh locus and remaining in the intellect possible
> Wherein hath he neither weight nor still-standing,   [c. 36]

—or, in the earlier version:

> From form seen doth he start, that, understood,
> Taketh in latent intellect—
> As in a subject ready—
> > place and abode,
> Yet in that place it ever is unstill,   ["Cavalcanti," *LE* 156]

The *subietto* or "subject ready" is bawdily correlated with the hips of Villon's once beautiful Heaulmière, "plump, firm and so well set / for love's great tournament" (Robert Lowell's translation)—a sensuousness not inconsistent, within the precincts of "the medieval dream" (as P. never tires of telling us), with "sheer love of beauty and a delight in the perception" (*P&T* 90). Accordingly, the next excerpt takes us in one leap from Villon's brothel to Plotinus' intellectualized definition of love as "hypostasis, essence proceeding from essence" (*Perì érotos, Enn.* iii.v.3), and to the metaphysical associations of "hypostasis" (cs. 76 and 81), eros being finally identified with *hierón*, Ka-ap's "temple." Love profane and sacred are thus again brought together—yet in the end the emphasis falls on "most noble" (*áriston*) *noûs*, on the voyager's "own mind," bearing him "thru these diafana" (c. 96) with the bright wings of the Spirit/gull. (The lines, of course, are also to be construed as a supplement to P.'s enquiry into the sources of "Donna mi prega," it being suggested that Plotinus' (?) "ouk aphistatai" is equivalent to Guido's "hath he neither weight nor still-standing," or, "neither weighed out nor hindered.") Having sketched this forbidding version of the poem's central mystery (Guido-Villon, the "moving" Queen regained in *RD*, *Th*'s temple), and proved to his (perhaps our) satisfaction that "the poem has a structure," the sorely tried combatant walks with his characteristic swagger—love's own "aloofness"—into the New Year, the Center which is also ("Nel mezzo del cammino") the Beginning.

14. Sounds in the Forest

The first canto of the poem's second century ushers us in fact into a new space, a new beginning, signalled by the dawn character: the Himalayan landscape, snow-covered and serene (for "Caritas leads to serenity"), which is the home of the Na-khi of Yünnan, their capital being Li-chiang. This is Pound's Tahiti, the virgin land to which no visitor has come, but for the rare emissaries of Peking ("Sail passed here in April; may return in October"— c. 49), and, more recently, the American Joseph Francis Rock (1884–1962), who, a geographer in the inclusive sense (for he was also a capable botanist, mineralogist, linguist, and anthropologist), gave decades of passionate and intelligent study to the exploration of the territory, and to the gathering and editing of Na-khi texts. Still more recently the region has been taken over by the soldiers of China, who put an end to a long decadence, but were, predictably, unwelcome to explorers of forgotten kingdoms like Rock (and P.), and even (to some extent) to the local population, which is of non-Chinese ethnical and cultural background, and had preserved some independence in its earlier vassalage to Peking. It is here that once a year the Muan-bpo or Sacrifice of Heaven was performed—a complex rite connected with a sacred enclosure within which a juniper stands for the emperor, the center of things, and two oak branches at its sides represent Heaven and Earth. In Pound the juniper is the *senhal* of the Na-khi and of paradise, a new Yggdrasil. Having encountered it, a secret pointer, in the opening lines of *Th* ("& on the hearth burned cedar and juniper"), we find it again—the first sign of the new world—planted into the *conversation* piece which announces, prosaically, Pound's Ithaca:

> Finding scarcely anyone save Monsieur de Rémusat
> who would understand him
> (junipers, south side) M. Talleyrand
> spruce and fir take the North

393

Chalais, Aubeterre,
        snow-flakes at a hand's breadth, and rain.   [c. 101]

This transparent instance of thematic construction (*a-b-a-b-a-b*—
a being France and more generally modern Europe, *b* the remote
world) provides us again with the key to the canto, which juxtaposes throughout the two levels, both of which in this case are
positive in connotation: Talleyrand (see *RD*), the hereditary master of Chalais, and Augustin Laurent de Rèmusat [1] are to Pound
worthy to inhabit his promised land beyond history; soon they
are to be joined by the Napoleon of the *Fifth Decad*. The description of the new world begins with the forces of vegetation and
with information about space—an absolute space, north and
south, and a particular and vital space from which the language
of the people (and of the poet) derives, like the Manners and
Customs, its unique savor—as stated explicitly in the parallel inception of a later canto:

> Na Khi talk made out of wind noise,
>   And North Khi, not to be heard amid sounds of the forest
> but to fit in with them unperceived by the game,
> But when the young lout was selling the old lout
>   the idea of betraying Mihaelovitch
> The air of the room became heavy . . .   [c. 104]

But here the European contributions have darkened considerably,
whereas in c. 101 the conjunction of Na-khi organic culture with
Napoleonic France and the connection between Talleyrand and
Chalais inspire Pound to return to what is nearly the beginning of
his quest for the promised land, at any rate to the origins of the
Cantos: the Provençal hours of June 1912 in which *P&T* and
"Provincia Deserta" were conceived:

---

1. The husband of Claire de Rémusat, whose *Memoirs,* tr. C. Hoey and J. Lillie (London,
1880), are the source of this passage and of others in the canto. P. may be conflating him
with his son, Charles de Rémusat, a political associate of Thiers, and the author in old age
of works on St. Anselm, Cherbury, and English philosophy—hence the lineage drawn in c.
100: "Erigena, / Anselm, / Cherbury, / Rémusat, / Thiers was against income tax." Cf.
Michaels, "Pound and Erigena," pp. 52–53.

At Chalais
              is a pleached arbour;
Old pensioners and old protected women
Have the right there—
              it is charity.
I have crept over old rafters,
              peering down
Over the Dronne,
              over a stream full of lilies.
Eastward the road lies,
              Aubeterre is eastward,
With a garrulous old man at the inn.
I know the roads in that place: [P 121][2]

Pound is "he who knoweth the roads," as he declared, quoting verbatim from the *Book of the Dead,* in "De Aegypto," a poem included in *A Lume Spento,*[3] and as he was to reiterate much more evocatively in the lines, already familiar to us, of that small jewel, "The Gypsy," which was also occasioned (as we learn from the epigraph) by the days of 1912:

The wind came, and the rain,
And mist clotted about the trees in the valley,
And I'd the long ways behind me,
              gray Arles and Beaucaire,   [P 119]

It is not difficult to recognize this landscape, or at least its epiphanic frisson, in the line, "snow-flakes at a hand's breadth, and rain"—even as we were made aware of it in c. 49 ("Rain; empty river; a voyage"), and, more distinctly, in *PC* ("and the rain fell all night at Ussel / *cette mauvaiseh venggg* blew over Tolosa"). Again, the elements place the individual in a universal perspec-

2. In his seminal essay, "The *Cantos:* Towards a Pedestrian Reading," *Paideuma,* 1 (1972), 61, Donald Davie points out that Chalais is placed not on the Dronne (like Aubeterre-sur-Dronne), but on the Tude. The "inn low by the river's edge" at the foot of the hill of Aubeterre is fondly remembered in cs. 76 and 80.

3. *P* 18. See E. A. W. Budge, *The Book of the Dead: The Chapters of the Coming Forth by Day* (London, 1898), ch. 78, pp. 135–36. Quoted in Peck, "Pound's Idylls," pp. 174–75.

tive, and he is carried away like "a leaf in the current" (c. 81): "Or le bagna la pioggia e move il vento." [4]

So we see that an old journey is superimposed upon the poet's newest enterprise; the former obtains as a cherished memory, the latter as text: Rock's perspicuous prose. [5] Both are concerned with a landscape which has seen much history—is in fact (as the familiar theme goes) a *measure* of history, of time:

> Trees line the banks, mostly willows. Kublai,
> Te Te of Ch'eng, called Timur, 1247, came hither
> Forest thru ice into emerald
>   in [*tan*] Tan (dawn, that is)
>   larix, corayana and berberis,
>   after 2 stages A-tun-tzu
>   a distance of one hundred *li*   [c. 101]

We recall the words intoned in c. 17: "Thither Borso, when they shot the barbed arrow at him"—and their echo in c. 91: "hither Ocellus / 'to this khan' "—as well as the more precise anticipation in c. 49: "In seventeen hundred came Tsing to these hill lakes." When he wrote this line in 1937 the poet could not know (but perhaps the poem knew) that in the end he would come to consider the "mountain lakes in the dawn" (c. 110) of the Na-khi. The new journey is undertaken under the auspices of the dawn, that is, in the sign ("hoc signo") which imports (among other things) the ability to *read* (c. 91). If one be "scientist" not only in the esoteric Poundian sense, as Rock was, one can read out the resonant Latin taxonomy of the plants and trees one sees— precise and magic names which the poet delights to take over. Finally the theme of the journey, with its "stages" of progress, comes to the fore, and a city is sighted—not Aubeterre or Borso's Venice or Brennus' Rome, but A-tun-tzu, a sizable village Rock encounters on his way. (For Rock's handsome *The Ancient Na-*

4. Manfredi on his bones ("Now the rain washes them and the wind moves them"), *Purg.* III.130. The line was well-known to P. for "vento" rhymes with "a lume spento."

5. See J. F. Rock, *The Ancient Na-khi Kingdom of Southwest China* (Cambridge: Harvard Univ. Press, 1947), I, 270; II, 281, 298, 316, 344–45. (References given in part in Davie, "Pedestrian Reading," 60*n*.)

khi Kingdom of Southwest China is a two-volume scientific account of the geographer's expeditions through the country,
equivalent to P.'s Provençal walking tours, and to Ulysses' periplus.)

Pound's earthly paradise, emerald in the dawn, is not a little
compelling on account of its unadorned sense of the sacred, of its
avoidance of rhetoric, and of its constant attention to the text
and to the sound of words in the memory ("Chalais, Aubeterre")—to data which are both "real" and evident, and yet elusive to the uninitiated or irreverent. (Not in respect to P.'s text,
for which no reverence is needed, but to the givens of existence.)
Thus it has been possible for *Th* to remain largely unread in these
twenty years since its publication—in fact this very canto has
been quoted as a comic instance of Pound's inability to "get
through even to himself" [6]—where it is one of his most naively
moving productions, a new "Provincia Deserta."

It is true that the appearance among the junipers of Napoleon,
and later of such fascist officials as Edmondo Rossoni and Carlo
Delcroix, arouses some perplexity—but only if we have not understood the rules of Pound's naive game. To tell him that these
phantasies are historically inadequate and even reprehensible
would be somewhat like telling Henri Rousseau that his land-
scapes lack perspective. Here for example is Napoleon, quite undistinguishable (be it not for the name of the battle) from Wang-
iu-p'u and others:

> KALON KAGATHON, and Marengo,
>   This aura will have, with red flash,
>   the form of a diamond, or of crimson,
> Apollonius, Porphery, Anselm,   [c. 101]

6. George P. Elliott, "Poet of Many Voices" (1961), Sullivan 252. The reference may be
unfair, for this is on the whole an engaging essay (and P.'s worst enemies always were—
and still are—the flatterers)—but the critic should learn to leave blanks for what he does
not know. Elliott could have found many better illustrations in *Th*. Donald Davie's dis-
missal of *Th* in *Poet as Sculptor* (1964), is more worrying. (Canto 101, he tells us, is
"mostly about the American Civil War"—p. 240.) In 1977 Davie was still claiming in
writing that P. had done badly by Rock, and that lines like the hypnotic "in ver l'estate,
Queen of Akragas / resistent, / Templum aedificavit / Segesta," are not "poetry" but the
"errors and wrecks" spoken of in c. 116.

The lawgiver is silhouetted again in the light—the color which is also form—and the dream wins the day, if anything connoting an engagement which we may want to share. Paradise is not of remote Yünnan, but something to be built in this world. The poet provides the inspiration, not of course the precise recipe, though he may have blundered into believing that he had also that to offer. The question of Pound's phantastic mimesis is in fact sensibly and accurately presented towards the close of the canto:

> and Joey said, "are they for real"
> > before primitives in the Mellon Gallery,
> Washington
> "Should," said H.J., "for humanity's credit
> > > feign their existence
> With the sun and moon on her shoulders,
> > the star-discs sewn on her coat
> > > at Li Chiang, the snow range,
> > > > a wide meadow
> > > > > [c. 101]

At the Mellon Gallery Joey[7] may have found angels, halos, and madonnas—images as "unreal" as the diamond aura enveloping the victorious lawgiver of Marengo, and yet true to a more profound notion of what is "real," as deviously claimed by Henry James for his characters (are these not, to some extent, instances of a "primitive" art?), and more convincingly shown by the Nakhi girl described subsequently (cf. the Venus "with golden / girdles and breast bands" of c. 1): she has sewn "star-discs" on her ceremonial garb as uncouthly as the poet has endowed his lawgivers with arcane halos, but what matters is the awareness of—and relationship to—the whole and the light that this imports; she is at one with the landscape against which Pound (who

7. "Joey is La Martinelli's kid brother, who was taken down to look at the paintings in the Mellon Gallery . . . I think what he meant was, 'Do they correspond to an external reality?' "—P. to Bridson, "An Interview with Ezra Pound," p. 176. Sheri Martinelli was one of P.'s St. Elizabeth's acolytes. The poet arranged for publication of some of her undistinguished drawings in *La Martinelli* (Milano: Scheiwiller, 1955), and contributed a preface which usefully glosses certain lines of *RD*.

is leafing through the fine illustrations of Rock's book) has placed
her, snow range and wide, speechless, meadow.[8]

The geographer's prose, terse and precise, and yet secretly
quickened by a passion for knowledge, for the discrete fact, is
ideally suited to go into the poem:

This mountain [Seng-ge ga-mu] is mirrored in the lake . . . No hunting
is permitted, and here roam many bears who live on the oaks, and often
come to the fields of the villages and eat their bread and peas . . . On
the top of this hill is a temple with a huge figure of Chenrezig with the
thousand arms and eyes (Kuan-yin of the Chinese) . . . Immediately
back of the main building there is a shrine dedicated to the mountain
goddess Seng-ge ga-mu . . . An incense burner belches forth white
smoke in the morning and evening, when pine branches are burnt as offering to the mountain goddess. . . . Junipers grow on all the lofty
peaks of the district of Yen-yüan, giving the latter a blue-green tint. The
dragon-like rivers flow zig-zag over its land. . . . Its passes over the
lofty peaks, covered with fragrant junipers, can safely be guarded by
one man. . . . The reason why so many places were called Tso (Bamboo rope) was because the aborigenes used rope bridges to cross the
large rivers . . .[9]

Pound lifts entire sentences, touching them up but slightly (as
when he introduces the esoteric first person plural), and places
them in a different context, teasing out their hidden symbolic
quality. He indicates, that is, what is essentially a way of reading,
of seeing the universal in the particular. Behind him is the Romantic tradition of epiphany, but there is a closer precedent that
he is not aware of: the Zen writing of Basho, who recounts in
words as simple and suggestive his journey along the Narrow
Road of the Deep North (*Oku no Hosomichi*), pausing to consider, much as Pound in "Provincia Deserta" and in the *Cantos,*
the spirit of the place. Again we come up against the fact that the

8. Rock, *Ancient Na-khi Kingdom,* i, pls. 76 and 77. The dto-mba spoken of in the next
two lines is a Na-khi exorcist. For the Henry James quotation see *K* 9.

9. Rock, *Ancient Na-khi Kingdom,* ii, 418, 412, 426, 444, 446. For the "hemp rope" in
the subsequent quotation see pp. 447*n* and 451.

landscape poetry of this self-styled Confucian is essentially Taoist
and Buddhist in spirit: [10]

> Obit 1933, Tsung-Kuan, for Honour.
>   Bears live on acorns
>   and come raiding our fields.
>   Bouffier,
> Elzéard has made the forest at Vergons
>   under Kuanon's eye there is oak-wood. Sengper ga-mu,
> To him we burn pine with white smoke
>   morning and evening.
>   The hills are blue-green with juniper,
> the stream, as Achilöos there below us,
>   here one man can hold the whole pass
> over this mountain, at Mont Ségur the chief's cell
> you can enter it sideways only, TSO [*tso*] is here named
> from the rope bridge, hemp rope? a reed rope?
>   and they pay the land tax in buckwheat.
> Food was in Tolosa, not chemical, and in Gubbio   [c. 101]

Though intact, the landscape has become anthropomorphic, allowing us to see gods at every turn, for instance a white goddess
in the smoke rising from the incense burner in the shrine of the
mountain- (and lion-) god (P., we notice, has changed both name
and sex of Seng-ge ga-mu)—at any rate the offering must be
placed in the context of those celebrated elsewhere in *Th*. Ache-
loüs, the "three-twisted river" of *WT* 5, would appear to be little
but Pound's associative response to Rock's zigzagging rivers, but
in fact refers us pointedly to the poet's alter ego, Heracles, and to
Greek myth. The superimposition of the peaks of Yen-yüan and
Montségur also carries ideogramic significance. (The aside on the
bridge recalls "the path wide as a hair" [c. 93] that the initiate
must go; the etymology of *tso* points back in import as well as in
sound to "Thusca quae a thure"—and etymology as such is much

---

10. This is not as inconsistent as P. would have thought, for (as Mancuso points out, p.
133) Confucian officials were apt to "cultivate the tao" at home and in old age. It is,
however, quite an inconsistency that P. should joke about Taoists "flying" and refer us in
the same breath to Muan-bpo, which "belongs to the same complex of magic-religious
beliefs" (Mancuso 136–37).

in the center of *Th.*) We realize that this composite landscape telescopes the principal agrarian civilizations of the poem: Greece, Provence, and then Napoleon's France and Mussolini's Italy. With this we can better appreciate the humane sprite to whom the sacrifice appears to be addressed: Elzéard Bouffier, who "made the forest at Vergons," in Provence, as reported by Jean Giono:

For three years he had been planting trees in this wilderness. He had planted 100,000. Of the 100,000, 20,000 had sprouted. Of these 20,000 he still expected to lose about half, to rodents or to the unpredictable designs of Providence. There remained 10,000 oak trees to grow where nothing had grown before. . . . He had once had a farm in the lowlands. There he had had his life. He had lost his only son, then his wife. He had withdrawn into this solitude where his pleasure was to live leisurely with his lambs and his dog. It was his opinion that this land was dying for want of trees. He added that, having no very pressing business of his own, he had resolved to remedy this state of affairs.[11]

Elzéard is definitely a Poundian—not a Wordsworthian—character, for he transforms, single-handed, a whole landscape: his reforestation brings water to dry wells and streams, people to the abandoned villages. The poet places him appropriately among the blessed "responsible for something more than their personal conduct," identifying him perhaps with the "Lion Mountain" Seng-ge ga-mu; he entrusts his oak wood to the compassion of Kuanon, and propitiates him with an offering of pine. (The passage also refers, in connection with the honor theme, to a Na-khi double of Elzéard, Tsung-kuan, a chief of the Yung-nin, and friend of Rock, who praises "his sense of justice and unimpeachable character.")[12] The elegy on the country landscape terminates with a recollection of the food of earlier days, a little banal but pointed (cf. the "bread of stale rags" of c. 45), for with it the voyager of 1912 and 1919, in Provence and in Umbria, claims a place among such Cathars (see the previous reference to

11. Jean Giono, "The Man Who Planted Hope and Grew Happiness," *Vogue,* 15 March 1954, p. 157.

12. Rock, *Ancient Na-khi Kingdom,* ii, 41.

Montségur) as Elzéard and Luigi: the bread he tasted as a young man is also "panis angelicus" (c. 93)—the secret of his power. (This is elaborated in the next canto: "Barley is the marrow of men, / 40 centess' in my time / an orzo.")

To conclude with Pound let us look at the last segment of his novel journey, which presents another minimal image of a world which is whole beyond confusion, and not devoid of tigers or (like the D.T.C.) of fragrant mint:

> Mint grows at the foot of the Stone Range
> > the first moon is the tiger's,
> > > Pheasant calls out of bracken
> Rossoni: "così lo stato . . ." etcetera
> Delcroix: "che magnifica!"
> > > > (prescrittibile)
> he perceived it:
> > The green spur, the white meadow
> > "May their pond be full;
> > The son have his father's arm
> > > and good hearing;
> (noun graph upright; adjective sideways)
> > "His horse's mane flowing
> > > His body and soul are at peace."   [c. 101]

The supposedly enthusiastic response of Rossoni and Delcroix (who may well have been humoring the eccentric foreigner) to Pound's account of Gesellite stamp scrip ("moneta prescrittibile"),[13] coalesces, instancing the "Breath of Nature" doctrine (*feng su* theme), with the pheasant's cry, and with the perception of the abundance of nature, which fills the family pond with water (or fish?), and the farm with strong sons of good hearing, capable that is of telling Na-khi talk amid sounds of the forest, and (P. implies) of good eyesight, for in the written language (as we gather) nouns are *differentiated* from adjectives by relative

13. "What Rossoni [minister of finance in several Mussolini governments] said was 'così lo stato . . .' That's where the state gets its cut . . . Rossoni saw the stamp scrip as a tax. . . . When [Carlo Delcroix, 'head of the Italian Veterans'—P.] first heard of stamp scrip, he beat on his head with his little wooden artificial arms and said 'che magnifica idea'— what a magnificent idea. He saw where it led and he grabbed a telephone . . ."—P. to Bridson, "An Interview with Ezra Pound," pp. 175–76.

position. Having thus touched upon the dictionary—the meaning of words—the canto closes with a traditional image of the hero, also borrowed from a Na-khi text [14]—in fact an equestrian statue of considerable contextual resonance. The "skilled" eye pauses at "horse" (see the finale of c. 97) and at "peace" (the very last word of 96), is reminded of the "conscience at peace" (*kuang ming*) of Kati/K'ang-hsi, and is lost in the "flowing."

As if obsessed by his yearning for "peace," the poet repeats the theme in the finale of c. 102 ("Domitian, infaustus / tried to buy peace with money"—the royal annals, we notice, continue to be told), and, indirectly, at the end of 103 ("the Mensdorf letter"— see above). The former of these variations may be taken to indicate that cs. 101 and 102 (like 47 and 49) are two of a set, and this would seem to be corroborated by the quality of the verse, distinctly superior as it is to that of the cantos immediately following. Yet a number of recurrent themes spanning the lot of these middle cantos of *Th* would suggest that they are to be taken as one episode proceeding without a break from the timeless world of c. 101 to the rather formless annals of 103, and thence rising again to the "mysteries" of 106, which will be dealt with in a separate chapter.

Canto 102, quite brief, is another description of the Ithaca of the *Cantos,* though offering only a glimpse of its central symbol ("south slope for juniper"). This time the emphasis falls upon the quest, the journey, the story of the "scientists"—in particular of Ulysses, who, having remained absent through the previous canto, becomes again, followed by a cohort of descendants, the focus of attention:

14. According to Carroll F. Terrell, "The Na-khi Documents I: The Landscape of Paradise," *Paideuma,* 3 (1974), 119, the source is Rock, *The Zhi Ma Funeral Ceremony of the Na-khi of Southwest China* (Vienna-Mödling, 1955), p. 197: "There are no more rocks in the path of your sharp sword . . . no dog in front of your horse to impede its way . . . You are on the way to the realm of the gods, your body and soul are at peace and the mane of your horse is beautiful." Na-khi texts, however, are repetitious and formulaic— thus P. could have picked up the augury somewhere else. The lines about mint, tiger, and pheasant, come instead from Rock, "The Romance of K'a-mä-gyu-mi-gkyi," *B.E.F.E.-O.,* 39 (1939), 143 and 151.

This I had from Kalupso
                    who had it from Hermes
"eleven literates and, I suppose,
                              Dwight L. Morrow"
the body elected,
                    residence required, not as in England
"A cargo of Iron"
                    lied Pallas
                              and as to why Penelope waited
keinos . . . eOrgei. line 639. Leucothoe
rose as an incense bush,
                    resisting Apollo,
                                        Orchamus, Babylon
And after 500 years
                    still offered that shrub to the sea-gull,
Phaeacians,
              she being of Cadmus line
The snow's lace washed here as sea-foam   [c. 102]

The stepped-down lines, somewhat reminiscent of Pound's edition of "Donna mi prega," suggest a relaxed yet powerful on-
ward movement, prepared to dreamily reconsider materials dealt
with elsewhere, and immediately qualified as Odyssean and hermetic (the references to Calypso—from *kalúpto*—and Hermes).
In Homer, Hermes communicates to Calypso, and the latter to
Ulysses, the "I" of the *Cantos,* that he must recommence his
voyage for the last time—but this message Pound replaces with
the immediate reason for *his* new trip (*Th*), namely the split between culture and government testified to by Cutting, and more
generally the split between culture and society, for American
senators (unlike English lords) are elected by actual constitu-
encies. (P. is also hinting at one of his favorite Mussoliniana,
quoted in cs. 77 and 99: "We are tired of a government in which
there is no responsible person having a front name, a hind name,
and an address.") Calypso, as readers of the *Odyssey* know, is almost a double of Circe—and it is the latter who in c. 47 instructs
the hero: "Knowledge the shade of a shade, / Yet must thou sail
after knowledge." But these first lines in which the poet acknowledges his source concern also the nature of myth, which is hear-

say, *Sagetrieb,* and hilarity. Pound had called attention several
times to Hermes' words to Calypso in *Od.* v.97–98, claiming
that they are finely ironic, "tricky as nature":

Possibly . . . I am so Xtian that a lying god tickles my funny bone.
> *You a goddess ask of me who am a god,*
> *Nevertheless I will tell you the truth.*
Goddess wd. know anyhow, so no use the habitual mendacity, put as
many folds on it as you like. [To W. H. D. Rouse, 6 June 1935, *L* 297.]

That Pound has this exchange in mind is shown by the subsequent reference to Athene's lie to Telemachus about carrying
iron (1.184). (The word is capitalized because of some "economic" notion: in c. 104 an instance of iron coinage is greeted
with cries of joy.) But if gods will occasionally lie, the poet is in
fact claiming that his message is truthful ("nevertheless I will tell
you the truth")—as he has done in two passages considered earlier, one of which, the prelude of c. 98, amounts to the text of
which this first page of c. 102 is the translation or parody, as indicated by the quotation from Cutting and by the sequel
(*krédemnon* theme). Likewise in c. 97, after putting the question,
"Chi con me?," the poet adds: "And the dogmatic have to lie
now and again / to maintain their conformity, / the chun tze,
never." (*Chün tze* is rendered as "man of breed" in *UP*.)
    These agile sentences amount, therefore, to a portrait of the
poet-protagonist and of the divine and communal world in which
he exists—an intent made apparent by the quotation (admittedly
difficult to recognize, but this is in keeping with the entire passage) of Penelope's praise of Ulysses (the wife's "waiting" being
another pointer to the voyage theme): "he (*keînos*) never did
(*eórgei*) any harm to any one"—not unlike the author of *PC*
("Neither Eos nor Hesperus has suffered wrong at my hands").
For a moment we suspect that some special meaning may be attached to the number of the line of which Pound lifts the first and
last word, or that there may be some reason for his inaccuracy—for he is looking at line 693—not 639—of *Od.* 4, a book
much quarried in *Th* (*diipetéos, dolicherétmoisi, tà ex Aigúptou
phármaka*).

The entrance of the double Leucò, who bodies forth the hero's inner good nature, his attention-reverence, and his mystical competence, launches the actual repeat of the latter section of the prelude of c. 98, which is tightened up and simplified, in form if not in content, and given more personal application, the method being only superficially similar to that of recurring clusters (Fortuna in c. 97, Gemistus-Plotinus-Anselm in 98). In fact Pound is reverting to the large-scale parody of Parts 1 and 2 of *HSM*, and of the two usury cantos—a parody which in both these instances attempted to compress and simplify the earlier text, but attracted new meaning in the process. An explicit bow to *HSM* is the use of Greek lettering in cs. 98 and 97 (the latter is to be parodied subsequently), and of Roman transliteration in c. 102, precisely as in the two parts of the earlier poem. Thus c. 102 is the final instance of a fascinating Poundian topos, the experimental reconsideration or rewriting of his own text. As in c. 51, the fact that the content is already familiar allows for greater relaxation and fluency—for a delight in words and images as such. As the fragmentary insights of c. 98 coalesce in a single discursive measure, the two Leucos become more closely identified. Already in c. 98 the "incense spike" ("virga turea"—*Met.* IV. 254–55) into which Apollo changes his beloved (who did not actually "resist" him—but then P. may want to conflate her with Daphne), is referred to as "an incense bush"; here we learn that the Phaeacians offer to the seagull-Leucothea "that shrub"—a designation purposefully vague to allow association with the incense. The Massiliots, that is, commit the "error" of c. 95 (" 'My bikini is worth yr/ raft.' Said Leucothoe")—they call something by the wrong name and take the girl-incense and the goddess-gull to be one person. In the land of Pound, where the first commandment is, "Call things by their names," this should be the unpardonable sin, and yet cs. 98 and 100 have provided justification for it, have indeed suggested that such controlled confusions ("et in nebulas simiglianza," "out of similitude into gathering") are the stuff of mythical and poetical imagination. In fact the "mistaken" Phaeacians are the very "scientists" capable of the most subtle discriminations (*dolicherétmoisi*, "thinning their oar-blades"), as between throstle's

note and banded thrush; they have pursued the discrete perception to the vanishing point, to the kernel of identity where metamorphosis occurs. Thus they may join the Na-khi in claiming
that they have not sinned by misnaming, the two meanings of the
phrase being equally applicable. The superimposition of Mediterranean colony and Himalayan people is finely intimated by the
pairing of sea foam (the element of Venus and Leucò—the
whiteness of *krédemnon*) and snow's lace, which does not occur
"there" (as in c. 98), but "here," for we are now "in" paradise.
(Cf. "The hills here are blue-green with juniper.") What was "anticipated" there, is realized here.

In the sequel of the repeat we return to the hero, but now the
mask of Ulysses coalesces with the face of the poet:

> [*pu*]   But the lot of 'em, Yeats, Possum, Old Wyndham
>   had no ground to stand on
> Black shawls still worn for Demeter
>   in Venice,
>   in my time,
>   my young time
>   OIOS TELESAI ERGON . . . EROS TE
> The cat talks μάω
>   (mao) with a greek inflection.
> Barley is the marrow of men,
>   40 centess' in my time
> an orzo.
>   At Procope, one franc fifteen for a luncheon
> and ten centimes tip for the waiter. Noi altri borghesi
> could not go down into the piazza. We thought we could
>   control . . . [c. 102]

The stand-in Orage is silently dropped, and it is Pound in person
who claims, under the tenuous cover of objective proposition,
preeminence among his former associates, as he returns, not
without nostalgia (cf. c. 26: "And / I came here in my young
youth"), to the inception of his career as an "initiate." The Venetian shawls, myth as a communal experience, have provided him
as far back as 1908 or earlier (P. had also been to Venice in 1898
and 1902) with the "ground" that his friends have lacked, mak-

ing him "such as to fulfil both deed and word," like Ulysses
(*"hoîos keînos éen telésai érgon te épos te"*—II.272). But misnaming has done its habitual good work in the quotation, changing word to love, the essential ground. That Venice provided inspiration in 1908 to the perplexed young man we gather from his
notebook, "At San Trovaso":

> Thou that hast given me back
>   Strength for the journey, . . .
> O Sun venezian, . . .
>   Alma tu sole!
> Cold, ah a-cold
> Was my soul in the caves of ill-fearing.   [*CEP* 246]

(These lines, bearing the title—itself a solecism—"Alma Sol Vene-
ziae," may be said to anticipate the linguistic medley and gram-
matic-orthographic inaccuracy of c. 102.) [15] This was the year in
which gondolas cost too much and in which the young gourmet
had to live upon barley soup—a detail which also finds its place,
together with Demeter and the cat, in the context of the mysteries, of the grain. (Incidentally, at Eleusis the initiates drank
mint and barley for wine, as this was the only refreshment Demeter had accepted when she came there on her quest.) [16] The
mawkish indication of the price of this and of another luncheon
gives us to understand that at the time the black shawls were
worn intolerance towards usury was still the norm ("In Byzantium 12% for a millennium"—c. 98), and functions as a protest
against the "bourgeois," who are forbidden the world of "black
shawls in the Piazza" (c. 98), the world of the poet and his Duce,
which they cannot control.

Under these Venetian and Eleusinian auspices the voyage prepared so far finally gets under way, and a number of different explorers step out from under the shadow of Noman. Pound keeps
to the route set in c. 98, from Yeats to truthful Nestor, yet he
multiplies his examples, adding notable material:

15. The style is delightfully parodied in Joyce's letter of 13 June 1925 to Harriet Shaw
Weaver, quoted in Read 232.

16. Karl Kerényi, *Die Mythologie der Griechen* (Zürich: Rhein-Verlag, 1951), Ch. 14.

And that ye sail over lithe water . . .
           under eyelids . . .
Winkelmann noted the eyelids,
      Yeats two months on a sonnet of Ronsard's.
"Jacques Père" on a sign near Le Portel,
      and belgians would pronouce it.
Eva has improved that line about Freiheit.
      "50 more years on The Changes"
or is said to have said that he could have.
Swan broke his knee cap on landing   [c. 102]

—and so on, with the emphasis shifting from "the intellectual struggle" (CV 327) to more traditional explorations. Yet in the meantime the journey after knowledge, "over lithe waters" (cf. c. 2), has been equated with the essential quest of the poet Pound, his (and Ra-Set's) voyage upon the surface of the marine eye of Aphrodite *elikobléphare,* "with slow-lifting eyelids" (c. 5)—an eye which is the symbol both of eros and of the awareness which perceives it, and, thinning the oar blades, expresses it. Its contemplative witnesses are Winckelmann (who dwells on the Greek adjective in *Geschichte der Kunst des Altertums*),[17] and the poet-translators who, by addressing—and in fact travelling upon—a text (as P. upon the *nékuia* in c. 1), summon the eyes to new life: Yeats who reads Ronsard; Shakespeare (or Jacques Père—see *ABR* 187) who, like Chaucer before him (and Le Portel's Swinburne after him), brings to England the Mediterranean melos, the music of Phaeacia (see "Cavalcanti," *LE* 199); the poet's friend Eva Hesse who "improves" in her translation one line of *PC* ("that free speech without free radio speech is as zero" / "dass Redefreiheit ohne Radiofreiheit gleich null ist"[18]—a Cervantesque reference within the poem to the poem's reception); and finally Confucius, who wishes he had fifty years to spend on the *I Ching,* the *Book of Changes* (A VII 16)—that is, upon those two

17. See J. Winkelmann (French spelling, used by P.), *Histoire de l'art chez les anciens* (Paris, 1802), pp. 459–60 (IV. iv. 20)—and Peck, "Pound's Lexical Mythography," pp. 26–27.

18. E.P., *Cantos 1916–1962: Eine Auswahl Englisch-deutsch,* ed. and tr. Eva Hesse (München: DTV, 1964), pp. 94–95.

grand themes, text and metamorphosis. (*I Ching, Metamorphoses, Cantos*—possibly a triptych?) The exploration within the eye, conducted with the white wings of time passing, is the undertaking of a lifetime (something for which, we recall, "there is no substitute"), and is expectably hindered by the conspiracy of ignorance:

> Took the Z for the tail of the KatZe
> vide Frobenius on relative Dummheit of pupil and teacher
> "The libraries" (Ingrid) "have no Domvile." Jan 1955
>   as was natural
>   "pseudos d'ouk . . . ei gar pepnumenos"
> seed barley with the sacrifice (Lacedaemon)
> But with Leucothoe's mind in that incense
>   all Babylon could not hold it down.   [c. 102]

As the story is told in *CV* 328, the pupil wondered whether *z* was Katze's tail and *k* his (possibly bewhiskered) head—a suggestion as fascinating to the structural and pictographic imagination of Frobenius and Pound (who, by the way, were both, in the opinion of the latter, cat-faced) [19] as it is "stupid" to the teacher, who is clearly not interested in the imagistic possibilities of the alphabet and in the mysteries of cats, and is accordingly to be judged the more stupid of the two. This kind of unconscious obscurantism is the unwitting ally of the deliberate suppression of information, since " 'To avoid other views' said Herbert (De Veritate) / 'their first consideration.' " It would be easier to underwrite this thesis did Pound not choose as an example of woeful censorship the unavailability in the libraries of such works as one Barry Domvile's autobiography, *From Admiral to Cabin Boy* (1947), which has been called "a comparatively mild piece of antisemitism." [20] The Homeric quotation which reintegrates this uneven cluster within the framework of c. 98 (it is transliterated, as called for by the method spoken of above) intimates that Domvile and the German pupil have been silenced because, like Cherbury and Nestor, "too intelligent to prevaricate" (c. 99), and this

19. See above, chapter 3, note 20.
20. Stock, *Reading the Cantos*, p. 111.

intelligence-sincerity is presently correlated with reverence for the forces of vegetation (the "intelligent" seed, precisely) and with a sacrifice in which these are called upon—the composite sacrifice of *Th* (performed by Phaeacians, Na-khi, Ulysses, Spartans), the chief purpose of which is to guarantee the accuracy of the instruments of expression (or "oars") of the celebrants. (Incidentally, the barley seeds are not offered by the Spartans—who, we recall, sacrifice upon Taygetus a horse to the winds—but by Penelope to Athene in *Od.* iv.761. The two offerings are connected by way of the seed-blowing Mount of c. 92.) The vegetal ceremony recalls, because of the association established earlier between the two Leucos, the story of the daughter of Babylon's Orchamus: it is her *mind,* her intelligence, that is manifest in plant life, and in this form nothing can suppress it. In other words, the explorer, having obtained the favor of the new fronds, "cannot fail to reach the glorious harbor" [21]—"*telésai érgon te épos te.*" Mind defeats Babylon with its "speed in communication"—by participating in the metamorphoses which link the human to the divine, culture to the animal and vegetal world. The seagull theme is omitted in this reprise, yet peace with the animals is conveyed in a different form, which refers us back to the eye from which this section of the journey started out:

> "for my bitch eyes" in Ilion
> copper and wine like a bear cub's
>   in sunlight, thus Atalant
> the colour as *aithiops*
>   the gloss probably
>   *oinops*
> as lacquer in sunlight
>   haliporphuros,
>   russet-gold
> in the air, extant, not carmine, not flame, oriXalko,
>   le xaladines
> lit by the torch-flare,
>   and from the nature, the sign.   [c. 102]

21. *Inf.* xv.56; tr. Robert Lowell, "Brunetto Latini," *Near the Ocean,* p. 111.

After all, the "fuss about Helen" (c. 98) had good reason, for the Achaeans journeyed to Troy on account of her "bitch eyes" (*"emeîo kunôpidos,"* as she herself puts it in *Od.* iv.145). For Pound *kunôpis* does not mean "shameless," as it is habitually translated in this passage, but is Homer's record of the eyes with which all poets are concerned—a record which he elaborates by referring to the wine and copper color contemplated in c. 97, and to another divine and zoomorphic maiden: Atalant, who was nursed by a she-bear, and whose eyes are accordingly a cub's. (The allusion pays homage to Swinburne, the author of *Atalanta in Calydon,* and the swimmer of Le Portel.) Thus the imitation of c. 98 links up with a reprise of the breakthrough of c. 97, with the enquiry into color conducted by Pound himself—a color which is now explicitly what had only been hinted at in the previous draft: color of eyes. The lines become again stepped-down, Cavalcantesque, hieratic—and the trend is again towards "abbreviation" (not amplification, as with the "explorers"). We need only note that as he pushes on with rapid strides in his work of transcription Pound is in danger of confusing his reader, for he seems to reverse the accurate diagnosis of c. 97, by stating that *aithíops* (with the implicit arcane pun) refers to the color of the eyes, while their gloss or luminescence is *oînops,* wine-like,[22] whereas in the "original" he had written: *"oînos aithíops* the gloss, probably, / not the colour." Actually both versions amount to the same, though the second, like the canto to which it belongs, is just a little cavalier. Pound has simply replaced *oînos* with "the colour as," and, conversely, "not the colour" with *oînops;* the central comment, *"aithíops* the gloss probably," he has left unchanged. In the second version the argument runs somewhat like this: the color (of wine, sea, eyes) is *as aithíops,* i.e., *as* something that burns/is warm; but for the color as such the Greeks have another word, *oînops,* hence *aithíops* (or *aîthops*)

---

22. This is in fact what John Peck (unaware, to boot, that *aithíops* is not the same word as *aîthops*) takes the passage to mean: "oinops being the gloss and aithiops the colour" ("Pound's Lexical Mythography," p. 24). Otherwise Peck's reading of the two passages is quite useful.

describes another quality of the luminous surface: "the gloss probably . . . as lacquer in sunlight."

After this slightly adjusted induction the two drafts run parallel, the second much compressed, with "in the air, extant" (for "exists in the air") as a precise pointer to the radiant world of the Cavalcanti essay: "The rose that [the magnet of the modern scientist] makes in the iron filings, does not lead him to think of the force in botanic terms [as P. does in *RD* and *Th*], or wish to visualize the force as floral and extant (*ex stare*)" (*LE* 154). With these words and their associations in mind we may go a little deeper into the "colour" of cs. 97 and 102, and see that it is the visible signature of the invisible virtue Pound had spoken of in 1913: "We might come to believe that the thing that matters in art is a sort of energy, something more or less like electricity or radioactivity, a force transfusing, welding, and unifying. A force rather like water when it spurts up through very bright sand and sets it in swift motion. You may make what image you like" ("The Serious Artist," *LE* 49). The other favorite image, first occurring perhaps in 1915,[23] is of course the floral one. The two are brought together in the finale of c. 74, a necessary prelude to c. 97, where we see how delicate a thing this apparently rough energy can be—Verlaine's water-jets, ecstatically sighing ("Claire de lune"), and a soft wind:

> Serenely in the crystal jet
>   as the bright ball that the fountain tosses
> (Verlaine) as diamond clearness
>   How soft the wind under Taishan
>   where the sea is remembered
>   out of hell, the pit
>   out of the dust and glare evil
>   Zephyrus / Apeliota
> This liquid is certainly a
>   property of the mind
> nec accidens est   but an element
>   in the mind's make-up

23. See "Affirmations: Vorticism," *New Age,* 14 Jan. 1915, pp. 277–78; quoted in Schneidau, *The Image and the Real,* p. 150.

           est agens and functions   dust to the fountain pan otherwise
                 Hast'ou seen the rose in the steel dust
                             (or swansdown ever?)   [c. 74]

This reminds us that at Pisa Pound can sum up much of the
poem—and the passage is a crucial synthesis—without putting
any strain upon communication. He can tell us, that is, that the
wind from the sea and the memories of the past bring much-
needed refreshment to his mind and body, prostrate in the glare
and dust of the D.T.C., and call upon the central symbols we
have spoken of, and many others: the water-jet balances the crystal ball of the *phantastikon;* the wind has witnessed the birth of
Venus and is soft as swansdown and cunnus; the D.T.C. is the
hell and "pitkin" of c. 1 made real; the poet rises "from under
the rubble heap" in anticipation of the ascent ("upon a Zephyr's
shoulder") to the aureate sky of c. 81, and of "the great flight" of
c. 90. The sequel defines the "liquid" (wind, water, color) in the
terms of Guido's canzone: it is not an accident in a subject (as
Dante and Cavalcanti defined love),[24] but an essential "element"
of the mind's world, the ground upon which everything ultimately rests. "The god is inside the stone . . . but there is never
any question . . . about the force being the essential, and the rest
'accidental' . . . The shape occurs" ("Cavalcanti," *LE* 152). If
the force be removed the bright sand and ball it had shaped and
set in motion falls back into dryness, "dust to the fountain pan."
But now the force is at work, and the shape occurs—the shape of
the goddess's rose.
    "And from the nature, the sign." We return to our comparison
of c. 102 with its "source," and note that, though he preserves its
verbal equivalent, Pound has dropped the striking ideogramic
image of *ling.* Consequently the cluster summoned by the rain
radical (Kuanon/Danae/Ra-Set on her tower/boat, and the sky-
fallen Nile) also falls out of the picture, and from the benevolent
lions we go directly to those other manifestations of mythologic

24. See *Vita nuova* xxv.1. The Latin comes from P.'s confusing discussion of "come in
subietto" (cf. c. 100) in "Cavalcanti," *LE* 175.

sensibility—the flickering spirits (Homer's, Dante's: color personified), and the "late" stars of Coma Berenices:

> Berenice, a late constellation.
>   "Same books" said Tcheou
> they ought to be brother-like.
>   Crystaline,
>   south slope for juniper,
> Wild goose follows the sun-bird,
>   in mountains; salt, copper, coral,
>   dead words out of fashion
> KAI ALOGA,
>   nature APHANTASTON,
>   the pine needles glow as red wire
> OU THELEI EAEAN EIS KOSMON
>   they want to burst out of the universe   [c. 102]

The mention of Berenice also looks back to the textual journeys,
"under eyelids," commended earlier, for as Yeats imitated Ronsard, so Catullus translated Callimachus. Hence, apparently, Mr.
Tcheou's remark that " 'These people . . . should / be like brothers. They read the same books.'/Meaning chinese and japanese"
(c. 88). Likewise Pound's redrafting of his own and others' texts
aims at brotherhood, benevolence, peace. (He may also be thinking of Santayana's pronouncement that it did not matter so much
"what books people read as long as they read the *same*
books.") [25] The following lines, taking us into Na-khi landscape
(with a hint at the crystalline *phantastikon*) seem to indicate that
the journey has reached its destination, the earthly paradise,
where we find the "salt, copper, coral" of the sea and of Venus,
and, ironically, the harbor of dead words out of fashion of c. 97.
There is of course no little life in the words of this canto, yet in
one sense they are in fact dead, that is, if we compare them with
"the unquenchable splendour and indestructible delicacy of nature," or with the glow of pine needles in the dawn or upon the
hearth (cs. 79 and 96). These things, Pound tells us with more

25. Quoted by Daniel Cory, "Ezra Pound: A Memoir," p. 33.

dead words, poorly transliterated from Plotinus or elsewhere, are ineffable (*áloga*) and most secret (*aphántaston*), yet are "not un-true'd by reason of our failing to fix [them] on paper" (*K* 52), and still must be attended with reverence and perseverance, not by evading the manifest universe.[26]

In fact Pound's mytho- (and logo-) poeia peters out as we come to the close of this otherwise sustained canto. With a few quotations from Ammianus he returns a little wearily to the history of kings, introducing Julian, who "built granaries," and was "naturally labeled 'apostate.'" (The previous pages, we gather, graph the emperor's state of mind.) The scene darkens further as he dies at an early age, and as we hear of Domitian try-ing, three centuries back, to buy peace with money, and this sets the lights for the subsequent segment—the most inchoate—of the journey of *Thrones*.

Canto 103 is the final installment of Pound's American annals, its suggestive inception ("1850: gt objection to any honesty in the White House") rhyming with the opening of c. 100, which antici-pates in form and subject matter this section of *Th*. It does not stay for long at any time with the subject, picking up other mate-rials from the diary of Madame de Genlis and elsewhere, and breaking through on two occasions into the mythical annals of the *Shu Ching*.[27] (The correlation of America and China is famil-iar from earlier "decads.") Likewise its close, repeating some-what the practice of the previous canto, goes on to recapitulate the Fortuna cluster and themes from the Deacon (Wodan, Fricco, Agelmund, Tuscany and incense, Brennus and wine—*oînos aîthops*). This suggests a consistent attitude to history remote and modern, but, as noted in connection with c. 100, Pound's reading of old annals and his doubtful insights into modern times will not coalesce, for the latter lack textual authority. Hence, for instance,

26. In c. 105 "ΕΑΕΑΝ" is given, in Greek alphabet, as *éen*, imperf. of *eimí*, but this would appear to be only an editorial emendation. It is more likely that P. was looking at *iénai*, inf. of *eîmi*, "I go" (then the quotation would mean: "does not want to go towards the cosmos")—or at *eáan*, inf. of *eáo*, "I leave" (but then the *eis* would be superfluous).

27. See Couvreur, *Chou King*, pp. 50–51, 58, 104.

his preoccupation at the time of publication with two lines on the second page of the canto: "France, after Talleyrand [,] started / no war in Europe." Finding that these did not agree with his slanted view of the origin of some of the wars of the last hundred years,[28] he had an errata inserted in the book, with the reading: "France, after Talleyrand [,] started / no war in Europe until '70." But he was not satisfied: he cast about for information ("Are you sure that France started no war in Europe until '70? And that Crimea is not in Europe??"), and eventually demanded the "black out" of the two lines.[29] Such are the liabilities of the self-appointed chroniclers of the tribe. Pound, we see, still thought of the poem as straightforward history, and not (as the symbolist Yeats remarked of his "system") as "stylistic arrangements of experience,"[30] and was foundering in the attendant perplexities, which would be comic were they not tragic, at a time when he had only a few months left before lapsing into permanent inactivity.

We suspect that the obscurity and disconnectedness, the unamusing inside jokes ("my ex-partner 'wuz / sekkertary / of State' "), and the jarring tough language ("I shall have to learn a little greek to keep up with this / but so will you, drratt you") of cs. 103–105, are all devices chosen by Pound, consciously or not, to prove to himself and to the reader that he knows what he is about, while in fact he is only waiting for the next moment of grace. But, unlike those professional double-dealers, Ulysses and the Cid, Pound will hide the truth even from himself, and this makes his plight more desperate, and singularly modern.

28. Cf. c. 104: "The Pollok was hooked by false promise: 'black sea' / 'help from the black sea' / only a pollok could have swallowed that promise"—and Malcolm Cowley's perceptive gloss: "Hitler was a martyr to the bankers. It was England, ruled by the usurocracy, which started the more recent phase of the war by urging the Poles to resist his reasonable demands." A Many-Windowed House: Collected Essays on American Writers and American Writing, ed. H. D. Piper (Carbondale: Southern Illinois Univ. Press, 1970), p. 190. Cowley has a just quarrel with critics who, like Hugh Kenner, thrive on P.'s lack of historical sense.

29. To Vanni Scheiwiller, 6 Dec. 1959. Accordingly, the lines were dropped in the Faber Cantos. But in recent American printings some bright editor has perpetrated the following emendation: "France, after Talleyrand started / one war in Europe."

30. Yeats, A Vision, p. 25.

With canto 104, an extensive assemblage of atomic facts that
does not yield any pattern, we are supposedly back in the promised land: it opens with Na-khi talk "not to be heard amid
sounds of the forest" (see above), deals briefly a page later with
Muan-bpo, without satisfying the expectation aroused in c. 98
(for this we will have to wait for cs. 110 and 112), invites us to
dissociate "pao[three] from pao[four]"—two tones like two birdcalls—
and closes with another quotation from the *Shu Ching*.[31] The
evocation of Muan-bpo indicates an awareness that, but for the
"force," the quality of the affection, the odds and ends of the
mind are dross, dust to the fountain pan:

> and there is
> > no glow such as of pine-needles burning
> Without ²muan   ¹bpo
> > no reality
> Wind over snow-slope   agitante
> > nos otros
> > > calescimus
> Against jade
> > calescimus,
> > and the jade weathers dust-swirl.   [c. 104]

Muan-bpo is conflated with the recurrent offering of "that
shrub"—cedar and juniper, pine and incense—of *Th*; belief, reverence, is the only criterion of truth: "If Muan-bpo is not performed, all that we accomplish is not real."[32] Against the autumn wind of c. 93, the dust-swirl, there is the *deus in nobis,* the
jade ("above crystal"—c. 94) of the initiate community—"nos
otros."

But through the remainder of the canto (five pages) the imagination does not take fire, though the materials are occasionally
lyrical and the characters benevolent: the sixteenth-century "me-
dico" Ambroise Paré; the seventeenth-century sinologue Prospero
Intorcetta, from whom "Webster, Voltaire and Leibnitz" (all lex-

31. See Couvreur, *Chou King,* pp. 44, 58, 66. Couvreur renders the characters which he
transliterates "foung huang lai [*not* li] i" as follows: "Les deux phénix viennent et s'agi-
tent avec élégance."

32. Rock, "Muan Bpo Ceremony," p. 41.

icographers to some extent) are said to derive "by phillotaxis / in leaf-grain," i.e. through the non-verbal tradition, the signatures of nature; [33] and Pound's "familiares" (a tag from cs. 20 and 90, now pointing not to "ferae" but to familiar ghosts):

> Iseult is dead, and Walter,
>   and Fordie,
>   familiares
> "And how my olde friend
>   —eh—eh
>   HOWellls?
> can" etcetera
>   Remy's word was "milésiennes"
> William's: monoceros,
>   vide his book plate.
>   The production IS the beloved.   [c. 104]

What is remembered is a turn of phrase—James's endless sentences—and *words* dead or alive like "milésiennes" [34] and Yeats's "monoceros" or unicorn. A few lines back Pound had reported the question: "What part ob yu iz deh POEM??"—and the last line may be the answer: the poem is the primary love object of the secretary of words. Yet in the disintegration of discourse shown by the context the pronouncement becomes unintentionally ironic. As the poem progresses there are always fewer words and complete utterances to the page, as if the resistance to be overcome in the writing became increasingly formidable. Pound's love of the word is clearly fretted with fear and frustration.

The annalistic mode is less prominent in this canto, though it includes an ineffectual attempt to "summarize" economic history on the lines of the "recapitulation" of c. 88, and alternates with some regularity visions of good and evil, or *panourgía*, "Adolf furious from perception" being among the champions of the for-

---

33. A library catalogue yields a Confucius, *Sinarum Scientia Politico-Moralis, a P. Prospero Intorcetta, siculo, S.J. . . . in lucem edita* (Paris 1672).

34. See 1 *HSM* 11, and "Rémy de Gourmont," *LE* 345. The other "familiars" are Ford Madox Ford, Iseult Gonne, and Walter Rummel—the pianist mentioned in c. 80 from whom P. may have picked up the Wagnerian leitmotiv technique (Stock, *Reading the Cantos*, p. 21).

mer, Disraeli ("bitching England") among those of the latter. In fact there is much fascism, anti-Semitism, and anti-Communism ("Homestead versus kolkhoz / Rome versus Babylon"—c. 103) in these cantos—another bad sign, for it indicates that the poet is not seeking, but falling back upon his opinions—and what opinions:

> Feb. 1956
> Is this a divagation:
> > > Talleyrand saved Europe for a century
> France betrayed Talleyrand;
> > > Germany, Bismarck.
> And Muss saved, rem salvavit,
> > > in Spain
> > > > il salvabile.
>
> [*chi*] semina motuum
> From Sulmona
> > the lion-fount—
> > > must be Sulmona, Ovidio's,
> Federico noted the hawk form   [c. 105]

Thus the opening of the last of the dark cantos, which returns, as the date indicates, to the annalistic form (the annals of the world, and the annals of P.'s writing). Semina, we recall, are associated with beer halls in c. 90 (and with *ling* in c. 104); but of course they also import the oneness of the rulers (all of them betrayed saviors, somewhat like their poet) with natural process and with metamorphic hearsay: hence the lion-fount (a royal and Dionysian symbol) Pound found in Ovid's Sulmona, and Frederick's (or Sargon's) hawk. In this instance mythopoeia may be said to prevail over bias, for the lines flow. This is generally true of the canto as a whole, which at least has a recognizable structure and subject, amounting to a portrait—a mask—of St. Anselm, one of the oar-thinners of c. 98, and a fascinating (and quite Poundian) character in his own right, being both a mystic and a rationalist of sorts, and an able politician as well. The canto comprises snippets from *Monologium* and *Proslogium,* and from Eadmer's biography of the saint (Anselm pragmatically indicates the spot where a well is to be dug, somewhat like Frobenius). It closes with an annalistic survey of medieval English history, extracted from William of Malmesbury's *Gesta Regum Anglorum*. The lot is quarried from *PL* [35] and rendered in Pound's acrid Americanese, quite unsure in tone, as we may well expect. For example, the question of investiture, which loomed large in Anselm's career, is referred to with, "And we bjJayzus reject your damn bishops"—and later we are informed that "Quendrida bumped off brother Kenelm." [36] Still, it is good, both for us and for the poet, to know where we are, and some of the matters touched upon are of relevance to the context of *Th*. (But this, it must be added, is also the case with the "sounds in the forest" and the "words" of c. 104.) Thus we hear of the archbishop's clarity and of his grammatical quest for the goddess of light: "digestion weak, / but had a clear line on the Trinity, and / By sheer grammar: Essentia / feminine / Immaculata." Also, his connections, by phyllotaxis perhaps, to the principals of Pound's "medieval dream," are explored—in particular his supposed agreement with the "rationalist" Cavalcanti (" 'rationalem' / said Anselm. / Guido: 'intenzione' ").[37] Hence the "luminous detail" which summarizes Pound's reading at the end of the canto: "Guido had read the Proslogion / as had, presumably, Villon." It is in fact not unlikely that the Florentine intellectual should have been familiar with Anselm (who is among the wise spirits in Dante's Heaven of the Sun)—but our primary concern is with the role of this historical surmise within the poem's imaginative structure. The statement, that is, must be read in the light of the final cluster of c. 100, where Guido and Villon also are associated; it suggests that the earlier juxtaposition was hardly a matter of bawdy contrast alone: after all, Villon, a 1452 graduate from the Sorbonne, must have been aware of theological speculation; the medieval dream, though embattled (*ABR* 104), is sustained—as again in 1959. The same can be said of the block of medieval

35. Vols. 158 and 179. See the chapter on Anselm in James J. Wilhelm's *The Later Cantos of Ezra Pound* (New York: Crowell, 1977).

36. For "Dalleyrand Berigorrr!"—the punch line of an anti-Semitic joke—see Stock, *Reading the Cantos*, p. 112.

37. See above, ch. 13, n. 6.

chronicle (chiefly from William of Malmesbury) that takes up
most of the canto's latter part (P. returning occasionally, and
again—as we know—in the end, to his main theme): a bare list-
ing of doubtful memorabilia, one to a stepped-across line, it is
appealing on account of its agreement with the annalistic undercurrent of *Th.* (The fragmentation and the drift towards a one-
word-to-a-line pattern, mentioned earlier, will also have been detected in the last quotations.) As usual, the chronicle also offers
material that claims attention in its own right:

> Charles of the Suevi
> > a noose of light looped over his shoulder,
> Antoninus declined to be God.
> Athelstan on occasion distributed,
> > Ethelbald exempted from taxes,
> > > Egbert left local laws,   [c. 105]

In the *Chronicon Centulense* of Hariulf, a 12th-century Flemish
abbot, Charles le Gros recounts a vision in which he is caught
up by "a spirit most splendid who held a ball of linen giving off a
ray of purest light, such as a comet"; as he hands him the roll
this personage says: "Take the thread of this burning ball and tie
it firmly to your right thumb, for it will lead you through the
labyrinthine woes of hell" (*PL* CLXXIV 1287). Pound overlooks
(or chooses to ignore) the Ariadne reference (to him equally attractive), and sketches a king who wields, rather than a saving
bikini, a "lasso of light" (as it is called in c. 104)—an image
delightful to meet in the labyrinthine halls of *Th,* and carrying
suggestions unequivocal and entertaining about the section's
ideal sovran.

Before leaving this uneven cluster of cantos it should be remarked that they form—with c. 106—a unit of verse to be taken
whole, for their cumulative effect largely depends upon a number
of themes, occasionally quite microscopic, that run in and out of
them (and—incidentally—suggest sequential composition). These
are the allusions to (and possible quotations from) Plotinus
(101–02, 104–05—besides 98–100); Charles le Gros (104–05);

the Na-khi (98, 100, 101–02, 104, 106); Luigi (97, 104, 106); "homestead versus kolkhoz" (103–04); young Ezra's cheap luncheons (101–03); the *Shu Ching*'s emperors (103–04); and Sulmona's Ovid (103–06). Concerning the latter the St. Elizabeth's prisoner significantly remarks: "Mirabeau had it worse, Ovid much worse in Pontus." Elsewhere he openly addresses the disjointedness and occasional aridity of his writing, laying them to the account of the very nature of his material ("We do NOT know the past in chronological sequence," he had pointed out in *K 5*):

> Fragmentary:
>> (Maverick repeating this queery dogmaticly.
>> mosaic? any mosaic.
> You cannot leave these things out. . . .
> They want to bust out of the kosmos   [c. 105]

An enquiry even approximate, mere indication of work to be done, is still preferable to acceptance of "what is already understood" (c. 96), or to (it comes to the same) evasion of the cosmos' irreducible intricacy. With luck the poet's mosaic may approximate in patches the golden vaults of Monreale remembered one canto back—a "topaz" or amorous structure a god may choose for a throne (see c. 88):

>   pen yeh
> Homestead versus kolkhoz,
>> advice to farms, not control
> tessera, Monreale,
>> Topaz, God can sit on.   [c. 104]

At his most liberal Pound can go no further than enlightened paternalism, which however takes care not to trouble the quiet farms where craft is transmitted from father to son (see c. 101), and where alone, in Pound's present view, the great art fit for the gods may come about. Meanwhile, to return to the earlier quotation, the ostensible reference to Lewis Maverick, editor of the

American abridgement of the "fragmentary" *Kuan-tzu*,[38] directs us to the eponymous text of canto 106, the remarkable poem (no mean repayment for the darker tracts of the journey) that we are to consider next.

38. Lewis Maverick, ed., *Economic Dialogues in Ancient China: Selections from the Kuan-tzu*, tr. T'an Po-fu and Wen Kung-wen (Carbondale, Ill., 1954).

15. A Late Mythologem

AND was her daughter like that;
Black as Demeter's gown,
              eyes, hair?
Dis' bride, Queen over Phlegethon,
5   girls faint as mist about her?
The strength of men is in grain.   [*kuan*] Kuan
NINE decrees, 8th essay, the Kuan   [*tzu*] Tzu

So slow is the rose to open.
A match flares in the eyes' hearth,
10   then darkness
"Venice shawls from Demeter's gown"   [c. 106]

Out of the chronicle and theology of c. 105 comes this mythological and legislative meditation, even as law and myth had emerged from the annals and economics of cs. 96 and 97, respectively. The pattern established there ("Who shall know throstle's note from banded thrush"—or *aîthops* from *aithíops,* color from gloss, *chen*[4] from *chen*[1]?) is adhered to, for light is demanded from the mythological memory as to the "similitude" and difference of Persephone and Demeter, daughter and mother, whom the first two lines balance against one another—goddesses aptly qualified by Dante's description of Bertran de Born: "And they were two in one, and one in two."[1]

Similitude is all we know of identity: Core emerges from the flux of language—the only noun in the first line—and before this is over she is said to be *like* something indefinite—an absentee referent of which various versions are given in the sequel, until we see that the comparison involves the gown of the mother on the one hand (a dark double of *krédemnon*) and the eyes and hair of the daughter on the other, and that what is being compared is a color, as in c. 97, which is also concerned with eyes. (Inciden-

1. *Inf.* xxviii.125, quoted by P. in the Browningesque "Near Perigord," the poem in which he compares himself to Bertran.

tally, *oînops* was occasionally used for blackness.)[2] That it is identity and not an answer that the poet is seeking is apparent from the sequel, which turns the lightly mentioned daughter into the awesome Queen and bride to Dis she was to become—actually a telescoping of mother and daughter, as well as a dark counterpart of the Queen of the third heaven.[3] Around her, like the shades about Tiresias (*aíssousin*), are the "girls tender" of c. 1, and the fairs (Tyro, Alcmene, Chloris, Ariadne) whom Persephone sends to meet Odysseus in *Od.* 11, and who are evoked in ur-c. 3 and elsewhere in the poem. They are the lesser incarnations of the queen, who, like Walter Pater's Mona Lisa, is "a perpetual life, sweeping together ten thousand experiences."[4]

Pound is undertaking anew in the mythological memory the voyage towards Persephone and finally Aphrodite on which he had set out in c. 1, as the parallelism between the two inceptions brings home:

2. Alice Elizabeth Kober, *The Use of Color Terms in the Greek Poets* (Geneva–New York: Humphreys, 1932), p. 86.

3. The lines are indebted to Arthur Golding's translation of *Met.* v.504–08, quoted in *ABR* 130:

> Now while I underneath the Earth the Lake of Styx did passe
> I saw your daughter Proserpine with these same eyes. She was
> Not merie, neyther rid of feare as seemed by hir cheere
> But yet a Queene, but yet of great God Dis the stately Feere:
> But yet of that same droupie Realme the chiefe and sovereigne Peere.

Golding's own version of Persephone's abduction P. quotes in "Notes on Elizabethan Classicists," *LE* 235–36—and made use of in the finale of c. 21. (Incidentally, the old man on the mule is also from Golding, "Address to Bacchus. ɪv," *LE* 237.)

4. *Studies in the History of the Renaissance* (1873), quoted in Praz, *Romantic Agony,* p. 253. If we read the famous passage again with the *Cantos* in mind we see that it prefigures the better part of P.'s phantasies about the lady: "Hers is the head upon which all 'the ends of the world are come,' and the eyelids are a little weary. . . . All the thoughts and experiences of the world have etched and moulded there . . . the animalism of Greece, the lust of Rome, the mysticism of the Middle Age with its spiritual ambition and imaginative loves, the return of the Pagan world, the sins of the Borgias. She is older than the rocks among which she sits; like the vampire, she has been dead many times, and learned the secrets of the grave; and has been a diver in deep seas, and keeps their fallen day about her; . . . and, as Leda, was the mother of Helen of Troy, and, as Saint Anne, the mother of Mary; and all this has been to her but as the sound of lyres and flutes, and lives only in the delicacy with which it has moulded the changing lineaments, and tinged the eyelids and the hands."

Aňd thén wěnt dówn tŏ thĕ shíp . . .
Aňd wás hĕr dáughtĕr līke thát . . .

(two iambs and an anapest, or rather the clause of a dactylic hexameter—arsis, trochee, dactyl, spondee—the latter foot short of a
syllable, which is to be reintegrated in the canto's final line: "Thĕ
ský ĭs léadĕd wĭth élm bóughs"). The Eleusinian implications of
the *nékuia* are stressed in Pound's rendering of the instructions
given Ulysses by Circe, "the trim-coifed goddess" (c. 1—cf.
"hair," 3)—"Ceres' daughter" being his addition to Homer's
lines (quoted in Greek in c. 39):

> First must thou go the road
>
> > to hell
>
> And to the bower of Ceres' daughter Proserpine,
> Through overhanging dark, to see Tiresias,   [c. 47]

As Persephone descends to the underworld in the autumn and is
resurrected with the new fronds of spring, so Ulysses—and the
sovran of *Th*—sails after knowledge and/or performs sexual intercourse in order that his land be fertile, the crops thick in his
death year.

This comes out in the peremptory assertion of lines 6–7, a dramatic "answer" (musically speaking) to the opening's subtle web
of questions. Investigation of the goddesses' feminine world and
refinement of language are, it is intimated, the "ground" of social
life—for "The strength of men is in grain"—and the foundation
of Law, as the latter apparent repeat from c. 102 ("Barley is the
marrow of men") turns out to be a borrowing from the "decrees" and "essays" of the *Kuan-tzu*, an "economic" work compiled around the third century B.C. and attributed to the semi-
legendary Kuan Chung, in which in fact we find that "The people
cannot live without grain to eat";[5] similar pronouncements occur
in the nine "regulations" (P. emphasizes the magic number) included in "Essay VIII: Basic Methods of Government."[6] As with
the *Sheng Yü*, Pound copies out the Chinese title of his new edict,

5. Maverick, *Economic Dialogues*, p. 70.
6. Ibid., pp. 57–59.

to make the correlation of Eleusis and Kung (cf. c. 52, and c. 47 vs 49) prominent, and to have us note that *kuan* is the character for "to govern" and includes (like *tso,* the initiate's bridge in c. 101) radical 118, "bamboo," the vegetal principle; and that *tzu* designates a boy but also, as in the names of Confucius and Mencius, a philosopher. The law is validated by the augury of the word, with its public and esoteric implications.

Having gone thus far into social consciousness, the poet returns, following the habitual *a-b-a-b* pattern, to his quest after "nothing but awareness," presenting us with the metapoetic import of the mythological motif: instead of Core, the resurgent rose of c. 74 ("so light is the urging"), its lightness turned to slowness. This is the slowness which is beauty (c. 87), as intimated by the sensuous sequence of o's and s's in l. 8, but also the beauty which is difficult ("Yeats two months on a sonnet of Ronsard's"): the following lines suggestively repeat the motif "For a flash, / for an hour. / Then agony," situating the flash in the eye (already mentioned in l. 3) of the lady—and of the poet, who can actually see her only in the brief moment of epiphany. It is just worth mentioning that these images, though securely repossessed by the poet's imagination, amount to decadent topoi. We think of the "rose dans les ténèbres" "seen" by Maeterlinck's (and Débussy's) Mélisande (P., who does not seem to have known where he was standing, called the opera *Pelléas,* in 1921, "that mush of hysteria"—*L* 178), and of Gourmont's *Litanies de la rose,* which bring together flower and eye: "Rose bleue, rose iridine, monstre couleur des yeux de la Chimère, rose bleue, lève un peu tes paupières" (quoted in Espey 73)—to say nothing of the symbol's more recent occurrences (Rilke's *Les Roses, Little Gidding*), and of the purported model both of Eliot and Pound: Dante.

As the light goes out (cf. c. 82: "a match on Cnidos") we are back in the darkness out of which the canto has arisen—precisely the blackness of Demeter's gown which now returns (for the dark is equivalent to the loss of Core), to be correlated with the shawls of Venetian women. Thus theme *a* expands to its original form (cs. 98 and 102), and incorporates as it were theme *b,* the social world.[7] The sequel elaborates this interaction so far only ideogramicly suggested making it known that the good government of the Republic of St. Mark and of all commonwealth must depend upon the "mysteries"—the metapoetic inquest:

> This Tzu could guide you in some things,
> > > but not hither,
> How to govern is from the time of Kuan Chung
> 15   but the cup of white gold at Patera
> Helen's breasts gave that.
> > > ὸ ϑεός
> runs thru his zodiac,
> > misnaming no Caledon,
> 20   not in memory,
> > > in eternity
> > > > and "as a wind's breath
> that changing its direction changeth its name,"
> > > > > Apeliota
> 25   for the gold light of wheat surging upward
> > > > ungathered
> Persephone in the cotton-field
> > > granite next sea wave
> is for clarity
> 30   deep waters reflecting all fire
> nueva lumbre,
> > > Earth, Air, Sea
> > > > in the flame's barge
> over Amazon, Orinoco, great rivers.   [c. 106]

The law of the poet who now addresses us directly incorporates old Kuan Chung's regulations but will not be limited by them: to travel, he tells us, "hither"—that is, to the promised land of *Th*—the *Kuan-tzu* is not sufficient; what we need is a shawl or a bikini, or a cup of white gold modeled upon the breast of Helen. The road to ROMA lies through AMOR, the love of the Cruel Fair,

---

7. In the typescript P. had indicated the source of the quotation of l. 11 in an additional line: "(thus Scarfoglio)." This was omitted perhaps to preserve the mythical concentration of the passage, or perhaps because Carlo Scarfoglio, a fellow commentator of P. at Rome Radio and the Italian translator of *CA*, changed his mind about fascism after the war, and this may have come to the poet's attention.

who calls here for the last time in the poem. The remarkable cup, which Pound appropriates as if to prepare to celebrate a synchretic mass, is spoken of in "Aux Etuves de Wiesbaden," the imaginary dialogue of 1917, where, in accord with Pliny (*HN* III. 81), it is said to have been "long shown in the temple at Lyndos, which is in the island of Rhodes" (*PD* 102)—and is mentioned again, in connection with "Tellus *géa* feconda," in Pisan cantos 77 and 79. Here it is apochryphally removed to the non-existent "Patera"—a portmanteau word which incorporates a sort of cup (*pàtera*) and indicates that it is dedicated to the cult of Apollo, who is worshipped "in Lycia, at Patara," as we find in *HSP* 1—but not in Propertius' Latin ("Lycio vota probante deo"— III.1). Pound probably picked up the connection from *Met.* I.516, and lifted the gloss into his *Homage*; forty years later he returned to the word because familiar, already written, and used it (in the portmanteau form "Patera") as a link between the two "guides" he would have us follow: the earthy goddess ("the breasts of Tellus-Helena"—c. 77) and the god (*ho theós*) of the precise definition, who wields the sun's lance "on the precise spot verbally." Accordingly in the sequel we find "the solar vitality" speeding through the zodiac whence he sees "all the earth and sea" (as Demeter remarks in the Homeric Hymn when seeking information from him about her lost daughter), and calling all objects with their proper names, as the Na-khi put it. Pound, who has sought earlier through similitude a definition for the eyes, "copper and wine like a bear cub's," of Atalant of Calydon, suggests that the god possesses the one and only definition of these, proof against misnaming, but that this is so only "in eternity," for in time and in memory (mythological and poetic) the name is bound to change according to direction as winds do if it is to be true to the color of nature. (The quotation from *Purg.* XI.101–02, which actually describes the fickleness of fame—"Thus one Guido has taken from another the glory of the language"—is made to import the *feng su* theme.) Pound, that is, will have it both ways: a definition precise in eternity, movable and tentative and metamorphic in time. ("Patera" and "Caledon" [for Calydon, or Calydonian] are instances of the latter.)

The wind's breath from the sun, Apeliota, may now usher us into the mystery of Tellus, and this will concern both the wheat and clarity. Instead of breathing upon Venus Anadiomene (or on her shell) as it is wont to, it turns the ungathered wheat into a sea, and from this Persephone (now mentioned for the first time) rises—to become the Venus of the underworld. The meadow through which she walks picking flowers will be a cotton field of the American South (which stood for "advice to farms, not control"), and her rape at the hands of Dis will be graphed by the wave running in granite of the Albigenses (who shared the Confederate philosophy and were likewise suppressed), a symbol of metamorphosis or sea change, standing "for clarity."

That the Excideuil image should stand for Core's abduction is of course only an impression, for the association between the South and Provence is enough to account for it. Yet in the sequel it becomes clear that we are looking again into the deep waters of an eye, and seeing there Ra-Set's barge with a mystical crew—the four elements. That is, we are witnessing at least three voyages: Venus upon her shell, Core descending to Hades and Phlegethon, Ra-Set in "the golden sun-boat." In fact, lines 17–34 comprise a single sentence which rings changes upon the first line of c. 98: "The boat of Ra-Set moves with the sun." The poet has found his way back to the vision of cs. 91 and 97, and his memory provides him freely with the essential, and emotionally precise, tags: words and phantasies which his mind has been turning about for a long time. So with the "new light" of which he speaks in a misplaced passage of SR ("[Juan de Mena] does not mention the appearance of the water, but suggests it in speaking of the sullen glow in the armor: 'Y dar nueva lumbre las armas y hierros' "),[8]

8. SR 34 and n. P. refers to his source as Mena, Muerte del Conde de Niebla—the Count being the "him" in the next quotation. This is actually an episode in a larger work, El laberinto o las trescientas (1444); the quotation is from copla 164.

P. seems to have been thinking of Mena's line when he wrote the "Canzon: Of Incense," which he published in 1910, like SR:

Thy gracious ways,
            O Lady of my heart, have
O'er all my thought their golden glamour cast;
As amber torch-flames, where strange men-at-arms

and again in ur-c. 2 (" 'Of sombre light upon reflected armour' /
. . . Full many a fathomed sea-change in the eyes / That sought
with him the salt sea victories"—*QPA* 26). Mena's line he associates with Arnaut's "remir contra·l lum de la lampa," and this
may be said to tie it up in c. 106 with the Albigensian wave, even
as it is used to materially describe, as a tag may, the otherworldly
lighting of the scene. That the Phlegethon, Nile, and "river of
crystal" should appear under the names of Amazon and Orinoco
may be thought of as a metacultural bonus. (At any rate, the
names are suggestive.)

With characteristic suddenness, the theme of the edict, and of
the things to which it may guide us, is now reintroduced. The
defense of Kuan Chung (who does not come out very well from
ll. 12–13) is taken on by the Master in person, as he does in
Analects xiv 18 (and c. 80) in response to a pupil's derogatory
remark:

35   "But for Kuan Chung we should still dress as barbarians."
        And if Antoninus got there, this was hidden
                Kuan, hidden   [*kuan* ¹]

Tread softly 'neath the damask shield of night,
Rise from the flowing steel in part reflected,
So on my mailed thought that with thee goeth,
Though dark the way, a golden glamour falleth.   [*CEP* 137–38]

Another poem in *Canzoni*, "Canzon: The Yearly Slain," is of relevance to the themes of c.
106:

The Maiden turns to her dark lord's demesne.

Fairer than Enna's field when Ceres sows
The stars of hyacinth and puts off grief, . . .
Fairer than these the Poppy-crowned One flees,
And Joy goes weeping in her scarlet train.

The faint damp wind that, ere the even, blows
Piling the west with many a tawny sheaf, . . .
This wind is like her and the listless air
Wherewith she goeth by beneath the trees,
The trees that mock her with their scarlet stain. . . .

Korè my heart is, let it stand sans gloze!
Love's pain is long, and lo, love's joy is brief! . . .

Crimson the hearth where one last ember glows! . . .
Blow! O ye ashes, where the winds shall please,
But cry, "Love also is the Yearly Slain."   [*CEP* 133–34]

Ad posteros urbem donat,
                                    coin'd Artemis
40   all goods light against coin-skill
        if there be 400 mountains for copper—
             under cinnabar you will find copper—
        river gold is from Ko Lu;
                                    price from XREIA;
45   Yao and Shun ruled by jade   [c. 106]

But it is now apparent (what was intimated as early as ll. 1–7)
that the distinction between "this Tzu" and Helen's cup, between
law and mystery, no longer obtains: Kuan Chung and his companions (Antoninus and the sovrans of *Th*) have not only instilled
the rudiments of civilization, but have indeed "got there" (or
"hither"—l. 13)—that is to the visionary locus described in the
previous lines—though information to this effect has been withheld, "hidden," both because the enemies of contemplation have
omitted it from their "records" (c. 97), and because "the mysteries *can* not be revealed." So much is imported by the subtle
pun on the lawgiver's name (comparable to *chen*[4] vs *chen*[1],
aîthops vs *aithíops*), Pound replacing *kuan*[3] ("to govern," as in
l. 6) by *kuan*[1] ("a gate . . . to shut or close"— M 3571), the first
character in the *Shih Ching* (" 'Hid! Hid!' the fish-hawk saith"),
which points to poetry as the handmaid of the mysteries and
graphs the "door" through which the sovran is initiated into
secret doctrine. It is on account of knowledge thus acquired that
he builds the temple city (Ecbatan, Wagadu), which (as Douglas
insisted) is an asset to future generations, even as *our* dress still
shows Kuan's influence, and as "This canal goes still to TenShi /
though the old King built it for pleasure" (c. 49). The coin (Antoninus'?) bearing the image of Artemis (virgin queen, cognate to
Core), exhibits the coalescence of "good" economics and venera-
tion, a thesis vindicated by the following handful of quotations
from the *Kuan-tzu:* [9] nature (or, rather, four hundred "Mounts")

9. "There are 467 mountains producing copper. . . . If there is cinnabar on the surface
there will be copper and gold beneath. . . . From the mountains in Ko Lu there came a
flood which washed down gold . . . When the demand for it becomes urgent, gold
becomes 'heavy'; when the demand slackens, gold becomes 'light.' The ancient kings es-

gives freely of grain as much as of precious metals ("Deus nec vendit . . . sed largitur"—c. 100), and the ideal economy is keyed to her "majestic rhythm," [10] leaving no place for usurious practice. (Price is set according to Aristotle's *chreía,* which P. takes to be actual use—as against artificially created demand.) [11] But this *natura* by which organic economy is governed is none but the goddess who wears gold, copper, and jade. (Cf. "vacuum" vs "inluminatio coitu" in c. 36.)

The first section of the canto comes to an end as its two themes are brought together in the prehistoric utopia of Yao and Shun (the earliest emperors) ruling with the exalted jade. The poet may now go as deep as he likes into arcanum without fear of being misunderstood: the middle section is given to "grain rite," the culminating sacrifice of *Th,* which is celebrated again by the "hunchback" Luigi (associated with Antoninus in c. 97):

> That the goddess turn crystal within her
> This is grain rite
>   Luigi in the hill path
>   this is grain rite
> 50   near Enna, at Nyssa:
>   Circe, Persephone
> so different is sea from glen that
>   the juniper is her holy bush
> between the two pine trees, not Circe
> 55   but Circe was like that
>   coming from the house of smoothe stone
> "not know which god"
>   nor could enter her eyes by probing
>   the light blazed behind her
> 60   nor was this from sunset.   [c. 106]

timated the degree of urgency, and issued decrees accordingly, raising or lowering the value of the middle money (adjusting to market developments?), regulating its value. . . . By regulating the degree of urgency (by increasing or decreasing government purchasing) with decrees, [they] could conserve the wealth of the state and at the same time make use of that wealth. . . . When Yao and Shun ruled as kings, they set all the land within the four seas in order. Their method was to use jade for Yü Shih in the north, and pearls for the . . . south." Maverick, *Economic Dialogues,* pp. 145–51.

10. *Oro e lavoro, SPr* 346.

11. *K* 54. Cf. c. 104: "in Xreia, to dissociate demand from the need."

Like Ra-Set, to whom she has become aligned in the previous alchemic scene, Core enters the protection of crystal, or (having "eaten the flame"—c. 39) conceives the body of light from the body of fire—the transubstantiation of the wafer in Pound's mass. With the abduction, said to have occurred "near Enna" in the *Metamorphoses,* and at Nysa in the *Hymn to Demeter,* the grain rite celebrates the seed entering the earth, the daughter becoming mother, or sexually expert. Thus Persephone, appearing as such for the last time in l. 51, is coupled with sensual Circe—a metamorphosis well prepared for by cs. 39 and 47, which are both Eleusinian and Circean. In the opening of the former a cat (elsewhere associated with Demeter) takes us from contemporary desolation to the hill paths of Liguria and Luigi (see l. 48), and therewith to Circe's hearth:

> Desolate is the roof where the cat sat,
> Desolate is the iron rail that he walked
> And the corner post whence he greeted the sunrise.
> In hill path: "thkk, thgk"
>   of the loom
> "Thgk, thkk" and the sharp sound of a song
>   under olives
> When I lay in the ingle of Circe
> I heard a song of that kind.   [c. 39]

We note in passing the familiar cluster cat-sunrise-fertility, and other evocative leitmotifs: the looms of Circe and of the silk weavers of Liguria (said to be hushed by usury in c. 51), and the Sirens' sharp song or *ligurè aoidé* (c. 20)—an apt metaphor of Pound's singing which also looks forward to the violin score of the *Chanson des oiseaux* given in c. 75 in the hand of the "Circe" of the *Cantos.*[12] A few lines down Pound quotes from Homer the witch's "house of smooth stone" (which is also to recur in the usura cantos, as well as in l. 56), and her parentage ("born to Helios and Perseis")—surely aware that Perse and Persephone, the brides of Helios (the sun of day) and Dis (the sun of night),

12. The score is signed O[lga] R[udge], and dated 28 September 1933. Gerhart Münch and Olga Rudge performed the *Canzone degli uccelli* in a Rapallo concert on 14 November 1933. Canto 39 first appeared in October 1934 (Gallup A37).

are ultimately one lunar goddess.[13] Accordingly, the crucial coupling of Circe and Persephone in the central passage of c. 106
mirrors the similitude and difference between mother and daughter with which we began. The two are unlike as Enna and Nysa,
sea and glen, pine and juniper—the passage is a set of dissocia-
tions—yet they are *like* each other, in the very words of l. 1. In
context both names serve (on good mythological evidence) as approximate definitions of the one goddess of vegetation, the
juniper and "holy bush" recalling the complex sacrificial
sequence of *Th,* and another heroine of the section: sea is "so different" from glen that the Phaeacians offer "that shrub" to Leucothea the gull, whereas the Na-khi worship the goddess in the
juniper—not a difference of any magnitude, but *a* difference, further blurred by "the two pine trees" between which the goddess
stands (in Muan-bpo the juniper is placed between two oak
branches). Three layers at least of meaning may therefore be distinguished in this grain rite, essentially a confrontation with the
lady: Persephone's story of abduction and initiation to sexuality,
an act of worship concerning the powers of vegetation, and the
quest of the proper definition and name of which the sacrifice is
always a correlative. As they watch Circe go to and fro at a great
web Ulysses' men wonder whether she be goddess or woman (*"è
theòs eè guné"*—c. 39), and Pound echoes this here using Acoe-
tes' words about Dionysus: "He has a god in him, / though I do
not know what god." [14] But the situation and question (compare
again ll. 1–5) are also topoi of the Stilnovo:

> Who is she that cometh, makying turn every man's eye
> And makying the air to tremble with a bright clearenesse
> That leadeth with her Love, in such nearness
> No man may proffer of speech more than a sigh?
>
> Ah God, what she is like when her owne eye turneth, is
> Fit for Amor to speake, for I cannot at all;

13. See Kerényi, *Mythologie der Griechen,* ch. 12: "The name of the queen of the underworld, Persephone, is related to Perse as an amplified form, or perhaps only as a more
solemn form."

14. Canto 2. Cf. *Met.* III.611–12.

Such is her modesty, I would call
Every woman else but an useless uneasiness.[15]

So the sister to Circe is also Guido's Primavera (the one who
shall come first, according to Dante's etymology), whose turning
eyes (cf. *elikoblépharos,* and ll. 3 and 9) become more ominously
forbidding in Pound's decadent imagination: "nor could enter
her eyes by probing" (cf. c. 91: "He asked not / nor wavered
seeing"); like her Tuscan counterpart, she is clothed in a trembling light, which, as we are pointedly told, is not the sunset's,
for of course the poet and his two chosen companions, the
hunchback and the cat, make their communion at sunrise—the
very time of day in which Core was caught up by her dark
lover:[16] in the end it is the lady herself that "sheds such light in
the air" (c. 6), being, both as Circe and as Leucò, the Mater Matuta, dawn personified. But wavering, asking, and probing is precisely what the poet—a negative theologian—has been doing
through this canto, painfully adding dissociation to dissociation
("not Circe . . . not know . . . nor could enter . . . nor was
this") and hardly coming any closer to a consummation. "It is
better to conceive a god by form," he had written in "Religio,"
"and, after perceiving him thus, to consider his name or to 'think
what god it may be' " (*PD* 97). In the sequel, "seeking the god's
name" (c. 97), he shuffles together Athene (Ulysses' chief patroness—*prónoia*—and a hypostasis [see cs. 81 and 100] of all
the hero's women), Perse(phone), Circe, Artemis (like Core, a
goddess of the moon, virginity, and vegetation; like Circe a
pótnia therôn—lady of the beasts), and Venus, who has been
linked to Circe as early as c. 1, and is accordingly worshipped
"By Circeo, by Terracina" (c. 39). All of which is in keeping with
the mythological evidence, though Pound, far from compiling a
theogony, is seeking in fear and trembling the lady's protection

15. "Cavalcanti," *LE* 199–200. An earlier, Victorian, translation of the sonnet appeared
in *Sonnets and Ballate of Guido Cavalcanti* (1912), and is quoted in Davie 104. In both
versions P. misunderstands l. 8, which seems to mean that "compared to her every other
[woman] calls for disdain." Also, the duplication of the phrase, to turn the eye, is clumsy,
and lessens the effect of l. 5.

16. Kerényi, *Mythologie der Griechen,* ch. 14.2.

(which he feels to be dependent on the success of his enquiry into memory), and soon blurts out the words addressed by the voyager and founder Brut to Diana in Layamon and in c. 91: "Help me in my need," "Counsel me where I may go."

> Athene Pronoia,
>   in hypostasis
> Helios, Perse: Circe
> Zeus: Artemis out of Leto
> 65   Under wildwood
>   Help me to neede
> By Circeo, the stone eyes looking seaward
>   Nor could you enter her eyes by probing.   [c. 106]

With the emergence of prayer Pound's "jagged" consideration of mythology and vision gives way to ritual chanting (the grain rite proper), the lines falling into stepped-down groups of three. The transition, however, is less perceptible than elsewhere, say in c. 81, where contemplation of the eyes led to "What thou lovest well remains" and "Pull down thy vanity." Canto 106 is concerned throughout with the coming of the lady; lines 46–60 make the transition from detached musing to immediate encounter; and the subsequent landscape with saint and worshipper fills in the background while the attempt to describe the goddess and enlist her help continues:

> The temple shook with Apollo
> 70   As with leopards by mount's edge,
>   light blazed behind her;
>   trees open, their minds stand before them
> As in Carrara is whiteness:
>   Xoroi. At Sulmona are lion heads.
> 75   Gold light, in veined phyllotaxis.
> By hundreds blue-gray over their rock-pool,
>   Or the king-wings in migration
>   And in thy mind beauty, O Artemis
> Over asphodel, over broom-plant,
> 80   faun's ear a-level that blossom.
>   Yao and Shun ruled by jade.

Whudher ich maei lidhan
                    helpe me to neede
    the flowers are blessed against thunder bolt
85   helpe me to neede
    That great acorn of light bulging outward,
            Aquileia, capparis, caltha palustris,
                ulex, that is gorse, hedys arachnites;
    Scrub oak climbs against cloud-wall—
90   three years peace, they had to get rid of him,
            —violet, sea green, and no name.
    Circe's were not, having fire behind them.
        Buck stands under ash grove,
            jasmine twines over capitals
95   Selena Arsinoe   [c. 106]

It is not of course the primitivistic chanting of the middle cantos,
nor the mellow music of the Pisan sequence, but a frail and somewhat "atonal" chain of minimal perceptions, employed with the
economy entailed by their scarcity. Fragments planted into the
cantos (100–05) leading up to this one (stone lions—symbols of
the king-initiate-poet—half-remembered from Ovid's Sulmona;
phyllotaxis or the ordering of leaves on stem) and basic motifs of
the poem ("ferae familiares," the "whiteness" of Guido and Car-
rara, dancing choruses of fauns and nymphs) coalesce with the
themes of the quasi-Circean apparition (68, 71, 82–85, 91–92)
and with several new notations (e.g., the "xoroi" of trees/fauns
and lions are enlarged by "hundreds" of unnamed creatures [wa-
terbugs?] over a familiar "rock-pool" [c. 91], and by "king-wings
in migration"—apparently a kenning for Monarch butterflies—a
suggestion I have from Eva Hesse, cf. the "many wings fragile"
of c. 92). These phenomena all conform to one phyllotactic structure (they are as it were the leaves of the world-tree), and are
contained as "beauty" in the mind of the lady, who now—in
keeping with the Brut theme and the vegetal burden of these
rites—is definitely the moon-goddess Artemis and her analogue
Fortuna, ruling with flowerlike eyes over the sublunary world.
(Line 84 is a novel "etymological" reading of the character *chen*

of cs. 86, 91, and 96.) The central theme of vegetation (we hear of trees, phyllotaxis, asphodel, broom-plant, blossom, flowers) culminates in a striking visionary image of fertility—the bulging acorn of light (86)—which is followed in turn by a second (cf. 61–64) roll-call of tentative "god's names," now directly culled from Latin botany, with a relish for their sonority, associations (aquila, arachne), and suggestions both of science and ritual (cf. previous gleanings from Rock).

Not all is well, however, with this fragmented visionary attempt, for it never wholly emerges from the agonizing darkness in which the canto set out. The much-suffering voyager continues in his need and in his doubts as to his destination ("Whuder ich maei lidhan"). As Fortuna, Artemis has been not a little "saeva" with his horoscope, as intimated by the unexpected reminder of the destruction of peace-seeking Edward VIII at the hands of the Enemy.[17] The poem's king is in fact throneless, and in the end he is still at a loss as to the name of the lady of the "ever-shifting" eyes (91—cf. the "triune azures" of c. 81 and the "violet, pervenche, deep iris" of c. 97). Indeed, the eyes have themselves become unnameable by line 92, where they are only pointed to by the genitive—a negative close to a vision that opened in the negative (54 ff.).

But line 92 is also the first of the canto's finale, cast in five groups of four lines (rather than three as heretofore); and the former of these "quatrains" (after referring apparently to Actaeon's fate—another connection between Artemis and Circe—and after offering a temple image of 1913 vintage), closes with a terminal, richly rewarding, *name,* a construct reminiscent of Ra-Set and Isis Kuanon: "Selena Arsinoe." The variant occurrence of the moon is in keeping with the previous prayer, whereas the

17. Line 90. P.'s account of the abdication is in agreement with Ribbentrop's memorandum to Hitler of 2 January 1938 ("Edward VIII had to abdicate, since it was not certain whether, because of his views, he would cooperate in an anti-German policy") but its source, quite untrustworthy (Eva Hesse, *Paideuma* 1: 86–88), is Fritz Hesse, *Hitler and the English,* tr. F. A. Voigt (London: Allen Wingate, 1954). Cf. c. 86: "as in the case of Edwardus / and von Hoesch [the German ambassador] on the telephone: / to good for three years, / or to evil / Eva's pa heard that on the telephone"; and Frances Donaldson, *Edward VIII* (London: Weidenfeld & Nicolson, 1974), pp. 201–02, 204.

entry of the Lagid queen Arsinoe II we are ready for only if we recall our reading into the background of the *oînos aithíops* cluster ("Bernice, late for a constellation"), of which Pound reminds us presently:

```
95                          Selena Arsinoe
          So late did queens rise into heaven.
                   At Zephyrium, July that was, at Zephyrium
                   The high admiral built there;
                                       Aedificavit
100   TO APHRODITE EUPLOIA
                   "an Aeolian gave it, ex voto
                   Arsinoe Kupris.
                   At Miwo the moon's axe is renewed
                                       HREZEIN
105   Selena, foam on the wave-swirl
                   Out of gold light flooding the peristyle
                          Trees open in Paros,
                                White feet as Carrara's whiteness
          in Xoroi.
110                         God's eye art 'ou.
                   The columns gleam as if cloisonné,
                          The sky is leaded with elm boughs.  [c. 106]
```

Arsinoe, who died on 9 July 270 B.C., was worshipped even in life as Arsinoe Aphrodite, and also called Zephyritis after the temple built in her honor on the promontory of Zephyrium near Alexandria by Callicrates, the "high admiral," here representing Ulysses who, having completed the long journey, renders thanks to Aphrodite Euploia or of the Good Voyage and builds her a temple, as anticipated as early as the close of canto 1.[18] It was in Callicrates' temple that Berenice offered in 247 as an "ex voto" (101) for her husband's return from the wars the lock which was to become a late constellation. These two offerings (cf. l. 16),

18. Venus' epithet and other details P. may have taken (directly or indirectly, by way of his edition—unidentified—of Callimachus) from an epigram of Posidippus (*Rhein. Mus.* 35: 91): "Propitiate for yourself this temple of Cyprian Arsinoe Philadelphus, set among earth and water. The admiral first placed there the goddess, lady of this beach of Zephyrium. She will grant a good voyage (*euplóien*) and in the midst of the storm becalm the sea in behalf of those who invoke her."

however, are conflated in Pound's finale with one less known, also memorialized by Callimachus: a nautilus presented to Arsinoe, as we find in Epigram 14, by a young girl, Selenaia, born in "Aeolian Smyrna," and "acquainted with virtue" (*esthlà hrézein*). This donation becomes the starting point for some momentous telescoping. We remember that old Kuan Chung's edict had to be taken together with the more subtle teachings of Helen's breast; likewise Callicrates and Ulysses, besides worshipping the goddess, are attended by her in the person of Selena(ia), whose nautilus—"foam on the wave-swirl" (105)—refers us in one breath to Leucothea's bikini and to the veil or *hagoromo* of the "moon nymph immacolata" (c. 80) who appeared to a fisherman by the "Windy [cf. Zephyrium] roads of the waves by Miwo," and, while performing a dance "symbolical of the daily changes of the moon," sang: "The jewelled axe takes up the eternal renewing, the palace of the moon-god is being renewed with the jewelled axe, and this is always recurring" [19]— which may be the first occurrence of the axe of *hsin*/make-it-new in Pound's *œuvre*—an occurrence possibly unintentional, for in 1914, when he published *Hagoromo,* Pound may not have been familiar with the relevant passage of the *Ta-hsüeh.* To repeat, the waxing moon's sickle functions as an ideograph of the make-it-new axe, and this is associated with the *hagoromo-nautilus-krédemnon* as it has been at the very first statement of the Leucothea motif: "get rid of paraphernalia" (c. 91). The axe clears away the "rubbish" so that "new fronds" (c. 97) may burgeon. So we finally come back to the goddess-as-tree, and to the reverence we owe her: "venerandam" in c. 1; "HREZEIN" (a verb which, taken alone, can mean "to offer sacrifice") in c. 106, where it is similarly emphasized by isolation from context (it does not conform with the "quatrain" scheme). The final lines bring the theme to the fore, by having the temple of Patara-Zephyrium flooded by the "gold light of wheat surging upward" (25)—which is also of course the element of Venus ("with golden

19. *Hagoromo, T* 308, 312. This reference Eva Hesse has pointed out to me. The nautilus per se is of course Venus' "concha" and "nautilis biancastra" (cs. 76 and 80), and the foam the element from which she rose.

girdles and breast bands"—c. 1)—and by presenting us again (cf. ll. 72–75) with the natural phenomena of which the temple is the crystallization: the emergence from trees of "goat-foot, with the pale foot alternate" (c. 4)—of dances the phyllotactic measure of which is to be carried over into the peristyle's "proportions"; and then "the sky leaded with elm boughs"—the stained glass of the *ara* which the *nemus* (see c. 79) *is*. Between these instances of the oneness of art and nature,[20] the poet speaks out in his own voice (not, as earlier, through the Brut persona) to the girl lately risen into heaven where she now rules as God's (*ho theós,* 17) own Sophia. She emerges again as eye (now merciful), awareness, hypostasis of the very "perception of relations" ("The Serious Artist," *LE* 52) that has given us this latter-day mythological song.

20. Notice the subliminal quotation of Gautier's "L'Art": "Lutte avec le carrare, / Avec le paros dur / Et rare / Gardiens du contour pur." With the columns-as-cloisonné of l. 111 (a simile enforced by alliteration), it functions as a timely reminder that P.'s mythologem, far from being a metahistorical thing, remains firmly inscribed within the poetics and estheticism of *Émaux et Camées* (and *HSM*).

16. The Edict

Angliae Amor

After the mystical travelling of c. 106, in the context of which the Law—the *Kuan-tzu*—performs an essential dialectic function, Pound closes *Thrones* with a final textual persona of a lawgiver, choosing for once a subject not eccentric—in fact the very origins of English and American legislation, and of the antiauthoritarianism by which it is marked:

> The azalea is grown while we sleep
> In Selinunt',
>   in Akragas
> Coke. Inst. 2.
>   to all cathedral churches to be
>   read 4 times in the yeare
>
> .   .   .
>
> And speaking of clarity
>   Milite, Coke, Edwardus
> "that light that was Sigier"   [c. 107]

The Mediterranean temples and the prophetic (and collective: "we") sleep of the previous canto give place to the speech of the Edict, similar in tenor to that of Yung Cheng ("Each year in the elder spring"—in the time, that is, of azaleas—"The herald shall invite your compliance"), and presently directed to other "cathedral churches," leaded with elm boughs. As he turns to Edward Coke—an "eternal light," like Dante's Siger (*Par.* x. 135)—and to *The Second Part of the Institutes of the Laws of England* ("Authore Edwardo Coke, Milite," as we read on the title page), Pound rediscovers England and the English language at the crucial stage, balanced in a splendid "flowering" between the Middle Ages and modern times, and chooses a hero most apt to body forth his world view. The great Coke (often referred to in the cantos of Adams—who had to come to terms with him as do most English and American students of law) is in fact "a man in love with the past," who gathered in his *Institutes*—as the title

suggests—the ancient statutes, chief among them Magna Charta,
and fought strenuously ("as for walls"—c. 98) for their text, illu-
minating it with his translations (from the Latin and Norman of
the old records), commentaries, and footnotes, often providing
etymologies no less fanciful than "Thuscia quae a thure" (c. 96).
Yet this traffic with the past, resulting in a most baroque and (to
the poet) delightful "feast of languages," is peculiarly Poundian
insofar as it is aimed at the building of the city of the future with
the occasionally healthy violence of the axe: Coke, the somewhat
overzealous guardian of the throne in the age of Elizabeth (he
was the savage chief prosecutor at the trials against Essex, Ralegh, and others),[1] was to become a major opponent of royal
privilege during the reign of "that slobbering bugger Jim First"
(c. 107), and a forerunner of the regicides of 1649 and of the
rebels of 1776:

In 1606 he was made Chief Justice of Common Pleas, and as such he
waged a difficult battle in defense of common law against ecclesiastic
jurisdiction and royal prerogative. In 1613, while Bacon became Chan-
cellor, he was promoted—*ut amoveatur*—Chief Justice of King's Bench.
He continued, however, to defend without relenting the common law
against the expanding jurisdiction of Chancery. To James I, who ordered that he submit, he answered that he was only doing what a just
and honest judge must. Consequently, in 1616, he was imprisoned in
the Tower by order of the Privy Council, with an order to revise the
"errors" of his *Reports*. Returning to Parliament, he became a leader of
the parliamentary faction, and, having taken part in the famous protes-
tation of 1621, was imprisoned for another nine months. In 1628, he
was, with Selden, one of the authors of the Petition of Right, one of the
great documents of English liberty. His chief work, the *Institutes of the
Laws of England*, finished around 1628, was published (with the excep-

1. Nevertheless in the late fifties P. was inclined to quote Coke in defense of his broadcasts: "When one knoweth of any treason or felony and concealeth it, this is misprision;
in case of misprison of treason the offender is to be imprisoned during his life . . . By the
common law, concealment of high treason was treason." 3 *Inst.* 36, quoted in Catherine
Drinker Bowen, *The Lion and the Throne: The Life and Times of Sir Edward Coke*
(1552–1634) (Boston: Little Brown, 1956), p. 219*n*. P. had been claiming for over a decade that "The treason was in the White House, not in Rapallo" (Cornell 103 and Norman 429). However, he forgot to put any reference to misprision into cs. 107–09.

tion of the first volume, 1628) posthumously by order of Parliament (ii, 1642; iii, iv, 1644).[2]

The Petition of Right, which sought confirmation of habeas corpus and forbade the levying of taxes without parliamentary consent, as well as the use of martial law in time of peace, had received upon its first submittal to Charles I (2 June 1628), an evasive answer, but five days later, under pressure from both Houses, the king yielded and gave his assent with the traditional formula: "Soit droit fait comme il est desiré." This final victory of Coke filled the city in the June dusk with rejoicing and bonfires (cf. c. 11), as we find in Sir Edward's biography by Catherine Drinker Bowen, *The Lion and the Throne* (a title which was bound to attract the author of *Th*),[3] and as reported ecstatically in c. 108 (the hands appear to be—so far as the poem's myth goes—Leucò's *phílai cheîres*—see c. 100):

> Enrolled in the ball of fire
> 　　　　　　　　as brightness
> 　　　　　　　　　　　　　clear emerald
> 　for the kindness,
> 　　　　　　infinite,
> 　　　　　　　　of her hands
> From the Charter to the Petition   1628
> 　　　　in June and toward twilight
> 　　　　　　　　DROIT FAIT   [c. 108]

Toward twilight, in the season "when rose is beginning," the season of *Th*, Justice is *done*.

Finally, Coke is a new interlocutor of the Queen, as Brut of Diana and Drake of "Miss Tudor" herself. In the *Institutes* Elizabeth is affectionately remembered as "Angliae amor" (an epithet P. lifts with his familiar anagram in mind), and as a wise ad-

2. Nicola Matteucci, *Antologia dei Costituzionalisti inglesi* (Bologna: Il Mulino, 1962), pp. 36–37. The order to publish 2 *Inst.*, the chief quarry of cs. 107–108, is the source of the words "Elfynge Cler[icus] Domus Com[mons]" printed in the margin of c. 108. It was issued on 12 May 1641. See the London edition of 1797, p. 745. Subsequent references, in text and footnotes, are to this edition.

3. Bowen, *Lion and Throne*, p. 503. P. noticed with pleasure that Bowen was also the author of a biography of John Adams.

ministrator of the country's wealth. (Among the deserts recorded
in her epitaph—as quoted in 2 *Inst.*, p. 577, and in c. 108—is the
"reducing of money to its proper value"—"Monetam ad suum
valorem reductam." This should be correlated with the economic
planning mentioned in the quotations from the *Kuan-tzu.*) She
was also, according to her admirer, a champion of Law:

And I well remember when the lord treasurer Burghley told Queen Elizabeth, Madame, here is your attorney generall (I being sent for) *qui pro
Domina Regina sequitur* [who prosecutes for his mistress the Queen],
she said she would have the forme of the records altered, for it should
be *attornatus generalis qui pro domina* VERITATE *sequitur* [who
prosecutes for his mistress the truth].[4]

This motif, which has much contextual resonance (Nestor, Cherbury, the *chun tze*), is picked up at the inception of the last canto
of *Th* ("Pro Veritate"), and placed side by side with another detail to Pound's liking, namely the enlightened provisions for
building of "Stat. de 31 Eliz.": "For every new cottage 4 acres." [5]
In hypostasis, Elizabeth is the queen of the flowers and temples
evoked at the outset of the Coke triptych—as well as a per-
sonification of Law, or of the Great Charter of the Liberties of
England:

> OBIT, in Stratford 1616, Jacques Père obit,
> >   In 33 years Noll cut down Charlie
> OBIT Coke 1634 & in '49
> > >   Noll cut down Charlie
> Puer Apulius . . . ver l'estate
> Voltaire could not do it;
> the french could not do it.
> >   they had not Magna Charta
> in ver l'estate, Queen of Akragas
> resistent,
> >   Templum aedificavit
> >   Segesta   [c. 107]

4. Coke, 3 *Inst.* 79; quoted in Bowen, *Lion and Throne*, p. 82.

5. See Stat. de 31 Eliz. 7 ("Concerning Cottages and Inmates"), 2 *Inst.*, pp. 734 ff. The
number before the sovran's name is that of the year of reign; the number that follows is
that of the law in that session.

These lines have been deemed "inexcusable," and therefore it is
worth pointing out that Pound, the lapse of tone in the opening
notwithstanding, is doing no mean job of historical and poetic
musing. Some light may be found in certain letters he wrote in
the fall of 1957 (which, incidentally, are good proof that these
cantos were drafted in St. Elizabeth's):

Sovereignty . . .
Shx/ against Unlimited.
   33 years from S's death to decapitation of Charlie . . .

[15 September]

Shx and Coke / law / sense of wrong in
unlimited monarchy / french revolution, Voltaire etc.
had NOT the Mag. Charta to stand on,
and J. Adams saw they wd flop. in short the
serious element in Shx   [14 December][6]

Pound takes sides with Noll (Cromwell), claiming that the king's
execution was but a consequence of the Bard's "serious element"
(see c. 93). He points out that both the Puritan and the American
revolution were conservative, they made new with good precedent, whereas the French had no sacred text to build on and
therefore ran to the excesses of the Terror and later of the Com-
mune, anticipating Communism. These value judgments are of
course short of unacceptable, but Pound is certainly being consistent with his ideology. He dreams of a utopian (and, of course,
metahistorical) symbiosis of throne, poetry, and shrine ("Puer
Apulius . . . ver l'estate . . . Templum aedificavit")—which he
takes to have been the aim of the revolutions of Coke, Adams,
and Mussolini—and which is unquestionably the aim of the
voyage of the *Cantos.* The lines build up an incantation—a
mantra—in which King and Queen, Frederick and Elizabeth,
stand out on the superb background of Agrigento and Segesta—
which is not described but consigned in the name: incantation is
not description, but it is—occasionally—poetry.
   It is interesting to note that, in the Hall of the *Cantos,* the
Coke balances the *Malatesta,* for seven cantos precede the latter

6. W. Moelwyn Merchant, "Souvenirs d'Ezra Pound," *L'Herne* 608 and 611.

and seven follow the former—a good opportunity to see in what direction Pound's style has developed. The trend is from persona to text, from portraiture to transcription: while cs. 8–11 are a full-blooded, if Vorticist, summoning of Sigismondo's flames and voices, cs. 107–09 are a mere trickle of words from only two sources (Coke and Drinker Bowen), juxtaposed with snippets from Leo the Wise and Wang-iu-p'u, and with breakthroughs to Mediterranean myth (essentially Provence) and to paradise. But the tendency to rely exclusively on text and vision is already prominent in the *Malatesta,* and in the *Coke* it has only been radicalized, burning out all that is not either writing or hypostasis, "that light that was Sigier."

The lawgiver's benevolence and peace of mind is admirably suggested by the recurrent breakthroughs of c. 107, the more satisfactory of the three given to Coke:

> Coke: the clearest mind ever in England
> vitex, white eglantine
>   as tenthril thru grill-work
>   wave pattern at Excideuil
> A spire level the well-curb,
>
>   ·   ·   ·
>
> had been a field full at Allègre
>   as 40 rising together,
>   the short tails.
>
>   ·   ·   ·
>
> The tapestries were still there in Chaise Dieu,
>   the sky's glass leaded with elm boughs.   [c. 107]

Human intelligence belongs among permanent things, among the clear outlines of plants and of the equally resurgent wave of Excideuil. It may also penetrate the submarine haunts of Venus, where "delicate / Algae reach up and out, beneath / Pale slow green surgings of the underwave" ("Sub Mare," 1912), recalling with good reason Guido's "diafan":

> Amphion not for museums
>   but for her mind
>   like the underwave

> Not the glitter 2 fathoms inshore,
> > the coral light sifting slowly mid sea-fans
> > > the great algae   [c. 107]

The theme of mind and perception is still foremost in the conclu-
sive vision of the whirlpool of light and of its builders—Cavalcanti's "river" (c. 91) and Dante's "lume in forma di rivera /
fluvido di fulgore" (*Par.* xxx. 61–62; cf. c. 39):

> So that Dante's view is quite natural:
> > this light
> > > as a river
> > in Kung; in Ocellus, Coke, Agassiz
> > > ῥεῖ the flowing
> > > > this persistent awareness
> Three Ninas from Gaudier
> > Their mania is a lusting for farness
> > Blind to the olive leaf,
> > > > not seeing the oak's veins.
> > Wheat was in bread in the old days.   [c. 107]

The blessed of Pound's Rose are such as have attended to things
and names:

> Cope is a hill
> dene: a valley, arundinetum
> drus is a thicket
> > Si nomina nescis perit rerum cognitio
> > > nemo artifex nascitur   [c. 109]

—as Coke remarks at the very outset of 1 *Inst.*, and often elsewhere: "The common law it selfe is nothing else but reason,
which is to be understood of an Artificial perfection of reason,
gotten by long study, observation, and experience, and not of
every mans natural reason, for, *Nemo nascitur artifex*" (1 *Inst.*
138). For Pound long study is closer to natural reason than Sir
Edward would grant, for awareness is "persistent" insofar as
it is always newly arising from signatures: the oak's veins (cf.
"Gold light, in veined phyllotaxis"—c. 106), and the olive leaf
which has the eye's glint. (Likewise Venus emerges from the

stone carved by Gaudier.) Accordingly, as in the close of RD
("Do not Hindoos / lust after vacuity?"), he turns against those
who have blinded themselves (and others) to all of this, and seek
what is far rather than the infinite to be found in the grain of
sand, or in a trade (*pen yeh*) come down through generations
of a family. Wang-iu-p'u had made a similar point in c. 99:
"2 incarnations [i.e., one's parents] in every home . . . and you
go up hill to seek wooden ones."

Even here there is no lack of traces of Pound's less savory attitudes, occurring whenever the obsession with the "perverters" (of
the Eleusinian bread, for instance) gains the upper hand, as is the
case in the following doggerel about the "decadence" of England,
which comes just before the finale of c. 107 quoted above:

> Flaccus' translator wore the crown
> The jew and the buggar dragged it down:
> "Devil in dung-cart" Gondomar
> And Raleigh's head on King James' platter.   [c. 107]

Horace's translator would seem to be Elizabeth (said to have
Englished Ovid in c. 85—translation is of course to P. a most exalted activity); the Jew is probably Roderigo Lopez, the queen's
surgeon and one of the victims of the "attornatus generalis"
Coke—but also Disraeli, mentioned in cs. 104 and 108; the
bugger, as we have seen, is the king who sent the poet and explorer to the block (P. chooses to ignore the part played by Coke
in Ralegh's affair); and Gondomar is the Spanish ambassador
known to the London populace as "devil in a dung-cart" because
"it was his custom to ride about . . . in a litter." [7] But of course
the passage is not "history" but the juxtaposition of ideas of
good and evil in a sordid dumb show. Likewise c. 108 includes
references, duly censored, to the anti-Semitic legislation of Edward I: "Divers [kings] had banished [the jews, and yet they re-
turned], but their usuries, no King before him" ("Stat. de Ju-
daismo," 2 *Inst.*, p. 507—the bracketed words are omitted by
P.). These are followed by a mention of "Uncle Carlo [Delcroix]"
(the fascist mediocrity of c. 101) and "Margarethe von Taufers"

7. Bowen, *Lion and Throne*, p. 417.

(alias Val di Tures, in the environs of which P.'s daughter was raised), which may explain what the "clean-up" may be for which they are praised in c. 92.

Canto 108 is the most reified and disintegrated of the triptych, little but a set of notes (with some calculation in the margin of the dates of the statutes, cf. c. 85), taken for the most part from Edward I's *Statutum de tallagio non concedendo,* which was much used by the parliamentary faction in its struggle against James and Charles. Here the poet finds corroboration for his (and Del Mar's) notion of coinage as a prerogative of the king, and—through the king—of the people, who may thus escape middlemen and usury (see 2 *Inst.,* pp. 574–76):

> 28 Edward I, a. D. 1300
> auxy soit signe teste de leopard
> and false stone not set in true gold
> Pertaine to the King onely
> to put a value to coin
> And to make price of the quantity   [c. 108]

The English lawgiver, like his Byzantine and Chinese counterparts, is concerned with the trueness of coin and stone, or of word and color—and the sign ("from the nature") of his sovranty—a leopard's head—proves that he belongs to the tradition of Sargon the Great, Antoninus Pius, Frederick II, and Venice-Sulmona.

The circle of *Th* may now close upon itself. After glancing at the *First Institute* and finding there the bit of geographic lexicography quoted earlier, as well as ("in the fine print") the statement that the law is above the king ("Nor can the King create a new custom"), and the "Mynes, Mynerals Precious Stones Quarries" of the *Kuan-tzu* (and of c. 98), Pound brings to a close c. 109 and this installment of the poem with a bird's-eye summary (this is not only a metaphor) of the themes which he has been considering:

> Wing like feldspar
>   and the foot-grip firm to hold balance
> Green yellow the sunlight, more rapid,
> Azaleas by snow slope.   [c. 109]

Crystal wing and prehensile foot would seem the prerequisites for
a journey which is to lead into new spaces of light and of rapid—
or divine—communication, among them the Na-khi's dawn
world, to which Pound removes the azalea said to grow as *we*
sleep by Selinunte in the triptych's incipit. To suggest the intensity of the communication he sought Pound reminded a correspondent that "The Chinese will send ONE IDEOGRAM." In fact, as
we read of the "Azaleas by snow slope," we are sure to perceive
a splendid ideogram (reminiscent of "midwinter spring") and to
recognize the calligraphy—again Zen-like—of the master. But
before moving ahead Pound looks back, with an obsessive hinting, at his trouble, summoning as in c. 106 a sovran dethroned
and fortuneless, and claiming as elsewhere to write an inside history to set against the records of officialdom:

> afraid he will balk and not sign mobilization,
> > got, said Monro, to get rid of him
> > > > > (Eddie)
> He has been around in the hospitals
> > Jury trial was in Athens   [c. 109]

The image lifted from the day's news is the more painful because
of its opacity. (It may be that with his insistent homage P. was
trying to establish contact with "Eddie," perhaps in view of some
kind of fascist coup in England. He was still to seek out Mosley
after his return to Italy. The psychosis is certainly prominent in
the line before last, where we find that the Enemy is doing away
with the good Duke.) To the end Pound's verse remains a hopeless tangle of myth and actuality, vision and squalor, and this
sorry veracity is one reason of its appeal.

The "dark shade of courage" (c. 90) is followed by freer
spirits: the queen of cottages and amor of England to the side of
the leopard-king, described as in the previous canto, with the difference that this time the feline sign occasions a leap back to the
origins of the secret and transparent tradition—to the Sicily not
of Frederick but of Pythagoras (linked with Taormina by
Heydon-P. in c. 91):

> Clear deep off Taormina
> > high cliff and azure beneath it

form is cut in the lute's neck, tone is from the bowl
Oak boughs alone over Selloi
                    This wing, colour of feldspar
                                    phyllotaxis   [c. 109]

From a "colour" as deep and clear as that of the Tyrrhenian contemplated from a "cliff's edge" in c. 76 (and as that of Garda) a
Venus may arise, or a philosophy, or a form perceived as music
(in accord with Pythagorean thought), suggested here with
Dante's images for the Eagle of Justice already quoted in c. 100.
Likewise Dodona's Selli (of c. 87 and *WT*) listen to, and interpret, the voices of the oak of Zeus (as P. watches the Washington elm boughs), and thus translate into the temporal terms of
life and culture the timeless vegetal pattern which the poet calls
phyllotaxis. Lastly—and this throws light upon the wing and the
foot-grip—Ulysses-Pound takes the advice of a seagull (here
conflated, perhaps, with a *migratory* "king-wing"/monarch—see
c. 106), as do the other initiates of "truth," of signatures, and of
reason:

Over wicket gate
                    INO Ινώ Kadmeia
Erigena, Anselm,
                    the fight thru Herbert and Rémusat
Helios,
          καλλιαστράγαλος Ino Kadmeia,   [c. 109]

This is the one occasion upon which Leucò is summoned by the
human name of Ino (the epithet, "of the fine ankles," is also
novel), but she is still identified (as at her very first entrance)
through her father, the founding hero (and poet) of cs. 4 and 93.
(The feldspar wing would appear the ultimate version of the
krédemnon which carried us into *Th.*) She rises, together with
Helios the King, over a symbolical wicket gate, reminiscent of the
rope bridge of c. 101 (in Coke's London, a wicket gate gave
access to the house of Essex, leader of an aborted coup) [8]—as if
she were indicating a point of passage to such as presently prepare to follow her directions—the four oar-thinning philosophers

8. Bowen, *Lion and Throne*, p. 131.

listed in the phyllotactic diagram of c. 100, to whom should be added the names called out in the parallel finale of c. 107 (Dante, Kung, Agassiz, Ocellus, Coke). Beyond the perilous passage the view opens over a city of temples, the Rome of the Middle Ages—which in the prelude of the section has been assigned to time past ("quae olim"), while now the tense is, possibly, the future:

San Domenico, Santa Sabina,
                    Sta Maria Trastevere;
                              in Cosmedin
    Le chapeau melon de St Pierre
          You in the dinghy (piccioletta) astern there!   [c. 109]

A French voice, in the fifth line of *Th,* censured in one breath estheticism and church politics—and it is again a French voice that in the line before last mocks what Pound (engrossed in his Pre-Raphaelite dream of the churches "where the spirit is clear in the stone") takes to be the baroque vulgarity of "the bowler hat of St. Peter's" (actually the work of Michelangelo) and of the "fat" church (see c. 52) of which it is the symbol. The suppression of the Albigenses was, we gather, but a temporary setback in the initiates' challenge of orthodoxy, while Ulysses-Dante-Pound salutes us with bravado (warning us once again in the words of *Par.* ii. 1), and sets his course towards further renaissances. In the last line it is just possible to discern Pound making sail for the last time, on 30 June 1958 as almost exactly fifty years back, for Europe and ROMA.

Part Five

Fragments of an Earthly Paradise

I hate and love. Why? You may ask but
It beats me. I feel it done to me, and ache.
                    —Pound, after Catullus, *T* 408

The crisis that release from imprisonment brought about in the old poet's life has been touched upon in connection with the genesis of *Thrones,* though it influenced the section only in the last stages of the preparation of the typescript and of publication: a more than usually high number of typos (e.g., in c. 102), and some disorder in cs. 103–09—this is the only evidence. Instead, in *Drafts & Fragments of Cantos* CX–CXVII (as P.'s notes for cantos 110–16 were editorially titled when they were published in 1969, ten years after they had been written down), we are immediately aware of a novel and painful emotional climate. The poet who had cheerfully left behind the milestone of c. 100 without so much as a second glance, and who, fifty pages later, surfaces unscathed, "aloof," from the "dark waves" that have more than once threatened to bring him under—this very poet realizes now that his work, and his life, are running out, and that the "enemy"—no longer the obsessive "they," but darkness, death, and a world of culture from which he is excluded—is gaining ground on all sides, to the point of reversing the positions defended so far against all odds, the essential premises of Pound's writing. So far the poet and the community which he imagines he represents have the right on their side, and the opposition, though substantial (Marx, Freud, etc.), remains essentially negligible, other; but now he becomes liable to the surmise that he himself is the other, and that he is alone: the collective first person plural of the initiates ("nos otros"—c. 104) disappears, but for a final transcription of the words of the Na-khi ("If we do not perform ²Ndaw ¹bpö [the Sacrifice of Earth] / nothing is

solid"—c. 112), and we are addressed by the first person singular
of one consciousness which is in the way of being quenched. In a
way this reminds us of the Pisan poem, with the difference that
fourteen years have elapsed and that the poet has little energy
left; furthermore the miracle of Pisa occurred because first the
War and then imprisonment severed Pound from his "world of
books gone flat" (Elizabeth Bishop) returning him to communal
experience—that of a country at war and that, even more intense,
of the prison camp—whereas in 1959 the old man is alone, and
the signals of danger come to him only from within. ·

Piecing together the often contradictory and tendentious evidence on this period, we gather that Pound continued his usual
boisterous self up to the latter part of 1959. When the *Cristoforo
Colombo* called at Naples reporters deceived him into giving the
fascist salute; then, from the port of Genoa, he reached the Tirol,
where he got *Th* ready for publication, gave interviews to right-
wing papers and to the BBC, and wrote a few notes. From here,
in the spring of 1959, he went down, in the company of his wife
and of a young friend, the Marcella of c. 113, his last love, to
Lake Garda and to the cities of northern Italy dear to his muse,
and eventually to Rapallo, where he rented an apartment and
spent the summer, writing his last lines, namely these cantos
110–16, the first of which may have been composed a few
months earlier. This season of poetry was not to survive the cold:
in February Pound was in Rome and granted Donald Hall his
Paris Review interview, which lacks the usual incisiveness and
pugnacity; he also appears to have shown him a typescript of the
last cantos, very close to their present form, judging from what
looks like a reproduction of the typescript, published surreptitiously in New York, 1967.[1] This is how a friend, who had seen
him a few months earlier in Rapallo, describes him at this time:

The following winter I was in Rome, and one afternoon in February
Ezra called me up at my hotel. He had changed considerably since I saw
him in Rapallo: he was frankly embarrassed by his erratic nervous condition. As he said: "One day I talk like a parrot and the next I can find

---

1. E.P., *Cantos 110–116* (New York: Fuck You Press, 1967).

nothing to say." All attempts to settle down again had failed during the recent months. For one thing, the young lady had returned to Texas and Ezra missed her. A source of stimulation had been taken from him, and after all those years of incarceration it was not encouraging to realise that the future promised little but a succession of grey hours. Ezra made an effort to be cheery which I found quite touching in the more level glow of my early memories of him. It was obvious that some profound emotional ebb-tide was leaving him stranded and incapable of any sustained concentration. The old trooper had lost all his bravado: he was thoroughly downhearted—*avvilito* is the Italian word for it.[2]

This psychological condition was to grow worse over the next couple of years, attended by infirmity of body, to settle in a cataleptic muteness lasting to the end, strangely reminiscent of "the Pythagorean time of silence" to which Pound refers his readers several times (for instance, at the beginning of c. 31). In these later years otiose questions concerning the *Cantos* from visitors were likely to be answered disparagingly ("I botched it"),[3] if at all. These and other statements that have been taken as palinodes carry small weight, being little but the expression of senile depression: in Pound, the man survived the poet. It goes without saying that the little writing he did in the sixties (chiefly letters and prefatory notes to reprints, produced after much coaxing) has no relevance to a consideration of the poetry, and a merely anecdotal bearing upon the history of the poet's attitudes to his work, for the man who wrote the book is not the "blown husk" of later years, much publicized insofar as no unsavory statement—and no poetry—was to be expected from him.

This crisis, as noted above, is clearly in the offing in cs. 110–16, though these were written under relatively serene circumstances. Its course is fully anticipated in c. 110, one of the more notable that Pound wrote, which opens with the same gaiety ("panache," P. calls it) of the finale of *Th*, to which it is closely linked in the way of themes, and becomes gradually more somber, drawing to a stalemate—the image of a little light in the darkness, which is to recur several times and eventually to termi-

2. Daniel Cory, "Ezra Pound: A Memoir," p. 35.
3. Ibid., p. 39.

nate the sequence, and with it the poem. A sequence which was intended as a "decad"—at least—and which editors of recent printings have attempted, rather artificially, to round out, by labeling as cantos 117–20 four fragments (totaling forty lines), the last of which is of doubtful authenticity.[4] No reader, however, can fail to notice that c. 116 has the look of a final rallying of forces towards a finale, and that the subsequent fragments are compelling reminders pointing to a future poetry which is also strikingly like the earliest work of Pound. But let us proceed in order.

4. "I have tried to write Paradise / Do not move / Let the wind speak / that is paradise.// Let the Gods forgive what I / have made / Let those I love try to forgive / what I have made." These lines originally appeared as part of a "Fragment from Canto 115," in *Threshold* (Belfast), 1962 (Gallup C1885), but were excised from the text in *Cantos 110–116* and in *D&F*. (Another interesting variant of c. 115 is printed in E.P., *Cantos 1916–1962: Eine Auswahl*, ed. Hesse, p. 188.) To take them out of their original context and to print them as a bathetic close to the *Cantos* is to defeat P.'s aim at some objectivity and reserve throughout the poem, and to mar the architectonics of the whole.

Another questionable decision of the editors of *D&F* is the insertion, between c. 116 and the so-called "Notes for cxvii et seq.," of two "Fragments of Cantos" of the war years (respectively from Gallup C1625 and from *L* 384), the former with the misleading superscript, "Addendum for Canto c"—as if c. 100 of *Th* were not a complete poem in its own right, wholly unlike the lines of 1942 (a repeat of the usury theme). In a critical edition these fragments should be printed not in the main text but in the apparatus, together with the *Versi prosaici* and other fugitive fragments of cantos.

17. A Quiet House

Thy quiet house
The crozier's curve runs in the wall,
The harl, feather-white, as a dolphin on sea-brink

I am all for Verkehr without tyranny
5   —wake exultant
                    in caracole
Hast'ou seen boat's wake on sea-wall,
                 how crests it?
What panache?
10   paw-flap, wave-tap,
              that is gaiety,
Toba Sojo,
         toward limpidity,
              that is exultance,
15   here the crest runs on wall   [c. 110]

The Roman churches whose names resound in the close of the previous canto, are telescoped in one "quiet house," a church more intimate and private, said to be the property of a "thou"— evidently Leucothea, who has just guided us to the city, or another incarnation of the *prónoia* (c. 106). Corroboration is available in the typewritten draft mentioned earlier, which reads:

Thy quiet house at Torcello,

        Alma Pulnoua

This tells us that it is a *white* goddess whom Pound is addressing, though her personal name is distorted or misnamed beyond recognition (perhaps P. was thinking of "Pronoia," or "Patrona")[1]—a corruption which may be the reason for its omission

1. "Patrona" is the reading (an editor's guess) in E.P., *Canto* CX (Cambridge, Mass.: As Sextant Press, 1965). This is an unauthorized printing based on the typescript later reproduced in *Cantos 110–116* (which had been circulating for some time among the tribe of P.), and carries therefore no textual authority. However, the person(s) who prepared *D&F* for publication accepted unwarily some of its readings, e.g., *chih* in l. 102, and *ching* in l. 128—characters which do not occur in the typescript.

461

from the accepted text. The poet or his editors have likewise excised from l. 1 the name of the small island which, until the eleventh century, was the chief center of the Venetian lagoon (a sort of ur-Venice), and is now almost deserted; in the apse of its imposing cathedral, rebuilt several times between the seventh and the eleventh century, is the striking mosaic of a *Virgo Lacrimans,* possibly the original of Pound's "Alma Pulnoua." These cuts do not alter the tenor of the opening, for the lady has already come in with the pronominal adjective of l. 1, and the setting is to be mentioned later on; the quiet house, however, stands out more nakedly at the center of attention—it is now more symbolic than descriptive (of a particular place). Ulysses dreamed of home for twenty years, and Pound is doing something of the kind, however difficult it may be for him and for us to decide where his true home be. (We recall that Leucothea, the "thou," is a projection of the inner nature of the voyager, whom we have overheard thouing himself and her in the close of c. 106, as he is to do again, and more fully, in c. 113: "God's eye art'ou, do not surrender perception"). At any rate this home (like the cathedral of Torcello and the temple of Euploia—almost an anagram of "pulnoua"—at Zephyrium) is not far from the sea, and is all decorated with marine ex votos. The crozier's curve running in the wall suggests that it is an expression of the Christianity of pre-Raphaelite times, when the spirit was clear in the stone and "the fat" had not "covered their croziers" (c. 52)—and rhymes with Excideuil's wave-pattern running "in the stone" (and through the poem: cs. 29, 48, 80, 106–07)—a senhal of the Albigenses as well as of something that flows but does not change (*"hreí* . . . this persistent awareness"—c. 107), of something that turns up always the same in the course of time: the goddess whose body is water, stone, and light. The other exhibit, the harl of a white feather, would seem to have fallen from the feldspar wing of the previous canto, and is a token of the white seagull-goddess and of her *krédemnon,* emerging from and diving under the water surface with the wavelike motion of a dolphin.

With this the house has passed from quiescence into animation—it has been thrown open upon an expanse of sea—and we

hear again the gay voice of our guide (who saluted us a few lines
back with, "You in the dinghy . . . astern there!") as it announces a final program of renewal and communication: "Verkehr without tyranny"—interaction and freedom as obtain among
the mobile materials of the poem. The man who addresses us objects to all kinds of censorship, he would have everyone determine
the way of his choice ("Oh how hideous it is / To see three
generations of one house gathered together!"—"Commission,"
P 89), as he has done for himself. He also advises us, "without tyranny," but with the friendly concern of Dante, "not to put
forth on the deep" on our own, and "to keep to [his] wake"—
which, he adds, is "exultant, in caracole," like Excideuil's wave.
Thus the inside of the church fades into the seascape of *Par.* II.
1–15—a text which spans the gap between *Th* and *D&F* as *Od.*
v. 345–46 has done between *RD* and *Th*—though the imitation
is made to incorporate with subtleness motifs which are wholly
Poundian: the wave which pursues its course both as water and
as stone ("on sea-wall"), and, indirectly, the rose which carries
much the same meaning, recalled through the Jonsonian turn of
phrase, "Hast'ou seen" (". . . the rose in the steel dust?"). Two
of the poem's dominant leitmotifs are thus superimposed in the
context of this joyous cavalcade through the sea (the dolphin
being a sort of sea horse), as the poet invites us to look, play, and
communicate in his company. His questions, in keeping with this
attitude, are masterful puns which telescope the various levels of
the narrative: "cresting" is an action appropriate to a wave, a
krédemnon, and a "plume or identifying emblem worn on a
knight's helmet";[2] "panache" indicates both the object of attention ("an ornamental tuft (as of feathers) esp. on a helmet"[3]—
from *pennacchio,* which in Italian is also used for a wave's cap of
foam), and the emotion of the observer and poet-voyager:
"aloof." Finally, it is hardly necessary to remind ourselves that
feathers are also used to write with, in order to see that the wake
which we are directed to attend is the written trace that the poet

2. *Webster's New Collegiate Dictionary,* s.v. "crest."

3. Ibid. s.v. "panache." Cf. Donald Davie, "Cypress Versus Rock-Slide: An Appreciation
of Canto 110," *Agenda,* VIII, 3–4 (1970), 20.

leaves behind, and which is in fact arranged here in wavelike fashion. By asking us to watch the wave and the resurgent rose Pound has always been directing our attention to the "patterns of recurrence" (Kenner) within his poem—his quiet house, which he now offers up as an ex voto to the goddess who is within himself—and "in nobis."

The rhyming of a "paw-flap" with the "wave-tap" that we have been following so far indicates that the "image" sketched by Pound's logopoeia (which, as Donald Davie points out, is also a fine instance of melopoeia and phanopoeia)[4] has attracted to itself a novel pictorial text, the *Choju Giga* ("Animal Scroll") of Kyoto, traditionally considered to be the work of a twelfth-century Buddhist monk, Toba Sojo, said to be the father of Japan's art of caricature.[5] In this delightful work, which has as much hilarity as religion (cf. c. 100), anthropomorphic rabbits, chipmunks, deer, etc., are seen sporting in the eddies of a stream and on its banks—paws and long ears gaily emerging from the water. The Buddhist monk who admits us to the 'sphere" of *D&F* is to be daringly and amusingly rhymed at the latter end of the sequence with another animal artist: Disney![6] Between these two there passes quite a throng of tutelary spirits—the facets (for the most part familiar) of the poet's complex but integral personality: Rock (110, 113); Brancusi (110, 117); Confucius, Napoleon, Orage, and Rothar (111); Agassiz (113); Mozart and Linnaeus (113, 115); Yeats (113–14); Voltaire and Bruno (114); Wyndham Lewis and Ovid (115); Mussolini and Justinian (116)—and, almost at the end, the "deep" humorist Laforgue.[7] The list,

4. Davie, "Cypress Versus Rock-Slide," pp. 20–21. See "How To Read," *LE* 25.

5. See Toba Sojo, *The Animal Frolic* (New York: Putnam's, 1954)—a children's book and probably P.'s "source."

6. "Disney against the metaphysicals"—c. 116. By "metaphysicals" P. means those whose "mania is a lusting for farness / Blind to the olive leaf " (c. 107). Apparently he did not see the sham in Disney's "nature"—indeed he was delighted with the schmaltzy squirrel-film, *Perri*.

7. "And I have learned more from Jules . . . since then / deeps in him." Hesse (p. 29) takes this to be a reference to the aquarium passage in the story "Salomé," and Davie agrees with her ("Cypress Versus Rock-Slide," p. 22). P., however, ignored the passage in his rendering of "Salomé" ("Our Tetrarchal Précieuse," *PD* 189–200), and there is nothing in the lines (which make good sense on their own) to support this reading.

which is not complete, is eccentric to say the least, but the quality
of the affection by which it is guided is not miserly—and this of
course is all that matters in the struggle to appropriate the cultural datum, to give meaning and value to language and its content—the poet's one essential function:

> But these had thrones,
>   and in my mind were still, uncontending—
> not to possession, in hypostasis
>   Some hall of mirrors.
>   Quelque toile
> "au Louvre en quelque toile"
>   to reign, to dance in a maze,
> To live a thousand years in a wink.   [c. 114]

The maze of culture is no longer—thanks to the poet's affection—a locus of death, where the mind does not move among relative values—which is what the uninitiated feels it is when first
glancing down the halls of the Louvre's Grande Galerie or long
library corridors. ("Amphion not for museums / but for her
mind"—c. 107.) Like Laforgue, Pound is confident that he will
find the eyes he is seeking somewhere among those paintings and
books,[8] on condition that he keep alive the vibrations of amor,
the *Verkehr* without tyranny—and without possessiveness and
jealousy—as he tells us here and in many other passages of *D&F*.
"Some hall of mirrors," he remarks wryly of Western culture,[9] as
well as of his poem, in which all personae resemble him "in
hypostasis"—and yet his affection and curiosity defeat the Man-
neristic frigidity of self-reflection. Accordingly, the autobio-

8. See Laforgue, "Complainte des consolations," quoted in *Make It New*, p. 166:
    Les Landes sans espoir de ses regards brûlés,
    Semblaient parfois des paons prêts à mettre à la voile . . .
    Sans chercher à me consoler vers les étoiles,
    Ah! Je trouverai bien deux yeux aussi sans clés,
        Au Louvre, en quelque toile!

9. Cf. the likewise colloquial comment in irritable c. 116: "and some climbing / before the
take-off, / to 'see again,' / the verb is 'see,' not 'walk on' / i.e. it coheres all right / even if my
notes do not cohere." Here P. is alluding to the last lines of *Inferno* ("salimmo su . . . e
quindi uscimmo a *riveder* le stelle")—the long climb from the pit of Hell to the shore of
Purgatory and to the top of the Mount, before taking off into space. He goes on to a melancholy comparison of Dante's first canticle with his attempted third one: "Many errors,/ a
little rightness, / to excuse his hell / and my paradiso."

graphic c. 114 we have been quoting terminates a few lines down
with the statement, simple and yet unhackneyed (if read with the
relevant lines of cs. 108–109 in mind): "And that the truth is in
kindness." There is in *D&F* a powerful and descriptive gnomic
strain, pre-Socratic in flavor.

We have "anticipated" a little—but now it may be easier to
follow the gradual darkening of the palette of c. 110, after its luminous inception: l. 4 is only the beginning of a struggle against
the poet's own "tyranny" which encompasses the whole of *D&F*,
choosing in c. 110 as a metaphor of the negative the mirror.
After revealing the exultance of Toba Sojo's animals (the non-
human life to which with the years the poet is increasingly attracted) the crest continues its course to become the "hellish
whirlwind" ceaselessly sweeping about Dante's lustful (see
Blake's illustration), among them two "troubled souls," the victims of tyranny, of the pain of love unfulfilled which is another
leitmotif—a lyrical one—of *D&F*:

15   here the crest runs on wall
          che paion sì al vent'
                          ²Har-²la-¹llü ³k'ö
          of the wind sway,   [c. 110]

Even more than the animals of the Japanese scroll, Paolo and
Francesca are summoned so indirectly that it is easy to pass over
the masterly "rhyme" made, like Na-khi talk, "out of wind
noise": on the one hand the courtly pair "that seemed so light
upon the wind," [10] on the other the Na-khi lovers who having
committed suicide are pacified with the ceremony called *Har-la-
llü k'ö,* or "Wind-sway-perform." Unmarried couples, Rock tells
us, would frequently resort to suicide when the girl became pregnant rather than face the community's censure, having been told
by the priests of an afterlife of bliss: they repaired to an alpine
meadow and after some days, when food had run out, took
their lives by poison, water, or hanging. *Har-la-llü k'ö* was performed in order to call back their souls and release them from the

10. "E paion sì al vento esser leggieri"—*Inf.* v.75. Quoted in *SR* 130.

power of demons.[11] By quoting in ll. 19–25 from the Na-khi literature concerning these haunting suicide pacts (also quarried for the close of c. 101), Pound (beside leading us once more to his promised land) suggests that *D&F* is to be a similar ceremony of purification and "pacification." (Cf. the deliverance of Tyro and Alcmene in c. 90.) The fitful to-and-fro movement of the sequence from positive to negative, elation to dejection, is accounted for by his being at one time the king and master voyager who greeted us above and an old man involved in a pathetic love affair unacceptable to his community, the termination of which is also to signify the end or suicide of his poetic career. The *Verkehr* he advocates in the passionate prologue is accordingly also the "free love" forbidden to the Na-khi lovers, to Paolo and Francesca, and finally to himself. The allusiveness with which he presents the suicidal pact is an indication of its intimate relevance.

When, in the Na-khi romance Pound is quoting, the girl K'a-mä-gyu-mi-gkyi has hanged herself from a yellow oak, her friend asks her: "If I gave you turquoise and coral eyes, will you again be able to see? If I attach the roots of the pine and the oak, will you be able to walk?" [12] Pound rearranges this question so that it will fit his Jonsonian pattern ("Hast'ou seen boat's wake?"), and replies that yes, it is possible to "rise" [13]—not beyond death but (as .imported by the wave pattern) beyond the Eliotic *fear* of death (c. 27). Only an eye unfettered by fear and by coercion, itself as deathless as the oak's seed ("Oak boughs alone over Selloi"— c. 109), can perceive the *forma* of the wave and of the rose:

can you see with the eyes of coral or turquoise
25   or walk with the oak's root?
     Yellow iris rise in that river bed
                   [yüeh$^{4.5}$ / ming^2 / mo$^{4.5}$ / hsien^1 / p'eng^2]   [c. 110]

11. Rock, "Muan Bpö Ceremony," p. 71*n;* and "Romance of K'a-mä-gyu-mi-gkyi," passim.

12. Rock, "Romance," p. 89. For ll. 19–23 see pp. 20*n,* 41–51.

13. Line 26. The verb occurs in the typescript but is omitted in *D&F,* thus depriving the line of some of its resonance and point. Therefore I have preferred the earlier reading.

The reply comes, first with extreme indirection, then more explicitly, from the forces of vegetation—iris, oak, and chiefly the juniper, senhal of the promised land. The irises are yellow so as to remind us possibly of the yellow oak and positively of the topaz irides spoken of with this very pun in *Mauberley*—that is, of the eye which is similar to the rose. The principal referent, however, is the iris Kakitsubata of the Nô of that name by Motokiyo, which Pound takes to be the story of a lady "who had identified herself with the Iris" on account of "an acrostic" on the flower's name composed by her lover Narihira, who was "the incarnation of a certain . . . high spirit," and "seems, after favour, to have been exiled from the court, and to have written poems of regret." [14] He laments that "The waves, the breakers return, / But my glory comes not again"—yet his occasional landscape verse has the power to manifest something as timeless as the waves:

The spirit [of the Lady Kakitsubata] manifests itself in that particular iris marsh because Narihira in passing that place centuries before had thought of her. . . . The Muses were "the Daughters of Memory." It is by memory that this spirit appears, she is able or "bound" because of the passing thought of these iris. [P. uses the sing. for the pl. throughout the play, as in l. 26.] That is to say, they . . . are the outer veils of her being. . . . She demonstrates the "immortality of the soul" or the "permanence or endurance of the individual personality" by her apparition—first, as a simple girl of the locality; secondly in the ancient splendours. At least that is the general meaning of the play so far as I understand it. [*Kakitsubata*, "Note," T 340.]

The quoted words may well be Yeats's, for some of these translations (or revisions of Fenollosa's notes) were drafted at Stone Cottage, and not a little influenced by the older man's interest in ghosts. Yet to Pound such phenomena are by no means supernatural: Kakitsubata becomes manifest because the journeying monk remembers the poem written for her by Narihira, just as the spirits of Provence appeared to Pound in their poetic individuality as he was walking the roads they had travelled: "I have thought of them living." (*Kakitsubata* was published in 1916,

14. *Kakitsubata*, T 332–33.

one year after "Provincia Deserta.") As with the wave and the rose, the ultimate import of the image is esthetic: only poetry can defeat death, on condition that there be an old monk to remember it.

There follows (ll. 29–31) a column of transliterations of characters, of which only the two first are identifiable with some confidence (for of course Mathews supplies a large number of alternative meanings or characters for every sound). *Yüeh* is probably "moon," and *ming* may be "bright" (as in cs. 84 and 100)—the first allusion (if that is what they stand for) to the lunar nature of the lady of the canto, shortly to be invoked as Artemis (a virgin, like Torcello's "Alma Pulnoua"). One reader, noticing that there are five transliterations, as many as the syllables in the names of Kakitsubata and K'a-mä-gyu-mi-gkyi, has submitted that Pound has written an "acrostic" of sorts or Chinese riddle in imitation of Narihira—but his suggestion, and the explication which he proceeds to give, are far-fetched to say the least.[15] The transliterations, therefore, are better left alone. Someone may stumble some day on a "source" (or on a manuscript in which the Chinese is written out)—if not, there is much in the *Cantos* that is incomplete and only illuminates the fitful condition in which the poem was written—and perhaps the condition of the modern world at large. At any rate it is clear that Pound continues to write with extreme subtlety, employing the method of c. 4—multiple allusion. The rhyming across different centuries and cultures of Paolo and Francesca and the Na-khi shepherds, of Disney and Toba Sojo, of K'a and Kakitsubata—these are the distillates of a fine poetic imagination which has no place for the gratuitous (in comparison the splices of c. 4 are quite mechanic)—only for the wonder, always new, of resemblances and differences.

The description of the Li-chiang landscape lifted from K'a's *Romance* in ll. 19–23 (which I have not quoted) leads smoothly, after a third call for a "further" reading ("They who are skilled in fire / shall read"—c. 91), to a celebration of Muan-bpo—Pound

15. See John Peck, "Landscape as Ceremony in the Later *Cantos:* From 'The Roads of France' to 'Rocks's World,' " *Agenda*, ix, 2–3 (1971), 56–58.

inserting a diagram of the sacred enclosure (the two oak branches that stand for heaven and earth, and in the middle the juniper that is a symbol of the emperor, and—to P.—of the goddess) within his house of writing, his church—which is therefore also placed in the center of things (the *chih*-gnomon of c. 85 recurs one page later), "nel mezzo" (c. 100). The significance carried by the sacred space within the cosmos is hinted at in the first line, which removes K'a's oak to Sumeru, the Olympus of Buddhists, and the Mount of the *Fifth Decad* and of *RD*. The oak is therefore a first figure of Yggdrasil, soon to be replaced by the juniper, focussed by the two oak branches in the enclosure of Muan-bpo as in that of the canto:

> Quercus on Mt Sumeru
>> can'st'ou see with the eyes of turquoise?
>>> heaven   earth
> 35   in the center
>>>>   is
>>>>>   juniper
> The purifications
>>   are snow, rain, artemisia,
> 40   also dew, oak and the juniper
> And in thy mind beauty, O Artemis,
>>   as of mountain lakes in the dawn,   [c. 110]

The recovery of the center (through the watching of shadows) and "the purifications"—in which various forms of water and vegetation are involved—induce the goddess of the house to become manifest, summoned by a plant which is hers by name (Artemisia, whose "strong, pungent odor" is in fact held by the Nakhi "to remove all impurities")[16]—a connection reminiscent of the one obtaining betwen Leucothoe and incense: "But with Leucothoe's mind in that incense / all Babylon could not hold it down" (c. 102). And in fact the poet addresses himself to the mind of the moon goddess, completing now the line of c. 106 with a pellucid comparison: the intellectual beauty which perceives relation is "as of mountain lakes in the dawn"—the dawn

16. Rock, "Muan Bpö Ceremony," p. 14*n*.

which has greeted us at the ingress of Na-khi land, in c. 101. This
Artemis is the *prónoia* who led Brut to England (addressed, as in
"Help me to neede" and in l. 1, in the second person)—she is the
one who at Ephesus "had compassion on silversmiths / revealing
the paraclete / standing in the cusp / of the moon." These comfort-
ing attributes underlie the subsequent change of her name to that
of Kuanon, and the allusion to the fingers whose "kindness, / infinite" is praised in c. 108—the fingers of Leucò, giving and receiv-
ing back (c. 100) the *krédemnon* of foam and silk:

> Foam and silk are thy fingers,
> > Kuanon,
> 45   and the long suavity of her moving,
> > willow and olive reflected,
> Brook-water idles,
> > topaz against pallor of under-leaf
> The lake waves Canaletto'd
> 50   under blue paler than heaven,
> the rock-layers arc'd as with a compass,
> > this rock is magnesia,
> Cozzaglio, Dino Martinazzi made the road here (Gardesana)
> Savoia, Novara at Veneto,
> 55   Solari was in that—
> Un caso triste e denho di memoria
>
> "Had I ever been in one?" i.e. a cavalry charge,   [c. 110]

With the transition to the third person the goddess recedes into
the landscape, no longer Himalayan but Italian, the Garda setting which the *Ur-Cantos* had taken as a point of departure:

> As well begin here, here began Catullus:
> "Home to sweet rest, and to the waves deep laughter,"
> The laugh they wake amid the border rushes.   [QPA 20]

—and to which (precisely as to a "home') the poet returns for
leave-taking. Oak and juniper fade into willow and olive, words
which reflect one another in sound (Kenner 546), and trees which
(like juniper and Artemisia) reflect the suave movement (again
the Stilnovo topos) of "her." We can also detect the glint of her

eye in the trembling of the olive leaf—one of the chief signatures
of the poem—"the pale under face of the leaves" [17] suggesting the
eyelid which frames the topaz iris, "clear as brook water" (*HSM*
and c. 29). Thereupon there is a coming forward of "such as will
increase our loves," the masculine and historical genii of the
place ("here"—cf. l. 15), which is taken as in c. 16 to be the setting or entrance of an earthly paradise, a Valley of the Princes
(like the one in *Purg.* 8):

> Then light air, under saplings,
> the blue banded lake under aether,
>   an oasis, the stones, the calm field,
> the grass quiet,
>   and passing the tree of the bough
> The grey stone posts,
>   and the stair of gray stone,
> the passage clean-squared in granite:
>   descending,
> and I through this, and into the earth,
>   patet terra,
> entered the quiet air
>   the new sky,
> the light as after a sun-set,
>   and by their fountains, the heroes,
> Sigismundo, and Malatesta Novello,
>   and founders, gazing at the mounts of their cities.
>   [c. 16]

Within a few lines our dreamer is listening to snatches of "Plarris
narrations": [18] "Galliffet led that triple charge . . . Prussians /
and he said / it was for the honour of the army." Over the years the
naively languorous, but pregnant, allegory of the early twenties
(we note the tree of the golden bough, signalling—as in the *Ae-
neid* and in c. 1—the entrance to the underworld) has been
purged of its quaint "visionary" machinery, and charged with
ambiguity: in 1959 Pound cites only the names of "the founders"

17. Allen Upward, *The New World* (1910), quoted in "Allen Upward Serious," *SPr* 408.

18. The "title," unlike others, is preserved (as "[Plarr's narration]") in the American text.
For Plarr and Galliffet see 1 *HSM* 7, *SR* 76, and Espey 92–96.

(the planners of the Gardesana occidentale—a spectacular motorway commissioned by Mussolini at the entreaty of D'Annunzio, who had built his bizarre villa-museum at Gardone)—and the sites of battles ancient and more recent, but always "honorable": Vittorio Veneto (1918), and, farther on, Galliffet's Sédan, and the steppe of Isbuschenskij (P.'s "Ibukerki"), where, in 1942, Count Alessandro Bettoni led one of the last suicidal cavalry charges.[19] Battles lost with "honour," except for Vittorio Veneto (where the Italians routed the Austrians)—but this also has a melancholy association: Solari neighbor Baicìn Solari (†1959), tree-planter (c. 87) and soldier, attracts Elpenor's epitaph from c. 1: "A man of no fortune and with a name to come."

```
        Bettoni, like Galliffet
                        (Ibukerki).
65      Cypress versus rock-slide,
            Cozzaglio, the tracciolino
                Riccardo Cozzaglio.
            At Oleari, the Divisione Sforzesca
            disobeyed into victory,
70          Had horses with them.                    [c. 110]
```

However remote from our taste, this cavalcade carries on the caracoling with which the canto began, and the themes of traditional epic ("de litteris et de armis, praestantibusque ingeniis"). Pound, who always "disobeyed," is still dreaming of victory, but he is also aware that this last cavalry charge is a bitter and quixotic affair: all that resists the rout—the rock-slide—is (as a perceptive reader has remarked) the cypress, a funereal tree[20]— and the trace of his song, as suggested by his epithet for the engineer Cozzaglio, apparently a hapax legomenon ("the little trace-maker"?). Likewise he takes advantage of the subtle rhyme between Elpenor's epitaph and the words with which Camões pref-

19. Information from Eva Hesse, "Anhang," in E. P., *Letzte Texte* (*Cantos CX–CXX*) *Entwürfe & Fragmente*, ed. and tr. E. Hesse (Zürich: Arche, 1975), p. 90.

20. Davie, "Cypress Versus Rock-Slide," p. 24. This reading, however, may be just a little over-ingenious, for P. could be pointing solely to Cozzaglio's use of "cypress versus rock-slide" along the Gardesana.

aces the tale of Inés de Castro (a subject already dealt with—like Garda and Kuanon—in the *Ur-Cantos,* as well as in cs. 3 and 30):

> *O caso triste, e dino de memória*
> *Que do sepulchro os homens desenterra,*
> *Aconteceu da mísera e mesquinha*
> *Que despois de ser morta foi Rainha.*

> A sad event and worthy of Memory,
> Who draws forth men from their closed sepulchres,
> Befell that piteous maid, and pitiful
> Who, after she was dead, was crownèd queen.   [SR 219]

—in order to give a turn for the worse to his ambiguous treatment of the lake, and to bring back the theme of violence against life and love, a violence of which he is the victim, but possibly also the author. Court jealousy prompts the assassination of Inés ("Jealousy, two stabbed her"), but king Pedro, "After uncommon quiet," commits in turn, in reprisal, a sin against nature: "A wedding ceremonial: he and the dug-up corpse in cerements" (ur-c. 2, QPA 27). Just so in c. 110:

> Felix nupsit,
>   an end.
> In love with Khaty
>   now dead for 5000 years.

> 75   Over water bluer than midnight
>   where the winter olive is taken
>   Here are earth's breasts mirroured
>   and all Euridices,
>   Laurel bark sheathing the fugitive,
> 80   a day's wraith unrooted?
>   Neath this altar now Endymion lies
>   KALLIASTRAGALOS
>   Καλλιαστράγαλος
>   [*hsin*] hsin
> 85   that is, to go forth by day
>   [*hsin*] hsin
>   That love be the cause of hate,
>   something is twisted,

Awoi,
90   bare trees walk on the sky-line,
            but that one valley reach the four seas,
mountain sunset inverted.   [c. 110]

It is difficult to make out, in the darkness that has suddenly come
down, what may be the cause of the conversion of love to hate
(87), for even the champion of *Verkehr* who muses of a valley
open to the four seas (see c. 99) shares some responsibility. The
most benevolent power in his universe, the undine "of the fair
ankles" (see c. 109), joins, in a graphic exorcism similar in import and form to the previous Muan-bpo, the vegetal renewal of
hsin and "lo jorn, der Tag" (c. 97)—a cluster familiar since c.
91—yet she cannot break the deadly pattern of the betrothals in
the previous lines: merging with the moon she joins her lover En-
dymion, forever asleep "neath this altar" (the altar of Muan-bpo
and of the "house")—or indeed drowned, as the echo of Ariel's
Dirge would suggest:

Full fathom five thy father *lies;*
        Of his bones are *coral* made;
Those are pearls that were his *eyes:*
        Nothing in him that doth fade
But doth suffer a sea-change
Into something rich and strange.
Sea nymphs hourly ring his knell:
Hark! now I hear them—Ding-dong bell.

In this way Pound allows us to look back to his question concerning the coral eyes as to a presage of Death by Water—a third
rhyme which, like the one involving Homer and Camões, does
nothing but make explicit (so to speak) relations which are
doubtless "out there," among things; having provided the reader
with a clue he leaves him the pleasure of alighting upon the perception which has been his (P.'s) starting point. But the import of
the rhyme Na-khi/Shakespeare (as of the rhyme Na-khi/Dante) is
unquestionably funereal: Ariel's rich and strange sea-change (recalled in the *Ur-Cantos* and in c. 92) is the very one that befalls
the corpse of Inés, and undeceives us as to the kind of eternity

earlier said to be provided by art. The same pattern ("Felix nup-
sit / an end") is readily discerned in the proffer of love for Kati, so
many thousand years dead, and in the allusions to Orpheus and
Euridice, and to Apollo and Daphne—a love which is of itself a
metaphor for poetry. Even as the earth's breasts (a memory of
Pisa) as mirrored in the lake are sterile, just so Daphne sheathed
by the laurels of verse acquires roots quite unlike the ones of
l. 25: she becomes a wraith "unrooted" from the day and transplanted surreptitiously into the gardens of night,[21] among waves
and roses that are all equally fossil:

> Daphné, les hanches dans l'écorce,
> Étend toujours ses doigts touffus;
> Mais aux bras du dieu qui la force
> Elle s'éteint, spectre confus.[22]

As earlier in the canto, Pound has remembered *Mauberley*
("Daphne with her thighs in bark") and its source, but rather in a
tragic than in an ironic key.

This is consistently a canto of inversions: love changes through
jealousy to hate and sterility (as in the tales of Inés and of
Awoi—another Nô heroine);[23] the elated opening, recapitulated
by the renewal character, turns out to be the prelude to an end;

21. See Davie ("Cypress Versus Rock-Slide," p. 25) on the "saturnine question-mark" of
l. 80.

22. Gautier, "Le Château du Souvenir," quoted in Espey 31. An "unsteady wraith" is
also to be found in *Kakitsubata*, as well as a "cracked husk of the locus" (*T* 338–40),
reminiscent of c. 115.

23. Awoi, in P.'s inaccurate reading of *Awoi-no-Uye*, is obsessed by "the demon of jealousy" ("This hate is only repayment / The flame of jealousy / will turn on one's own hand
and burn"), until a priest performs an exorcism. (Cf. c. 77: "Awoi's *hennia* plays hob in
the tent flaps . . . Lo Scirocco è geloso.") Of relevance to c. 110 are also the following
lines by the Chorus:

> Hateful, heart full of hate,
> Though you are full of tears
> Because of others' dark hatred,
> Your love of Genji
> Will not be struck out
> Like a fire-fly's flash in the dark.   [*T* 328]

Awoi-no-Uye and *Kakitsubata* are printed and discussed together in *"Noh" or Accomplishment* (*T* 323–40).

even the "mountain lakes in the dawn" which brought us to
Garda are reflecting—and *inverting*—by the end of the lacustrine
episode, a mountain sunset. We now realize that "Thy quiet
house" is a phrase as ambivalent as everyone's attitude to the
"home," a womb easily transformed by just a little additional
"quiet" into a foreign and ghost-ridden thing, as Freud showed
in his discussion of the contraries *heimlich* (homely) and *unheim-
lich* (uncanny), which have it within them to become syn-
onyms.[24] Accordingly the house-canto, after changing into the
lake that twists all things "out of natural measure" (c. 36), is finally identified as a tomb and associated with the mausoleum of
Galla Placidia (see cs. 21 and 76) and with Byzance, the symbol
of Yeats's art "out of nature," heretofore the antithesis of
Pound's unartificial paradise:

>   La Tour, San Carlo gone,
>   and Dieudonné, Voisin
> 95   Byzance, a tomb, an end,
>   Galla's rest, and thy quiet house at Torcello
>   "What! What!" says the auzel here,
>   "Tullup" said that bird in Virginia,
>   their meaning?
> 100   That war is the destruction of restaurants
>   Quos ego Persephonae
>   [*chih*]   chih
>   not with jet planes,
>   The holiness of their courage forgotten
> 105   and the Brescian lions effaced,
>   Until the mind jumps without building
>   [*chih*]   chih
>   and there is no *chih* and no root.   [c. 110]

Propertius boasted of three books that he would take, "my not
unworthy gift, to Persephone"[25]—but Pound, in this last and disconsolate "Ode pour l'election de son sepulchre," uses the quotation sardonically, and throws in with the books his peculiar bric-

---

24. Sigmund Freud, "The Uncanny," *Standard Edition,* XVII (London: Hogarth Press,
1955), 217–52.

25. *HSP* 6 and Prop. II. 13. The words had also served as an epigraph to *Canzoni,* 1911.

a-brac: cherished restaurants (his distaste for "the dinner scene" should, however, be borne in mind), the undecipherable speech of birds—the same birds which he, a follower of Arnaut and Jannequin, had sought to render onomatopoeically, perpetrating an additional forgery—and which he still attempts to dissociate, as "throstle's note from banded thrush." The world of jet planes in which (as he remarks bathetically) [26] the courage of the resisters mentioned previously (and of Brescia, "the Lioness of Italy") has been forgotten, is actually the correlative (and this is a novel and painful confession) of the condition of his mind, which "jumps without building"—the time of road-making is over. This brings to mind the final words of *The Waste Land* which have been mocked in c. 8, somewhat prematurely, as it now appears:

> From time's wreckage shored,
>   these fragments shored against ruin,
> and the sun [*jih*] [27]
>   new with the day.
> 115   Mr Rock still hopes to climb at Mount Kinabalu
>   his fragments sunk (20 years)
>   13,455 ft. facing Jesselton, Borneo,   [c. 110]

26. But see W. C. Williams, "For Eleanor and Bill Monahan," *Pictures from Brueghel*, p. 85:

> The moon which
>   they have vulgarized recently
>   is still
> your planet
>   as it was Dian's before
>   you. What
> do they think they will attain
>   by their ships
>   that death has not
> already given
>   them? Their ships
>   should be directed
> inward upon   But I
>   am an old man. I
>   have had enough.

27. Here and elsewhere the editors of *D&F* have added to the character the transliteration and tone number as in Mathews—a mistake for these signs are often mental images not to be sounded in reading.

The sun is new every day . . . Pound continues to murmur, as if to ward off the end, his ensign *jih hsin,* but is hardly comforted: the "Mount" which, like his persona Rock, he still hopes to climb, is much too high.

There remains the conviction that the fragments can return to the surface, "resurgent *eikones*" (c. 76), at a remove of twenty or three hundred years, as was the case with Rock, whose studies were jeopardized when in 1943 the ship that carried his manuscripts was torpedoed "and twelve years of work were sent with it to the bottom of the Arabian sea,"[28] and who about twenty years later was to come back to life through Pound's poem, also if this cannot mean very much any longer. All that remains of the stirring and changeable world of life of which the *Cantos* have often made us more aware is a glimmer of light in the midst of Francesca's "infernal windstorm that never rests" (*Inf.* v.31):

```
120    A wind of darkness hurls against forest
                    the candle flickers
                            is faint
       Lux enim—
                    versus this tempest.
125    The marble form in the pine wood,
                    The shrine seen and not seen
       From the roots of sequoias
                            pray    [ching]    pray
                        There is power
130    Awoi or Komachi,
                    the oval moon.                         [c. 110]
```

"But light"—the textual fragment comes to the poet's aid—"per se omnem in partem se ipsam diffundit"—expands of its own accord through all space.[29] In the distance there may still be the promised land, seen and not seen: a "pineta" (c. 90), a marble form, a shrine—the House. Like Prospero at the end of the *other*

28. Rock, "Muan Bpö Ceremony," p. 2. P.'s "20 years" could also be a mistake for (or a rounding out of) Rock's "twelve years of work."

29. Robert Grosseteste, *De Luce,* quoted in "Cavalcanti," *LE* 161, and in c. 55. Cf. c. 113: "That the body is inside the soul— / the lifting and folding brightness [v. "Phanopoeia" 2, *P* 169] / the darkness shattered, / the fragment."

Tempest, with a gesture moving in its simplicity, Pound *prays* to his goddess, both vegetal (*ching,* it will be recalled, is "reverence" for that kind of energy) and lunar, by the roots of sequoias (see c. 87), and invoking as precedents Awoi, delivered from jealousy through prayer, and Ono no Komachi, gathered to her lover after death through the offices of a monk.[30] Wielding his old talent for form, he comes round in the end to his point of departure, namely the confrontation with "the female principle of the world":[31] the moon which is oval like the egg of generation, and like "the face-oval beneath the glaze," contemplated by the minor poet Mauberley at the expiration of his textual career.

30. See *Kayoi Komachi, T* 226–31. The crucial *ching* should again be compared with "Venerandam" in c. 1 (and with *hrézein* in c. 106).

31. Williams, "For Eleanor and Bill Monahan," p. 86. This principle, the poet adds (and his friend P. would agree at least in part), "is my appeal / in the extremity / to which I have come."

18. The Image and the Circle

O light eternal, that dost dwell only in thyself, alone dost comprehend thyself, and self-comprehended, self-comprehending, dost love and send forth gladness!

That circling, which so conceived appeared in thee as a reflected light, beheld awhile by my eyes, within itself, of its own color, appeared to me painted in our own image, wherefore my sight was all committed to it.

As is the geometer who sets himself to square the circle, and does not find, by thinking, that principle whence he lacketh, such was I at this new sight; I would have wished to see how the image conveneth to the circle, and how it is contained; but for this my wings were unfitted, save that my mind was smitten by an effulgence, wherein its will came to it.

        —*Par.* XXXIII. 124–41, as translated in *SR* 153

The themes of *Drafts & Fragments* are all embedded in the remarkable first canto of the sequence. In particular the fragments of cs. 111 and 112 (which add up to just over eighty lines) have the form of lucid postscripts to the matters we have been dealing with. The first comprises some annotations on history and law (Napoleon, Talleyrand),[1] indicating that Pound persisted to the end in his prosaic and "objective" intent, followed by another confrontation with the ambiguous revelations of the "water bluer than midnight." Speaking schematically, it could be called a portrait of the lawgiver and of his Egeria. The "more poetic" section, following upon the barest transcription, commences by revealing the precise nature of the "ground" upon which Orage, unlike "Yeats, Possum and Wyndham" (c. 98), stood:

1. Talleyrand's "Confucianism" is intimated by bringing his name together with the characters *wu hsieh szu* ("Have no twisty thoughts"—*A* II 2), which are printed (in Chinese) at the end of *CA*. Thus "(heart's field)," the "etymology" of *wu,* should be moved up one line. See Hesse, "Anhang," p. 79.

> A nice quiet paradise,
>> Orage held the basic was pity
>> *compassione,*
>>> Amor   [c. 111]

Pound's preoccupation for his "paradise," reiterated in the same form in c. 116, is of little interest, for it is none but he who has conceived the naive project of writing about heaven before the event, and it is silly that he should now tell us how difficult it is. However, the familiar histrionics are sharpened by irony ("nice"), and by the crucial reference to "quiet," which allows us to identify this locus as the "house." The subsequent transition to the waters of night (which are this time the sea's) is prefigured by the earlier metamorphoses of that "sacred" edifice. Love and compassion are the attributes of the undine, the *krédemnon,* and yet their emergence turns out to be hardly settled in the context of the ambiguities of the real:

> Gold mermaid up from black water—
>> Night against sea-cliffs
>>> the low reef of coral—
> And the sand grey against undertow
>> as Geryon—lured there—but in splendour,
> Veritas, by antithesis,[2] from the sea depth
>> *come burchiello in su la riva*
> The eyes holding trouble—
>> no light
>>> ex profundis—
> naught from feigning.
> Soul melts into air,
>> anima into aura,
>>> Serenitas.
> Coin'd gold
>> also bumped off 8000 Byzantines
> Edictum prologo
>> Rothar.   [c. 111]

2. Thus the typescript. The printed text has "anthesis" (Greek for "flowering"), which also makes some sense (see c. 91: "& light then / as the holly-leaf"), and which P. did not care to correct in the *D&F* galleys, but is by far less persuasive (for verity is precisely the *antithesis* of Geryon's fraud).

Though Leucò or her fellow mermaid are gold that gathers light in the gloom, and though "splendour" is the word upon which fifteen pages on the poem comes to an exalted close, the subtle comparison with the Geryon of cs. 49, 51, and 97, who emerges, "as at times wherries lie ashore,"[3] from the chasm of Dante's eighth circle, poses the possibility of a final "inversion," of a frightening confusion of verity and fraud, natural process and usury. We are delighted by the decisive "sincerity" of the poet, who, after much simplistic partitioning, confesses that he does not know what the word coming to him from the sea depths ("ex profundis") will import. The eyes from which he expected relief darken, gold is shown to take human life (the coiner may be Abd-el-Melik of c. 97), the "prologue" to Rothar's Edict[4] enters into a desperately ironic relation with what is after all "a tomb, an end." There is more "serenity" in the thirty lines "From c. 112," which are all lifted from Rock's Muan-bpo essay, and are Pound's final gesture in that direction. For a close he turns, with a pun on a Na-khi pictogram,[5] to "fate's tray," the winnow of Fortuna, which perhaps will sift the wheat from the chaff, allowing him "to confess wrong without losing rightness" (c. 116).

A new departure is signified by cs. 113 and 114, which are more complex and fragmented than the ones immediately previous. In the former Pound turns immediately, with a happy con-

3. "Come talvolta stanno a riva i burchi"—*Inf.* xvii.19, and *SR* 133. P. may have changed "burchi" (pl.) to "burchiello" (sing. and dim.) under the influence of Giovanni Giudici's translation of *HSM*, first published in *Il Verri* for June 1959. Here "Coral of Pacific voyages" is rendered by "Burchiello nel Pacifico" (*OS* 223).

4. P.'s source (*History of the Lombards* iv. 44), quoted correctly in c. 103, reads: "in sui edicti testatus est prologo." This, however, does not quite warrant correction in the text of "Edictum" to "Edicti" (as in E. P., *Letzte Texte*, ed. Hesse, p. 16): P. may have wanted the sound of the nominative, or just not cared enough to check—at any rate his "errors" give us the texture of his brush stroke.

5. "A large winnowing tray made of the small bamboo (Arundinaria) *¹mun*, here it stands for *²mun* a fate, a life, the Chinese *ming*"—Rock, "Muan Bpo Ceremony," p. 71. (Incidentally, *ming* is the character "forcedly translated" as "Fortuna" in c. 86.) P. transcribes as follows: "Artemisia / Arundinaria / Winnowed in fate's tray / [*²mun*]neath / luna [moon pictogram]." In the typescript there is an additional line to the canto: "Until Di Marzio [prob. the editor of *Meridiano di Roma*] quotes Guicciardini" (for the latter see c. 92). Thus the Na-khi walking tour leads to fascist "honour" and revanchism.

trast, from the "luna" of the previous finale to the sun, who
"runs" (c. 106) through the twelve *houses* of the zodiac:

> Thru the 12 Houses of Heaven
>   seeing the just and the unjust,
>   tasting the sweet and the sorry,
> Pater Helios turning.
> "Mortal praise has no sound in her ears"
>   (Fortuna's)
> θρῆνος
> And who no longer make gods out of beauty
> θρῆνος   this is a dying.
> Yet to walk with Mozart, Agassiz and Linnaeus
>   'neath overhanging air under sun-beat[6]
> Here take thy mind's space
> And to this garden, Marcella, ever seeking by petal, by leaf-vein
>   out of dark, and toward half-light
>
> And over Li Chiang, the snow range is turquoise   [c. 113]

Calling upon the manifold consciousness of the "father," who is
as blissful and indifferent as Fortuna to mortal praise and blame
(see c. 100), Pound-Heracles seeks to escape the uncanny quiet of
his house and tomb, yet at once the funereal theme is sounded
again, defining the loss of the esthetic and mythical dream
sketched in the opening. However, these dialectics lead to a positive and unexceptionable synthesis: a space of the *mind* (the relevance of this theme in the later cantos has already been noted)
which is truly human: the world of Mozart and Linnaeus (and, to
a lesser extent, of Agassiz), distinguished by attention to process,
phyllotaxis ("leaf-vein"), and by the persistent enquiry ("ever
seeking") which one appreciates in these cantos. But then Li-
chiang's turquoise range ("can'st'ou see with the eyes of turquoise?"— c. 110) casts its shade upon the poet's loving invitation to Marcella (see c. 47: "Never idle, by no means by no wiles
intermittent"), intimating the deadly import of the latter. A uni-
vocal unriddling of human affairs is by now out of the question,
the "truth" being the endless cycle of loss and retrieval:

---

6. This doubtful line does not occur in the typescript.

> The hells move in cycles,
>   No man can see his own end.
> The Gods have not returned. "They have never left us."
>   They have not returned.
> Cloud's processional and the air moves with their living. [cf. c. 3]
> Pride, jealousy and possessiveness
>   3 pains of hell
> and a clear wind over garofani   [carnations] [c. 113]

Still, Pound's protest against all kinds of oppression, as well as against the "fear" which is "father of cruelty" (c. 114), stands out clearly defined, and valid:

> Error of chaos. Justification is from kindness of heart / and from her hands floweth mercy.
>   As to sin, they invented it—eh? / to implement domination
>   And for a little magnanimity somewhere, / And to know the share from the charge / (scala altrui)   [c. 113]

And so to the closing salutation of the poet, still homeless and dying "upon another's stairs,"[7] his consciousness however to the last "une conscience occupée—jamais vide—la conscience d'un homme au travail jusqu'à son dernier souffle":[8]

> And in thy mind beauty, O Artemis
>   Daphne afoot in vain speed.
> When the Syrian onyx is broken.
>   Out of dark, thou, Father Helios, leadest,
> but the mind as Ixion, unstill, ever turning.   [c. 113]

Stillness and unstillness are the two poles of attraction (of familiar contextual significance—"the dimension of stillness") among which in the course of D&F the mind's paradigm hesitatingly runs on, in anticipation of the fatal rupture of the Syrian onyx.[9]

---

7. "Thou shalt make trial of how salt doth taste another's bread, and how hard the path to descend and mount upon another's stair (lo scendere e 'l salir per l'altrui scale)"—Par. XVII.58–60, and SR 148.

8. Gaston Bachelard, Poétique de la rêverie (Paris: Presses Universitaires de France, 1961), p. 47.

9. Cf. HSP 6: "Nor will you be . . . too weary / To place the last kiss on my lips / When the Syrian onyx is broken." The last line of the canto echoes "The Coming of War: Actaeon" (1915): "Unstill, ever moving" (P 107).

Canto 114, the more telling lines of which have been discussed in the foregoing chapter, is largely concerned with "the fight against jealousy," with special regard to sexual custom and family ambience—the House.[10] It should be read bearing in mind (for several personal allusions) the 1920 *Indiscretions* and the conflictual private life led by Pound, who now appears to pronounce himself for certain experiments in promiscuous community[11]—a final gesture towards enlightened law-giving before the well-known envoi of cantos 115 and 116. The glosses provided so far should suffice to an understanding of the latter's form and substance, though these are of themselves perspicuous:

> The scientists are in terror
> > and the European mind stops
> Wyndham Lewis chose blindness
> > rather than have his mind stop.
> Night under wind mid garofani,
> > the petals are almost still   [c. 115]

A subtle dialectic has come to obtain between the desire to persevere at all costs—so that the European mind may continue to function (a phrase both pathetic and grandiose, for P. is chiefly thinking of his own intermittent intelligence—yet his awareness of stoppage may be accurate enough)—and the lure of motionless lake water, of petals by this time "almost still." Himself a "thin husk" rather than a Lorenzaccio (c. 7), the poet listens to the immemorial music of wind, light, and tide, moving upon the Torcello lagoon. "Wave falls," he had written, "and the hand falls." Yet the wave rises again:

> A blown husk that is finished
> > but the light sings eternal

10. This reading was suggested by Eva Hesse in 1974, and reiterated in her "Nachwort" and "Anhang" to E. P., *Letzte Texte*. The conclusions she draws from her collation ("Nachwort," pp. 75–77) of the first part of c. 114 with the dialogues by Bruno there quoted (*La cena delle ceneri, De l'infinito universo e mondi, Lo spaccio de la bestia trionfante*), are less convincing.

11. If "the man of Oneida" is a reference not only to a Loomis uncle of the poet but also to the founder of Oneida Colony, where "complex marriage" was practiced (Hesse, "Anhang," p. 94).

> a pale flare over marshes
> > where the salt hay whispers to tide's change
> Time, space,
> > neither life nor death is the answer.
> And of men seeking good,
> > doing evil.
> In meiner Heimat
> > where the dead walked
> > > and the living were made of cardboard.
>
> > > > > > > > > [c. 115]

The house as possession has decidedly become the place that converts good to evil, committing its owner to the love of death. So
much is imported by the close, which should not be mistaken for
a vain reaffirmation of the poet's power to resurrect the dead.
Throughout *D&F* he has denounced the wooing of Inés (whether
the suitor be himself or another) for what it is: violence, tyranny,
inversion. But then it is surely not Pound's pronounced nostalgia
that claims, and holds, our attention, but his position as a persistent—if at times unconscious—witness to the contemporary predicament.

In the final canto the mind of Ixion confronts with "gaiety"
the mind of the god who *comes* in marine guise, attended by the
dolphins of c. 110, to greet the voyager, or to bring him the
"gentle death" Tiresias had promised Ulysses:

> Came Neptunus
> > his mind leaping
> > > like dolphins,
> These concepts the human mind has attained.
> To make Cosmos—
> To achieve the possible—   [c. 116]

And, again as in c. 110, the poet addresses to the reader his familiar query:

> I have brought the great ball of crystal;
> > who can lift it?
> Can you enter the great acorn of light?
> > But the beauty is not the madness

> Tho' my errors and wrecks lie about me.
> And I am not a demigod,
> I cannot make it cohere.
> If love be not in the house there is nothing.   [c. 116]

There is a touch of truculence in the challenge to "lift" the great ball—which is at one time the acorn of light of c. 106, Pound's *phantastikon,* the divine vision, and the poem as distinct from its compiler, now beached among errors and wrecks—but this false note is made good by the eventual reprise, beautifully articulated, of the basic theme: the House reattaches itself, beyond (and through) negation and loss, to "the drawing of this Love" (*Little Gidding*)—to a post-Christian eros [12] in the absence of which nothing can be said to exist ("without ²muan ¹bpo / no reality"—cs. 104, 112). Thereupon Pound recalls, endearingly, Laforgue and Disney, the squirrels and elms of St. Elizabeth's, and closes, like Dante, with a statement of impotence that opens the way to "atasal" (c. 76), "union with God"—that is, the revelation of a splendor beyond (one's own) death granted to *WT*'s "demigod" Heracles:

> But to affirm the gold thread in the pattern
> 　　　　　　　　　(Torcello)
> al Vicolo d'oro
> 　　　　　　(Tigullio).
> To confess wrong without losing rightness:
> Charity I have had sometimes,
> 　　　　　I cannot make it flow thru.
> A little light, like a rushlight
> 　　　　　　　to lead back to splendour.   [c. 116]

By piecing together such traces or writings as Torcello's golden thread of mosaic and the Vico dell'Oro of old Rapallo (a final

---

12. However, one is also reminded of the final words in Valéry's *Cahiers:* "Le mot Amour ne s'est trouvé associé au nom de Dieu que depuis le Xrist"—as well as of a passage of Alain translated extemporaneously by P. in September 1960: "The spirit will be able (will know enough) to deprive itself of power, of every *kind* of power. That is the highest Kingdom. Now Calvary announces this very thing, in so eloquent, and so violent a way, that I will add no commentary whatsoever" (quoted in Cory, "Ezra Pound: A Memoir," p. 36).

and quite novel bit of archeological "rhyming") one may find one's way *back* from time's ruins to the City of Deioces, Venus' (Notre Dame la Daurade's) golden river of love—Paradise lost and regained. But that love is the last essence of the mirthful goddess of c. 1 is only to be learned by other, more elusive, "traces"—the flashes of personal charity in one's life: "J'ai eu pitié des autres . . ." It is these that ultimately do the building.[13]

The three fragments printed at the end of *D&F* under the editorial heading, "Notes for Canto cxvii et seq.," may have been written before the final struggle recorded in c. 116, yet their present location is fortunate (as is not the case with c. 120 so-called). They pass over the otiose question whether the *Cantos* are a ball of crystal or a wreck, and look *beyond* the poem, thus providing it with the open-ended and relaxed finale that it needs. The first of the set is readily identified as a footnote to c. 110's envoi, with its talk of "the marble form in the pine wood" and "the shrine seen and not seen":

> For the blue flash and the moments
>   benedetta
> the young for the old
>   that is tragedy
> And for one beautiful day there was peace.
>   Brancusi's bird
>   in the hollow of pine trunks
> or when the snow was like sea foam
>   Twilit sky leaded with elm boughs.
> Under the Rupe Tarpeia
>   weep out your jealousies—
> To make a church
>   or an altar to Zagreus Ζαγρεύς
> Son of Semele Σεμέλη
> Without jealousy
>   like the double arch of a window
> Or some great colonnade.   [c. 117]

13. The draft of the passage in the typescript reveals a P. as irritable as Heracles in his agony: "Charity is what I've got—damn it, / I cannot make it flow thru. / A little love like a rush light / to lead back splendour . . ." (the dots are P.'s).

While "blessing" the companion and anima of his last verse Pound is aware of the culpability of his senile attachment (usury, we recall from c. 45, "hath brought palsey to bed")—an attachment which is also, so far as it involves "jealousy," the cause of the conversion of love into hate. Yet he savors the extraordinary gift of the "benedetta": one whole day of peace,[14] as memorable as two crucial epiphanies of his later poetry: the elm boughs leading the autumn sky in c. 106, and the foam-*krédemnon* changing to snow in c. 98. In this *quiet,* only very slightly disturbed by the references to the Tarpeian Cliff and to the double arch associated in c. 4 with another suicidal love, Pound meditates his last project: to build a house free of jealousy, a temple which the poet himself, a feline god, may inhabit with his Mother.[15] This project is not unlike the one announced, after a memorable pause, at the end of the subsequent somber fragment, which mourns the death of love, and with it of life ("m'amour, ma vie," in the typescript):

> M'amour, m'amour
> > what do I love and
> > > where are you?
> That I lost my center
> > fighting the world.
> The dreams clash
> > and are shattered—
> and that I tried to make a paradiso
> > > > terrestre.   [c. 117]

The diagnosis is dispassionate: Pound has worn himself out in a frightful and ridiculous tourney with windmills, and yet his unrealized plan for an *earthly* paradise is more compelling than the dependable accomplishment of such as never lose themselves.

In the end, having regained his confidence, the poet rises from his own "failure" and sets out, comforted by memory, towards a world which is truly new—the world of man, the temporal *image*

14. Cf. "Erat Hora" (1911): "Nay, whatever comes / One hour was sunlit and the most high gods / May not make boast of any better thing / Than to have watched that hour as it passed."

15. According to Stock 577, in 1958 P. considered building on a cliff in the environs of Merano a three-columned temple, like the one graphed in cs. 97 and 100.

the arcane interaction of which with the timeless *circle* Dante had
sought to apprehend at the supreme moment:

> La faillite de François Bernouard, Paris
> or a field of larks at Allègre,
>> "es laissa cader"
> so high toward the sun and then falling,
>> "de joi sas alas"
> to set here the roads of France.
>
> Two mice and a moth my guides—
> To have heard the farfalla gasping
>> as toward a bridge over worlds.
> That the kings meet in their island,
>> where no food is after flight from the pole.
> Milkweed the sustenance
>> as to enter arcanum.
>
> To be men not destroyers.   [c. 117]

Bernouard, it will be recalled, was the first printer of the XXX
Cantos: Pound reaffirms his material and collective conception of
the poetic artifact. ("And as to who will copy this palimp-
sest?"—he wonders in c. 116.) "Lie quiet"—we think we hear
him say, as in c. 1—"Divus, Bernouard, and Pound." The old
man dies in order that the new man may be born—indeed the
end is no longer the vain emptiness of death but an excess of joy,
the "gaiety" of c. 110: the lark falls "ab la dolchor qu'al cor [li]
vai" (c. 91)—from the sweetness that goes to her heart. With a
happy gesture the *Cantos* hark back, while running out, to the
springtime of modern Western poetry—Bernart's song—and to
the dawn of the vocation of the poet Pound: the roads of Provence as he saw them around Midsummer Day, 1912. His
guides in this first and last journey are "tous les influx de vigueur
et de tendresse réelle" (Rimbaud): two mice, a moth, and the butterflies or *"king*-wings" (c. 106) that feed on milkweed and meet
in their island, preparing for the great migratory flight.[16] That the

16. Cf. the close of c. 109. A different interpretation of "kings," less functional to the
context, was suggested to me by Dorothy Pound. A contributor of *Edge* for Sept. 1957
provided the following information: "In February this year a group of about 60 bankers,

arcanum to which they point the way is revealed in the end as a
fully human world has been indicated above—and the Dantean
source of the last statement (*Par.* v.80) should be borne in mind.
It is only a hypothesis, a promised land at the threshold of which
this huge Browningesque machine must come to a stop—like the
prehistory of the tribe, or of modern consciousness, which we
may take it to be. Of course, the better part of the job remains to
be done.

------

economists and planners from the United States, England and other countries held what
can only be described as a secret meeting at St Simon Island off the coast of Georgia. . . .
It was at Jekyll Island [!] off the coast of Georgia in 1910 that a group of bankers held a
secret meeting to plan the United States Federal Reserve Board system which became law
on December 23, 1913."

Index